Reproducing Gender

Reproducing Gender

POLITICS, PUBLICS, AND

EVERYDAY LIFE AFTER SOCIALISM

SUSAN GAL AND GAIL KLIGMAN, EDITORS

PRINCETON UNIVERSITY PRESS

PRINCETON, NEW JERSEY

Library of Congress Cataloging-in-Publication Data

Reproducing gender : poliitics, publics, and everyday life after socialism / Susan Gal and
Gail Kligman, editors.

p. cm.

Includes bibliographical references and index.

ISBN 0-691-04867-3 (cloth : alk. paper)—ISBN 0-691-04868-1 (pbk. : alk paper)

1. Women—Europe, Eastern. 2. Women—Europe, Eastern—Social conditions. 3. Birth
control—Europe, Eastern. 4. Women's rights—Europe, Eastern. 5. Europe, Eastern— Social
conditions—1989.

I. Gal, Susan, 1949– . II. Kligman, Gail.

HQ1590.7.R46 2000

305.42'0947—dc21   99-041739

This book has been composed in Adobe Caslon.

The paper used in this publication meets the minimum requirements of
ANSI/NISO Z39.48-1992 (R1997) (*Permanence of Paper*)

www.pup.princeton.edu

Printed in the United State of America

1 2 3 4 5 6 7 8 9 10
1 2 3 4 5 6 7 8 9 10
(pbk.)

Don't talk to me about cosmetics, money is the best face-cream.

—woman cannery worker

Young capitalism is usually an enterprising man who either tries to dispossess you of your apartment or your land. He knows best, he knows that he deserves it, and that everything can be arranged. He visits offices, looking for legal possibilities, and Mrs. W. from [the town of] Jozefyów is trembling.

—Polish magazine

As a matter of fact, we write what they want us to write, and then we go ahead and do what we want.

—NGO leader on obtaining foreign funding

CONTENTS

IN THE EARLY 1990s when we began this work, the subject of gender was hardly recognized as a focus for research on East Central Europe. We were fortunate nevertheless to enjoy the strong support of a number of institutions and individuals who were convinced of the need for an initiative such as ours. We thank Jason Parker and the Joint Committee on Eastern Europe of the American Council of Learned Societies, who encouraged us to develop our ideas into a project. The Open Society Institute of Budapest, Hungary, generously funded most of the research. We especially appreciate the patience and encouragement of Katalin Koncz, Diane Cullinane, and Emily Martinez. Sydel Silverman and the Wenner-Gren Foundation for Anthropological Research provided important additional funding for ethnographic research. We were pleased to have been selected as the first recipients of the foundation's program for International Collaborative Research.

It is never easy to coordinate a collaborative project. This one was particularly complex. It included participants living on three continents and in more than ten countries, during a period when new communications and banking systems in East Central Europe were just being established. We could not have managed without the administrative support of the Center for the Study of Women at the University of California, Los Angeles, and especially the dedication, responsibility, and good humor of Dawn Waring and Van Do-Nguyen. Many thanks as well to Anne Ch'ien and Mark Bunting of the University of Chicago. Two workshops were crucial to realizing the joint effort: Most importantly, they enabled participants to engage in intensive discussion and fruitful debate. The conference center at Il Ciocco in the hills of northern Tuscany made these meetings as much an aesthetic and culinary pleasure as an intellectual event. Bruno Giannasi handled organizational details and resolved all manner of emergencies with hospitality and charm. In like fashion, Doru Afloarei of Dream Tours International, California, won our admiration for his unflappable and good-natured efficiency in arranging travel for the second workshop. The Collegium Budapest/Institute for Advanced Study provided a congenial setting in which to finish the manuscript.

In addition to those represented in this volume, the following researchers were associated with the project at various phases, and we thank them for their participation and contributions: Marina Blagojević (Serbia), Maria Čermáková (Czech Republic), Daša Duhaček (Serbia), Dorothea Gyriecz (Austria), Smaranda Mezei (Romania), Silva Meznarić (Croatia), Maxine Molyneux (United Kingdom), Stefka Naumova (Bulgaria), Hanna Navarová (Czech Republic), Anna Okruhlicova (Slovakia), Vesna Pusić (Croatia), Sabine Röhl (Germany), Jirina Šiklova (Czech Republic), and Anna Titkow (Poland). We especially wish to express our gratitude to Dorothy Rosenberg for her constructive intellectual role and collegiality.

Revisions of several chapters benefitted from the careful attention of Rita Bashaw, Eva Fodor, Robert Levy, and Elizabeth Stephenson. We owe special thanks to Laurie MacDonald Brumberg for her meticulous and invaluable editorial assistance in preparing the final papers for publication. This was a process that required not only tolerance in the face of the pressure of deadlines, but also skill in standardizing notes and bibliographies containing references in no less than nine languages. Mary Murrell of Princeton University Press often cheered us by expressing enthusiasm for this project.

All of the participants in this volume have valiantly endured the communicative and logistical difficulties that are inevitable in a project involving many years and great distances. We are grateful to them and express our thanks. For those who live in East Central Europe, the transformations discussed in this book have been as much a part of their everyday lives as they have been the focus of research. We ourselves have learned a great deal from all of the participants— in conversations, from the papers, and through the process of working together over these years.

Finally, we thank each other. A serendipitous combination of intellectual affinity and optimism linked to a historical moment brought us together. Mutual respect and tolerance as well as continuing intellectual engagement have kept us going. No small measure of good will and appreciation for the absurd have gone into making our collaboration work.

Susan Gal and Gail Kligman
Budapest 1998

Reproducing Gender

INTRODUCTION

SUSAN GAL AND GAIL KLIGMAN

WHY WAS ABORTION among the first issues raised, after 1989, by virtually all the newly constituted governments of East Central Europe? In Romania, liberalization of abortion was the second decree issued by the provisional government upon the fall of the Ceaușescu regime. Abortion's legality in East Germany and its restriction in West Germany almost derailed German unification. In Poland the question has become virtually a permanent feature of the parliamentary agenda. But abortion was only one of a range of issues associated with sexuality and human reproduction that have taken center stage in the years since 1989. In the former Yugoslavia, rape was a weapon of war. Because women who had been raped and the children that resulted from rape were ostracized and rejected by their own ethnic groups, rape was also and intentionally a tool of "ethnic cleansing" through its tragic reproductive consequences. Unwanted babies became a political issue in Romania and Germany as well, but in different ways. A private adoption market in babies, not all of whom were unwanted by their birth mothers, emerged in Romania. The rate of voluntary sterilization increased dramatically among east German women, and this produced a political scandal when it was noticed and labeled a "birth strike" by the mass media.

Throughout the region, democratic institutions were being created, fiscal and constitutional crises threatened, and legislative politics were being rethought in dramatic ways. Yet, among these weighty concerns, the leaders of the new states (themselves mostly male) also heatedly debated questions of "proper" sex, women's roles, birthrates, fertility control, and childcare. This book began with our own wonder at this phenomenon and our conviction that exploring it would lead to a deeper understanding of how institutional change is occurring in the region.

Questions of sex, gender, and reproduction, however, have not been high on the research agenda in the decade since the end of state socialism. Most scholars of and in the region have more vigorously explored economic and political processes such as marketization and democratization. We argue, in contrast, that in the understanding of these apparently ungendered processes a consideration of gender is crucial. This is because a gendered perspective highlights aspects of the post-socialist transformations that have been taken for granted, thereby recasting and sharpening our understanding of change. Thus, for instance, democratization comes more clearly into view if we ask how "politics" itself is being redefined as a distinctively masculine endeavor. Similarly, if we examine how women and men are differently located in the emerging national economies, we foreground the usually unremarked yet pervasive and often feminized phenomenon of small-scale marketization.

To generate such novel analyses, however, we need fresh evidence. That is why, in 1992, we (Susan Gal and Gail Kligman) saw the need to expand our own ongoing research into gender and reproduction in Hungary and Romania with more broad-scale, empirical and comparative work. At the urging of the American Council of Learned Societies, we conceived a plan for a research project that would include scholars and evidence from most of the countries of the region. This book is the result of that extended collaborative enterprise. Unlike many recent collections on gender and post-socialist transformations, it is not an edited volume in the traditional sense. Rather, the fourteen studies included here emerged from a single project with a common set of conceptual assumptions, paired with a commitment to interdisciplinary approaches and multiple methodologies.[1]

We began with the observation that the economic and political processes of the "transition" in Eastern Europe are not gender neutral and that one of our primary tasks would be to explore the various ways in which gender has been a factor in the current transformations.[2] In addition, an interest in the intertwined relationship between public discourse about sex and reproduction on the one hand, and the everyday practices of gender on the other, constituted the overarching conceptual commitments shared by all participants. Because the countries of East Central Europe are not monolithic, nor is the rubric "women" a homogeneous social category, another of our premises was that comparative research (not only across countries but across social strata and economic sectors) would be essential. It was also clear that any single project would have to be selective in the issues addressed.

The fourteen chapters in this volume are organized into three parts: Reproduction as Politics, Gender Relations in Everyday Life, and Arenas of Political Action. These chapters are unified not only by the fundamental conceptual framework with which we started, but also by further common definitions, themes, and goals. Taken together, all the chapters present evidence to strengthen the emerging scholarly view that, with important variations from country to country, women have experienced the political-economic changes since communism differently than men and have been differentially affected by them. Documenting such changes in a range of contexts has been one of our primary aims. But we are not arguing simply for the study of differences between men and

[1] This introduction began as a much longer chapter that, in addition to outlining the collaborative project's basic framework, located its findings in historical context. The manuscript's reviewers, however, as well as Mary Murrell, our editor at Princeton University Press, suggested that a shorter introduction would serve the chapters better, obviating concerns about the book's length and price. At the same time, they persuaded us that the original essay also merited publication. Thus, we have further developed our earlier introduction into a companion volume, *The Politics of Gender after Socialism*, that complements the collaborative book's case studies. Directly emerging from the research project, it expands on historical and comparative issues, thus broadening the context in which the studies may be understood.

[2] "Transition" merits quotation marks because, in concert with other recent research, the approach of this book rejects many of the early assumptions of transitology. For a review of these assumptions and criticisms, see Róna-Tas 1998.

women in the region. On the contrary, these contributions all reflect the view that looking at post-socialism from the perspective of gender relations is important because it promises to clarify the means by which changes are occurring in politics and economics as broadly understood.[3]

Gender is defined here as the socially and culturally produced ideas about male-female difference, power, and inequality that structure the reproduction of these differences in the institutionalized practices of society. What it means to be a "man" or a "woman," to be "masculine" or "feminine," varies historically. Such cultural categories are formed through everyday interactions that are framed within larger discourses and within specific institutions. We argue that there are reciprocal effects here: Not only do the ideologies and policies that states produce circumscribe the range of possible relations between men and women, but ideas about the differences between men and women shape the ways in which states and economies are imagined, constituted, and legitimated.[4] Drawing on case materials, the chapters provide strong examples of how gender relations both form and are formed by different kinds of states, different kinds of economies, and different forms of political action.

It is important to remember that, while the category of gender is central to social life, gender arrangements are diverse. One of the important lessons of the studies gathered here is that if there ever was a single gender regime of state socialism, it has long been replaced by many different ways of understanding the relations between men and women. Scholars agree, nevertheless, on some of the broad features of socialist gender orders. There was an attempt to erase gender difference (along with ethnic and class difference), to create socially atomized individuals directly dependent on a paternalist state. Yet women in socialism were also sometimes constituted as a corporate category, often becoming a special object of state policy, with ministries or state offices dedicated to what was defined as their concerns. Women's full-time participation in the labor force was dictated by the state, on which women were more directly dependent than they were on individual men. In short, the ideological and social structural arrangements of state socialism produced a markedly different relation between the state, men, and women than is commonly found in classic liberal parliamentary systems, in various kinds of welfare states, and in other political forms. Gender as an organizing principle, and gendered inequality, are present in all these systems, but with profoundly different configurations.

Socialist gender arrangements themselves varied significantly over time and space. Indeed, socialist regimes were often characterized by contradictory goals

---

[3] There is a growing literature on the situation of women in the region. See, for instance, Corrin 1992; Rai et al. 1992; Einhorn 1993; Funk and Mueller 1993; Moghadam 1993; Posadskaya 1994; Rueschemeyer 1994; and Renne 1997. In contrast, the gendering of social processes has so far received little attention.

[4] This definition relies on Joan Scott's (1988) influential essay. We have also been stimulated in thinking about the effects of gender on post-socialist politics by several traditions of feminist work on states, including Pateman 1984; Connell 1990; Gordon 1990; and related work on forms of patriarchy (Walby 1990).

in their policies toward women: They wanted workers as well as mothers, token leaders as well as quiescent typists. While officially supporting equality between men and women, the regimes often countenanced and even produced heated mass media debates about issues such as women's ideal and proper roles, the fundamental importance of "natural difference," the deleterious effects of divorce, or labor-force segregation—such as the feminization of school teaching or of agriculture. These debates revealed the paradoxes and contradictions in official discourses, as well as the pervasive tensions between daily life and governmental images claiming to represent it.[5]

The varying relations between official discourses and the everyday practices of men and women are a central theme of this book. It is our point of departure that in socialism, social actors reacted as much to the representations of themselves in official communications as to the often unforeseen consequences of state policies. The development of more open public spheres since 1989, and the arrival of capitalist mass media, have swept away censorship and "official" discourse in this classic sense. There are now numerous alternative narratives—ways of looking at the world—that vie for popular attention and attempt to achieve persuasiveness and thus domination. Most of the studies in this book describe the way changing images of men and women are ubiquitous in the debates of politicians, social and medical experts, and literary figures, as well as in popular common sense. Yet the apparent plurality and openness of mass media veil the fact that certain issues remain undiscussed, some perspectives suppressed. Furthermore, as many chapters show, the disjuncture between such public discourses and ordinary practices in a multitude of contexts, far from disappearing, now takes quite different shapes and continues to be crucial for understanding change in the region.

Another common theme is the importance of seeing the post-1989 period not simply as a break with the past, but also in part a continuation of it. Thus the gender relations of the socialist period form, in each study, the necessary background against which to understand the present. Furthermore, just as the dramatic ruptures of 1989 do not vitiate the importance of long-term social and cultural continuities, so the relative isolation of East Central Europe in the Cold War period must not prevent us from seeing the crucial role of Western images and global economic institutions in shaping the region's past and present. From Eastern perspectives as from Western ones, the Cold War constructed a world that appeared split into two. Yet, in retrospect it is clear that East and West were intimately intertwined and reciprocally defined each other.[6] As several chapters

---

[5] Among the studies addressing gender relations under state socialism, we have relied on Kligman 1988, 1994, 1998; Gal 1994, 1996; Ferree 1995; Lampland 1995; Verdery 1996; Ferge 1997; Fodor 1997; and Wolchik and Meyer 1985. Many of the works cited in footnote 3 also provide valuable information on the socialist period.

[6] This is as true about recent and historical images of East and West within East Central Europe (Gal 1991), as it is about long-standing imaginings in Western Europe about the East (Wolff 1994; Todorova 1997).

show, understanding the current imagery and presence of the West in East Central Europe is indispensable for explanations of ongoing changes.

Because the combination of conceptual agreement and methodological and disciplinary diversity that characterized this project is unusual, we feel it is important to discuss the project's development in some detail. In planning the work, we envisioned three phases.[7] First, we invited twenty-four specialists from the region as well as from the United States and Britain to a four-day workshop in Italy in 1993, with the aim of detailing the project's conceptual framework. At the end of intensive discussion, participants decided on a number of broad research themes, around which the three parts of this volume are organized: (1) the ways in which discourses and public arguments about reproduction and sexuality are related to issues of women's rights, democracy, civil society, nationalism, and public policy; (2) the processes by which the marketization of the economy has differentially affected men's and women's subjectivities and the everyday relations between the genders; and (3) the ways in which political identities have been created and political mobilization has occurred in the period since 1989. Participants later submitted proposals outlining research projects of their choosing on one or another of these three questions and within the broad conceptual framework established at the workshop.

We also discussed methodologies and sources of data. In contrast to the design of many other comparative projects, ours was not based on standardized research methods or instruments. Rather, scholars used sources of evidence most familiar to them through their own disciplinary training. Thus, legal scholars provided judicial and legislative evidence; ethnographers and sociologists collected qualitative and quantitative materials ranging from in-depth interviews and fieldwork observations to survey data. This diversity of methodologies and types of evidence prevents standardized comparisons, but instead acknowledges that such comparisons will be meaningful only after the basic contours of historical change are sketched. Hence, organizing the project around the use of uniform questionnaires or statistical sampling seemed premature. We began with a more open-ended, exploratory strategy in which methodological diversity is a strength of the project. While this strategy precludes predictive kinds of generalization, it nonetheless enables generalizations about the ways in which gender is a feature of processes of transformation. This methodological diversity allows us to question empirically what may otherwise be assumed about phenomena very much in flux. Similarly, it enables us to examine these phenomena from different perspectives and to thereby grasp different dimensions of what is a complex reality.

With the participants' research proposals in hand, we embarked on a fundraising effort to support the second and third phases of the project. In the course of fundraising, some of the original participants found they were unable to continue in the project; other researchers were invited to join. From the project's

---

[7]The initial meeting that set the agenda for this project was held in June 1993. Funding for the research phase was secured in summer 1994. The manuscript was submitted in June 1998.

inception the goal was to achieve broad coverage of the region and to include scholars from East Central Europe as well as American and Western European scholars with expertise in the region. Yet it proved impossible to recruit participants from every one of the post-socialist states, and equally impossible to include studies of every country. It was not our intent that, of the former Yugoslavia, only Serbia be represented in this volume;[8] however, our own networks did not then extend to Bosnia or Macedonia, for example, and our further efforts to contact possible participants in a timely manner proved futile. This was also true of Albania. We regret that these countries are not discussed in this volume. Although originally there were researchers from Croatia, the Czech Republic, and Slovakia reporting on their own countries, none of them was able to see the project to its conclusion. The Czech and Slovak cases are nevertheless included, analyzed by an American scholar.

Despite changes in the final list of participants, the following countries are represented: Bulgaria, the Czech Republic, Germany, Hungary, Poland, Romania, Slovakia, and Yugoslavia (Serbia). We deliberately chose to include the former German Democratic Republic in this project, just as we decided to exclude the countries of the former Soviet Union. Both these decisions were shaped by conventional Cold War political geography.[9] We reasoned that German unification did not erase the recent past, as has sometimes been assumed by those who no longer include the eastern provinces of Germany in the study of postsocialism. The inclusion of the former Soviet Union would have enlarged the size and scope of the project, which were already daunting from an organizational perspective.

Over the course of a two-year period, participants pursued their research, many in frequent consultation with us.[10] A second workshop was convened in June 1996. Preliminary papers of the research results were circulated in advance, presented at the workshop, and debated. Sessions were structured so that researchers writing on different countries or from different perspectives but engaging the same issues were asked to comment directly on each other's work.

The ensuing discussions were intense and often heated, yet critically constructive. Points of comparison and difference that were not explicit in the papers

---

[8] Unfortunately, the report on Croatia could not be completed without further delay to the overall project. Nevertheless, we thank Rutvica Andrijašević and Petar Teofilović for their translations.

[9] We resisted suggestions from funders to include Ukraine, Russia, the Baltics, and also Vietnam and Cambodia as "transitional" countries. In a similar vein, we are well aware of the important comparisons that should be made between changing gender relations in Eastern and Western Europe and, indeed, of the constructed nature of the East/West divide. We take up these latter comparative issues in the companion volume.

[10] As the list of authors indicates, some of the participants conducted their research with coworkers who were not, however, directly involved in the larger project. We find it interesting that, despite a general focus on gender, the research topics individually formulated by a number of participants reflected the issues concerning the "transition" that dominated research in their respective countries. For example, the Poles raised different aspects of "new gender contracts," the Hungarians (and the American working on Hungary) chose topics relating to economic stratification, and the Serbs focused on violence and nationalism.

emerged through discussion. There were substantive disagreements among participants that at times reflected analytical differences; at others, differences in political positions. These disagreements did not only represent what some have characterized as an East-West divide; there were also lively tensions expressed among participants from the region and within single countries. For example, while some viewed society as comprised of rights-bearing individuals, others thought it to consist of personified collective groups. The discussions proved particularly instructive for us, the project's co-directors, in our daily review of substantive issues in relation to the project's overall conceptual framework and its ongoing refinement. This helped us on the last day, as we met individually with each participant to offer suggestions for gathering additional evidence, sharpening analytical points, and responding to comments raised in the discussion sessions and in informal conversations.[11]

The final phase took almost two years and consisted of a process of rethinking and revision for publication. This process was more demanding than any of us in the project had anticipated. For example, while the new communications technologies make such an international project more feasible, they cannot alleviate misunderstandings, time pressures, and genuine differences of perspective. Among the problems encountered were language and translation difficulties and those generated by different traditions of scholarly exposition. They made all of us more aware of our assumptions about how to frame an argument and about the challenges of writing for international audiences. These conflicts have had their ultimate compensations, especially in the increased clarity they have brought to the conceptual formulations in each chapter. If such a project appears, in retrospect, overly optimistic and its logistic requirements byzantine, we did not anticipate such complexities at the time. Doubtless we were as intoxicated as our East Central European colleagues by the euphoria of the early 1990s, when everything seemed possible. That mood has long been replaced by more sober assessments, which the studies here reflect.

While all of the studies address the overarching themes of the project, each of the book's three different parts engages directly with more focused issues. The chapters in Part One are devoted to discussions of Reproduction as Politics. According to liberal theory, as well as sociological common sense, reproduction is part of the private sphere of domesticity and family, not the public sphere of politics, civil society, and state-formation. Yet, as the chapters in this part show, the politicians, publishers, and media consumers who constituted the first democratic parliaments and public spheres of 1989 indeed discussed such private issues.

This heightened interest in abortion and related issues is best understood with the aid of feminist theory, which has long argued that the private/public distinction is less a straightforward description of social domains than an ideologized dichotomy that produces the appearance of separation between activities that are

---

[11] As part of the cooperative effort, several participants took the initiative to send written comments to others. For this we are grateful.

nonetheless closely linked.[12] The flurry of public discussion about reproduction is an instance of the politics of reproduction, a field that studies the "intersection of politics and the life cycle" (Kligman 1992:364). It takes as its object of study the "seemingly distant power relations [that] shape local reproductive experiences" (Ginsburg and Rapp 1991:313) and investigates how "state policy and ideological control are experienced in everyday life" (Kligman 1998:3). Indeed, the laws, regulations, and administrative machinery that the new states are installing will have long-range repercussions for the ways in which women in East Central Europe give birth and for how people practice contraception, raise their children, and imagine their own and their children's futures.

The politics of reproduction encompasses not only how distant power relations affect individual and local reproductive practices, but also how political process itself is shaped through the discussion and control of reproduction. To highlight the relationship between reproductive issues and political processes, we emphasize how debates about reproduction "reveal the ways in which politics is being reconstituted, contested, and newly legitimated" (Gal 1994:258), in short, how the public discussion of reproduction makes politics.

This is precisely Eleonora Zielińska's point. In her study of the abortion debates, she argues that struggles around the Polish government's attempts to prohibit women's access to abortion are not entirely about abortion. Rather, the debates reveal what is at stake in creating a newly democratic state. They make visible the influence of the Catholic Church on state governance and highlight the many contradictions between the government's stated moral goal of banning abortion and its other policies, for instance, its unwillingness to support better contraception or to stem the wave of abortion tourism. Zielińska draws on parliamentary debates, public opinion polls, and her own participation as a legal advisor to show how political actors—individual politicians as well as groups— are defined and socially constituted in the very process of the abortion debate, as is the relationship between the state and its citizens and the position of Poland within Europe.

Sharon Wolchik looks at the other side of the politics of reproduction: the ways that state policies influence everyday reproductive decisions, in this case in the Czech and Slovak Republics. She starts with the communist era, showing the strong effects of Marxist-Leninist ideology on conceptualizations of women roles, and hence on policies affecting women. Wolchik argues that, more recently, direct interventions designed to influence reproduction have had less impact on reproductive decisions than have the broader changes in social and economic policies characteristic of the post-socialist era. For instance, restriction of social welfare supports, although gradual and partial in the Czech Republic, has never-theless contributed to lowered birthrates. Similarly, political changes allowing a broader range of opinion have contributed to breaking the hegemony of pro-

[12] The feminist literature on public/private is voluminous. See di Leonardo 1991 for a critical review of the anthropological work on this issue. Political theorists have also made important contributions in thinking about this dichotomy, as have social historians. Fraser 1989 and Phillips 1991 provide critical discussions of recent European and American social theoretical contributions.

natalist thinking. In this renewed debate on population, some women and women's groups have entered into public debate for the first time, although nonelite women remain depoliticized.

The next two chapters, both on Germany, complement each other. Although dealing with quite different empirical materials—one on abortion, the other on sterilization—they both illustrate how images of reproduction make politics, as such images are deployed for political purposes, especially in the differential valuation of "East" and "West." Eva Maleck-Lewy and Myra Marx Ferree show the complex ways in which the abortion debate shaped German unification. Through public talk about abortion, political identities based on East-West differences emerged, and the category of "women" became a political identity in the New Federal States. The issues were very differently framed in the old and new states. In the West, the abortion debate revolved around the role of the state and engaged mostly the political parties. In the East, the debate centered on self-determination for women, the meaning of democracy, and what positive lessons could be learned from the G.D.R. experience.

The East-West divide was similarly relevant to panicked discussions about low birthrates and sterilization in the German media. As Irene Dölling, Daphne Hahn, and Sylka Scholz show, eastern women's choice to be sterilized was explained by the media as both a sign and a result of their being "eastern." The media described the women involved and the East itself as chaotic, an impoverished region filled with barren, selfish women who were lazy and incompetent. The West, by contrast, was represented as the modern ideal: orderly, self-reliant, individualistic, family-oriented, self-controlled, and self-aware. Such moral and political allegories were all the more powerful for being veiled and implicit. Yet there was a significant gap between media discourse and everyday practice: The hundreds of eastern women interviewed by Dölling and her co-workers gave many reasons for choosing to be sterilized, none of which matched the media images. The reasons ranged from resistance to the new restrictive abortion legislation, to the wish to limit already ample families, to the attempt to coordinate careers and families in the new context of no state support. Significantly, through their representations, the media managed to hide the ways in which sterilization choices were linked to post-socialist changes.

Part Two, Gender Relations in Everyday Life, moves from reproduction to gender relations broadly defined. The chapters examine the routine ways in which men and women interact with each other in social institutions, for example, in the division of labor in households, in sexual relationships and friendships, and within different sectors of the economy. The characteristic structures of feeling that orient what men and women expect out of life are discussed as well, as are the changes occurring simultaneously in the institutions and routinization of work; in images of masculinity, femininity, and marriage; and in narratives about life course and life strategy. These studies show how gender relations are intertwined with the region's newly expanding market economies, producing different outcomes for men and women, and for images of masculinity and femininity. At the same time, they pose the question of how marketization itself is gendered: how ideas and expectations about men and women are among the factors shaping economic change in the region. Of the many aspects of economic change, several of these studies examine the increasing disparity in incomes and the shift in the ways stratification is ordered and justified. It emerges from these chapters that in the current restratification of society, gender plays a subtle but crucial role, so that examination of gender relations allows us to better understand how the growing disparity happens and what forms it takes.

Mira Marody and Anna Giza-Poleszczuk compare Polish women's magazines of 1974, the height of the socialist period, with those that appeared in 1994, in order to explore the changing images of masculinity and femininity available to Polish men and women. They argue that there is currently a tense relationship between the ideals presented in mass media and the practices of women and men in their everyday lives, a tension that differs from the discrepancy between ideals and practice present during socialism. Not only are there conflicting demands from a variety of institutions (the Church, a new privatized corporate sector, the legal system) but the identification of men and women's "proper" responsibilities has itself become a contentious public issue. In the socialist era women were seen as mothers and workers; gender relations were represented as a compromise between the female "brave victims" responsible for everything and everyone and their men, who acted like dependent "big children." By contrast, the post-1989 male image is of market-oriented, aggressive independence, while femininity consists of ambitious and commodified sexuality. Individual men and women of different ages struggle with these images, sometimes taking advantage of the possibilities they offer, sometimes resisting the new demands.

Definitions of masculinity and femininity are also changing in Hungary. Although motherhood remains central to all the women studied, life history interviews and ethnographic observation allowed Katalin Kovács and Mónika Váradi to find, as well, systematic differentiation among women in their under-standing of femininity. Kovács and Váradi document the linkage between women's gender ideals and emerging class differences between managerial elites, entrepreneurs, and manual industrial workers. Each social stratum showed a distinct and characteristic understanding of femininity and masculinity. Women's cultural ideals and expectations about femininity and gender relations materially shaped their chances for social mobility. For instance, women who demanded emotional support from husbands, and divorced women who refused such support, were utilizing an effective strategy for upward mobility. At the same time, these gender ideals—of partnership and mutual support—were becoming the symbolic markers that, along with other cultural emblems such as consumption patterns, signal and justify the new class status that these women have attained.

Women's work and recent patterns of social mobility are also the themes of Julia Szalai's contribution on "marketization from below," based on a wide range of sociological evidence from Hungary. Szalai argues that activity in the second economy of socialism was everyone's mode of filling familial and societal needs unmet by the socialist state. It simultaneously provided women with valuable experience they could later use in a market economy to develop a much-needed small-scale service sector. Szalai argues that the new capitalist market "liberated" women, allowing their unpaid work in the second economy to be turned into remunerative jobs. Small-scale marketization was thus feminized in Hungary. But women's new jobs have varied a great deal in quality, ranging from well-paid contractual positions to a variety of insecure, unprotected, part-time or day-labor jobs. Those with more education who were better paid gained more advantageous arrangements; others faced unemployment, lack of benefits, and ultimately social marginalization. Thus the expansion of job opportunities for some has been accompanied by ever-increasing social insecurity or polarization.

Finally, Adriana Băban's contribution on sexual and reproductive relations in Romania again takes up the question of female subjectivities, exploring Romanian women's sense of self. She documents the legacy of Ceauşescu's brutal, coercive banning of abortion, a policy that misappropriated women's bodies in the interests of the state. Using in-depth interviews, she describes the effects of this policy on women's intimate lives and their relation to their own bodies, to motherhood, and to their reproductive capacities. Starting with attitudes toward the newly available option of abortion (the "gift" of democracy to women), Baban describes women's continuing alienation from their bodies, their reluctance to communicate about sexuality, and their fears of men and of sexuality itself. She calls for more education about contraception and more responsible use of the new option of legal abortion.

Part Three—Arenas of Political Action: Struggles for Representation—returns, more explicitly, to politics. It has been widely remarked that the number of women representatives in the parliaments of East Central Europe plummeted just as these parliaments gained a measure of real power after 1989. But national parliaments are hardly the only venues for political action. On the contrary, to understand the forms of women's action in the public sphere, an expanded conceptualization of the "political" is required, one that does not focus exclusively on legislatures and party politics, but attends as well to a wider range of forums—regional and local government and nongovernmental organizations (NGOs) such as self-help, charity, health, and women's organizations—in which women in some countries have been relatively more active in the socialist as in the post-socialist periods.[13] The chapters in Part Three map out the emerging pattern of men's and women's participation in an expanded public sphere, distinguishing between "arenas" of action: parliamentary activities, local government, newly forming civil society, international organizations, and mass media.

In each of these arenas, questions of "representation" arise, in both senses of the term. Who speaks on behalf of women, or for issues that concern women particularly, and how are men and women portrayed in debates and discussions? In the studies dealing with reproduction as politics, we have already seen that discussions of abortion, population, and sterilization have contributed to making

[13] Studies by Regulska 1995; Graham and Regulska 1997; Waylen 1994; Szalai 1991; Fuszara 1991; and Molyneux 1994 have analyzed post-socialist politics. See Phillips 1991 on the broader debate about women's political participation. Kligman 1996; Gal 1996; Scott et al. 1997; and Watson 1993 have all discussed the dilemmas of women's prominence in civil society.

politics by defining the identity and legitimacy of political actors (women's groups, individual politicians, "Easterners" vs. "Westerners"). Here we turn to related questions: How is the post-socialist political process itself shaped by gender? How do ideas about gender affect political inclusion and exclusion?

Małgorzata Fuszara notes that parliaments are now the major law-making and policy-making organs in the region. Whatever other forms of action are available to women, their continued exclusion from formal, institutional politics remains a serious dilemma. Contrary to the arguments of male politicians, right-wing groups, and even some sociological surveys, women's absence from formal politics in Poland has not been due to women's own preference for the home, nor due to women's general view that "men are better at politics." Opinion polls have shown that many women want to be involved in formal politics, are educated enough to do so, and are willing to vote for female politicians, including those who raise issues most interesting to women, issues that have been absent from platforms and party programs. Fuszara argues that women's low participation has been due to men's dominance in party politics, especially in the wheeling and dealing that leads to nominations. Men in such positions have ignored the importance of the women's vote and have not allowed female candidates to represent women's issues, which therefore have been absent from platforms and party programs.

Joanna Goven also focuses on a parliament—not the gender of its members but the gender bias of its debates. In the face of budget deficits and pressures from the World Bank to reduce social spending, the socialist-led Hungarian Parliament of 1994–1998 argued about the proper form of a new family leave policy. Although the language of rights was pervasive, "women's rights" (as opposed to those of "mothers" or "families") were nowhere mentioned or considered, which in turn allowed Parliament to ignore the need for extra-domestic daycare. The local discourse on gender constrained the way in which international pressure was translated into policy. More generally, Goven shows how ideas about men and women shaped a policy process, which in turn defined what would count as societal needs. This gendered policy process also reconstructed citizenship: Despite newly expanded political rights, only some categories of people were understood to be deserving of entitlements, support, and dispensations; others were ignored or defined as undeserving.

As we turn from parliaments to the NGOs of what has been termed "civil society," it is important to note a historical shift in the region. Before 1989, when parliaments were weak and had relatively large numbers of women members, participation in civil society meant participation in secondary economic activities or in dissident activities. Prominent dissidents were mostly men, and it was they who articulated the meanings of civil society and of anti-politics against the state. Women were primarily support personnel, crucial but less visible and less acknowledged. "Anti-political" agendas focused on questions of universal human rights and citizenship. As parliaments have come to dominate the public sphere, quite different gender codings have emerged. The overwhelming maleness of parliaments (in membership and discourse) now contrasts with the relatively greater presence of women—and women's issues—in the nongovernmental organizations that dominate the weak civil societies of the region.[14]

Laura Grunberg (on Romania), Krassimira Daskalova (on Bulgaria), and Zorica Mršević (on Yugoslavia) provide richly detailed chapters about the diversity, nature, and operational problems of such organizations. In Romania, women comprise over half of NGO participants, but Grunberg's surveys and interviews with leaders of women's NGOs show the organizations to be largely ineffective. Due to the legacy of communism these NGOs have been overly oriented toward the state, responding to its agendas while unsure about their own. The relative lack of domestic financial support has compelled them to seek funding from international agencies, which have often set agendas irrelevant to local circumstances. The language of international agencies has rarely translated well into the everyday lives and problems of Romanian women. Furthermore, as Daskalova also shows for Bulgaria, despite the apparent diversity of women's NGOs, their claims about women's needs have been all alike and, sadly, match conservative, state-defined views about motherhood and about women as subordinate objects of social protection. Daskalova shows how the conditions of women in Bulgaria, as well as the discourses about them, constrain the possibilities of action for women's NGOs in Bulgaria.

But not all women's NGOs fit this mold. The Belgrade hotline against domestic violence, like many other women's NGOs, was created through the efforts of feminists from the former Yugoslavia and supported by foreign money, in this case small infusions of funds from Western friends and colleagues. But quite unlike most Bulgarian and Romanian women's NGOs, the Belgrade hotline was oriented to local problems, effective in action, and independent in formulating policies. At a time when war in the Balkans gained even international attention, domestic violence was still unrecognized as a social problem inside Yugoslavia. The women who organized the hotline spoke out against both. They helped hundreds of women struggle against male bias in law courts, as well as among police, family, and medical personnel. The hotline's most important accomplishment, however, was to introduce the issue of domestic violence into public discussion through the mass media. They helped redefine it from an accepted practice to a crime and substantially increased public awareness of it.

The Belgrade hotline's consciousness-raising activities provide one example of the mass media as an arena of political action. The German debates about reproduction, discussed in Part One, provide another. More complex is the case discussed by Jasmina Lukić, who shows how regime-controlled newspapers and magazines helped foment the Yugoslav war and naturalize the break-up of federated Yugoslavia by drawing on accepted images of mythic mothers and their

---

[14]We put "civil society" in quotes because it has become more of an ideologized phrase than an analytical category. We also note that even oppositional politics has become a morally tainted form of action that people deeply distrust in many of the countries of the region, although local action often seems more acceptable. But there is much variation in this. Even within the studies in this volume, Fuszara and Zielińska report relatively high interest and participation in politics, as do Lukić and Mršević. In contrast, both Grunberg and Daskalova report widespread distrust and condemnation.

patriotic brave sons. The independent press presented opposing opinions toward the war and often undermined nationalistic boundaries established by Serbian leaders. Nevertheless, the independent press, Lukić argues, also relied on traditional images of women to construct and symbolize what it considered to be a better world. Thus, both the independents' and the nationalists' agendas were made more persuasive by reliance on implicit and deeply accepted gender stereotypes. Only the publications of the small feminist organizations produced a more fundamental critique: They rejected both the war and the gender stereotypes that allowed it to be naturalized.

Read in light of each other, the chapters in Part Three show how different arenas of political action have come to be coded as male or female. Ideas about gender difference, in each of these arenas, can shape what is defined as societal needs, societal goals, and the requirements and entitlements of proper citizenship. Furthermore, the case of Belgrade newspapers provides an extended example of a process evident in the German, Polish, and Romanian cases as well: Exclusionary politics are often articulated through ideas about gender. Such metaphorical use of gender stereotypes to talk about other matters strengthens the force of the stereotypes themselves.

In concluding this introduction, we return to the impulse that initiated the project itself. The book covers a broad range of topics, providing much detailed evidence about women's and men's new circumstances in post-socialism.[15] We have highlighted a number of common patterns and regularities; the chapters themselves provide additional information that merits further comparative attention. More importantly, all the studies in our collaborative project have explored the complex relationship between ideas and practices of gender on the one hand and broad political-economic change on the other.

First, the studies show that varying state ideologies and policies, and the diverse incentives of market economies, differentially circumscribe the life possibilities for men and women and constrain relations between them. State policies and market forces reach far into intimate life and shape gendered subjectivities.

Equally noteworthy are the inverse effects we have documented. Discourses of gender influence the ways in which states and markets are imagined and constituted. In Germany, for instance, public discussions of sterilization and abortion implicitly legitimated western forms of political practice as orderly and rational, while defining anything eastern as chaotic and backward. Or again, assumptions about gender differences have had an impact on the formulation of social policies in Hungary, the Czech and Slovak Republics, and Poland, and through such policies have affected the reconstruction of citizenship. Economic changes are also shaped by cultural ideals about male–female relations. For instance, expectations about men's role in marriage have contributed to women's social mobility in Hungary, and the emotionally supportive marriage is becoming one of the cultural emblems of the new entrepreneurial class. Finally, several

---

[15] Nonetheless we do not address all important issues. For instance, although homosexual practices, prostitution, and international trafficking in women, children, and men are gaining public attention in the region after decades of silence, these issues are only touched upon.

chapters have documented how assumptions about gender difference—in Poland, Romania, Bulgaria, and Serbia—have contributed to a division of political labor in which men dominate in national-level politics while women, if active, participate in NGOs and local organizations. In sum, the practices of gender, and concomitant ideas about the differences between men and women, have fundamentally shaped the broad social changes that have followed the collapse of communism.

BIBLIOGRAPHY

Connell, R.W.
  1990   The State, Gender and Sexual Politics. Theory and Society 19:507–544.
Corrin, Chris, ed.
  1992   "Superwoman" and the Double Burden: Women's Experience of Change in Central and Eastern Europe and the Former Soviet Union. Toronto: Second Story Press.
di Leonardo, Micaela, ed.
  1991   Introduction. *In* Gender at the Crossroads of Knowledge: Feminist Anthropology in the Postmodern Era. Pp. 1–50. Berkeley: University of California Press.
Einhorn, Barbara
  1993   Cinderella Goes to Market: Citizenship, Gender, and Women's Movements in East Central Europe. London: Verso.
Ferge, Zsuzsa
  1997   Women and Social Transformation in Central-Eastern Europe: The "Old Left" and the "New Right." Czech Sociological Review 5(2):159–178.
Ferree, Myra Marx
  1995   Patriarchies and Feminisms: Two Women's Movements in Post-Unification Germany. Social Politics (Spring):10–24.
Fodor, Eva
  1997   Power, Patriarchy, and Paternalism: An Examination of the Gendered Nature of State Socialist Authority. Ph.D. thesis, University of California, Los Angeles.
Fraser, Nancy
  1989   What's Critical about Critical Theory? The Case of Habermas and Gender. *In* Unruly Practices: Power, Discourse, and Gender in Contemporary Social Theory. N. Fraser, ed. Pp. 113–143. Minneapolis: University of Minnesota Press.
  1997   Rethinking the Public Sphere: A Contribution to the Critique of Actually Existing Democracy. *In* Justice Interruptus: Critical Reflections on the "Postsocialist" Condition. N. Fraser, ed. Pp. 69–98. New York: Routledge.
Funk, Nanette and Magda Mueller, eds.
  1993   Gender Politics and Post-Communism: Reflections from Eastern Europe and the Former Soviet Union. New York: Routledge.
Fuszara, Małgorzata
  1991   Legal Regulation of Abortion in Poland. Signs 17(1):117–128.
Gal, Susan
  1991   Bartok's Funeral: Representations of Europe in Hungarian Political Rhetoric. American Ethnologist 18:440–458.

1994   Gender in the Post-Socialist Transition: The Abortion Debate in Hungary. East European Politics and Societies 8(2):256–287.

1996   Feminism and Civil Society. *In* Transitions, Environments, Translations: Feminisms in International Politics. J. Scott, C. Kaplan and D. Keates, eds. Pp. 30–45. New York: Routledge.

Ginsburg, Faye and Rayna Rapp
1991   The Politics of Reproduction. Annual Review of Anthropology 20:311–345.

Ginsburg, Faye and Rayna Rapp, eds.
1995   Conceiving the New World Order: The Global Politics of Reproduction. Berkeley: University of California Press.

Gordon, Linda, ed.
1990   Women, the State, and Welfare. Madison: University of Wisconsin Press.

Goven, Joanna
1993   Gender Politics in Hungary: Autonomy and Antifeminism. *In* Gender Politics and Post-Communism: Reflections from Eastern Europe and the Former Societ Union. N. Funk and M. Mueller, eds. Pp. 224–240. New York: Routledge.

Graham, Ann and Joanna Regulska
1997   Expanding Political Space for Women in Poland: An Analysis of Three Communities. Communist and Post-Communist Studies 30:65–82.

Kligman, Gail
1988   The Wedding of the Dead: Ritual, Poetics, and Popular Culture in Transylvania. Berkeley: University of California Press.

1992   The Politics of Reproduction in Ceauşescu's Romania. East European Politics and Societies 6(3):364–418.

1994   The Social Legacy of Communism: Women, Children and the Feminization of Poverty. *In* The Social Legacy of Communism. J. Millar and S. Wolchik, eds. Pp. 252–270. Woodrow Wilson Center Series. New York: Cambridge University Press.

1996   Women and the Negotiation of Identity in Post-Communist Eastern Europe. *In* Identities in Transition: Russia and Eastern Europe after Communism. V. Bonnell, ed. Pp. 68–91. Berkeley International and Area Studies, University of California.

1998   The Politics of Duplicity: Controlling Reproduction in Ceauşescu's Romania. Berkeley: University of California Press.

Lampland, Martha
1995   The Object of Labor: The Commodification of Labor in Hungary. Chicago: University of Chicago Press.

Marody, Mira
1993   Why I Am Not a Feminist: Some Remarks on the Problem of Gender Identity in the United States and Poland. Social Research 60(4):853–864.

Moghadam, Valentine, ed.
1993   Democratic Reform and the Position of Women in Transitional Economies. Oxford: Clarendon Press.

Molyneux, Maxine
1994   Women's Rights and the International Context: Some Reflections on Post Communist States. Millennium: Journal of International Studies 23(2):287–313.

Pateman, Carole
  1988   The Sexual Contract. Stanford, CA: Stanford University Press.
Phillips, Anne
  1991   Engendering Democracy. University Park, PA: Pennsylvania State University Press.
Posadskaya, Anastasia, ed.
  1994   Women in Russia: A New Era of Russian Feminism. London: Verso.
Rai, Shirin with Hilary Pilkington and Annie Phizacklea, eds.
  1992   Women in the Face of Change: The Soviet Union, Eastern Europe, and China. New York: Routledge.
Regulska, Joanna
  1995   Women's Participation in Political and Public Life. Background Document EG/EGM 95, #10. Strasbourg: The Council of Europe.
Renne, Tanya, ed.
  1997   Ana's Land: Sisterhood in Eastern Europe. Boulder, CO: Westview.
Róna-Tas, Akos
  1998   Path-Dependence and Capital Theory: Sociology of the Post-Communist Economic Transformation. East European Politics and Societies 12(1):107–131.
Rueschemeyer, Marilyn, ed.
  1994   Women in the Politics of Post-Communist Eastern Europe. Armonk, NY: M.E.Sharpe.
Scott, Joan
  1988   Gender and the Politics of History. New York: Columbia University Press.
Scott, Joan with Cora Kaplan and Debra Keats, eds.
  1997   Transitions, Environments, Translations: Feminisms in International Politics. New York: Routledge.
Szalai, Julia
  1991   Some Aspects of the Changing Situation of Women in Hungary. Signs 17:152–170.
Todorova, Maria
  1997   Imagining the Balkans. New York: Oxford University Press.
Verdery, Katherine
  1996   What Was Socialism, and What Comes Next? Princeton, NJ: Princeton University Press.
Walby, Sylvia
  1990   Theorizing Patriarchy. Oxford: Blackwell.
Watson, Peggy
  1993   The Rise of Masculinism in Eastern Europe. New Left Review 198:71–82.
Waylen, Georgina
  1994   Women and Democratization: Conceptualizing Gender Relations in Transition Politics. World Politics 46:327–354.
Wolchik, Sharon L. and Alfred G. Meyer, eds.
  1985   Women, State, and Party in Eastern Europe. Durham, NC: Duke University Press.
Wolff, Larry
  1994   Inventing Eastern Europe: The Map of Civilization on the Mind of Enlightenment. Stanford: Stanford University Press.

PART ONE

Reproduction as Politics

CHAPTER 1

Between Ideology, Politics, and Common Sense: The Discourse of Reproductive Rights in Poland

ELEONORA ZIELIŃSKA

OF THE PARLIAMENTARY STRUGGLES that have dominated public life in the independent Republic of Poland since 1989, none has been more divisive than the "abortion battle." The rhythm and shifts of the abortion debate have closely followed major political changes and can be charted according to the rise and fall of three presidents, four Parliaments, and eight governments. Until 1993, the "post-Solidarity" political parties, named after the 1980s anti-communist opposition, held power. After the 1993 parliamentary elections, the "post-communist" parties controlled parliament. In September 1997, the post-Solidarity parties again assumed power. During these years, abortion was delegalized, then liberalized, and is once again headed for restriction.[1] To state the obvious, legal abortion is an issue especially susceptible to politicization; in post-communist Poland this has been the norm.

Issues associated with procreation and women's reproductive rights, particularly the permissibility of abortion, belong to a set of concerns that remain historically and comparatively vital and that often become the topic of impassioned public debate at times of crisis or societal transformation. Generally speaking, periods of intense public attention to reproductive issues precede legislative changes.[2]

I express special gratitude to Gail Kligman for her generous and competent contributions to the final preparation of my text.

[1] Editors' note: At the time this was written, demands to restrict Poland's liberal abortion law were growing. In December 1997, Parliament approved a ruling by the Constitutional Tribunal that invalidated the most recent amendments and further restricted Poland's abortion laws.

[2] During the French Revolution, the code passed in 1791 by the Constituent Assembly granted a woman immunity if she aborted a pregnancy (Code Penal de 1791, part 2, title II, section 1, art.17). Tendencies toward decriminalization were also present in Russia during the October Revolution (see Postanovlienije Narodnowo Komisariata Zdrowohranienija i Justicji, sec. 8 XI, no. 90, published in *Sbornik Ukazow RSFSR* 1920:471). The same was true in Spain during the period of revolutionary struggle; in 1936, abortion during the first trimester was legalized in Catalonia (see Decret pel qual es regulada la inruptio artficial de l'embaras, Diari Oficial, sec. 1, no. 9, published in *Generalitat de Catalunya* 1937:114–115). The most dramatic example is Romania, where in December 1989, almost the day after the Ceauşescu regime was overthrown, the extremely repressive abortion legislation was repealed (Order no. 605 of the Minister of Health, Dec. 27, 1989; see also Kligman 1998). A similarly liberal law was passed in Bulgaria in 1990 (Ministry of Health and Social Care, Decree no. 2, February 1, 1990; see the English translation in *International Digest of Health Legislation* [hereafter *IDHL*] 1990, 41[4]:624).

Throughout history, the liberalization of abortion laws has reflected a popular sentiment that the prohibition of abortion is oppressive, discriminatory, and in violation of women's control of their own fertility. In other former Soviet Bloc countries—Hungary and Lithuania, for example—campaigns to restrict abortion rights have failed. Poland is a striking exception. While the recriminalization of abortion has been variously motivated, first and foremost has been the conviction, expressed by many politicians, that abortion must be stopped and that banning it is the most effective way to do this. Several moral, demographic, and practical concerns underlie this belief (e.g., the need to protect conceived life, the need for increased population growth, and the need to resolve transition-related labor force problems by redomesticating women—that is, by sending them "back to the home and children").

Some politicians claim that a majority among Polish society wants a ban on abortion (there is little evidence, however, to support this claim). When introducing more restrictive legislation, parliamentarians have invoked this argument to demonstrate their "responsiveness" to voter demands. Indeed, putting abortion on the parliamentary agenda may be instrumental in forging a politician's public persona. The way in which a politician handles this issue may reveal his or her vulnerability to external influences, most notably to the Catholic Church; alternatively, it may reflect a propensity for conformism or a determination to participate in public life and political maneuvering.

Still others assume that the constant presence of abortion on the parliamentary agenda has little to do with abortion itself. They argue that debates about abortion serve other ends. For example, because abortion provokes an emotional response, it is viewed as a surrogate topic by which attention can be drawn away from the enduring socioeconomic problems generated by the transition.[3] Similarly, abortion has become a "symbolic test, a focus of the many dilemmas of supporters of personal freedoms and supporters of traditional norms" (Sadurski 1993). The abortion controversy ignites other sociopolitical disagreements about, for example, the role of the Catholic Church in the polity and society, the character of demographic and social policies, sexual education, contraception, healthcare, and the national budget (Pawlak 1991:128). It also raises fundamental questions about the role of women in society, the principle (and understanding) of gender equality, and the way women's rights, including reproductive rights, are situated in the hierarchy of socially accepted values. From this perspective, the abortion debate represents a coded discourse that reflects fundamental concerns, including the shape of the state itself, the state's obligations to society (and vice versa), the rule of law, and, last but certainly not least, the scope of the protection of civil rights and fundamental freedoms. In short, the abortion debates are both an element of and a means for shaping politics (Gal 1994:285). Because abortion focuses attention on crucial issues of human and societal reproduction, scholars

---

[3] This process of symbolic substitution also works in relation to other highly charged legislative endeavors such as the official name or symbols of state or legal responses to "coming to terms" and "settling scores" with the communist past.

may view the debate as a litmus test of the kind of democracy being institutionalized in Poland.

In this chapter, I analyze abortion and abortion debates as a way to explore
the development, and gradual institutionalization, of democratic practices in the
Republic of Poland. To this end, I first review Poland's major abortion legislation
through the summer of 1997, emphasizing the post-1989 parliamentary debates.
I then present the key actors in these debates. To illuminate the context in which
rhetorical battles and legislative changes have unfolded since the collapse of
communism, I examine recent demographic trends and society's attitudes toward
abortion and related practices. Finally, I discuss the implications of recriminalizing abortion for Polish society and for Poland's evolving democracy.

I have based my research on an analysis of parliamentary documents, reports
of governmental and nongovernmental organizations regarding the application
of the anti-abortion law, press reports, and participant observation in my capacity
as an expert on legislative matters. I have also drawn data from official statistics
and from public opinion polls on the legal availability of abortion and usage
of contraception.

POLAND'S ABORTION LEGISLATION: PAST AND PRESENT

Poland has traditionally had liberal abortion legislation.[4] In 1932, after long and
heated discussions dominated by physicians, criminologists, and journalists, the
idea that the fetus was a human being who thus deserved complete protection
was abandoned in Poland's penal legislation, and women were guaranteed the
right to abortion for medical and legal reasons (that is, rape and incest; see
Peiper 1933:628). After World War II and until 1956, despite the political
transformation of Poland, these provisions remained unchanged. In 1955, abortion was liberalized in the Soviet Union as part of the post-Stalinist liberalization
of social and political life; voices calling for further liberalization were soon
heard in Poland as well (see Wolińska 1962:12–15). In 1956, a new law was
introduced, which, in addition to maintaining medical and legal indications for
abortion, included a woman's difficult living conditions as legitimate cause for
terminating a pregnancy, provided that a physician performed the abortion. The
1956 law decriminalized self-induced abortion and abolished penalties for women
seeking clandestine abortions.[5]

---

[4] The 1818 Penal Code reflected the relatively humanitarian approach to abortion characteristic
of the Enlightenment. Abortion was considered a crime only if it was performed without the woman's
consent and was punishable by three to ten years' imprisonment (art. 130). In other cases, abortion,
even if self-induced, qualified as a misdemeanor and was punishable by one to three years at a
detention house (art. 323).

[5] Regarding the 1932 Penal Code, see articles 231–234. The draft had included legitimate social
factors described as "the difficult economic situation of a woman." Regarding 1956, see Law no. 61,
of April 27, 1956, determining the conditions under which termination of pregnancy is permissible.
Dziennik Ustaw Polskiej Rzeczypospolitej Ludowej (*Journal of Laws,* hereafter Dz. U.) 1956, no. 12;

Over the next twenty years, abortion legislation was revisited, usually in the context of demographic policy. However, in contrast to developments in other socialist countries, Poland's abortion law did not change (see Kligman 1998). The 1969 Penal Code reaffirmed the 1956 abortion regulations, meaning that the state's pro-natalist policy was managed primarily through propaganda measures and economic incentives. A constitutional provision calling for special protection of motherhood was introduced, and maternal benefits were increased.[6]

With the advent of Solidarity in 1980, the Polish anti-abortion movement emerged from inside church walls and mounted a public campaign. Reacting to these developments, the Minister of Health and Social Welfare changed the executive regulation, making gynecologists-obstetricians the exclusive providers of abortion.[7] The ministerial instruction issued in 1981 made access to abortion more complicated and required doctors to provide contraceptive counseling.[8] However, with the imposition of martial law in December 1981—an act that harkened back to the Stalinist era—public debate on abortion and other critical issues ceased.

In 1989, while Poland was still under communist rule, seventy-eight deputies introduced the first anti-abortion bill in the Sejm (then the one body equivalent to today's lower chamber in the Polish Parliament; see *Tygodnik Powszechny* 1989, no. 10). The draft law on "the legal protection of the unborn from the moment of conception" banned abortion in all circumstances and mandated three years' imprisonment for both the woman and the provider. The proposed law provoked massive public debate. Faced with protests and street demonstrations shortly before the crucial June 4, 1989, elections, the communist Parliament decided to shelve the anti-abortion law (Zielińska 1990:64–69).

The Post-1989 Transition

Before turning to the tumultuous post-1989 history of abortion legislation, mention should be made of the deeply rooted prejudices against women in Polish society, the related gender stereotypes that have surfaced during the first eight years of transition, and the broad features of the abortion debate itself. Women are perceived as sex objects or as biologically determined creatures whose primary

English translation in *IDHL* 1958, 9(2):319. Passage of the abortion law was aided by a comparatively good demographic situation, on the one hand, and the difficult living conditions of a considerable number of Poland's inhabitants, on the other. Furthermore, the growing demand for labor necessitated an increase in the number of female wage laborers, which, in turn, was facilitated by liberalized abortion. See Zielińska 1987:263–267.

[6] See Law no. 94 of April 19, 1969, published in Dz. U. 1969, no. 13; English translation in *IDHL* 1971, 22(4):971; the constitutional amendment (Law no. 36 of February 16, 1976; published in Dz. U. 1976, no. 7) concerned article 5, item 7 and article 78, item 1 of the Polish Constitution; on benefits, see Law no. 188 of December 17, 1974; published in Dz. U. 1975, no. 34.

[7] Law no. 110; published in Dz. U. 1980, no. 26.

[8] Instruction no. 11/810 of September 1981 of the Ministers of Health, Transport, National Defense and Internal Affairs on the termination of pregnancy in social health service establishments (published in *Dziennik Urzędowy Ministerstwa Zdrowia i Opieki Społecznej* 1981, no. 11).

contributions to society are as mothers and wives. A moral double standard functions with respect to male and female sexual behavior. The latter are expected either to be virgins or wives and mothers.

According to sociological studies, the abortion debate has its own vocabulary and rules of discourse. The categories invoked in these discussions articulate one set of values in self-righteous opposition to all others, most notably, pro-life versus pro-choice values. (Although pro-life advocates were the first to resort to this rhetorical style, those supporting abortion have also adopted it, if to a lesser extent.) Such categorical polarization reflects two different worlds in which conflicting semantic codes are used and in which abortion is differently understood. Each "side" characterizes its own positions as good, correct, and based on objective and irrefutable knowledge, while denouncing their opponents' views as bad, wrong, and based on subjective and questionable assumptions. Pro-life proponents invoke the symbolic force of totalitarianism, Hitlerism, Stalinism, and the like to argue against liberalized abortion, while pro-choice supporters castigate their foes as defenders of traditionalism, fanaticism, "Iranianism," and totalitarianism as well. Other discursive strategies used by all participants include exclusion of inconvenient topics, selective representation of issues, and denial or minimization of an issue's existence or importance. Such tactics have led to the emotional representation of this issue, which in turn has both fostered group solidarity and hindered intergroup communication (see Matuchniak-Krasuska 1991:101). Under such conditions, consensus has become less feasible. Instead, the terms of debate have raised questions about Parliament's real aims and also about whether the abortion debate might serve ends other than providing a reasonable solution to the problem of abortion in Poland.

From early on, those who supported the anti-abortion law defined the moral framework of all relevant parliamentary debate. To these opponents of abortion, any law that permitted "murder" was morally unacceptable. Thus, with supporters of liberalization ipso facto construed as immoral, the chances for constructive discussion were automatically obviated. Even though both sides agreed that abortion is evil, that it should not be used as a means of fertility control, and that steps should be taken to limit its frequency so as to better protect the unborn, the protagonists were unable to compromise on their fundamental differences regarding how best to protect the unborn.

Proponents of the ban have invariably resorted to arguments about the unborn child's inalienable right to life and the moral norm of "Thou shalt not kill" (yet these same advocates of a fetus's rights neglect women's rights altogether). They also argue that the repeal of the 1956 law would constitute an important step toward de-communization and de-Stalinization and would bring the Polish legal system into conformity with Christian values. Supporters of the anti-abortion law denounce their opponents for sponsoring parliamentary initiatives that they deem dangerous to society's moral fiber. They condemn, for instance, what they see as "express" divorces, the "glorification" of sexual "deviation," the demoralization of young people through sex education, and the undermining of parental rights with respect to their children's upbringing (see *Trybuna*, April 11, 1996).

Those opposed to recriminalizing abortion have argued that the proposed restrictions will jeopardize Poland's admission to the European Union; they note, for example, that no similar legislation exists elsewhere today except in Ireland (see *Kultura* no. 15, 1989, Kubicki interview). They have also underscored the basic discrimination against women that the law would create,[9] as well as the health risks that would certainly result if women were compelled to seek unsafe abortions. Those opposing the anti-abortion proposal have also countered with assertions that the "rights" of the fetus are equal to those of a person. Insisting that no empirical evidence exists to support this claim, they argue that it merely expresses a moral belief. They also note that the bill's authors were guilty of wishful or magical thinking, inasmuch as the latter treated the law as if it were a magic spell that would make an undesirable social phenomenon simply disappear. Yet as the history of abortion makes clear, banning abortion does not eradicate its practice.

Moreover, opponents of the anti-abortion proposal(s) have questioned the legitimacy of the Catholic Church's attempts to legislate what amounts to its own ideology.[10] Indeed, they argue that if current trends continue, Poland may become a theocratic state. They caution that a ban on abortion would likely be accompanied by initiatives that would undermine the state's ideological neutrality. Notably, these initiatives could include policies requiring religious education in public schools, national conformity with "Christian values" in the educational system as well as radio and television media, or the elimination of practices deemed "contrary" to Catholic teaching, such as artificial (or what is generally referred to as "modern") contraception, new reproductive technologies, civil marriage, and divorce—all of which point to the breaching of boundaries between church and state.

1989–1993

Several months after the 1989 elections, in which Solidarity was victorious, the anti-abortion campaign started anew. The Episcopate Family Council urged Parliament to continue work on the anti-abortion bill, reintroduced by thirty-seven senators in December 1989. A modified version passed in the Senate in September 1990,[11] but its supporters failed to get it accepted in the Sejm before the new elections of October 1991 (see also Szawarski 1990:4).

While the debates in Parliament raged on, access to abortion was in fact being restricted by the "one small step at a time" method. In April 1990, the Minister

[9] It should be mentioned that the abortion debate has exposed the patronizing attitude of male deputies and senators toward women, as well as their consistent tendency to treat women instrumentally. See Fuszara 1994:64. She quotes a senator who admonished women, "Saying that my womb is my business is very inelegant and ladies don't talk that way."

[10] Even proponents of the unconditional protection of life voiced reservations about the proposed legislation and suggested a *vacatio legis* of up to six years to bring up a new generation of women in a moral climate unfavorable to abortion. See Safjan 1989:48.

[11] Senate's draft, Parliamentary print no. 553. The final draft was approved in April 1991 by the Extraordinary Parliamentary Commission. See *Gazeta Wyborcza*, April 25, 1991.

of Health and Social Welfare issued a new executive regulation (Law no. 178 of April 30, 1990; published in Dz. U. 1990, no. 29) requiring that a woman consult three physicians and a psychologist before she could terminate a pregnancy. Also introduced were a twelve-week limit for legal abortion due to a woman's difficult living conditions and a conscience clause for physicians. The latter enabled a physician to refuse to perform or assist an abortion. In that same year, 1990, the Ministry of Health instituted payment for the costs of an abortion and hospitalization in a state hospital; these expenses had previously been covered by insurance (see Płakwicz and Zielińska 1994:189).

Challenging the regulation before the Constitutional Tribunal, the Commissioner for Civic Rights argued that the Ministry did not have the authority to regulate these matters because the latter were clearly "reserved" for an act of Parliament. The Tribunal nonetheless upheld the regulation on grounds that a physician's right to refuse could be interpreted according to the constitutional principle of freedom of conscience, inasmuch as the contested regulation merely repeated an existing norm in the legal system. Although the Tribunal admitted that such repetition was improper, it ruled that it was not unconstitutional as no new legal norm had been established.[12]

The Tribunal expressed another controversial opinion: It held that a physician's judgment that continuation of a pregnancy might endanger a patient's life or health should, in ethical terms, be considered tantamount to performing an abortion. Moreover, the Tribunal stressed that women in Poland never had the right to abortion. Observing that the 1956 law only spelled out conditions for the permissibility of abortion in the interest of protecting women's health, the Tribunal concluded that the contested ministerial regulation did not violate women's rights.[13] A Ministry of Health commentary stated that "a woman has full freedom to decide about her motherhood only to prevent a pregnancy. Once conception has taken place, the will of the woman ceases to be an exclusive or decisive factor in regard to termination of pregnancy" (Krotkiewska 1956:8).

These first steps toward restricting access to abortion were followed by others. On December 14, 1991, the National Convention of Physicians, the highest self-governing body of the medical profession, approved a new Code of Medical Ethics. Physicians were forbidden to perform abortions for any reason other than risk to the woman's life or health or if the pregnancy resulted from a criminal offense.[14] Physicians and lawyers alike criticized the new code. Lawyers emphasized that the 1956 law permitted abortion for social reasons or in the event of

[12] See Decision of the Constitutional Tribunal of January 15, 1991 (*Ustawa* [law; hereafter U.] 8/90). Careful analysis of the norms under question suggests that this claim is not true. For additional information, see Garlicki 1994:15.

[13] For a critique of this ruling, see Zielińska 1991:116.

[14] This went into effect on May 3, 1992. Article 38 of the Code of Medical Ethics allows that prenatal diagnostic procedures may be carried out only where the associated risk to the fetus or the woman is not disproportionate to the anticipated benefits. "The identification of developmental abnormalities or genetic disorders does not constitute a basis for termination of pregnancy." The code also obligated a physician to protect the life and health of a human being from the moment

fetal deformity. Moreover, they argued that a situation should not be created in which a physician, who was obeying the law, could be brought before the medical board for violating its own code of ethics and then deprived of his or her license to practice medicine.[15]

The Commissioner for Civic Rights appealed to the Constitutional Tribunal for review of these sections of the Code of Medical Ethics, observing that while the code was addressed specifically to physicians, it necessarily affected women's legal access to abortion. The Commissioner stressed that since physicians also had the exclusive right to perform legal abortions, the ban imposed on medical personnel thus deprived women of the possibility of obtaining a legal and safe abortion in cases of difficult living conditions or fetal malformations.

On October 7, 1992, the Tribunal sidestepped the question of whether the abortion provisions of the ethics code were contrary to law, holding that the challenged norms were of a purely ethical character and that its own competence to review regulations was confined to provisions containing legal norms. Hence, it upheld the code's provisions, recommending that Parliament address the apparent inconsistencies between the relevant legislation and the new provisions (see U. 17/92; Zielińska 1992:25). Although the majority opinion was criticized in four dissenting opinions as well as by many independent experts, it had by then become clear that the Constitutional Tribunal supported anti-abortion measures, even at the expense of its professional reputation. As a result of this ruling, physicians were faced with a difficult dilemma: Should they follow the 1956 law still in force or the provisions of the Code of Medical Ethics? In view of this murky legal situation, it is not surprising that many physicians, fearing professional reprisals, refused to perform abortions, regardless of their legality.

Deeming this circumstance to be incompatible with the newly introduced constitutional provision declaring Poland to be a "democratic state of the rule of the law respecting the principles of social justice," the Commissioner for Civic Rights again addressed the Tribunal. In March 1993 the Tribunal held that a physician who performed an abortion in conformity with the law but in violation of the applicable provisions of the Code of Medical Ethics cannot be subjected to disciplinary action by the chamber of physicians. However, the practical implication of this ruling was virtually nil because the regulations of the Code of Medical Ethics concerning abortion were changed at the next National Convention of Physicians.[16]

---

of conception and granted the right to refuse to perform artificial fertilization procedures. Code of Medical Ethics, December 13, 1991; published in English in *Kennedy Institute of Ethics Journal* 1993, 2(4):371–383.

[15] *Gazeta Wyborcza*, December 18, 1991. For a comparative discussion of the double bind in which physicians were potentially placed, see Kligman 1994 and 1998 on this issue in Ceauşescu's Romania.

[16] See judgment of March 17, 1993 (*Wyrok* [verdict; hereafter W.] 16/92), published in Dz. U. 1993, no. 23, item 103; and the Code of Medical Ethics, December 13, 1991, revised December 14, 1993. The general clause concerning a physician's obligation to protect life and health dropped the phrase "from the moment of conception" in favor of a more general rule stating that when undertaking medical procedures on a pregnant woman, a doctor is at the same time responsible for the health and the life of the child (arts. 37 and 38). And, in a special chapter on "Procreation,"

In the meantime, the debate in Parliament continued. One of the victorious parties of the 1991 elections, the Christian-National Union (ZChN), proposed a very restrictive abortion bill. It declared that each human being has a right to life from the moment of conception, and it proposed a penalty of up to two years' imprisonment for a medical practitioner terminating a pregnancy except when necessary to save the woman's life. This draft reintroduced penalties for self-induced abortion and also prohibited anyone from causing harm or damage to the fetus. In the spring of 1992, a group of parliamentarians introduced a counterproposal that provided for sexual education, the right to family planning, and access to abortion as a last resort, as well as for the regulation of "artificial procreation." During this period, a bill proposing a national abortion referendum was also introduced. In July 1992, both it and the revised abortion proposal were rejected, while the 1991 anti-abortion draft was forwarded to a special commission.

At last, on January 7, 1993, the Polish Parliament passed a new abortion law, the Law on Family Planning, Legal Protection of the Fetus and the Conditions of Permissibility of Abortion, which became effective on March 16, 1993 (see Law no. 78; published in Dz. U. 1993, no. 12; hereafter, this law will be referred to as the anti-abortion law or the 1993 law). The new law severely limited the availability of abortion, prohibiting legal abortions for social reasons and prohibiting abortions performed by doctors in private practice. Although less restrictive than originally intended, the law was much more restrictive than the 1956 legislation. Parliament also adopted some of the wording of the counter bill by, for example, changing the title. In the end, the 1993 law was an artificial merger of two bills representing diametrically opposed ideologies. The pro-life forces found it too liberal; the pro-choice, much too restrictive. Lawyers, regardless of their moral judgment of abortion, were troubled by the law's legal inconsistencies and internal contradictions.

The 1993 abortion law not only declared that the life and health of the unborn should be protected from the point of conception; it also stipulated up to two years' imprisonment for anyone (except the pregnant woman) who "causes the death of the conceived child" (see art. 149a of the Penal Code). The law provided that in especially justified cases, the court had the right to withhold penalty toward any offender found guilty of voluntarily causing the death of a conceived child. Causing the death of a conceived child against the will or without consent of its mother is punishable by six months to eight years' imprisonment (new art. 149b of the Penal Code), and causing injury or endangering the life of a conceived child is punishable by up to two years' imprisonment (new art. 156a of the Penal Code). At the same time, it clarified that a physician is not guilty of an offense if the abortion was performed in a public hospital for medical and legal reasons

---

the physician was obligated to act with special attention to the process of reproducing human life, providing full information on the process of fertilization and birth control (according to the current state of medical knowledge) to patients interested in these issues and to inform patients belonging to increased risk groups about the diagnostic and therapeutic procedures of modern medical genetics, including the potential risks associated with prenatal testing (art. 38).

or if there was a known fetal malformation. An abortion may be granted for medical reasons if two other doctors have confirmed that the pregnancy endangers the life or seriously threatens the health of the pregnant woman; for legal reasons, if there is a justified suspicion, confirmed by a public prosecutor, that the pregnancy has resulted from a criminal act; and because of fetal malformations, if the result of prenatal diagnostic examinations, confirmed by two doctors' opinions, indicates the existence of serious and irreversible damage to the fetus. A new regulation (see art. 23b of the Penal Code) banned any experiments on the fetus other than those conducted to protect its health or that of the mother. This did not, however, apply to prenatal diagnostic exams if the risk of miscarriage was not noticeably increased. Also excluded from the ban were conditions relating to fetal malformations. For example, if the family of the conceived child carried a genetic disorder, if there was a suspicion that the fetus suffered from a genetic disorder that could be cured or remedied, if the consequences of the disorder might be limited during the prenatal period, or if a serious fetal deformity was suspected, then such experiments or exams were allowed.[17]

In addition, the law required state and local government agencies to provide assistance for "pregnant women, the conceived child and its mother"; to ensure that schools educate students about "sexuality, conscious and responsible parenthood, the value of the family and of conceived life" (schools have also been obligated to give assistance to students who become pregnant); and to guarantee free access to "the methods and means of birth control" to all citizens. Moreover, the Ministers of Health, Education, and Justice were required to report to the Sejm in 1994 on the effectiveness of the law's implementation in its first year— a requirement that was amended in 1995 to include subsequent years.

Not surprisingly, passage of the 1993 abortion law did not end the abortion debate; instead, it marked the conclusion of another round in what may be viewed as an ongoing series of rhetorical battles on this most volatile of issues.

1993–1997

The victory of post-communist and leftist parties in the September 1993 parliamentary elections provided hope for the return of a more liberal abortion law. In part, the electoral success of these parties was influenced by their positions on church-state relations and on abortion. Public opinion polls indicated that the populace was wary of the Catholic Church's intrusion into their private sexual lives. In 1994, the Parliamentary Women's Group attempted to amend the anti-abortion law to include access to legal abortion for social reasons. However, then President Lech Wałęsa refused to sign the amendments passed by both houses of Parliament, while the Sejm failed to collect enough votes to overturn the presidential veto. In November 1995, the leftist opposition party,

---

[17] It should be mentioned that the Civil Code was also modified. Unborn children gained legal capacity with the reservation that their financial rights and obligations be executed on the condition that they are born alive (Civil Code, art. 8, para. 2). Children who live could also demand compensation for prenatal damages (Civil Code, art. 446).

Labor Union, proposed—once again unsuccessfully—to put the permissibility of abortion to a national referendum by attaching this question to the referendum on privatization to be held in December 1995. But in March 1996, another draft amendment liberalizing the 1993 law was introduced. As a result of strong support from the Democratic-Left Alliance and from several very skilled and active deputies, the post-election liberalizing amendments were approved by the Sejm. Although the higher chamber rejected this amendment, the Sejm garnered a two-third's majority to overrule the Senate's veto.

The law of August 30, 1996, considerably modified the anti-abortion law of 1993. Significantly, reproductive rights are explicitly mentioned in the preamble.[18] Nonetheless, in the spirit of compromise, this principle is preceded by recognition of the fundamental value of life, as well as by the assurance that the care for human life and health is the basic obligation of state, society, and citizens alike. The 1996 law reintroduced social factors, such as difficult living conditions, as legitimate causes for abortion in addition to medical and legal reasons. Moreover, doctors were again permitted to perform abortions in their private practices. Reduced payment schedules for certain contraceptive pills were also incorporated into the new legislation. At the same time, certain positive provisions of the 1993 law were retained, notably those regarding sex education in schools, free access to contraception, and assistance for pregnant women.[19]

However, the 1996 law is not as liberal as the 1956 law. For example, a twelve-week time limit has been stipulated for abortions that are performed for social or legal reasons. Also, a woman's decision to terminate a pregnancy must be fully informed and carefully weighed, meaning that she must submit to mandatory consultations and a waiting period of three days. Harsher penalties are meted out for illegal abortions performed after the fetus is considered viable outside the women's womb (approximately after the twenty-fourth week of pregnancy).

In January 1997, President Aleksander Kwaśniewski signed the 1996 amendments liberalizing the anti-abortion law. But the abortion saga did not stop there. Already in December 1996, a group of senators appealed to the Constitutional Tribunal, contesting the proposed amendments. On May 28, 1997, one day before Pope John Paul II's visit to Poland, the Tribunal ruled that most of the 1996 amendments were unconstitutional because they conflicted with the fetus's constitutionally protected right to life. This ruling was very controversial because the 1952 Constitution, modified in 1992 and then in force, did not explicitly mention *any* right to life, least of all that of a fetus. Nevertheless, the Tribunal decided that the unborn's right to life could be drawn from the general principle that Poland is a democratic state that abides by the rule of law.[20] It also ruled

---

[18] The respective provision reads as follows: "Everybody has the right to responsibly decide about having children as well as the right to information, education, counseling and the means enabling them to exercise this right."

[19] The 1996 law also altered the Civil Code, denying the legal capacity of the unborn as well as potential demands for compensation for prenatal damages. See note 17.

[20] The new Constitution of April 2, 1997, in force since October 17, 1997, provides for the explicit guarantee of the legal protection of everyone's lives and does not single out the unborn (see art. 38).

that the provision permitting abortion on "social grounds" was incompatible with the constitution because of its vague formulation and failure to protect the rights and liberties of the unborn (see *Rzeczpospolita*, June 19, 1997). According to the Tribunal's reasoning, the life of the unborn may be adversely affected by the subjectively determined evaluation of the pregnant woman's difficult living or psychological situation. The Tribunal further declared that a woman's right to decide about reproduction is valid only until conception (see Kroner 1997; Lang 1994:4).

Although the Democratic-Left Alliance proposed that there be a national referendum on the permissibility of abortion for social reasons (see *Rzeczpospolita*, May 30, 1997), Parliament again voted this idea down (*Rzeczpospolita*, June 19, 1997). In part, this may reflect the Catholic Church's influence in Parliament. The Church has always steadfastly opposed a vote on a "moral" issue, claiming this to be "not only anti-Christian, but anti-Polish and inhuman as well." At the same time, however, the Church's resistance to a referendum may stem from its ability to more easily influence the vote of 460 deputies and 100 senators than 20 million Poles who are eligible to vote on this issue. As will be discussed below, support for the Church's position is in fact hardly clear-cut. As is well known, the politics of abortion in Poland are exacerbated by the influence of the Pope. Given that a post-Solidarity opposition now has a parliamentary majority, it is unlikely that the Constitutional Tribunal's decision will be rejected in Parliament.[21]

Here, it is important to note that limitations on the right to abortion have been accompanied by attempts to restrict additional aspects of reproductive practice and knowledge ranging from contraceptives to new reproductive technologies. Sterilization for nonmedical reasons remains quite controversial, as does the use of certain contraceptives that may act as early abortifacients. Assisted reproduction, a new field of medicine, is growing fast in Poland. However, no specific legal regulations pertaining to this field have been introduced. The media has reported widely on the emerging controversies over artificial insemination techniques, particularly the freezing and transfer of embryos for implantation. The inclusion of sexual education and information in the public school system is another topic of heated debate. All of these issues are closely linked to the abortion debate, forming part of the broader discourse on reproductive rights.

ACTORS IN THE ABORTION DEBATE

The efforts to liberalize or restrict abortion have involved both governmental and nongovernmental actors. Among the public authorities most active in the battle for reproductive rights are the Ombudsman for Civic Rights; the Government Commissioner for the Family and Women; the Parliamentary Women's Group (which consists of approximately forty-five deputies and senators); most

---

[21] Editors' note: The decision was, in fact, approved.

of the deputies from the Democratic-Left Alliance (the so-called post-communist party that was in power from 1993 to 1997); some deputies from the Polish Peasant Party (which until 1993 was a member of the ruling government coalition); the majority of deputies from Labor Union (UP)—the opposition party to the post-communist government (now without parliamentary representation); some deputies from the opposition post-Solidarity party Freedom Union (UW); and the current president, Aleksander Kwaśniewski.[22]

In addition to political figures, many participants in what is labeled civil society are engaged in the battle over abortion. Most of the pro-choice women's organizations are associated with the Federation for Women and Family Planning; these include both feminist organizations and others such as the Young Women's Christian Association. The Federation seems to play the leading role in the fight for reproductive rights in Poland. Here, it should be noted that the women's movement in Poland has developed over the last eight years. Instead of one token communist organization, there are now nearly two hundred associations representing different political views and organizational goals. Initially, threats to women's rights including their reproductive rights strengthened the women's movement. However, conflicts within groups have contributed to divisions among and between organizations.

The activities of the afore-mentioned governmental organizations and nongovernmental organizations (NGOs) have been supported by a number of lawyers, mostly from Warsaw University and Toruń University, and by a small group of philosophers, social policy specialists, sexologists, and many prominent and respected gynecologists and geneticists from leading Polish medical institutes.

On the other side of the barricade are small but very vocal right-wing parties and powerful interest groups that describe themselves as Christian or nationalist. (Until the 1993 elections, they were among the majority in Parliament; between 1993 and 1997, they generally lacked parliamentary representation, but in 1997 they formed an electoral coalition with Trade Union Solidarity and regained power.) They claim among their ranks physicians' self-governing bodies, the Chairman of the Constitutional Tribunal, the Chief Justice of the Supreme

---

[22] The current president, Aleksander Kwaśniewski, made a campaign promise to sign legislation amending the anti-abortion law of 1993 by making abortion permissible on social grounds. When asked if abortion should be penalized, he said it should be legal for medical reasons, in cases of fetal defects, and for social reasons. His attitude is based more on social and economic factors than on the recognition of a woman's right to choose, which gives cause for concern as to whether he will sign a law that leaves the final decision on abortion to the woman. Responses to a Federation for Women and Family Planning survey show that only two serious candidates in the 1995 presidential election declared they would sign legislation liberalizing the anti-abortion law. One said this would depend on the actual wording of the law. The only woman candidate, Hanna Gronkiewicz-Waltz, Chairwoman of the National Bank of Poland, was opposed to such legislative changes. She was also against safeguarding reproductive rights in the Constitution and providing special programs for women, including an ombudsman for the equal status of women and men; she favored parental consent for sex education at school, a pro-natalist policy, and the signing of the concordat agreement with the Vatican. Asked about the role of women, she said they should be primarily wives and mothers, although more and more are choosing to have a career. See the *Bulletin of the Federation for Women and Family Planning* 1995, 2 (Autumn).

Court, former President Lech Wałęsa, and the hierarchy of the Roman Catholic Church.

Pro-life NGOs are associated with the Federation of Movements for the Defense of Life. In contrast to pro-choice organizations, which have been divided by rivalries and conflicts, the pro-life movement has grown and consolidated itself in the 1990s, thus acquiring considerable resources and organizational skills.[23] Currently the Polish Federation of Movements for the Defense of Life lists as member organizations ninety-two representatives of foundations, associations, and pro-life and pro-family movements from all over Poland. (In the unofficial Report on Polish Women prepared by the Federation for the U.N. Fourth World Conference on Women held in Beijing in 1995, no data on the actual members of these organizations are provided.)

The increasingly vocal anti-abortion movement has a number of prominent activists, among them a well-known priest, doctors, and several women who run homes for single mothers. During the protests against the liberalization of the law in 1995, the anti-abortion movement collected 800,000 signatures in support of their position, whereas pro-choice organizations managed to collect only 2,500. Prior to the Senate vote on the 1996 amendments, an estimated 30,000 proponents of restrictive abortion legislation demonstrated in Warsaw, as opposed to 100 supporters of the amendments.

As is generally known, the Polish Catholic Church is the main proponent of anti-abortion policy. Since 1989, the public role of the Catholic Church has expanded, making it the single strongest and best organized institution in the country. Many politicians and political parties fight for the church hierarchy's "blessings" and are afraid to openly oppose it. (This includes politicians from the Democratic-Left Alliance.) It is believed that nobody wins in Poland if the Roman Catholic Church is against them (see Matynia 1996:397; Nowicka 1996c:23). Not surprisingly, the Church has been unequivocal in its support of the most restrictive versions of anti-abortion draft laws. For example, it has repeatedly organized prayer vigils and urged the faithful to lobby Parliament for the "defense of life." (Note that approximately 90 percent of the population declare themselves to be Roman Catholic.) Priests have participated as experts in all public and parliamentary discussions, and Cardinal Józef Glemp has met regularly with deputies just before decisive votes. Deputies who have openly declared their opposition to the anti-abortion bill have been criticized in church

---

[23] The Catholic Church's financial and organizational support was not only motivated by a moral imperative. Through the signature-collecting campaigns held all over Poland, the church was able to gain data on "election geography," that is, the localization of its supporters in the 1997 parliamentary elections. It should be noted that foreign anti-abortion organizations contribute strategy recommendations and informational materials to the Polish anti-abortion movement although there is no evidence indicating how much support is provided.

In the 1980s, anti-abortion activities in Warsaw involved three groups with an estimated membership of fifty, plus several dozen more sympathizers. The movement believed that moral values were best influenced in the family. See Drążkiewicz 1988:111.

sermons in their electoral districts.[24] Indeed, the Pope's visit in 1991 was nearly suspended because the Polish Parliament reached no "proper" consensus on protection of the unborn. For the Pope, abortion is a favored topic. During his visit to Poland in June 1997, he declared that the world had become the arena for the "defense of life" and that "a civilization which rejects the innocent deserves the name of barbarous." He approvingly recited Mother Teresa's statement, "If a mother is allowed to kill her own child, what could stop you and me from killing each other?" (see *Rzeczpospolita,* June 5, 1997).

After the Sejm passed the draft of the new amendment in September 1996, the Catholic Church forcefully vented its condemnation. "A nation which kills its own children is a nation without a future. There is no rule of law in a state which permits the murder of innocents," admonished the Pope. One bishop warned that passage of the amendment "seriously threatens the possibility of good relations between the Church and the current Sejm. This decision is participation in a crime. It is a horrible thing to observe people who for months on end, in cold blood, plan the murder of hundreds of thousands of human beings. I would not hesitate to call this a crime against humanity" (Montgomery 1996:1– 3). Another bishop expressed admiration mixed with regret for the mothers of those deputies who voted for liberalization because these women had not aborted. According to this bishop, Poland would have been better off had these deputies not been born. Another member of the Church hierarchy remarked, "[T]he Church in Poland has gone into mourning because of the criminal law passed by the Sejm" (see Noszczyk 1996:2).

This effort to demonize parliamentary deputies who support abortion rights soon reached new heights. Cardinal Józef Glemp insisted that "there can be no place at the altar for people who say 'yes' to death."[25] The prior of the Jasna Góra monastery condemned pro-abortion deputies for treason of the motherland and said they had "divested themselves of the moral right to represent Poland" (Wołk Laniewska 1996). "Parliamentarian, Thou Shall Not Kill!" urged the Catholic daily *Słowo Powszechne.* The Bishop-Chaplain of the Polish army, who is paid from the state budget, called the vote odious and humiliating and compared abortion to a world war.

By stoking the fires of the abortion debate, the church and politicians associated with it have instrumentally promoted what they consider to be the moral renewal of society and Christian values. Indeed, some view the Church's leading role in Polish society as part of the Vatican's strategic goal to re-evangelize Europe, with Poland serving as the model Catholic state. At the same time, however, critics of the Church have questioned why the Church hierarchy is so principled in the case of Poland yet accepts the legalization of abortion elsewhere, most

[24] See also *Gazeta Wyborcza,* March 25, 1996, on the pilgrimage in the defense of life and the prayer "for solidarity with every conceived child."

[25] When the most prominent and respected Polish gynecologist was killed in a car accident in May 1997, the Catholic hierarchy refused to officiate at the religious funeral. The physician had openly declared his opposition to the banning of abortion.

notably in Italy, the very seat of the Vatican. The Church's initial reaction to the 1997 law was addressed to the Polish Parliament. Some left-oriented political commentators see the liberalization of abortion as an indicator of state sovereignty and parliamentary integrity. They suggest that the Church fears that the legalization of abortion might signal the potential rejection of the concordat agreement or passage of a law on equitable taxation of the Church (which the Church wants to prevent at all costs; see Gadzinowski 1996).

In addition to the Church's exercise of its moral authority, medical practitioners have also taken active roles for or against abortion. As evidenced in the Medical Code of Ethics, a substantial number of physicians, especially those representing the Chamber of Physicians or the Catholic Association of Polish Physicians, assume it to be their exclusive right to decide on abortion. When the 1996 amendment entered into force, the executive body of the Polish Chamber of Physicians issued a statement encouraging physicians to refuse to perform abortions for reasons of conscience. But it is not only physicians who have opposed abortion. Midwives and nurses are also found among abortion's opponents. Such is their influence that in several cases, doctors have been unable to assemble a team to perform the procedure.

While the disciplinary courts have been lenient toward those physicians who have violated the 1993 law, rarely convicting them on infringement grounds alone (see, for example, Gubiński 1996:163), the majority of gynecologists are reluctant to take a public stand on abortion.[26] This may indicate that they do not want to openly support the maintenance of legal abortion; alternatively, it may mean that they have a practical interest in the delegalization of abortion because their incomes increase as a result of the "risk tax" for performing illegal abortions (see Błachut and Krajewski 1991:36–47).

The media has also been influential in the abortion debates. In the beginning of the anti-abortion campaign, the media (except the Catholic media) seemed to be more sympathetic to the opponents of the draft. However, when chided by the Polish Episcopate, some of the media adopted a more reserved position. Some nationwide dailies such as *Gazeta Wyborcza* or *Rzeczpospolita* are objective in reporting on abortion. However, public television, especially Channel 1, present biased programs.[27] Channel 1 still devotes eleven times as much coverage in its evening news to groups that oppose abortion rights than to those who support it.

To be sure, the Catholic media has occupied a key position in the anti-abortion campaign. The popularity of Radio Maryja (the broadcast station St. Mary)

---

[26] The Court's leniency may be explained either by disagreement among members of such courts about the prohibition or by general tolerance toward colleagues found guilty of professional misconduct.

[27] For example, on the day of the first reading of the 1996 bill liberalizing the anti-abortion law, Channel 1 of Polish Television broadcast "The Silent Scream." In the discussion following the movie, biased statements about "the murder of unborn children" and assertions that adoption would solve the problem of abortion predominated. The Federation for Women and Family Planning sent a letter of protest to the Director of Channel 1 demanding objective reporting on abortion and the broadcasting of the American film by Dorothy Fadiman, "When Abortion Was Illegal." Thus far,

since 1993 is a phenomenon in and of itself warranting sociological study. Its programs have mobilized listeners to participate in various activities such as organizing rescue actions outside abortion clinics. Radio Maryja has also broadcast the names of "bad doctors," that is, those who perform abortions.

PUBLIC OPINION ON ABORTION

Both before and after the passage of the anti-abortion law, numerous public opinion surveys were conducted on the issue. These surveys have varied in form, ranging from "public consultations"—letters sent to the Sejm about the Senate's 1991 anti-abortion proposal—to polls on the permissibility of abortion and surveys on attitudes to abortion.[28] Recent survey results shed light on the claims made by some that the battle to ban abortion reflects the will of the electorate.[29] For example, polls conducted just after the 1993 law delegalized abortion for social reasons revealed that half of those surveyed thought the law should be changed.[30] In 1994, 58 percent favored modifying the law, 19 percent agreed with it, and 22 percent expressed no opinion.[31] In 1996, 52 percent favored changing the law, 29 percent opposed change, and 19 percent had no opinion.

Among the group who supported change, 83 percent tended to believe that the activities of the Catholic Church were not beneficial to society, 75 percent were rarely or never religiously observant, and 72 percent held left-leaning political preferences. Also, men were somewhat more likely than women to favor liberalization of the law (55 percent and 50 percent, respectively); conversely, 32 percent of women compared with 25 percent of men supported the anti-abortion law. Those opposed to changing the law included the elderly, health pensioners, and residents of rural areas, including farmers. Those who were religiously observant clearly favored the ban (58 percent; of the religiously observant, only 12 percent favored changing the law).[32]

---

this has been to no avail (see *Trybuna*, April 11, 1996). However, management changes in public television give hope for a modification of programming and information policies.

[28] On permissibility of abortion, see the OBOP survey commissioned by *Gazeta Wyborcza*, March 25, 1996 (a cross-country representative sample of 1,079 Poles age 16 and older). On attitudes about abortion, see the Central Statistics Office 1995:135–137, 236. The latter was conducted by the Institute for Social Studies of Warsaw University using a cross-country representative sample of 2,000 adults age 18 and older. In 1992, 1,647 persons completed and returned questionnaires; in 1993, 1,649; and in 1994, 1,647.

[29] See CBOS 1996. The survey report was based on a cross-country representative sample of 1,256 Polish adults.

[30] See the 1993 CBOS survey, conducted among a national representative sample of 1,076 Polish adults.

[31] CBOS 1994. The survey report was based on a national representative sample of 1,209 Polish adults.

[32] On the 1996 survey, see note 29. On voters favoring change, for example, 71 percent among Democratic-Left Alliance voters, 69 percent among Labor Union voters, and 68 percent of those who voted for Aleksander Kwaśniewski in the 1995 presidential elections were in favor of changing the 1993 abortion law. In a March 1996 OBOP poll, 62 percent of respondents also supported change.

TABLE 1.1
Public Opinion Regarding the Permissibility of Abortion (Percentages)

Should abortion be:	Nov 1990	Sept 1991	Sept 1992	April 1993	May 1994	July 1994	Oct 1995	March 1996
Permitted without restriction	19	22	26	23	18	22	18	13
Permitted, with exceptions	34	35	35	41	42	37	36	41
Forbidden, with exceptions	26	22	22	20	22	21	23	29
Forbidden in any circumstance	14	12	10	10	9	14	14	10
Not sure	7	9	7	6	9	6	9	7

Sources: CBOS Polling Center Surveys, Warsaw.

Although there has been some variation, all polls demonstrate that support for extreme positions has systematically declined since 1990. For example, in March 1996, only 10 percent favored a total ban on abortion—a drop of 4 percent since August 1994. Public support for unconditional access to abortion has also decreased in the past few years, from 26 percent in 1992 to 13 percent in 1996 (see Table 1.1). In general, most Poles believed in 1996 that abortion should be legal with certain restrictions (42 percent in 1996 and 36 percent in 1997);[33] 50 percent held that social reasons should be legitimate grounds, while 37 percent opposed social reasons as legitimate cause for legal abortion (see Table 1.2). Prior to the passage of the 1996 bill liberalizing abortion, polls indicated that the expectations of those favoring liberalization were more radical than the Labor Union's proposed amendments. (This was also confirmed in the Polish General Social Survey.) The proposals maintained the general prohibition but included social reasons as legitimate cause. Voters, however, supported legalization with certain restrictions (see Tables 1.1 and 1.2). In a 1997 survey, 37 percent of men and 33 percent of women indicated unequivocal support for a woman's free choice in the first weeks of pregnancy; 30 percent indicated some support.[34]

Data show a clear hierarchy with respect to the approval of reasons for legal abortion (see Table 1.2). Most approve legal abortion if the mother's life is in danger (90 percent in 1991; 88 percent in 1996), although there is lower approval if her health is at risk (83 percent in 1991; 78 percent in 1996) or if the pregnancy resulted from rape or incest (73 percent in 1991; 75 percent in 1996). Least

[33] According to a 1997 CBOS survey, conducted among a national representative sample of 1,108 Polish adults, 14 percent supported unconditional access to abortion; 36 percent, legal abortion with certain restrictions.

[34] The question was, Do you agree or disagree with the sentence: Women should have the right to abortion in the first week of pregnancy. Fourteen percent of respondents were unequivocally against, of whom 11 percent were men and 17 percent women. 1997 CBOS survey, conducted among a national representative sample of 1,102 adult Poles.

TABLE 1.2

Public Opinion Regarding the Permissibility of Abortion in Various Situations (percentages)

Should abortion be legally permitted when:	May 1991		March 1992		March 1996	
	Yes	No	Yes	No	Yes	No
The mother's life is in danger	90	7	88	6	88	7
The mother's health is at risk	83	12	82	11	78	14
The pregnancy resulted from rape or incest	73	17	80	11	75	13
It is known that the child will be born severely handicapped	67	21	71	15	65	20
The woman is in a difficult financial condition	49	41	47	39	50	37

Sources: CBOS Polling Center Surveys, Warsaw.
Note: Answers of "I don't know" were omitted.

approval was expressed for cases in which it had been determined that the child would be born severely handicapped (67 percent in 1991; 65 percent in 1996; see OBOP 1996, note 28). Over the last four years, public approval of abortion for genetically related reasons has declined, as has pregnancy resulting from rape or incest (CBOS Polling Center 1996).

These findings do not differ widely from those of the Polish General Social Survey in which the attitudes of married women toward abortion were studied over the three-year period from 1992 to 1994 (Central Statistics Office 1995). Generally, liberalization of abortion to accommodate a woman's choice was broadly accepted (45.4 percent in 1992; 51.6 percent in 1993; 52 percent in 1994),[35] which accounts for one difference from the CBOS polls regarding the approval of abortion for social reasons. In the General Social Survey, while the percentages fluctuated, they did not decline (53.7 percent in 1992; 57.5 percent in 1993; 57.7 percent in 1994).

It should be mentioned that the results of public opinion polls and attitude studies must be interpreted with standard methodological caution. For example, a decline in liberal attitudes to abortion may be related to an intensification of anti-abortion propaganda. Or too much propaganda may produce the opposite effect, signaling disapproval of the state or church's intrusion into private life. But even with these considerations in mind, it has been repeatedly demonstrated that a majority of Poles favor liberal abortion policies.[36] Politicians active in the abortion debate are clearly not listening to the voters' will, as has consistently

[35] 1994 CBOS survey. The question was: Should abortion be a legal option for married women who do not want to have more children?

[36] The public opinion polls of November 1996 show that 58 percent favored the 1996 amendments and 33 percent were opposed. See November 1996 CBOS survey, based on a national representative sample of 1,110 adult Poles.

been the case with respect to the issue of holding a national referendum on abortion. Despite the collection of three million signatures in 1992, Parliament rejected all draft proposals. The reasons appear to be based more on political interests than on those of the electorate.

DEMOGRAPHIC FACTORS AND THE PRACTICE OF ABORTION BEFORE 1993 AND AFTER 1996

During the thirty-seven years in which the liberal 1956 law was in force, the estimated abortion rate in Poland was much higher than in the West, lower than in the former Soviet Union, and more or less the same as in Bulgaria, Yugoslavia, and Hungary (Zielińska 1986:268). Official statistics rarely indicated more than 140,000 abortions per year.[37] Nonetheless, it must be kept in mind that abortion statistics are notoriously unreliable. The official statistics do not, for example, reflect abortions performed by private doctors who, to avoid taxes, did not report them. The estimated number of abortions varies according to the source. In the 1970s, the Catholic Church maintained that there were 600,000 to 1 million abortions annually. But the majority of Polish demographers claimed that the annual figures were between 300,000 and 500,000 abortions and that most of them (90 percent) were performed because of the woman's difficult living conditions (Okólski 1988:208).

Following the introduction of restrictions on abortion in the early 1990s, the number of reported abortions dropped. For example, in 1990, there were 59,417 abortions officially registered; in 1991, 30,878; and in 1992, 11,640. These figures are important because they clearly indicate that the 1993 anti-abortion law was approved at a time when the number of reported abortions was systematically falling (Okólski 1993:7). After the 1993 law came into force, the numbers decreased dramatically: In 1993, only 777 abortions were recorded; in 1994, 782; and in 1995, 559. The majority of these abortions were performed for medical reasons (e.g., the mother's life or health was at risk): In 1993, there were 736 abortions; in 1994, 689; and in 1995, 519. In 1993, there were also 32 abortions performed because of fetal malformation; in 1994, 74; and in 1995, 33. Abortions because a pregnancy had resulted from a criminal offense accounted in 1993 for 9 abortions; in 1994, 19; and in 1995, 17. To be sure, the same reservations regarding statistical reliability apply to post-1989 data. It is clear to everyone except the Board of the Federation of Movements for the Defense of Life that the official data do not reflect the real scope of abortion as practiced in Poland today.[38]

[37] See Statistics of the Ministry of Health and Social Welfare. The highest number of legal abortions was in 1962, when 199,429 were registered. After 1967, the number did not exceed 150,000; after 1980, the number dropped to approximately 138,000 per year, with further declines recorded in 1987 (122,536) and 1989 (83,000). Approximately half of the registered abortions were performed in public hospitals.

[38] The government reports summarizing the effects of the anti-abortion law after one year note that these numbers pertain only to abortions performed in hospitals. It is "believe[d] that abortions

While the number of abortions have declined, so have the number of births. This trend began in the mid-1980s (with 677,000 births in 1985), reaching, by 1994, the lowest number of live births since World War II (483,000 live births; see Central Statistics Office 1995:2) followed by yet another decrease in 1995 (to 433,000). This continuous decline may be attributed only in part to changes in the age structure of women in their childbearing years. Moreover, marriage patterns have not changed in Poland, and more than 90 percent of births occur within marriage. The fertility rate has continued to decrease (from 76 live births per 1,000 women in 1980 to 58 in 1991; 53 in 1992; 51 in 1993; 49 in 1994; and 43 in 1995), as has the ratio of children per woman (1.85 in 1993; 1.80 in 1994). In view of this, perhaps the lowered number of abortions may be better understood as a consequence of increased contraceptive knowledge and effective usage of contraceptives or of unreliable official data.[39]

Recent studies demonstrate that effective contraceptive usage remains very low in Poland (see the following section). Hence, the official statistics warrant scrutiny. In its 1996 report on the effects of the anti-abortion law, the Federation for Women and Family Planning attempted to construct a more realistic estimate of the number of annual abortions. Confidential data obtained from an "abortion tourism" agency indicated that it organized 1,500 abortions abroad during the two years of its activity. A review of print media advertisements suggests that there were at least twenty similar agencies operating in Poland. Estimating 800 "tourist abortions" arranged per agency, this adds 16,000 abortions performed abroad on Polish women to the official statistical total. And this total does not take into account the "abortion tourism" of women living in border areas whose travel to foreign clinics is not organized by any agency. Furthermore, the Federation's analysis indicates that some 30,000 abortions are performed in doctors' private offices, bringing the estimated number of annual abortions to 40,000 or 50,000; this represents five to seven times more abortions than those listed in the official statistics (see Nowicka 1996b:4).

Demographers' attempts to estimate the number of abortions for the beginning of the 1990s yielded similar results. These studies, based on analysis of comparative data, have shown that the hypothetical lower limit on the number of abortions is five times that of the official data (Jóźwiak and Paradysz 1993:38). Jóźwiak and Paradysz, although highly critical of official statistics for those years, nonetheless acknowledge that the public debate may, over time, influence birth control attitudes and behavior (see Jóźwiak and Paradysz 1993:32 and also note 39).

However, as clarified by the demographic data, the restrictive abortion law has not significantly altered the frequency of abortion. The Ministry of Health

---

are still performed in doctor's private offices." See the Ministry of Health and Welfare 1994:37. Nor do these figures include abortions resulting from abortion tourism. Yet the Federation of Movements for the Defense of Life concludes from evaluating the report on the functioning of the anti-abortion law that: "Thanks to the introduction of the law many children's lives have been saved." See Federation of Movements for the Defense of Life 1994:3.

[39] On fertility rates, see the Central Statistics Office 1996:2, 62. Also, while restrictive legislation also has an impact on fertility behavior, it is not an empirical cause of change in fertility behavior. See, for example, Kligman 1998 on Romania.

(for which the official statistical data are compiled) has not commented on the evident trends revealed earlier in this discussion, nor has it initiated any reliable study of the effects of the anti-abortion law. This lends further credence to the assumption that the introduction of the anti-abortion law had little to do with the actual limiting of the practice of abortion in Poland.

Until 1993, abortions were performed in public hospitals, in "physicians' cooperatives" (semi-private outpatient clinics), and in physicians' private offices. If performed in a public hospital, the procedure was, until 1990, free of charge (i.e., covered by insurance). Although before 1990 private abortions were quite expensive (equivalent to approximately one month of an average salary), women who could avoid public hospitals did so because of the lack of choice regarding medical procedures, the lack of privacy, and poor sanitary conditions in the public hospitals. The restrictions introduced in 1990 did not particularly affect the abortion options of better-off women; nevertheless, poor women's access to safe abortions was significantly diminished.

However, access to abortion became more difficult for all women after the 1993 anti-abortion law was passed. Abortions could only be legally performed in a public health institution. Invoking the conscience clause, some large public hospitals refused to perform legal abortions, even when the hospital was the only provider in the area. Although individual doctors may claim this right, a hospital, ward, or department head may not do so in the name of all physicians. In Cracow it was reported that several doctors used the conscience clause to avoid performing abortions at the public hospital but invited women to their private offices for the procedure (this being more lucrative for physicians).

In addition to such problems, some women, especially those living in small towns or rural areas, have found it difficult to obtain the physicians' certificates necessary for a legal abortion to be performed. Doctors are reluctant to issue them because abortion tends to be frowned upon in such locales (see Nowicka 1994, 1995:45). For the women, this has meant paying the high costs of abortions performed in private practices. Physicians' fear of public condemnation was frequently encouraged by the actions of priests employed as hospital chaplains who, after acquiring information from attendants or nurses, then pressured doctors. In one well-known case, a 41-year-old mother, Grażyna Z., was partially paralyzed and was admitted to a hospital with a suspected brain tumor. The woman already had seven children and was eight weeks pregnant. Surgeons and neurosurgeons issued a certificate stating that the pregnancy should be terminated because it endangered the patient's health. Nonetheless, before the abortion was performed, a male nurse informed a priest about the scheduled procedure. The priest then pressured the patient and her husband against termination of the pregnancy.[40] It should be added that in small towns and rural areas, women do

[40] Another statement followed in which abortion was not recommended. At a different hospital where a woman was diagnosed with a brainstem abscess, no one discussed the issue of her pregnancy with her, despite knowledge of its existence. She was diagnosed (by computer tomography and electromagnetic resonance) and treated (with antibiotics) as if she was not pregnant. The woman gave birth in December 1995 and died when the child was one month old. See *Na Żywo*, February

not generally have access to prenatal exams (to determine if there are fetal malformations) because medical professionals in these areas often do not have the necessary knowledge or skills.[41]

According to the Federation for Women and Family Planning, women whose pregnancies are the result of rape or incest have found it hard to obtain an abortion in part because they have had difficulty in obtaining affidavits from public prosecutors attesting that a crime had been committed (Nowicka 1996b:4). Ministry of Justice data indicate that twenty-eight such documents were issued in 1993 and twenty-four were issued in 1994 from the offices of public prosecutors.[42] Several of these pertained to cases of incest, statutory rape of a minor (under 15 years of age), and sexual assault on a mentally retarded individual.[43] In its 1994 report, the Ministry of Health and Social Welfare also noted its intervention into a case in which doctors refused to perform an abortion for such reasons. As a consequence, the minister issued a circular to surgeon generals and heads of medical academies informing them that they must properly execute the law and that women who are permitted by law to have an abortion must not face obstacles. Yet the report also remarked that there had been no formal complaints by women in 1994 regarding such obstacles, and only one was recorded in 1995. The Ministry interpreted this as evidence that women's legal rights were being respected.[44]

Regarding social factors as a legitimate cause for an abortion, many public hospitals have announced they will not perform abortions on these grounds despite reliberalization of the law in 1996.[45] Again, it is poor women who pay the consequences, sometimes with their lives.

Many gynecologists with private practices have continued to perform abortions, regardless of the legality. Prices vary in Poland by region and in accordance with the method used, the stage of the pregnancy, and the facilities available. After abortion was recriminalized in 1993, the cost increased several times to include a "crime tariff." In general, the cost was two to four times the minimum monthly salary (U.S. $300–$1,000 in the years 1993–1996). Despite the illegality of performing abortions in private offices, doctors advertised their services publicly.

6, 1966. In March 1996, the Catholic Information Agency reported on the "baptism of the child the doctors sentenced to death," without mentioning the death of the mother. See *Bulletin of the Catholic Information Agency,* March 12, 1996. The child's ultimate fate is unknown to me.

[41] According to the Ministry of Health, access to testing was sufficient and, in general, unrestricted. In 1994, 1,137 such examinations were performed, and fetal malformations were found in 27 cases. The Federation for Women and Family Planning does not agree with the Ministry of Health's evaluation of availability of prenatal testing. For additional details, see Nowicka 1996b:13.

[42] See Council of Ministers 1994:35.

[43] See Ministry of Justice 1994:10.

[44] See Ministry of Health and Social Welfare 1994:7; Council of Ministers 1994:9.

[45] According to the report of the Ministry of Health, presented to Parliament in February 1997, of a total of 435 public hospitals in Poland, 209 do not perform such abortions. In twelve of forty-nine administrative provinces not one public hospital would perform abortions. Abortions are performed in all hospitals in only fourteen administrative provinces. See the report, *Abortion in Poland: Latest Developments,* prepared by the Federation for Women and Family Planning.

The following advertisements appeared in *Gazeta Wyborcza* (March 22, 1996:42): *All procedures*; *Procedures with anesthesia*; *Menstrual induction, IUDs, procedures*; *Gynecological office. All procedures. Lowest prices*; *Gynecologists–absolutely everything*; and *Gynecologists–full range of services*. Even though this publicity is for illegal services, it has not provoked any serious reaction from the prosecutor, the Ministry of Health, or the Chamber of Physicians.

Doctors are not the only ones who advertise illegal services. Abortion tourism agencies also do so openly. Most of the organized trips are to Poland's eastern and southern neighbors: Ukraine, Lithuania, Russia (Kaliningrad), Belarus, and, until the first criminal cases against doctors, the Czech Republic and Slovakia (see later in this section), where abortions are cheaper than those performed illegally in Poland or in the West (approximately U.S. $200). There is little quality control on abortions performed abroad. In some border areas of Poland (e.g., Gdańsk, Cracow, Katowice) there have been reports of women seeking medical care for complications following "tourist" abortions. Women who go abroad are not only at risk because of the conditions in which the procedure is performed, but also because of the means of transportation back to Poland, which may contribute to post-abortion complications.[46]

But not everyone can afford private abortions in Poland or elsewhere. Limited access to legal abortion has led to an increase in maternal deaths caused by unsuccessful self-induced abortions, in spontaneous abortions or miscarriages,[47] and in the number of abandoned children. For example, after the initial restrictions in 1990, four maternal deaths because of secondary complications were reported in one of Poland's major cities. No such cases had been reported during the preceding twenty years. The Ministry of Health data for 1994 show an increase of hemorrhaging among pregnant women. The report also notes that pregnant women between the ages of 35 and 45 tend to already have several children. These women often suffer from multiple medical problems that place them and their fetus's health at risk. Their mental health has also been negatively affected by the fear of pregnancy.[48] Medical conditions prevent some of them from using modern contraceptives, and others suffer the consequences of ineffective natural methods. Limiting sexual relations with their husbands has caused marital problems. Relatedly, Pawelski (1994:195) commented that many women had strong emotional reactions to the 1993 law and the state's intrusion into their private lives. They experienced fear and guilt, even when they were not at risk of unwanted pregnancy. This, in turn, became a source of sexual tension for couples. "Induced frigidity" was among the most frequently observed disorders among women who sought therapy (Pawelski 1994:194–196). Yet the Board of the Polish Federation of Movements for the Defense of Life dismisses the

---

[46] On abortion tourism ads, see *Gazeta Wyborcza*, March 22, 1996:36, and Nowicka 1996b:13; on post-abortion tourism risks, see Ministry of Health and Social Welfare 1994:8.

[47] For example, official data revealed an increase of 1,255 spontaneous abortions in 1993 for a total of 53,148. By 1995, the official number had dropped to 45,308. Whether the anti-abortion law is the cause of these fluctuations has been the subject of dispute.

[48] Ministry of Health and Social Welfare 1994:8.

negative influence that the abortion ban has had on women's psychological health, stating that, to the contrary, the law has decreased the incidence of "post-abortion syndrome."[49]

Whether the law has mitigated the post-abortion syndrome or not, it is clear that mothers are having difficulties caring for their children. The problem of unwanted children may be assessed in part by looking at the figures on newborns abandoned by their mothers in hospitals. In 1995 there were 738 cases of infant abandonment by single mothers as well as by those with many children. While the causes of child abandonment are many in this period of transition, the fact that the 1993 law limited women's options to control their fertility cannot be excluded as an important contributing factor.[50]

Not surprisingly, illegal abortion is becoming more common, as is usually the case when abortion is criminalized. An assessment of criminal proceedings sheds some light on the increased frequency of illegal abortion. (Government reports rightly suggest that the figures are probably much higher than those construed from a review of criminal proceedings.) For example, based on information provided by public health institutions regarding the admission of women for miscarriages, there were fourteen formal cases in 1993, thirty-eight in 1994, and forty-nine in 1995; based on information provided to the authorities by common-law husbands, husbands, and grandmothers about the termination of pregnancies by their common-law wives, wives, or granddaughters, eleven cases were initiated in 1993, twenty-six in 1994, and eighteen in 1995. In cases in which discarded fetuses were later discovered around sewage plants, garbage dumps, or parks, nine women were investigated in 1993, twenty-two in 1994, and eleven in 1995; criminal proceedings also resulted after police learned of a woman's death or found her body.[51]

Thus far, the courts have issued verdicts on six of these cases. One was on that of Paweł M., who had assaulted and then thrown his pregnant common-law wife out of an apartment window. She suffered multiple injuries, including rupture of the spleen and internal hemorrhaging, which caused the death of a 20-week-old fetus. The defendant was sentenced to three to five years' imprison-

[49] See Federation of Movements for the Defense of Life 1994: 2.

[50] On infant abandonment, see the Council of Ministers 1995, and the 1996 Annex, Tables 5 and 6. No nationwide data is available for the early years of the transition. However, figures for Warsaw (city and province combined) illustrate what has most likely been a generalizable increase throughout the country: In 1992, there were 22 such cases; in 1993, 49; and in 1995, 76. See also the Ministry of Health and Social Welfare 1994:8; the Council of Ministers 1995:10; and the Council of Ministers 1996 Annex, Tables 5 and 6. On child abandonment, see data from the Bureau of Computer Studies of the Department of Statistics of the National Police Headquarters. There has also been a slight increase in infanticide, although this is not a common practice. On infanticide, data from Ministry of Justice records show 59 cases in 1992; 56 in 1993, 52 in 1994, and 42 in 1995.

[51] In one case, the husband notified the police after finding his wife's dead body in their apartment. The postmortem showed that she died from hemorrhaging in the course of aborting a three- or four-month-old fetus, with the additional possibility of a pulmonary embolism. The postmortem also found that an unidentified foreign object had been introduced into the vagina to induce the miscarriage. See the Ministry of Justice 1994:11.

ment and ordered to pay a 100 Polish złoty fine to the Social Aid Committee. There are other cases of violence against women resulting in the death of a conceived child.

Legal proceedings have also been introduced against suspected accomplices to abortion. For example, three Cieszyn residents were accused of providing assistance to at least two hundred unidentified women who traveled to the Czech Republic where they had abortions (see Council of Ministers 1995:34). Their cases were widely publicized, in part because evidence was based on 45 ninety-minute cassette tapes, seemingly obtained from police phone taps. This suggested a pressing need to amend the Penal Code; according to article 198 of the Penal Code, such an act was lawful. According to the Polish Constitution, the same act was a clear violation of the right to privacy (see Ratajczak 1995). The defendants each received one-year prison sentences, which were suspended for two of them. The public also was informed of the criminal punishments against doctors in Slovakia and the Czech Republic who had performed abortions on Polish women; the laws in these countries do not permit abortions on foreigners (see Maćkowiak 1996).

The increases in child abandonment and in maternal mortality caused by abortion-related consequences and illegal abortion are all well known and predictable effects of banning abortion (see Kligman 1998). In view of the alleged rationale for the restrictive legislation—to curtail or eradicate abortion—one can but wonder at the relatively weak response of the Polish authorities to illegal abortion and abortion tourism. Again, this confirms that the introduction of the restrictive abortion policy has been used primarily to achieve goals other than that of limiting the practice of abortion itself.

OTHER MEANS OF DISCOURAGING ABORTION

Other practical means may be instituted to encourage childbearing and rearing and to discourage abortion, among which are financial assistance for pregnant women and women raising children, sexual and contraceptive education (and provision of and access to contraceptives), and information about assisted reproduction (or new reproductive technologies). The 1993 law called for social assistance for pregnant women and those raising children. However, budgetary constraints have been claimed by many local communities as the basis for refusing to make these payments. In response, the Commissioner of Citizens' Rights, considering this an unnecessary violation of privacy, noted that women had the right to challenge the government for any delays in their benefits (Ratajczak 1995). This led some legal scholars to conclude that denying women in difficult living conditions legal access to abortion, while at the same time claiming that there are insufficient funds to distribute the mother/child benefits incorporated into the 1993 law, should be perceived as a violation of the constitutional principle of social justice (Lang 1994:9). It should be mentioned that, in some countries, financial assistance for pregnant women and mothers has contributed to a reduction in the number of abortions (Maćkowiak 1996). Again, the disjunction between abortion discourse and practice in Poland is evident.

It is widely recognized that access to and use of modern contraceptives is an important factor in the reduction of abortion as a method of fertility control. But contraception is not customarily used in Poland even by young married couples, and those who do use contraceptives do not do so effectively. A government report noted that only 2.2 percent of Polish women use hormonal contraceptives; sterilization is virtually nonexistent (Kowalska 1993:66). Other sources maintain that no more than 6–8 percent of the population uses modern contraceptives, and 40 percent or more have never used any method of contraception.[52] The most frequently mentioned reasons for such limited use of contraception are: (1) no habit of using contraceptives (cited by 41 percent of those surveyed in a public opinion poll); (2) religious considerations (cited by 39.2 percent); (3) shame involved in buying contraceptives (cited by 35 percent); (4) fear of negative side effects (cited by 28 percent); (5) lack of information (cited by 23 percent); and (6) lack of trust in their effectiveness (cited by 15.4 percent). Limited availability and the high price of contraceptives were also cited by 5.1 percent and 9.2 percent of those surveyed, respectively.[53] Fears are exacerbated by lack of objective information about the pros and cons of particular contraceptives. The media and Catholic organizations have also conducted an anti-contraception campaign. A Ministry of Education approved textbook states, "Contraception, which destroys fertility, is harmful to people because it destroys their health," and "women who use contraception, risking all its harmful effects, feel hurt and used" (see Ombach 1994:93). Another says, "Any agent harming the reproductive functions (e.g., using contraceptives) has side effects on other organs of the body, and the stronger the agent, the more powerful that effect" (Król 1993:138). Nonetheless, pharmacy employees have observed that the anti-abortion campaign has resulted

[52] Calculations on hormonal contraceptive use were based on the sale of contraceptives in pharmacies. This does not account for black-market sales, for which no statistical data are available. Council of Ministers 1994:19. A 1993 nationwide CBOS survey showed that 63 percent of couples with children were not using any method of contraception. For a report on these findings, see CBOS 1994. According to a 1995 survey (based on a representative sample of 1,111 Poles over the age of 15), 44.3 percent have never used contraceptives; 41.5 percent use them only from time to time. See *Mareco Poland* 1995. Some of these results were published in the Council of Ministers 1996:14.

[53] *Mareco Poland* 1995:138. Based on this poll the Ministry of Health claimed that pharmacies were adequately supplied with contraceptives. Five percent of survey respondents noted that in their neighborhoods, they had difficulty acquiring condoms; 9.4 percent reported difficulty obtaining the pill; and 11.4 percent reported difficulty acquiring IUDs. Approved contraceptives include all types of IUDs and the postcoital pill. The Board of the Polish Federation of Movements for the Defense of Life has contested the promotion of IUDs, which they claim act as an early abortifacient, thus violating article 1, paras 1 and 2 of the 1993 law.

There has been discussion of offering rebates on contraceptives to address the cost factor; however, this is a controversial issue on both financial and religious grounds. Catholic circles claim, for example, that supporters of the regulation have been bribed by the pharmaceutical lobby. Finally, price reductions for pills were introduced in the 1996 law.

in increased contraceptive usage, which was affirmed by the 1994 Council of Ministers' report about the effects of the 1993 law. It states that the law changed women's attitudes about contraception; more of them are seeking information from their doctors (see *Polityka* no. 5, 1993; Council of Ministers 1994:19). No empirical studies have been conducted to confirm these observations. Meanwhile, the Catholic Church ardently attempts to convince young persons and adults that modern contraception is immoral and shameful. Women complain that doctors do not provide adequate information about or refuse to prescribe contraceptives (which violates the Code of Medical Ethics). The lack of will exhibited by public authorities with respect to counteracting the anti-contraceptive propaganda of the Catholic Church suggests that abortion and abortion-related statistics will not disappear in the near future, whatever the hopes of those who oppose abortion.

Comparative studies of the international literature make clear that education about sexuality and contraception contributes to reduced abortion. Research into the attitudes of Polish youth toward sex leaves many questions unanswered. This is largely because of the cultural taboo of discussing sex in public—with friends, family members, or school counselors (Kowalska 1993:49). It should not then come as a surprise that sex education in schools is a controversial topic. After extensive debate, the Sejm did include a provision in the 1993 law requiring the Ministry of Education to introduce classes "on human sexuality, family values, conceived life, and birth control" (art. 4). And indeed, sex education has been incorporated into the broader topic of education about love and responsibility, and it is taught primarily as a part of classes such as biology or Polish literature. Teachers are required to seek assistance from specialists and to consult with parents about the subject matter.

Opinions vary on the effectiveness of sex education so introduced. For example, the Government Commissioner for Women and the Family, the Council of Ministers, and the Federation for Women and Family Planning have concluded, upon reviewing the survey results (see Trawińska 1995), that the Ministry of Education's efforts are inadequate (see Nowicka 1996b:9).[54] The vast majority of textbooks approved by the ministry are based on the Catholic Church's teachings on family planning. These books are one-sided and perpetuate stereotypical images of human sexuality while ignoring modern advances in contraception.

---

[54] This research was conducted on a nonrepresentative sample of teachers from 707 schools: elementary (61.7 percent), high school (15 percent) and vocational (22.5 percent) who were very critical of the Ministry's activity. "The only way to describe what is going on is to say it's chaos, both from the point of view of organization and the selection of topics. Neither the teachers nor the students have any systematic access to information, and what they learn is not systematically evaluated. What's more, the effects of instruction are not verified; this is true not only of testing changes in attitude, but also the facts learned" (Trawińska 1995). Among the teachers who present this material are counselors (22.6 percent); teachers of Polish (19.2 percent); biology (24.6 percent); mathematics, history, physical education, and religion (2.5 percent). Among respondents, 60 percent believe that they and their colleagues lack the necessary qualifications. Their negative self-evaluation is reflected in teenagers' still widely held beliefs in various myths, including first intercourse does not result in pregnancy and contraception and masturbation are harmful.

Despite widespread criticism and many recommendations that they be withdrawn from the list of Ministry-approved textbooks, they continue to be recommended for use in schools. Politicians, again, are sensitive to Church approval.[55]

The Board of the Polish Federation of Movements for the Defense of Life, on the other hand, fully supports the effort made by the Ministry of Education to live up to the requirements of the law. It has also protested against people who favor irresponsible sexual behavior and groups that promote "negative" attitudes, such as the Sami Sobie youth movement and graduates of a university sex-educators' course.[56]

The restrictive abortion provisions have also had an impact on other reproduction-related practices. Those seeking help for infertility problems have been affected by the anti-abortion law. For example, frozen human embryos were found at one private infertility clinic. A director of the Health Department reported this to the local prosecutor's office as an infraction of articles 23b, 149, and 156 of the Penal Code. Collecting and storing additional embryos violated the ban on embryo experimentation. The prosecutor's office rejected the argument, as did the Warsaw Chamber of Physicians. However, the legality of certain medical procedures remains unresolved, such as whether the law applies to human embryos outside the woman's womb or, depending on the response to this concern, whether an embryo, which consists of several cells but has not been implanted, can be considered a conceived child under the Penal Code and whether the doctor is liable.[57] Clear regulations are necessary in the highly controversial realm of assisted reproduction, whose "touchy" relationship to abortion legislation is self-evident.

[55] See the Neutrum Association report, 1996:29. For example, Cardinal Glemp condemned recommended textbooks on human sexual life as being "full of pornographic accents." *Rzeczpospolita*, May 30, 1997. So too, did Adam Strzembosz, the President of the Supreme Court. *Rzeczpospolita*, May 26, 1997.

[56] This is an alternative youth health movement's sex education program that was denied government funding for the 1993–1994 school year.

[57] The legal literature is divided. See Majewski and Wróbel 1993:137; Buchała 1994:188–189; and Zielińska 1995:26. However, even those authors who take the position that the Penal Code applies to the embryo are sharply divided over the legal classification of in vitro fertilization and over the doctor's potential liability. Buchała argues that in vitro fertilization is punishable based on article 149a of the Penal Code. To support this argument, he quotes an unspecified source, at the same time admitting that "the law doesn't address" the legality of such medical procedures. The author also expresses the view that while in vitro fertilization is illegal, the implantation of embryos is not necessarily so. His final opinion is that until medical technology makes it possible to obtain a successful pregnancy from the artificial (in vitro) fertilization of a single ovum, such fertilization is punishable based on article 149a. Buchała also states, however, that these technological advances cannot be pursued, since "in-vitro fertilization is banned, regardless of its objective." He does not state his position on the question of freezing and storing additional embryos for possible future implantation. In light of this, his position should be confronted with current medical knowledge in the area of assisted reproduction.

Majewski and Wróbel take a different view on this subject. In their opinion, "Art. 149a § 1 of the Penal Code does not seem to fully apply to a ('spare') human embryo created by artificial fertilization." The authors do not believe that a "person performing artificial fertilization can be punishable for omission of duties based on art. 149 § 1 of the Penal Code." They support their

CONCLUSION

The battles to ban abortion are a revealing means through which to view the process of transition from communism to democracy since 1989. The Polish case demonstrates that some politicians make deliberate, instrumental use of the issue of abortion. It has even been said that some of them suffer from a disease described as the "abortion syndrome," which manifests itself as a need to introduce this subject into the parliamentary agenda at least once a year; its symptoms become more pronounced whenever an election is in the offing. The abortion debate is the best test of a politician's attitudes toward the Catholic Church, the electorate, the party caucus, or colleagues. Since party discipline is usually enforced during voting on this issue, it is a convenient bargaining chip to gain particular concessions or political support on other matters.

In contrast to other countries in which abortion policies were shaped for political ends (see Kligman 1992:373; 1998), the Polish case demonstrates "the shaping of politics through . . . discussion of abortion" (see Gal 1994:260, 285) as well as the creation of political groups through these discussions (also see Maleck-Lewy and Ferree, this volume). The abortion debate is thus central to the process of democratization itself—to what models of democracy and the state will be institutionalized, to the ways in which the legal system and rule of law will function, and to the degree of direct citizens' participation in government. As this chapter has emphasized, the abortion debate in its various versions and the activities of the political actors engaged in it have not represented the expectations of the Polish electorate. Public opinion polls repeatedly show that the majority of Polish citizens do not favor a ban on abortion. Moreover, the political debates are not foremost about finding effective ways to reduce or eliminate the practice of abortion, legal or illegal.

The abortion debate is a noisy discursive struggle, but it is also one that has real empirical consequences—a fact that the proponents of restrictive abortion policy apparently either fail to see or simply ignore. As the data analyzed in this chapter demonstrate, the 1993 law was not only ineffective but also unjust. Increasing numbers of Poles are living in poverty, and women are heavily represented among their ranks. It is this increasing number of poor women who have been most adversely affected by the inability to obtain a legal abortion for social reasons. And while the law may have forced women to give birth, it did not create effective mechanisms to ensure that government agencies would fulfill their financial obligations and that mothers faced with difficult living conditions could manage to rear their children. The 1993 anti-abortion law itself was

opinion by arguing that even if the person performing in vitro fertilization can be assumed to have a special obligation to prevent the death of an embryo (which they see as doubtful), then responsibility for omission does not apply since in this case, there is no action aimed at preventing death. Considering this situation from the point of view of deliberate action leads, in the authors' opinion, to "the paradoxical conclusion that the action resulting in the conceived child's death" is the fertilization itself (Majewski and Wróbel 1993:37–38).

criminal in its consequences. It resulted in massive resistance through abortion tourism and illegal abortion. The law's hypocrisy was revealed in its protection of conceived life, as a noble and absolute goal, at the expense of the actually existing conditions of everyday life.[58]

Despite the empirical evidence regarding the deleterious effects of restricting abortion, Parliament did approve the Constitutional Tribunal's June 1997 decision before the December 17 deadline, which means that the 1993 anti-abortion law is again in force (and almost all of the 1996 amendments are invalid).[59] To be sure, a national referendum will not be held for the reasons already discussed, nor is legislative compromise in the offing, again for the reasons elaborated throughout this chapter. Regrettably, the prognosis is not optimistic. The legal battle over abortion is a highly politicized process that serves interests perceived to be far greater than those of enhancing women's control of their fertility. Although the battle is waged in a democratically elected Parliament, in Poland, democracy remains "democracy with a male face."

BIBLIOGRAPHY

Błachut, Janina and Krzysztof Krajewski
  1991   The draft law on legal protection of a conceived child: some criminal policy and criminological remarks. Państwo i Prawo 5. (In Polish).
Buchała, Kazimierz
  1994   Commentary to the Penal Code, Second Edition. Warsaw: Wydawnictwo Prawnicze [Legal Publishing House]. (In Polish).
CBOS Polling Center
  1994   The family: a theoretical or actual value. Warsaw: CBOS Survey Report (November). (In Polish).
  1996   Attitudes toward legal permissibility of abortion and possible change of the law. Warsaw: CBOS Survey Report (April). (In Polish).
Central Statistics Office
  1991   Poland's demographic situation in the 1990s. Warsaw: Central Statistics Office. (In Polish).
  1996   Statistical yearbook, volume LVI. Warsaw: Central Statistics Office. (In Polish).
  1994   Polish general social surveys. Warsaw: Central Statistics Office. (In Polish).
  1995   Polish general social surveys. Warsaw: Central Statistics Office. (In Polish).
Chałubiński, Mirosław, ed.
  1994   Politics and abortion. Warsaw: Agencja Scholar. (In Polish).
Consortium of Women's NGOs
  1995   The Situation of Women in Poland: Report to the UN Fourth World Conference on Women in Beijing. Warsaw.

[58] Editors' note: This brings to mind the disjunction between the Communist Party's representations of their achievements and the "actually existing socialism" that people experienced in their daily lives.

[59] The decisions taken by the Constitutional Court in Poland are not final; in principle, approval by the Sejm is required. However, if the Sejm fails to take any decision within six months, the Court's decision is upheld.

Council of Ministers
  1994   Report on the second year of the execution of the law of January 7, 1993.
         Warsaw. (In Polish).
  1995   Report on the third year of the execution of the law of January 7, 1993. Warsaw.
         (In Polish).
Drążkiewicz, Jerzy
  1988   Testimony and assistance: On anti-abortion movements in Warsaw. Warsaw:
         Uniwersytet Warszawski. (In Polish).
Federation of Movements for the Defense of Life
  1994   A year after the law. How law protects life: evaluation of the functioning of
         the January 7, 1993 law. Warsaw: Federation of Movements for the Defense
         of Life. (In Polish).
Fuszara, Małgorzata
  1993   Abortion and the Formation of the Public Sphere in Poland. *In* Gender Politics
         and Post-Communism: Reflections from Eastern Europe and the Former
         Soviet Union. Nanette Funk and Magda Mueller, eds. Pp. 241–252. New
         York: Routledge.
  1994   The Abortion Debate and the Shaping of the Political Scene in Poland after the
         Fall of Communism. *In* Politics and Abortion. M. Chałubiński, ed. Warsaw:
         Agencja Scholar. (In Polish).
Gadzinowski, Piotr
  1996   The squeal of a sovereign parliament. Nie 38. (In Polish).
Gal, Susan
  1994   Gender in the Post-Socialist Transition: The Abortion Debate in Hungary.
         East European Politics and Societies 8(2):256–287.
Garlicki, Leszek
  1994   The Constitutional Court in Poland. Unpublished manuscript.
Gubiński, Arnold
  1996   Commentary to the code of medical ethics. Warsaw: Naczelna Izba Lekarska.
         (In Polish).
Jóźwiak, Janina and Jan Paradysz
  1993   The demographic aspects of abortion. Studia Demograficzne 1. (In Polish).
Kligman, Gail
  1992   The Politics of Reproduction in Ceauşescu's Romania: A Case Study in Politi-
         cal Culture. East European Politics and Societies 6(3):364–418.
  1994   The Social Legacy of Communism: Women, Children and the Feminization
         of Poverty. *In* The Social Legacy of Communism. J. Millar and S. Wolchik,
         eds. Pp. 252–270. Woodrow Wilson Center Series. New York: Cambridge
         University Press.
  1998   The Politics of Duplicity: Controlling Reproduction in Ceauşescu's Romania.
         Berkeley: University of California Press.
Kowalska, Irena
  1993   The problems of abortion in light of attitudes and behavior about birth control.
         Studia Demograficzne 1. (In Polish).
Król, Teresa
  1993   On the road to adulthood. Warsaw: AND. (In Polish).
Kroner, Jolanta
  1997   The conceived child malprotected. Rzeczpospolita (May 30). (In Polish).

Krotkiewska, Lidia
 1956   Conditions for the permissibility of abortion: Texts and commentary. Warsaw: Ministerstwo Zdrowia [Ministry of Health]. (In Polish).
Lang, Wiesław
 1994   Procreation Rights. Unpublished manuscript presented at the conference "Women in the Family and Public Life." Warsaw.
 1997   Opinion prepared for the Ministry of Justice on the constitutional claim of senators concerning the 1996 legal amendments to the anti-abortion law of 1993. (In Polish).
Maćkowiak, Tadeusz
 1996   Illegal abortion. Gazeta Wyborcza (January 16). (In Polish).
Majewski, Janusz and Włodziemierz Wróbel
 1993   The legal protection of the conceived child. Państwo i Prawo [State and Law] 4. (In Polish).
Mareco Poland
 1995   Contraception: Availability and obstacles to use. Mareco Poland [Marketing Research]. (March). Warsaw. (In Polish).
Matuchniak-Krasuska, Anna
 1991   The categories and rules of the Polish abortion discourse. *In* Somebody else's problems: On the importance of the unimportant. M. Czyżewski with K. Dunin and A. Piotrowski, eds. Pp. 100–122. Warsaw: Ośrodek Badań Społecznych [Institute of Social Surveys]. (In Polish).
Matynia, Elżbieta
 1996   Finding a Voice: Women in Postcommunist Central Europe. *In* The Challenge of Local Feminisms: Women's Movements in Global Perspective. Amrita Basu, ed. Pp. 374–404. Boulder, CO: Westview Press.
Ministry of Health and Social Welfare
 1994   Report on the execution of the law of January 7, 1993 (April). Warsaw. (In Polish).
Ministry of Justice
 1994   Report on the execution of the law of January 7, 1993 (April). Warsaw. (In Polish).
Montgomery, Katarzyna
 1996   Permitting abortion. Gazeta Wyborcza (August 31). (In Polish).
Neutrum Association for a Neutral State
 1996   Respecting the freedom of conscience and religion in public schools. Neutrum Association Report (February). Warsaw. (In Polish).
Noszczyk, Jack
 1996   A church in mourning. Gazeta Wyborcza (September 2). (In Polish).
Nowicka, Wanda
 1994   Report no. 1 on the consequences of the law of January 7, 1993. Warsaw: Federation for Women and Family Planning. (In Polish).
 1995   Report on the Consequences of the Anti-Abortion Law in Poland. Review of Sociology 1.
 1996a   The Effects of the 1993 Anti-Abortion Law in Poland. Entre Nous 8:34–35.
 1996b   Report no. 2 on the consequences of the law of January 7, 1993. Warsaw: Federation for Women and Family Planning. (In Polish).
 1996c   Roman Catholic Fundamentalism Against Women's Reproductive Rights in Poland. Reproductive Health Matters 8:21–29.

OBOP
  1996   OBOP survey report on attitudes toward permissibility of abortion. Warsaw:
         OBOP. (In Polish).
Okólski, Marek
  1983   Abortion and Contraception in Poland. Studies in Family Planning
         14(11):263–274.
  1988   Population, reproduction, and the modernization of society: The Polish syn-
         drome. Warsaw: Książka i Wiedza. (In Polish).
  1993   Abortion in the light of various fields. Studia Demograficzne 1. (In Polish).
Ombach, Marina
  1994   In search of true love. Warsaw: AWK-MAG. (In Polish).
Pawelski, Arnold
  1994   Abortion, value systems and guilt: A sexologist's comments. *In* Politics and
         Abortion. M. Chałubiński, ed. Warsaw: Agencja Scholar. (In Polish).
Pawlak, Wojciech
  1991   The abortion controversy or the art of parliamentary heuristics. *In* Somebody
         else's problems: On the importance of the unimportant. M. Czyżewski with
         K. Dunin and A. Piotrowski, eds. Pp. 123–151. Warsaw: Ośrodek Badań
         Społecznych [Institute of Social Surveys]. (In Polish).
Peiper, Leon
  1933   Commentary to the Penal Code. Warsaw. (In Polish).
Płakwicz, Jolanta and Eleonora Zielińska
  1994   Abortion in Poland. *In* Abortion in the New Europe: A Comparative Hand-
         book. B. Rolston and A. Eggert, eds. Pp. 199–213. Westport, CT: Green-
         wood Press.
Plenipotentiary for Family and Women
  1995   Report on the UN Fourth World Conference on Women in Beijing. Warsaw:
         Government of the Republic of Poland.
Ratajczak, Aleksander
  1995   A democratic state of law in a totalitarian wrapper. Rzeczpospolita (November
         11). (In Polish).
Sadurski, Wojciech
  1993   How we are seen in the West. Rzeczpospolita (January 23–24). (In Polish).
Safjan, Marek
  1989   On the legal protection of the human in *statu nascendi*. *In* The legal protection
         of the unborn child: The dispute over the draft law. Warsaw: Biblioteka Nurt.
         (In Polish).
Smoliński, Zbigniew
  1973   The current situation and perspectives on women's fertility in Poland: A family
         survey. (In Polish).
Szawarski, Zbigniew
  1990   Poland moves against abortion. Bulletin of Medical Ethics 62.
Trawińska, Maria
  1995   Pro-family and sex education in the Polish school system. Warsaw: Agencja
         Promo-Lider. (In Polish).
Wolińska, Helena
  1962   The termination of pregnancy in penal law. Warsaw: Wydawnictwo Prawnicze
         [Legal Publishing House]. (In Polish).

Wołk-Laniewska, Alina
    1996   A church of confrontation. Przegląd Tygodniowy 36. (In Polish).
Zielińska, Eleanora
    1986   Penal law assessments of abortion: A comparative study. Warsaw: University
            of Warsaw Press. (In Polish).
    1987   European Socialist Countries. *In* Abortion and Protection of the Human
            Fetus. S. Frankowski and G.F. Cole, eds. Pp. 241–334. Boston: Martinus
            Nijhoff Publishers.
    1990   Abortion: conditions of legality in Poland and the world. Warsaw: Wydawnic-
            two Prawnicze [Legal Publishing House]. (In Polish).
    1991   Glossary to the decision of the Constitutional Tribunal of January 15, 1990.
            Państwo i Prawo [State and Law] 7. (In Polish).
    1992   Constitutional Standing of the Code. Bulletin of Medical Ethics 82.
    1993   Abortion Legislation in Eastern Europe. Criminal Law Forum 4.
    1995   On the interpretation of penal regulations of the protection of the conceived
            child. Państwo i Prawo [State and Law]. (In Polish).

CHAPTER 2

Reproductive Policies in
the Czech and Slovak Republics

SHARON L. WOLCHIK

REPRODUCTIVE POLICIES IN THE Czech and Slovak Republics, as elsewhere, are among those areas of public policy that span the gap between the private and public spheres of life. Reproductive decisions are obviously among the most private decisions men and women make. At the same time, however, the choices individuals and couples make regarding the number of children they will have and when and the kinds of contraception, if any, they will use are influenced in important ways in all societies by political, social, and economic factors.

These include, most directly, legislation regulating women's access to abortion and the availability of contraception. They also include the impact of other public policies that determine access to childcare, maternity benefits, and broader social welfare policies. Economic factors, including those that have an impact on the standard of living and availability of employment, also play a role in reproductive choices, as does the impact of the broader social and intellectual climate, including the terms in which citizens and political leaders conceptualize reproductive rights and choices as well as popular conceptions of women's roles and the gender division of labor within the home.

As in other post-communist states, reproductive decisions and policy making in regard to reproduction in the Czech and Slovak Republics have been influenced by the legacy of the communist period in terms of changes in women's roles and popular attitudes regarding gender roles and reproductive issues and by the nature of the political and economic transition from communist rule. The impact of these factors has been most evident in the area of abortion rights, where there have been efforts to enact laws that would restrict women's access to abortion. It is also evident in other areas that influence reproductive decisions, including accessibility of contraception, the financial situation of families, the availability of childcare, popular and elite perceptions of gender roles, and the terms in which reproductive issues are defined.

This chapter examines these issues by focusing on the making of reproductive policies in the Czech and Slovak Republics since the end of communist rule. After presenting a brief overview of reproductive trends and policies in Czechoslovakia

I would like to acknowledge the research assistance provided by Nancy L. Meyers, Spencer Smith, and Jay Honigstock. I would also like to thank the MacArthur Foundation, the Woodrow Wilson Center, The International Research and Exchanges Board and the Institute for European, Russian during the communist era, I turn to an examination of reproductive policies during the post-communist era and the factors that have influenced policy making in this area since 1989. Central issues to be examined include the way in which political leaders, women activists, and broader groups of women conceptualize issues related to reproduction; the impact of reproductive policies on reproductive trends and women's choices in this area; the influence of "transitional politics" on policy making in this area, including the role of experts and organized groups, such as women's and religious groups; the impact of privatization of medical care and social welfare reform on reproductive behavior and attitudes; and the impact of women's continued exclusion from policies on reproductive policy making and decisions. I also discuss regional differences and differences in popular and elite perspectives on reproductive issues in the Czech and Slovak Republics. As my discussion illustrates, debate and discussion about reproductive issues in the post-communist period have been confined largely to the elite level. The issues involved, including efforts to restrict women's access to abortion in Slovakia, are controversial. However, they did not serve, as in many other post-communist countries, to mobilize large numbers of women to take a greater role in politics.

Reproductive Trends and Policies: The Communist Legacy

Reproductive trends in the first half of the communist period in Czechoslovakia reflected the impact of the modernization strategy political leaders followed after 1948 as well as the very high levels of employment of women in the main child-bearing ages. As Tables 2.1 and 2.2 illustrate, birthrates began to decline in Czechoslovakia in the 1950s and continued to be low throughout the 1960s. Pro-natalist measures adopted in 1970 led to a short-term increase in the number of births, but the birthrate declined again in the last decade of communist rule.

Policy making in the area of reproductive policies was determined by the nature of the political system and the impact of changes in the political climate on the way in which communist ideology influenced the policy-making process in this and other areas. Changes in the overall political climate also affected the extent to which groups and individuals outside the top party leadership could have an influence on policy.

Regulations governing access to abortion were liberalized in 1954 and again in 1957. As in other communist countries, contraceptives were not widely available and levels of use of any form of contraception were very low. In these circumstances, abortion became the main means of birth control. As Table 2.3 illustrates, the number of abortions increased rapidly in the late 1950s and 1960s and remained high throughout the communist period.

Rates of abortion were highest in the large cities. They were also somewhat higher in the Czech Lands than in Slovakia, where levels of development and

and Eurasian Studies at The George Washington University for their support of part of the research on which this article is based.

TABLE 2.1
Live Births, Deaths, and Natural Increase per 1,000 Population, ČSSR, Selected Years
(Aggregate Data)

	Live Births	Deaths	Natural Increase		Live Births	Deaths	Natural Increase
1920	26.4	18.3	8.1	1966	15.6	10.0	5.6
1930	21.8	13.9	7.9	1967	15.1	10.1	5.0
1935	17.0	13.3	3.7	1968	14.9	10.7	4.2
1940	20.6	14.0	6.6	1969	15.5	11.2	4.3
1945	19.5	17.8	1.7	1970	15.9	11.6	4.3
1946	22.7	14.1	8.6	1971	16.5	11.5	5.0
1947	24.2	12.1	12.1	1972	17.4	11.1	6.3
1948	23.4	11.5	11.9	1973	18.9	11.6	7.3
1949	22.4	11.9	10.5	1974	19.8	11.7	8.1
1950	23.3	11.5	11.8	1975	19.6	11.5	8.1
1951	22.8	11.4	11.4	1976	19.2	11.4	7.8
1952	22.2	10.6	11.6	1977	18.7	11.5	7.2
1953	21.2	10.5	10.7	1978	18.4	11.5	6.9
1954	20.6	10.4	10.2	1979	17.9	11.5	6.3
1955	20.3	9.6	10.7	1980	16.3	12.2	4.1
1956	19.8	9.6	10.2	1981	15.5	11.8	3.8
1957	18.9	10.1	8.8	1982	15.2	11.7	3.5
1958	17.4	9.3	8.1	1984	14.7	11.9	2.8
1959	16.0	9.7	6.3	1985	14.5	11.8	2.7
1960	15.9	9.2	6.7	1987	13.8	11.5	2.3
1961	15.8	9.2	6.6	1988	13.8	11.4	2.4
1962	15.7	10.0	5.7	1989	13.3	11.6	1.7
1963	16.9	9.0	7.4	1990	13.3	11.7	1.7
1964	17.2	9.6	7.6	1991	13.3	11.5	1.9
1965	16.4	10.0	6.4				

Sources: Srb, Demografická příručka, p. 83; Statistická ročenka ČSSR 1970:91 and 1976:85; see also sources for Table 2.3.

urbanization were lower than in the Czech Lands during the early part of the communist period and where the influence of the Catholic Church remained greater (see Heitlinger 1979 and 1987, esp. chapter 3; also David and McIntyre 1981:232–234).

In the late 1950s, policy makers were hampered in responding to the declining birthrate by the fact that it conflicted with expectations created by the official ideology. Thus, Marxism-Leninism held that population growth would increase under socialism, as couples and families benefitted from the end of economic scarcity. Specialized experts, including those whose job it was to monitor population trends, such as statisticians and demographers, were aware of the decline in the birthrate, but were not part of the circles that made policy, nor, given the way in which demographic trends conflicted with the country's official ideology, were they able to bring such trends to the attention of political leaders or lobby for measures to counter them effectively (Heitlinger 1979; Wolchik 1981b).

TABLE 2.2
Live Births, Deaths, and Natural Increase per 1,000 Population, ČSR and SSR,
Selected Years

	ČSR			SSR		
	Live Births	Deaths	Natural Increase	Live Births	Deaths	Natural Increase
1945	18.2	17.3	0.9	23.7	19.5	4.2
1946	22.1	14.1	8.0	24.2	14.0	10.2
1947	23.6	12.0	11.6	25.8	12.2	13.5
1948	22.2	11.4	10.8	26.5	11.9	14.6
1949	20.9	11.8	9.1	26.4	12.1	14.3
1950	21.1	11.6	9.5	28.8	11.5	17.3
1951	20.6	11.4	9.2	28.7	11.5	17.2
1952	19.7	10.7	9.0	28.3	10.4	17.9
1953	18.7	10.7	8.0	27.5	9.9	17.6
1954	18.1	10.7	7.4	26.8	9.5	17.3
1955	17.7	10.0	7.7	26.6	8.8	17.8
1956	17.2	9.9	7.3	26.3	8.7	17.6
1957	16.3	10.4	5.9	25.3	9.3	16.0
1958	14.8	9.8	5.0	23.9	8.2	15.7
1959	13.4	10.1	3.3	22.3	8.6	13.7
1960	13.3	9.7	3.6	22.1	7.9	14.2
1961	13.7	9.9	3.8	20.8	7.5	13.3
1962	13.9	10.8	3.1	19.8	8.1	11.7
1963	15.4	10.4	5.0	20.4	7.7	12.7
1964	15.9	10.5	5.4	20.1	7.6	12.5
1965	15.1	10.7	5.5	19.3	8.2	11.1
1966	14.4	10.8	3.6	18.5	8.2	10.3
1967	14.0	11.1	2.9	17.4	8.0	9.4
1968	13.9	11.7	2.2	17.0	8.5	8.5
1969	14.5	12.2	2.3	17.7	9.0	8.7

continued

Liberal access to abortion was justified in part by reference to its impact on women's equality. However, as with other policy measures that affected women's status, this measure was adopted without any real consultation of women or input from women's groups. The women's committees attached to communist organizations were abolished in Czechoslovakia in the early 1950s as the Stalinist system was consolidated, and, as in other communist countries, the single official women's organization that was allowed to exist served to mobilize women to carry out objectives determined by the leadership rather than to articulate or defend women's interests (Heitlinger 1979; Scott 1974; Wolchik 1981a, b).

As the result of the liberal abortion law, as well as the housing shortage, high levels of employment of women, and the very difficult economic situation of young families, the birthrate continued to drop in the late 1950s and early 1960s (see Table 2.1). However, it was only in the period of theoretical renewal at the elite level that was the prelude to the political reforms of 1968 that demographers

TABLE 2.2 (cont.)

	ČSR			SSR		
	Live Births	Deaths	Natural Increase	Live Births	Deaths	Natural Increase
1970	15.1	12.6	2.5	17.8	9.3	8.5
1971	15.7	12.4	3.3	18.2	9.4	8.8
1972	16.6	12.1	4.5	19.1	9.0	10.1
1973	18.3	12.5	5.8	20.0	9.4	10.6
1974	19.4	12.6	6.8	20.8	9.6	11.2
1975	19.1	12.4	6.7	20.6	9.5	11.1
1976	18.5	12.4	6.1	20.8	9.5	11.4
1977	17.9	12.4	5.5	20.6	9.7	10.9
1978	17.4	12.4	5.1	20.4	9.8	10.6
1979	16.7	12.4	4.3	20.3	9.7	10.6
1980	14.9	13.1	1.8	19.1	10.1	8.9
1981	14.0	12.7	1.4	18.6	8.7	6.1
1982	13.7	12.6	1.1	18.2	9.9	(8.3)
1983	—	—	—	—	—	—
1984	13.3	12.8	0.5	17.7	7.6	5.5
1985	13.1	12.6	0.5	17.4	10.1	7.3
1986	—	—	—	—	—	—
1987	12.7	12.3	0.4	16.1	10.0	4.9
1988	12.8	12.1	0.7	15.9	10.0	5.9
1989	12.4	12.3	0.1	15.2	10.2	5.0
1990	12.6	12.7	0.1	15.1	10.3	4.8
1991	12.6	12.1	0.8	14.9	10.3	4.5
1992	11.8	11.7	1.3	14.1	10.1	4.0
1993	11.8	11.4	0.8	13.8	9.9	3.9
1994	10.4	11.4	−0.1	12.4	9.6	2.8

Sources: Srb, Demografická příručka, p. 83; Statistická ročenka ČSSR 1970:91 and 1976:85; see also sources for Table 2.3.

and statisticians, as well as economists and other specialists, were able to discuss demographic trends honestly and call for change in the country's reproductive policies. Aided by the brief ideological thaw that followed the 22nd Congress of the Communist Party of the Soviet Union in 1961, specialists in a variety of areas began to come to terms with the distortions that had occurred in the country's intellectual life as the result of the consolidation of the Stalinist system. This process was most evident in the area of the economy, where a negative growth rate in 1961 spurred party leaders to give economic experts more freedom in the hopes of finding a remedy for the country's economic malaise (see Šik 1967; Skilling 1976; Kusin 1971, and 1972). However, it came to involve other specialists as well.

As in other areas of life, discussion of the country's demographic situation originally remained confined to the elite level. Demographers, statisticians, economists, and other specialists debated the causes of the declining birthrate and

TABLE 2.3
Abortions in ČSSR, ČSR, and SSR, 1953–1994

	Abortions in the ČSSR		Abortions in the ČSR		Abortions in the SSR	
	Number	Per 100 Live Births	Number	Per 100 Live Births	Number	Per 100 Live Births
1953	30,566	11.1	25,175	14.4	5,391	5.4
1955	35,087	13.1	25,850	15.4	9,237	9.7
1958	89,076	37.5	67,643	47.2	21,433	22.7
1960	114,602	52.2	85,213	65.5	29,389	32.9
1965	79,591	34.1	58,554	39.4	21,037	24.7
1970	99,766	43.3	71,893	48.3	27,873	34.3
1975	81,671	28.0	55,511	28.8	26,160	26.6
1980	100,170	40.0	68,930	44.6	31,240	32.6
1985	119,325	49.7	83,042	60.9	36,283	40.0
1986	124,118	52.5	83,564	74.2	40,624	46.6
1987	159,316	73.8	109,626	76.4	49,690	58.9
1988	164,730	75.9	113,730	85.4	51,000	61.0
1989	160,285	76.6	111,683	86.7	48,602	60.4
1990	159,705	75.5	111,268	84.9	48,437	60.3
1991	148,222	—	103,124	79.4	45,902	—
1992	135,815	—	93,435	76.5	42,626	—
1993	—	—	69,398	57.1	38,815	—
1994	—	—	53,674	50.2	34,883	—

Sources: Aleš 1993:230; Český statistický úřad 1994:85; Federální statistický úřad, Český statistický úřad, Slovenský štatistický úrad 1967:94; Federální statistický úřad, Český statistický úřad, Slovenský štatistický úrad 1968:102; Federální statistický úřad, Český statistický úřad, Slovenský štatistický úrad 1972:116; Federální statistický úřad, Český statistický úřad, Slovenský štatistický úrad 1978:108; Federální statistický úřad, Český statistický úřad, Slovenský štatistický úrad 1984:108; Federální statistický úřad, Český statistický úřad, Slovenský štatistický úrad 1989:112; Růžková and Aleš 1995:231, 245; Srb 1967:118; Štatistický úrad Slovenskej republiky 1993:116; Tirpák and Adamica 1995:261; Vývoj společnosti ČSSR v číslech 1965.
Note: Data for the period 1953 to 1960 include spontaneous abortions.

assessed the potential benefits of various remedies at specialized professional conferences and on the pages of small-circulation specialized journals (Heitlinger 1979; Wolchik 1983).

The rehabilitation of the social sciences in the mid-1960s allowed demographers and sociologists to conduct additional empirical studies of the causes of the decline in the birthrate. These once again highlighted the impact on birthrates of the uneven pattern of change in gender roles, particularly the high levels of women's employment outside the home, and the stressful situation of young families (Prokopec 1962; Srb et al. 1959:228–231; Wolchik 1983:117–124; Heitlinger 1979:177–189).

The number of groups involved in the discussion about reproductive issues increased in the mid to late 1960s. Specialists, particularly those involved with the State Population Commission established in the late 1950s, continued to play the dominant role in defining policy alternatives in this area. Similarly, women's views on reproductive issues continued to reach policy makers primarily in mediated form, as specialists and professionals interpreted the results of survey research to the Communist Party's gatekeepers who gathered information for policy makers. However, with the spread of nonconformist ideas among Party-related intellectuals in the mid-1960s and the reestablishment of a mass-based women's organization in 1966, women's activists also articulated their perspectives more directly (see Scott 1975; Wolchik 1981b:372–388; Heitlinger 1979:68–76). Through seminars, such as the one organized in 1966 on the role of women in socialist society, and articles in both the specialized and mass circulation press, women intellectuals active in the Official Women's Committee cooperated with specialists in challenging the official approach to women's issues and drawing attention to previously undiscussed aspects of women's situations. As in other areas of life, Communist Party-affiliated intellectuals took the lead in this effort.

In the course of the political reforms of 1968, when censorship in effect ceased to exist in Czechoslovakia, women's leaders explicitly identified the women's organization as an interest group to articulate and defend women's interests vis-à-vis Party and state authorities. They also called for a thorough reexamination of women's situation under socialism and for greater attention to women's preferences in the making of policies in all other areas (Švarcová 1964b:16, 1964a:5, 1965). They also participated in the increasingly open debate concerning all aspects of women's lives that developed in the course of discussion of economic reform and demographic policies. Originally centered on the consequences of women's employment for reproductive trends, this discussion also included consideration of other negative effects of the elite's emphasis on women's economic roles, the value of women's employment outside the home, and the difficulties women faced in performing their multiple roles (see Wolchik 1981b; Scott 1975; Hietlinger 1979).

As I have demonstrated at greater length elsewhere, many different perspectives were articulated in the course of these discussions. However, although women activists continued to defend women's right to work, discussions of women's issues came to be dominated by a focus on women's maternal roles. In reaction to the previous focus on women's roles as economic producers, leaders of the women's organization, as well as specialist elites, argued that the state should recognize the social importance of motherhood and reward women for the contribution they made to socialism by having and raising children (for examples, see Háková 1966:547–565, 1967:3).

The August 1968 invasion of Czechoslovakia by Warsaw Pact troops, which signaled the end of the reform era, also brought about the end of the efforts by women's leaders to define women's organizations as interest groups to defend women's interests. Women leaders who had supported the broader political reforms were removed from their positions, and open advocacy of women's interests once again became impossible. Many of the specialists involved in discussion of reproductive policies were also victims of the massive personnel purges that removed most supporters of the reforms from their positions.

However, the new approach to reproductive issues articulated during the course of the late 1960s continued to inform reproductive policies adopted after that time. The pro-natalist policy measures adopted in the early 1970s were based largely on the work of the specialists centered in the State Population Commission and reflected both positive incentives and negative sanctions to encourage population growth. The new measures were decidedly pro-natalist. During the height of the reform period some demographers as well as economists argued that the country had to learn to produce what it needed with the population it had and supported the efforts of economists to reform the economy. However, after the end of the reform period, it was not possible to articulate such views. In the interest of increasing population growth, both paid and unpaid maternity leaves were lengthened, and a variety of measures, including increased children's allowances, low interest loans for young families, increased priority in obtaining apartments for young couples who had children, and state subsidies for many of the items, such as children's clothing and equipment needed for young children, were adopted to decrease the expense of childbearing for young couples (see Heitlinger 1979, chap. 7; 1976:123–135). Many of these were similar to those being enacted elsewhere in the region (see David and McIntyre 1981:232–234).

Although abortion remained legal, the leadership also enacted a variety of measures designed to limit abortion for reasons other than the health of the mother. These included restrictions on access to abortion for social reasons, a category that accounted for 80 percent of all abortions in 1970 (see Heitlinger 1979:187). The abortion commissions that women were required to appear before in order to obtain permission for abortion were instructed in the early 1970s to restrict abortions for all but health reasons; however, most women who persisted were able to obtain permission (see Heitlinger 1979:187).

The new model of a socialist woman that continued to inform policy making in regard to reproduction and other issues of particular concern to women recognized the importance of women's maternal and domestic roles for society. According to this model, women were no longer expected to contribute to society in all areas throughout their life spans. Rather, it was expected that women would emphasize different roles at different stages of the life cycle. Thus, young women would obtain their educations and contribute to society by working; they would then focus on their maternal roles and, supported by maternity leave and mothers' allowances, remain at home to take care of small children. Once their children reached school age, women would once again become workers.

The leadership did not take seriously the problems for women's equality that this model, which presupposed that women would be out of the labor force for an extended period of time while rearing children, posed. Measures to allow women to keep their qualifications current, for example, so as not to fall behind their colleagues while at home with young children, were never implemented. Nor did the leadership or specialists who advocated pro-natalist policies consider the impact that reemphasis of women's maternal roles would have on women's perceptions of their own roles and aspirations or on the perceptions others would have of young women.

In the 1980s, certain demographers began questioning the wisdom of pro-natalism. These questions did not arise from concern about the impact of pro-natalism on women, but were connected instead to the growing realization among experts that the economy was in need of serious change. Zdeněk Pavlík, for example, argued that Czechoslovakia needed not more people but a more efficient economic system that would allow the country to produce what it needed with the population it had. Other experts noted that pro-natalist policies had in fact had an impact largely on the timing rather than the number of births; that is, young couples had their children earlier than they might have otherwise, but they did not have more children than they had originally planned (Kuchár and Pavlík 1990:299–309).

Widespread opposition to the abortion commissions and their ineffectiveness in reducing the rates of abortion led to their abolition in 1987. These commissions, which consisted of local officials, doctors and other medical personnel, and social workers, required women to appear to justify their requests for abortion in all cases except those involving a threat to the health of the mother, and were widely despised by women. They were also ineffective, as most women who repeated their requests were eventually allowed to end unwanted pregnancies (Wolchik 1983; Heitlinger 1976). Only 1.3 percent of requests were refused in 1986, for example (Aleš 1990:293). As Tables 2.1 and 2.2 illustrate, the number of abortions increased following the abolition of the abortion commissions, and the birthrate continued to fall in both the Czech and Slovak areas in the last years of communism.

THE POST-COMMUNIST ERA: REPRODUCTIVE TRENDS AND POLICIES

The end of communist rule in Czechoslovakia has been followed by important changes in both reproductive trends and policies in Czechoslovakia and its succes-sor states. The process by which policies in this area as well as in others are made has also been influenced in significant ways by the nature of the political and economic transitions from communist rule.

In both the Czech Lands and Slovakia, the end of communist rule has been followed by a further sharp drop in the birthrate. These trends, which have also occurred in other post-communist states, were evident most immediately in the Czech Lands. As Table 2.2 illustrates, the decline in births, which occurred in both the Czech Lands and Slovakia, became particularly sharp in 1994 in the Czech Lands. In that year the region experienced its lowest birthrate since statistics on natality began to be recorded in 1785 (Růžková and Aleš 1995:241). This decrease occurred despite a sizeable increase in the number of women in the most productive childbearing years in 1994, a fact that had led experts to predict an increase in births in that year. The decline in births was greatest among women in the youngest age groups (Růžková and Aleš 1995:242; Tirpák and Adamica 1994). The main exception to the decrease in the fertility of women in the Czech Republic occurred in the case of the Romany population. The average number of children of 40-year-old Romany women was more than twice that of Czech women of that age and 1.7 times greater than that of Czech women 20–30 years old (Fialová 1994:163). The birthrate continued to decline in 1995 in the Czech Lands (Český Statistický Úřad 1996:95). The decline was less dramatic, but the birthrate also fell in Slovakia.

There has also been a significant drop in marriages in both the Czech Republic and Slovakia since 1989 and an increase in the age of first marriage for both men and women. Thus, in the Czech Republic, there were 90,953 marriages in 1990 (8.8 per 1,000 population) and 58,440 in 1994 (5.7 per 1,000 population) (Růžková and Aleš 1995:239). In 1995, there were 54,956 marriages (Český Statistický Úřad 1996:105). The age of first marriage increased from an average of 21.4 years in 1990 to 24.0 years for women in 1994 and 23.9 to 26.2 years for men. These figures are still lower than in other developed Western countries, but it is clear that trends in the Czech Republic are coming to approximate those in other parts of Europe (Růžková and Aleš 1995:239). Divorces, in contrast, have remained at almost the same level (Růžková and Aleš 1995:240; see also Rychtaříková 1995:157–172).[1] Experts expect that both the number of couples who are living together without being formally married and the number of children born out of wedlock, which equaled 12.6 percent of all births in 1993 (Fialová 1994:163), will continue to increase in the Czech Republic (Fialová 1994:164; Rychtaříková 1995:159).

In Slovakia, the number of marriages declined from 40,435 (7.6 per 1,000 population) in 1990 to 28,155 (5.3 per 1,000 population) in 1994 (Tirpák and Adamica 1994:254). In 1995, there were 27,489 marriages (5.1 per 1,000 population) (Štatistický úrad Slovenskej republiky 1996:154). Divorce levels remained stable during this period (8,867 in 1990, 8,666 in 1994, and 8,978 in 1995) (Štatistický úrad Slovenskej republiky 1996:154); given the lower rates of marriage, the rate of divorce per 100 marriages increased from 21.9 in 1990 to 30.8 in 1994 (Tirpák and Adamica 1994:256).

In contrast to the trends in the communist era, the number of abortions also dropped dramatically. As Table 2.3 demonstrates, in the Czech Lands, abortions per 1,000 live births decreased rapidly from 90.1 in 1991 to 60.5 in 1994. The number of artificially induced abortions followed a similar trend. There were 85.2 such abortions per 100 live births in 1989; 83.4 in 1990; 81.7 in 1991; 76.5 in 1992; 58.2 in 1993; 50.2 in 1994 (Růžková and Aleš 1995:245); and 50.1 in 1995 (Aleš 1996:241). In absolute terms, there were approximately half as many abortions in 1994 as in 1991. In Slovakia, the number of abortions also dropped substantially and reached the lowest level per 1,000 population since 1977 in 1994 (Tirpák and Adamica 1994:260). The number of abortions dropped to 35,879 in 1995 (Štatistický úrad Slovenskej republiky 1996:159).

Demographers attribute these rapid changes to a number of factors. The decline in the birthrate in the Czech Lands in part reflects a rapid increase in the age of men and women at first marriage, which now approximates the norm

---

[1] In 1995 there were 31,135 divorces in the Czech Lands. See Český statistický úrad 1996:107.

in other developed European countries. It also reflects both the positive and negative impacts of the economic changes since 1989 on young people and young families. On the positive side, certain demographers attribute the drop in the birthrate and the decision to marry later to the new opportunities available to young people to travel, gain new qualifications, and work abroad (Růžková and Aleš 1995:239). These trends also reflect the more difficult economic situation of young families that has resulted from the shift to the market, including the end of certain government subsidies, such as low interest loans to young couples in 1991; the need for families to take greater responsibility for their own welfare; and the reform of the social welfare system from one of universal coverage to one based on need.[2] Families with two or more children or single parents, which had been most likely to be in poverty before 1989, faced the most difficult economic situations (Kroupová and Huslar 1991:171).

The economic hardship many families experienced, especially in the period immediately after the end of communism, and the increase in unemployment, which was particularly severe in Slovakia but also affected many families in parts of Bohemia and Moravia, also contributed to the hesitancy of young men and women to start families. Finally, the increased cost of many of the consumer durables and services needed for raising families, including childcare, also played a role (Růžková and Aleš 1995:242; Tirpák and Adamica 1994:257; Rychtaříková 1995).

The rapid drop in the birthrate and in the rate of abortions also reflects changes in the use of contraceptives in both the Czech Republic and Slovakia. Despite the fact that it was one of the most developed countries to become communist after World War II, levels of contraception remained very low in Czechoslovakia throughout the communist period. Studies of men's and women's reproductive behaviors indicate that this situation resulted from a variety of factors, including limited knowledge about modern methods of contraception; lack of availability of certain contraceptives, such as birth control pills; the high cost of certain contraceptives; and the fact that, in contrast to abortion, which was free under the communist government, all contraceptives cost something. The fact that available contraceptives, such as condoms and IUDs, were uncomfortable to use and unreliable, as well as fear about the health consequences of certain methods, such as IUDs, also contributed to the low use of contraception (see Heitlinger 1979; David and McIntyre 1981:232–234).[3]

Experts at the State Statistical Office concluded that the greater use of modern contraceptive methods was the most important factor in explaining the rapid drop in the number of abortions and that the institution of a fee for abortions not required for health reasons contributed in only a secondary way. As evidence, they cited the continued substantial decrease in the numbers of abortions between 1993 and 1994, for example, after the change in the cost of abortion. Support

---

[2] See Kuchařová and Lhotská 1995:164–169 for a discussion of the differences in the situation of different kinds of young families. See also Kroupová and Huslar 1991:149–178.

[3] See Kayal 1994 for interviews with women who discuss these difficulties.

for this conclusion is reflected in the fact that contraceptive use increased by several times in the Czech Republic in the early 1990s (Růžková and Aleš 1995:245).

Studies of reproductive behavior and of women's situations conducted since the end of communist rule provide additional insight into the factors that govern reproductive choices in the Czech Republic and Slovakia at present. A study of 1,072 women between the ages of 15 and 44 in Czechoslovakia carried out for Dr. Radim Uzel, a gynecologist who was at the time head of the Institute for the Care of the Mother and Child in Prague, found that 27.1 percent of Czech and Slovak women used "effective women's contraception," such as IUDs and birth control pills; an additional 28.6 percent depended on condoms. Half the sample in Slovakia and 40 percent in the Czech Lands used methods experts considered unreliable or did not use any form of contraception.[4]

A study of reproduction and health in the Czech Republic conducted by the Czech Statistical Office and the Institute for the Care of the Mother and Child in cooperation with the United States Center for Disease Control and Prevention and the World Health Organization found that 66 percent of all pregnancies were planned in the Czech Republic. Most unplanned pregnancies ended in abortion (Goldberg et al. 1994:33). Approximately 69 percent of married or previously married women used some kind of family planning. Seventy five percent of couples with two or three children used some kind of contraception, but only 29 percent of couples without children did. Women with higher education were significantly more likely to use contraception (Goldberg et al. 1994:34). Coitus interruptus, condoms, and IUDs were the most commonly used contraceptives among married women, accounting for three-quarters of all contraceptives used. Only 8 percent of married women used birth control pills. Among unmarried women, coitus interruptus and condoms were the most commonly used methods (Goldberg et al. 1994:34).

Most of the women surveyed in the 1995 study who indicated that they did not use contraceptives were either pregnant or had very low levels of sexual activity. Most of the others who did not identified fear of negative effects of various contraceptive methods on their health as the main reason for not using contraception. The authors of this study note that religious beliefs accounted for less than 1 percent of the reasons for not using contraception, even among Roman Catholic women (Goldberg et al. 1994:34, also their Table 2.6). Use of birth control pills has increased dramatically in the Czech Republic since 1989, in part as the result of greater availability due to the entry of foreign producers into the Czech market. By 1994, an estimated 8 percent of women in the Czech Republic used birth control pills (Kayal 1994).

A study carried out in Slovakia in 1995 found that most women (62 percent) felt that a two-child family was an ideal family; 23 percent thought that an ideal family should have three children (Bútorová 1996:38–39). The study found that 87 percent of women and 84 percent of men agreed with the notion that

---

[4] "Lack of Education on Contraception Causes High Abortion Figures," *ČTK National News Wire*, May 14, 1992.

responsible people use contraception and plan their families (Bútorová 1996:46). When asked which methods of contraception they would recommend to their friends, 83 percent of women in the fertile ages indicated that they would recommend condoms; 52 percent birth control pills; and 48 percent IUDs; 45 percent indicated that they would recommend coitus interruptus and 43 percent the rhythm method. However, medical experts estimate that less than 6 percent of Slovak women actually use birth control pills (Bútorová 1996:44).

As these trends and studies illustrate, reproductive decisions continue to be influenced in important ways by public policies. The latter, in turn, have been shaped by the nature of the new political system that has emerged, the impact of the economic transition, and the legacy of the communist period.

REPRODUCTIVE POLICIES: THE POLICY-MAKING FRAMEWORK

Policy making in regard to reproductive issues in the post-communist period has reflected the impact of several partially contradictory developments, perspectives, and views. These include the open challenge to pro-natalism by certain demographers and other specialists in population matters, the efforts of economic reformers who advocated a rapid move to the market to shift responsibility for the well-being of families to individuals rather than the state, and the ambivalent popular reaction to many aspects of the communist legacy. Elements of the latter that were particularly important included not only inconsistencies in popular attitudes regarding individual and state responsibilities but also attitudes toward the pattern of change in gender roles that had occurred under communism and perspectives on desirable gender roles.

The nature of transition politics in Czechoslovakia and later its successors and the impact of the shift to the market on elite and popular perceptions have also had an impact on legislation that influences reproductive choices. Overall, at the policy-formulation stage, a wider group of actors has been involved in the making of reproductive policies than were involved during the communist era. These include political leaders and bureaucrats; medical, demographic, and economic experts, as well as those involved in the making of social policies; representatives of the Catholic and other churches; women's activists and groups; and representatives of other nongovernmental organizations. Public opinion as reflected in social science research has also played a role in policy formulation.

The more open nature of the policy-making process and the larger number of actors involved have given women more avenues through which to articulate their preferences in regard to reproductive policies and to play a role in the process. However, despite the repluralization of politics that has occurred since 1989, policy making in the area of reproductive policy is still largely the affair of political elites. As the discussion that follows illustrates, women's low level of representation in positions of political power and the lack of ties between women's groups and legislators have limited women's direct influence on decisions in this as in other areas. Women still tend to be seen, as they were during the communist period, as resources to be mobilized in many discussions of reproductive policies, to the extent that they are explicitly considered at all.

The politics of transition have had an important influence on women's opportunities to articulate their political views, organize politically, and pressure political leaders; they have also influenced women's levels of representation in political elites and the ability of women leaders to articulate policies of particular interest to women. The move to the market and the hardships it has created for many women and their families, at least in the short run, have also had consequences for reproductive decisions.

Discussion of reproductive issues in the immediate post-communist period also took place in a climate in which many men and women questioned or rejected the approach to women's issues and roles that had prevailed during the communist era. This reaction reflected the state's appropriation of the goal of women's equality and the difficulties many women and their families experienced as the result of the uneven pattern of gender-role change that occurred under communism. It was evident in the view, shared by many women activists, that levels of women's employment were too high and that the previous approach had given too much emphasis to women's economic roles at the expense of their maternal roles (Wolchik 1993:29–47, 1994:3–28). However, as in the case of attitudes toward the role of the state, where many citizens felt that the role of the state should be reduced but did not want to see many aspects of state-provided services and guarantees changed, attitudes toward women's roles also reflected the internalization of certain aspects of the communist experience. These were particularly evident in attitudes toward employment, where studies have found that women have other motivations for working in addition to economic necessity (see Čermáková 1995; Bútorová and Čermáková 1996; Maříková 1996).

The sections to follow examine the influence of these factors on several aspects of reproductive policy-making. These include the reconsideration of pro-natalism; changes in social policies that affect reproduction; and changes in regulations regarding abortion. As my discussion illustrates, direct interventions designed to influence reproduction have had less impact on demographic trends and reproductive decisions than the impact of broader processes of economic, social, and political change.

Pro-Natalism Reconsidered

With the end of censorship those experts and specialists who had begun to question the wisdom of pro-natalist policies gained the opportunity to articulate their views more openly. Other specialists also expressed their views about the value of the pro-natalist measures enacted in the 1970s and 1980s and about the compatibility of a state population policy and a democratic, individually oriented political system and market economy. Some of the most interesting contributions to this debate were expressed in articles in the main demographic journal, *Demografie*, in the early 1990s. Sparked by an October 1990 article challenging the utility of population policy in the new political and economic conditions, this debate centered around several main issues. The first concerned the utility of the package of measures adopted in the 1970s to stimulate the birthrate. Opinion in this respect was divided among those, including most of the demographers involved in the discussion, who argued that the pro-natalist policies adopted had been a useful mechanism to influence population developments and those who felt that such policies had merely affected the timing, but not overall number of births or family plans for children.

Not surprisingly, many of the demographers who had been involved in designing the pro-natalist policies of the 1970s defended their utility. Citing evidence from a survey of demographers, sociologists, doctors, and other experts involved in population politics conducted in 1982, Vladimír Srb, one of the architects of the pro-natalist package, noted that over 97 percent of those experts felt that population policy had a very great (49 percent) or great (48 percent) significance for society. However, the same survey also reflected a division of opinion among experts concerning the utility of population policies. Sixty-five percent found the measures necessary. However, 26 percent of those surveyed found them ineffective, and 6 percent found them useless (Srb 1992:53).

Aligning himself with those who felt that a population policy, particularly one that was "pro-natalist, and dynamic" and separate from the broader sphere of social policy, was necessary, Srb noted that population policy is often justified by the need to regulate the reproduction of the population so as to preserve a proportion of basic age categories of the population with the goal of optimizing the economic, social, and cultural development of a given society. "The goal," in his words, "is the creation of conditions for families, so that they can realize their reproductive goals (how many children and when)." Noting that it is also necessary to pay attention to the "qualitative side" of population issues, Srb reaffirmed his belief in the need for a population policy that would be "institutionalized" once again (Srb 1992:53–54).

Other demographers, such as Milan Kučera, have argued that the focus of population policy is the future of the country and that its goal should be "the creation of a stable age structure of the population without large waves of births, with greater emphasis than previously on ensuring the health of the population, including decreasing death rates and increasing the life span" (Kučera 1992:235). Claiming that population policy cannot be subsumed under social policy, which focuses primarily on the socially needy, or family policy, which is differentiated according to various lifestyles and different kinds of families, Kučera argues that the time frame of demographic policy is longer term and that it must be concerned with developments 30 to 60 years in the future. Conceding the need for a change from the previous approach of subsidies and agreeing with the view that reproduction should be seen as the individual's responsibility, he notes that

> every government in every period has been involved fundamentally in the development of the population—either actively, directly or indirectly, or through its lack of interest (thus mainly negatively). A democratic government must pay attention to the population development of its country just as it does about its environment, even if it doesn't have

the time or means to do so at the moment. To not have children or to have few children means to lose the future: this is true in the case of the reproduction of individuals just as in the case of the reproduction of the nation, and more so if the nation is a small one. (Kučera 1992:235).

Kučera also called for demographers to prepare a position regarding the country's population policy to be presented to the government and representatives of all political parties and movements (Kučera 1992:235).

These perspectives have been challenged on several grounds by other demographers and sociologists. Milan Aleš, for example, has argued that political leaders did not pay any attention to the deliberations of the State Population Committee during the communist period but were interested primarily in using pro-natalist measures not so much as to consciously influence population growth as to demonstrate their ability to rule and claim the increase in births as evidence of the success of "normalization" (Aleš 1992:54–55). Noting that other democratic states do not hesitate to enter into the life of individuals by enacting measures, such as lower taxes, children's allowances, and parental leave, that have an impact on parenting, he argues that these policies are not an active population policy, but rather part of social policy that is concerned with upholding the minimum standard of living of citizens who otherwise would be handicapped as the result of parenthood: "Population development is undoubtedly markedly influenced by social policy, but it is, however, its side product." Aleš also articulates a number of practical impediments to a specific population policy, including the difficulty of forecasting and affecting long-term trends such as birthrates and migration. He argues that most current politicians have never thought very much about population policy or taken steps to promote it in practice. Aleš also raises objections to the new focus on the "quality" of the population and notes that it will be very difficult to identify who is the more valuable element of the population and warns of the racist uses of such terms (Aleš 1992:54–55).

Ladislav Rabušic notes that two different views have developed concerning population policies: that of demographers, who see the need for a separate, although reformulated, population policy, and that of those who take a more sociological perspective, who would like to see population policy replaced by family policy or social policy. He notes that the sociologically oriented point of view regards the reproductive behavior of individuals as "a social affair, which is, as is well known, influenced by their interests, value orientations and also by structural factors encompassing the whole social, economic, and political framework, in whose space every one moves and acts socially" (Rabušic 1992:56). From this perspective, the questions to be asked concerning the declining birthrate involve the reasons why the value of families and children is decreasing and why "this value, which has up to this point been a stable value of human existence all of a sudden is being replaced in first place by other values, by other life goals, which the society did not have earlier."

In contrast to the perspectives of the demographers outlined earlier, Rabušic emphasizes the importance of the changes in the forms of intimate relations and partnerships as one of the most important factors. Noting the diversification of family forms that has occurred in other developed societies, which now include unmarried cohabitation, couples who live apart, purposefully childless marriages, homosexual unions, and marriages with children, he questions whether the state can influence the reproductive behavior of individuals living in such diverse arrangements by means of an explicit population policy.

He also argues that the institutionalization of a population policy would reduce the level of responsibility of families in the area of family planning: "Social change such as we are experiencing now," he claims, "is among other things influenced by the extent to which the people of that state understand that they themselves have responsibility for their own life, for its quality, and its standard of living. The choice of the number of children is a choice of a lifestyle, a personal and independent choice, during which it is necessary to weigh only one's own forces and abilities" (Rabušic 1992:56–57). For this reason, Rabušic argues, population policies must be changed to family policy that will respect variations in the family behavior of individuals. Such a family policy, he claims, would be one of the forms of a social safety net and a form of social policy (Rabušic 1992:57).[5]

Other observers have argued that previous population policy was not effective, in that it did not prevent the decline of births, and in some cases was counterproductive because it led to discontinuities in the age structure of the population. Still other objections to the adoption of an active population policy include the view that it cannot be effective because it intrudes into a markedly private sphere of behavior and the belief that population policy influences primarily the behavior of those groups of women with the lowest educational levels (Řezníček 1992:144).

Noting that population policy, as well as social policy, was made in Czechoslovakia by a narrow circle of specialized experts "oriented in existing western models with little regard for the given tradition, reality, wishes, and possibilities of the population," one of the participants in this debate noted that all of the contributors to the debate to date had been "theorizing men." He called for efforts to ascertain the views of working women and for a representative study of the views of mothers, and perhaps fathers, about the real impact of population policies on their reproductive decisions (Řezníček 1992:144).

The contributions to the debate by two women that were printed in the same issue of *Demografie* present very different perspectives from those articulated here. The first, by an author who identifies herself as a woman, mother, and grandmother who has also been involved as a sociologist with population policies for the previous ten years, questions whether population policy should be institutionalized in a democratic state. She also asks who will set the goals for population development and according to what criteria and who will determine who will benefit from efforts to improve the "quality" of the population. Noting that "the number of children in a family is determined by the lifestyle of the parents, which reflects their preferences for certain values," she argues that the number

---

[5] For another argument that population policy should be seen as a part of social policy, see Řezníček 1992:143–144.

of children should "correspond to such a lifestyle rather than to some unclear need of a higher whole or so-called higher interests" (Freiová 1992:146).

Sociologist Jiřina Šiklová, who was instrumental in the founding of the Prague Gender Studies Center and has written extensively about women's issues, objected to the assumption that population policy is of necessity pro-natalist, rather than anti-natalist. Emphasizing the concern of experts in other parts of the world about the negative effects of overpopulation, she notes that "population measures are part of the programs of many political parties despite the fact that almost no one can justify why precisely in our country, in the ČSFR, we should desire an increase in the population" (Šiklová 1992:147). She calls for demographers and other experts, as well as political leaders, who are no longer required to tell the Party leadership what it wants to hear but are responsible to the voters, to make sure people know about the negative effects of population growth as well as about the social cost in terms of the need for social support of pro-natalist measures that are used by groups that are "less socially able" (Šiklová 1992:147–148). She also argues that spending on education can be seen as part of population policy, in that demographic developments put pressure on educational institutions to educate students, and notes that failure to invest sufficiently in education will later require more investment in remedial social programs and centers (Šiklová 1992:148).

Social Policy and Social Welfare Reform

As noted earlier, certain experts have come to see population policy as properly part of social policy. As in the area of reproductive policy more directly, a variety of understandings have been articulated concerning the nature and the scope of social policy that are desirable in Czechoslovakia and its successors. Supporters of economic reform and the rapid recreation of a market economy, who advocated a marked reduction in the government's responsibilities for providing social welfare and ensuring an adequate standard of living for all citizens, also supported a changed approach to population issues that would reduce the role of the state in this area.

However, as in the area of social welfare reform more generally, where efforts to move to a means-based system provoked protest and led to the adoption of gradual changes, the country's leaders moved cautiously in changing policies that affected reproduction.[6] The system of family benefits was extensive under communist rule when average transfers per child per month equaled approximately 15 percent of an average monthly salary by 1989, an amount equal to 9.7 percent of total government expenditures (see Kroupová and Huslar 1991:151–153). Although the new concept of family and social policy envisions a reduction in universal benefits coupled with social assistance programs for those groups in

---

[6] See Vobruba 1993:167–180; Večerník 1993:181–202; and Konopásek 1993:203–224 for recent discussions of social policy in the Czech Republic. See also Nesporová 1993:83–94; Kroupová and Castle-Kanerová 1992, chapter 4, for analyses of the changed approach to social policy since 1989.

the population most in need of help, political leaders moved slowly to implement these changes.[7] Maternity benefits were not only retained after 1989, but were also extended to include women who were at home. Maternity leaves were also changed to parental leaves, and thus in principle became available to men who assumed full-time care of infants and young children. The 900 crowns per month that a parent received for caring for children at home, however, was below the lowest pension.[8]

Children's allowances also remained universally available rather than being based on need. In the Czech Republic, these were increased again in mid 1993.[9] From April 1993, compensatory contributions of 220 crowns per month for one child were stopped for families whose incomes exceeded twice the minimum living standard.[10] Trade union officials who demanded that the government increase funds for the needs of children noted that the real value of children's allowances decreased by one-third to one-half by June 30, 1993, due to the increase in prices and cost of living.[11] New regulations adopted in 1993 shifted the basis for assigning benefits from the number of children in the family to the age of children. However, families were guaranteed that the contribution they received would not be less than the amount they received prior to the adoption of the new system.[12] Serious financial problems resulting in part from corruption and the collapse of several state banks in spring 1997 resulted in cuts in social spending as well as other austerity measures. In September, the Czech Parliament passed the government's proposal to cut the amount spent on children's allowances by raising the threshold for receiving them. To receive such allowances, which previously were available to all families whose income was three times above the poverty level, a family must now have an income 2.2 times above the poverty line. This measure, which went into effect on October 1, 1997, was expected to reduce the proportion of families receiving the supplement from 96 to 75 percent, thereby saving approximately 300 million crowns in 1997.[13] In Slovakia, reform of the social welfare system has taken place more slowly as the result of the different orientation of the Mečiar government.[14]

[7] See Musil 1995:423–434; Rys 1995:197–208; and Hart 1995: 209–220 for discussions of popular attitudes toward social policy reform.

[8] "Mateřská a 'otcovská' dovolená," *Lidové noviny*, October 4, 1993, p. 7.

[9] kjk, "Více peněz na děti," *Práce*, March 5, 1992:1–2; "Government Increases Some Social Allowances," *ČTK*, May 5, 1993; ika, "Přídavky na děti se zřejmě proti úvodnímu návrhu zvýší," *Lidové noviny*, September 9, 1993:2; ika, "Výplata přídavků na děti podle nové úpravy by neměla být ohrožena," *Lidové noviny*, September 18, 1993:2; ika, "Přídavky na děti podle věku," *Lidové noviny*, October 14, 1993:3.

[10] šb, "Od dubna vyšší životní minimum," *Lidové noviny*, January 6, 1993:12; ika, "Rodinám s nízkými příjmy," *Lidové noviny*, April 10, 1993:12.

[11] "Government Creating Anti-Population Climate," *ČTK*, September 6, 1993.

[12] ika, "Přídavky na děti se zřejmě proti původnímu návrhu zvýší," *Lidové noviny*, September 9, 1993:2.

[13] Simonik 1997.

[14] Luboš Juřina, "The Deadline for Social Reform, as Announced in the Government Program, Will Probably Not Be Met," *Trend*, February 1, 1995:14A.

In both the Czech Republic and Slovakia, discussion of social policy reform has been complicated by the differential birthrates of the Romany population. In Slovakia, statements such as the one by Prime Minister Vladimír Mečiar in September 1993 concerning the need to reduce family allowances to reduce the reproduction of "socially unadaptable and mentally backward" groups of the population have stirred controversy and provoked charges of racism.[15] In the Czech Republic, discussions of these issues have been more veiled. Certain experts and politicians have related reform of social policy to the quality of the population and to the reproductive patterns of socially weak segments of society. The shift to age of children rather than number of children in the family as the basis for assigning children's allowances indirectly addresses this issue, as large families are found primarily among Romanies in the Czech Republic. As in the communist period, the phrase "families with many children" continues to be a code for Romany or Gypsy families.

The main area of change in social policies that affect reproduction occurred in those policies in which the state subsidized goods and services for infants and children. These included low interest loans for young families guaranteed by the state; very low cost, subsidized children's clothing and equipment; and public childcare (Kroupová and Huslar 1991:151–152, 172–173). Low interest loans were eliminated for young families in 1991, and most subsidies were eliminated in the early 1990s. The lack of resources of municipal governments led to the closing of many childcare facilities and to the introduction of fees at others.[16] Coupled with the closing of many facilities previously operated by factories or economic enterprises, the latter change led to difficulties for many working parents in obtaining low cost or affordable childcare for their children. These difficulties have been particularly great for parents of the youngest children.[17] The number of places in nurseries for children up to 3 years of age, for example, declined from 78,555 in 1989 to 58,699 in 1990 and 17,210 in 1991. The decrease was particularly great in Slovakia, where the total number of public nurseries declined from 618 to 16 between 1989 and 1991 and the total number of places for children from 166,218 to 582.[18] The number of places in kindergartens also declined, although not so precipitously, from 11,380 schools with 636,622 places in 1989 to 10,924 schools with 512,503 children in 1991.[19] The number of

[15] "Slovak Government Considers Lowering Family Allowances," *ČTK*, September 3, 1993; "Mečiar: Social Policy to Curb Romany Birth Rate," *ČTK*, Prague, September 3, 1993, as reported in *FBIS-EEU-93-172*, September 8, 1993:16–17; "Remarks Trigger Protests," *ČTK*, September 6, 1993, as reported in *FBIS-EEU-93-172*, September 8, 1993:16–17.

[16] tos, "Školy nemají prostředky na svou další existenci," *Lidové noviny*, June 9, 1993:3; ria, "Kolik zaplatíme za školy," *Lidové noviny*, September 3, 1993:2; kva, "Školy podraží, učitelky ale nezbohatnou," *Lidové noviny*, September 7, 1993:2; kva, "Málo soukromých mateřských škol," *Lidové noviny*, September 8, 1993:2; "Na školky se zatím přispívat nebude," *Lidové noviny*, October 22, 1993:21.

[17] ria, "Jesle k nezaplacení, a tedy ke zrušení," *Lidové noviny*, August 4, 1993:2.

[18] Federální statistický úřad, Český statistický úřad, Slovenský štatisticky úrad 1992, p. 589.

[19] Federální statistický úřad, Český statistický úřad, Slovenský štatisticky úrad 1992, p. 553.

children of kindergarten age (3–5 years) who are in kindergarten decreased from 89.0 percent in 1990 to 84.4 percent in 1992, but increased to almost the same level (88.9 percent) in 1994. Almost all kindergartens previously operated by economic enterprises and cooperatives have closed or been terminated. Only 1.6 percent of all children in kindergarten were in private or church-run programs in the mid-1990s (Bulíř 1995:309–310).

In line with the new approach to family and social policy, the state has continued to support single-parent families within the framework of social assistance in both the Czech and Slovak Republics. Such families, most of whom are headed by women, were hit disproportionately by the economic changes, and many found themselves below the poverty line.[20] State support for such families continued to be higher than for families with both parents.[21] Mita Castle-Kanerová argues that discussion of family policy in the period immediately after the end of communism was informed by a very conservative view of family relations. Thus she notes that the 1990 proposal for a new social security system

> highlights the negative impact of the old system on families' "spiritual function," as well as on their roles in education and socialization. A very detailed and deeply conservative discussion follows. There is to be a revival of the "primary mutual solidarity," of family "sovereignty," of expanding the space for "family creativity," etc. The existential burden is to be removed in order to allow the family to flourish. As if economic freedom was the key to solving all other problems. Gender politics is conspicuously absent. (Castle-Kanerová 1992:113)

Similar perspectives have been evident in discussions of revisions of the law on the family in the Czech Republic and social policy reform in Slovakia.[22]

Abortion

In addition to changes in social and family policy, there have been several attempts to regulate access to abortion since 1989. In both the Czech Lands and Slovakia, these included increases in the cost of abortion. In Slovakia, the government of Ján Čarnogurský also made an effort to enact a much more restrictive law that would have outlawed most abortions. Conservative political forces, including religious organizations and religiously based political parties, participated in these discussions in both the Czech Lands and Slovakia. However, in neither case did such groups succeed in eliminating women's access to abortion.

Most men and women in both the Czech Lands and Slovakia opposed the idea of restricting access to abortion. However, many men and women also felt

---

[20] See Večerník 1995:87–100 for an analysis of the changing basis of poverty in the Czech Republic after 1990.

[21] Ministry of Foreign Affairs of the Slovak Republic, Center for Strategic Studies of the Slovak Republic 1995. See Večerník 1995:99 for analysis that highlights the fact that families with children have now moved into the lowest positions on income indicators.

[22] See ika, "Nový zákon o rodině je nutný," *Lidové noviny*, January 26, 1994:2; ika, "Nový zákon o rodině má být už letos," *Lidové noviny*, January 21, 1994:2; and Eva Martínková, "Mladé rodiny jsou nejohroženější," *Lidové noviny*, May 7, 1993:1–2.

that levels of abortion were too high. As Table 2.4 illustrates, surveys conducted by the Institute for Public Opinion Research in Prague since 1990 have consistently found that men and women in the Czech Republic feel that women should have the right to decide about having an abortion. Only 3–5 percent of respondents reject abortion in all instances; 9–10 percent feel that abortion should be allowed only if a woman's life is threatened.

Differences in the views of men and women on these issues are not statistically significant. However, support for women's right to abortion varies by age, educational level, size of place of residence, and religious affiliation. Thus, in 1995, 72 percent of younger people agreed that women should always have the right to decide about abortion; 48 percent of those over 60 agreed. Fifty-eight percent of those with elementary education support this right, compared to 67 percent of those with high school educations and 63 percent with university educations. Approximately 56 percent of respondents who live in villages with up to 2,000 inhabitants agreed with this right, compared to 68 percent in cities over 100,000 population. Most strikingly, only 44 percent of Catholic women supported women's right to decide in all circumstances, compared to 73 percent of women who identified themselves as nonbelievers.[23]

Other surveys of popular attitudes toward abortion confirm the general acceptance of women's right to decide. A 1991 study conducted by the Institute for Public Opinion Research in Czechoslovakia, for example, found that 61 percent of the population of Czechoslovakia thought a women should decide about having an abortion. Twenty-three percent felt that abortions should be allowed only for health and social reasons, 11 percent only if a woman's life were in danger. Four percent wanted to outlaw abortion. Respondents in the Czech Republic were more supportive of women's right to choose (63 percent) than those in Slovakia (56 percent), but differences were not great.[24]

TABLE 2.4
Attitudes toward Abortion in the Czech Republic

	1990	1992	1995
Women should always have the right to an abortion	60%	64%	63%
Abortion should be allowed only when health or family reasons warrant it	26%	23%	25%
Abortion should be allowed only when the mother's life is endangered	9%	10%	9%
Abortion should be banned	5%	3%	3%

Source: Institute for Public Opinion Research, Prague.
Note: Sample size approximately 1,000 in all cases.

[23] "Názor veřejnosti na interrupce," Prague, IVVM, October 26, 1995.
[24] "Názory na interrupce," *Lidové noviny*, August 10, 1992:12; and "Abortion Decision Rests with Woman, a Majority Say in Poll," *ČTK*, April 30, 1991.

A 1993 study of women's reproductive behavior in the Czech Republic found that 85 percent of those surveyed favored women's right to decide to have an abortion under all circumstances. In contrast to the 1995 survey just discussed, however, this study found that a large majority of Catholic women (83 percent) also agreed with women's right to choose. Non-Catholic women who identified themselves as believers also generally agreed with this right, although to a lesser degree: 72 percent (see Table 2.5; also Goldberg et al. 1994:38). As Table 2.6 illustrates, a large proportion of those who do not agree with allowing women

TABLE 2.5
Percent of Women Respondents Age 15–44 Who Think That Women Should Always Be Able to Decide Whether to Have an Abortion (by Selected Characteristics)

Characteristics		Percent	Number of Cases
Total		85.2	(4,497)
Republic	Bohemia	86.4	(2,737)
	Moravia	83.4	(1,760)
Size of Place	Less than 5,000	84.1	(1,472)
	5,000 to 19,999	87.1	(967)
	More than 20,000	88.2	(2,058)
Age	15–19	82.5	(662)
	20–24	84.3	(756)
	25–29	86.9	(828)
	30–34	88.0	(720)
	35–39	84.8	(805)
	40–44	85.9	(726)
Marital Status	Currently married	86.0	(3,217)
	Previously married	87.9	(355)
	Never married	82.5	(925)
Education	Primary	78.8	(738)
	Secondary, no diploma	84.0	(1,779)
	Secondary, diploma	88.9	(1,601)
	Any university	91.0	(379)
Religion	None	87.4	(2,867)
	Catholic, attend mass	70.8	(256)
	Catholic, do not attend mass	85.7	(1,134)
	Other	72.1	(226)
Household Income	3,000 or less	77.4	(188)
	3,001–7,000	83.6	(1,885)
	7,001–10,000	87.8	(1,278)
	More than 10,000	87.9	(803)
	Not stated	82.3	(343)

Source: Table 22, 1993 Czech Republic Reproductive Health Survey. Czech Statistical Office, WHO Collaborating Center for Perinatal Medicine/Institute for the Care of Mother and Child, Prague, and Centers for Disease Control and Prevention, USA, January 1994.

unrestricted access to abortion nonetheless support a women's right to choose if her life is endangered, there is a fetal defect, the pregnancy endangers a women's health or is the result of rape. A survey conducted by STEM in 1994 found that religious belief reduced support for abortion to some extent. However, 31 percent of those who identified themselves as believers definitely agreed and 35 percent tended to agree with abortion on demand (a total of 67 percent).[25]

A recent study of women's situations in Slovakia provides information on the proportions of men and women who approve of women's right to choose an abortion in particular circumstances. Approximately 90 percent of men and women surveyed in June 1995 approve of a woman's right to have an abortion when the mother's life is threatened, 83 percent when the woman has been raped, and 82 percent when it is likely that the child will be handicapped. Fifty-nine percent approve when the pregnancy is unwanted for whatever reason, 55 percent when families will have difficulty caring for the child for social reasons, and 50 percent when parents do not want another child. Forty-six percent approve when the women is a minor, 31 percent when the child was conceived out of wedlock, and 23 percent when the woman is unmarried (Bútorová 1996:41). Based on their responses to these circumstances, approximately 40 percent of women and 42 percent of men are classified as approving of women's right to choose abortion; 51 and 52 percent hold "hybrid" positions in which they approve in certain circumstances and disapprove in others; and 9 and 6 percent are opponents of abortion. Support for women's right to choose abortion is greatest among those who have higher education, who are between 25 and 44 years of age, and who are not religious. Thus, 34 percent of those who classify themselves as deeply

TABLE 2.6
Opinions on Whether Women Should Be Able to Have an Abortion under Given Circumstances, among Respondents Who Think There Should Be Restrictions on Whether Women Can Have Abortions (Percent Distributions)

| Circumstance | Whether Women Should Be Allowed to Have an Abortion under the Given Circumstance | | | | |
	Yes	Depends	No	Not Sure	Total
Woman's life is endangered	90.7	2.5	4.3	2.5	100.0
Fetal defect	73.9	9.8	10.9	5.4	100.0
Woman's health is endangered	71.5	10.8	12.4	5.3	100.0
Pregnancy resulted from rape	71.0	7.8	14.9	6.3	100.0
Woman/couple cannot afford a baby	15.6	18.1	55.5	10.9	100.0
Woman is not married	8.3	18.2	70.3	3.3	100.0

Source: Table 23, 1993 Czech Republic Reproductive Health Survey. Czech Statistical Office, WHO Collaborating Center for Perinatal Medicine/Institute for the Care of Mother and Child, Prague, and Centers for Disease Control and Prevention, USA, January 1994.

Note: n = 657. This table does not include the 85.2 percent of respondents who said that women should be able to decide whether to get an abortion under any circumstances.

[25] "Most Czechs for Abortion, Divorce but Split on Prostitution," ČTK, March 22, 1994.

religious and 7 percent of those who say they are religious are opponents of abortion. Of those who are not religious, only 1 percent are opponents (Bútorová 1996:42).

Debate about the revision of the 1986 law on abortion began soon after the end of the communist system. The impetus for reconsideration came from religious leaders and leaders of religious parties who opposed the law on moral grounds. In November 1990, the Bishops' Conference sent a letter to the Federal Assembly and the legislatures of the Czech and Slovak Republics requesting that they eliminate legal abortion (Červenková 1990:16). This action was followed in December 1990 by a pastoral letter demanding the end of abortion.[26] In February 1991, the Bishops' Conference sent a more moderate appeal to the Czech Ministry of Health restating the position of church leaders against abortion. However, noting that the CNR would not pass a rigorous anti-abortion law and that it was necessary to assess the situation realistically, the proclamation called for the use of moral education and the provision of social supports for pregnant women rather than the outlawing of abortion (Červenková 1990:16).

In March 1991, Deputy Prime Minister of the Czechoslovak federal government Jozef Mikloško established a consultative commission on abortion that included representatives of the Ministries of Health, Education, Youth and Physical Training, and Labor and Social Affairs, as well as members of Parliament and representatives of churches and civic organizations.[27] The Ministries of Health of the Czech and Slovak Republics began drafting new legislation to combat the high rates of abortion in October 1991.[28]

Government action to amend the laws that governed abortion followed somewhat different paths in the Czech Republic and Slovakia prior to the end of the common state. These differences reflected some of the ways in which society and politics differed in the two areas. In the more secularized Czech lands, parties affiliated with the Church were the junior partners in the ruling coalitions. In Slovakia, religion is a more important influence on everyday behavior, and the Prime Minister from 1990–1992 was a former Catholic dissident. The Minister of Health was also a Catholic activist. Thus, the Czech Minister of Health proposed a modification of the law whose primary significance was an increase in the fee for abortion for nonmedical reasons. In April 1992, the Slovak Minister of Health, who was a member of the Christian Democratic Movement, proposed a law on the defense of human life in the provision of health services that would have reestablished abortion commissions and seriously restricted women's right to abortion.[29] The fall of Ján Čarnogurský's government as the result of the June 1992 elections prevented the implementation of the proposed Slovak law; as a result, the 1986 law remained in force in Slovakia.

[26] "Catholic Bishops Demand Ban on Abortion," *BBC Summary of World Broadcasts*, January 5, 1991.
[27] "Commission Is Set Up in Czechoslovakia to Deal with Abortions," *ČTK*, March 27, 1991.
[28] "1986 Law on Abortions Too Benevolent, Slovak Minister Says," *ČTK*, February 13, 1991.
[29] Irena Jirků, "Interrupční zmatky," *Mladá fronta dnes*, October 15, 1992:16. "Vladný navrh 279. Zákon o ochrane ľudskeho života pri poskytovani zdravotnickej starostlivosti," Bratislava, March 1992.

In the Czech Republic, the implementation of fees for abortion took place in the context of a broader revision of prices for healthcare services. The introduction of 2,500 or 3,000 crown fees for abortion for nonmedical reasons in 1992 was justified primarily by reference to the negative impact of repeated abortions on women's health and the cost to the state of paying for these procedures.[30] Supported by a number of women parliamentarians who were also gynecologist-obstetricians, the change in the regulations that went into effect imposed a fee for abortion other than those for health reasons, a sum equivalent to approximately a month's salary.[31]

A variety of actors became involved in the discussion of abortion rights in both the Czech Republic and Slovakia. These included political leaders, particularly those affiliated with Christian parties; state officials, including those in ministries responsible for health, education, and youth; church leaders; and experts and specialists in the areas of health, education, and social policy. Representatives of nongovernmental groups, including Christian and other women's groups, various right to life associations, professional associations, and planned parenthood groups also participated in these debates.

One of the earliest public manifestations of the extent to which opinion was divided on this issue occurred in response to a letter by Radim Uzel, a doctor who worked at the Institute for the Care of the Mother and Child in Prague and became one of the main activists in planned parenthood groups, published in *Lidové noviny* in March 1990. Attributing the threat to access to abortion to Christian groups and political parties, Uzel linked the 1986 law on abortions to U.N. documents that Czechoslovakia's leaders had signed that guaranteed citizens the right to family planning. He also sought to dispel fears that the decline in the birthrate would pose a threat to the well-being of the country and argued that the problem lay not with the abortion law but with the health consciousness of the population. The real issue, as he identified it, was not restriction of women's right to abortion, but rather the need for measures to increase knowledge about responsible choices and access to contraceptives.[32] A controversial figure because of his creation of the Independent Erotic Initiative and unorthodox methods of getting publicity for his cause, Uzel has become an outspoken promoter of contraception who has advocated, among other things, free contraceptives for all women under the age of 21.[33]

---

[30] See Irena Jirků, "Kdy, jak a kolik zaplatíme za zdravotní péči," *Mladá fronta dnes*, October 17, 1992:7.

[31] In early July 1993, the cost of an early abortion was raised to 2,831 crowns, and an abortion between eight and twelve weeks was raised to 3,459 crowns. "Pevné maximální ceny na interrupce," *Lidové noviny*, July 12, 1993:2. See also Ivana Karásková, "Poplatky za interrupci nesmějí být trestem," *Lidové noviny* October 5, 1992:3, for the efforts of the Society of Czech Gynecologists-Obstetricians to postpone the introduction of fees for three months. See also kar, "Jaké poplaty za interrupce," *Mladá fronta dnes*, October 5, 1992 and ika, "Interupce: úmava cenu," *Mladá fronta dnes*, October 7, 1992:3.

[32] Radim Uzel, "Chyba není v interrupci," *Lidové noviny*, March 7, 1990:2.

[33] ria, Černý trh s antikoncepcí," *Lidové noviny*, April 30, 1993:2, and sb, "Strana NEI žádá svobodu interrupcím," *Mladá fronta dnes*, November 16, 1992:3.

Publication of Uzel's article provoked 170 replies from readers. Most of these (87 percent) were vehemently against abortion. Five percent were classified as "tolerant" by the author of an article introducing excerpts from a few of them, and 8 percent agreed with the existing law. Most of the letters were from men between the ages of 25 and 50. Very few specialists or women replied. Of those specialists who did, 90 percent favored retaining liberal access to abortion.[34] Thus, the view expressed by the majority of letter writers differed markedly from support for women's right to abortion evident in the public opinion polls discussed earlier.

Public support for retaining women's right to abortion was clearly among the factors that influenced discussion of the revision of the law on abortion at the elite level. The proceedings of the March 25, 1991, meeting of the commission established under the auspices of the Division for Education, Culture, and Health of the Office of the Federal Government provide some insight into the perspectives of the groups involved. In the course of the meeting, a medical doctor associated with the movement for life argued that contraception should be seen as an early form of abortion and called for outlawing abortion.[35] Another woman, who was affiliated with the Christian Democratic Association of Women in Slovakia, argued that abortion was equivalent to the genocide of the nation and argued against abortion for any reason. However, all of the other forty-five participants in the discussion agreed from the outset that it was not possible to outlaw abortion. There was also general agreement that the number of abortions was too high. Perspectives differed, however, on the nature of abortion and the most feasible ways of reducing the high numbers of abortions. As one would expect, religious spokespersons, as well as those affiliated with various right to life groups and Christian members of Parliament, argued that abortion should in fact be seen as "ending" a new life rather than "interrupting" pregnancy. Representatives of pro-life groups stressed the need to inform the public about the risks of abortion. Several also noted that abortion should not be seen as a form of contraception and argued that propagation of contraception led to the development of a "contraception mentality" that in turn led to abortions. Advocates of this position also called for use of "natural" family planning methods.

Many of the medical experts who participated in the debate emphasized the need to retain legal abortion as well as increase knowledge about and the availability of contraceptives. Several speakers, including one associated with the Organization of Marital and Family Counselors, pointed to the need for better services for pregnant women as well as for social and economic help for women in order to allow them to make a free choice in regard to abortion. Other experts emphasized the need to increase education for parenthood.[36]

[34] Petra Procházková, "Interrupce, ano či ne?" *Lidové noviny*, April 14 1990:4.

[35] "Záznam z jednání poradní komise pro otázky interupce s místopředsedou vlády ČSFR RNDr. J. Mikloškem, DrSc., konané dne 25. března 1991 na Úřadu vlády ČSFR v Praze," mimeograph, Prague, March 25, 1991:6.

[36] "Záznam," 1991:7–8.

Members of the Czech Obstetrical Gynecological Society expressed similar sentiments in their position on the revision of the law. Among other points, they emphasized the far greater risks women face from pregnancy than from very early abortion and argued, "We do not have either a health or a moral right to require a woman to undergo a 100 time greater risk of death from unwanted pregnancy and maternity."[37]

A medical doctor who served as advisor to the Czech Minister of Health expressed a hybrid of these views. Observing that the Ministry had already prepared a proposal for change in the Czech Republic, she noted that the new law would change the terms in which abortion was discussed to indicate that abortion was the end, or killing, of the fetus. She expressed the view that, although it was not feasible to outlaw abortion during the first twelve weeks, the terms governing when it was permissible for women to have abortions should be carefully defined. She also called for free women's contraceptives to be made available to women as soon as possible as a short-term measure and for education on responsible parenting as a long-term measure to reduce the high number of abortions.[38]

The comments of representatives of women's groups reflected the more general division of opinion among women. Thus, the representative of the Czech Women's Club argued that there was a general lack of respect toward women in society and that an educational program should be undertaken to make sure that everyone understood that men bear some responsibility in reproductive decisions. The representative of the Czech Union of Women, the continuation of the old official women's organization, agreed with these views and emphasized the fact that fees for abortion would have to be waived for women with lower incomes or be subsidized at least partially. In a position paper on the issue, Union spokeswomen also used the fact that an embryo is part of a woman and cannot exist without her as justification for women's right to reproduction and abortion as part of their right to self-determination. They also pointed to other factors that limited women's right to reproduction, including unhealthy environmental and working conditions and economic conditions that made it difficult for women to contemplate responsible parenthood.[39]

The most unqualified defense of women's right to choose came from an expert affiliated with the Sexology Institute of the Medical Faculty in Prague. Arguing that women must retain the right to decide about abortions and have the right to protection against unwanted pregnancies, he called for increased sex education and contraception to decrease the abortion rate.[40]

In light of the later efforts of the Slovak government to restrict abortion, the positions of the representatives of the Slovak government are of interest. One,

[37] "Stanovisko výboru české porodnicko—gynekologické společnosti k současnému Zákonu 66/1986 Sb. o umělém přerušení těhotenství," p. 2.

[38] "Záznam," 1991:11.

[39] "Stanovisko ČSŽ k interrupcím," January 1, 1991.

[40] "Záznam," 1991: 9.

who worked in the Ministry of Education's ethics department, noted that society must make it clear that it tolerates but does not recommend abortion. The other, Dr. Vránová, who was Secretary of the Slovak government's Committee for Women and the Family, emphasized that all children had a right to be wanted. She argued that state policies concerning social care for families should not be reduced to social assistance and urged that steps be taken to change the law on adoption to make it easier for couples to adopt unwanted children.[41]

At present, then, women retain the right to abortion in both the Czech Republic and Slovakia. Religious groups continue to call for the end to legal abortion in both countries,[42] but to date have had little success in persuading public officials to enact restrictions. Many opponents of abortion have shifted the bulk of their efforts to encouraging government officials to create better conditions for young families and increase support for mothers who will give their children up for adoption.

IMPLICATIONS FOR OUR UNDERSTANDING OF GENDER POLITICS AND THE POLITICS OF TRANSITION

As this consideration of some of the main elements of reproductive policies in Czechoslovakia and its successors illustrates, issues that affect reproduction have been influenced by many of the same factors that have shaped policy making in other areas since the end of communism. One of the most important of these is the relatively small role women in both the Czech Lands and Slovakia play in politics. As numerous studies have documented, the marginalization of women from the exercise of effective political power that occurred under communist rule has continued since 1989 (Wolchik 1993:29–47, 1994:3–28; Einhorn 1993; Wolchik et al. 1994; Čermáková and Navarová 1990). Although women who have become political leaders since the end of the communist system have educational levels closer to those of their male counterparts and are thus more likely than their communist predecessors to have the skills needed to be effective political leaders, they are few in number and must deal with the widespread notion that there is no need to pay special attention to women's particular interests in policy making.

Analysts have offered a variety of reasons to account for women's lower levels of interest in politics. For our purposes, these are less important than the implications of women's limited participation in the exercise of political power for policy making. Because women leaders are few in number and because they are not supported by large women's movements outside Parliament, they are often marginalized in policy decisions. The efforts of Catholic women parliamentarians in the Czech Republic did not succeed in establishing a ministry to deal with

[41] Ibid., 11.
[42] See "Apostolic Church Rejects Abortion as Means of Social Aid," *ČTK*, March 16, 1993; "Slovakia: Catholic Bishops Seek Reform of Abortion Law," *BBC*, November 13, 1995; "Cairo Was a Display of Selfishness—Vlk" *ČTK*, September 22, 1994.

women's and family issues in the 1990–1992 period, for example. Instead, a commission on women's issues was set up to advise the government (interview with Dr. Ivana Janů, Prague, June 1992). In Slovakia, a Committee for Women and the Family was established as part of the government. However, it served largely to provide materials to support the actions of the government. It had no independent budget or powers and, in the words of one of its officials, little influence on social and family policy. The irrelevance of this body to policy making is reflected in the fact that it was not even asked to take a position on the government's proposed law to restrict abortion radically in 1992 (interview with Dr. M. Malevecková, Bratislava, March 1992).

Efforts by political leaders and conservative groups to restrict abortion led individual women to intervene in the policy-making process as specialists, political leaders, and representatives of women's groups. Women have also participated in the debates about abortion, family policy, and other issues related to reproductive policy that have taken place in the print and other media. Women activists on both the conservative and liberal or feminist sides of the issue have also organized numerous public discussions, roundtables, and seminars about these issues for their members and the broader public. However, women have not been mobilized to enter the political arena in large numbers in connection with any of these issues. There were no demonstrations of women in Slovakia, for example, when the Slovak government proposed its very restrictive abortion law in 1992.

In the case of pro-natalist policies and social policy reform, part of the reason for women's lack of involvement may lie in the fact that decision making has taken place largely at the elite level.[43] It may also reflect the fact that, although they may disagree with particular changes in individual aspects of social policy, most women in both the Czech Republic and Slovakia feel that individual families rather than the state should be responsible for the well-being of children (Bútorová 1996; Čermáková 1996).

In the area of abortion policies, the proposed changes may not have mobilized women because they felt that restrictions were unlikely to be enacted. Most women in Slovakia, including intellectual women who supported free access to abortion, were not concerned about the restrictions on abortion proposed by Ján Čarnogurský's government in 1992 because it appeared quite likely that his government would be defeated in the June elections, for example.[44] In this situation, then, where there is an absence of a dramatic, realistic challenge to women's reproductive freedom, reproductive policies are unlikely to serve, as they have elsewhere in the region, as a means of increasing women's interest in politics or in the development of a large women's movement in the Czech Republic or Slovakia.

Although the lack of a real threat to access to abortion means that reproductive policies narrowly defined are unlikely to mobilize women, issues related to the

---

[43] See Kroupová and Castle-Kanerová 1992:115–116 for the argument that a broad public discussion has not taken place.

[44] Interviews with Olga Plavková, Soňa Szomolanyi, Etela Farkašová, and Zora Bútorová in Bratislava, June 1992.

broader social and economic context that affect reproductive decisions may spark greater interest on women's part. As recent cutbacks in social spending, including children's allowances in the Czech Republic, suggest, the real threat to women's reproductive freedom will come from social and economic developments that may limit women's ability to have children by their impact on the family's livelihood and standard of living.

To date, women have not taken to the streets or engaged in other forms of collective action to protest or to attempt to influence these developments. However, the threat of strikes by public sector employees in the Czech Republic, many of whom are women, particularly in health and education, indicate that such issues have the potential to mobilize women. Should some form of protest or collective action develop among women, nonetheless, it is likely that they will frame or articulate their demands as family issues that affect society as a whole, rather than as gender issues that relate to women's particular situation or interests.

BIBLIOGRAPHY

Aleš, Milan
    1990   Populační vývoj v Československu v roce 1986. Demografie 29(4):293.
    1992   Populační politika: ano či ne? Demografie 34(1):54–55.
    1996   Populační vývoj v České republice v roce 1995 (Z roční zprávy Českého statistic-
            kého úřadu). Demografie 38(4):293.
Bulíř, Michal
    1995   Mateřské školy v letech 1990–1994. Demografie 37(4):309–310.
Bútorová, Zora
    1996   Ona a on na Slovensku. Bratislava: Focus.
Bútorová, Zora and Marie Čermáková
    1996   Rodina a zaměstnané ženy I. Data & Fakta 1.
Castle-Kanerová, Mita
    1992   Social policy in Czechoslovakia. *In* The New Eastern Europe. Social Policy
            Past, Present, and Future. Bob Deacon, ed. London: Sage.
Čermáková, Marie
    1995   Gender, společnost, a prácovní trh. Sociologický časopis 31(1):724.
    1996   Rodina a zaměstnané ženy. I. Data & Fakta 1:1–4.
Čermáková, Marie, and Hana Navarová
    1990   Ženy a volby. Prague: Czechoslovak Academy of Sciences, Institute of Soci-
            ology.
Český statistický úřad
    1994   Statistická ročenka České republiky. P. 85. Praha: Český spisovatel.
    1996   Statistická ročenka České republiky. Praha: Scientia.
David, Henry P. and Robert J. McIntyre, eds.
    1981   Reproductive Behavior: Central and Eastern European Experience. New
            York: Springer.
Einhorn, Barbara
    1993   Cinderella Goes to Market. London: Verso.
Federální statistický úřad, Český statistický úřad, Slovenský štatistický úrad
    1992   Statistická ročenka České a Slovenské Federativní Republiky. Pp. 553, 589.
            Prague: SVET.

Fialová, Ludmila
  1994   Reprodukce v rodinách a mimo ně. Demografie 37(3):159–164.
Freiová, Eliška
  1992   Co může a co smí populační politika? Demografie 2:145–146.
Goldberg, Howard with Jaroslav Kraus, Ivan Tomek, and Petr Velebil
  1994   Průzkum reprodukce a zdraví—ČR 1993. Demografie 36(1):30–39.
Háková, Libuše
  1966   Ženy v sociální struktuře naší společnosti. *In* Sociální struktura socialistické
          společnosti. Pavel Machonin et al., eds. Pp. 547–565. Prague: Nakladatelství
          Svoboda.
  1967   Naš rozhovor s Irenou Durišovou. Vlasta 22:3.
Hartl, Jan
  1995   Social Policy: An Issue for Today and the Future. Czech Sociological Re-
          view III(2):209–220.
Heitlinger, Alena
  1976   Pro-Natalist Population Policies in Czechoslovakia. Population Studies
          30(March):123–135.
  1979   Women and State Socialism: Sex Inequality in the Soviet Union and Czechoslo-
          vakia. Montreal: McGill-Queen's University Press.
  1987   Reproduction, Medicine and the Socialist State. New York: St. Martin's Press.
Kayal, Michele
  1994   Eroding an Abortion Culture. The Prague Post, April 20 (Online. Lexis/
          Nexis Academic Universe. 26 May 1999).
Konopásek, Zdeněk
  1993   O dvojí univerzalitě institucí welfare state. Sociologický časopis 29(2):203–224.
Kroupová, Alena and Mita Castle-Kanerová
  1992   Social Policy in Czechoslovakia. *In* The New Eastern Europe: Social Policy
          Past, Present and Future. Bob Deacon, ed. London: Sage.
Kroupová, Alena and Ondřej Huslar
  1991   Children at the Turning Point: Economic Reform and Social Policy in Czecho-
          slovakia. *In* Children and the Transition to the Market Economy: Safety Nets
          and Social Policies in Central and Eastern Europe. Giovanni Andrea Cornia
          and Sándor Sipos, eds. Pp. 149–178. Brookfield, VT: Gower.
Kučera, Milan
  1992   K populační politice—bez závěru. Demografie 3:235–236.
Kuchár, Ivan and Zdeněk Pavlík
  1990   Optimalizace kvality populace. Demografie 29(4):299–309.
Kuchařová, Věra and Věra Lhotská
  1995   Ekonomická situace mladých rodin. Demografie 37(3).
Kusin, Vladimír V.
  1971   The Intellectual Origins of the Prague Spring: The Development of Reformist
          Ideas in Czechoslovakia, 1956–1967. Cambridge: Cambridge University Press.
  1972   Political Grouping in the Czechoslovak Reform Movement. New York: Colum-
          bia University Press.
Maříková, Hana
  1996   Rodina a zaměstnané ženy II. Data & Fakta 2 (February).
Martínková, Eva
  1993   Mladé rodiny jsou nejohroženější. Lidové noviny, May 7:1–2.

Ministry of Foreign Affairs of the Slovak Republic, Center for Strategic Studies of the Slovak Republic
  1995   The National Report on the Status of Women in the Slovak Republic to the Fourth U.N. Conference on Women in Beijing. Bratislava: Ministry of Foreign Affairs and the Center for Strategic Studies of the Slovak Republic. February.
Musil, Libor
  1995   Statusová solidarita a česká sociální politika. Sociologický časopis 31:423–434.
Nesporová, Alena
  1993   The Czech and Slovak Federal Republic: Labor Market Trends and Policies. *In* Structural Change in Central and Eastern Europe: Labour Market and Social Policy Implications. Georg Fischer and Guy Standing, eds. pp. 83–94. Paris: OECD.
Prokopec, Jiří
  1962   Vdaná žena v rodině a zaměstnání. Zprávy státní populáční komise 2:1–63.
Rabušic, Ladislav
  1992   Populační či rodinná politika? Demografie 1:56–57.
Řezníček, Ivo
  1992   Česká, slovenská, případně romská populační politika zdola? Demografie 2:143–144.
Růžková, Jiřina and Milan Aleš
  1995   Populační vývoj v České republice v roce 1994. Demografie 37(4):237–253.
Rychtaříková, Jitka
  1995   Sňatečnost svobodných v České republice dříve a dnes. Demografie 37(3):157–172.
Rys, Vladimír
  1995   Social Security Developments in Central Europe: A Return to Reality. Czech Sociological Review III(2 Fall):197–208.
Scott, Hilda
  1974   Does Socialism Liberate Women? Experiences from Eastern Europe. Boston: Beacon.
Šik, Ota
  1967   Plan and Market Under Socialism. Eleanor Wheeler, transl. White Plains, NY: International Arts and Sciences Press.
Šiklová, Jiřina
  1992   K diskusi o populační politice. Demografie 2:147–148.
Simonik, David
  1997   One Out of Five Czech Families to Lose Child Care Supplements. Carolina 258, September 12 (electronic journal).
Skilling, H. Gordon
  1976   Czechoslovakia's Interrupted Revolution. Princeton: Princeton University Press.
Srb, Vladimír
  1992   Potřebuje Československo populační politiku? Demografie 1:64–66.
Srb, Vladímír with Milan Kučera and Dagmar Vysušilová
  1959   Průzkum manželství. Demografická příručka 228–231.
Štatistický úrad Slovenskej republiky
  1996   Štatistická ročenka Slovenskej republiky 1996. Bratislava: VEDA.
Švarcová, Helena
  1964a   Jak je to s ženskou otazkou? Vlasta 10.

1964b Názory, polemika, kritika. Vlasta 5.
1965 K postavení ženy v socialistické společností. Zprávy státní populační komise 4.
Tirpák, Michal and František Adamica
1994 Populačný vývoj v Slovenskej republike v roku 1994. Demografie 36(4):254–266.
Večerník, Jiří
1993 Utváření nové sociální regulace v České republice. Sociologický časopis 29(2):181–202.
1995 Změny v rozdělení příjmů domácností 1988–1992. Demografie 37(2):87–100.
Vobruba, G.
1993 Nadnárodní sociální politika v procesu transformace. Sociologický časopis 29(2):167–180.
Wolchik, Sharon L.
1981a Demography, Political Reform, and Women's Issues in Czechoslovakia. *In* Women, Power and Political Systems. Margherita Rendel, ed. London: Croom Helm.
1981b Elite Strategy toward Women in Czechoslovakia: Liberation or Mobilization? Studies in Comparative Communism 14(2 and 3, Summer/Autumn):23–42.
1983 The Scientific-Technological Revolution and the Role of Specialist Elites in Policy Making in Czechoslovakia. *In* Domestic and Foreign Policy in Eastern Europe in the 1980s. Michael J. Sodaro and Sharon L. Wolchik, eds. Pp. 111–132. New York: St. Martin's.
1993 Women and the Politics of Transition in Central and Eastern Europe. *In* Democratic Reform and the Position of Women in Transitional Economies. Valentine M. Moghadam, ed. Pp. 29–47. New York: Clarendon.
1994 Women and the Politics of Transition in the Czech and Slovak Republics. *In* Women in the Politics of Postcommunist Eastern Europe. Marilyn Rueschemeyer, ed. Pp. 3–28. Armonk, NY: M.E. Sharpe.
Wolchik, Sharon L with Zora Bútorová and Jan Hartl.
1994 Citizen Attitudes toward Politics in the Czech Republic and Slovakia. 1994 Data Files. [Ženy a volby. Marie Čermáková, ed. Prague. Unpublished study.]

CHAPTER 3

Talking about Women and Wombs:
The Discourse of Abortion and Reproductive Rights
in the G.D.R. during and after the *Wende*

EVA MALECK-LEWY AND MYRA MARX FERREE

AT THE TIME OF GERMAN unification, protests against West Germany's effort to extend its own restrictive abortion law to the former German Democratic Republic (G.D.R.) drew international attention. While many had expected Cold War–related issues such as NATO membership to complicate the unification process, it was in fact the regulation of abortion that threatened to derail negotiations. To avoid an impasse, changes to the abortion law were postponed for two years, during which time the Bundestag (Parliament) was to hammer out a new draft. The first proposal put forward was challenged on constitutional grounds and modified in response to the Constitutional Court's objections. The legislation ultimately adopted modified the state's role, but generally affirmed its regulatory powers. For West German women, it improved access to abortion; for East German women, it was symbolically degrading and created new obstacles to abortion. In the course of what became a nearly five-year-long debate, the meaning of the G.D.R. experience and women's role in society moved to the center of the political agenda.

In this chapter, we address the abortion debate as an example of political discourse that shaped German unification. We rely on Jenson's definition of discourse as "beliefs about the way politics should be conducted, the boundaries of political discussion, and the kinds of conflicts resolvable through political processes. . . . Its major impact is to inhibit or encourage the formation of new collective identities and/or the reinforcement of older ones" (Jenson 1987:65). Focusing on the way this discourse developed in the former G.D.R., we examine women's actual experiences with abortion and also look at the ways in which Eastern responses to the West's devaluation and erasure of G.D.R. experience shaped the post-transition debate. We conclude that the abortion discourse crystallized collective identities based on gender, but also based on East-West differences. While the practical consequences of the new law are varied, the symbolic significance of the abortion controversy lies in three related develop-

The authors thank Irene Dölling, Susan Gal, Donna Harsch, Gail Kligman, Carol Mueller, Dorothy Rosenberg, and Silke Roth for their comments and suggestions on an earlier draft.

ments: the imposition, by West Germany, of boundaries on political discussion; resistance by East Germans, expressed in an evolving democratic discourse; and changes, especially in the East, in the perception of women as political actors.

From a West German perspective, East German resistance to the terms of debate has been variously interpreted as ignorance of parliamentary procedure, inexperience with democracy, and even as a lack of ethical socialization (see, for example, Schäuble 1991). We understand such interpretations to be themselves a part of the discourse we analyze. The boundaries of political discussion accepted by West Germans were, to say the least, questionable to East Germans. For instance, why should protection of the unborn (an abstract right) be regarded as central? What places criminal law, rather than women's rights, at the center of debate? If East Germans viewed legalized abortion as a positive aspect of the G.D.R. experience, why was this not given more credence and respect? Because most East Germans—especially women—fundamentally rejected the premises of Western discourse, redefining the issue in Western terms meant narrowing the universe of discourse available to East Germans. It also demonstrated the West's rejection of G.D.R. perspectives and collective identities.

In the following section, we review the nature and history of the abortion issue in Germany, paying particular attention to women's different experiences in the East and the West. We then turn to the process of unification, examining ways in which certain actors and discursive possibilities became dominant during the transition period (in German, this is referred to as the *Wende*, or turn-around). We emphasize the unification process as a shift in the "political opportunity structure," that is, a change in formal rules, partisan alignments, and cleavages within and among elites that together constitute the "dimensions of the political environment" and open or close "the gates of opportunity" for social movements (Tarrow 1994:18). After discussing our research strategy and materials, we address the changing nature of abortion discourse in selected East German newspapers.

ABORTION LAW AND REFORM IN THE TWO GERMANYS

After World War II, in both East and West Germany, the legal point of departure for regulating abortion was Paragraph 218, part of a nineteenth-century criminal code that defined abortion as a felony. Feminists of the Weimar period made a strong push to abolish Paragraph 218, but their efforts failed. Nazi abortion law sharply distinguished between "worthy" and "unworthy" life, forbidding abortion in the former case but demanding it in the latter (Koonz 1986). In 1950, the G.D.R. substantially rewrote its civil and criminal codes, replacing Paragraph 218 with new regulations that continued to define most abortions as illegal (Maleck-Lewy 1994). For its part, the Federal Republic of Germany (F.R.G.) resurrected the pre-war criminal code, including Paragraph 218. In response to the Nazi experience, it also adopted a provisional constitution explicitly charging the state to uphold "respect for all human life." It deferred promulgation of a formal constitution until such time as Germany's eastern section (the original Soviet occupation zone) was reintegrated—a time that became increasingly unimaginable as the reality of two states became more fully established.

In the 1970s, a wave of abortion reform swept through much of the industrialized world, including the two Germanys (Dahlerup 1986). In 1974, West Germany passed a law permitting first-trimester abortions. The Constitutional Court overturned this law in 1975 on grounds that it gave inadequate protection to unborn life. In 1976, Parliament returned with a "compromise" that specified four conditions under which an abortion could be legally performed. These conditions included a pregnancy resulting from rape or incest; a medical condition that endangered a mother's life or physical health; eugenic concern in the case of known fetal deformity; or an unspecified "social emergency."

Even after this reform, West Germany's abortion law was among the most restrictive in Europe. Although most abortions (80 percent or more) were performed on grounds of a "social emergency," the regulations were burdensome (a woman needed the permission of two doctors and was required to seek counseling and observe a three-day waiting period), access was uncertain (especially in Catholic areas), and the window of opportunity was always in danger of closing (an increasing number of charges were brought against women for illegal abortions, and doctors were occasionally prosecuted for certifying an emergency too readily). Particularly in southern regions where Catholics dominate the political process, abortions were not only difficult to obtain but were potentially risky. In 1988, a Memmingen doctor was prosecuted for unwarranted use of the social emergency clause; his confidential records were opened and the names of women for whom he had performed abortions were publicized (Friedrichsen 1991). Many women, after being denied an abortion in a conservative jurisdiction, went to Holland for the procedure; occasionally, these women were subjected to mandatory gynecological examinations when crossing the border back into Germany (Maleck-Lewy 1994).

In the face of such harassment, the demand to legalize abortion remained a litmus test of feminism in West Germany. However, abortion reform made little or no headway in the decade preceding unification. Feminists argued for the repeal of Paragraph 218, but their efforts were routinely ignored. By contrast, opponents of abortion gained strength in government, even as popular opinion turned against the methods available to enforce the criminal abortion statute. Anti-abortion forces brought a case to court that threatened to abolish insurance coverage for abortion and, some argue, even challenged the limited availability of legal abortion. It was widely agreed that one in four pregnancies ended in abortion, frequently because the social emergency clause was generously interpreted or because women would travel abroad if denied an abortion in Germany. Indeed, both sides agreed that illegal abortions were common in West Germany, and relatively few were prosecuted. By 1989, West Germany's abortion law was being depicted as an example of political hypocrisy.

The G.D.R.'s 1972 abortion law also passed as part of the international reform movement and tried to address a similarly unsatisfactory experience with criminalized abortion. As Harsch later detailed, the very restrictive abortion regulations of 1950 (Gesetze über Mütter-und Kinderschutz und die Rechte der Frau) had troubling consequences: Because women would travel to socialist states with more liberal laws, or attempt the operation themselves, the (illegal) abortion rate remained high, while approximately sixty deaths each year were attributed to illegal abortions (Harsch 1997). Generally speaking, it was believed that difficult living conditions prompted women to seek an abortion. A "silent liberalization" began to take place around 1965, as commissions increasingly approved women's requests for abortion. The typical petitioner was an employed, married woman with more than the average number of children, who argued that the social burden on her family was insupportable (Harsch 1997; Maleck-Lewy 1994). More women also began to argue that their right to study or to work was being violated, and the number of petitions continued to rise. Evidently, in the late 1960s and early 1970s, the discussion of abortion reform in both socialist and nonsocialist countries heightened women's dissatisfaction with the status quo and made doctors and politicians more willing to consider alternatives (Harsch 1997; Ankum 1993).

Yet issues surrounding abortion seemed to highlight conflicting public interests; on the one hand, socialist policy demanded full employment for both women and men, yet a drop in the birthrate would be considered a threat to the state's survival. A mechanism was thus sought to respond to this contradiction. While avoiding public discussion of the issue, the national legislature officially legalized first-trimester abortion in 1972. In a unique gesture, given the G.D.R. political context, the Christian Democrats cast a minority vote against the law. Even so, there was no public debate. Accompanying legislation made birth control pills available at no cost and allowed for second-trimester abortions, upon recommendation of a hospital committee, when the medical condition of either the mother or fetus was believed to outweigh the health risks of a late-term abortion.

Beginning in the early 1970s and intensifying over the next decade, the G.D.R. also implemented an extensive set of social supports to encourage motherhood. This included paid leave for childbirth and for the care of sick children, virtually free public childcare, and hot school lunches. While the birthrate rose, so too did legal abortions, until the rate approximated what previously had been the rate of legal and illegal abortions combined; after that, the abortion rate began to drop (Hennig 1990; Ockel 1992). By the 1980s, approximately one in four pregnancies ended in abortion—roughly the same ratio as in the F.R.G.

The 1975 publication of Charlotte Worgitsky's novel *Meine Ungeborenen Kinder* [My Unborn Children] offered a limited opportunity to discuss the nature of a woman's choice in seeking an abortion (Worgitsky 1975). The circumstances of the novel, which compel the protagonist to abort several pregnancies, are used as a vehicle to explore questions that women commonly struggled with in silence and shame. For example, when is abortion a responsible choice? How is sexual repression associated with unwanted pregnancies? When and how do women actually decide to have an abortion? By 1989, women in the G.D.R. had a generation of experience with legal, first-trimester abortions, but they had only a modest start in evaluating the social meaning of that experience. Despite a general sense that the abortion law helped women, there was concern about the lack of public discussion on this issue and the limited availability of counseling.

The merger of East and West Germany might have enlarged the space for dialogue and public debate. For West German feminists, there was an early window of opportunity to reform abortion law in the direction of East Germany's liberal statutes. Indeed, lessons might have been drawn from the G.D.R.'s effective combination of legalized abortion and public incentives for childbirth. For women in the East, the overthrow of the repressive communist regime promised not only an opening for public discussion but also a long overdue opportunity to evaluate the G.D.R.'s experience with liberalized abortion laws. However, the political opportunity structure of the F.R.G. shaped the course of the *Wende* and imposed severe constraints on the universe of acceptable political discourse.

Abortion Reform during the Unification Period

In November 1989, the sudden overthrow of the G.D.R.'s Communist Party leadership by grassroots protestors presented West Germany's conservative government[1] with a new and welcome opportunity. Eager to sign a unification treaty, the West Germans hastened to advance talks. In the summer of 1990, when G.D.R. negotiators balked at accepting the F.R.G. abortion law, the two parties struck a deal to postpone legislation until late 1992. By this time, lawmakers were to draft a law that "better guaranteed the protection of unborn life and a constitutionally correct management of a conflict situation for pregnant women than is the case in either part of Germany at this time." The language is more telling than was generally recognized at the time. It did not mention women's right to self-determination, it placed a premium on protecting the life of the unborn, it defined unwanted pregnancies as "conflicts," and it failed to specify who would manage such conflicts, although it demanded that resolutions be "constitutionally correct." Moreover, the body of law that set the parameters of reform was the F.R.G. constitution. In part, this was because the West German government used the urgency of unification to effectively incorporate the G.D.R., as five "New States," into the largely unmodified Federal Republic. It also had used the negotiations as a way to fend off liberal demands for constitutional reform. While the particular phrase in the treaty relevant to abortion seemed to demand "protection of unborn life" and respect for "the situation of pregnant women," it set the terms of debate in a West German constitutional framework, thus placing woman and fetus, West and East, on unequal footing. While reserving substantial powers for the Constitutional Court, the treaty defined Parliament as the primary actor in developing a single, national abortion law.

[1] In 1989, the F.R.G. government represented a coalition among the CDU, the CSU, and the FDP.

For the two years before the joint legislature would pass a new abortion law, the existing statutes of both the "old" and "new" states remained in effect. The question of whether or not West German women might benefit, even temporarily, from the availability of legal, first-trimester abortions in the "new" states was debated under the rubric of *Wohnort/Tatort*—that is, whether the law should be applied on the basis of a woman's residence or the location of the act ("scene of the crime"). One side argued that if legal abortions, performed in East Germany, were universally available, it would be too easy for West German women to circumvent the law. The other side countered that few West Germans would resort to "unsanitary and inconvenient abortions" in the East when they could travel just as easily to the Netherlands (Riemer 1993). The "scene of the crime" rule prevailed for the interim period.

As the new abortion law was being formulated in 1991 and 1992, each party submitted a proposal to Parliament. Other proposals came from an anti-abortion wing of the Christian Democratic Party (CDU) and from a multiparty coalition spearheaded by women legislators (the *Gruppenantrag* [group bill], or so-called compromise). The latter proposal, which ultimately passed, legalized abortion for any reason during the first trimester, but required counseling and a waiting period. To make childbirth a more feasible option, it also included public incentives such as increased funding for kindergartens. Technically, members of Parliament were released from the obligation to vote by party, but in fact, the parties wielded considerable pressure.

Early on, West German politicians and commentators acknowledged the constitutional constraints to which new legislation was subject, yet many hoped that, with a new configuration of justices, the Court's thinking had changed since 1974. Few East Germans understood the role of the Constitutional Court as a political actor in the West, and few seem to have interpreted the phrase "constitutionally correct" as particularly significant. Because the stated goal was to draft a new law, political parties naturally took the lead in shaping the abortion agenda. This was typical for a strong party state, in which party discipline and competition defined most issues (Young 1996). Although the East German human rights movement, including the women's movement, had been instrumental in overturning the G.D.R. government, these groups won only eight seats in the unified German Parliament.[2] Approximately half of the East German representatives were affiliated with the Christian Democrats, making this the single strongest party in the former G.D.R.

Initially, the parties to the left, including the Social Democratic Party (SPD), the Alliance 90/Green Party, and the Party of Democratic Socialism (PDS), demanded unqualified access to abortion during at least the first trimester and

---

[2] East German feminists, formally members of the Independent Women's Association (UFV) rather than a political party, were part of this reform movement. The feminists who won seats were, for parliamentary purposes, affiliated with different groups, for example, Christina Schenk with the Alliance 90/Greens, Petra Bläss with the PDS, and others with the SPD. The West Greens had failed to win the necessary 5 percent of the vote to be included in this parliament.

social measures to support mothers and children.[3] The Liberal Party (FDP) demanded some form of counseling but opposed increases in state support. The CDU and their more conservative Bavarian allies, the Christian Social Union (CSU) were split—some wanted to retain the existing set of conditions under which abortion would be permitted, and some pushed to eliminate the social emergency "loophole." Since it was clear that none of these proposals could win a majority, women from the liberal end of the CDU joined women from the FDP and SPD in drafting a compromise. Their proposal combined limited social support with a provision for mandatory counseling and a waiting period, but it left the ultimate decision, during the first trimester, to the woman. Both the formation of a multiparty coalition and the prominence of women legislators in this ultimately successful initiative were highly unusual in German politics (Mushaben 1993).

Although Parliament was the central stage upon which abortion reform was debated, a grassroots feminist lobbying effort was also conducted in both eastern and western Germany. Nevertheless, with the parties' virtual monopoly on political space (even in terms of sponsoring allegedly "grassroots" demonstrations), the influence of such movements was limited (Rucht 1996). In this instance, feminist advocacy was notably unsuccessful. Looking closely at the parliamentary debates, several analysts (Berghahn 1995; Mushaben, Giles, and Lennox 1997; Sauer 1995) have noted that political discourse patronized and marginalized women, even though women legislators played a prominent role. The SPD slogan was "help, don't punish," which many legislators used to cast women as helpless victims, suffering from psychological conflict and economic stress. Their arguments suggested that few, if any, women would choose abortion absent conditions of acute economic necessity. Women legislators actively distanced themselves from the "types of women who would choose abortion," depicting them as confused and needy and proposing to "help rather than punish" them. Although legislators were primarily concerned with the most appropriate and effective means to protect unborn life, the constitutional basis for providing such protection was scarcely debated.[4] The very name of the committee in charge of drafting the law was the Special Committee for the Protection of Unborn Life, a designation to which none of the major West German parties objected.

Both sides in the debate invoked the problem of West German women circumventing the law either as evidence of the futility of criminalized abortion or as support for a more rigorous law stringently enforced. For West Germans who

---

[3] The Social Democratic Party (SPD), the second largest party in the former G.D.R., led the push for abortion reform in the 1970s. The Alliance 90/Green Party represents human rights groups, and the Party of Democratic Socialism (PDS), nearly all of whose supporters are in eastern Germany, is a reformed and rechristened version of the former Communist Party.

[4] The notion that the fetus was a constitutionally protected human life was in principle highly debatable, as feminist legal scholars had long pointed out (see, for example, Frommel 1994). As the U.S. Supreme Court found women's right to decide about abortion covered under the "penumbra" of a nonspecific right to privacy, the F.R.G. Constitutional Court found the state's obligation to protect the fetus in a nonspecific clause about respecting human life.

wanted to entice rather than coerce women to bear children, abortion law became a vehicle for making claims on the state to offer "alternatives to abortion." This meant providing social benefits, such as enhanced childcare, that could be justified under the rubric of "help rather than punish." While these social support measures were an improvement for women in the West, they represented a substantial cutback in support for families with children compared to G.D.R. standards. From an East German perspective, it was ludicrous to define such cutbacks as "help," but this view was marginalized by the dominant western discourse.

As time went on, the East German experience with legalized abortion was invoked less as a positive "accomplishment" than as an indication of what an immoral government could allow to happen (Mushaben et al. 1997; Riemer 1993). In general, the unification treaty did not treat G.D.R. laws and policies as anything other than transitional arrangements to be phased out on different schedules; the G.D.R. abortion law was cast as the last remnant of a "failed system" that was both economically and morally "bankrupt." The West's negative evaluation of the former regime extended to everything associated with the G.D.R., so that PDS support for any proposal or action could be politically damaging. Support for abortion was no exception, a fact that compelled the Social Democrats to distance themselves from the PDS position—as well as from the G.D.R. abortion law.

Outside of Parliament, feminist activists who mobilized on behalf of a woman's right to a self-determined pregnancy found themselves surprisingly divided and ineffective. A variety of reasons have been advanced for this. First and most important, women's experiences were different in the East and the West. Legal abortion was an old right and a new issue for East German feminists; it was not among their primary concerns during the *Wende*, and it was only one of many ways in which women were losing ground as a result of unification (Wuerth 1994; Ferree 1994). For former G.D.R. feminists, as Wuerth has shown, self-determination with respect to abortion paralleled self-determination with respect to democracy; it was considered an individual's fundamental political right. By contrast, legal abortion was a new right and an old issue for West German feminists. The shift in opportunity structure, brought about through unification, held out the prospect that women might gain the right to choose—a right they had never before enjoyed. Yet the campaign for abortion and the argument that abortion rights are central to feminism had been an ongoing concern for decades. In the West German feminist discourse of the late 1980s, as Ullrich has shown, the abortion issue was linked to concerns about new reproductive technologies and the ethics of decision making. As a result, it developed more as a social-medical issue about women's participation and informed choice than as a political issue about liberty and self-determination, as it previously had been defined (Ullrich 1994). The combination of different political experiences and different ways of framing the issue led to tensions and conflicts within the women's movement that may have hampered mobilization (Ullrich 1994; Wuerth 1996).

The Group Bill (developed by women politicians and supported by the SPD, the FDP, a small portion of the Western CDU, and a considerable number of the Eastern CDU) was also seen by many Western feminists—including Alice Schwarzer, the prominent publisher of the feminist magazine *Emma*—as "better than nothing." Feminist party activists were under tremendous pressure to follow their party in supporting the compromise measure (Wuerth 1996). Many West German feminists believed that a battle in the streets over abortion would only undermine the work of women in Parliament and put even the compromise at risk. Although the Greens and the PDS did not officially support the compromise, they let it be known that their members would vote in sufficient numbers to ensure the bill's passage.

East German feminists did not view the compromise as an "improvement" since, for women in eastern Germany, it would mean a decline in living conditions and a loss of self-determination. In Parliament, Christina Schenk and Petra Bläss (East/UFV) argued that abortion was not about the "protection of life" by whatever means. Taking a strong social constructionist position, they argued that the nature of a fetus depends on the meaning that a woman imparts to it. As Schenk put it, "The embryo may be a child to her, a person from the beginning, loved from the first moment, because she wants it and waits longingly for it. But it also may be for her—and I know what I am saying—a parasitical mass of cells" (Mushaben et al. 1997). Several female supporters of the compromise denounced this position as immoral (Mushaben et al. 1997). According to these authors, the parliamentary discourse was itself premised on the maternalist assumption that all women hope to bring a fetus to term and that any woman for whom abortion is not a terrible ethical conflict is immoral and frivolous (Sauer 1995). The efforts made by Schenk, Bläss, and a few SPD women to redefine this issue failed. Thus women's claim for self-determination, first signaled by the unification treaty, was finally marginalized by the parliamentary debate. Moreover, the prominence of western feminists in supporting the Group Bill established abortion as an issue of ethics and moral choice. This situated East German feminists, and others who defined abortion within a framework of rights, outside the realm of effective political discourse (Wuerth 1994).

In sum, the unification process itself had important consequences for abortion law reform and shaped the contours of political discourse in the new Germany. The mandate to devise a national abortion statute, as articulated in the unification treaty, placed the issue squarely within the party-dominated parliamentary arena and affirmed the ultimate authority of the West German Constitution. The very language of the treaty was evocative of West German discourse, and the SPD's "help rather than punish" rhetoric lent credence to the view that abortion is an immoral act. It also identified the state—not the pregnant woman—as the primary decision maker. In addition, the social provisions that constituted state "help" represented a net loss for women in eastern Germany. Despite the implications for women in the East, the fact that this was a "women's bill" put pressure on West German feminists to accept the legislation as a "small improvement," which merely divided and weakened the women's movement. Gradually, the unification process unraveled all the G.D.R. "accomplishments" that had supported mothers and children. Access to abortion, rhetorically discredited and legally dismantled, was the final casualty. Although the door opened in 1989–

1990 to the possibility of reform, it closed in 1991–1992 when all things connected to the G.D.R. were abandoned wholesale. In western discourse, the association of legalized abortion with the East German experience simply cast women's reproductive rights as a component of a "bankrupt" and "immoral" state that no politician would risk defending.

In May 1993, the Constitutional Court overturned the June 1992 abortion law on grounds that it gave insufficient protection to human life. The Court insisted that abortion remain a felony unless justified by rape, incest, birth defect, or threat to a woman's life, but allowed that women who undergo mandatory state-licensed counseling (which must be directed toward preserving the life of the child and may not be carried out by any person or organization that provides abortions) would be exempt from the threat of legal prosecution.[5] Nonprosecution was justified in the court decision by the presumed "mental crisis" experienced by the pregnant woman and also by the need to secure her cooperation in the counseling process. The Court further defined the act of persuading a woman to have an abortion as a prosecutable offense. Because abortion remains a criminal act, it is not covered by the state health plan, although low income petitioners who meet the strict abortion criteria may apply for social welfare to cover the cost.

In the summer of 1995, Parliament passed a modified law that strengthened the state's ability to exert moral pressure on both abortion providers and women seeking abortions. It required abortion counselors to be state tested and certified every two years and to report in writing on the substance of each counseling session. In conservative Catholic states such as Bavaria, women have always found it difficult to find a doctor or hospital willing to perform an abortion. This obstacle was compounded in 1996, when Bavaria passed a law forbidding outpatient abortions and allowing police to search doctors' homes and offices for evidence of illegal abortion (*Der Spiegel* 32, 1996:579).[6] In the "new" states, abortions continue to be performed in public hospitals and by most doctors, and financial aid is provided to the extent that the law permits. The much-discussed measures to "help" women and families have not yet been fully implemented. The legal right of all children to attend state-financed preschool from age 3, supposedly introduced in January 1996, has largely been deferred because city and state governments claim not to have the requisite funds.

TRACING THE DISCOURSE: NEWSPAPERS IN THE G.D.R.
AND THE NEW FEDERAL STATES

To understand the range and development of specifically East German discourse among opinion leaders in the general population (as opposed to legislators and movement activists), we turn to newspapers with a predominantly East German

[5] Thus abortion was not "legalized" but merely "decriminalized," while its moral wrongfulness was actively affirmed.

[6] Abortions are also defined as illegal if the woman fails to give a reason (thus putting the law in direct contradiction to the federal rule), if the abortion is unreported, or if the doctor derives more than 25 percent of his or her income from performing abortions. This sweeping rule completely

readership published between January 1989 (the year of the *Wende*) and December 1993 (when the parliamentary debate ended). From the first mention of unification until the final court decision, abortion was a frequent topic in the mass media.

Because television and radio broadcasts have not yet been systematically archived, we were unable to include the full range of debate in our sample. Being restricted to print media, we selected sources that would be roughly parallel in East and West Germany, and thus excluded the glossy news and human interest magazines that are unique to the West. We selected two East German papers that have relatively wide circulation and dissimilar readerships; both date back to the independent G.D.R. and have continued to publish in the post-unification period. We attempted to locate every article and letter about abortion in both papers throughout the period of debate.[7]

In the days of the G.D.R., *Die Neue Zeit* (NZ) was identified as the "Central Organ of the CDU"; it was typically read by members of that party and by those who identified as Christians. It printed CDU materials and reported on discussions within the East German churches. With the merger of the East and West German Christian Democratic parties, *NZ* changed its masthead to "Berlin's Newspaper for Germany." As a consequence of privatization in the East, the publishing group that puts out the *Frankfurter Allgemeine Zeitung* (FAZ) bought the paper and hired a West German editor-in-chief. Besides losing readers in the East, it failed to attract West German readers and finally stopped publishing in 1993. Between 1989 and 1993, there were 59 articles or letters to the editor on the subject of abortion.

Neues Deutschland (ND) was the most widely distributed paper in the G.D.R. Called the "Central Organ of the SED" (the ruling Communist Party), it published all government proclamations and, in this sense, was an official state paper. With the transformation of the G.D.R. in 1989, the paper lost its official role and became independent in 1990. Although circulation has declined steadily, ND remained in 1996 the most widely read newspaper in the former G.D.R. states. The paper's readership tends to be well educated and to vote strongly for the PDS (the SED's reformed successor). The paper presents itself as "a politically left-leaning, pluralistic forum" with "particularly extensive coverage of the new Federal States and Berlin," (that is, of the former G.D.R.). In the 1990–1993 period, there were 91 articles and letters about abortion (there were none in 1989).

We also examined selected articles in the *FAZ*, which is published in the relatively liberal western state of Hessen, but takes a notably conservative editorial position. Unlike our East German sample, we included only 50 percent of the available articles on abortion, which we had assembled from another project;[8]

---

overrides the confidentiality of patient records and has outraged doctors; its constitutionality remains to be tested.

[7] Because German newspapers, though archived, are not indexed, this required direct review of every issue of each paper for the entire period studied.

[8] The sample of FAZ articles was collected by a research team at the Wissenschaftszentrum Berlin. Headed by Friedhelm Neidhardt, the team is systematically coding abortion discourse in

the sample excluded letters to the editor. Since we focus specifically on the perspective that former G.D.R. citizens brought to the abortion debate, on how it conflicted with the dominant western discourse, and on how this conflict was managed, we examine only those articles that characterize the East German experience or otherwise illustrate a particularly eastern frame of reference. Given space limitations and the scope of the present analysis, we do not directly discuss the western discourse here.

Rather than count specific words, phrases, or semantic units in the manner of a formal content analysis, we conducted an intensive, qualitative analysis of the texts. Though we did count articles of specific types, we focused particularly on identifying changes in the themes expressed and examining the points at which these variations occurred. Because the two East German papers differ sharply in terms of their readership and central concerns, we present our findings in terms of themes most frequently developed in each paper. We begin, however, with a broad overview of the changes in both papers.

Change and Commonality

It is notable that both East German papers use the distinctive phrase *Schwanger-schaftsabbruch* [termination of pregnancy] rather than the word abortion. In West German discourse, by contrast, the word *Abtreibung* [abortion] is used occasionally, but it is more common to refer euphemistically to "a pregnant woman in a situation of need" or to a "conflict pregnancy." Although the East German papers shifted their focus over time, they continued, throughout the period of debate, to frame the issue as the "termination of pregnancy." Thus the very act of defining the subject betrays an enduring gap between East and West. Eastern discourse focuses on the condition (pregnancy); Western discourse focuses on the woman and further attributes "conflict" and "need" to any woman facing an unwanted pregnancy.

In 1989 and 1990, when *NZ* opened a discussion about abortion among its (primarily) eastern readers, the paper's position reflected the views of its readers and was consistent with a Protestant understanding of ethics. The tendency of both staff articles and letters to the editor was to affirm liberal pluralism. Only one article presented the official position of the East German bishops. Several pieces sought to evaluate—at an individual as well as a social level—the G.D.R. experience with legal abortion. Yet by 1991, the lines of disagreement had begun to crystallize. Distinctions were drawn between official Protestant and Catholic positions, as writers either attacked or defended the first-trimester rule (upheld in the G.D.R.), the allowable exception rule (followed in the F.R.G.), and the proposed alternatives, including the Group Bill. Increasingly between 1991 and 1993, the papers reported—with little comment—on official church or party positions. In 1992, two articles vehemently refuted charges in the western press (namely by the news magazine *Der Spiegel*) that G.D.R. hospitals practiced

West Germany and the United States from 1962 to 1994. We examined only the years between 1989 and 1993 and looked only at references to the G.D.R. and its abortion laws.

infanticide (drowning babies in buckets). Over the course of five years, the voices represented by the paper changed from those of individual readers and journalists to party (CDU) and church spokespersons—in other words, mainstream political and religious "experts."

Consistent with past practice in the G.D.R., *ND* carried no articles at all about abortion in 1989. Because abortion was defined as neither a political issue nor a moral problem but as a medical and social fact, public discussion was discouraged. The first article, which appeared in 1990, reported on a sociological conference in Leipzig and provided facts about the number of abortions taking place and who was having them (March 16, 1990). Approximately half of the articles published in 1990 were devoted to the problem of how to retain the trimester rule. There also were several announcements, particularly in 1990 and 1991, of public demonstrations against Paragraph 218, followed by extensive coverage of these events. At the time, these demonstrations were seen as a strategy not for retaining the trimester rule, but for influencing the formulation of the Group Bill. By 1992–1993, the paper was publishing letters and articles contending that abortion law reflected male domination over women's lives. Likewise, it began articulating the view that the political debate itself should be a lesson in how little women count in the F.R.G. In time, these positions were defined as "oppositional" to the parties and to institutionalized parliamentary process in the F.R.G.

As this brief examination suggests, the two former G.D.R. newspapers differ, but they also resemble one another in important ways. They used a common language to frame the abortion issue, and both papers gradually shifted toward polarized positions. In both cases, the institutional concerns of party and church became increasingly evident, displacing the sense of self-reflection that immediately followed unification. Yet despite their similarities, the differences between these papers caution us against assuming that a single, consistent G.D.R. perspective exists either in the media or among the general population. Taken together, the content of these papers reveals the distinctiveness of G.D.R. discourses in relation to those representative of the F.R.G.

Die Neue Zeit: Christianity and Ethics in the East

Die Neue Zeit's thematic focus indicates the paper's effort to formulate and represent a Christian perspective on abortion. Certain key aspects of the East German experience provide an instructive context for this. By 1989, Christians were a minority in the G.D.R. (75 percent of the population belonged to neither the Protestant nor the Catholic Church, compared to 20 percent in the F.R.G. who were similarly unaffiliated). Most Christians in East Germany were Protestant. Moreover, the Protestant churches sheltered, and in some cases supported the activities of, political dissidents. Although the G.D.R. was formally based on the principle of separation of church and state, the regime in fact demanded that its citizens receive political, nonreligious education. Gradually, the churches, and religious influences generally, were weakened. When abortion reform was introduced in 1972, both the Protestant and Catholic Churches spoke out against it, but neither could make their objections public. Discussions among Christians about abortion were confined to individual parish communities. Even so, abortion was seldom discussed in the final years of the G.D.R. It was a new issue, especially for younger people.

The CDU-East was the second strongest party in the G.D.R., but was more an "accompaniment" to the Communist Party than a true opposition. It approached the 1989 transition as an opportunity for "revitalization on the basis of a Christian perspective and democratic principles." For the West German Christian Democrats and the Federal Government, this "reforming" party was their most significant partner in negotiating the terms of unification, and the CDU-East drew the highest number of East German votes in constituting the new Parliament. Supported by leading figures in the East German churches and challenged by its "sister party" in the West, the CDU-East understood much sooner than other groups in the East that it had to deal with abortion and with the attitude of its members toward this issue. In a position paper written in late 1989 and published in *NZ*, the CDU-East challenged its constituents to discuss "the protection of unborn life" (January 27, 1990). The outcome of this discussion formed part of the new party program, a draft of which was published in *NZ* in March 1990.

The CDU-East presented itself as a G.D.R. mainstream party with a liberal, democratic/pluralist position. In its draft program, the CDU-East clearly stated that "forbidding abortion and threatening punishment are not helping life." Although this expressed a majority opinion within the CDU-East, the formulation nevertheless situated the CDU-East in opposition not only to a minority of its own members, but also to the churches and to the majority in the CDU-West. In a section entitled "Protection of Unborn Life," the CDU-East party program begins, "the protection of unborn and born life is a great responsibility for society and for parents. When a request for a termination of pregnancy is made, helpful counseling must precede this decision in conscience. Society must create conditions in which the life of the child will be chosen and in which that life can be led in humane conditions" (*NZ*, March 17, 1990).

Such a formulation puts the question of protecting unborn life in a different context than that assumed by the CDU-West. The CDU-East does not deny the importance of responsibly exercising individual conscience. While it casts abortion as a special situation in a woman's life and in her relationship with her partner, it does not define this situation as an emergency or crisis. It does not impute severe moral conflict. Thus, conscience is defined as the freedom and right of the individual to decide either for or against an abortion. Elsewhere in the program, the decision to abort is defined as a principle of liberty. In addition, the CDU-East emphasized society's responsibility for protecting unborn life. It demanded better counseling, which it took to mean counseling in which the moral as well as the medical implications of abortion are discussed. At this stage in the debate, the CDU-East argued that counseling would have to be voluntary to be helpful (March 17, 1990).

In response to the party's request for discussion, many letters appeared in *NZ* from readers and members of the CDU. Some of these early letters were from East German women who displayed no particular religious background (June 6, 1990; June 20, 1990a). The printed discussion among readers in 1990 centered upon the relationship between a Christian perspective and abortion and drew particularly upon the opinions of ministers and doctors (both women and men). Readers posed two questions: What is the theological-ethical view regarding protection of unborn life? And what legal and political conclusions should Christians draw from the fact that they live in a society made up of people with varying viewpoints?

The timing of the discussion is important. This exchange took place in response to a specific challenge and within a particular political context, namely one in which a nondemocratic authority structure had been recently overthrown and not yet been replaced by a new, let alone legitimate, authority. In addition, this was the first time that a Christian perspective on abortion was presented in print.

NZ published readers' letters under the heading "Raising Awareness of Responsibility for Life: For and Against § 218." Notably, even those letters stating that fetal life is a gift from God and must be protected do not claim the absolute right to do so under any circumstances; this would, as they say, "disqualify all other understandings of values as immoral." Instead, readers assert that Christian ethics demand "tolerance, respect and responsibility in dealing with others" (June 20, 1990b). One advocates "respect and tolerance for the decisions of conscience of those who think otherwise," adding, "however much Christians might feel that the value of life is inviolable, they must also recognize that the world in which one lives is not perfect and that bad relationships, abandonment, violence and killing exist." Later she argues, "we Christians know that God turns in love particularly to people in their failures. When a woman decides to abort, she will have to live with this burden, but we may not exclude her from the love that God in Christ showed to all the guilty and burdened" (July 25, 1990).

There was also consensus among readers that protection of life, as a social obligation, requires women and men to act conscientiously so that abortion is not used as a method of birth control. The "responsible exercise" of abortion rights is repeatedly demanded but is interpreted in various ways, including the need for more equality and partnership in relationships, better sex education (in social studies and not just biology classes), encouragement of youth toward more interpersonally aware and responsible relationships, and better counseling for women with an unwanted pregnancy (e.g., January 27, 1990a; June 20, 1990b).

We believe that this initial discussion reflects, in part, the historical position of Christians as a minority in the G.D.R., sensitized therefore to the need for tolerance among "those who think otherwise." It also reflects a welcome change from the G.D.R. context in which there could be no open discussion or acknowledgment of an ethical dimension to this choice. Although two readers argued vehemently that abortion is killing and as such is indefensible, others claimed that "abortion poses a deep ethical challenge to society that in principle may not be treated as private"; they proposed a humane acceptance and recognition of women's difficulties: "In this tension between ethics and human need we do not stand apart. We cannot in our actions draw on simple formulas or absolute certainties" (July 25, 1990).

This moral consideration led readers to the conclusion that women's liberty is at stake (June 20, 1990a). While one woman minister argued that "the self-determination of the woman over her body must remain a legally protected right," (July 25, 1990) a male CDU activist wrote, "not with restrictive measures, but only with social support and sensitive pastoral care can one change the values that people employ in the decision about unborn. . . . The equality of women and men in creation is reason for Christian Democrats particularly to advocate the equality and value of women! We Christian Democrats should separate ourselves from undemocratic traditions in this regard" (January 27, 1990b). This libertarian-democratic argument was especially significant to readers considering abortion in the context of the overall transition to democracy, which this writer defined as "a legal system that places individual people in central position." He then asked, "why, then, are they on one hand emphasizing the right of the individual but on the other hand destroying the most significant accomplishment of the G.D.R. in securing individual legal rights, the law about termination of pregnancy? The individual person, in any case not the individual woman, would then no longer be central" (January 27, 1990b).

In the summer of 1990, the incorporation of the G.D.R. into the F.R.G. was negotiated, and, through this process, abortion discourse in the East and the West took on a new political dimension. In East Germany, the debate itself assumed new meaning. Up to that point, East Germans were simply reaching toward some understanding about abortion and about the ethical and legal dimensions of the law in a society developing toward democracy; after unification, the parameters of debate changed abruptly to reflect western priorities. Questions concerning the constitutionality (according to the F.R.G. Constitution) of East and West German statutes became paramount. In summer 1990, *NZ* published its last major article defending the trimester rule and voluntary counseling. Both the nature of the discussion and the participants in it had changed.

In November 1990, *NZ* reported for the first time on an action of the Roman Catholic Church. Under the headline, "Yes to unborn life: two thousand march through the city center," the paper depicted the placards used in a Berlin demonstration (e.g., "unborn children: the price of German unity?") and cited a bishop's claim that the number of abortions in the G.D.R. were especially high and that "killing is not a solution" (November 23, 1990). With these and later reports, a Roman Catholic position on abortion was presented, not just in the *NZ*, but in the East German media generally, for the first time.

Both the Catholic and Protestant Churches sponsored conferences and special activities, such as the Catholics' "Week for Life," that specifically targeted East Germans "in the hope [that] information and enlightenment would have an effect especially at the grassroots" (June 8, 1991). They reported disappointing results: There had "not yet been wide engagement" because there was "at this time little feeling for the theme." Some Catholic parishes tried to anchor the topic in local issues—such as violence, anti-foreign feeling, or ecology—to stir more of a response, and they distributed an abundant supply of materials produced by the Church.

By June 1991, this mobilization was viewed, in part, with concern. An editorial in *NZ* portrayed the activities of the churches and the extensive debate among the parties as taking on "the characteristics of a war of religion" because, in principle, "a compromise is not possible. It is becoming clear that unconditional availability of abortion, as in the former G.D.R., will not be the law in unified Germany" (June 7, 1991). The consequences of the Catholic Church's strong involvement became a topic in itself for *NZ*. While characterizing both churches as having a shared commitment to "born and unborn life," one writer defined the Catholic position as more "hard-line." *NZ* remained more sympathetic to the Protestant position, which it described as support for "situation ethics, which is more attentive to the situation-specific conflicts of the woman, her partner, and family. The church accepts a decision process between acceptance and rejection of a developing human life, even when abortion remains only a last recourse, and always sinful." The "differences in life circumstances" are issues that "ethical, legal and theological evaluations must take into account" (June 7, 1991; June 22, 1991). Unlike the western discourse, this language defined "conflict" as more than simply what a woman experiences.

Beginning in 1991, media coverage reflected the West's increasing dominance over abortion discourse. West German commentaries were published with increasing frequency, despite the fact that the paper's western readership was negligible. Unlike the earlier letters, articles often expressed abstract and uncompromising "pro-life" positions, depicting women as merely "confused" and "suffering" (e.g., March 21, 1991; July 3, 1991; August 27, 1991).

By 1992, *NZ* was reporting primarily on the political-tactical maneuvering of the parties, and published relatively few editorials or letters. A spokesperson for the Protestant Church, objecting to the focus on a "new formulation of a criminal law on termination of pregnancy," argued that this was an ineffective means to protect life compared to "changing consciousness and building consciences along with measures of social support" (June 7, 1992). Yet despite such objections, the discourse had shifted to the parliamentary-legal process and to the issue of criminalization—in other words, it had been recast into an essentially West German mode. Although it once had been a public forum, *NZ* no longer expressed or helped to shape a distinctively East German consciousness. This changed perspective, as well as the paper's ultimate collapse, is indicative of the exclusion of East German discourse from the "unified" mainstream.

Socialism and Democracy in Neues Deutschland

The social and political context of *ND* also reflects the distinctive experiences of the G.D.R. Newly independent of the SED, *ND* was publishing articles in 1990 that reflected a need to come to terms with the past and to identify what was valuable and what needed to be changed. One early article traced the moral reasoning behind the Party's support for legalized abortion in the 1920s and emphasized that "the Communist Party was far from recommending abortion as an ideal . . . but the doors of the clinics were open to the daughters of refined society while the proletarian women were handed over to dangerous quacks" (June 14, 1990). A lengthy interview with the G.D.R.'s representative in International Planned Parenthood, herself a physician, interprets G.D.R. history with abortion law positively. She makes clear both her criticism of the G.D.R. and her support for the trimester rule, saying

> Even though I don't like that famous term "accomplishment," I nonetheless see the trimester rule as one of the few real accomplishments that we had. . . . [E]ven among us the trimester rule was very controversial . . . but when the woman simply isn't up to raising a child, I see the trimester rule as a humane one and under these conditions I would defend it. For I tell you, it is nonetheless true that to forbid something is not actually to hinder it. . . . It's a mystery to me why all these years we were not allowed to publish the numbers (abortion rates) for they weren't bad, even in international comparison. One in four pregnancies on average today ends in a termination, which is exactly the same rate as in the F.R.G. (September 1–2, 1990)

Other articles also assert this comparability as a virtue of the trimester rule; one states, for example, "The relation of abortions to births was 1 to 3 in the old-F.R.G. despite its abortion paragraph, exactly the same as in the former G.D.R. Paragraph 218 thus protects no unborn life but endangers mothers" (February 25, 1991; see also July 16, 1991).

Given the impending move toward unification, there also was an effort by readers, authors, and activists to take the measure of the changing political opportunity structure. *ND* published interviews with CDU politicians Christa Schmidt and Dorothee Wilms, and also with Alice Schwarzer and Christina Schenk, feminists from the West and East, respectively. By this point, the collection of tens of thousands of signatures, street demonstrations, and demands for a popular referendum appeared to have the potential to derail the treaty and the two-year moratorium was put into effect. Only one person writing for *ND* warned that the treaty's language of a "constitutionally correct" decision effectively put the embryo ahead of the woman, suggesting a legal basis for "compulsory mother-hood" (September 23, 1990). Thematically, writers in this period were especially concerned to situate abortion as an issue that is preeminently about democracy and human rights, the two rallying cries of the reform movement that toppled the government. There were calls for a referendum (June 18, 1990). The headline of one article illustrates the political context: "Paragraph 218 and the emergency operation on the unification treaty—be one country, but without one Memmingen case" (September 1–2, 1990).

Articles favoring the G.D.R.'s trimester rule championed it on grounds that it respected women's right to self-determination. Much of the language used casts the 1972 law as an "accomplishment" and characterizes the proposed restrictions as "backward." An article headlined "The Inquisition Returns via Paragraph 218" calls it "not one step backward but a hundred," and argues that "Eastern women do not want to give up rights once guaranteed. . . . Retaining the discriminatory Paragraph 218 deserves no comment other than that by Kurt Tucholsky:

"The old order which still exists today as in the past both took and gave to the German—took from him his freedom and gave him power over others" (February 25, 1991). A restrictive abortion law is thus interpreted as coercion and as a threat to democracy. Another article argues, "Women will be left behind as has happened so often already. The right to a self-determined pregnancy that had been realized in the G.D.R. and envied by many women in the old federal states is already in extreme danger" (May 7, 1991). The general theme of these articles is captured in one headline: "Evaluate democracy also on the basis of §218" (June 14, 1990).

The perception of abortion as a kind of test regarding the nature of unification grew as the prospects for maintaining the G.D.R. law worsened. Loss of abortion rights became tied to a general sense of loss—of status and identity as an East German, and of the social benefits of the G.D.R.; "as *Ossis* we are labeled as second-class citizens in the unification treaty. . . . Soon we will find abortions harder to get . . . yet no one asks about the conditions for already born life" (March 8, 1991). The abortion question is a "test of power in all of Germany that is destroying the social benefits achieved in the former G.D.R. . . . and a test of the true content of democracy in Germany (May 7, 1991).

In 1990 and early 1991, demands to keep the trimester rule were increasingly coupled with expressions of uncertainty about how it could be retained; by mid-1991 it seemed evident to many authors that the trimester rule was not politically viable. The practical impossibility of getting a trimester rule in the new Germany led many of those writing in the East German papers to radicalize their positions. Women of the PDS begin to advocate for women's absolute right to self-determination throughout pregnancy (which was never even considered in the G.D.R.) rather than assert their original position, which was that anything worse than the G.D.R. law would be unacceptable. Four articles make a case for this position, which was adopted by a majority at the June 1991 PDS Party Congress. The argument was that "mere reform" of Paragraph 218 would still "deny a woman the right of self-determination over her pregnancy and thus over her entire life plan, by securing the state's control over her reproductive ability" (July 3, 1991a). Petra Bläss, a prominent feminist in the PDS parliamentary delegation, went so far as to assert that "a time-limited right to self-determination isn't one" (May 14, 1991a). A minority continued to assert that a trimester rule is "more medically and ethically sound and not inconsistent with the principle of women's self-determination" (July 3, 1991b). The majority position, however, was not a proposal with a realistic chance of passage; it was defended as a nonnegotiable statement of principle about women's self-determination. Neither was it a newly invented position; it was a principle borrowed from the hopeless efforts of the West German feminist movement in the 1980s.[9] As one author argued,

---

[9] *Ersatzlose Streichung*, or total removal of Paragraph 218, has been the official position of the West's Green Party since its first party congress and is a frequent demand of the autonomous feminist movement, including Schwarzer's *Emma*.

Three-quarters of East German women favor retaining the trimester rule, which however is vehemently rejected by politically active West women. . . . Women mostly approve of such limits in order to have a means of restraining the "others," the so-called casual, irresponsible, immoral women. . . . For women and men with leftist sentiments, who claim emancipated people free of relationships of domination show solidarity in dealing with each other, I find such an orientation telling. . . . If in our image of free and self-determined people we actually proceed immediately to the idea that maybe some people will misuse this freedom, we will end up again with a utopia surrounded by a Wall. . . . That such a proposal (for the complete elimination of §218) will play no role in Parliament should not dishearten us. (May 24, 1991)

Principled statements with no real chance of practical success had characterized what might be an "oppositional stance" in the G.D.R. (Miethe 1996). In the abortion debate, the adoption of such unrealizable principles by *ND* and by the PDS represented, in part, a claim to a new oppositional identity in relation to the F.R.G. For example, recounting a conversation with three women PDS leaders, an interviewer cited them as variously pointing out how "as a left opposition, we are challenged precisely in this burning political issue" and that the stance of the party "has to do with our understanding of opposition and thus also of politics" (May 29, 1991). This sense of being "oppositional" was shared by readers, one of whom noted that the "principled position in our abortion bill is necessary to our status as opposition" (June 25, 1991). It is important to note that by taking a stance in opposition to the F.R.G. does not mean that readers are sympathetic to the old G.D.R. As one reader writes, she found "with bitterness" the G.D.R. to be an intrusive guardian [*vormundschaftlicher*] state, but sees "the high aspirations to democracy of the F.R.G." undercut by its even more intrusive guardian role in criminalizing abortion, and concludes "a humane purpose sanctifies no inhumane means. That too is a bitter lesson from the G.D.R. past" (May 14, 1991b).

But where being "oppositional" in the G.D.R. would unleash a repressive state response, being "oppositional" in the F.R.G. often means being ignored. A sense of being cast into the political wilderness, of not being able to stimulate discussion or provoke repression, was increasingly evident in 1991 and 1992, as the protest demonstrations that had worked in 1990 were suddenly treated as irrelevant. As political maneuvering to build parliamentary majorities becomes more important not only to the parties but to West German feminists, a sense of futility increasingly characterizes abortion articles in *ND*. One rages that "even the name of the 'Special Committee for the Protection of Unborn Life' formed in Parliament by the CDU, CSU, FDP, and the SPD already shows what its result will be" and approvingly quotes Christina Schenk, a feminist affiliated with the Alliance 90/Greens parliamentary group, as saying that "the claim to domination of the clerical, conservative, rightist politicians is similar to that of the SED" (September 27, 1991). Another argues, "People who take democracy and the inviolability of human dignity seriously must be concerned about Memmingen [i.e., the prosecution of a doctor who performed abortions] . . . while the actual Memmingen witchcraft trial continues, the political witch-burners are trying to push together the ugliest possible consensus." After reporting the status of parliamentary debates, the article concludes, "Many persist in the mistaken feeling that this process would be democratic. Memmingen will be back soon" (November 28, 1991). Another article reports critically on the mobilization of the Catholic Church and other anti-abortion forces, referring to them as "witch hunters in black and red robes" and looking for their Nazi roots (December 27, 1991).

As a party, the PDS in 1991 and 1992 is also in the process of defining itself in relation to potential constituencies. Compared to other parties, East or West, women are better represented in the PDS both as voters and as members (Schröter et al. 1996), and the visibility of gender, feminism, and women in *ND* is striking, especially in relation to West German media norms. Terminology that is radical and rare in the West (e.g., "patriarchy," "male domination") is present in the framing that *ND* journalists employ to describe the losses women are experiencing as a result of unification, of which the loss of abortion rights is depicted as emblematic. That conditions for women and children in the former G.D.R. are getting worse is cast as part of the hypocrisy of the government and its "pro-life" forces, while the "credibility of left politics rests on its answer to the critical question of what stance it takes to the self-determination of women" (May 24, 1991). Paragraph 218 is interpreted not only as a general loss of democracy, but also as the specific oppression of women, setting self-determination against paternalism (May 22, 1992, for example). The intertwining of democracy in principle and women's rights in practice remains a consistent theme in *ND* throughout the period, but as the decision in Parliament becomes imminent, there is a growing sense of fatalism that "a twenty-year-old right of East German women is going to be taken away" (June 19, 1992).

In 1992 the focus shifts to the parliamentary debates themselves, and most articles are concentrated in the period immediately before and after the vote is taken. Although demonstrations are called for and reported, the legislation itself is the focus. Representative Christina Schenk, who is given a front-page spot to editorially sum up its effects, sarcastically defines it as offering "coercive counseling through which women who lived in the G.D.R. finally will be put in the position to make responsible decisions" (June 27–28, 1992). The sense that the legislative decision repudiates women's experience of and in the G.D.R. is strong. As the Constitutional Court affirms this decision in 1993, it is also announced as "ending twenty-one years of woman-friendly practice in East Germany" (June 16, 1993). The repudiation of women's history of self-determination as responsible actors is framed as a rejection of the positive collective identity of East German women as a whole. The decision is framed as "a demeaning judgment about women in the former G.D.R. It suggests that they acted without a conscience for the past twenty years when, as the law allowed, they decided for themselves for or against the birth of a child" (June 23, 1993).

In the wake of the Court's 1993 decision, the sense of loss of rights thematically predominates, but the imputation of psychological conflict and hence of guilt to women who want to abort is also contested actively. One journalist writes about "women who find themselves with a conflict pregnancy—so the official language goes" (June 16, 1993a), while an editorial asks bluntly, "How much conflict does a woman have to show in order not to be taken for hard-boiled, unfeeling, or without conscience?" (June 16, 1993b). Others speak of the state's effort to get into women's heads and "brainwash" them into guilt.

A focus is also put on the F.R.G. in relation to other systems. Five different articles report on abortion laws in other countries, each one pointing out how backward the F.R.G. is in comparison (June 16, 1993d–g). These articles can be read as efforts to separate the F.R.G. from the West in general, as a way of facilitating criticism of the F.R.G., and as indirect refutation of the West's charge that the PDS was backward and was only promoting "G.D.R. nostalgia" by supporting the trimester rule. Locating both "backwardness" and male dominance as specific characteristics of the F.R.G. allows the PDS to present itself as a generally "progressive" force, which is where it is attempting to position itself in the overall landscape of unified Germany in the mid-1990s.

Overall in the period we see *ND* as increasingly taking an openly polemic and political stand. Throughout the entire 1990–1993 period it publishes no article or letter to the editor written from a "pro-life" perspective, but it clearly defines itself as "oppositional" vis-à-vis the dominant F.R.G. political discourse, which it casts as nondemocratic. *ND* consistently uses the phrases "termination of pregnancy" and "right to self-determination" and actively contests the language of "help" and "conflict" that both the legislature and the court endorse. In short, it articulates a feminist and "Eastern" identity that in part has been formed by the rejection and failure of its self-determination discourse.

CONCLUSIONS

Despite the different constituencies that each of these two former G.D.R. news-papers addresses and the different focus of their concerns, the abortion discourse that developed in East Germany has specific characteristics that set it apart from the dominant frames of reference employed in West Germany. In the West, the debate centered in the parties and revolved around the role of the state, as guardian, to offer "help" or "punishment" to a woman experiencing a "conflict pregnancy." In the East, the debate reflected the ways in which lessons from the G.D.R. past would be incorporated into the present, and the issue crystallized around the meaning of democracy and self-determination for women. As Gal argues in regard to Hungary, "The abortion debate turns out not only to be very much about abortion, but also an argument in absentia with communism . . . a contest for control of the emerging principles of political rule" (Gal 1994:260). Both the Christian ethics of the *NZ* and the "oppositional" stance of *ND* are political claims that actively challenge elements of G.D.R. history, but also take issue with the newly dominant practices of the F.R.G. A key conceptual element in both forms of post-socialist discourse is the definition of democracy and its relation to reproductive politics. For *NZ*, the meaning invested in democracy is that of liberal pluralism: tolerance for a diversity of opinion, stress on the individual rather than the state as the locus of moral choice, the end of moral and political absolutism, and freedom of choice for women. For *ND*, democracy is more an investment in substantive rights: self-determination for women, quality of life for children, and open and effective political opposition. While the discourse of *NZ* leads to the *conclusion* that women must be free to choose, realizing this right is the *premise* on which *ND*'s evaluation of democracy rests. For both former G.D.R. papers, the focus on democracy reflects a concern for putting practical limits on the state—that is, of insuring a nontotalitarian mode of governing. In these papers, readers and journalists alike associate the state's claim to decide for women with an anti-individual, and hence potentially totalitarian, impulse. Both papers actively challenge the inconsistency of a liberal state that claims to respect the individual, yet sees pregnant women as less than full persons and accepts limits to the autonomy of women that it rejects for other classes of people (c.f. Bordo 1995; Berghahn 1995).

Contrast these definitions of democracy with the West German emphasis on formal institutional procedures, such as voting and majority rule. Within the bounds of due process, the state is free to act, and social or political minorities are expected to accept the legitimacy of the state's actions. In the case of abortion, clear majorities of public opinion in the East and the West favored a trimester rule similar to that of the G.D.R. Thus it was not majoritarian principles as such, but acceptance of the processes by which the F.R.G. parties and Constitution operate that gave the decision democratic legitimacy. The empowerment that individuals experienced in the social movements that overthrew the SED government and in the consensus-seeking roundtables that proliferated during the transition encouraged citizens of the former G.D.R. to imagine democracy as something other than a clash of parties and partisan interests. The abortion decision thus became emblematic of the "democracy deficit" believed by many women and men in the G.D.R. to be characteristic of the unification process (Maleck-Lewy 1995; Berghahn 1995).

Unlike the situation in some other post-socialist states, women played an obvious and even leading role in the abortion debate in Germany, both East and West. Although women were the spokespersons in the parliamentary debates, the range of their discourse remained limited by the earlier Constitutional Court decision and by the priorities of West German political parties. In the G.D.R., abortion had been a medical or social issue, not a politicized women's issue (Hennig 1990). In the new Germany, this changed. In the context of the unification process, contested definitions of women as ethically responsible or irresponsible, as self-determining or "in conflict" were politically central. In this struggle, the evaluation of women's lives and choices became a metaphor for the evaluation of the G.D.R. as a whole. As Gal argues, "Rather than the shaping of reproductive practices for political ends, we see the shaping of politics through the coded discussion of reproductive practices" (1994:285). At the same time, however, the focus on abortion as the crucible for such political identification made "women" a political identity that had not existed in the G.D.R.

But the assumption that "women" constitute a single category with a common interest or set of representatives is also called into question in this account. Defense of individual rights and autonomy enters into parliamentary and popular discourse as an "eastern" perspective and is either discounted or discredited by advocates of a maternalist view. The latter view defines women's primary role as childbearer and casts the state as a benevolent protector and guardian; it is a stance that many politically active women in West Germany were willing to take, if only for short-term strategic reasons. Yet this position effectively erases a generation of women's experience with self-determination and returns them to the status of morally incompetent actors, a lesson that is not lost upon either *NZ* or *ND* readers. Thus, while "women" became a political category central to the debate over abortion policy, women's actual interests were divided between East/West even more than along feminist/nonfeminist, or Christian/non-Christian lines.

This examination of the discourse about abortion in the former G.D.R. reveals the emergence of a distinctive eastern perspective about democracy and about women. These views represent efforts to come to terms with political experiences—both the good and bad of socialist history and the swallowing of the G.D.R. by the F.R.G. through unification. The defeat of the "G.D.R.-style" trimester rule, in the context of the discourse surrounding it, thus becomes an occasion for the formation of collective identities as *Ossis* [Easterners], as women, and as distinctively Eastern women. Abortion is surely a women's issue, but it is also a fundamentally political issue of transition that cannot be ignored.

BIBLIOGRAPHY

Ankum, Katherina von
   1993   Political Bodies: Women and Re/Production in the G.D.R. *In* Women in German Yearbook. Vol. 9. Jeanette Clausen and Sara Friedrichsmeyer, eds. Pp. 127–143. Lincoln: University of Nebraska Press.
Berghahn, Sabine
   1995   Gender in the Legal Discourse of Post-Unification Germany: Old and New Lines of Conflict. Social Politics 2(1):37–50.
Bordo, Susan
   1995   Are Mothers Persons? Reproductive Rights and the Politics of Subject-ivity. *In* Unbearable Weight: Feminism, Western Culture and the Body. Susan Bordo, ed. Pp. 71–97. Berkeley: University of California Press.
Dahlerup, Drude
   1986   Introduction. *In* The New Women's Movement: Feminism and Political Power in Europe and the United States. Drude Dahlerup, ed. Pp. 1–25. Beverly Hills, CA: Sage.
Ferree, Myra Marx
   1994   "The Time of Chaos Was the Best": Feminist Mobilization and Demobilization in East Germany. Gender & Society 8(4):597–623.
Frauen gegen den §218 Bundesweite Koordination
   1991   Vorsicht "Lebenschutzer!" Die Macht der organisierten Abtreibungsgegner. Hamburg: Konkret Literatur Verlag.

Friedrichsen, Gisela
  1991   Abtreibung: Der Kreuzzug von Memmingen. Frankfurt: Fischer Taschen-
              buch Verlag.
Frommel, Monika
  1994   Warum ist die Abtreibung noch immer ein politisch brisantes Thema? *In* Ohne
              Frauen ist kein Leben: Der §218 und moderne Reproduktionstechnologien.
              Zentrum interdisziplinäre Frauenforschung, ed. Berlin: Verlag Christine
              Hoffman.
Gal, Susan
  1994   Gender in the Post-Socialist Transition: The Abortion Debate in Hungary.
              East European Politics and Societies 8(2):256–287.
Harsch, Donna
  1997   Society, the State, and Abortion in East Germany, 1950–1972. American
              Historical Review 102(1):53–85.
Hennig, Gert
  1990   Wieder §218? Erfahrungen eines Frauenartzes. Berlin: Dietz.
Jenson, Jane
  1987   Changing Discourse, Changing Agendas: Political Rights and Reproductive
              Policies in France. *In* Women's Movements of the United States and Western
              Europe. Mary Katzenstein and Carol McClurg Mueller, eds. Pp. 64–88. Phila-
              delphia: Temple University Press.
Koonz, Claudia
  1986   Mothers in the Fatherland: Women, the Family and Nazi Politics. New York:
              St. Martin's.
Maleck-Lewy, Eva
  1994   Und wenn ich schwanger bin? Frauen zwischen Selbstbestimmung und Bevor-
              mundung. Berlin: Aufbau Taschenbuch Verlag.
  1995   Between Self-Determination and State Supervision: Women and the Abortion
              Law in Post-Unification Germany. Social Politics 2(1):62–75.
Miethe, Ingrid
  1996   Von der Opposition zur Position: Das Politikverständnis bürgerbewegter
              Frauen der DDR vor und nach der deutschen Vereinigung. Unpublished manu-
              script.
Mushaben, Joyce
  1993   Concession or Compromise: The Politics of Abortion in United Germany.
              Paper presented at the American Political Science Association, Washington,
              DC, 1993.
Mushaben, Joyce, Geoffrey Giles, and Sara Lennox
  1997   Women, Men and Unification: Gender Politics and the Abortion Struggle since
              1989. *In* After Unity. K. Jarausch, ed. Pp. 137–172. Providence, RI: Berghahn.
Ockel, Edith
  1992   Anzahl der Lebendiggeborenen und Schwangerschaftsabbrüche von 1973–
              1989 in der ehemaligen DDR. *In* Ende der Selbsverständlichkeit? Die Ab-
              schaffung des §218 in der DDR: Dokumente. Kirsten Thietz, ed. Pp. 118–119.
              Berlin: BasisDruck.
Riemer, Jeremiah
  1993   Reproduction and Reunification: The Politics of Abortion in United Germany.
              In From Bundesrepublik to Deutschland. Michael Huelshoff, Andrei Markov-
              its and Simon Reich, eds. Ann Arbor: University of Michigan Press.

Rucht, Dieter
   1996   The Structure and Culture of Political Protest in Germany since 1950. Paper
           presented at the Tenth International Conference of Europeanists, Chicago.
Sauer, Birgit
   1995   "Doing Gender": Das Parlament als Ort der Geschlechterkonstruktion. *In*
           Sprache des Parlaments und Semiotik der Demokratie. Andreas Dörner and
           Ludgera Vogt, eds. Pp. 172–99. Berlin: Walter de Gruyter.
Schäuble, Wolfgang
   1991   Der Vertrag: Wie ich über die deutsche Einheit verhandelte. Stuttgart:
           Deutsche Verlags-Anstalt.
Schröter, Ursula with Renate Ullrich and Dietmar Wittich
   1996   PDS und Feminismus: Politische Akteurinnen und feministische Politikan-
           sätze in der PDS. Study no. 30. Berlin: Institut für Sozialdatenanalyse.
Tarrow, Sidney
   1994   Power in Movement: Social Movements, Collective Action and Politics. New
           York: Cambridge University Press.
Thietz, Kirsten
   1992   Ende der Selbsverständlichkeit? Die Abschaffung des §218 in der DDR: Doku-
           mente. Berlin: BasisDruck.
Ullrich, Kerstin
   1994   Abortion Discourse in Germany and Ireland. Unpublished manuscript. Euro-
           pean University Institute.
Worgitsky, Charlotte
   1992   Meine ungeborenen Kinder: Entstehung und Wirkungsgeschichte. *In* Ohne
           Frauen ist kein Leben: Der §218 und moderne Reproduktionstechnologien.
           Zentrum für interdisciplinäre Frauenforschung, ed. Berlin: Verlag Christine
           Hoffman.
Wuerth, Andrea
   1994   The Reunification of Germany and the Politics of Abortion: An Examination
           of the Abortion Rights Campaign. Paper presented at the Ninth International
           Conference of Europeanists, Chicago.
   1996   National Politics/Local Identities: Abortion Rights in Post–1989 Berlin. Paper
           presented at the Tenth International Conference of Europeanists, Chicago.
Young, Brigitte
   1996   An Illiberal German State: The "Fraktionsstaat." Paper presented at the Tenth
           International Conference of Europeanists, Chicago.

CHAPTER 4

Birth Strike in the New Federal States: Is Sterilization an Act of Resistance?

IRENE DÖLLING, DAPHNE HAHN, AND SYLKA SCHOLZ

IN DECEMBER 1994, *Esprit*[1] magazine published an article entitled "Birth Strike: What Will Become of the Future?" A photograph, probably taken the night the two Germanies were united, accompanied the article. In the foreground stood a young woman, isolated and holding a baby on her arm. In the background was a crowd, marching under a black-red-and-gold flag from the Brandenburg Gate toward the Reichstag. The only identifiable figures in the group were male. The woman, nestling her blanketed baby, appeared sad—stern even—as she gazed in the direction of the crowd.

To understand this photograph, we need to know that *birth strike* is a term frequently used to describe the declining birthrate in eastern Germany since unification. In 1989, 198,922 children were born in the German Democratic Republic (G.D.R.); in 1993, live births totaled only 80,500. "At 0.7 percent, [eastern Germany] currently has the lowest fertility rate in the world" (*Die Zeit*, October 7, 1994). At the same time, women in the East are being sterilized with increasing frequency. In Brandenburg, the only state in the new Federal Republic of Germany (F.R.G.) to maintain a statistical register of sterilizations, the procedure was performed 6,224 times in 1993, up from 827 in 1991. In this context, the 1994 publication of a photograph taken in 1990 carries a message: As represented by the woman standing apart from the crowd, German unification[2] has not had a positive effect in terms of fertility or an abundance of children.

The "demographic collapse," which *Der Spiegel* (38, 1993) reported as unprecedented in twentieth century German history, has in fact become a frequent topic in the mass media. As in other formerly socialist countries, reproduction (and reproductive behavior) is a highly contested subject—both emotionally and politically. We argue here that reporting on women's reproductive behavior activates a political discourse that symbolically delegitimizes the old social order and helps

---

[1] *Esprit* is the journal of the Democratic Women's Union, the successor organization to the Democratic Women's Union of Germany. This was the only women's organization that existed in the German Democratic Republic.

[2] In German, the term "unification" also has a sexual connotation; it can mean "sexual intercourse," "to sleep together," or "to consummate a marriage." The unification of the two German states has frequently been symbolized with the image of marriage.

to imagine and interpret the new. The discourse of gender plays an important part in this process: Norms of femininity are (re)produced and measured against an accepted "standard" of reproductive behavior, while interpretations of the (old and new) social order are sexualized. Moreover, by genderizing contemporary social problems and conflicts and discursively linking them to women's reproductive behavior, this process establishes a hierarchical symbolic order. We hypothesize that these are the actual reasons for the widespread media attention given to the declining birthrate, reproduction, and sterilization. Indeed, women's true motives for not bearing children or for being sterilized are probably uninteresting to the media. It is not surprising that their stories are rarely heard.

After a three-year study, we found an unmistakable discrepancy between the representation of women being sterilized and women's self-professed motives for undergoing the procedure. This discrepancy itself reveals the discursive marginalization of eastern German women—the facts of their decision are not only subject to interpretation, but incidental to the discourse. In our opinion, this suggests that the discourse itself reflects much broader social relationships. Both the women we interviewed and the media linked voluntary sterilization to the economic, social, and political disruption of transition. Yet while women explained their decision as a response to new constraints in their daily lives, the media seized upon the issue as a way to discuss population policy, socialism versus capitalism, East versus West, the future of eastern Germany or the future of the new integrated state. The women we interviewed never talked about a birth strike, yet this term has become common currency in the media. Significantly, the notion of a birth strike dates back to the early 1900s and is linked to the feminist and syndicalist discourse of that period.[3] It evokes fears of the German people dying out, of a future threatened by female sexuality run amok, and of (individual) stubbornness or collectively organized resistance. The contradictions between sterilization as a discursive event on the one hand and as a woman's decision on the other are documented in the results of our investigation.

To begin, we use the tools of discourse analysis to evaluate media reports about "sterilization in the East" and the alleged birth strike. In this part of our analysis, our goal is twofold: First, we want to determine who takes part in the discourse, in what context, and with what intent; and second, we want to know whose interpretations tend to be accepted as legitimate. Our objective is to unravel the various themes that are linked together and to show how—by embedding them in various discourses (some of which have a long history)—they are used to interpret social change.

---

[3] The term *birth strike* appeared for the first time in France in 1870 and derives from the Parisian Marie Huot's concept of a "strike of the bellies." It was taken up by the syndicalist workers' movement and transformed into birth strike. Mixed with socialist ideas, the term was applied in Germany by the Social Democratic doctors Bernstein and Moser, who in 1910 began, through public lectures and pamphlets, to inform working-class women about birth control methods and called for a birth strike. The birth strike was declared a decisive strategy to ensure the cultural rise of the working class. In their propaganda, women were made central figures in the effort to cure social misery through birth control. At the same time, a state policy against voluntary birth control began (for a

After examining the ways in which sterilization is represented in the media, we look closely at women's actual decisions to undergo this procedure. With the empirical results of our study in Brandenburg, we compare the media accounts with women's stated motives and ask whether—and from whose perspective— the term birth strike is justified.

The Magdeburg Scandal: "Afraid of Unemployment, Women Undergo Sterilization"

Media reports of the rising number of sterilizations and the declining eastern German birthrate, like the one used for the title of this section,[4] began to appear in late 1989–1990. Yet it wasn't until May 1992 that what might be called a full-blown media campaign began, triggered by a single event. Even today articles occasionally appear on this subject. As part of a weekly series entitled "Labor Market Policy is Women's Policy," Editha Beier, an Equal Opportunity Officer[5] for the city of Magdeburg, publicly reported that in the state of Sachsen-Anhalt, employers were pushing women to be sterilized as a condition of getting (or keeping) a job. Editha Beier and her co-workers brought the following facts to public attention:

> During office consultations, several women confided that they had been steri-lized following their (potential) employer's request for proof "that they were unable to sustain future pregnancies." One of Ms. Beier's co-workers recalled having met "several such young women" in the hospital (*Magdeburger Volks-stimme*, May 20, 1992).
>
> These women had requested and been given certificates by the Magdeburg Medical Academy verifying that the procedure had been performed.
>
> Elsewhere in Sachsen-Anhalt, an Equal Opportunity Officer reported that "childless women from 19 to 33 years of age" were being sterilized "out of fear of unemployment." On their own initiative, women were providing proof to that effect in their job applications. The Officer "had been aware of [such cases] for some time."
>
> A similar report in a rural district stated that, in response to her job application, an electronics technician "was told . . . to send her husband. The young woman decided to be sterilized and then return to the employer with the certificate" (*Magdeburger Volksstimme* May 20, 1992).

---

full discussion, see Bergmann 1992). In the articles we analyzed, the term *birth strike* alluded to these events.

[4] Title of an article in the *Süddeutsche Zeitung*, May 23, 1992.

[5] Equal Opportunity Officers are employed at the state and municipal levels, as well as in private enterprises, and are assigned the task of ensuring equal treatment for men and women. Their authority is differently defined in individual states and municipalities. The appointment of Equal Opportunity Officers was a demand made, primarily by women, during the transition period (1989– 1990) in the G.D.R. With unification of the two German states, the West German model of

These cases were all discussed in the context of a rising number of sterilizations performed in the Magdeburg Medical Academy (1,200 sterilizations in 1991 compared to 8 in 1989). The same facts and examples were repeated—often word for word. Increasingly, reports began to question the accuracy of the women's charges. Several factors encouraged this. First, the women involved each chose to remain anonymous. Also, it was unclear from Editha Beier's account whether the employers had actually coerced the women (perhaps by threatening their jobs) or if the women had decided of their own volition. Nevertheless, media interest in the "sterilization scandal" continued. The press linked sterilization to a variety of new social ills, and the incident itself became a triggering mechanism for the discursive treatment of other issues "in the air."

A brief look at the political and socioeconomic context following German unification helps illustrate why certain themes were addressed in the media. By 1992, eastern Germany was nearing a state of crisis. Many unprofitable enterprises either shut down or streamlined their operations by eliminating jobs. By October 1992, 16.2 percent of the active workforce was unemployed; of this group, over 60 percent were women. According to the Federal Statistical and Labor Office, estimates of hidden unemployment (i.e., people engaged in involuntary part-time work, work in the second economy, retraining, or early retirement programs) would put the percentage at 38.5 percent (these figures have remained nearly unchanged). For many in the former G.D.R., economic hardship was compounded by the uncertainty and sense of anomie that resulted from a collapse of social norms and the loss of networks previously taken for granted. High expectations for an improved standard of living, a West German system of justice and administration, and opportunities for democratic action ran headlong into the reality of declining economic opportunity.

Politicians, especially those in the ruling parties[6] eager to maintain their power and position, were under pressure to deal swiftly with this crisis. They needed to preserve the impression that daily life was better in the new Federal State than it had been in the "illegitimate G.D.R." Scandals could be quite useful for this purpose.

Many eastern women experienced the consequences of unification as particularly negative and far-reaching—these women were frequently referred to as "the losers of unification." Not only were they more likely than men to lose their jobs, but they also were less likely to be hired. Moreover, as socialist labor policies were revoked, benefits and special services suspended and daycare centers closed, it became increasingly difficult for women to balance work and family. Statistics also showed a sharp decline in marriages and births and a drop in the divorce rate. Not least among the changes that specifically affected women was the

---

Women's Affairs Officers was carried over to the East. However, the name Equal Opportunity Officer was retained in the new states.

[6] The new states were all governed by the Christian Democratic Party (CDU), in some cases in coalition with the Free Democratic Party (FDP). Exceptions to this were Brandenburg, which was governed by the Social Democratic Party (SPD), a dominated coalition that included the FDP and the Greens; and Berlin, which was governed by a CDU/SPD coalition.

elimination in 1992 of the G.D.R.'s liberal abortion law. This had allowed women to terminate a pregnancy during the first trimester, at no cost and without having to speak with a counselor in advance. At the same time, women in eastern Germany faced fewer obstacles to sterilization under the new system. To be sure, changes in the abortion law and the more liberal approval process for sterilization encouraged more women to exercise this option.[7]

Amidst the disruption and uncertainty of profound institutional change, talk about the winners and losers of German unification, as well as western standards of normalcy, gender roles, and women's (potential) role in political and economic life, were all popular themes under public discussion. When the story broke about a "sterilization scandal," it provided a useful venue to link these issues to the "birth strike" of eastern German women.

UNRAVELING THE DISCOURSES

We tried to reconstruct the media campaign as comprehensively as possible for our analysis. For the period from May 18, 1992, to June 18, 1992, we evaluated twenty-seven periodicals (nineteen regional, national, and foreign newspapers, plus eight magazines, including women's magazines). Thirteen of the nineteen newspapers and one magazine reported, at least once, on the "sterilization scandal." For the period from June 19, 1992, to February 1995, we used the newspaper collections of the Chair for Population Science at Berlin Humboldt University and of the Berlin Feminist Health Center; we also scanned selected newspapers and magazines printed in 1994.[8] Stories about the "sterilization scandal" reflected

[7] According to a 1969 regulation issued by the G.D.R. Ministry of Health, sterilizations were to be performed only in exceptional cases when medically indicated, and even then only on condition that the woman had already given birth to at least two children. The procedure was performed approximately three to four times per year at large clinics, and this remained relatively constant until the mid-1980s. A change in this practice occurred around 1987–1988, when the approval process was liberalized, possibly due to the procedure's acceptance in other European countries as a method of birth control and family planning. A clear rise in sterilizations was evident in the G.D.R. until 1989–1990.

As this article goes to press, there is no legal regulation of sterilization in the Federal Republic of Germany. The only law that applies in this matter is paragraph 226a of the Criminal Code (StGB = Strafgesetzbuch), which addresses "physical injury with the permission of the injured." The costs of sterilization are currently paid through mandated insurance.

[8] Our analysis includes a total of 47 articles, which can be divided into four categories: (1) Articles that report directly on the May 1992 "sterilization scandal" in Sachsen-Anhalt. These appeared primarily during the four weeks after the triggering "discursive event" by Editha Beier (21 articles total). (2) Articles in which sterilization is not the main theme, but is discussed in connection with demographic developments and the declining birthrate in eastern Germany or the situation in the labor market. Some articles (thirteen total) appeared at the same time as the articles in category I, while others appeared one to two years later. (3) Articles on sterilization that make no direct reference to the Magdeburg events, but report generally on sterilization in the East and explore the possible reasons for it. Seven such articles appeared between 1990 and 1994. (4) Articles about the operation and its (primarily psychosomatic) side effects. Out of five articles, three appeared in 1992 and one each in 1993 and 1994.

a broad spectrum of political views, ranging from conservative to liberal, left-alternative to socialist. Openly right-conservative or right-wing publications are not represented in our sample.[9]

To evaluate the media campaign, we rely on the conceptual assumptions and terminology of discourse theory.[10] Upon this basis, we have isolated the lines of discourse described below. Individual articles contain intersecting lines of discourse, which may form knots of mutually reinforcing or even contradictory arguments and images. Persons quoted in the media often invoke different themes as well. In teasing out the lines of discourse, we were particularly interested in metaphors and interpretive patterns. We wanted to know who took part in the discourse and with what authority and power they participated. We identified the following participants:

Equal Opportunity Officers, having triggered the discursive event, were most heavily represented from mid-May to mid-June 1992. Afterward, their presence diminished substantially. Having limited authority and resources, this group is on the periphery of political power. Within the discourse structure, we can classify them as protagonists of a feminist counterdiscourse.

When the story broke, *politicians* reacted with outrage and threatened legal action if evidence of coercion was discovered. Because none of the women filed complaints or revealed their identity, no further comment was required. The politicians' presence also declined with time.

The presence of *experts*, notably *physicians* and *psychologists*, was consistently high and increased over time. *Social scientists* and *counselors* can be included in this group, and they are most heavily represented in articles of type 2 and 4 (see footnote 8).

The *women* themselves hardly appear (six times altogether). Three articles, which include interviews by western German journalists, reveal a marked East-West bias.

The goal of our analysis was to dissect the lines of discourse brought into play by the triggering event (information about employers demanding the sterilization

---

[9] The famous *Frankfurter Allgemeine Zeitung*, a relatively conservative newspaper, did not participate in the media campaign, but neither did *Emma*, the feminist magazine.

[10] We will borrow from discourse theory in our analysis of the media campaign. Following Foucault, and also Peter Schöttler, we understand discourse to mean: "a certain linguistic materiality which is institutionalized in one form or another as a societal manner of speaking, with as it were, built-in power and resistance effects" (Schöttler 1989:102). We assume that participants in the discourse with different political, ideological positions can confront one another by taking different discursive positions on the field of the same system of collective symbols that constitute a culture (Link 1984:68). Discourses have a history (genealogy) that must be reconstructed if one wishes to grasp their current content. Furthermore, discourses are structured by lines of discourse that appear on different discursive levels (science, politics, media, daily life, administration, etc.), affect one another, and (can) be taken up by one another (see Jäger 1993:181). Discursive knots and collective symbols "which meander between the discourses" (Jäger 1993:181) establish a connection between different special discourses in an interdiscourse, in which the proximity to the interdiscourse of the different discourses (scientific, political, etc.) varies. Discursive events are "events which have been given great discursive prominence

of female employees). The central point was to discover how cultural patterns of perception and interpretation are discursively activated and reproduced as legitimate and self-explanatory by a range of participants who often think of themselves as politically opposed to one another.

The Discourse of Order

The notion of order is central to the culture of modernity (to which both capitalist and socialist societies belong). In our collective imagination, the alternative to order is *chaos*: indefinite, indistinguishable, absurd, incompatible, ambiguous, ambivalent (Bauman 1992:17). Thus, social change and shifting power balances are registered as disruptions, or *disorder*. The notion of order, we posit, precedes reflection and judgment and exists at all levels of discourse, from the common to the scientific.

In the media coverage surrounding the Magdeburg incident, what was scandalous for politicians was the disrupted image of a *legal order* that is designed to protect against coercion. In fact, politicians had been aware of the complaints for some time prior to Ms. Beier's disclosure. It was only amidst the publicity, however, that "legal measures" were proposed and those employers accused of coercion were depicted as "the lowest of the low" (*Neues Deutschland*, May 21, 1992). Thus, in the public sphere, politicians appear as the guardians of order. A comment by Governor Münch emphasized that order requires separating the old from the new. "If the accusations were true," he said, "it would be a scandal. It is not possible that the methods of totalitarian regimes have been practiced in Sachsen-Anhalt" (*Tageszeitung* [*taz*], May 20, 1992). In other words, the rule of law bears no resemblance to state socialism.

Although the Equal Opportunity Officers were among the political opposition, they too reproduced the discourse of order. This is clear in a statement by Editha Beier in which she calls the "sterilization scandal" a "symptom of an environment which is currently forcing [women] to extremes" (*Neue Zeit*, May 23, 1992). She demanded a political response on grounds that sterilization represented, first and foremost, structural discrimination against women. For her, the question of coercion was of secondary importance. Nevertheless, by speaking about "extreme" behavior, she too formulated her argument within the discourse of order; that is, she invoked a gender order in which the norm (or nonextreme behavior) is female fertility and childbearing.

In countless articles, journalists and experts referred to eastern Germany as chaotic or as a disaster area (*Der Spiegel* 38, 1993). The contrast and use of hyperbole confirm the superiority of the new (western) order and situate (potential) threats to that order firmly within the East.[11] When women are portrayed

---

and which influence to a greater or lesser degree the direction and quality of the line of discourse to which they belong" (Jäger 1993:181).

[11] This double meaning should be seen against the backdrop of crisis and symptomatic western German attitudes; the cost of the reconstruction in the East, which must be (co)paid by the western German population, is, to some degree, compensated by this feeling of superiority.

as solely responsible "for an unprecedented demographic collapse" (*Der Spiegel* 38, 1993), they symbolize the East's (psychological, social, and somatic) impoverishment; like a barren woman, the East can have no future.

When the media reported on sterilization as a woman's attempt to keep her job, they suggested that eastern German women were revealing their attachment to the old system. The media derided their "damned, anticipatory obedience" (*taz*, Feb 21, 1994) and suggested that their concern about job security was a virtue that not only contributed to the G.D.R.'s forty-year endurance, but also was hopelessly old-fashioned. In this sense, sterilization, which is final and irreversible, is associated with an *outmoded* woman whose character is *externally determined* (authoritarian/totalitarian). This is contrasted with the *internally determined*, self-reliant *modern* woman who makes decisions based on a set of options, and thus acts, according to current sociological terminology, in an *individualized* manner. Their desire to work also identifies eastern German women as utterly behind the times: The alleged decision to sacrifice their fertility for a job identifies them with a system in which paid labor for the collective good carried the highest value.[12] This alleged collectivism also represents what is outmoded (socialist), disorderly, and chaotic. Whether impelled by socioeconomic conditions or behavioral idiosyncrasies, these women faced an uncertain future.

A less dramatic disruption of order appears in the line of discourse that links sterilization to a temporary catching-up phase. Early on, physicians and other experts theorized that the rapid rise in sterilizations was a response to restructuring, namely, that it represented the exercise of newly won individual rights following the restrictive legacy of the G.D.R. (see, for example, *Magdeburger Volksstimme*, May 20, 1992). Journalists and various experts tended to genderize this argument. Characterizing sterilization as an overzealous attempt to catch up, they blamed women for upsetting (at least temporarily) "the natural balance" of reproductive order. This argument shifted the Equal Opportunity Officer's charge of structural discrimination outside the center of attention.

In terms of the increased sterilization rate, the East's need to catch up assumes an overtone of unbridled female sexuality that has escaped state control and legal order. If women want to indulge but also avoid the cost of the pill, or—as one student put it—"really have fun" (*Der Spiegel* 38, 1993), it conjures up a popular media image of the *Ossis*, who irresponsibly live beyond their means and want the benefits of western prosperity without hard work and without having to worry about future consequences.

---

[12] An article in the *Mitteldeutsche Zeitung* on May 20, 1992 judges sterilization to be a perfidious "entrance fee to the labor market." The shift of moral disapproval from the employers to the women is revealing. Of course, employers coercing women to be sterilized should also be rejected as perfidious but, "What is really terrible is that women believe that they have a chance of getting a job only if they never bear a child" (*Mitteldeutsche Zeitung* May 20, 1992). This sentence is ambiguous: It contains both a condemnation of the women who are ready to sacrifice their fertility for a job, and it warns against the naive belief that women can assure themselves entry to the labor market by giving up children. Here too the cultural pattern is reproduced according to which women are defined first and foremost by their ability to bear children.

Discursively, order is imposed on the East by superimposing images of what is normal on what is already presumed to be chaotic. It was emphasized, for example, especially in 1993–1994, that the number of sterilizations performed in eastern Germany—although higher than in the West—nevertheless was within a "normal" range for West European countries. Similarly, the alleged birth strike was sometimes characterized as an adjustment to the West German model, and thus simply a shift in childbearing practices. Even at this level of discourse, however, women as independent, self-willed subjects are marginalized, and any (possible) elements of resistance are overshadowed.

The Discourse of Population Policy

Because all modern societies need to maintain a stable population, regulating population growth is an important aspect of state power (Foucault 1983). In addition, population policy discourse is closely connected to the forms of collective representation that accompany nation building. In this context, the term birth strike is highly loaded because it signals a threat to the nation's collective *We.*

Together with the discourse of order, the population policy discourse occupied a central place in press reports of the "sterilization scandal." Early on, attention focused on the link between sterilization and the labor market. A striking shift occurred several weeks later when reports noted an inverse relationship between the rate of abortion and sterilization, while the birthrate continued to decline (*Neue Zeit*, June 27, 1992; *Deutsches Allgemeines Sonntagsblatt*, July 17, 1992). Reports on the declining birthrate in the five new states also appeared with increasing frequency (*Berliner Zeitung*, April 24, 1992). As the media campaign continued, population policy reports also began pointing to the rising number of sterilizations.

Research publicized in the feminist counterdiscourse (*Junge Welt*, June 6, 1992; *Neue Deutschland*, April 18, 1994) revealed no direct connection between sterilization and the birthrate. The media, however, continued to publicize the image of a sterilized, childless woman.

One characteristic of the population policy discourse was the invocation of the danger of a *dying nation.*[13] Attention focused on East-West comparisons and new images of the "enemy." Population experts were the primary spokesmen for this line of discourse, which was the most heavily influenced by scientific discourse.[14]

Researcher's calculation that the population of the new states would decline 20 percent by the year 2010 were connected to the gloomy and depressing image

---

[13] The threat of the nation dying out, within the context of a declining birthrate, was the central theme of population policy discourse in the Federal Republic during the 1960s and 1970s (see Beck-Gernsheim 1984).

[14] A study conducted by two population scientists at the Berlin Humboldt University, Rainer Müntz and Ralf Ulrich, played an important role in this. From early 1994, all the predictions made by these two scientists were presented in the media (see Münz and Ulrich 1994).

of contemporary eastern Germany. Cities were described as "open air museums" (*Die Zeit*, October 7, 1994), and there was talk of depopulated streets and squares. Formulations like "creeping depopulation," "the East Germans are slowly *dying* out," and the "bleeding dry" of a "desolate land" (*Die Zeit*, October 7, 1994; *Freitag*, August 12, 1994; *Der Spiegel* 38, 1993; *Die Woche*, July 28, 1994, and August 4, 1994) tied the present plight to poor long-term prospects. Since the current decline in births would produce another low birthrate in twenty-five to thirty years, in the long term—according to predictions—the new Federal States would become a land of the elderly, its population senile (*Der Tagesspiegel*, January 6, 1994; *Berliner Zeitung*, June 21, 1994).

Women, who are said to be causing this "unprecedented demographic collapse," are indirectly blamed for the short- and long-term social consequences: In the short term, they are responsible for the closing of kindergartens and the firing of daycare workers, teachers, doctors, and other caretakers; in the long term, they are responsible for falling purchasing power and municipal tax revenues, particularly in those (rural) regions where the population decline is most severe.

The changing image of the enemy within population policy discourse is striking. In the 1970s in the Federal Republic, emancipated (which usually meant professional) women were blamed for the declining birthrate registered at that time. They were charged with "insufficient motherliness, lack of consideration and modesty, increasing professional ambition, overblown striving for self-realization; in short, striving for their own money and for recognition" (Queisser et al. 1992:14). Emancipated women were also held responsible for the (projected) aging of society and high unemployment rates, and blamed for threatening the German nation. In the current population discourse, no reference is made either to this earlier discourse or to its background, and the dying East is never interpreted as a threat to the German nation. The image of the enemy shifted from the emancipated, western woman to the sterilized eastern woman, both unwilling to give birth. But the eastern woman, who clings to the notion of combining work and motherhood, also represents the old system.

Within this discourse, the central lines of discrimination no longer run between men and women, but between western women and eastern women. Individual (western) women and the counterdiscourse of western feminism are subsumed within a single homogenous image. "The West" becomes a model according to which family takes precedence over professional pursuits, and any effort to combine them is an individualized choice.

The Medical-Scientific Discourse

The overwhelming importance of medical-scientific discourse in the West hardly needs emphasis (Honegger 1991; Duden 1991; Laqueur 1992). Physicians and psychologists increasingly dominated the sterilization debate in a number of ways. First, despite their lack of empirical evidence, physicians presumed to know why women in the East were being sterilized. The elaboration of potential medical motivations put individual decisions, rather than social structural factors, in the foreground. Moreover, when gender stereotypes are reproduced by "demi-gods in white coats," they acquire a kind of scientific legitimacy. The pairing of femininity with fertility establishes certain natural, fixed, and essential character-istics that women cannot ignore with impunity.[15] These stereotypes can be found as frequently in feminist papers (*Neues Deutschland* and *taz*, for example) as they are in conservative papers. Finally, by portraying male sterilization as risk-free and female sterilization as complex and dangerous, physicians and psychologists perpetuate the image of an unreasonable woman who does not consider the consequences of her actions. This is also the image of an incompetent woman who must be told by experts what the possible consequences of her decision could be.[16] What's more, by establishing the criteria by which sterilization requests are deemed acceptable or unacceptable, physicians define both what it is to be "a [normal] woman" and how long the ability to bear children is subject to social control.

The Discourse of Modernization and Individualization

The concept of modernization, borrowed from German sociology, is often used in journalistic discourse to specify supposed differences in East and West Germany's stages of development (Hradil 1992). For instance, freedom (e.g., choice of contraceptive methods) is regarded as a sign of modernity but not of traditional or less modern socialism. A slightly different sense of the modern comes from "individualization theory" (see Beck 1986; Beck and Beck-Gernsheim 1994), which holds that the achievement of individualism is a central feature of moder-nity. For example, one sociologist remarked, "[In the East] there used to be pre-ordained life histories" (*Der Spiegel* 38, 1993). Yet these "histories" have been made obsolete by the leap to a modern, more individualized society. The insecurity this produces can "explain" (or excuse) the desire of eastern German women to be sterilized. Reversing the equation, physicians assert that individualization con-notes egoism and the loss of commitment to social relationships. Women who bear fewer children are cast as egotistical, as suffering from a "prosperity syn-drome" (*Neue Zeit* June 27, 1992) that contributes to the decline of civilization (see also Miegel and Wahl 1994).

The Feminist Counterdiscourse

It is important to note that there were discussions of the sterilization issue in the mass media that explicitly argued against some of the discourses outlined in the last sections. A number of such counter-themes emerged in feminist writings from both eastern and western Germany. But in other ways this feminist discourse

---

[15] This warning is impossible to overlook in headlines like "Wenn Sterilisation bereut wird. Wer nicht selbst entscheidet, leidet seelisch mehr [sic!]" [When sterilization is regretted. Those who do not decide for themselves suffer more psychological harm] (*Tagesspiegel*, June 7, 1992); "Ein Zurück gibt es nicht mehr. Die Sterilisation der Frau führt zur dauerhaften Unfruchtbarkeit" [There is no way back. Sterilization of women leads to permanent infertility] (*Berliner Zeitung*, June 4, 1992).

[16] The majority of the articles we found in our research describing the sterilization procedure do not refer to a "sterilization scandal." Since they were published at the same time, and in some cases

simply reproduced the dominant lines of argument, and it too was heavily marked by polarizing East-West stereotypes. The feminist counterdiscourse is associated with the new women's movement that developed in West Germany in the 1970s and questioned the stereotypical images of motherhood and femininity in its critique of patriarchy. For a time, writing from the women's movement gained a firm place in the West German media. In the fall of 1989, a women's movement emerged in the G.D.R. and picked up many of these same issues. After unification, however, the women's movement quickly declined in the East. Today, several activists work as Equal Opportunity Officers and, from these positions, continue a feminist counterdiscourse.

The themes mentioned specifically in this counterdiscourse are equal rights and equal opportunity for women and—above all—women's right to self-determination. Editha Beier, for example, argued that the demand for female employees to be infertile fits into a catalogue of discriminatory practices that includes preferential firing and asking job applicants about their intentions to get pregnant. Sterilization was just another indication of structural gender discrimination; the scandal that it signified was the expulsion of eastern German women from the labor market. Some people noted that gender discrimination is characteristic of all modern societies. Speaking about the West, one woman commented, "It makes your hair stand on end, what the employers get away with" (*Frankfurter Rundschau*, July 10, 1992).

In another counter-theme, eastern women journalists emphasized the autonomy and responsibility displayed by women who are sterilized, noting that they are driven by the goal of economic independence. This image directly undermined the dominant view of immature women who thoughtlessly give up their fertility (*Junge Welt*, June 6, 1992, and August 22, 1992; *Neues Deutschland*, April 18, 1994). One journalist cited a female gynecologist from Brandenburg: "Most of the women who choose the operation for irreversible infertility have thought carefully about this step" (*Neues Deutschland*, April 18, 1994). Finally, some eastern feminists linked sterilization (in eastern Germany) to the "reform" of Paragraph 218, which abolished the G.D.R.'s abortion law. Again, the discussion emphasized women's right to make free, self-determined choices.

Here, another connotation of the term birth strike should be mentioned. This is the notion of women's subversive, and organized, resistance against unreasonable demands and cultural attributions. This image contrasts sharply with the modernization discourse, in which voluntary sterilization is an act of individualization, that is, women's professed desire for socioeconomic mobility, for flexibility in arranging their hours and working environment, and for the freedom to determine the trajectory of their own life/fertility cycle.

In western Germany, women journalists showed empathy yet maintained a clear distance. Their articles not only reproduced East-West stereotypes, but also certain arguments found within the dominant discourses. The "Eastern Woman" emerges as a cliché: She is insecure, suffers from fear of the future and a lack of

---

appeared next to articles about the "sterilization scandal," their location demonstrates their intent and effect in this context.

social confidence. By choosing sterilization, eastern women are said to be looking for a sure thing (*taz*, February 21, 1994). They are portrayed as inflexible, unwilling to face risk, and incapable of adjusting to change. These images are strikingly evocative of modernization discourse; because eastern women are not sufficiently individualized, they are not modern. Moreover, by allowing such "serious intervention in their own bodies," eastern women demonstrate that they lack body-consciousness or, by implication, that they lack consciousness of their feminism. "The women in the former G.D.R. . . . accepted interventions in their own bodies with far fewer reservations [than their sisters in the West]" (*taz*, February 21, 1994). These depictions contrast sharply with the image of western women, who are seen as strong, flexible, achievement-oriented, and politically conscious. Again drawing from the modernization discourse, there is an allusion here to the catching-up phenomenon: Eastern women are supposed to want what western women already have. "It's no wonder that the women in the East are now seeking 100 percent reliable contraception which their sisters in the West have long had" (*taz*, February 21, 1994). Just as in the official discourse, eastern German women are portrayed as outmoded representatives of the old order.

Another feature of East-West stereotyping is the selective use of interviews to support a given image. In the few articles that contained firsthand accounts, journalists clearly preferred to interview unemployed women. Invariably, they lived in "cold, gray, endless suburbs," were married and had several children, consistent with the G.D.R. norm, early in life (see *Deutsches Allgemeines Sonntags-blatt*, July 17, 1992; *Freitag*, March 4, 1992; *Zitty*, 7, 1994). Significantly, when western journalists refer to eastern women as "the losers of unification," the counterdiscourse begins to mimic the official discourse (*Die Zeit*, July 16, 1993). That is, both lose sight of the fact that the transition, with all its problems, has brought new opportunities to women in eastern Germany.

We found only one article written by a western journalist (*Freitag*, May 28, 1993) that breached this stereotype of East-West polarization. Noting women's general frustration about the abortion issue and the resurgence of gender discrimination since unification, she called upon eastern and western women to join, not in a birth strike, but in a strike against male domination.

Discourse, Media, and Constructed Identities

Before examining the actual motives of women who were sterilized, it seems useful to summarize the results of our media analysis. The discursive event—the 1992 "sterilization scandal"—proved an effective medium through which several highly charged topics could be symbolically knotted together. Public discussion was never simply about sterilization. Instead, the "sterilization scandal" evoked a host of other issues, including the definition of femininity, the scientifically and medically determined norms of motherhood, and, most strikingly, the contrast between eastern and western Germany. This latter discourse revolved around images of women as symbols of modernization and individualization, in both the positive and negative sense. If we are correct, and sterilization became a coded way to talk about other politically important topics, then it is no surprise that the women involved were rarely interviewed or quoted publicly. Although supposed facts about their motives and behavior were central to the arguments outlined here, women's actual motivations were not considered and, indeed, had little relevance.

In the next part of our study, we turn away from the media images and look at the actual considerations cited by women who were sterilized after 1990. It is interesting to compare our results with the "facts" presented in the press. Did these women think of their decision as a form of birth strike, as resistance—individual or collective—to an untenable social order, or as an act of individualization? In our opinion, this question can only be answered by paying careful attention to the life situation and decision-making process of the women themselves. Each of these interpretations, namely individualization, birth strike, and resistance, is symbolically linked to the discourses outlined earlier. A note on usage: We use birth strike, in the traditional German sense, to mean politically organized, collective resistance against conditions perceived to be intolerable. We use the term *resistance* as it is defined in feminist literature (see Honegger and Heintz 1981:9ff). Typically arising from women's sense of isolation, it can mean either a collective or an individual act, or it can be directed inward, as in the case of anorexia. For women socialized in the G.D.R., we believe it is most useful to focus on individual resistance that, commonly understood, need not be political.

VOLUNTARY STERILIZATION: THE CASE OF BRANDENBURG

To test the veracity of the media reports, we interviewed a group of women in Brandenburg[17] and asked what led to their decision to be sterilized. We began the empirical study in 1993 and completed it in 1995. Familiar with the 1992 press campaign, we were interested in the following questions:

1. What is the social background of the women who opted for this procedure? We wanted to know about their age, education or vocational training, current employment, marital status, and number of children.

2. What form of contraception had been used previously, and which partner was responsible?

3. What kinds of considerations led to their decision to be sterilized?

4. How was the decision made? What was the initial impetus, and how much decision-making time passed prior to sterilization?

5. Did their physician influence their decision in any way, and if so, how?

---

[17] Brandenburg has a population of 2.5 million and an area of 29,000 square kilometers. Berlin, administratively an independent city-state, is located in Brandenburg's geographic heart and is now the German capital. During the G.D.R. period, a significant proportion of economic activity was based on agricultural production. Of 180,000 previously employed in agriculture, only 35,000 earn a living in farming today. In addition, there are a few large industrial enterprises (steel production, mining, textiles) that have been greatly reduced in size as a result of the structural changes in the last five years. Prior to 1990, 107,000 people were employed in these industries; today only 24,000 jobs remain. Women's rate of participation in the labor force, which in the G.D.R. period was about

In Brandenburg, the rising trend in sterilization did not begin immediately after the changes in 1989 and 1990, but developed somewhat later. Between 1991 and 1993, statistics show a 750 percent increase. Official statistics for 1993 show 6,224 sterilizations were performed in Brandenburg, to which approximately 1,000 outpatient procedures must be added. These calculations indicate that more than 7,000 sterilizations per year were performed in a population of 524,000 women of childbearing age (ages 15–45).

Clinics were selected in twelve locations that were geographically, economically, and demographically representative for the state of Brandenburg. In these twelve clinics, we asked the medical personnel to distribute a standardized questionnaire to women entering the Gynecology Department to be sterilized. A total of 1,000 questionnaires were distributed, with the proportion distributed to each clinic corresponding to the number of sterilizations performed in that clinic in 1993. The distribution of questionnaires began in April 1994 and ended one year later in April 1995. Of the 1,000 questionnaires distributed, 405 were usable, representing a return quotient of 40 percent.

The questionnaire consisted primarily of questions regarding motivation and social position.[18] Based on our evaluation of the theoretical literature and the media reports, as well as several conversations with gynecologists, we developed a list of eighteen motivations,[19] classified according to the following factors:

1. Family structure (e.g., "I'm too old for another child")
2. Social-economic constraints (e.g., "Contraceptives are now much too expensive")
3. Health risks associated with reversible contraceptives (e.g., "I've used all the other contraceptives long enough")
4. Exercise of new rights (e.g., "I thought about sterilization in G.D.R. times, but it was much too complicated")
5. Economic independence (e.g., "In my current job I cannot afford a[nother] child")

---

86 percent (see Winkler 1990:64), fell to about 60 percent as a result of the economic collapse. At the time of our study, the unemployment rate for women in Brandenburg was 21 percent.

[18] The questionnaire addressed the following topics:

Current employment and principal (current or previous) employment
Education and technical or professional training
Changes in employment during the previous 12 months
What first led to consideration of irreversible contraception?
Time between the first suggestion and the operation
Reasons for deciding to have the operation
Previous method(s) of contraception
Pregnancies, births
Problems and risks associated with previous pregnancies and births
Partner (length of time together, characterization of the relationship)
Was sterilization of the male partner considered?
Age, marital status, number of persons in the household, place of residence (village, town, city), religion, income

[19] Initial screening results prior to the study revealed that no woman had been sterilized at the demand of or under pressure from her employer. In preliminary interviews, the medical directors in

6. Medical concerns (e.g., "The health risk of an abortion is too great for me")

7. Changes in the abortion law (e.g., "After the Karlsruhe decision, I wanted an absolutely reliable form of contraception")

We included a section for women to list any considerations not specified on the questionnaire. We scored the responses according to the following scale: Decisive, Important, Less Important, Meaningless, Does Not Apply. Each reason was ranked in order of importance based on the value of the median.

Because the questionnaires could not elicit the breadth of information needed to evaluate the decision-making process, we also conducted a series of interviews. Our interviewees were selected from responses to a newspaper advertisement; also, each questionnaire contained a letter outlining our intentions and interest in interview subjects. Of approximately 160 women who were willing to be interviewed, we chose 28 using a random selection method and conducted conversations with them lasting, in some cases, several hours. We transcribed the interviews and evaluated them using standard content analysis.

We wanted to develop a typology (see Mayring 1993) that would encompass several factors, including women's motivation to be sterilized, their life history and current living situation, and their strategy of action. In the biographies of G.D.R. women, we compared the following structural elements: employment history; life plans, including priorities for work and family; reproductive behavior, including the way in which motherhood is integrated into their life; and the effects of motherhood on their employment history and current employment status.

Our goal was not only to find out why women undergo sterilization but also to analyze the differences between their stated motivation and the picture painted in the public discourse. We therefore paid particular attention to how our results either supported or (more often) seriously contradicted the assumptions and assertions made in the media.

Age and Family Size

In the media, it was repeatedly claimed that young, childless women in the East were using sterilization to resist motherhood. We wanted to know if this explanation, which undergirds the image of a "dying East" corresponded to women's actual motivation and life situation. Analytically, our first step was to correlate social structural factors, such as age and family size, with the reasons "I am satisfied with the size of my family" or "I feel too old for a(nother) child."

The average age of the women in our sample was 36.[20] As illustrated in Table 4.1, nearly 90 percent were over 30. The percentage of women under 25 (0.3

---

the Gynecology Department also dismissed employer pressure as a reason for sterilization. They offered as evidence the fact that no woman had requested certification of infertility. We therefore did not include on the questionnaire an explicit question about this issue.

[20] Comparisons with various countries showed that the average age of sterilization (median) lies between 35 and 38. For England and Wales it is 36.7; for France, 38; for the United States, 35 (see Kettin and van Praag 1985:228).

TABLE 4.1
Distribution of the Sample Group by Age

Age Group	< 25 Years	26–30	31–35	36–40	41–45	> 46 Years
Percentage	0.3	13.0	33.6	33.1	17.2	2.8

percent) was insignificant. For the younger group, sterilization played virtually no role as a contraceptive method. Our study confirmed that the discourse about childless women being sterilized is false. All the women included in the sample had given birth to at least one child. A large percentage had two or three children. Demographic analyses from the period prior to 1989 clearly demonstrate the prevalence of the one- or two-child family and also indicate that the average woman's childbearing years had ended by age 30. This is confirmed by the results of our investigation.

Table 4.2 compares the family size of women in our sample to a representative average among comparable age groups (see Trappe 1995:105).

An overwhelming number of the women surveyed indicated that family planning was a principal consideration in their decision to be sterilized: 60.5 percent rated it Decisive, and 20 percent rated it Important. A woman's age at the time of her decision was also an important factor. Approximately 35 percent of the women felt they were too old to have another child and rated this as Decisive in their decision; 19 percent rated age as Important.

Partnership, Birth Control, and Responsibility

We started from the assumption that women typically expect—as was common in the G.D.R.—to have one or two children in their third decade and that contraception would be an important part of their life planning. We suspected that responsibility for contraception could be measured according to one's choice of method. We further assumed that choosing sterilization as a contraceptive method indicated one or another partner's acceptance of responsibility. We therefore asked whether the possibility had been discussed of the male partner being sterilized and, if so, why it was decided that the woman would undergo the procedure.

TABLE 4.2
Distribution of Children

Number of children	Representative Average	Research Sample
No children	6.9%	–
1 child	32.5%	20.1%
2 children	48.2%	54.3%
3 children	9.0%	15.1%
4 or more children	3.4%	4.5%

Based on our data sample, approximately 75 percent of the women who were sterilized were married. At the time they were questioned, 14 percent were divorced and another 3.5 percent were married but separated from their spouse. Three quarters of the women who responded Not Married, Widowed, or Separated had entered a new relationship, meaning that a total of 96 percent lived with long-term partners. This highlights one contradiction between the press reports and women's lives. Women involved in long-term, happy relationships do not easily fit the image of a chaotic East.

Our research also indicated that in most cases the possibility of the male partner being sterilized was not considered. Indeed, nearly 70 percent reported that this option was never discussed. Among those who had discussed it with their partners, a decision was not hard to reach. Despite the fact that male sterilization is technically a simpler procedure, it was only in the rarest cases that this was considered a viable option. According to the women in our sample, reasons for this included: "He's afraid that he would no longer be potent," "He wouldn't have done it anyway," "Perhaps he'll find a younger woman and will want to start a new family with her," or "I'm the one who gets pregnant, not him."

Finally, the women in our sample had all used, for several years, other forms of contraception. Of the 405 women questioned, over 50 percent (221) had used the pill, approximately 20 percent had used an intrauterine device (IUD), and 20 percent had used condoms. While so-called "natural methods," were used by a small percentage of women, other methods were rare. During the G.D.R. period, gynecologists generally did not recommend diaphragms or condoms because of their limited reliability, but they did recommend, and freely provided, the pill and the IUD. The conclusion that women bore primary responsibility for birth control is supported by the fact that over 70 percent used a long-term form of contraception, designed specifically for women.

Professional Skills and Employment Status

One assumption promoted by the media was that the women being sterilized were unemployed, unskilled, and/or socially disadvantaged. Another was that women in the former G.D.R. were excessively work-oriented and would pay any price to keep their jobs—even sacrifice their fertility.

The first assumption is simply false. Statistics for Brandenburg put women's unemployment at 21 percent (Landesamt für Datenverarbeitung und Statistik 1994). In our sample, 21.7 percent were unemployed, meaning that unemployed women are not overrepresented in the research population. Highly qualified professional women[21] were, however—39 percent compared to 26 percent among the general population. Finally, 58 percent of the women sampled had completed vocational training, which means that only 2.7 percent were unskilled.

---

[21] "High professional qualifications" included technical school, technical university, and university degrees. Journeyman certification is included in the category "occupational training."

Our analysis reveals that there is a group of unemployed women who have limited resources and for whom sterilization is a remedy for a difficult socioeconomic situation. The primary reasons these women choose sterilization are: (1) Contraceptives are no longer covered by insurance and are therefore too expensive and (2) cuts in state aid to families make the cost of another child too high. The relationship between unemployment, low income, and sterilization as a cost-free method of contraception proved highly significant for unemployed women. A factor analysis confirmed this result. Motivations cited by these women included: "Contraceptives are much too expensive today," "Support for families with children is much too low," and "Raising a child is much too expensive today; I cannot afford it." For unemployed women, sterilization can hardly be characterized as the kind of unbridled consumption portrayed in the media.

The second assumption, that the strong work ethic of women in the former G.D.R. influences their decision to be sterilized, is partially correct. Although most women in the research group were professionally minded, the importance they attached to a career as part of their own identity varies significantly. This was shown most clearly in our analysis of the interviews and will be described later. Nevertheless, a differentiated examination shows that there is a group of women for whom the decision was highly influenced by job-related concerns. A factor analysis for this group revealed the following motivations: "In my current job I cannot afford to have another child," "I was afraid of not being able to find another job or losing the job I have now," "I want to maintain my economic independence," and "I want finally to do something for myself . . . to travel, to buy things." The group citing this motive represented employed women with a relatively high level of income.

Initial Impetus and Decision-Making Time

Press reports tended to characterize the increase in voluntary sterilization as a new trend or an exercise in frivolity. We therefore asked who or what initially suggested sterilization and how much time passed between that moment and the actual procedure. Tables 4.3 and 4.4 illustrate the results.

Approximately one-third of the women received the first suggestion from either their gynecologist or general practitioner. This fact points to women's dependence on medical experts with respect to this issue. When the impetus comes from a

TABLE 4.3
Initial impetus (n = 402)

Initial Impetus	Percentage
Regular doctor	3.0
Media	6.9
Husband/partner	11.6
Regular gynecologist	27.7
Women friends/acquaintances	31.9

TABLE 4.4
Decision-Making Time: Initial Impetus to Sterilization (n = 400)

Time Period	Percentage
Up to 6 months	41.8
6–12 months	25.3
1–2 years	21.8
2–3 years	4.8
More than 3 years	6.5

doctor, it is accompanied by a short decision-making period. One-third of the women noted the impetus as a recommendation by women friends and acquaintances. Within well-functioning women's networks, information about other women's experiences is passed along tested channels and is highly valued. In our sample, fewer than 12 percent received the impetus from their husbands or partners, and only 6.9 percent received it from the media.

Table 4.4 demonstrates that, for most women, relatively little time passed between first suggestion and actual sterilization. Again, several variables must be considered in relation to one another. Family size and a woman's age—the two most decisive factors behind a decision to be sterilized—both proved highly significant in terms of decision-making time. For 67 percent of the women, the time between first impetus and sterilization was one year or less. This length of time can be attributed neither to women's frivolity nor to a fashion trend, but it is explained by a woman of a particular age group having reached optimum family size and trusting in the recommendations of her doctor and the advice of women friends, colleagues, and neighbors.

Response to the Changed Abortion Law

One striking result of the questionnaires is the number of women who responded that "revision of the abortion law" influenced their decision. This factor was listed by 57 percent as Decisive or Important, irrespective of age or income level. This suggests the possibility of individual resistance, a point we confirmed in our interviews and which we will describe in more detail below.

Summary of the Questionnaires

Our empirical investigation revealed clear discrepancies between the media coverage of sterilization and the real life circumstances of women who opted for this procedure. On average, women who were voluntarily sterilized were approximately 36 years old, had one or more children, and lived with their partner in a long-term relationship. These women had reached their desired family size and considered themselves too old to have more children. Professionally, they were more highly qualified than the national average, and nearly all had completed vocational or professional training. After years of using reversible contraceptives, many women regarded sterilization as a way to avoid the side effects and uncertainty associated with other methods.

Other motivational groupings can be identified, including: (1) socially disadvantaged women who chose sterilization because of financial hardship and lack of state support—the decisive factor for these women is the now obligatory high cost of contraception; and (2) career-oriented women beyond the childbearing phase who are actively involved in their work and have a high level of income.

Birth Strike: Resistance or Individualization?

The questionnaires provide only a starting point for interpreting possible patterns of resistance or individualization. To address these issues more fully, we conducted twenty-eight thematically structured interviews and analyzed them using a structural typology. From the questionnaire data, we first identified several dimensions of a woman's experience that were germane to her decision (career or family orientation, priorities regarding motherhood/family or employment, career prospects, ability to balance work and motherhood, motivating factors, experience with reversible contraceptives). We then identified three character-types and classified the interview data according to the following typology.

Type I: Family-Oriented Women

The women in this group were between 33 and 35 years old and described themselves as living happily in a long-term relationship. Their household income tended to be high, and they might be described as well-situated. As far as we could determine from the information available, these women came from large, more traditional families, which is to say that they grew up in an agricultural or religious environment. Born between 1959 and 1961, their family orientation was likely reinforced by G.D.R. family policies of the 1970s and 1980s (see Helwig and Hildegard 1993; Trappe 1995).

Both family and career are highly valued by these women, although their life choices tended to support family as their highest priority. Their self-image was strongly shaped by their role as mother and family protector. At most, these women wanted two children.

> My qualifications are just right for me to be able to manage my work and my family. If I had gotten a college degree, I would have to be more committed to my career and would not have had as much time for my family. And that wouldn't suit me, so I'm happy as I am.

Rather than question their responsibility for family and childrearing, these women integrated it positively into their self-image.

> Back then I really didn't think about it. Later the role of mother became more important for me, I'd have to say that. So, I'd give up my job for my children. . . . Yes, I'm more mother than woman.

They felt best within their families. Problems about combining work and motherhood rarely entered into their personal reflections. Their primary reason for working was to gain social recognition and new contacts.

> I am happy in my job and I am happy as a mother. A little more at work, you get more recognition there, have your own money, you aren't dependent on anybody.

Another said,

> Well, you really didn't have to worry a great deal about education and training. It all went more or less automatically. University. Getting accepted really wasn't a problem . . . the first child at 19, that's why she's already so big. And everything worked out okay. The second came three years later, was no problem. And the most important thing was really the children, that they grew up healthy and it all worked out okay.

Of the six women in this group, four had a technical school certificate, one had a college degree, and one had a journeyman's certificate. After the changes, with the exception of one woman who was unemployed, they all maintained jobs within their field. The majority were working in the civil service, where labor force reductions have thus far been less drastic. In terms of employment, they did not experience the transition as a discontinuity.

Had nothing changed in 1989, this group still would not have wanted a larger family and would have considered sterilization a viable form of contraception. Two motivating factors were absolutely decisive for this group. The first was family planning.

> I was always afraid of a pregnancy and didn't want more children. These days you don't have time for more than two children.

The second was that they believed they were too old to have more children.

> Well, since I've reached the age and the matter of children, it has to come to an end, because to start all over again at 34 and have another child, when I already have two, it's no longer a question. And that drew the line.

For this group, sterilization cannot be interpreted as an act of (individual) resistance. These women viewed sterilization simply as a method of fertility control; it was not a statement against changed political or economic conditions. Neither can it be described as an act of individualization since, for them, the decision fit quite naturally into a pattern of life decisions.

Type II: Socially Disadvantaged Women

These women were financially insecure, either because their husband's income was insufficient or because they were (both) unemployed and had only their monthly unemployment or welfare payments. The families of this type were also deeply in debt. Based on information provided about family of origin, these women had several siblings and grew up under modest conditions. Work and family held roughly equal positions in their life stories. They worked to provide family income and to make social contacts. Their preference was for no more than two children.

> I mean, I did grow up, we were four girls at home, but I always said, four children, you never want to have that many. Two in any case. I couldn't imagine a life without children.

These women—despite their preferred family size—typically gave birth to more than the average number of children. All described serious problems in combining work and motherhood, which they related to a large family and to conflicts with their partner.

For these women, the image of a harmonious family life contrasts sharply with their experience. During the interview, many women described a pattern of abuse and violence. Probably as a result of this experience, a striking number of women in this group had broken relationships behind them, in some cases several.

> But, oh well, since things went so wrong with my first, well, it's just normal to want to have children together. And then after my third arrived things got really bad, somehow, my husband treated the two big ones a little unfairly, sometimes he even hit them and things like that. We had to make it clear to him that he wasn't allowed to do that. With the help of the child welfare service, too. Oh well, and then he completely spoiled my third. And so I thought, this can't go on this way, we have to do something about it . . . and then I got pregnant. . . . Okay, I said, then I'll take another one. Well, and because of it things got better.

When women entered into a new relationship, they wanted, and generally had, a child with this partner. The motivation behind this may have been to reestablish family harmony or to start a family with a "biologically shared" child.

The employment histories of women in this group are marked by frequent changes, sometimes into unskilled jobs. Although all had completed journeyman training, it qualified them only for poorly paid, gender-typed jobs. After 1990, all of the women in this group were dismissed from their jobs and had been unemployed for several years by the time of the interview. With low-level qualifications and several relatively young children, their chances of reentering the labor market were very poor.

> I've applied a few times already. The chances are simply bad. I mean, I'm already 38, you're not young anymore, you're not old yet, sort of in the middle, the children are still. . . . The [employers] only see the number of children, they don't even ask how old they are or whether they can take care of themselves already. . . . Well, if you already have three or four kids and aren't so young anymore, you're the first to go. It's actually very sad, I have to say. But what can you do? You have to cope with it.

They often decided to be sterilized because of the high cost of contraceptives:

> The pill is very expensive. And since we had a monthly loan payment of 1,500. . . . I couldn't afford the pill.

Another reason given was the difficult economy and lack of social or financial support for families with several children:

> A child should have nice things and the way it is now for my children, I can't do anything special with them during summer vacation because we don't have any money, it makes me suffer, I'd never do it again. I'm certainly not going to have another child when I already can't manage. When you think it over, groceries, those are huge expenses, it's not just 3 marks 10 like we used to pay.

This group has been the most seriously affected by the reduction or elimination of material and nonmaterial transfers and of other support mechanisms typical for large families in the G.D.R.

For this group, sterilization cannot be regarded as an act of individualization. Because of their social position, these women already had limited options in the G.D.R.; following unification their situation only deteriorated. In the G.D.R. their opportunities were shaped by their classification as a "child-rich" family. In the new Germany, their job qualifications have been devalued and they have been compelled to work below their skill level. Their chances on the labor market are limited, and their exclusion from productive work throws them back exclusively upon their families.

For women of this group, sterilization can be regarded as a form of resistance. Because of their limited room to maneuver, it offered a rare opportunity for independent decision making.

> I said, so do I have to pay for it, too? She [the gynecologist] says, "Yes, you have to pay." So I said, No, I won't do it . . . you don't have the dough anyway, I said and then I asked the guy from the [insurance company] is it free? Yes. Well, then we know what we have to do.

Their resistance was directed against the new abortion law and the subordination of women that comes with it. It also was a form of resistance against the power hierarchy that existed within their most intimate relationship.

> I told my husband a story about something else. I didn't tell him anything about it, because back then we were still at one another . . . so for God's sake, I don't want another kid. And four really are enough. Still, I have to say, you should do it all over again.

Type III: Career-Oriented Women

The women in this group were highly qualified and generally held professional positions. Their income level was higher than the other two groups. Their priority was to be autonomous and to do interesting, demanding work. As one respondent replied, "I always wanted to have a profession, to be independent."

Having children and combining work and family had always been a part of their life plans. Although this produced many conflicts, it became easier to balance as their children grew older.

> For me, my profession came first. I couldn't imagine already being, or wanting to be a mother at 19 or 20. For me, it was out of the question, I have to say. . . . When I

met my husband in my mid-twenties, it then became clear to me that sometime in the next two or three years I would begin a family, and then I really wanted to have children. And actually it was the right time for me personally. I had been able to develop myself professionally and had taken advantage of it for myself. And then I thought, now it's about time to want to have a child and as soon as possible. And that's how it turned out.

These women tended to be in less conventional relationships than women in the other groups. Half of them had been divorced and were either in a long-term relationship with a new partner or living alone with their children. They often attributed their divorce to their own need for self-determination and to their husband's inability to sustain an egalitarian partnership. These women typically had one or two children who, in most cases, were 13 or older at the time of sterilization.

> It could also be because I am an emancipated woman. Maybe that's one of the reasons. If I weren't so involved in life, with [both] feet, after all, it's a male profession, if I were to subordinate myself just a little, that would have pleased him. But since I always tried to get my own way or to say, that will be done this way and this the other. Maybe that's why it didn't work out.

According to the women who were in a relationship at the time of our interview, the male partner also tended to have a good job and earn a high income.

All but one of the women in this group had a technical or university degree. Following unification, they typically passed through a sometimes critical reorientation phase, but they were generally able to consolidate their professional position within four or five years. They can be classified in three subgroups according to their situation at the time of the interview:

> The first and largest group (nine women) completed some form of professional requalification (this might have meant additional training or simply an orientation to new western standards). They all advanced to higher positions with a corresponding increase in salary. They were professionally successful women.
>
> A second group (three women) also advanced to mid- or high-level positions, but experience their current situation as extremely negative. Although they are professionally successful, they have young children and their family life is a source of pressure. They noted that the problems are exacerbated by conflicts in their relationship.
>
> The women in a third subgroup (three women) were enrolled in a retraining program that would qualify them for work at a lower level than what they were doing before the changes. They agreed to retraining because they want to take advantage of every opportunity and in no case want to be limited to home and family. They will need to be resourceful to establish themselves professionally.

These women decided on sterilization because of their strong orientation toward work and because they knew another pregnancy would create new conflicts in their lives. The risk and uncertainty of reversible contraceptives contributed to their decision. Once again, women in this group felt they were too old to have more children.

> Well, I was pretty clear about it, I didn't want any more children under the new conditions. I was just in the midst of an occupational change and about to begin in this office and the boys are big and healthy.

For the women in this group, one might say they achieved a level of individualization after 1989. Given their strong orientation to work and a career, their education and professional training, and their more varied living arrangements, these women meet the criteria outlined in current theories of individualization. Another sign of individualization is that these women display a high degree of health consciousness, expressed here as a critical perspective on reversible contraceptives. It's probably also true, however, that events in their lives after 1989 built on a foundation already firmly in place during the G.D.R. period. With educational opportunities, and in some cases help from their families, these women had long been able to choose from a broad spectrum of possibilities. Throughout their professional development, they have sought demanding work and a high degree of freedom and flexibility. The ability to take advantage of opportunities is part of their social capital and this, under the new circumstances, gives them more room to maneuver than the women of the other types.

PARAGRAPH 218: THE ABORTION LAW

In our evaluation of both questionnaires and interviews, "changes in the abortion law" proved to be non-specific to any group as a motivating factor. Most women totally rejected the new regulations, which demand compulsory counseling prior to the procedure and removed public financing. In their criticism of the new law, women pointed primarily to the control it imposes on their personal decisions.

> Well, I think that it is treating women like children. This whole regulation, this "must let themselves be advised on this question, whether to carry a pregnancy to term or not." I'm sure there are situations which could be a conflict, in the moment when a pregnancy is first established. For me, however, it is out of the question that the surrounding circumstances also have to be in favor, whether I bring up a child or not. ... I think, I don't have to make a special trip to a conflict counseling session and bare my soul and describe my psychological condition. I must retain the ability to make up my mind for myself.

Under the new law, women display a heightened sense of fear about having to carry an unwanted child to term. Most women do not want to risk this situation.

> And then came this idiotic discussion: Paragraph 218 or not, back to the Middle Ages. ... Especially with the pill or IUD they say it still could happen sometime or other or you get to menopause and stop taking the pill and then I'm supposed to let

someone or other tell me, maybe in my mid-forties, you have to have the child; today you really don't know anymore how the law is going to be interpreted and I didn't want to let these old men decide for me.

CONCLUSIONS

Our interviews and questionnaires show decisively that voluntary sterilization cannot be characterized as a birth strike in eastern Germany. However the media construed women's motivations, the women who were actually sterilized offer no support for this interpretation. There is, however, some evidence that both resistance and individualization played a part in some women's decision. We have argued that media representation of this phenomenon—which focuses heavily on the chaos threatening western German order and uses gendered ideas and images to discursively control the chaos—is more about interpreting social change than it is about the lives and decisions of women being sterilized.

By contrast, the women in our study gave concrete reasons—differentiated by social position—for their decision. The profound social transformation since unification has jeopardized or completely undermined many of the things these women previously took for granted, including the ability to raise a family and have a career, develop professionally, maintain a certain standard of living, and plan for the long term. These women (prematurely) sacrificed their fertility to protect the welfare of their children and families. It was a gesture of control, exercised to ameliorate conditions that threatened their livelihood and that they could not manage in any other way. These conditions included deleterious changes in the labor market, social welfare cuts, and rent increases.

Sterilization can also be understood as a differentially motivated form of individual resistance, although it is not resistance in the usual political or collective sense. A woman might resist a situation that threatens her job opportunities or, like the women of Type III, she might resist efforts to deny her self-determination. Indeed, certain decisions, like abortion and contraception, were seen in the G.D.R. context as self-evidently a matter of personal choice. A woman might resist what she experiences as injustice, like the Type II women whose disadvantaged social position—already established in the G.D.R. period—made them vulnerable to impoverishment.

Voluntary sterilization also reflects the structural problems of eastern German women. It might be a form of resistance, but it is nevertheless an individual act directed against one's own body. It calls attention to the very limited sphere of decision making that women in modern societies generally have. In the case of state-socialism, it also underscores the obstacles to collective action posed by the lack of civil society. In general, when the political space for participation does not exist, women's only recourse may be to individual forms of *resistance*. For women of the former G.D.R., the legacy of long internalized modes of reacting continues to hamper collective organization. Avenues to decision making remain limited, and, under the current conditions, one might say that the problem has grown worse.

It is only among women of Type III that we can speak of individualization, and for them it has a decidedly gender-specific meaning. For a woman to be autonomous, to set a high standard and take advantage of professional opportunities, means—much more than it did in the G.D.R.—choosing between a career and children. These two expectations are now less compatible than ever. For women in the new federal states, being sterilized symbolizes this structural problem. It is the price that women must pay for their careers.

BIBLIOGRAPHY

Newspapers/Media

Berliner Zeitung (Berlin)
  4/24/1992   Im Kreissaal bleiben die Betten leer. Geteiltes Deutschland: Geburtenrückgang im Osten—Babyboom im Westen.
  6/4/1992   Ein Zurück gibt es nicht mehr. Die Sterilisation der Frau führt zur dauerhaften Unfruchtbarkeit.
  6/21/1994   In den Zahlen steht die Zukunft.
Deutsches Allgemeines Sonntagsblatt (Hamburg)
  7/17/1992   Der Wende-Knick.
Esprit (Berlin)
  1994   Gebärstreik. Was wird aus der Zukunft? (December)
Frankfurter Rundschau (Frankfurt/Main)
  7/10/1992   Frauen unter Druck gesetzt.
Freitag (Berlin)
  3/4/1992   Die Ostalgikerin.
  5/28/1993   Gau—die größte anzunehmende Unzumutbarkeit.
  8/12/1994   Sterben die Ostdeutschen langsam aus?
Junge Welt (Berlin)
  6/6/1992   Keine Skandale.
  8/22/1992   Meine Entscheidung.
Magdeburger Volksstimme (Magdeburg)
  5/20/1992   Was ist wirklich dran am "Sterilisationsskandal" von Sachsen-Anhalt?
  5/20/1992   Frauen-Kritik an Landespolitikern.
Mitteldeutsche Zeitung (Halle)
  5/20/1992   Perfider Verzicht.
Neues Deutschland (Berlin)
  5/21/1992   Frauenkliniken in Sachsen-Anhalt bestätigen: Mehr Sterilisationen.
  4/18/1994   Heißt das Motto Arbeit statt Kinder?
Neue Zeit (Berlin)
  5/23/1992   Kein Mann wird gefragt, ob er noch Kinder zeugen wolle.
  6/27/1992   Stets ein Kompromiß der Unzulänglichkeiten.
Der Spiegel (Hamburg)
  1992   Alles über den Kopf, no. 22.
  1993   Lieber einen Hund, no. 38.
Süddeutsche Zeitung (Stuttgart)
  5/23/1992   Aus Angst vor Arbeitslosigkeit. Frauen lassen sich sterilisieren.

Tagesspiegel (Berlin)
　6/7/1992　Wenn die Sterilisation bereut wird.
　1/6/1994　Kitas in Ruheplätze umbauen?
Tageszeitung [taz] (Berlin)
　7/19/1991　Sterilisationskurve geht steil nach oben.
　5/20/1992　Schicken Sie besser Ihren Mann für den Job.
　2/21/1994　Aus Zukunftsangst auf Nummer sicher.
Die Woche (Hamburg)
　7/28/1994　Ein Volk unter Schock.
　8/4/1994　Ein Land verödet.
Die Zeit (Hamburg)
　7/16/1993　Geld oder Leben.
　10/7/1994　Land ohne Kinder.
Zitty (Berlin)
　1994　Der Absturz der Mütter, no. 7.

Books/General

Bauman, Zygmunt
　1992　Moderne und Ambivalenz: Das Ende der Eindeutigkeit. Hamburg: Junius
　　　　Verlag.
Beck, Ulrich
　1986　Risikogesellschaft: Auf dem Weg in eine andere Moderne. Frankfurt/Main:
　　　　Suhrkamp Verlag.
Beck, Ulrich and Elisabeth Beck-Gernsheim
　1994　Riskante Freiheiten. Frankfurt/Main: Suhrkamp Verlag.
Beck-Gernsheim, Elisabeth
　1984　Vom Geburtenrückgang zur neuen Mütterlichkeit. Frankfurt/Main: Fischer
　　　　Verlag.
Bergmann, Anna
　1992　Die verhütete Sexualität. Hamburg: Rasch und Röhring Verlag.
Duden, Barbara
　1991　Der Frauenleib als öffentlicher Ort: Vom Mißbrauch des Begriffs Leben.
　　　　Hamburg, Zürich: Luchterhand Verlag.
Foucault, Michel
　1983　Sexualität und Wahrheit. Bd. 1: Der Wille zum Wissen. Frankfurt/Main:
　　　　Suhrkamp Verlag.
　1991　Die Ordnung des Diskurses. Frankfurt/Main: Fischer Verlag.
Helwig, Gisela and Maria Nickel Hildegard
　1992　Frauen in Deutschland 1945–1992. Bonn: Bundeszentrale für politische
　　　　Bildung.
Honegger, Claudia
　1991　Die Ordnung der Geschlechter: Die Wissenschaft vom Menschen und das
　　　　Weib. Frankfurt/Main: Campus Verlag.
Honegger, Claudia, and Bettina Heintz
　1981　Listen der Ohnmacht: Zur Sozialgeschichte weiblicher Widerstandsformen.
　　　　Frankfurt/Main: Evangelische Verlagsanstalt.
Hradil, Stefan
　1992　Die "objektive" und die "subjektive" Modernisierung: Der Wandel der west-
　　　　deutschen Sozialstruktur und die Wiedervereinigung. Aus Politik und Zeitge-
　　　　schichte: B29–30, S3–14.

Jäger, Siegfried
  1993   Kritische Diskursanalyse: Eine Einführung. Duisburg: DISS Studien.
Ketting, Evert and Philip van Praag
  1985   Schwangerschaftsabbruch: Gesetz und Praxis im internationalen Vergleich. Tübingen: DGVT.
Landesamt für Datenverarbeitung und Statistik
  1994   Bevölkerung und Erwerbsleben im Land Brandenburg 1993: Ergebnisse des Mikrozensus. Potsdam: Landesamt für Datenverarbeitung und Statistik.
Laqueur, Thomas
  1992   Auf den Leib geschrieben: Die Inszenierung der Geschlechter von der Antike bis Freud. Frankfurt/Main: Campus Verlag.
Link, Jürgen
  1984   Über ein Modell synchroner Systeme von Kollektivsymbolen sowie seine Rolle bei der Diskurs-Konstitution. *In* Bewegung in Stillstand und Metapher. Jürgen Link and Wulf Wülfing, eds. Pp. 63–92. Stuttgart: Klett Cotta Verlag.
  1986   Noch einmal: Diskurs. Interdiskurs. Macht. kultuRREvolution 11:4–7.
Mayring, Philipp
  1993   Qualitative Inhaltsanalyse: Grundlagen und Techniken. Weinheim: Deutscher Studienverlag.
Miegel, Manfred and Stefanie Wahl
  1994   Das Ende des Individualismus: Die Kultur des Westens zerstört sich selbst. Bonn: Aktuell Verlag.
Münz, Rainer and Ralf Ulrich
  1994   Was wird aus den neuen Bundesländern? Demographische Prognosen für ausgewählte Regionen und für Ostdeutschland. Berlin: Humboldt-Universität Lehrstuhl für Bevölkerungswissenschaft.
Queisser, Hannelore with Christiane Schmerl and Lindy Ziebell
  1992   Lebensplanung ohne Kinder. Frankfurt/Main: Fischer Verlag.
Schöttler, Peter
  1989   Mentalitäten, Ideologien, Diskurse: Zur sozialgeschichtlichen Thematisierung der "dritten Ebene." *In* Alltagsgeschichte: Zur Rekonstruktion alltagsgeschichtlicher Erfahrungen und Lebensweisen. Alf Lüdtke, ed. Pp. 85–136. Frankfurt/Main: Campus Verlag.
Trappe, Heike
  1995   Emanzipation oder Zwang: Frauen in der DDR zwischen Beruf, Familie und Sozialpolitik. Berlin: Akademie Verlag.
Winkler, Gunnar (ed.)
  1990   Frauenreport '90. Berlin: Verlag die Wirtschaft.

PART TWO

Gender Relations in Everyday Life

CHAPTER 5

Changing Images of Identity in Poland:
From the Self-Sacrificing to the Self-Investing Woman?

MIRA MARODY AND ANNA GIZA-POLESZCZUK

> Men are stupid, stuuupid . . .
> Yeah . . . they can think only about their work. They're stupid . . .
>
> I'm simply a feminist . . .
> Me too.
>
> . . . and any young girl is able to make fools of them.
> —*Conversation between two elderly Polish women*

IN TIMES OF MAJOR systemic upheaval—such as Poland experienced following the 1989 transition from state socialism—the study of gender provides a particularly illuminating perspective on social change. Gender is one of the broadest identity concepts. Not only is gender implicated in discussions about sexuality and reproduction; it also underlies many assumptions about work, leisure, political activity, religion, family relations, and socioeconomic relations. Careful analysis shows that while femininity and masculinity, including "styles" that differentiate one sex from the other, are often ascribed to biological differences, they are in fact constrained and constructed by specific economic, political, and social forces. But the effect also works in the other direction. Reconstructing gender practices provides an insight into the broad spectrum of social processes that shape expectations and requirements related to male and female identities. Forms of gender identity are never incidental; they disclose the sociocultural pressures and circumstances under which men and women live.

Although most Polish women understand gender as a biological attribute rather than a socially constructed identity (Marody 1993), there is little doubt that the rapid institutional changes precipitated by the transition to democracy and a free market have changed the social context in which men and women understand and carry out their social roles. Among those institutions that have changed fundamentally we must include labor markets, national and local political organizations, and legal systems. From the beginning, institutions such as the Catholic Church have strongly influenced the transition. By exercising political pressure, the Church has tried to transform gender-related legal regulations and to shape public discussion about women's status in society, their rights and duties as citizens, and their biological responsibility to reproduce the nation. The mass media, another crucial institution, has been equally important in producing ferment around gender roles. The opening of the mass media to private sector interests and foreign investment has introduced new images and models of gender identities, propagating ideals of masculinity and femininity that challenge older visions of manhood and womanhood.

This chapter aims to document how identities in Poland have changed since the transition. Specifically, we hope to trace the tense relationship between idealized images of women and men available in media representations and the practices of women in their everyday lives. We are witnessing today the beginning of a process that Ginsburg and Tsing (1990) have called "negotiating gender," although in the Polish context, this process is perhaps more volatile and less legalistic than "negotiation" implies. On the one hand, men and women are confronted by conflicting ideas and demands emanating from a variety of institutions. Indeed, the identification of men and women's "proper" responsibilities has become a contentious public issue. On the other hand, we see individual men and women struggling to make sense of recent changes—some resisting, some taking advantage of emerging opportunities, and many both resisting and accepting different aspects of the new vision. The long-term effects of this process will change not only hegemonic ideals of female and male identities, but also the everyday relations between men and women.

Put another way, we assume that the process of gender formation draws on two main sources. The first is the world of everyday practice, in which individuals are confronted with a set of factors that shape the available possibilities for action. This includes the size and shape of the labor market, the level of salaries and wages, the adequacy of public services, the legal regulations of marriage, social welfare, and childcare facilities, among others. The second is the world of discourse, contained in traditional and popular culture, mass media reporting, and especially advertising. The world of everyday practice defines the range of opportunities and constraints that shape individual actions; the world of discourse offers idealizations of appearance, personality, and behavior that become attached to gender and gender relations. Thus, to understand and describe the process of changing gender identities now taking place in Poland, we have to refer to two sources of material: the symbolic imagery offered to the public (together with the language in which one talks about gender and gender relations) and the hard facts of life that are the hammer and anvil of gender formation.

Our first goal, then, is to document ideals about femininity and masculinity. For this we turn to popular women's magazines. It is an important cultural fact that there are no "men's magazines" to which we could turn for a parallel investigation, although women's magazines provide much information about expectations and images of men. This asymmetry is also evident in the fact that women, far more than men, have been targets of public debate concerning gender role identification. Our second goal is to chart the nature and magnitude of changes in gender ideals, and for this purpose we systematically compare magazines published in the socialist period with those produced after several years of "transition." Finally, we juxtapose the imagery of gender identities presented in magazines with data about the actual economic and political pressures under which people acted in Poland. For this we use sociological surveys, statistics, and general social and economic indicators to examine the opportunities open to men and women and the types of relations that exist between them.

Our choice of research design has two advantages. First, it allows us to contrast cultural images and social contexts in two historical periods. More importantly, it directly taps one of the major forces producing the changes we are investigating. The "press" is by no means the same institution in these two periods and systems. In the first period, we are considering a situation in which the press was largely controlled by the ideological policies of a centralized state. In the second, it is not the state's ideology and policies but market principles, the ideology of the market, competition among domestic and foreign magazines, and advertising that drive the mass media. We can thus ask a number of crucial questions: Do the principles and logic of each social system—state socialism and free-market economy—create distinct relationships between discourse and practice, particularly as they pertain to gender identity? Under each system, what is the disjunction between reality and representation, and how does it matter in women's everyday lives?

WOMEN'S MAGAZINES

Content analysis of popular women's magazines provides our basic source of data. Such magazines allow us to trace the relationship between discourse and practice in at least one public forum. In photos, advertisements, and journalistic accounts, readers see the "woman" they should strive to be. Articles and fiction pieces also show journalists' and editors' sense of what a woman's life goals and expectations should be. Here, the tone of women's magazines is often explicitly didactic. A look at these writings also allows us to infer certain institutionalized patterns that journalists often assume but do not discuss. Our reading of women's magazines also includes letters to the editor. These highlight the problems and topics raised by female readers themselves. We are aware that publication of readers' letters is a matter of editorial policy and that the content is not freely shaped by readers. Nevertheless, even a biased selection of letters provides invaluable access to a forum in which some women have articulated their problems.

To place gender ideals and images within the context of systemic constraints and opportunities that most readers actually experienced at the time, we've used a combination of sociological surveys and economic and political indicators to depict "real life" conditions in Poland during each of the periods we consider. Such broad-based sociological data also help to illuminate the ways in which those constraints and opportunities color the relations between men and women, creating structural status differences based on gender. Thus, although we cannot have direct access to readers' responses, we can infer their general socioeconomic circumstances. This allows us to identify many of the ironies, paradoxes, and incompatibilities between ideals and genuine possibilities.

Since our focus is on the change in women's gender identity that has occurred in Poland since the transition, this chapter is divided into "before" and "after" snapshots of the change, showing perceptions of gender identity during the communist period, and then after socialism's demise. We chose two women's magazines, *Przyjaciółka* [Woman's Friend] and *Kobieta i Życie* [Woman and Life], and one magazine for girls (*Filipinka*), all of which have been published since the 1960s. *Przyjaciółka* was circulated mainly in small towns and villages, whereas *Kobieta i Życie* was addressed primarily to urban women. We analyzed the 1974 and 1994 annual run of each magazine. Information about each copy was systematically recorded in a specially designed "table of contents" according to the following categories: title of a contribution, author, summary of problems, conclusions, descriptions of women and men, and the percentage of magazine space given to the contribution. This register enabled us to estimate more precisely changes in the stress put on specific issues (such as marital problems, sexual problems, or housekeeping advice), shifts of interest, and changes in ideal or "problem" characteristics imputed to women and men.

We turned to the magazines' 1974 issues to reconstruct ideals of woman's identity already established during the communist period. We wanted to examine a "mature" form of the pattern, that is, one well past the formative stage, and one that arguably was the starting point for current changes. The year 1974 was also a relatively prosperous one in Poland, which means that problems specific to the economy of shortage do not skew our results, since such articles are not much in evidence in these issues. The 1994 issues served as a source of information about the new process of gender negotiation, which was well underway by this time. Additionally, our analysis included the independent findings of Beata Łaciak (1995), whose content analysis included a broader range of women's magazines published since 1990.

WOMEN'S IDENTITY UNDER SOCIALISM

Three basic factors influenced the processes of gender negotiation during the socialist period. First, official state policies directly shaped female roles by attempting to forge a "New Society," and they indirectly affected women by controlling and limiting the public spaces in which individuals were allowed to act. Second, traditional patterns of gender relations—that is, those that predominated in the immediate pre-socialist era—persisted. Despite the state's effort to dominate all realms of life, the "new" socialist society could never fully eradicate traditional forms of social behavior. Third, trends and changes in global culture, imported largely from the West, offered alternative role models for women.

Throughout the communist period and into the transition, all three factors—state, cultural tradition, and external influences—interacted with each other, creating conflicting demands and providing contradictory images from which women could forge their own sense of gender identity.

Women's Official Image: Employee and Mother

In the official politics of the communist regimes, distinctly women's issues were raised twice, and in both cases were closely connected and subordinated to the broader political, ideological, and economic problems facing the regimes. The first episode started at the beginning of the post-war period and was aimed at the occupational activation of women. Apart from doctrinaire reasons, such as communism's long-standing commitment to full and compulsory employment and to women's equality, there were practical motivations to this policy: Women were an important source of labor in a post-war economy suffering a relative shortage of workers.[1] This was due in part to enormous population losses suffered in World War II. But it was produced as well by the new industrialization policy that created huge labor demands. The government actively encouraged women to take jobs. In part, this took the form of public urging in the media; it was otherwise achieved through the imposition of material constraints. Except for work in certain strategic blue-collar jobs (mining, for example), wages and salaries were quite low. Men were unable to fulfill their role as breadwinners, and family income had to be supplemented by women's income. Faced with such extreme economic hardship, many women had no choice but to take on wage labor.

Nonetheless, although the state guaranteed women an equal right to work, women were not treated equally in their work. Throughout the communist period, Polish women were generally not given leadership positions or promotions, and worst of all, there was no pay equity. Women's wages were 20–40 percent lower than those of men working in the same positions. According to studies done in the early 1980s, in all occupational categories, except the professions, gender influenced earnings more significantly than education, occupational position, age, job tenure, or membership in the Communist Party (Siemieńska 1990).

At the same time that the state was encouraging women to join the workforce, another issue became a matter of state policy: motherhood. By the early 1960s, it had become clear that the socialist state would be unable to develop the wide-reaching social policies earlier envisioned, not the least of which was an agreement to help women by assuming some of the responsibility for their families. The post-war baby boom, which lasted until 1958, created an enormous demand

---

[1] That the "occupational liberation" of Polish women was not the result of their own political struggles but occurred basically by coercion (Titkow 1995) is doubtless one important factor in the current situation and attitudes about Polish women. Another is the fact that the communist regime, in its plans for social change, was interested primarily in women's economic role and not in a more thoroughgoing change in gender relations.

for social services that the state was unable to supply.[2] As an alternative, the government—primarily between 1960 and 1965—tried to decrease the birthrate. It promoted birth control, advertised contraceptives, and established the Conscious Motherhood Association, a network of family planning centers. These efforts, reinforced by broad societal changes and by certain external influences, were so successful that, by the early 1970s, government officials had grown alarmed by Poland's declining birthrate. As a consequence, the government developed a pro-natalist policy that promoted a "2 plus 3" family model and introduced paid maternity leave and special credits for young families.

Just as labor policies defined women exclusively as workers, so did pro-natalist policies and the new propaganda define women exclusively as mothers. The picture of a woman who wants to work—even in such male jobs as a tractor driver, doctor, or postal worker—was simply changed to depict the woman *and* her children. In the state's essentializing vision, women were workers and mothers, nothing else. And while the government encouraged each, they did little to help women coordinate the two roles, except to reemphasize a traditional image of the self-sacrificing Polish mother who subordinates her needs and aspirations to the needs of family and country (Titkow 1995).

One finds a clear reflection of this picture in our women's magazines from 1974. There are only two salient roles in which women are portrayed—employee and mother. Women's social identity is most often described as *wife, mother, worker, citizen,* and *breadwinner.*[3] Consistent with this image, women who work and are upstanding citizens also have happy marriages, strong families, and admirable children. Other kinds of women were presented as negative models and were held up to suggest the looming threat of what might go awry. These were *potential rivals, mistresses, divorcees, hussies,* and *bimbos.* Most frequently, women were characterized as *hard-working, kind, economical, clever, reasonable, experienced, resourceful,* and *organized.* But they were also referred to as *lonely, depressed,* and *tired.*

In the articles and stories we analyzed from this period, the average heroine is a shop assistant, teacher, nurse, white-collar worker, occasionally a doctor or a skilled worker. She usually begins her career following secondary or even primary school, and then supplements her education by attending night school. Even if she has a high level of education, she usually is not very ambitious. Her primary asset and life goal is her family. Indicative of this image is the phrase, "I was not tempted to make an academic career; I wanted to be a good doctor who efficiently helped people."

In such idealized scenarios, the heroine invariably quits her job after giving birth and stays at home to raise her family. "I have dedicated my life to my

[2] The birthrate increase lasted until 1958 and had its peak in 1953 (19.5 per 1,000). Between 1958 and 1964, the birthrate fell rapidly (from 18 to 10 per 1,000; it was still higher than the average for European countries). This level persisted until the mid-1980s when it again started to increase (Okólski 1992).

[3] These are the actual words (translated from Polish) used to describe women in the magazines we analyzed.

children and family, for whom I have taken full responsibility," says one protagonist. However, this self-sacrifice is not presented as purely altruistic, but as a kind of delayed self-fulfillment. She says about her children, "I believe they will achieve what I could not." When pushed to specify the kinds of achievements her children will make, she can only reply, "They will certainly be citizens of good standing." Again, the job of motherhood is to produce respectable citizens for the state.

According to the magazine articles, the heroine's job, even if she continues to work after having children, is not as attractive as other forms of self-fulfillment because she knows that her chances for promotion are slim. "I began to work as a simple clerk, today I have an independent post in the office. Whom can I become more? An Assistant Director? There is an Assistant Director. A Director? There is one. Both the Assistant Director and Director are still young. It means that there are no more rungs on the ladder of my career." She works because she has to. The family could not make ends meet on her husband's salary alone.

In magazine stories, the rare women who do not forfeit their ambition and become involved in their career usually pay a high price. One might infer that when the state's dual interest in promoting women's employment and motherhood conflicted, motherhood was given higher priority, at least in this period. The job market was presented as offering little opportunity or fulfillment for women. To be sure, there may have been some truth in these images. Women were portrayed as having to work much harder than male colleagues, having to fight for even the smallest bit of respect in the workplace, suffering a beleaguered family life, and having to cope with stress and conflict at work and again with husband and children at home. As a final blow and result of these sacrifices, women were then shown to be abandoned by their husbands, who had taken up with a "nice little woman," stupid but smart enough to keep saying, "Sweetheart, how clever of you!"

Ironically, the dilemmas of juggling work and family are often seen to result in the destruction of the family. According to the magazine stories, the main threat for a Polish woman and her family is an unmarried woman, a woman who craftily snatches a husband from the wife. Compared to the heroine, she is usually younger, more stupid, and, unfortunately, more attractive. The heroine who takes care of her family does not have time to take care of her own appearance. Most important, however, this "other" woman has more patience with men and can appreciate their foibles. The husband does not play a very significant role in the story—he is, rather, a dupe or a bit of property that belongs to one woman but is stolen by another who dares to become interested in a married man.

In the 1974 women's magazines that we reviewed, there are no positive images of a divorced woman. Divorced women are portrayed either as unhappy or as wicked and crafty. Divorce is seen as a particularly dramatic event in a woman's life, not only because it destroys her main achievement—the family—but also because it changes her social image and status. She becomes a potential trouble-maker for her social environment, which is portrayed as a community of families, and she is treated with disdain as a potential rival and "the other."

   More to the point, the magazines provide no advice to women who might need or choose to divorce, blaming them—not their husbands—for the failed marriage. Indeed, divorce itself is presented as an anomaly. If only a woman had focused on her family, the argument goes, she would not be in this situation. Marriage crises can be avoided through planning and a proper assessment of problems. "Anna's marriage was saved when she became aware of what her husband expected from her, that is, which of his desires were not satisfied." Anna's desires are taken for granted—she wants to have children and to bring them up without too many problems. "Sooner or later everyone starts a family." Husbands are seen as more or less the same and are viewed as playing no real role in the success of the marriage or the family. Discussions of men's roles and about problems, such as domestic violence and alcoholism—which often cause women to leave their husbands—are largely ignored.

   Although focused on traditionally female goals, the idealized woman presented in the magazines is nearly devoid of any feminine or even individual features. It is difficult to find information about her age, physical appearance, and inner problems or about her feelings and behavior except as they relate to family or work. She is, above all, a social being: one element of several different social structures (family, company, planned economy, and socialist society) that demand "rational" behavior from her. Even such fundamental practices as eating and nourishment are "rationalized" to fit and justify the particular, idealized logic of the (shortage) economy: "The norm of protein consumption is half a gram per one kilo of body weight. A Pole consumes 46 grams daily, which is exactly what he needs. Every gram above that norm is a blameworthy waste." Similarly, there is a social logic to every activity; she should remain active—jogging or walking on weekends—because her work requires that she be in good physical shape. While raising children, she should remember that the state needs not only managers and engineers, but also housekeepers and secretaries.

   Likewise, reproduction is presented as a function of state necessity and is discussed largely in the language of production: In the magazines we reviewed there are many alarming articles about the decreasing birthrate. "We are efficient in our work, but ineffective in giving birth." The language of production is also used in discussing problems of sexuality, although these are addressed only rarely. One article summarizes: "What you have said, Doctor, [referring to a well-known sexologist] leads to a conclusion that a successful sexual life is an *additional* domain in which one should *invest* her/his psychological energy, imagination, and *work*. How is it feasible in the 20th century, under the present circumstances [e.g., with women overworked and tired] to come home and undertake a new, difficult *task* [e.g., having sex]? What you have talked about, all this absorbing play is good, but only during summer holidays." The hierarchy of "tasks" is clearly articulated: "If a woman is to be [sexually] ingenious, always attractive . . . well-dressed, clean, cheerful, and at the same time the home is to be kept in order—such a woman will end up quickly in a dark grave." Because nobody wants to "end up in a dark grave" and the home must be kept in order, the implicit message is to forget about such unproductive things as sexual satisfaction or postpone them until the summer holidays.

The image of a rational woman focused on her job and family is also part of the socialization model promoted in the girls' magazine *Filipinka*. "Filipinka has many times and in different ways encouraged you to be ambitious . . . in the sense of seizing the hard-earned opportunity to play a useful role in society and in a job. And this is the precondition of happiness and satisfaction." Thus, girls' ambition is implicitly defined as limited; it is merely a synonym for doing one's best. Girls are cautioned to avoid aiming too high. If you failed the university entrance exams, do not worry. You can be useful and creative as a dressmaker or shop assistant. What is really important is the welfare of society, and individual happiness can follow from personal commitment—to whatever one does.

Although the most important domains for this commitment are, of course, occupation and family life, they are not often discussed in *Filipinka*. Rather, it is taken for granted that everyone works and has a family. *Filipinka* does not offer its young readers models of the good employee and mother; in fact, it avoids difficult issues of all kinds. Instead, didactic stories focus on keeping girls young. The magazine's typical heroine is "always busy, engaged in school activities, enthusiastic, a bit crazy, but skilled and full of initiative, a nice colleague." Any "individualizing" behavior, whether reading ambitious books or listening to jazz, is kept within the limits of social convention.

There is a rather surrealistic and fantastic quality to the ideals presented by these magazines, if one remembers the social circumstances in which they were written. In 1974, *Woman and Life* and *Woman's Friend* were telling women to be brave, yet one detects a quiet undercurrent of women's exhaustion and helplessness. In 1974, *Filipinka* was telling young readers to be happy, but one has a nagging sense that the magazine is arguing against the grain of readers who are too bored, shy, and lost to feel the excitement of youth that *Filipinka* so desperately tries to purvey. However, in both cases the hidden message is the same: *You can manage your problems if you accept the reality of the system and of your place within it.* What that reality meant was only superficially discussed or mentioned in passing. The message was simply that there is a presumed "right" way to do things. It is only by searching carefully that one finds, in these magazines, traces of another reality. For example, in 1974, readers of *Woman and Life* sent in letters to the editor as a way to protest an absurd regulation requiring that the cost for sewing services be calculated according to the length of seams and the threads used in them. Meanwhile, oblivious to such mundane dilemmas—which affected daily life deeply indeed—*Filipinka* published a story about scouts building tourist huts in Bieszczady, a desolate mountain region beyond the reach of its readers.

GENDER RELATIONS: "BRAVE VICTIM" AND "BIG CHILD"

While the socialist state took great interest in shaping women's roles vis-à-vis work and motherhood, it was silent on gender relations broadly defined. A patriarchal model of family was presumed by both the state and society: The man was head of the household and the primary wage earner; the woman was a housewife and domestic caretaker. While the government tried in the early 1950s to promote the "modern family," an arrangement in which partners share duties and responsibilities, the attempt was met with widespread resistance and was soon abandoned.

Explanations for the persistence of the patriarchal family can be found, at least in part, in Poland's pre-war social structure and in the country's changing demographics both during and after the war. Before the war, approximately 70 percent of the population lived in the countryside; during the war, the urban intelligentsia suffered disproportionate losses, so that the post-war population was comprised mainly of peasants. Between 1946 and 1983, six million people migrated from the countryside to the cities, accounting for a 42 percent increase in the urban population. By one estimate, the number of contemporary Polish families who do not have at least grandparents living in the countryside is only 15 percent (Wasilewski 1986). Not surprisingly, social models of family organization have remained closely linked to the rural peasantry.

While demographic factors provide one explanation for the continued persistence of the patriarchal family, this model persisted, on a symbolic or representational level, because there was no real alternative. The socialist government, failing in its attempt to redefine men and women's social roles, began instead to reinforce pre-war conceptions of gender. Nevertheless (and ironically) the continuing official emphasis on a "traditional" family model, together with the changing socioeconomic conditions created by communism, altered family life and fundamentally changed the structural conditions that shaped relations between the sexes.

First of all, the so-called "occupational activation" of women, in conjunction with the state policy of keeping wages low, led to significant changes in the actual economic relations between men and women. Because men could no longer be the sole, or even primary, providers for their families, they lost the base of their authority as head of the household. Meanwhile, women gained new educational opportunities and social networks, and, thanks to an indulgent divorce law, they could more easily extricate themselves from unwanted relationships. Yet, the persistent discrimination against women in the workplace, not to mention the generally low wages paid to employees of both sexes, hardly made the choice of career over marriage a viable option (Giza-Poleszczuk 1993). Consequently, women gained social duties and responsibilities outside the household, without much help in performing the traditional ones inside it, whereas men lost their elevated status as family providers, without gaining alternative sources of social importance.

This discrepancy between the symbolic ideal and actual gender roles created significant tension between men and women and ushered in a new stage that was not about "negotiating" as much as "hard bargaining" over gender relations (Ferree 1990). By the early 1970s, worsening economic conditions exacerbated the problems between the sexes, with women and men scraping to make ends meet, making alliances out of sheer economic necessity, and continually facing chaotic, unstable, and often untenable economic conditions. Whereas in 1966 it took an average of 63 minutes to do the daily shopping, by 1970 that time had increased to 94 minutes (Smulska 1985). Nevertheless, the ratio of women's to men's contributions to household chores remained 4:1 (Siemieńska 1990). Thus, despite women's increasing significance as wage earners, they still bore the brunt of household work.

Interestingly, in the women's magazines of the period, some articles touted the value of partnership within the family. They were not warmly received. In a rare example, *Woman and Life* published a piece in 1974 that compared men's and women's relative contributions to the household economy. The value of women's household activities, including cooking, cleaning, washing, ironing, and taking care of children, was estimated according to average market prices for these services. When this amount was added to a woman's average job income, the total was much higher than the average man's salary.

The article elicited a heated response from men. In letters sent to the publisher, many tried to prove that the calculation was wrong, pointing to the value of their own household work, such as doing small repairs, washing dishes, and painting. But more importantly, many women also reacted negatively. In several letters to the editor, women blamed the journal for "disturbing their husbands' peace of mind," and asked the magazine to leave "our dear pets" alone.

To understand such a reaction from women who, on other occasions, had complained of being overworked and undervalued, it is best to look more closely at male–female relations during this period. Schematically, the 1974 magazines reveal two levels of discussion that roughly correlate to divisions between public and private. In those articles that address women's role in the public sphere— that is, in their working lives—men are seen to be rivals. Women must fight to be acknowledged as equals and accomplished workers. "A man can have a moment of weakness; he can fail to succeed in something," says one article. "A woman has to be alert all the time, or people will say she is a sissy, she didn't manage." A female doctor was quoted to say, "I was always put in the worst kind of work. They did not allow me to perform surgery. Everyone would wait to catch my mistakes. To be acknowledged in work, a woman professional must be ten times better than a man."

In contrast to the combative language used to describe relations between women and men in the working world, a very different kind of language is used to describe gender relations in the home. Here, women talk about the need to bring up their husbands, to raise them as they would a child. "Knowing my husband well," a wife is quoted as saying, "I knew that he had a lot of merits and that I would be able to bring him up, to raise him." This can include both formal and informal education. The articles describing such actions emphasize the need to finesse changes in male behavior, rather than challenge men directly, which might hurt their pride. Indirect methods seemed to be preferred. One woman is quoted as saying about her husband,

> Since he kept saying that marriage wasn't slavery and everybody should behave according to one's own will, I decided to show him that I was also free. One evening I put the

children to bed, and before my husband was ready to go out I told him that today it was my day off. He thought I was joking, but I really went out and spent the night with my colleague from work. . . . In the morning I went directly to work. At home, when he asked me about this, I repeated his words about the freedom of spouses. And it worked. Next evening he didn't go out and observed my doings. This month he brought me at last his whole salary.

In other instances, women talk about helping their husbands through night school or making bargains in which men are given special allowances (the right to buy a motorcycle, for instance) in exchange for taking the initiative to improve the family's economic status. "I promised him that I would do anything to buy him a motorcycle if he only passed the first grade of technical school." Such strategies demand, however, constant control and initiative. "I read books aloud for him, made summaries, drew him into discussions, controlled his homework, and sometimes wrote them myself for him." In many cases, the task of improving a husband's qualities requires real sacrifice. "At the beginning we were in a very difficult situation. My husband was ill since he [had just undergone] a serious surgery. Nothing, however, frightened me. I was ready to work in order to provide for both of us. . . . My husband recovered some time later. He graduated from the university." Certainly, this was made possible by her hard work, which often tested the limits of physical endurance: "How many sleepless nights and miles walked in fall rains and winter snow!" In letters to these magazines, women consistently portrayed themselves as sacrificing everything for the family, consistently portraying their role as the gentle and wise mother who rears not only her children, but her husband, too.

The theme that women are more clever than men, and especially more mature, is one that is also emphasized in the girls' magazine *Filipinka*. Often, it is invoked when "explaining" sexual behaviors or as part of an official response to changes in sexual patterns. Whether because of western influence or because of communist policies that encouraged women's independence (e.g., divorce laws, employment), there is evidence that by the 1970s there were significant changes in sexual/reproductive behavior among younger people. A retrospective study comparing the dates of marriage with the dates of a first child's birth showed that by the 1970s, there was an 8.3 percent increase in the number of children born before marriage and a 35.3 percent increase in those born during the first eight months of marriage (Giza-Poleszczuk 1993). Viewed together with a 7 percent increase in births among women aged 15–19 and a growing rate of abortion, the data indicate that patterns of sexual behavior were shifting significantly.

Yet the editors of *Filipinka* seemed to willfully ignore these trends. They advised girls not to pay too much attention to boys. As far as sexual behavior was concerned, the magazine stressed that girls should seek their boyfriends' "respect" by disallowing touching before marriage. In this situation, "the girl should be the restraining factor because girls are more mature," having gained a sense of responsibility for their actions sooner than boys. Thus, despite social trends to the contrary, the magazine stressed the importance of keeping sexuality within marriage. In sexual ideals, as in much else, the official line encouraged the centrality of family.

At least as it was shown in the socialist period women's magazines, this stereotypical Polish family was composed of a strong woman and a weak man. Men were portrayed as "big children" dependent upon their wives for coaching and support. Their accomplishments could all be attributed to their wives' self-sacrifice. Before all else, the heroine of the women's magazines thinks of her family's well-being, even at the expense of her own health. Frequently, this sacrifice is accompanied by complaints that men are ungrateful and would leave their faithful wives for other women. In the end, the self-sacrificing wife is hailed as a "brave victim." The officially supported image of the Polish mother is insinuated into the magazine's portrayal of women as beleaguered at home and exploited at work, always sacrificing for the good of the family and society. There is, however, a reward: the belief that *he would not have become what he is without her.* A woman's husband is indebted to her not only for all her household work, but also for his social status and personal importance. Even if he leaves her, the heroine knows that he would be unsuccessful and helpless, like a child, without her own sacrifice, maturity, and cleverness.

It should be remembered that the "brave victim" identity was not just given to women, but was also shaped by them. As one reader of *Filipinka* wrote in a letter tinged with irony, "[Mother] keeps complaining that she is tired. Sure, she is. Does she sit for a moment, read a newspaper? Oh no. She has always something to do, of course for us, not for herself. And then she reminds us that she is sacrificing herself for our sake." Women willingly assumed the role of the victim; what we must ask is, why?

When speaking of the "brave victim," we might stress either "brave" or "victim." One could emphasize a woman's sacrifice and the burden of dividing her life between job and family (brave), or one might focus on the wickedness of a male world in which a woman is discriminated against both as an employee and as a woman (victim). Following the cultural logic of such labels, one could argue that the notion of "bravery" provides supplemental gratification, making bearable such onerous tasks as "carrying heavy bags full of shopping, suffering from lack of sleep, and being terribly tired," simply to have some "justifiable sense of being an indispensable manager of family life" (Titkow 1995:318). Perhaps the sense of *victimhood* encourages a kind of self-respect.

We argue that the "brave victim" image also gave women a kind of moral upper hand in their domestic lives, especially when considered in conjunction with the relatively high level of education that these women achieved (United Nations 1991). Certainly, women were victims of the social system, they were discriminated against in the world of politics and work, they were responsible for most domestic work, and they often suffered from physical violence at home. Nonetheless, it seems to us that the "brave victim" identity gave women some justification for—and pride in—their situation; they were sacrificing themselves for the greater good. And this conferred upon them a sense that they were the real authority in the private sphere, the real head of the family.

What were men's possibilities in the same period, and how did they respond to the "brave victim?" First, in objective terms, men were victims of the system, too. Because the public sphere was so thoroughly controlled by the Party, men who were unwilling to become communists, for instance, were often blocked in their professional ambitions. Second, as we have noted, men were often frustrated at home because the legal and economic structures of socialism prevented them from fulfilling their role as head of the family—a role demanded by pre-war traditional values. Finally, the state-controlled mass media provided little in the way of an idealized image of masculinity. The "heroic socialist worker" was not relevant to the domestic scene. At home, men could not even play the martyr, since women had already taken that role. They thus had few options: They could feel guilty and submit to a wife who supposedly knew best what was good for the family or they could rebel against the "big child" role.

Judging by the evidence we analyzed, there were several forms of such rebellion, revealed most poignantly in letters to the editor. In the 1974 magazines, many women complain that their husbands drink, do not care about children, and do not give them the money necessary for everyday living. "He drank and wasted [money] and I, with my little salary, had to make ends meet." This form of rebellion—a refusal to participate in family life—can be interpreted as an attempt to compensate for the undermined position of family head. Another form of rebellion was to maintain and even exaggerate the patriarchal model, although it did not fit the new circumstances in which women's wages made important contributions to the family's income. Thus, women also complain that husbands behave as sovereigns whose will must be immediately satisfied. "He works for 16 hours a day, absorbed by plans, perspectives, urged with deadlines. . . . We do not see him, but when he comes home at last, the children must run with slippers for daddy and the wife must make the bed so he can regenerate [his] working power for tomorrow." Frustrated with this attitude, women note that they are also working and are equally entitled to "regenerate their working power."

In sum, the "new society" created by state socialism was new economically and, to some extent, new in terms of its legal regulations. It substantially changed the material conditions in which the vast majority of Poles lived, and it noticeably altered women's economic contribution. But many pre-war notions persisted in the symbolism and ideology of gender during the communist era. The image of the stalwart Polish mother, admonitions against premarital sex, pro-natalism, and the fundamental idea that the family is the center of life were all drawn from popular cultural ideals that existed long before the advent of communism. Although communist ideology claimed to be creating new forms of social ties, it nevertheless endorsed the ideal of a patriarchal family.[4]

---

[4] We have argued elsewhere (Marody 1993; Giza-Poleszczuk 1993) that the state's support of "family," and of the sacrifices women should make for family, was also motivated by an explicit calculation that this would stabilize economic and social reproduction, which was endangered by the inefficiency of the communist public service sector.

Generated by the conditions of state socialism—that is, in response to material needs and ideological contradictions—the gender identities of "brave victim" and "big child" helped to unite couples around a common goal: ensuring the well-being of the family and children. Yet these images blocked the development of new gender constructs within marriage (or alternative images of gender relations) that might have been more congruent with women's increasing education and contribution to the family budget and men's declining opportunities in the public sphere.

Gender and Transition: The New Woman and the Old

What happens to the "brave victim" image—not to mention all of the women who have styled themselves after it—when socialism is replaced by free-market capitalism and when the media are no longer state-controlled but run as a set of distinct, private sector businesses? In the new Poland, the "brave victim" image, crafted in reaction to the limitations and demands of state socialism, no longer serves its intended purpose. Three shifts are important here. First, the range of available commodities and services has expanded to a degree previously unknown. Second, the position of women in the labor market has changed dramatically; unemployment has grown significantly at the same time that a plethora of career opportunities have opened up, giving women entirely new choices. Third, the symbolic sphere of culture has expanded enormously in the past years, and now offers women a variety of "model" lifestyles that challenge the one we described earlier.

Today, women must choose between the old and the new—between roles that undoubtedly will take them in opposite directions. Economically, the abundance of goods and services stands in stark contrast to the "economy of shortage" that marked the period before the transition. This eases the burden of daily work needed to maintain a family and, indeed, seriously diminishes the importance of the family as an economic unit. Women no longer have to wait in line, carry heavy bags, or do everything themselves. But the abundance of goods is also a temptation to buy, and it puts pressure on limited family budgets. Women must either economize, choosing to forego newly available commodities, or must earn more money in order to purchase the goods and services now flooding the Polish market.

Yet, women who choose to earn face a formidable obstacle in the bifurcated labor market. On the one hand, unemployment is growing, and women are disproportionately affected. Women have a hard time finding jobs, especially if they have small children or other demands that restrict, or are perceived to restrict, their ability to work consistent hours. Yet, at the same time that the demand for unskilled or moderately skilled labor is decreasing, there is growing demand for highly skilled workers. One result is the emergence of a new class of professional women whose investment in education and training has finally begun to pay off. But such careers usually demand significant personal conces-sions, making it almost impossible for women in Poland to combine career and family. Many women, especially younger women, must choose between the two.

Besides the structural and economic changes that are redefining women's roles, the explosion of advertising and media images that accompanied the opening of markets has significantly transformed symbolic representations of women, creat-ing new images for women to aspire to, and hence affecting the real life choices they make. Previously, women responded to a state-dominated media that not only encouraged them to be workers and mothers but, before all else, to be *subservient to the "collective needs" of family and society*. Now, the media is no longer an agent of the state, and women are responding differently. Accentuating the values of free-market capitalism, the mass media today are largely funded by advertisers who aim to sell consumer goods rather than state policy. Even so, there are many kinds of consumers. For example, advertisements often depict women as *responsible consumers* whose market behavior is based on planning, rational evaluation, and economic calculation. Other times, advertisements as-sume women's individualism, creating a world of female needs, comforts, and desires.

In the service of consumerism, the new women's magazines—many trans-lations of Western publications—are introducing Polish women to different models of masculinity and femininity, which stand in stark contrast to both traditional Polish and socialist era images. Julia Wood, in her summary of popular imagery in the western mass media, writes,

> Typically men are portrayed as active, adventurous, powerful, sexually aggressive, and largely uninvolved in human relationships. Just as consistent with cultural views on gender are depictions of women as sex objects who are usually young, thin, beautiful, passive, dependent, and often incompetent and dumb. Female characters devote their primary energies to improving their appearance and taking care of homes and peo-ple. (1995:235)

The difference between this and the "brave victim–big child" pattern is espe-cially striking.

Yet, there are also counterpressures to gendered consumerism. The Catholic Church continues to produce images of women as mothers and "vessels of the nation." And irrespective of the motivation for this model, it has not been lost on political leaders that its acceptance by the population would contribute to solving the unemployment problem. Since half the employed persons in Poland today are women (45.5 percent of the labor force in 1995), their retreat from the labor force would increase the number of jobs available. While men may not want many of these feminized and low-paying jobs, the general idea has politi-cal appeal.

But if post-1989 images of women present a new ideal of gender, what are these contrasting images, and how do women react to their symbolic appeal?

Individualization: Success and Personality

During the communist period, the most general characteristic of women's identity formation was its collectivist bias. A woman was not seen to have her own personality. Instead, she was described through her social context; her aspirations for self-development were transferred onto the lives of her children, and her needs were subordinated to the interests of her family and, ultimately, to the needs of society or state policy. The images presented in women's magazines after 1989 present a very different model.

The "new woman" is first and foremost portrayed as an individual. The focus is on self-fulfillment and individual success. In all domains, from career to sexuality, the shift toward individualization is evident, while collective goals and responsibilities are downplayed. For example, in *Your Style*, a magazine targeted to an affluent and upscale market, women are presented as successful professionals who are active, glamorous, and dedicated to their careers. They are usually shown to be in their mid-40s, very smart, and attractive. More significantly, these women are encouraged to develop social graces and intellectual interests; youth and beauty, while important, are not enough to make a "new" woman. According to one article, "The most popular are those who are newly employed—but not those who work in the telephone unit or with the photocopier. . . . The women most sought after are not only attractive and fashionably dressed, but they have a high IQ, know how to make brilliant conversation, and have a sense of humor."

By contrast, *Woman's Friend* and *Woman and Life* continue to target middle-class and lower-class women,[5] building on the more traditional image of a home-maker. Although articles about housekeeping in the 1994 issues of *Woman's Friend* appear half as many times as in 1974, they still predominate. Nonetheless, major distinctions are made between the "new" and "old" woman, even when the emphasis is on the domestic sphere. The "new" woman, although she cares for her family, does not forget about herself. The publishers of *Woman's Friend* declare that their mission is to promote a modern lifestyle, to advise women about how to care for themselves with minimum expense, and about how to relax, dress, and cook—all so that a woman can say about herself, "I am practical and modern." The new image of a woman's family responsibilities and duties no longer demands complete sacrifice. On the contrary, even if a woman quits working to raise her family, it is argued, she should not neglect her own personal development.

Other magazine stories portray women who successfully do it all. A typical protagonist in the post-transition magazines is a journalist—as one article put it, "a true TV star, but also a wonderful wife and mother." The story continued, "Home and family are at least as important as her job." One woman interviewed

[5] We use the terms "middle class" and "lower class" as simple shorthand for income differences. The social structure of Poland is being fundamentally transformed, and it would be difficult to characterize emerging strata or classes in more detailed terms.

by the magazine said, "I care for my job because it gives me satisfaction. But if I were forced to choose between my job and my family, I would choose the family." The ideal for the "new" woman is to link a happy family life with a successful professional career. The article finishes by urging women to seek more than just success; "for real happiness," it says, "a woman needs the satisfaction of both work and a loving family."

Nowhere is the symbolic shift in women's aspirations more evident than in the magazine articles that depict a young heroine. Łaciak reports on a magazine interview with one young woman who says, "I am not ready to make such a decision—to find a husband, to have children, and to give up my job. I have worked too hard for all this" (Łaciak 1995:235). Careers are perceived in purely individualistic terms: as a prize for individual talents and effort, and not as the result of excellence in implementing collective goals. Professional success is located almost exclusively in the domains of business and the culture industry (for example, among TV stars, singers, and actresses). A woman's success is understood to put her husband in a difficult position; thus the best combination is if they are both successful or run a business together.

The individualization of women's identity is particularly visible in the representation of sex. In *Woman's Friend*, sexuality was covered three times more frequently in 1994 than it was in 1974. In *Woman and Life*, coverage is less frequent, but here too, two striking changes are evident in the way that sexuality is addressed. First, it is increasingly presented outside the context of marriage, and second, the problems related to a woman's sexual life are discussed less than sex itself, which is now treated as an important domain of activity.

The articles appearing most frequently focus on sexual technique, including ways to avoid routine and boredom or increase satisfaction. More important, they stress women's right to sexual satisfaction. The new woman is not just the object of a man's sexual fulfillment, but his partner in reaching mutual pleasure while building a deep relationship. The emphasis on sexual pleasure stands in sharp contrast to the "sex is yet another task" message of the 1974 magazines. Consistent with this shift, articles about contraceptives are twice as frequent in the 1994 issues of *Woman's Friend* than they were in 1974. Partnership in sexual life, say the magazines, is built on mutual recognition of the different needs and reactions experienced by men and women. Thus, it is no longer just biological differences, but psychological differences that are discussed. In fact, both *Woman's Friend* and *Woman and Life* carried three times as many articles about such gender-based dilemmas in 1994 than they had in 1974. Authors focused on ways to avoid conflict and misunderstanding and urged readers to respect women's and men's unique characteristics.

The model of the "new" woman now put forward is based on an individualistic belief in self-expression, rather than on the old notion that women should provide for others first (family, state, society, and economy). "You are exceptional!" reads a title on the cover of *Your Style*. "You deserve it!" declares an advertisement. A woman is now presented not as an element of the social and family network, but as an individual, a unique psychological unit requiring recognition and respect.

"A woman should actively shape her life, broaden her [mental] horizons, develop interests, and strive for perfection" (Łaciak 1995:239). A woman's social worth is no longer based on her complete self-sacrifice. She is encouraged to make demands on others and to strive for herself. Paradoxically, these new virtues are promoted not as being important in themselves, but primarily as a means to attract men.

Discovering Femininity

The most striking change in the content of the magazines we analyzed is the return of "femininity" and, with it, a return of elements from the "old-style" patriarchy. By "femininity" we mean particular standards of character and physical attractiveness stereotypically ascribed to women. Without a doubt, physical attractiveness is portrayed in the majority of women's magazines as the most prized feature a woman can possess. We see this not only in advertisements, but also in advice columns ("you can be more beautiful") and in the increasing number of articles that feature famous actresses and models. If, in the communist period, women were presented as devoid of physical features, the "new" woman is described first in terms of her appearance and her dress.

Attractiveness is recognized as a key factor behind a woman's "success," both with men and in the labor market. Polish newspapers are full of classified ads offering jobs to young, attractive women. Companies now demand dress codes and teach their employees how they "should" look. An article in one magazine reads, "In one of the companies in Warsaw, women are required to wear clothes made from high-quality fabrics. In another, girls are asked to sign, in addition to their job contracts, an agreement to always have painted nails and depilated legs."

In the upscale magazine *Your Style*, it is taken for granted that women value and will spend time at being attractive—striving toward a standard of beauty largely defined by advertisements of glamorous, thin, young models. "To be a genuine, modern woman, you have to find time for yourself." However, in publications for the less affluent, *Woman and Life* and *Woman's Friend*, beauty is treated with ambivalence. While they criticize the superficiality of physical attractiveness, these magazines nevertheless reinforce images of beauty based on slenderness, youth, and fashion. A common strategy for reconciling these seemingly contradictory messages is to wrap beauty in the familiar package of personal health. One article begins, "I will certainly disappoint all those who expect that I will be writing about cosmetics and make-up. Of course, they matter for a woman who would like to look cared for, but health is most important." Despite her disclaimer, the author continues, "The basis for health and beauty is a slim figure, a young firm body with peach-colored skin, and a young looking face without wrinkles."

Polish women have revived this definition of femininity with mixed feelings. On the one hand, the magazines seem harmless and fun—it can be interesting to read about new fashion, to learn how to care for one's hair, to know which exercise routines promote a better figure. But this image of the "new" woman undermines all the values that marked the "old" woman as a brave victim. A columnist for *Woman and Life* revealed her bitterness toward the new standards of attractiveness when she described a scene in which a man rudely pushed her off a bus: "I am sure if I wore at least black stockings as my [fashionable] 'femininity banner,' my bus misogynist would feel like a superman who opens the door, falls to my feet, and proposes an exciting weekend in Anin."

Coming after years of what may be called the "a-sexualization" of communist era images of women as workers and mothers, the new emphasis on sexual attractiveness undermines women's position in relation to men. Besides working as mothers, housewives, and wage-earners, women are also expected to spend time on their appearance. The new feminine ideal suggests an interesting shift: Instead of sacrificing themselves to serve the needs of family and society or to "manage" men, women should now subordinate themselves to male desires and standards of beauty. Schematically, one might say that in the "brave victim/big child" model, both men and women sacrificed themselves to the inefficiencies of the socialist state and economy, although women found a kind of moral strength in their victimhood. By contrast, women, according to the new model, are valued primarily as pretty objects. Because a woman's worth is now determined by her desirability to men, the new ideal of femininity reinforces male dominance.

The Revival of Masculinity

One of the most striking and, we would argue, significant changes in the post-1989 media is the "male comeback." Whereas men had largely disappeared from communist era women's magazines, the new enthusiasm for Western capitalist values corresponds to a burst of enthusiasm for a particular type of man. He is shown in advertisements as strong, attractive, individualistic, and dominating and can be seen to embody the vision of the post-transition world. Men are no longer discussed in terms of "dear pets" or "big children." The men presented in women's magazines (TV stars, journalists, and businessmen) earn a lot of money, dress well, and are self-confident and independent. They can cook for themselves and do not need a wife to run their household. More to the point, these men are always shown with a beautiful woman at their side, a companion to enhance the man's image.

The new man emerging in both advertisements and articles in women's maga-zines is certainly desirable to Polish women—at least to some Polish women. But it is ironic that the women who want such a man at home have to use the old methods to "make" one. Although we can draw only upon anecdotal data, wives are often the ones pushing their husbands into the public sphere and to make a name for themselves in the new capitalist system. According to a friend of ours who runs an employee search and selection agency, half of the resumes and inquiry letters sent to his company by men are actually sent by their wives. Several psychologists have pointed out that many of their male patients are brought in by wives who demand, "Do something with him. Motivate him." This change was astutely captured by the well-known Polish cartoonist Andrzej

Mleczko, who depicted an ordinary man sitting in an armchair with his newspaper, his wife prodding, "Don't just sit like that! Look at Wałęsa, what he has achieved! Do something!"

Ironically, this new man is also threatening to women. One article reads, "Young capitalism is usually an enterprising man who tries to either dispossess you of your apartment or your land. He knows best, knows that he deserves it, and that everything can be arranged. He visits offices, looks for legal possibilities, and Mrs. W. from Jozefów is trembling." Poor Mrs. W. understands neither those young men nor the new reality. She reads women's magazines and sees herself as a victim of the transformation, which she believes is depriving her not only of her apartment but also of her status as a Polish mother.

By redefining men as no longer in need of a wife's "protection," the new system has again opened the process of gender bargaining. As we have shown, the "brave victim/big child" imagery was rooted in the institutional conditions of the communist political and economic system, but it was maintained and simultaneously reinforced by everyday relationships between men and women. It was through a web of daily interactions that underlying systemic patterns were experienced. The imagery kept its power because there were neither symbolic nor material resources available through which women and men could imagine their lives independent of the other sex, or imagine a different set of arrangements, based upon different assumptions.

In sum, the old virtues and assets, which previously bolstered women's self-esteem, are losing their importance as a means for dealing either with the new conditions or with the new man. Different assets have become important: age, education, computer skills, fluency in languages, personal attractiveness. It is not surprising that women feel both challenged and threatened. For some, mostly younger women, there are new opportunities. For others, especially those who forged their identities in the pre-transition world, the changes are probably threatening. Importantly, the very same can be said of men; the "big child" or even "rebellious big child" model does not fit the new imagery. Moreover, as participants in the ongoing changes, we sense that it is not only women who feel the basis of their womanhood or femininity threatened. As the comments in current magazines suggest, men feel their masculinity threatened not only by the demands of these new images, but also by the direct, everyday demands placed upon them by wives and girlfriends.

Conclusions: From Self-Sacrifice to Self-Investment?

Having presented the range of new imagery evident in the magazines of 1994, we now turn in closing to sociological survey research, contrasting media images with the opinions expressed by respondents in a nationally representative sample. We then offer some conclusions about the media and changing gender expectations. Although the magazines seem neatly different in the two periods we examined, the surveys present a more complicated picture. In the 1990s, socially accepted norms for women in Poland are inconsistent and contradictory. This indicates that, despite the media's clear imagery, people are ambivalent about the role women should adopt in the current circumstances.

On the one hand, we have a set of attitudes that seem to go together; they tie women to households and children and men to wage labor. In one opinion poll, 47.3 percent of respondents agreed (strongly or rather strongly) that, "If a married woman's job demands too much of her time, keeping her away from home, she should give up her job." Only 20.5 percent felt the same way about men. Of the respondents, 54.5 percent also agreed (strongly or rather strongly) with the opinion that, "If there is unemployment in the country, men should have more rights to jobs than women." A full 75.3 percent accepted the opinion that, "It is necessary for women to have children in order to gain a sense of fulfillment" (Marody 1994). Approximately 50 percent of those polled believe that, "Most men are better suited emotionally for politics than most women" and that, "Women should take care of their homes and leave running the country to men" (Cichomski and Sawiński 1993).

On the other hand, and despite the results described here, the model of a family in which only the husband works, leaving the wife to take care of the home, was accepted by only 23.5 percent of respondents (more often by men; n = 1,698). And 55.9 percent of those questioned accepted a model in which both spouses share housework and childcare (Marody 1994). In other ways, too, there are signs that the family is not central to all respondents. Only 19 percent of respondents believe that it is wrong (always or almost always) to have sex before marriage, and only 27 percent wanted "to make divorce more difficult to obtain than it is now" (Cichomski and Sawiński 1993). Finally, there was widespread acknowledgment, among all parties polled, of the social discrimination that women face. Also, women were perceived by members of both genders as having fewer opportunities to learn new skills, get a job, or receive a promotion.

As we have demonstrated, the inconsistency in opinions about women's role in Poland is, in part, a legacy of the socialist state. It attempted to mobilize women into the labor force, but it neither provided the social support that this required nor offered an alternative image of femininity. A parallel case can be made for men, whose material conditions were substantially changed and for whom there appeared no new imagery depicting masculinity in the domestic realm. Even so, other survey research suggests that the current changes do not have parallel effects on men and women. Men seem more accepting of the new definition of femininity; they welcome a sexually attractive, witty, and professionally successful woman. Women are more dubious.

For instance, responding to the survey question, "What do men expect from women in Poland nowadays?"[6] women consistently overestimated the emphasis that men place on housekeeping. Despite the new imagery, women believed that they were expected to be perfect housekeepers and to sacrifice their own needs

---

[6] In research conducted by the firm GfK Polonia for a woman's magazine in 1993.

to their family's interests; indeed, women cited such expectations significantly more often than men declared them. On the other hand, women tend to underesti- mate men's respect for a woman's intelligence and professional success. More men expect these traits from women than women believe they do.[7]

The incongruity between 1994 media images and survey results echoes—albeit in a different tone—the disparity between the images purveyed by communist era magazines in 1974 and the practices evidenced by letters to the editor and statistical information about gender in that era. In both periods, there is clearly a sizable gap between public discourse and practice, or between "reality" and "representation." But it is also the case that the content and structure of this gap is importantly different in the two periods; the representational terrain has shifted along with the social system. In the communist era, the mass media functioned in the service of a state hoping to produce workers and mothers. Media stories were didactic and often bland, acknowledging and valorizing women's heavy burden while denying the larger social structure—an economy of shortage— that created them. The old media addressed women in a depersonalized way, identifying them as a kind of fulcrum on which balanced larger social forces; the woman it most idealized was the "common woman" with everyday struggles and needs, bravely running a household, raising children, and working a job. Implicitly or explicitly, self-sacrifice was touted as the road to satisfaction.

By contrast, the new advertising-based, capitalist, mass media seeks to encour- age consumerism. As analyses of the media in Western Europe and the United States have emphasized, this is most often achieved by creating a sense of need or a desire for unattainable personal traits that commodities promise to supply. Far from encouraging material self-denial, magazines use seductive, glossy images to evoke fantasy and desire. In our estimation, these images bear less resemblance to the everyday lives of most Polish women than did the communist era stories we analyzed. In the new formula, every woman should try to be extraordinary: She should be attractive, successful, and elite and should reach for beauty, affluence, and happiness. Presumably, the first condition leads to the other two, and all three can be achieved through consumption. Whereas the old media generalized, the new media individualize. Yet they do so not by rewarding individ- uality, but by creating stereotypes of a new "ideal," which can be purchased on the market.

The strikingly different goals and methods of the media during these two eras point to some of the challenges facing women since 1989. Both the imagery of the new media and the constraints produced by the increasing importance of private corporate employment pose new dilemmas for women's daily lives. Women must adjust to new values that do not reward them for being a self- sacrificing mother or a brave victim—both roles to which many women have dedicated their lives. More generally, the transition period has inverted the

---

[7] We note that these results are suggestive but hard to interpret. The seemingly distinct perceptions between the genders may reflect different attitudes, or it might be indicative of a domestic division of labor in which men take housekeeping so much for granted that they do not even consider it important, assuming women are by nature responsible for and good at housekeeping.

emphasis on self-sacrifice in private and victimhood in public that was both a value and a necessity under state socialism. Moreover, the state and the (much older) patriarchal culture congratulated—or at least consoled—women who accepted the role of "brave victim" as a practical strategy.

Since 1989, the image of woman most idealized—and indeed glamorized—has been that of the successful professional whose happiness is derived not from self-sacrifice, motherhood, or victimhood, but from success in the "outside" world. For the few women who are relatively young, have the requisite job skills, and are unburdened by children, the post-1989 transition has been filled with rewards and opportunities. These women have been able to reject the "brave victim" frame of reference and are finding satisfaction in their new jobs and careers.

Nevertheless, this is a relatively small new elite. For many other women—retirees and pensioners, unskilled and nonprofessional workers, mothers struggling to raise their families—the new ideal is not a woman that they recognize or hope to become. Most women have neither the means nor the opportunity to meet the new standard of an attractive, intelligent, admired woman or a "rational manager." Whereas the old "brave victim" image provided some comfort to these women by affirming their struggles, the new images of success largely deny the validity of their lives; by downplaying the importance of the work they have done, the new images deny them moral power. Whereas the discourse of the socialist state emphasized a role for women based on labor and sacrifice and subordinated both men and women to the inefficiencies of the state, the new discourse of advertising emphasizes a role for women based on beauty (as judged by men) and individual success (as defined by patterns of consumption). For many women, this emerging model of femininity only undermines their efforts toward self-recognition.

BIBLIOGRAPHY

Cichomski, Bogdan and Zbigniew Sawiński
   1993   Polish General Sociological Surveys 1992–1993. Warsaw: University of Warsaw Institute for Social Studies.
Davis, James A. and Tom W. Smith
   1992   General Social Surveys 1972–1992. Chicago: National Opinion Research Center.
Erikson, Eric H.
   1950   Childhood and Society. New York: Norton.
Ferree, Myra Marx
   1990   Beyond Separate Spheres: Feminism and Family Research. Journal of Marriage and Family 52(4):866–884.
Ginsburg, Faye and Anna Lowenhaupt Tsing
   1990   Introduction. *In* Uncertain Terms: Negotiating Gender in American Culture. Faye Ginsburg and Anna Lowenhaupt Tsing, eds. Pp. 1–16. Boston: Beacon Press.

Giza-Poleszczuk, Anna
  1993   The Strategies of Family Formation: Poland and Western Countries. *In* The
          Transformation of Europe: Social Conditions and Consequences. Matti Ales-
          talo et al., ed. Pp. 219–233. Warsaw: IFIS Publishers.
Łaciak, Beata
  1995   Wzór Osobowy Współczesnej Polki [Role Patterns of the Contemporary Pol-
          ish Woman]. *In* Co to Znaczy Być Kobietą w Polsce? [What Does it Mean
          to be a Woman in Poland?]. Anna Titkow and Henryk Domanski, eds. Pp.
          233–244. Warsaw: Institute of Philosophy and Sociology, Polish Academy
          of Sciences.
Marody, Mira
  1993   Why Am I Not a Feminist? Social Research (4):853–864.
  1994   Life Strategies in the Emerging Capitalist Economy and the Role of Gender.
          Polish Sociological Review (2):103–111.
Okólski, Marek
  1992   Anomalies in Demographic Transition in Poland. Geographia Polonica 59:27–
          35.
Siemaszko, Andrzej
  1988   Co Polacy Potępiają? [What Do Poles Condemn?]. Polityka, February 27,
          Pp. 1, 4.
Siemieńska, Renata
  1990   Płeć, Zawód, Polityka [Gender, Occupation, Politics]. Warsaw: ISUW.
Smulska, Grażyna
  1985   Rynek i Konsumpcja w Roku 2000 [Market and Consumption in the Year
          2000]. Życie Gospodarcze 56:7.
Szelényi, Iván and Robert Manchin
  1988   Socialist Entrepreneurs: Embourgeoisement in Rural Hungary. Madison: Uni-
          versity of Wisconsin Press.
Titkow, Anna
  1995   Status Evolution of Polish Women: The Paradox and Chances. *In* The Trans-
          formation of Europe: Social Conditions and Consequences. Matti Alestalo et
          al., eds. Pp. 316–338. Warsaw: IFIS Publishers.
United Nations
  1991   The World's Women: Trends and Statistics 1970–1990. Social Statistics and
          Indicators, Series K, Number 8:101. New York: The United Nations.
Wasilewski, Jacek
  1986   Społeczeństwo Polskie, Społeczeństwo Chłopskie [Polish Society is a Peasant
          Society]. Studia Socjologiczne 3:39–56.
Wood, Julia
  1995   Gendered Lives: Communication, Gender and Culture. Belmont, CA: Wads-
          worth.

CHAPTER 6

Women's Life Trajectories
and Class Formation in Hungary

KATALIN KOVÁCS AND MÓNIKA VÁRADI

THE STUDY OF SOCIALIST and post-socialist stratification is a major scholarly industry in Hungary. Yet the position of women in these processes has rarely been posed as a central question, and ethnographic evidence, as a result, is quite rare.[1] Even students of gender have concentrated on differences between men and women and on gender patterns vis-à-vis the state. They have neglected stratification among women and the effects of gender on social stratification. In contrast, our study addresses differences *between* women in an eastern Hungarian agro-town. Our aim is to understand how the ongoing restratification of Hungarian society is, in part, a gendered process. By focusing on the life trajectories of women in several social strata, we highlight the systematic variation in their images of femininity and their cultural understandings of relations between men and women. We argue that women's expectations and ideals about gender intersect with economic and political processes, thus producing new patterns of class formation.

In the course of ethnographic fieldwork in this town, we identified three emerging strata for comparison: (1) a local managerial/institutional elite, (2) entrepreneurs and administrators, and (3) manual industrial workers who are increasingly impoverished and socially isolated.[2] This three-way classification of women is based in part on their occupations, and hence on their relations to

I am grateful to Mónika Váradi for her tremendous work in conducting interviews and co-writing the first version of this material. I benefitted greatly from the comments of Irene Dölling, Susan Gal, Myra Marx Ferree and Júlia Szalai.

[1] For example, the work of Szelényi 1995, Szelényi et al. 1988, Juhász, and their colleagues (e.g., Szelényi and Kostello 1996), both inside and outside of Hungary, has been especially influential, particularly the notions of embourgeoisement and socialist embourgeoisement. Although rarely discussing women, this work does mention the role of culture and women in family strategy and provides inspiration for our exploration of life histories. The statistical work of Andorka, Kolosi, and their co-workers includes women as a demographic category. In this tradition, the work of Koncz on women's participation in the labor force is especially helpful. But this approach does not document variation or strategies within any category. At a certain point in the 1970s, work on stratification was critical and even politically daring because it presented evidence about the failure of a socialist egalitarian dream. The work on poverty, which later became an issue in *samizdat* literature, was particularly important.

[2] Those remaining or returning to agriculture, or taking it up for the first time, constitute another important and contrasting group. We leave them out only because of lack of space.

production. But to understand the interactions of class and gender, it is equally important to examine the formation of class differences as a cultural process in which class consciousness is produced through consumption, sociality, taste, and definitions of the self.[3] Differences in gender relations and cultural ideals about masculinity and femininity contributed to the making, historical consolidation, and legitimation of new classes in western Europe. Inspired by students of West European class formation, we focused on ideas and expectations about relations between men and women, marriage practices, and patterns of individual and family consumption. By grouping entrepreneurial women with women administrators and contrasting this group to both manual workers and women attached to the managerial elite, we highlight lines of fissure based not only on work and production, but also on the cultural aspects of class.

This approach does not assume that current Hungarian class formation is a mirror or recapitulation of earlier historical processes. On the contrary, it is the difference between this and other cases, both historical and contemporary, that illuminates the relationship between gender ideals and practices on the one hand, and class formation on the other. The particularities of the contemporary Hungarian case, in contrast to historical examples, stem in part from factors such as the accessibility of Western media, the role of foreign investment, and international political pressure. But equally important are the constraining effects of Hungary's socialist past as it relates to gender. In planning our study, we were especially interested in the possible effects of earlier policies that aimed to socialize the functions of the family and to turn men and women alike into homogenous "workers." Another crucial question concerned the fate of the ideal of gender equality—a legacy of socialist ideology—since the dominant public discourse in Hungary at the time of our investigation was markedly conservative, taking as its ideal the subservient homemaker who lives through and for her husband.

To chart various models of femininity, work, marriage, and consumption, we have relied on in-depth interviews, oral life histories, and ethnographic observations. But fine-grained analyses such as we are attempting need to be contextualized. Just as the women we interviewed must be seen as part of the social and historical fabric of the town in which they live, so the town—here called Karikás—must be regarded as a part of the broader Hungarian context. We have used published survey data and opinion polls as well as local documentary sources to identify statistical patterns of male/female employment, political participation, and attitudes toward politics and the economy in Hungary generally as a baseline for our discussion.

The chapter is divided into several sections. First, we briefly describe the town, our sample, and our methods. Then we provide a picture of men and women in the Karikás economy, examined in the larger Hungarian context, before taking up gender differences in political activity, again showing how the town we have chosen fits into national patterns. Finally, against the background of these differences, the last section develops an ethnographic account of stratification

---

[3] Pierre Bourdieu's work is an excellent example of this, although he does not often discuss gender.

among three groups of women: wives of the local managerial elite, entrepreneurs and administrators, and manual workers. We compare their social origins, major life experiences, and also their ideals and assumptions about femininity, child rearing, relationships with men, body care, and consumption. Our conclusions outline the ways in which differing ideals and expectations shaped the life trajectories of the women in our study and thus affected their chances for social mobility. At the same time, these ideals and expectations became the cultural markers and sustaining rationale for emerging social classes.

The Locality and the Study

The town we selected for research is located east of the Danube in Hungary's Great Plain. With 27,000 inhabitants, Karikás is large enough to have considerable social stratification. In 1995 and 1996, we interviewed sixty women, each for about five hours. The women were selected as part of a snowball sample designed to represent the full range of social groups characteristic of Karikás and of rural Hungary.

All sixty women were between the ages of 35 and 55, and thus presented a range of experience from both before and after 1989. Included were ten blue-collar workers at a local cannery, fifteen white-collar clerical-administrative workers, seven teachers, nine high-ranking public servants, thirteen entrepreneurs, and six farmers. We worked with each woman to complete a questionnaire, compiling information about her and her husband's family and friendship networks, education and work experiences, leisure activities, body care, and consumption patterns. In a second meeting, we recorded her life history. In most cases we were able to interview the women in their own homes and could therefore observe the environment in which they lived. Even with respect to the thirteen women who preferred to be interviewed at their workplace (mostly teachers, white-collar workers, and entrepreneurs), during the course of our fieldwork and participation in local events during 1996, we were able to observe them in various domains of Karikás public life.

Historically, Karikás is an agro-town, surrounded by scattered agricultural settlements. It is still true that a relatively high percentage of the population (about 30 percent) works in agriculture. Ten percent live outside of town in isolated settlements. Nearly everyone farms a small plot or garden—a legacy of both the socialist second economy and earlier traditions—and this helps considerably in meeting subsistence needs and providing supplemental income. Karikás is also an educational center; it boasts eight lower level schools, a secondary grammar school, two vocational high schools, and a teacher's training college that attracts people from all over the country. Since 1989, some schools have been returned to the Calvinist Church, making Karikás once again a center of Calvinist activity. Finally, besides the employment opportunities in agriculture, town administration, public health, and education, industry has been an important source of jobs. The cannery was by far the most important, employing more people than all other manufacturing firms combined. In recent years, however, each of these three sectors—agriculture, public administration, and industry—has suffered a tremendous loss of jobs. Unemployment affected men first in 1992–1993, when skilled workers were laid off, but male and female unemployment in Karikás has been roughly equal since 1995. As we will discuss below, "entrepreneurship" constitutes another large employment category in Karikás and includes a diverse work force.

Men and Women in the Economy

In Hungary, women's employment has dropped by 20 percent in the last decade. According to a survey conducted by the Central Statistical Office, only 61 percent of Hungarian women were employed in 1995. The percentage in Karikás is considerably lower (55 percent). A national survey of women found that two-thirds of those interviewed thought women should be involved in wage-earning. Yet among these, 60 percent said that women should not be employed full-time. The gap between women's ideals and their choices is revealed in the responses of women who were active wage-earners at the time of the survey. Only 10 percent said they would be willing to move from full-time into part-time jobs; of this group, 88 percent claimed this was because their income was essential to their family's survival (Frey 1996). Again, the Karikás data are quite similar; not one among the actively employed respondents mentioned a desire to work part-time. Even those who had left the labor market were still working but were in "black" or "gray" areas that are not officially registered.

A closer look at industrial employment in Karikás reveals a pattern of differences between men and women. As with most Hungarian food-processing firms, the Karikás cannery produced for the Soviet market. After 1989, it faced an extremely difficult financial situation, and half of its workers were laid off. These job losses, however, were not counterbalanced by an increase in private sector employment. In 1992, two of the cannery's divisions were bought by French firms; the remainder underwent a "manager-employee buyout" in which roughly half the stock remained state owned and 51 percent was turned over to managers and workers. The French firms were relatively small, and one relied primarily on seasonal labor. (Until recently, those in seasonal work could count on unemployment benefits; by 1994–1995 benefits were reduced to a very small income supplement.) Only that part of the cannery owned by workers and managers continued to employ a sizable labor force (1,100 people), but this too was partly seasonal. Although the factory has always employed equal numbers of men and women, men have predominated in management.

Employment patterns in other industries and in the state administration mirrored those in the cannery. In 1995, men occupied two-thirds of the managerial posts—and the most lucrative jobs. This had been a consistent pattern since before the transition. Only in feminized occupations such as public health, education, and municipal administration did women hold top leadership positions. Even in small-scale gardening enterprises, men routinely occupied managerial and decision-making roles, with women seen as regular helpers rather than equal partners.[4]

One other major source of employment in Karikás, which has increased substantially since 1989, is entrepreneurship. This is a heterogeneous census category that represents full- and part-time work and includes merchants and small artisans, professionals pursuing work for their own profit (e.g., notary, bookkeeper, pharmacist), and persons who have moved into new occupations. For some, entrepreneurial work may provide supplementary income; for others, it may be a sole source of support. Examples include teachers and administrators working as part-time AMWAY or Avon agents or members of the "new rich" operating services such as Volkswagen dealerships, gas stations, or beauty parlors. Most entrepreneurs, however, are small retailers and traders. In 1995, there were 1,198 registered entrepreneurs in Karikás. Men far outnumbered women in every form of entrepreneurship, with the exception of bookkeeping. The reasons for this imbalance are revealing. Men have taken up entrepreneurial activity after being fired from jobs. So far, women have exercised other options, especially maternity leave, to avoid official unemployment. Also, women carry out a range of services for others, such as caring for children or for the sick and elderly, housecleaning, or contributing to small-scale agricultural production. Although each of these jobs creates income, they are usually pursued outside the formal umbrella of registered entrepreneurship. Although we cannot estimate the proportion of Karikás women who work in these jobs, we do know that this pattern was common even before the transition, particularly among young and middle-aged women who are classified in the census as "housewives."

One respondent, for example, a skilled worker formerly employed by the cannery, was dismissed from the permanent staff when the factory was privatized, but was lucky enough to find a job as a cleaning woman in the local archives. Besides working in this officially registered position, she cleaned the apartments of the town's wealthier stratum on a regular, although unofficial, basis. Both she and her single mother had always supplemented the family income with such hidden service work. That this was a well-accepted practice is indicated by the fact that among her clients were the notary and the town's central administrator.

In sum, men who work in public institutions, industry, and private entrepreneurship fill the best positions in the local economy. If anything, the imbalance between men's and women's employment patterns has only become more severe since the transition. Statistics for differential income reflect this as well. According to a national study for 1995, men in the legal economy earned, on average, 10.5 percent more than women (Frey 1996). Women in Karikás do not, however, perceive this to be a problem. As elsewhere in Hungary and other post-socialist

---

[4] It is noteworthy that women were not always and everywhere restricted to secondary positions in the agricultural second economy. Őrszigethy (1986) found the opposite situation before the transition in a region close to the Budapest conurbation zone. There men commuted to industrial work in the capital, while women remained in the village employed by agricultural cooperatives and managed the auxiliary household production on their own.

countries, gender inequalities of pay and position are not seen as a political issue (Gal 1996:79–80; Watson 1996). In part, this is because they are hard to perceive, since gender segregation in the labor force makes it appear that men and women simply perform different jobs that deserve different levels of remuneration. Also, income differences are often excused by referring to women's lesser experience or lesser qualifications due to time lost through maternity leave. It is an interesting phenomenon that women generally believe it is the men who have suffered most seriously from the effects of emerging capitalism, both locally and nationally.

Men and Women in Politics

The question of what counts as a publicly recognized problem brings us squarely to the issue of women's participation in the political arena, where such problems are formulated. Since the 1989 transition, women in Karikás have acted in concert with women across Hungary and the rest of the region; they have, on the whole, withdrawn from politics. This occurred in several different ways. In 1989, just before the changes, women held leading positions in all municipal administrations. Moreover, women and men shared in almost equal numbers the top posts in municipally run institutions, such as the primary and secondary schools, public health, and social and cultural institutions. Following the changes, women's equal representation disappeared, as men took over in the technical and finance departments of town administration. Within the elected town council, the change has been much more dramatic. In 1989, 22 percent of the council was made up of women (thirteen out of fifty-eight). By the second multiparty election in 1994, and partly as a result of changed electoral districts, only three women were elected to a council of twenty-three; two were from the conservative Smallholders Party, and one was from the Socialist Party.

Yet these figures do not accurately represent the complex relationship of women to politics in Karikás, or the ways in which women perceive their political role. There are numerous women in town who are politically active as candidates for office (fourteen in the last election, or 20 percent), as leaders of political parties (two of the four active parties), and as presidents or active members of civic organizations. Furthermore, in contrast to those women who were active before 1989 but have withdrawn from public life, those who have recently entered politics are often committed to conservative parties (e.g., Smallholders, Christian Democrats). Their personal and family histories in part explain this.

Take, for example, Margit, executive secretary of the local chapter of the Smallholders Party. Now in her sixties, she came from a wealthy peasant family, and her experience is not unusual for this stratum. As she tells it, she married a man from a similarly well-to-do peasant family, but in 1952, within a year of her marriage, the family's entire property was confiscated, her father was imprisoned, and she was labeled a "kulak whore." Not only did she enter the ranks of unskilled labor at the cannery, she also endured the humiliation of having to be hidden by her co-workers when the Party secretary came to inspect. She now says, "I am proud. All our property was taken away, just like everyone in our class, so we had to change, and yet we stayed afloat." With education she slowly rose through the ranks, all the while maintaining her parents' work ethic. Her marriage failed, so she raised her daughter alone and managed over the years to start life anew several times, finally becoming a high school principal and remarrying at age 49. Margit also experienced the collapse of socialism as a new start—a kind of late revenge. As she put it, "It was a great feeling; I started to feel like a full person again."

But Margit and other women who are politically active are ambivalent about their positions. The president of the local chapter of the Christian Democrats was among our respondents, yet she avoided telling us this, despite the fact that our questionnaire specifically asked about it. Another woman, an energetic teacher, organized the post-socialist Association of Large Families, a group with a predominantly female membership, and was known to be the motor behind the group. Nonetheless, she pushed her husband to be president, saying, "He will at least be respected by the authorities with whom the association must negotiate." Women's organizations, such as the Calvinist Women's Association, were unlike other civil society initiatives in that they reflected a typical female ambivalence in their very structure. This group, for instance, did not even register itself officially, arguing that it was not strong enough to take on a public role.

Women often said that they had no time for politics. Yet clearly there is more involved than this. That the tenor of local politics is uncongenial to most women is revealed by one candidate for municipal office, who said, "I was nominated by the Agricultural Association. I accepted it because I liked them, and it was quite in line with my skills, but I was still glad I wasn't elected in the end. I would not have had enough patience to sit through their endless discussions." As she implied, it was the futility of these discussions—quite apart from their length—that alienated her. Even Margit, the Smallholders' executive secretary, who is manifestly political, whose appearance is strong, bony, and almost masculine, and who acknowledges that her interests and lifestyle are far from "feminine" by local definitions ("I am not the mother or housewife type at all") nevertheless avers, "I don't consider myself a political person. There are more men who have a talent for politics. I have a more peaceful character. I am shocked by these hard, coarse, masculine political battles."

Women's sense that their womanhood is antithetical to politics has most likely been influenced by the emerging definition of political activity itself. As Gal has argued, the discourse of politics in Hungary since at least the early 1980s—adopted by most new political parties—relies on a gendered definition of public action, so that "by various logics, men are public figures and women, as a social category, are depoliticized" (Gal 1996:79). The result is that women do take on political roles, but they do not feel well suited to the job. They see themselves, instead, as socially active, politically conscious, sometimes strong and powerful, but fundamentally private individuals. Neither do they organize to help themselves as women. The organizations made up largely of women work for other goals. One helps large families; another, the Calvinist Women's Association, performs church-sponsored charity work, such as giving presents to newly baptized babies. As Gal suggests, "Women in the post-socialist societies feel a sense of equality with men . . . that they retain from the official ideology of state socialism. Relying on this, and being as eager as anyone else to be part of a capitalist democracy, women too want to think of themselves not as some special category of person but primarily as "individuals" and equal "citizens of a new society" (1996:79).

But not all women are equally interested in politics, even in this ambivalent, somewhat contradictory way. As one might expect, women in different strata are differently oriented to politics. For most entrepreneurs, municipal administrators, teachers, and even leading public servants, political activity means watching the nightly news and participating in campaign rallies when famous national politicians visit. Admittedly, their participation is often motivated more by the celebrity value of the visitor than by their own party sympathies. But even these political interests were entirely missing from the lives of workers and low-level clerical employees. This is, perhaps, predictable. As of 1995, no party on the Hungarian political scene acted as a labor party or represented the interests of workers. There was not even a legitimate language for describing workers' claims, except perhaps the rhetoric of the immediate communist past (see Rychard 1996:477). The only women who were positively interested in politics were self-employed farmers. As smallholders who have started afresh, they are precisely those whom the Smallholders Party seeks to represent.

Such diversity among emerging new classes is not limited to political interests and participation but is manifest in other cultural realms as well, especially in terms of expectations about gender relations. Thus far, we have discussed the ways in which men and women in Karikás are differently positioned in the community's economy and political life. We will now switch gears to focus on women in different walks of life and the ways in which their divergent gender attitudes and practices enable mobility, thus contributing to and legitimating their social positions.

CLASS FORMATION THROUGH WOMEN'S EXPERIENCE

For the women of Karikás, womanhood consists, ideally, of four kinds of responsibilities: to work for a living, to maintain an effective and efficient household, to financially assist one's children, and, for those who are married, to satisfy one's husband. Virtually all the women we spoke to would like to fulfill these apparently self-imposed requirements. Not everyone succeeds. But more important, the imagined ways of fulfilling these responsibilities and, equally telling, the range of available options vary substantially according to a woman's place in the social hierarchy. Our research suggests that a woman's social mobility (upward or downward) often depends on how she defines, imagines, and practices these ideals.[5] Of course, the direction of causality is difficult to demonstrate with ethnographic and observational materials, but we believe the patterns we have discovered are extremely suggestive. None are completely new, and all have roots in the socialist past. In what follows we portray the contrasting ideas, lives, and practices of women in three selected social groups: the emerging local elite, entrepreneurs and administrators, and manual workers.

Before detailing these differences, however, it is important to state broad unifying beliefs and practices. Women in Karikás accept as inevitable that they, as women, have to work harder than men do. Indeed, national statistics indicate that women shouldered three-fourths of the burden of housework in 1995 and spent three times more time on childcare than men did (Frey 1996). These figures indicate a considerable recent increase in men's participation in such duties, probably a side effect of increased male unemployment. Our data from Karikás match these national statistics; household work and childcare are mainly women's work, although most of the women we talked to regarded caring for children not simply as work but as the giving and getting of love. Most women remembered their three or more years of maternity leave as a "heavenly" time, the happiest period of their lives. Only a very few women put their young children into nurseries, explaining their preference for returning to work by saying, "I'm not good with babies" or, "It's better for babies in nurseries, where professionals take care of them." Similarly, only a handful of men participated in housework, which usually took the form of grocery shopping, weekly housecleaning, and, occasionally, cooking. Even those women with the highest ranking administrative or teaching jobs, and those with the strongest sense of autonomy, dedicated themselves to the care of their children and households. Typical is the vice principal of the local teachers' college who spent an entire day, every week, preparing five days' worth of carefully cooked and packed food for her daughter to take to university, 100 kilometers away, where she was a medical student. Within these broadly similar ideological or cultural beliefs, however, there are important differences.

Local Elites

Over the last twenty years, geographic stratification has been reshaped in Karikás, but the changes are far from complete. Well-to-do families and those in leadership positions live in large homes in a separate part of town or in newly refurbished houses on the main streets; formerly owned by wealthy peasants, these homes are now admired for their architectural and historical charm. Families of more modest means live in smaller, new houses or in state housing projects. In such projects, however, small but upwardly mobile entrepreneurs can often be found living next to workers and the unemployed. Despite a tendency toward segrega-

---

[5] It has become routine to talk about the importance of symbolic capital, in Bourdieu's (1984) sense, to understand social mobility. Gender ideals might work in a similar way, sometimes inherited from parents and often giving actors resources in their efforts to engage with life possibilities.

tion, there is still substantial interaction among the loosely defined groups we have outlined here.

Overall, Karikás has not developed an exclusive post-socialist local elite to replace the old *nomenklatura* and party hierarchy. Rather, there are small circles of informally connected individuals who are often found at the same public functions, including fundraisers and charity balls, party get-togethers, hunting clubs, and other local organizations. For our purposes, industrial managers, politicians, and clergy form one analytically interesting group that we will contrast, from the standpoint of gender relations, to another elite group, comprised of municipal administrators and successful entrepreneurs. We discuss this group in the next section.

By 1995–1996, the chief managers of industrial concerns were among the richest and most important people in town, employed at the cannery's successor firms. They were all men and, as in the rest of the country, they came from the ranks of former second and third echelon managers who were able to rise due to the privatization and splintering of their firms. Several of these men were active in local and even national politics, but in sharp contrast to the socialist period, their post-socialist political activity did not directly influence their economic success. One of these men, a member of the liberal Free Democrats, was elected to Parliament as early as 1990. In contrast, another was widely known to have quite conservative views. He was on good terms with prominent right-wing local politicians and was presbyter of the Calvinist Church. The mayor of Karikás (who is not officially linked to any party but has leftist leanings) must also be listed here because of his influential position and widespread networks. The Calvinist clergy also belong in this grouping.

The form of gender relations among this group emerges most clearly if we examine the wives of these men and their ideas about marriage and about themselves. For example, Rózsa is the wife of a top manager. At 42 she is a shy, reserved person, the daughter of a Calvinist pastor. She was religious enough by inclination to have been among the few who went to church even during the socialist period. She teaches mathematics in the vocational high school and paints as a hobby. She relies on hired help to clean their home, which is filled with her canvases. Even in the new era, Rózsa is withdrawn and rarely goes to public functions, let alone participates in organized community life as one might expect of the wife of a prominent manager. Quite the opposite of a "public person," she has tried instead to diminish her public presence, wearing shapeless, dark dresses whenever she ventures out of the house.

Erzsi, another manager's wife, was similarly withdrawn from public life, but for somewhat different reasons. Her husband, fifteen years her senior and previously married, is also a member of Parliament. Erzsi lives in a rather isolated, large house, equipped with a swimming pool and decorated with hand-carved folk furniture and paintings by modern Hungarian artists. She and her husband vacation in Italy during the summer and ski during the winter. Previously, Erzsi worked at the cannery (where she met her husband), first as a clerk, then as a salesperson, and again as a clerk. Three years ago, at her husband's suggestion, she left her part-time job and has since occupied herself with housework, driving her daughter to private lessons, taking aerobics classes and jogging to lose weight, as well as making weekly visits to the hairdresser, masseuse, sauna, and cosmetician. She goes to the theater with women friends and considers herself a happy, satisfied person. Although she rarely sees her husband, it was clear that appearing fresh and attractive for him in the morning is one of her responsibilities. In this context, she considered a beautiful and well-toned body to be a "product" for which she had to "work." If anything was wrong in this picture for her, it was the time and effort she devoted to constant care and management of her body, which she nevertheless considered flawed and inadequate.

Judit was quite a different case, but with telling parallels. She is the wife of the town mayor. A lively, public-spirited person, she had been a middle-ranked municipal administrator when she quit her job to help her husband in his gardening/produce business, presumably to increase their income. She has since worked extraordinarily hard, without paid help, to maintain the children and the household while tending to tomatoes and the other vegetables they sell. She does virtually all the physical work and takes great pride in feats of hard labor, which even endanger her health. Her admiring husband approves and restricts his own participation to managing the financial end of the business and fulfilling his mayoral responsibilities. It was Judit who had the interest and ambition to reenter public life, but instead of doing it herself, she pushed her gardener/entrepreneur husband to run for mayor. This is not to say that her husband, a man in his forties, was not also interested in this kind of conspicuous public service. He responded eagerly to pressure from his wife and friends to run for office, in part because it presented a test through which he could challenge himself to succeed. Previously, he had become a leading local entrepreneur; now he would take on the task of administering the whole town. He did not take easily, however, to the socializing and communicating that went with the job—tasks more suited to his wife's ambitions.

A final example is the town's Calvinist clergy. One pastor's remarks were typical: "Men are different from women. . . . [I hate] women who want to act like men. The whole society has to be blamed because women do not want to be real women." His wife shared this view. "My job," she said, "is to make sure that he can do his job without any problems or difficulties, to allow him to carry out the task God and the Church have given him. He lives in the family, but he is still independent. I have decided to do this. I was given to him as his helping hand; it is not a burden that I live in this family as a servant." Another Calvinist pastor was herself a woman, but she suffered the disapproval of her male colleagues (pastoral posts have been open to women in the Hungarian Calvinist Church since 1981). She teaches at the Calvinist college, has two children, and has written a book entitled *Home, Homemaking and Nation*, published in 1990 by the Church Media Department. It is perhaps not surprising that the book outlines the proper (asymmetric) relationship between men and women in marriage, modeled after that between the head and body of Christ in the Church. It details the necessary subjugation of women; as the Church owes obedience to Christ, so do women owe obedience to their husbands.

While these women are quite different in many ways, they exemplify a pattern of gender relations in which women, while often retaining waged employment, nevertheless subordinate or redirect their own ambitions and autonomous activities—especially public ones—in order to put their husbands in the foreground. They willingly, often gladly, take direction from their husbands and adopt a dependent role as helpmate, trophy, or servant, with the apparent approval and satisfaction of their successful or religiously committed husbands. This pattern is usually considered a return to earlier forms, and certainly it is sometimes legitimized by allusions to the past. But the context in which it currently operates fundamentally changes the meaning of these forms. Indeed, the details of everyday practice signal an important difference. The activities in which women are engaged—skiing, publishing religious books, being pastors, doing aerobics for self-improvement, or engaging in agriculture despite holding degrees in higher education—hardly fit any earlier pattern. The current tendency is not, therefore, a revival of traditional nineteenth-century or pre-war bourgeois models. Rather, it is an amalgamation that, whether justified by religious precepts or secular images of commodified bodies, becomes the symbolic mark of high social status, part of the new elite's self-definition. Importantly, it also reflects an ideological commitment diametrically opposed to the former socialist system.

Entrepreneurs and Administrators

Willingly subservient wives nevertheless constitute a very small proportion of women in Karikás. We turn now to the educated, upper echelons of entrepreneurs and the similarly educated administrators employed in industry, education, or the municipality. For this group, images of marriage and what they can rightly expect from a husband are systematically different, as are their backgrounds and their attitudes toward their own bodies.

Our interviews revealed that the nine administrators in our sample—one might call them public servants—were autonomous, self-confident women with strong personalities. Often ambitious, they demanded what they called "partnerships" with men, along with romantic love. They did not always succeed, of course, but their vision of what we would call gender relations often contributed importantly to their life course and thus to their patterns of mobility. These women came from artisan, merchant, or bureaucratic families, occasionally from rich peasant backgrounds, and most of their own mothers worked outside the home. Professionally, they began in low-level clerical positions, and through perseverance, correspondence courses, or night school, they each earned the diploma or advanced certification necessary to move into a higher level administrative job. Within our sample, vocations of this type included chief librarian, municipal office manager, chief notary, and town clerk. Some women moved in and out of teaching positions as well. Such movement-by-stages through educational advancement was the typical path of social mobility for most people in the last decades of state socialism.

The women we interviewed who fell into this category wanted not only to achieve specific career ambitions, but also to make happy marriages and to be mothers. Nevertheless, they all had been divorced, at their own initiative, and it was among this group that we found the few women who put their infants into nurseries. As these women explained, they could not endure living with husbands who raised obstacles to their ambitions or refused to be true "partners." What women meant by this term was simply working together at the difficult task of raising small children and gaining their husbands' support of their careers. While claiming their own independence, these women could not tolerate their husbands' gestures of independence from the marriage—for example, the beer drinking after soccer, card playing into the night, or the situation in which "he goes to take out the garbage in the afternoon and doesn't come back till 11 at night because he's been getting drunk with his friends." They were particularly unwilling to put up with such behavior if they felt themselves tied down to small babies or to the demands of the husbands themselves. One woman recounted, "When we first got married, my husband wouldn't allow anyone around me, neither men nor women, no circle of friends at all. All he cared about was the stew on the table and a clean shirt on his back. My whole life revolved around making a variety of stews for him and baby food for the kid. By the end I could hardly eat from rage and exhaustion." Another, in similar circumstances, recounted an epiphany, "When my little girl was born I thought, well I've given birth to a servant-to-be. Because a person is turned into a chambermaid when she gets married. As they say, a clean shirt and a warm cunt—that's all men want."

Both these women divorced while their children were young and raised them alone or with the help of their parents. They were willing to serve their children but not their husbands. They were willing to give up their marriage, but not their professional life. Interestingly, even after such negative experiences, these women retained their ideals about marital partnerships. Six of our respondents remarried, again for love, and with considerable success. Virtually all claimed to be happy. The second set of husbands included men who were themselves devoted to their careers as administrators or entrepreneurs. Nevertheless, the men were the ones who accommodated to the women's requirements and successfully adjusted themselves to previously established mother–child routines. One woman explained with satisfaction, "My husband is a very helpful partner, he really does his best in everything." She had two small children when they met, and her mornings of hectic preparation for school and work were an enormous burden. "I said to him, 'I'm easy to get along with, except in the morning, when there is so much to do!' And then he just took over the entire morning routine from me, he just did everything." It is not at all that such husbands literally take on half of housework or childcare (only six out of sixty respondents reported husbands who shared housework and childcare, and none shared equally). Rather, they were willing to be emotionally supportive of their wives' ambitions and to make special gestures to help. At least to this extent, some men in Karikás shared these women's ideal of marital partnership, while others did not.[6]

Marriages based on an ideal of partnership were even more common among respondents who were entrepreneurs. As noted earlier, this occupational category is especially diverse. Most entrepreneurs left previous jobs and entered this field after 1989, a challenging move that required initiative and a sense of self-possession. As one such woman said, "So far, [in life] I've always been able to get whatever I've wanted." In most cases, however, people did not become entrepreneurs voluntarily, but were forced to do so by the loss or transformation of earlier jobs. Sometimes a woman continued with her regular job, while her employer simply disappeared (as in state-owned hairdressing salons or hospitals). In other cases, entrepreneurs learned entirely new skills, following the logic of private business. Among the most successful were those who were already deeply involved in socialism's second economy, often as a family sideline, while some family members kept jobs in the state economy (Szelényi et al. 1988). Although artisans, craftsmen, and wealthy peasants were somewhat overrepresented among the parents of today's entrepreneurs, we found no clear link between a woman's social background and her decision to become an entrepreneur. However, most of these women had mothers who were themselves salaried workers. Particular gender ideals, family support (parents who gave money or provided childcare), and large social networks (including previous clientele or foreign friends) contributed powerfully to these women's ability to become and remain entrepreneurs. The women in this group have the most extensive social networks beyond their family ties, and most live in what they consider a full partnership with their spouse or live-in mate.

While many entrepreneurs are poor, uneducated, and struggling, they share social traits with the educated, upper echelon we focus on here. Kinga, for example, was a dentist who had not given up her practice. But five years ago, with the help of an Austrian acquaintance who acted as investor, she and her husband opened a Volkswagen car shop in the county seat some kilometers from Karikás. The Austrian had first come to Hungary to hunt, met Kinga's father, and later had his teeth fixed in Kinga's private dental clinic. Kinga, her husband, and the Austrian own equal shares in the car dealership. Each year the business

---

[6]It is worth mention that many of the teachers in our sample endured a somewhat different version of this marital dilemma. Often they rose slowly through the ranks, studying at night, but all the while shouldering the housekeeping and care of little children. Many of the teachers stayed in marriages where the husbands offered no support at all for such endeavors and, indeed, were sometimes hostile to them. Most difficult were cases in which the wife's social status as teacher rose above that of a skilled-worker husband. Such discrepancies caused serious tensions within marriages and families. These women often felt that in addition to their other burdens they also spent their energies on maintaining an emotional "balance" with their husbands, by supporting the man's dignity, pushing themselves into the background, and understating their own achievements. Unlike the administrators and entrepreneurs, these women could not demand "partnerships," although they clearly believed in them. Unlike the conservative elite, they practiced a kind of self-effacement, while clearly not believing in it.

has grown spectacularly, so by the time of our interview they had eighty employees. Kinga's in-laws lived close by and helped considerably with the two children. The couple relied on each other, establishing a division of labor in the business, and they hired regular, frequent help to care for their large house, which was elaborately decorated with antiques, and for the two or three cars parked out front.

Kinga and her husband consider themselves partners, struggling toward common family goals. As she noted, "If you look around, you see that a lot of marriages end in divorce . . . but this is not so for us. I think we have a better relationship since we got involved in business." Indeed, Kinga thought there were many things she did better than her husband, and so she took over more of the business tasks. To cope with the stress of risk-taking, to succeed at challenging work, and to make a well-deserved profit in the family enterprise were among the goals that seemed to strengthen these relationships. Importantly, the men agreed to family expenditures that benefitted their wives, for instance spending money on hired help or labor-saving devices. Indeed, among entrepreneurs, 60 percent of the respondents said they were happy with their marriage, compared to 43 percent within the sample as a whole. It was also among entrepreneurs and administrators that we met the most open and flexible women, willing and able to engage in a nonconformist lifestyle. In this group were several unmarried women who lived with a lover. Two women lived apart from their husbands, each maintaining a separate household in another city. Apparently without jealousy, both partners in these cases provided for the other and for the children, and responsibilities varied depending on which household the family was in at any given time. The women in this group also spoke of extramarital affairs without stigmatizing them; it was simply a reality of life that could as easily occur to them as to their husbands. As one said, this is something that "can be part of the cards one is dealt."

Like Kinga, many women in the entrepreneur and administrator group, even those who were not educated, were vehemently committed to providing their children with a level of education that would ensure them a place at the university. People went to great lengths to achieve this, often amassing a crippling debt. These women also sought to provide their children with a house or apartment—a goal that is extremely difficult to achieve given current economic circumstances.

This group of women—entrepreneurs and public servants—also had quite distinct views of their own bodies and selves. They are regular clients at the hairdresser's, cosmetician's, solarium, and sauna. Unlike most women in Karikás, they engage in sports, they swim or attend aerobics classes, and they care about their health. But unlike the manager's wife described earlier, for whom bodycare is a form of work, these women do not consider care of their bodies to be a way of fixing something wrong or of compensating for their dependent status vis-à-vis their husbands. Rather, like expenditures for clothes or an investment in their business, they consider the consumption of such services to be an essential part of their more or less consciously formulated and formalized public relations activities. Simply, they believe that looking good increases their chances to sell a product or to practice their occupation. Similarly, they believe that consumption of mass media, because it is so closely linked to business, plays a role in maintaining a sense of autonomy. These women would purchase a variety of magazines, old and new, but primarily those that met the needs of their clients. Invariably, however, they would read the magazines before placing them in a waiting room. Unlike workers (who will be discussed below), women entrepreneurs watched more news programs and less entertainment television, and they read science fiction or bestsellers (e.g., Danielle Steele, Robin Cook) and not romance novelettes. Some also read poetry, classic literature, or philosophy.

Except for these relatively solitary entertainments, men and women spent their free time together, usually amongst family and friends, most often to celebrate name days and holidays. While this is generally true of all strata in Karikás, the recent drop in salaries has limited such activities for most middle-income families. Among the groups we consider here, only top administrators and entrepreneurs continued an active and lively round of get-togethers, and in so doing were able to foster the extended family and friendship networks so necessary for their economic success. The men in this group also engaged in separate activities in which women did not directly participate. For several decades, a "club" has existed in the pub of the state socialist "House of Culture," to which men from the middle and upper echelon went, often daily, to drink, chat, and discuss politics. These men also participated on sports teams sponsored by the municipality and in private hunting clubs.

In sum, the leisure activities, media consumption, and personal care practices preferred by women in this group, as well as by their husbands and male counterparts, suggest the making of a class culture—that is, a sense of distinction, value, and taste—that sets them apart from other strata and, in their own eyes, is justified by and explains their success. A more important aspect of this culture is a form of femininity imagined as autonomous and independent, yet in need of moral support. This ideal is congruent with expectations about "partnership" in male–female relations. These are certainly important as a symbolic aspect of class formation; to treat one's husband or wife in a particular way becomes a marker of being the "right" kind of person. But it is significant that the gender ideals that these women maintain contribute materially and quite directly to making their entrepreneurial activity possible. By rejecting husbands who lacked the qualities they need in a partner, top administrators and entrepreneurial women made strategic (although risky) moves toward upward mobility. At the same time, the businesses that these women ran and the salaries they earned gave them the autonomy and the wherewithal to make such choices—that is, to dispense with men who did not meet their requirements.[7]

---

[7] Individual differences remain. A very few women consider themselves tragically crippled by their marriages because their husbands undermine their dignity and self-confidence. Even though they long for autonomy, these women do not leave, however, because they consider themselves too old or too tied to the children.

Manual Workers

Our final category provides a stark contrast to the other two. Most manual laborers [*munkásasszony*] at the cannery came from poor peasant or landless laborer backgrounds and entered the cannery after primary school to supplement the family income. Most have worked at the cannery all their lives. Although wage labor is generally considered alienating and exploitative (see Lampland 1995), it nevertheless is seen as an improvement over the uncertainty and poverty of agricultural labor. In the factory, women felt more secure in the value of their labor ("If you worked hard, you could do all right"). Furthermore, women's actual memories of their youth at the cannery in the 1960s and 1970s belie the abstract condemnation. The cannery provided a kind of surrogate family, and the women we spoke with shared warm memories of the youth brigades and of elder factory workers who taught them as second mothers. "It was harder in the old times, because there was more heavy manual work . . . but we just did it. . . . We were not emotionally drained but physically . . . then you worked and joked around too; even though you were breaking your back you did so happily." In the 1960s and 1970s, the general manager was a father figure who encouraged women to improve their status through education. By taking courses, for example, a woman might advance to the level of skilled worker (which was better paid) or move out of the factory altogether. Single or childless women were favorite targets, especially for political training in Marxist-Leninist colleges, because it was presumed that they "had time." One woman recounted, "I figured out I had taken seventeen years of courses while working in the cannery. At that rate, I could have graduated from a university by now!"

The cannery's role as substitute family was particularly important because workers' ties to their real families were often brittle or lost altogether. These women reported the highest incidence of suicides, alcoholism, and work-related disabilities in their family of origin. In contrast to the other groups we have discussed, where extended family networks provided important support, women in this group often lost touch even with siblings once they went off to work. Women explained this by saying, "All my brothers and sisters had their own troubles."

Most often, marriage ties were also made within the factory, as young people frequently met at factory-organized outings. Indeed, at every step of life, the cannery provided aid and support. This included providing subsidized first apartments, state-supported loans for new families, and discount prices for buses and vacation hostels. Factory cohorts stuck together, celebrating name days and often planning joint summer holidays. Since workers often lived in the same housing project, young families relied not on kinship networks, but on their neighbors for favors, childcare, and sociality. This further tied cannery workers to one another and to the factory. But the factory held claim over workers in a negative way, too. Unlike women in other walks of life, workers could not participate in the second economy of late socialism because the high season of the cannery overlapped with the high season of agricultural labor in the second economy.

This left workers all the more reliant on wages and further isolated them from the social networks that the second economy both relied on and fostered.

While these circumstances gave workers a strong sense of belonging and protection, they also encouraged dependence on the factory. In a different sense, so too did the strong pressure to join the Communist Party. Many rejected the Party for religious reasons or simply to counter the coercion. For others, however, membership was a real honor, and it certainly was indispensable to anyone who wanted to rise in the ranks. But there were other advantages as well. "There were meetings of the members every two or three months, and they weren't bad. We heard a lot about what was going on in the factory, things you wouldn't know otherwise, because they were about economic policy. . . . And you could say what you wanted. They at least always wanted to know what we thought were the problems."

Following privatization of the factory, however, these circumstances changed drastically. With restructuring, many workers were fired, and the factory lost its paternalistic function. Workers felt increasingly insecure, afraid they might slip into the poverty that many remembered from childhood. Distrust grew common, the old sense of camaraderie was lost, and workers no longer met socially. "Now everyone has their own protected space and is careful never to teach someone else how to handle a machine. There is a lot of professional jealousy going on here," one cannery woman told us. "We are afraid of each other. Someone might report on you; there have been strange incidents, thefts, and people getting fired when accused of stealing. It is another way of getting rid of people." Co-workers started avoiding each other outside of work. "If you have a problem, you tend to withdraw, for if you look around, all you see is misery."

Although nominally they were shareholders in the cannery, workers felt much less a part of the enterprise than in the years of consolidated socialism when the factory was a paternalistic employer. "We get so little information, we just assume there's something wrong again, but we don't know what." They noted that the distance between workers (even as shareholders) and management was widening, not only monetarily, but also in terms of information and values. They saw the world dividing into the few with a lot of money and the many, including themselves, with less and less. They also were experiencing the cultural devaluation of labor itself, both for its own sake and as a guarantee of a livelihood. "I was raised to do hard, manual work. That's what I know how to do, that is how I want to earn my living. And now all I hear is that everyone is supposed to be an entrepreneur. Well, I'm not cut out for that. Even if I had the capital, I'm not like that, not so brave, and wily, and convoluted. Some people are born to work, not everyone can be an entrepreneur. And this new system, it humiliates and ruins those who work." For women workers, and also their husbands, who have neither links to the second economy nor recourse to an extended family or social network, the post-socialist loss of the factory's multifarious support system has been catastrophic. Many are on the verge of poverty.

In our sample, marriages among workers were particularly unstable; 50 percent among these respondents were divorced, several more than once. This is well above the sample average of 23 percent. Most often, the women had abandoned husbands who drank, acted aggressively, or physically abused them and their children. Divorce was a way to escape a situation they experienced as unbearable. Even in the best of circumstances, marriage created the double burden of wage labor followed by housework, childcare, and inevitable money worries; it marked a sharp end to a relatively carefree girlhood, when there was some money to spare for new dresses and plenty of parties, holidays, and dances with co-workers. Most factory women remembered their early, unmarried years at the factory as the happiest times of their lives. After a first divorce, some of our respondents lived alone for as many as twenty years. Sometimes another man would not tolerate the woman's children. Many women did not want to remarry and simply refused all offers. "I've got a lifetime of hatred for men. . . . I couldn't imagine a stranger walking around here in my house." Another said, "We must work, and after that our private life just has to be put aside. Who's even in the mood for that? We come home exhausted, do the housework, and are happy to fall into bed to rest." Marital difficulties were linked to money. "There is no way a poor man can be happy, because sooner or later there will be such tensions and fights around money. . . . You might think you are happy, but then the screaming about money starts, because in this world money is the first thing." Only two women spoke of their husbands as people with whom they had joint plans or with whom they wanted to work together to realize some future goal.

Among workers, general expectations about husbands and marriage were markedly different than those displayed by women of the two groups previously discussed. Going back even to their family of origin, these women had no experience with the kind of family in which father is the "breadwinner" and mother is the "housewife." Nor have they ever imagined their husband as partner, not even as a "partner in struggle" for a better life. Although they might have married for romance and youthful attraction, they reported considerable hostility toward their spouses. Generally, their expectations amounted to little more than wanting men to earn some money and not to leave the heaviest physical labor for women. One woman summed it up by saying, "My little sister has no water in the house, so she has to bring it in huge cans, meanwhile her husband sits and watches TV. Even when the food is cooked, he won't even take it out of the fridge. . . . This I consider brutal, totally brutal. We were talking the other day, and I said, if I had to choose, I'd take men's work any day, rather than this women's work, where you just work constantly, continuously. . . . I said, if I could just have been a man, I'd fuck over the men, just like the men fuck over women." Nevertheless, it was not disappointment of even these minimal expectations, but the unbearable abuse, that generally led to divorce.

Although working women held a significantly different view of marriage than women in the other groups, their expectations of motherhood were remarkably similar. These women were devoted to the care of their children, and their ideal of providing for a child's long-term prospects paralleled that of the other groups. But raising children, often alone, was extremely difficult, not least because factory wages were so low. Women were thus forced to take on extra jobs, usually weekend work or night shifts on a three-shift system, to scrape together money for their children's needs. Even so, they rarely succeeded. "My only wish is to secure an apartment for my child, so she could start her life in earnest. This is all I wish for." Others tried to provide their children with educational opportunities so they did not have to be manual laborers. But in fact, most of the children of women workers entered the factory. Some mothers, despite their own lack of education, were quite intent upon teaching their children the advantages of learning over labor. But in practice, for these children to be apprenticed to a shopkeeper required considerable education and upward mobility and demanded an enormous sacrifice from their mothers.

Low wages and poverty were, of course, the most important determinants of women workers' consumption patterns. Yet even within such constraints, it is important to note women's personal needs, desires, and values—in short, the ways in which women workers thought about their bodies and their selves. Decades of three-shift labor have taken their toll of abuse on women's bodies. Their faces are heavily lined, compared to women of the same age in other walks of life, yet they were not interested in the newly available cosmetics and creams that are so attractive to other women. As one worker said, "Don't talk to me about cosmetics and creams. Money is the best face cream." The cannery rented space to hairdressers and cosmeticians, whose services were cheaper than those available in town. But women did not frequent these establishments. They cut their hair short and wore kerchiefs while working in the cannery. Such neglect of their bodies, however, felt to be necessitated by work, went much deeper; at the time of our research, there was not one among the women workers who was healthy, who did not have arthritis, sclerosis, curvature of the spine, varicose veins, or gynecological or gastric disorders. But these problems were a low priority compared to the desperation of needing to earn money, keep the household together, and support children. As one woman said, "I have a gastric ulcer. Sure, it hurts. Sometimes it hurts so badly it throws me into convulsions, but I keep telling myself, I don't care; if everything in there rots, I still don't care."

Only through leisure do women workers turn away from this ethos of self-neglect. They find time to watch *Dallas* and other TV series, to read cheap romance novels (such as *Romania*, *Julia*, and *Tiffany*, which are targeted to a female audience), and to read women's magazines. Books and magazines are shared among co-workers and friends and between mothers and daughters, even though they are not often immediately relevant to these women's lives. "I like to read recipes," said one woman, "even though I've never seen a nutmeg in my life." The books, the movies, and the magazines are easy to read and easy to forget, and thus conducive to reuse; one woman revealed that she had "two sacks of *Tiffany* saved in the closet." Women were fairly conscious of the role that such diversions play in their lives. "I like to watch karate and romantic films, it is just great that in these films everything is smooth and wonderful, while life itself is a piece of shit." The movies, magazines, and romances provide consolation and a measure of comfort.

Unlike the entrepreneurs and administrators, who are now making their way within the nascent social classes emerging in the post-socialist period, industrial workers constitute a group that was largely created by, and achieved consciousness through, state socialism. The paternalistic practices of that system produced a group of women especially dependent on the factory—and thus on the state—with no social or financial resources outside it. During the final years of state socialism, skilled (and sometimes even unskilled) men could participate in the second economy, for instance, by subcontracting within their state-owned firm; women, however, who were relatively unskilled, could not. Moreover, because the factory functioned as a substitute for family and social networks, women had little opportunity or incentive to acquire alternative supports.[8] Factory perquisites, as long as they existed, benefitted women. Indeed, such state supports allowed women to leave abusive husbands, to live alone and support their children, and to dispense with elaborate expectations about male–female relations. But once the supports were withdrawn, women found themselves dangerously isolated. Their wages were inadequate, they were bereft of social networks, and they also, often, lacked the kinds of cultural expectations—for personal autonomy, "bravery," and initiative or for partnership relations with men—that might allow them to make a different kind of working-class life.

CONCLUSIONS

This chapter has focused on systematic differences among women in their ideas about themselves and their relations with men. We have identified three quite different patterns of gender relations (and gender ideologies) that coexist in one Hungarian town. We believe there are others, too; our study aimed not to be exhaustive but to sketch certain broad contrasts. In any case, if ever there was a single "gender regime of socialism," it is long gone. The three patterns we describe characterize discreet parts of an emerging post-socialist hierarchy. In trying to understand this hierarchy, we assume that new classes are formed not only by new relations to the means of production, but also by people's changing relations to consumption; this involves ideas about identity, commodities, tastes, styles, and values. We have argued that women's ideas about femininity, their sense of self, and their expectations about relations with men are closely linked to class formation.

This relationship is manifest in two distinct ways. First, certain gender ideologies are characteristic of a specific emerging class, thus distinguishing it from other strata or class fractions. Gender ideals become structured markers of distinction and difference, parallel to the cut of clothes, the details of social manners, or the organization of meals. Like these other markers, the way a man treats his wife, for instance, can help identify his place in the social order. Thus, the manager and parliamentarian who asked his wife to quit her job and to busy

---

[8] It is interesting to note the irony that in U.S. capitalism, it is the working class that typically has an extended social network, on which they rely to make their relatively meager resources stretch to fulfill norms for family provisioning that the American working class seems to share with middle classes. In contrast to the case we describe here, in the United States, extended kinship, neighborhood, and friendship networks are working-class and emphatically not middle-class phenomena.

herself caring for their child, their home, and herself was surely aware of the high status and anti-socialist import of these gestures. The implicit message, which is supported by pre-socialist and Western models, is that only a rich and powerful man can afford such a wife.

Similarly, the moral support provided by many entrepreneurial husbands is, we believe, emerging as part of the positive self-image held by Hungarians in small to medium-sized businesses. But gender arrangements also justify and legitimate whichever social position people claim for themselves. So, for example, the Church elite understand women's subservience as a positive value that not only characterizes their beliefs and practices but also shows them (as followers of holy law) to be especially fit for the positions they hold. It is for this reason that a woman can be a Calvinist pastor and author, yet write a book that directly contradicts her own social position by arguing for the necessity and correctness of women's dependence and subservience to men. In a similar way, when women entrepreneurs and high-ranking public servants understand their trips to the cosmetician, the solarium, and exercise class as investments in public relations for their businesses, these practices become not simply self-care, but outward evidence of the rightness and deservedness of any business success they experience.

Second, it is clear from our research that the practices associated with some of the gender ideologies we have charted are themselves materially involved in women's mobility, and thus in the making of classes. The most striking cases are those of entrepreneurs and high-ranking public servants, whose ideals about husbands as "partners" enable them to reject men who do not hold such values or who will not support—financially, emotionally, or by helping with housework and childcare—a woman's educational ambitions or desire for upward mobility. Expectations about one's ability to choose or refuse a mate thus become tied to movement into a social position and are also characteristic of that position. The women workers provide a negative example of this same process. Their downward mobility has been produced largely, of course, by the tragic loss of the factory support they had learned to expect in the previous system. But in addition, the paternalistic dependence created by their relations to the factory also encouraged the development of minimal expectations about men. They now have very few cultural bases on which to imagine or build a future that would involve husband–wife cooperation.

We conclude with two noteworthy ironies concerning the legacy of state socialism in current processes of restratification. Like many students of Hungarian restratification, we have found that today's local elite come from at least two different backgrounds. Some are former socialist technocrats or *nomenklatura* who managed to retain, and in some cases improve on, the position they held under the old system; others are the new entrepreneurs, most of whom started their business in the second economy. In our research, it was members of the managerial elite who subscribed to beliefs (strengthened by religion and anti-socialism) about women's subservience and self-effacement, creating an amalgam of gender practices that is unprecedented in its present form. It relies in certain particulars on practices of the socialist period, yet it presents and legitimates itself as something entirely old, a revival of a "traditional" pattern. The members of this managerial category differed considerably from the entrepreneurial elements of the new elite, who, although perhaps drawn to furniture in the "folk" style and other forms of nostalgia, laid no claim to "tradition" concerning relations between men and women.[9]

Second, the industrial workers who were most closely tied to the main institution of state socialism—the factory—have, unsurprisingly, suffered the most from the fall of the system and are likely to be even more endangered, impoverished, and socially isolated in the future precisely because of the patterns of dependence created by socialist paternalism. The same loss of dignity and sense of exclusion that we found, even among those women who have managed to keep their jobs, has been reported for industrial workers in other post-socialist contexts as well (see Dölling 1994; Spulbeck 1996). In contrast, women who were further removed from the central institutions of state socialism or who had escaped them are actually benefitting from some of the gender patterns produced by state socialism. Indeed, state socialist policies designed to weaken families and to socialize their functions fostered (sometimes inadvertently) women's independence and autonomy. That men and women are in some sense equal or "the same," or are at least capable of working in intimate "partnership," is part of a socialist ideal, even if it was honored more in the breach during the past forty-five years. Certainly it was not a feature of any pre-socialist Hungarian tradition, nor has it been powerfully present in the Western mass media recently flooding the country. Thus, while it is certainly the expansion of the market and capitalist social relations that have enabled entrepreneurial women's success, their participation, as women, in building a decisively anti-socialist order is also importantly based on their expectations about gender relations. In this sense they are, ironically, the unacknowledged ideological heirs of socialism.[10]

BIBLIOGRAPHY

Andorka R. with T. Kolosi and György Vukovich
   1991   Social Report 1990. Budapest: TÁRKI.
Bourdieu, Pierre
   1984   Distinction: A Social Critique of the Judgement of Taste. Richard Nice, transl.
           Cambridge, MA: Harvard University Press.
Buchowski, Michal
   1996   The Shifting Meanings of "Civil" and "Civic" Society in Poland. *In* Civil
           Society. C. Hann and E. Dunn, eds. London: EASA Routledge.

---

[9] Scholars arguing for the dual source of the post-socialist elite include Róna-Tas 1994 and Szelényi and Kostello 1996; the role of the second economy is foreshadowed in Szelényi et al. 1988. Our material suggests not only that these two origins are marked by different patterns of gender relations, but also that they may rely on quite different cultural allies (e.g., with different links to religious spokesmen). It is among former members of the *nomenklatura* that we find some of the least egalitarian gender ideals.

[10] We thank Susan Gal for pointing out this final irony in the patterns we have documented.

Dölling, Irene
 1994   Women's Experience "Above" and "Below." The European Journal of Women's Studies 1(1):29–42.
Ferree, Myra Marx
 1990   Beyond Separate Spheres: Feminism and Family Research. Journal of Marriage and Family 52(4):866–884.
Frey, Mária
 1996   A nők helyzete a munkahelyen és a háztartásban [Women's situation in the workplace and the household]. Összefoglaló a "Közösen a Jövő Mukahelyeiért Alapitvány" támogatásával lebonyolitott felmérés zárótanulmányából. Budapest: Munkaügyi Minisztérium, Kézirat.
Gal, Susan
 1996   Feminism and Civil Society. Replika (Special Issue):74–83.
Kovács, Katalin and Mónika Váradi
 1996   Middle Class and Working Class Women in Rural Hungary. Unpublished manuscript.
Lampland, Martha
 1995   The Object of Labor: Commodification in Socialist Hungary. Chicago: University of Chicago Press.
Őrszigethy, Erzsébet
 1986   Asszonyok férfisorban [Women in men's roles]. Magyarország felfedezése. Budapest: Szépirodalmi Könyvkiadó.
Róna-Tas, Ákos
 1994   The First Shall Be Last? Entrepreneurship and Communist Cadres in the Transition from Socialism. American Journal of Sociology 100(1):40–69.
Rychard, Andrzej
 1996   Beyond Gains and Losses: In Search of "Winning Losers." Social Research 63(2):465–485.
Spulbeck, Susanne
 1996   Anti-Semitism and Fear of the Public Sphere in a Post-Totalitarian Society. *In* Civil Society. C. Hann and E. Dunn, eds. London: EASA Routledge.
Szelényi, Iván
 1995   Menedzser-Kapitalizmus [Manager-capitalism]. Magyar Lettre Internationale 19(Winter):21–29.
Szelényi, Iván and Eric Kostello
 1996   The Market Transition Debate: Toward a Synthesis? American Journal of Sociology 101(4):1082–1096.
Szelényi, Iván with Robert Manchin et al.
 1988   Socialist Entrepreneurs: Embourgeoisement in Rural Hungary. Madison: University of Wisconsin Press.
Utasi, Ágnes with András Gergely and Attila Becskeházi
 1996   Kisvárosi Elit [Small city elites]. Budapest: Politikatudományok Intézete.
Watson, Peggy
 1996   Civil Society and the Politics of Difference in Eastern Europe. *In* Transitions, Environments, Translations: Feminisms in International Politics. Joan Scott, C. Kaplan, and D. Keates, eds. Pp. 21–22. New York: Routledge.

CHAPTER 7

From Informal Labor to Paid Occupations: Marketization from below in Hungarian Women's Work

JÚLIA SZALAI

PRIVATIZATION IS USUALLY REGARDED as the primary means by which command economies are transformed into market-regulated systems. While the transformation of large-scale, socialist industrial enterprises has attracted considerable attention, much less notice has been given to what might be called "marketization from below," that is, the dramatically altered economic and social arrangements being created in post-communist societies as diverse groups adapt to the changed conditions of daily life. In Hungary over the past decade, these changes have affected all aspects of people's lives, including work-related and household economic strategies, deep-rooted values of social relationships, habits of family life, and parents' plans for their children's future.

To better understand the pervasive changes in Hungarian society, as well as the resulting tensions arising therein, it is critically important to identify newly emerging and highly varied labor market options and arrangements. Specifically, it is important to examine the ways in which a changing blend of market forces and state actions have produced different patterns of employment and unemployment for male and female workers. Upon close examination it becomes clear that, in response to economic restructuring, Hungarian women are actively developing a small-scale service sector. Skills and expertise that, by necessity, had been exchanged by women informally and unofficially in the socialist economy are entering the cash nexus as paid occupations. Even so, these work arrangements are unusual, rarely registered, and difficult for statistical surveys to detect. Women often hold regular jobs, and at the same time balance multiple part-time, often short-term, contractual or consulting work in service industries of many kinds. Although the development of small-scale business follows routes and rules different from the more visible privatization of large firms, I argue that this widespread process of "marketization from below" has equally important implications for Hungary's economy and society and for the opportunities available to women in both arenas.

The two principal aims of this chapter are to explore changes in women's position in the post-1989 labor market and to situate controversies associated with these changes in a historical and comparative context. In the first section, I discuss women's present position in the Hungarian labor force. Then, using a range of statistical and qualitative evidence, I piece together a picture of women's current work strategies and the varied forms of their paid labor. The analysis presented in these two sections illustrates that women's strategies, as well as their contribution to the emerging service sector, owe a great deal to their earlier experiences in the flourishing informal economy of late socialism. In those years, the tacitly permitted and temporary withdrawal from compulsory eight hour workdays, facilitated by a diverse set of social entitlements, enabled women to turn an otherwise disadvantageous position in the socialist labor market to their own advantage. Against this background, I will highlight the differential long-term effects of these practices on men and women's employment in the sphere of organized labor today.

In the third section, I examine the consequences of Hungary's changing labor market from a different perspective. Here I argue that the multiplication of a range of job opportunities offers one of the most important means for achieving household security and that women are the major actors in these newly developing work arrangements. Still, not all workers can combine traditional forms of employment with these new sources of livelihood; hence, the current circumstances are producing an increasingly stratified, polarized labor force. I discuss the process by which this bifurcation takes place and note the marked and steadily growing inequalities in daily living conditions.

My second goal in this chapter is to locate the current changes in historical and comparative perspective. The marketization of skills and services that were previously exchanged informally within and between households is hardly unique to post-communist transformation, as the vast literature on the twentieth-century welfare state attests. The same thing happened in Western economies as the service sector expanded following World War II. Many post-war states, by committing themselves to support full employment and expanded public services, created a market for certain skills that facilitated women's entry into the labor force. New jobs in education, health services, and care for children and the elderly were constructed as "women's work," and thus presented employment opportunities specifically for women.

With this framework in mind, I conclude with a brief historical overview of women's post-war employment in Hungary. This is important because, despite similarities in the quantitative measure of women's increased participation in the labor force, the political implications of and socioeconomic motivations for women's employment were markedly different under socialism. The juxtaposition highlights the fact that simply discussing the effects of "state" and "market," according to their broadly perceived functions, is inadequate. It is crucial to also specify their role and function in given periods and societies. In Hungary, where intrusions by an all-encompassing communist state could be quite harsh, compulsory employment had the ironic effect of pushing women's unpaid labor back into the home and linking it to the kinds of informal networks characteristic of small communities. In this "private sphere" women could demand and ensure an acceptable quality of service; this was impossible in the state sphere, where formal criteria rather than sensitivity to actual needs dictated standards of service delivery. Women's withdrawal into their homes and local communities had equally significant political implications. Because the family was the only recognized unit that escaped direct state interference, women's "retreat" constituted the only legitimate way to avoid, or at least mitigate, the state's otherwise permanent control over daily life.

By contrast, it is now the market that "liberates" much of women's informal labor, rendering it legitimate and openly exchanged as paid labor. Again, both narrow economic as well as broader political aspects of transformation are influential. One can argue that different variants of the state—for instance, the communist or welfare state—have differently affected women's participation in the labor force. Likewise, the particular form of marketization is a variable that influences labor force configuration. Despite expectations, marketization in contemporary Hungary is clearly providing women with a wider range of suitable work arrangements than they had before.

However favorable this particular consequence, it is just one side of the ongoing story. The other is the marked differentiation among work opportunities available to women; at one end of the spectrum are well-paid jobs and clearly defined contractual positions, and at the other are a variety of insecure, unprotected, part-time or day-labor jobs. The more advantageous arrangements are concentrated among women who are better educated, better paid, and better off, whereas women who are less educated and lack either skills or family backing are forced to the margins, where they face a higher risk of unemployment and the disastrous long-term threat of social exclusion. Hence, the expansion of women's job opportunities has contributed both to the segmentation of the labor market broadly understood and to the ever-increasing polarization of the social structure.

Where Are the Women?

In contrast to most post-communist countries in the region, open marketization has not been accompanied by deterioration in Hungarian women's job opportunities. At least in terms of employment, it seems that the changes of the past decade have worked more to the detriment of men. Skills that were valued under socialism and found in many male-dominated jobs have been seriously devalued and are often unmarketable in the new environment. For many men whose qualifications embodied security, stability, and prestige under the old regime, marketization has meant ruin for their careers and future prospects. Thousands of men have failed to adapt to the new socioeconomic conditions of post-1989 Hungary (Laky 1997; Sík and Tóth 1997).

The results have been disastrous. Sociographic reports from northern Hungary, once the heart of a now collapsed steel industry, or from once thriving settlements in what today are silent coal mining regions, paint a gloomy picture of impoverished, seriously ill, middle-aged men walking from pub to pub throughout the day. At best, they can hope for casual work in agriculture during the peak summer months; however, even this pays too little to sustain them for the rest of the year. Starvation among the children of these workers is relatively widespread. It is little wonder that many of these children lack even a primary school education—despite the fact that, by law, it is compulsory. At 12 and 13, children leave school to assist in and around the household while their parents are away and to earn money to help cover their family's immediate needs (Lippai 1996; Pető 1997). Between 1985 and 1994, in parts of the country where heavy industry and mining had once been concentrated, mortality rates for men in their forties grew to be twice the national average. Statistics indicate an increased incidence of alcoholism, frequent mental disorders, and the rapid spread of all varieties of respiratory disease (Central Statistical Office [hereafter CSO] 1986, 1995a, b, c; 1996a). There appears to be limited hope that the situation will improve. Annual labor power surveys show that unemployment rates in these regions are more than double the national average. Moreover, the proportion of those who are "permanently unemployed" is steadily increasing. In this same northern region in 1995, 52 percent of the registered unemployed had been on the dole for more than two years; the national average was 38 percent at the time (Laky 1997).

To be sure, large numbers of female jobs have also been hit by economic restructuring. Under socialism, unskilled and semi-skilled industrial labor was heavily feminized in state-run enterprises. With the collapse of socialism, the majority of these jobs have proved superfluous. Nevertheless, women's options seem to be different from men's. Although the workplaces in which women were concentrated under socialism have disappeared faster than others have (Laky 1997), unemployment rates for women have remained consistently below the respective rates for men. Already in 1990, census data had registered a substantial self-reported unemployment rate of 10.3 percent among men, but only 1.7 percent among women (CSO 1992c). While unemployment has increased significantly since then, gendered differences continue to favor women. According to the latest findings of the Household Panel Survey for 1996, the unemployment rate was 14.0 percent among men and only 9.4 percent among women (Sík and Tóth 1997).

In view of the declining opportunities for regular employment, one would expect women to have returned on a massive scale to traditional housekeeping roles. However, the labor power surveys do not confirm such expectations. On the contrary, the number of housewives between the age of 14 and 55 declined from 5 percent in 1989 to 3.8 percent by 1992. Although annual labor power surveys show a distinct increase since then (with figures of 12 and 13 percent for 1995 and 1996, respectively), other studies demonstrate that "housewives" often work for wages in the unregistered "gray" zone of the economy. Taking this into account, the number of full-time housewives appears to be on the decline (CSO 1996b; Laky 1997).

If they are no longer counted among regular employment statistics, yet are neither unemployed nor swelling the ranks of full-time housewives, where, then, are those masses of women who so recently constituted the feminized socialist labor force? As I will show, women have not disappeared from work. In recent years, their presence within the labor force has actually grown stronger. Yet, women's economic performance remains largely unmeasured and underregistered in labor statistics and economic surveys because many of the jobs they perform can neither be classified as "employment" or "entrepreneurship," nor conceptualized in terms of traditional "household duties" or "leisure activities." Moreover, the organizational settings in which most women's labor takes place, as well as the forms of work and relations of cooperation and coordination, remain in a state of flux.

Although women's work often escapes statistical measurement, it would be a mistake to classify it as "illegal." The motives behind it are usually different from those that drive the "black economy." While the latter is built on practices of tax evasion or on semi-criminal activities—made possible, in part, by chaotic legal provisions together with poor government surveillance and control—women's unregistered work is generated by different conditions.

The bulk of women's activities derive from traditions of the informal economy under socialism, which, to a great extent, were based on unpaid labor. Although cash exchange was becoming more common by the end of the socialist period, large segments of the informal economy still functioned according to the principle of eliminating, or at least reducing, the role of money. Participation was regulated by the strict discipline of mutual exchange of labor and favors within family, kin, neighborhood, and occupational networks. Unpaid labor was variously motivated. For example, it was sometimes inspired by the strong drive to modernize one's lifestyle and buying habits or was a way to compensate for artificially low wages and salaries, as well as the limitations created by state prohibition of capital accumulation. Through the exchange of unpaid work, different households, the members of which might have a variety of different skills, could rely on each other for services that were unavailable in the formal economy.

In other cases, unpaid labor functioned as a form of assistance to community-based institutions, or what in other systems would be called "volunteerism." Amid chronic shortages of money and commodities, people were able to offer their labor as a form of charitable donation to churches and religious circles or to support those engaged in politically dangerous underground activities. They might also help in providing childcare, education, or healthcare—areas that were chronically underfinanced, understaffed, and underequipped by the socialist state. Whatever the purpose, all such work took place in a domain that was "unofficial" and thus informal. Neither the legal institutions nor the economic regulations of the socialist system took explicit notice of them, although they were tacitly considered at all levels of decision making.

With the turn toward open marketization, a variety of these previously unpaid, informal activities have entered the world of paid labor. Whether work is performed on a temporary subcontracted basis or through consulting agreements for part-time work or services delivered, these activities are important elements in the expansion, through noninstitutionalized paid labor, of the previously underdeveloped tertiary sector.

The transformation of formerly unpaid work into paid labor is a dynamic feature of marketization from below. Because it is often manifest in second and third jobs, marketization from below contributes not only to transforming informal economic activities into formal ones, but also to a merging of the two. This curious integration of the once separated formal and informal economies is occurring primarily in the service sector in which, to reiterate, women are the principal actors. As previously noted, because women's paid activities are often neither regular nor stable enough to be correctly registered, it is difficult to estimate the actual value of their economic contribution. Yet, by drawing on several indirect measures and the results of numerous studies, it is possible to identify three emerging trends in the labor market: (1) a growing service sector is among the most important changes in Hungary's modernizing economy; (2) women's overrepresentation in this sector has been a catalyst for small-scale marketization from below; and (3) the unconventional forms of women's participation in paid labor is altering women's position and status in post-communist Hungarian society.

RESTRUCTURING, THE SERVICE SECTOR, AND NEW FORMS OF WOMEN'S WORK

Labor market statistics collected since 1989 allow us to make certain generalizations about the effects of restructuring on the Hungarian economy and labor force. However, because data gathered before and after 1989 are not directly comparable, longitudinal changes are more difficult to document.[1] Nevertheless, even rough and aggregate comparisons show two distinct trends.[2] First, there has been a sharp decline in what previously were customary forms of employment, namely, full-time jobs in large, state-run enterprises and organizations. Since 1990, 1.4 million registered workplaces have disappeared. Second, there has been a major shift in the sectoral composition of the labor market. For example, the combined share of employment in industry, construction, and agriculture dropped from 60 percent in 1980 to 40 percent in 1994. At the same time, the service

[1] This is because regular manpower and labor market surveys were reorganized according to entirely new principles in the early 1990s. Since the old categories were more restrictive than the new ones, counting a narrower band of activities as "employment," the scope of the economically active population has been enlarged merely by modifications of measurement. Thus, it might well be the case that the indicators of growth in economic activity are simply statistical artifacts. At any rate, it is now impossible to sort out the relative impact of redefining employment versus genuine restructuring of the labor market.

[2] For the following overview, I made use of the annual manpower balances and the quarterly manpower surveys of the Central Statistics Office for 1992, 1993, 1994, and 1995. These surveys are run on a randomly chosen, nationwide representative household sample. All adult members (ages 15–74) are interviewed about their gainful activities during the week preceding the survey. The sample size is 25,000 households on each occasion (thus, the surveys report the data of circa 50,000 adults). One-sixth of the sample is rotated on each sample selection; thus, each household remains in the sample for five subsequent surveys, providing data for follow-up within a period of fifteen months. To identify key trends in the data, I have also drawn on studies by Laky 1995a, 1995b, 1996, 1997; Tímár 1994; Czakó and Vajda 1994; and Ványai and Viszt 1995.

sector expanded dynamically. The latest manpower surveys indicate the speed of these changes. While the total number of employees in industry, construction, and agriculture dropped from 2 million to 1.6 million between 1993 and 1995, the number of those in services grew from 2.4 to 2.5 million. A breakdown of these figures reveals that the growth was due to the rapid expansion of services that were nonexistent, seriously underdeveloped, or understaffed during the socialist period, including banking, public administration, social security, preventive medicine, welfare assistance, and adult education.

This important sectoral shift largely resulted from women's move out of dying industries into more modern segments of the labor market. Of course, women's increased participation in service work is not an entirely new phenomenon. As indicated by census data from 1970, 1980, and 1990, women constituted the major source of labor for the gradual expansion of healthcare, education, social services, and administration even during the decades of socialism. The gendered character of these industries may be seen from a summary of statistical data. While the total number of those working in healthcare, education, and culture grew by 48 percent between 1970 and 1990, this increase was produced almost exclusively by women: Men's participation grew by 10 percent in these fields, while women's grew by 72 percent. Similarly, over these two decades, the number of those working in financial administration and banking grew by 24 percent, out of which the differential growth rates for women and men were 30 and 5 percent, respectively (CSO, 1992a; for an analytical discussion, see Vági 1985). However, restructuring since 1989 has intensified the gendered character of the service sector. First, women are now strongly represented at all levels in these segments of the labor market (Nagy 1997; Frey 1997). Second, as the opportunities for gainful employment have become more varied, it is primarily women who are taking advantage of them (see below; also Laky 1995b; Frey 1997).

Recent survey data are also suggestive with respect to men's and women's changing occupations and opportunities (CSO 1994c). The expansion of a feminized service sector has made upward occupational mobility a possibility for women en masse, meaning that the economic restructuring of this sector has been more favorable toward women than men. There has also been increasing differentiation among and between women and men. Within the service sector, skilled and highly educated women have profited more than unskilled women, but the latter have benefitted in ways that their male counterparts have not, due to the lack of a similar boom in highly masculinized sectors of the economy. Unskilled and less educated men have fallen more rapidly into long-term unemployment. For example, a comparison of first and current jobs shows that all cohorts of unskilled female workers experienced greater career advancement than unskilled men have. Among women under 30, 16 percent of those who began working in an unskilled industrial job had shifted to the service sector by 1993, while the comparable figure for men was only 7 percent. In agriculture, the tendency is similar: Approximately 6 percent among young female agricultural laborers moved to service work by 1993 compared to a 1 percent relocation rate among men.[3] By the mid-1990s, as a result of both long-term patterns and recent trends, women constituted 50–73 percent of the labor force in the fields of healthcare, education, banking and financial services, catering, real estate, advertising, business consulting, and the rapidly expanding public and social services (CSO 1992a, 1995c, 1996b; see also Hrubos 1994).

In addition, there has been a pronounced shift in workers' use of time at the workplace. To understand the nature of these shifts, it is first necessary to understand the conceptualization of "work" applied in employment statistics. Under socialism, categories of statistical measurement followed from the ideological assumption of compulsory full employment. Hence, labor market surveys only counted compulsory, full-time work registered at a regular workplace as "employment." Other labor activities did not officially exist.[4] Yet, as is well known, broad segments of the labor force were engaged in secondary economic activities after their "compulsory full-time work," or, in many instances, even during their official work time. Some of these activities were unpaid; some were illegal; some were in state-authorized private enterprises such as household agriculture. Moreover, the annual contribution to the GDP from secondary economic activity was manifest through widespread reconstruction projects and newly built dwellings, in the "surprising" surplus of income from agricultural export to both the East and West,[5] or in the less evident, although equally important, improvement in such areas as the quality of healthcare and care for the elderly. Even though it became increasingly difficult to deny the existence of marketable informal work, neither the time spent working in the informal economy nor the steady expansion of work in this sphere appeared as productive labor. Official acceptance (including statistical recognition) of the informal economy remained formally in abeyance.

In 1992, statistical categories of "employment" were replaced by those currently used in international practice. Following recommendations from the International Labor Organization (ILO), "economic activity" and "status in the labor market" began to be measured separately. The very meaning of employment had changed; those who performed paid work for at least one hour in the week preceding the survey were considered "employed." With this change in measurement criteria, those arrangements and forms of work, which by and large had gone unrecognized under socialism, became visible. Practices, which before had seemed to be responses to the failures of socialism, began to be marketized.

---

[3] In showing the relative mobility of unskilled young women compared to their male peers, the other side of the picture is equally important; the rate of those who not only started their working life in unskilled industrial work but were also doing it at the time of the survey was 49 percent among young men, but only 32 percent among young women. Similarly, among young, male, agricultural laborers, 77 percent were still in the same job, while only 48 percent among women were.

[4] There were, however, other types of investigations into people's working behavior and way of life (the most important among them were representative time-budget surveys, conducted regularly by the Central Statistical Office). I draw upon results from these surveys later in this section.

[5] It should be noted that the scope of private agricultural production was different from cooperative production. For example, gardening, raising pigs, and cultivating fruit were all typical of the former, while growing wheat was typical of the latter.

Indeed, marketization has generated a constant increase in the number of jobs performed by individuals in various flexible arrangements. Now that statistical categories reflect work practices with greater accuracy, it is possible to more precisely chart marketization from below and the gender differentiation that shapes it.

Although labor market experts insist that part-time employment has not expanded in Hungary, annual labor power surveys present a different picture. Statistics indicate a steadily growing number of people whose weekly work time, at a registered place of employment, is less than forty hours. Quarterly surveys, conducted in 1992 and 1993 according to ILO conventions, indicate that the number of people who worked fewer hours than their "accustomed" working time rose from 120,000 to 250,000 within one year. Analysis of the data reveals that women in particular reported to work less frequently. From women's responses to questions about the cause of this contraction in their work week, it is clear that neither sickness nor newly introduced measures by their employers accounted for the change. Instead, women reported that the decrease in their work time was a "personal decision."

Other studies clearly indicate that shortened hours at the primary place of employment do not mean an overall decrease in the time devoted to gainful activities. On the contrary, the ratio of those engaged in multiple concurrent jobs has been increasing over the past decade and has been especially strong among women: Between 1986 and 1993, the proportion of those working for a cash return outside of regular employment grew from 4.8 to 9.9 percent among women, while remaining at a level of 8.4 percent among men (Vajda 1996; Kuti 1996).

For many, irregular "excursions" away from regular jobs slowly developed into systematic absences, resulting in a significant reduction of working time at a primary job. The number of people working "regularly shortened weekly working hours" increased from 216,000 to 226,000 within a single year. Furthermore, although there was a decline from 67,000 to 42,000 of those who claimed that they generally work less than forty hours a week because their employer was unable to underwrite contracts for a longer period, there was an increase from 43,000 to 94,000 in the number of those who considered this "shortened" work week to be their "full" working time. The increase in the number of workers who claimed such a reduction in their work week can be attributed to the expansion of female employment with shorter working hours. While the number of men who regularly worked less than forty hours a week fell from 79,000 to 77,000 in the one-year period between the labor power surveys of 1992 and 1993, the number of women increased from 136,000 to 149,000. These developments point to a gradual change in the interpretation of "full-time employment" and also make clear that women are the major agents of this change.

Qualitative studies suggest that there are deliberate strategies behind these figures. In an attempt to adjust to changing economic conditions, women juggle their primary jobs with temporary forays into better paid—although less secure—

areas of the labor market. Using all manner of excuses, they occasionally withdraw from their "first" job to take up short-term contracts or perform day labor for immediate payment. Bargaining for better pay is usually easier and more favorably negotiated in the face-to-face interaction characteristic of small-scale private businesses, one-time contracts, temporary assignments, or other forms of casual work. However, these noninstitutionalized types of gainful work lack job security and protection. By contrast, although fixed employment is often underpaid, it gives women access to a variety of entitlements such as guaranteed social security and free healthcare, as well as continued access to information and social networks. Hence, the safest and most profitable solution for women proves to be a combination of several forms of work with different conditions and types of return; the gradual decline in women's worktime at their primary place of employment has undoubtedly facilitated this (Szalai 1991; Frey 1996; Vajda 1996). It is nonetheless important to note that women's expanded job options do not necessarily yield significantly greater income. The opportunity to combine main and secondary jobs is unevenly distributed among women; moreover, many women pursue such strategies more out of necessity to maintain family living standards than out of choice.

Besides allowing women a greater level of flexibility, reduced working hours also introduced the possibility for women to learn new skills. Women seem particularly eager to take advantage of educational opportunities, and demand for the mushrooming number of training programs in various service and business fields is apparently growing. Interest seems to be greatest among the least educated; a comparison of national time-budget surveys for 1986 and 1993 shows that the average amount of time devoted to learning increased only among persons with no more than an eighth grade education. Moreover, in this realm, women were consistently more active than men. Among men with only elementary schooling, the average time spent in one form or another of adult education grew from 158 to 184 minutes per day; among women, the increase was much sharper, growing from 174 to 293 minutes per day (CSO 1994a; see also Hrubos 1994).

Yet organized training of this kind is not the only or perhaps even the most important source for acquiring the skills needed for new jobs. A life history and occupational career survey conducted in 1996 among a sample of 250 freshly minted social workers points to the significant role played by women's activities in the informal economy (Horváth and Lévai 1996). Some 70 percent of those interviewed were women who had moved from blue-collar work or administrative jobs to recently created community-based institutions of social service provision. When asked when and how they acquired the skills they needed for their new occupations, two-thirds of the women reported that much of their expertise came from a decade-long exchange of personal services in the informal economy.[6] A

---

[6] Informal learning was all the more important because, up until 1985, formal training in social services did not exist. Many women acquired informal "training" during the period of young mother-

series of interviews with both male and female entrepreneurs also showed the marked impact that the knowledge, capital, and personal relations accumulated through the informal economy had on those entering into post-1989 businesses (Czakó and Vajda 1994).

It is also important to ask about the kinds of employment opportunities that, by simultaneously attracting women and reducing labor costs for those who would employ them, are paving the way for women's participation in the labor force. At present, due to the gaps in available statistical data, it may only be said that most semi-institutionalized positions, which have come into being in response to open marketization, did not exist in the formal socialist economy. Activities such as domestic and foreign stock brokerage, financial assistance, preventive medicine, welfare assistance, and adult education and training have emerged to meet new and growing demands. Job opportunities have also been created in church and religious organizations, trade unions, and in the more than 30,000 emerging nongovernmental organizations (NGOs) and other civic groups. Political advising and consulting have also become highly sought after at both the local and national levels.

Post-1989 social structural changes have also given rise to new occupations in the field of welfare provision and regulation; women fill the ranks of those being trained for these jobs. There are now thousands of women who hold onto their primary jobs but work part-time as welfare officers and social workers. Women may also be contracted to provide personal services within the rapidly expanding network of family help centers, shelters and daytime warming rooms for the homeless, clubs for unemployed youths, training and retraining programs, and mobile catering. Moreover, welfare services have recently expanded into the traditional institutions of healthcare and education, thereby increasing job possibilities for those with appropriate qualifications. However, it is important to emphasize that these jobs generally do not come in the form of full-time employment with a single employer. When long-existing healthcare and educational institutions take on recently trained social workers, for example, they may contract informally for services, on a one-time basis, or to licensed entrepreneurs (Horváth and Lévai 1996).

IMPLICATIONS FOR SOCIAL STRATIFICATION

As I argued in the previous section, the strategy of multiplying labor force participation by juggling various configurations of paid work is a widespread phenomenon in contemporary Hungary, and women are the major actors in this process. Taking on multiple jobs represents an attempt to accommodate to or take advantage of the changing structure of production. Employers and enterprises use

---

hood; while on childcare leave, these women would collectively organize neighborhood playhouses, babysitting, catering, or nursing for the sick. Other women gained experience through voluntary work in family help centers or community clubs. Still others mentioned parents' associations as the major context in which they had learned about providing assistance and support to families in crisis.

and benefit from flexible labor as an employment strategy that lowers costs. At the same time, individuals who rely on a multiple job strategy to balance income and security are better able to guard themselves and their families against the unfavorable effects of rapid economic change, such as inflation, the discontinuation or restriction of maternity or sick leave, and even layoffs. But here it is important to recognize that the door is not equally open to all strata of society to engage in such activities. In order to see the marked social stratification produced by differential access to multiple labor force participation, it is necessary to analyze statistical evidence that is differentiated according to household composition rather than gender.

The importance of a multiple job strategy can be gauged by one relatively visible measure: the high incidence of part-time entrepreneurship. Over 400,000 small businesses (amounting to some 10 percent of the economically active population) are run on a part-time basis by people otherwise regularly employed. These part-time enterprises operate mainly in trading, brokerage, counseling, transport, and repair services and make significant financial contributions to household income. As the findings of a 1993 survey demonstrate, 20– 27 percent of monthly earnings for part-time entrepreneurs was derived from informal business activities (Czakó and Vajda 1994).

Indeed, income earned from entrepreneurial and other activities outside of regular employment seems to represent a rising proportion of household budgets. According to the annual household panel survey for 1991 through 1996, revenue from these sources grew from 13.5 to 16.8 percent of the average Hungarian family's monthly income (Sík and Tóth 1997). The changing composition of monthly household budgets further indicates the importance of the multiple job strategy. Data from subsequent family budget surveys suggest that wages from occasional work, ad hoc contracts, casual work, and a wide variety of entrepreneurial activities are, in the aggregate, playing an increasingly important role in people's livelihoods. In 1989, the proportion of earnings derived from (nonagricultural) work pursued in addition to a regular job represented 3.2 percent of a household's average monthly revenue; by 1995, the proportion had grown to 10.1 percent, with approximately two-thirds of it drawn from entrepreneurial activities (CSO 1993a, 1996c). A more detailed breakdown of the data shows that such income plays a very different role in the livelihood of various social groups. Moving up the income scale, the significance increases greatly, in both the absolute sum and its proportion within the total monthly household budget. For households in the lowest income decile, fees and wages from jobs outside established (traditional) workplaces made up only 8.3 percent. For households in the highest income decile, the corresponding figures are the opposite. In this group, earnings derived from temporarily contracted entrepreneurial and other nontraditional jobs made up 16.8 percent of revenues in addition to returns from full-time employment. The sharp differences in the composition of these budgets may be attributed to the fact that the proportion of unemployed workers is 17.6 percent in the lower income group, compared to only 1.9 percent in the higher income group. Moreover, 18.1 percent of members in the former group are still full-time employees with regular jobs, compared to 54.1 percent in the latter. The 1992 data of the Hungarian Household Panel reflect similar trends. The portion of monthly revenue derived from contracted temporary jobs and casual work was 19.1 percent for private entrepreneurs, 16.6 percent for those in (regular) employment, 13.1 percent for the unemployed, and only 2.9 percent for pensioners (Spéder 1992).

Two parallel tendencies seem to be at work. On the one hand, as I have noted, the contraction of "classical" forms of full-time employment apparently has not narrowed the breadth of gainful activities. On the other hand, access to nontraditional forms of work seems to show signs of significant segmentation. The rapidly expanding arena of part-time, temporary, contractual, and occasional work is accessible mainly to higher-earning and entrepreneurial subgroups in the population. In contrast, it seems that unskilled workers—especially men— who become unemployed are often unable to find work even in unfavorable conditions. The result is that some people have good access to a variety of jobs, while others are excluded from practically all kinds of work and are thus rapidly marginalized. An example of such exclusion can be seen among a group of men in southern Hungary who had been laid off from industrial work. At the time of the survey, all had been unemployed for at least twelve months, meaning that they confronted the expiration of their unemployment benefits. Only 9 percent were able to earn occasional income from casual or day labor jobs, thus making up the loss of their benefits; none of the men had any hope of being reemployed (Horváth et al. 1992). Hence, stratification of the labor market means not only differential access to "better" and "worse," "more secure" and "less secure" work, but often a difference in the chance to engage in *any* form of gainful activity. For the time being, it appears that the emergence of new work arrangements does not serve those who fall out of jobs in the ever contracting sphere of regular, full-time employment. Instead, those groups who already occupy the strongest positions take up most new opportunities and, in so doing, successfully defend themselves against the losses caused by diminishing returns in the "old" state-socialist occupations.

HUNGARIAN WOMEN'S WORK IN HISTORICAL PERSPECTIVE

It is certainly not my aim in this chapter to evaluate the economic significance of women's expanding service work. However, in the wake of post-1989 changes, it may be stated that women's increased economic participation has contributed to bringing the structure of the Hungarian labor market, and of the entire economy, closer to the prevailing patterns of the developed world. As has been shown in the preceding sections, these structural changes have resulted from two simultaneous processes: the erosion and contraction of "traditional" sectors of socialist production and the dynamic unfolding of a wide range of new occupational opportunities. With respect to the factors motivating recent changes in the pattern of women's labor, the latter development seems to be more consequential for the "boom" in the service sector.

But before more closely examining Hungarian women's changing use of time, space, skills, and the means at their disposal, it is useful to review certain basic features of women's situations during the post-Stalinist years that gave rise to the informal economy and to women's participation in it. This historical overview is all the more important because long-term tendencies inform current processes of economic restructuring. Despite the fact that, quantitatively, the sectoral composition of the contemporary Hungarian economy resembles that of the West, the differences between the two systems are still fundamental. A major distinction may be seen in the supply of labor. I show in detail that the "opening" and marketization of Hungarian households, and the resulting conversion of what previously had been informal unpaid activities into paid labor, function today (at least to an extent) as a substitute for those roles that, in the West, were historically filled by a reserve army of "nonworking" women. It is well documented in the extensive sociological and historical literatures that it was mainly the millions of housewives, formerly outside the world of organized labor, whose mobilization facilitated the steady expansion of the service sector beginning at the end of the nineteenth century (for detailed discussions of these historical developments, see Oakley 1974; Pahl 1984; Brenner and Laslett 1989).

In contrast, comparable resources for economic restructuring were not available in Hungary at the start of the service industry's rapid growth. Instead, due to women's compulsory full-time employment under socialism, the significant restructuring of their home-based work provided the basis for expansion. By the 1980s, when the tertiary sector began to expand, former "housewives" had long been absorbed into socialist production. Women's labor was largely tied down in unskilled jobs in heavy industry, construction, and agriculture or in untrained white-collar work in state and enterprise administration.

However, women's involvement in the formal sphere represents only one side of the story of socialist production. There were also tasks that *had* to be performed (e.g., care for children, the sick, and elderly; catering; household accounting) but which production in a command economy failed to resolve adequately. In the decades of late socialism, the structural tension between the population's demands and the unsatisfactory level of provisions to accommodate them was the major factor giving rise to the informal economy. Here, a brief review of well-known phenomena and processes is in order.[7]

By the late 1970s and early 1980s, the adult population was "fully employed," meaning that expanded employment was no longer a hallmark of socialist industrialization. Yet, among the Hungarian labor force, overall worktime continued to increase. As the data series of subsequent time-budget surveys reveals, this increase was owed exclusively to intensified work in the informal economy.[8] The

---

[7] The phenomenon of the Hungarian informal economy has an enormous literature, in Hungary and abroad. Here I am only summarizing and highlighting particular aspects. Throughout the 1980s, Hungarian periodicals such as *Medvetánc*, *Századvég*, and *Magyar Füzetek* dealt extensively with the second economy. For a more recent overview, see the collected writings of Kemény 1991.

[8] In part, the number of hours spent working overtime grew. But more important was the steady rise in the amount of time devoted to activities in family-based production. This rise was made possible by cutting the hours that people spent at their workplaces (CSO 1987).

gradual shift in working time from the formal to the informal economy was achieved by making use of the numerous possibilities for temporary withdrawal from compulsory employment. By taking advantage of these officially sanctioned exit strategies, workers did not openly give up participating in the socialist domain. Such opportunities came in the form of extended or newly introduced entitlements pertaining to social security, for example, paid childcare leave and job protection until the child reached 3 years of age; additional, legally guaranteed paid sick days for mothers of young children (until age 14); liberal access to disability pensions that permitted a limited number of monthly working hours; and various early retirement programs for those working in conditions of "extra danger."

At the time, expanding the scope of centrally distributed benefits also served a number of political and economic interests. The various entitlements helped to harmonize the Communist Party's attempts to maintain strict control over wages with enterprise managers' conflicting drive to raise the earnings of their most productive workers. The expansion of entitlements also helped the Party realize its mammoth program to "catch up with the West by the 1990s through a steady rise in living standards." Moreover, long-sought political gains at last seemed within reach; by allowing people to occasionally withdraw from their workplace, where Party control was experienced most directly, the new entitlements facilitated a tacit compromise between totalitarian rule and the Hungarian people's demands for personal freedom—demands never forgotten since the 1956 revolution. However temporarily, the intensity of the state's daily control over peoples' lives was greatly reduced. Furthermore, people did not lose their positions in the formal sphere, nor did the unspoken acceptance of their temporary exit damage the ideological concept of compulsory employment. In cases of "nondeserving" behavior, entitlements could easily be withdrawn by the authorities; no fora existed for legal protection against such arbitrary decisions. Perhaps the most meaningful advantage to those who made use of these entitlements was that they could suddenly devote time and energy to activities based on their own decisions. Although the income derived from social security benefits remained 30–60 percent below that of average earnings from full-time employment, the financial loss was readily compensated by a better and more purposeful utilization of time, skills, and energy.[9]

Most important for our discussion, it was mainly women who used these benefits to temporarily withdraw from formal employment (CSO 1986–1993). There was a certain logic to their decisions. First, since women's wage levels remained approximately 30 percent below those of men, the relative loss in income suffered as a result of the wage-benefit differential was less for women than it was for men (CSO 1985). Second, temporary exit from full-time work eased the conditions and daily living constraints experienced by the hundreds of thousands of people who performed hazardous, unhealthy work on overused, unpro-

---

[9] For a detailed discussion of this, including the improved division of tasks and duties among various members of family-run businesses, see Szalai and Orosz 1992.

tected industrial assembly lines in an endless sequence of alternating daytime and nighttime shifts; women were certainly overrepresented in this group (CSO 1985). Third, as workers who might otherwise be stuck in unskilled manual or administrative jobs with minimal prospects for upward mobility, withdrawal from employment served as a breakthrough in this hopeless situation; it opened a gateway to learning and to new skills that would later enable occupational change via the informal economy and personal networks. As a consequence, the ratio of those taking part in one or another program for temporary exit was steadily increasing among working women, while it remained at the same level among men. Between 1971 and 1989, the proportion of those temporarily unemployed rose from 7 to over 12 percent among working age women, but remained around 9 percent each year among men (Laky 1996). The time-budget data show the outcome of these changes from another perspective: Between 1977 and 1986, the labor time spent at workplaces of the formal economy decreased by 7 percent, whereas the labor time spent by social security recipients on small-scale agricultural production and on construction or services in the informal economy grew by 80 and 136 percent, respectively (CSO 1987; see also Neményi 1994).[10]

The use of social security benefits to temporarily withdraw from employment enabled numerous families to simultaneously contribute to and benefit from a complex network of informal services. In this way, broad strata of society were able to satisfy—even if it took intensive work to do so—the more or less "Westernized" consumer aspirations that socialist production did not so much as attempt to fulfill. Unmet needs were especially great with respect to infrastructural facilities and a wide range of services that would provide comfort and personal care. Because socialist production was driven by the obsession with quantitative growth at all costs, these areas had been chronically neglected.

It is hardly surprising, therefore, that the major foci of productive activity in the informal economy were services and labor-intensive infrastructural development. All of these activities were performed by family members within the household, harking back to peasant traditions of pre–World War II Hungary. The organization of these informal economic activities was managed through what comparative, international time-budget data series demonstrate to have been a "more balanced" division of labor between the sexes than exists in the West, through longer paid and unpaid working hours, less leisure time, and constant "availability" based on mutual help (Babarczy et al. 1991).

The informal economy grew as a result of both constraints and choices. Constraints arose first the inflexible working hours of state employment, as well as from the ever poorer quality of commodities and the low standard of services within the state-controlled sphere and the constant shortage of access to them. Home-based unpaid work constituted a feasible means to satisfy the population's strong claim for modernization; this was the driving force behind

[10] The corresponding figures for those in full-time employment also indicate some increase, although on a more modest level. Time devoted to informal agricultural production rose by 9 percent over the period in question, while the respective growth rate in construction and other productive services was 40 percent.

"embourgeoisement" during the post-1956 rule of the Communist Party (named after its leader as the "period of Kádárism"). As a result of the popular commitment to such initiatives, the informal economy ensured a level of performance that was closer to the Western standard than to the rival system of state-organized production. It is important to note that these higher standards were achieved through an exceptional diversity of skills and knowledge, which cut across the traditional division of labor between the sexes. Women who had more and better opportunities for temporary withdrawal from the formal workforce became experts in construction or repair services as naturally as in agricultural production, sales, or administration. Similarly, if the rational division of roles required it, men increased their share of care-related activities such as cooking, caring for children (especially school-age children), attending nursery school meetings, or visiting sick relatives. These examples do not imply that traditional patriarchal relations disappeared from the life of Hungarian families. Nevertheless, flexibility and purposeful adaptation to changing conditions were high priorities in the face of constant pressure and the desire to improve the quality of life. This high degree of adaptability was the secret source of the surprisingly high performance of the informal economy.

The outstanding productivity associated with the informal sphere applied to the modernization of housing, to the infrastructure, and to a whole series of personal services—particularly in the realms of child rearing and caring for the sick. Several studies convincingly demonstrate the differences between performance of the formal and informal spheres of production. A survey of young school children found that those who attended school after years spent at home with their mother performed significantly better in subjects based on creativity, fantasy, and independent thinking than those who attended school after three to four years of institutional care where, as a rule, rigorous supervision and basic shelter substituted for education and caring (Vekerdy 1984). The higher standards of care provided in the informal sphere were also demonstrated in reports about the effectiveness of home-based medical care or about the rates of full recovery for psychiatric patients attending community-based self-help groups compared with those in long-term hospital care within the state-run system (Levendel 1987).

Intensified work in the informal economy resulted in a significant transformation of the consumption patterns of Hungarian households. Beginning in the 1970s and for the ensuing ten to fifteen years of relative prosperity, there was a substantial increase in the time and money spent on construction. These investments served functions of production and consumption alike: They contributed to the expansion of available space for service work in individual apartments and also made daily living more comfortable and more modern. Home building became a mass movement, clearly driven by Western norms of comfort and taste. Out of the 980,000 apartments built between 1971 and 1989, more than 70 percent were constructed exclusively by families on the basis of the large work-exchange system of the informal economy (see Kenedi 1981). Census figures are revealing with regard to the remarkable increase in housing standards achieved through informal production. Within a single decade, the average floor space of apartments increased by 17 percent, from 59 square meters in 1980 to 69 square meters in 1990. In 1980, 51 percent of apartments had at least some conveniences; by 1990, this had grown to 73 percent. The proportion of third, fourth, or additional rooms increased from 24 percent in 1980 to 40 percent ten years later (see Farkas and Vajda 1992 for a detailed discussion).

Apart from meeting the obvious need for shelter, the spatial expansion and modernization of households facilitated a variety of uses. Time-budget data indicate the marked increase in childcare provision, teaching, nursing, administration, and organizational services that women on temporary leave from employment (usually on maternity leave) began to offer in their modernized homes for others in the community. The influence of Western-style aspirations was also manifest in the proliferation of privately built holiday homes. These new holiday homes made it possible for many to spend leisure time in a manner previously restricted to the privileged strata. Furthermore, such second homes could easily be transformed from "dead capital" into business resources providing, for example, seasonal catering services or lodging.

The rapid spread of household appliances, electronic devices, personal computers, and automobiles in Hungary is another indicator of the mass transformation in consumption patterns and lifestyles, the direct and indirect effects of which have been equally important. Not only did people acquire new possessions, but with them, new knowledge and skills.[11] This transformation of consumption patterns and skills occurred in Hungary with a "universalization" similar to that described in the scholarly literature on post-war economic development in the West (Oakley 1974; Pahl 1984; Brenner and Laslett 1989). Census data and household surveys clearly show the narrowing of the traditional rural-urban gap and of the differences between the various occupational strata with respect to the standard of housing, the quality of communal infrastructure, and the level of household comforts.

Together with the narrowing of differences in material consumption, there was also a convergence in cultural habits, including fashionable ways to spend leisure time, preferred holiday activities, tourist destinations, and forms of entertainment (CSO 1987, 1992a, 1993a). In all of these ways—the patterns of everyday life, taste, habits, and aspirations—Hungarian society in the 1970s and 1980s began to resemble the West in one important aspect: Through expansion of the informal economy, a broad "consumer middle class" arose that largely shared Western norms of modernity.

Despite these similarities, there were nonetheless deeply rooted differences that generally stemmed from the divergent roles played by "state," "work," and

---

[11] The most eloquent example of this, perhaps, is the rapid development of information technology now taking place in Hungary, the basis for which was clearly created by the movement of private imports in the 1980s. Not only did this establish a modern infrastructure for personal computer networks, thus encouraging the small business fever of the 1990s, it also expanded women's expertise in the now fashionable occupations of program organizing, accounting, tax consultancy, administration, book and magazine publishing, and printing.

"home" in Western capitalist and East European state socialist societies. Whereas the post-war Western state generally played a key role in incorporating women's unpaid home-based services into paid female labor in an expanding tertiary sector, in Hungary, the socialist state's policy of compulsory full employment forced unpaid female labor back into the home.[12] The rigid economic policy of industrialization failed to keep up with the modernization of consumer needs in society. Thus, services provided (mainly) by women were channeled toward the informal economy and therefore centered on the household and the intracommunity exchange of unpaid labor. In this respect, the most important novelty of the post-1989 economy has been the "melting" of constraints on marketizing labor and services; the rapid mobilization of previously dead capital has become a major vehicle of marketization from below and, as such, has been a principal factor behind the transformation from a command to a market-based economy.

Thus, there has been an impressive and efficient transformation of resources, which formerly were used exclusively to satisfy personal and family needs, into productive capital: Apartments—or parts of them—are "home" to a variety of consumer and personal services; holiday homes serve as bed and breakfasts; telephones are now tools for brokers and salesmen; personal computers are used to administer small businesses; washing machines are the capital for small cleaning businesses; and well-equipped kitchens are used for catering services.

This heightened entrepreneurial activity is not, however, occurring in any customary sense of regular or even part-time employment. As I have argued, new jobs are not evenly distributed among a growing number of employees, but rather, those already employed are engaged in multiple forms of labor. Teachers do cleaning after school hours, university lecturers add to the family income with sales work or nightwatches, healthcare workers become taxi drivers in the evenings, journalists do bookkeeping and brokerage on weekends, office workers organize catering services. Because women have accumulated knowledge and skills in many of these areas, they are the ones primarily entering these paid services. Thus, as the state continues to withdraw from both production and all-embracing welfare policies, a market is being created for services that women formerly provided, through their unpaid labor, in the informal socialist economy. This trajectory is in sharp contrast to the Western state's role in broadening women's opportunities for gainful work.

CONCLUSIONS: THE ROLE OF MARKETS AND STATES IN WOMEN'S WORK

In post-1989 Hungary, expansion of the service sector is taking place largely without new investments. The majority of new jobs, having emerged through the marketization of women's skills and expertise, are still home-based and, therefore, do not include social security benefits. To be sure, women are not a

---

[12] For a detailed discussion of the post-war Western economies, see Esping-Andersen 1990; for an overview of the departures between East and West, see Vági 1985.

strong presence at the top end of the newly expanding, lucrative, large-scale services such as banking and stock brokering; rather, they are heavily represented in small-scale services at the lower echelons. Among the buyers of these services are former state enterprises and public institutions, which, having broken into smaller constituent units, require far more in the way of services than they did before. Each newly established small company, for example, requires bookkeeping, administration, cleaning, and delivery services. An increased demand for services in the form of part-time labor or casual work (usually performed by women) has also grown among a very prosperous upper stratum of private households. And new service-related job opportunities have emerged in the greatly expanded civil segment of local governments and NGOs.

However, the transformation of the service sector from informal to wage labor has taken its toll on the consumer middle class of the late socialist years. In post-1989 Hungary, even in the recent years of sharp economic decline, those who have access to multiple job opportunities have been able to substantially improve their living conditions. The less fortunate have had to abandon their former aspirations, sell their valuable goods, move out of the apartments that once represented their steady advancement, and confront a future in which their days slowly end in poverty. Increasing poverty and the need to "manage" and "control" it reflect the transformation of Hungarian society into a more highly differentiated class society and, ironically, have given rise to occupational opportunities for women who enjoy better educational and living conditions.

There is a rapidly increasing need for what are considered to be traditional domains of female expertise, especially care-giving and assistance for the poor. Although the professionalization of social work is still at an early stage, there are clear signs of upward social mobility for women entering the institutional sphere of care provision (Horváth and Lévai 1996). To be sure, budgetary struggles over the distribution of scarce state funds impede the process. Nevertheless, it may be said that marketization and privatization contribute importantly to the sharp differentiation of society-wide social relations. Thus, the success of women aspiring to middle-class positions in the expanding spheres of social services and community-level public administration is largely dependent on the failure of an ever increasing number of poor to adapt to living conditions in Hungary today.

Clearly, these developments resemble the patterns that earlier prevailed in Western economies. In both cases, women's wage labor increased dramatically after World War II, and women are concentrated at the small-scale or lower ends of the service sector. But, as I have tried to show, Hungarian women reached this position by a very different route, have markedly different forms of engaging in gainful activities today, and attach different values to *home* and *work*. These differences suggest that, when looking at the expansion of women's paid labor, we need to distinguish between different kinds of *states* and *markets* and the roles that each has played in the historical formation of women's work.

In most of Western Europe, the expanding welfare state was an important economic actor, drawing women into social service and clerical work after World

War II. In the process, many previously home-based activities, especially care for the young, the sick, and the elderly, were transferred from household to wage work in the world of socially organized labor. The welfare state thus contributed not only to women's employment, but also to their independence and autonomy from family and household, which is represented by paid work in the "public" realm.

In Hungary, the post-war state was of a very different kind, as was its role vis-à-vis women. True, women's entry into the world of paid employment paralleled similar developments of the period. However, due to the Party-state's policy of compulsory employment, their entry was largely an outcome of harsh enforcement. Both employment policy and its focus on heavy industry were driven by the dictates of totalitarian rule and quantitative economic growth at all cost. Thus, not only were socialist workplaces experienced as politically oppressive, being the long arms of the Communist Party, but broad strata of women also had sound economic reasons to question the rationale behind their compulsory employment, since it required them to fill the lowest ranks of state enterprises. At the same time, the socialist economy could not satisfactorily provide for consumer demand, which eventually was met by tacitly allowing the growth of a home-based, informal economy. When possibilities for work in the informal economy arose, women took advantage of the opportunities in ever increasing numbers. The Party-state thus created the circumstances for women's temporary withdrawal from the labor force and for the use of their "liberated" time to develop a service sector in the unofficial, informal economy. While employment at socialist workplaces was for many women a source of oppression and deprivation, labor in the private sphere was perceived as the basis for self-determination and independence—at least from the state. In contrast to women in Western Europe, many Hungarian women, during the socialist period, found the household to be the site of increasing autonomy and substantial economic contribution.

Thus, in Hungary, it was not the state that provided women with a sense of economic sovereignty, and it is even less so today. As women's skills and expertise are marketized, that is, turned into sources of cash income, into paid occupations with public recognition, it is the market that becomes the midwife for women's current, indeed *second*, entry into the world of paid work in the post-war period. This conversion is one of the driving forces of marketization from below, and it is the rapid contraction of state involvement in employment and production that created the socioeconomic space for it.

But if we had to distinguish among different types of states in order to understand women's employment in Hungary, we also have to distinguish types of labor markets. Expansion of the service sector (both public and private) in much of Western Europe involved the creation of new places of employment. Service jobs were sometimes part-time and were often low-paying and low-skilled "junk jobs." Still, they were permanent and had legal protections. In contemporary Hungary, on the other hand, many of the jobs available to women in the new market economy are occasional, one-time, cash-payment, or otherwise irregular. Paradoxically, the multiple job strategy that served as a protection against the socialist state is now, with little alteration, a protection against the excesses of a market economy. Yet, despite the access to higher income that such irregular jobs provide, they do not give security or legal protection. They thereby threaten to make the women who take them second-class workers. Furthermore, because these jobs are not distributed among a growing number of employees, the current pattern of marketization is contributing to increasing bifurcation, even income polarization, of the population. Those with jobs have the networks and skills to get more jobs. Those without, especially in the sharply contracting industrial sector, drop into dead-end unemployment and poverty. It is hard to avoid the conclusion that the current pattern of marketization from below, in conjunction with the continuing withdrawal of the state from both production and welfare, is contributing not only to the recommodification of women's work within one stratum, but also to the increasing segmentation and economic polarization of Hungarian society as a whole.

BIBLIOGRAPHY

Babarczy, Ágnes with István Harcsa and Hannu Paakönnen
    1991   Time Use Trends in Finland and Hungary. Helsinki: Central Statistical Office of Finland.
Brenner, Johanna and Barbara Laslett
    1989   Gender and Social Reproduction: Historical Perspectives. Annual Review of Sociology 15:381–404.
Central Statistics Office (CSO)
    1985   Foglalkoztatottság és kereseti arányok: 1982, 1983, 1984 [Employment and Earnings: 1982, 1983, 1984]. Budapest: KSH.
    1986   Demográfiai Évkönyv 1985 [Demographic Yearbook 1985]. Budapest: KSH.
    1987   Időmérleg: 1977 és 1986 tavasza [Time-Budget: Spring 1977 and 1986]. Budapest: KSH.
    1992a   1990 Évi Népszámlálás 3 kötet [1990 Census, Vol. 3]. Budapest: KSH.
    1992b   A negyedévenkénti lakossági munkaerő-felmérés adatai [Quarterly Manpower Survey]. Budapest: KSH.
    1992c   A nemzetgazdaság munkaerőmérlege 1992, január 1 [Annual Manpower Balance]. Budapest: KSH.
    1993a   Családi költségvetés 1989, 1991 [Family Budget 1989, 1991]. Budapest: KSH.
    1993b   A negyedévenkénti lakossági munkaerő-felmérés adatai [Quarterly Manpower Survey]. Budapest: KSH.
    1993c   A nemzetgazdaság munkaerőmérlege 1992, január 1 [Annual Manpower Balance]. Budapest: KSH.
    1994a   A magyar társadalom életmódjának változásai I: A társadalmi idő felhasználása [Changes in the Way of Life of Hungarian Society I: The Use of Time]. Budapest: KSH.
    1994b   A negyedévenkénti lakossági munkaerő-felmérés adatai [Quarterly Manpower Survey]. Budapest: KSH.
    1994c   A nemzetgazdaság munkaerőmérlege 1992, január 1 [Annual Manpower Balance]. Budapest: KSH.
    1995a   Demográfiai Évkönyv 1994 [Demographic Yearbook 1994]. Budapest: KSH.

1995b   A negyedévenkénti lakossági munkaerő-felmérés adatai [Quarterly Manpower Survey]. Budapest: KSH.

1995c   A nemzetgazdaság munkaerőmérlege 1992, január 1 [Annual Manpower Balance]. Budapest: KSH.

1996a   Statisztikai Évkönyv 1995 [Statistical Yearbook 1995]. Budapest: KSH.

1996b   A nemzetgazdaság munkaerőmérlege 1992, január 1 [Annual Manpower Balance]. Budapest: KSH.

1996c   Családi költségvetés 1995 [Family Budget 1995]. Budapest: KSH.

Czakó, Ágnes and Ágnes Vajda
1994   Kis-és középvállalkozók [Small and Medium Entrepreneurs]. Budapest: Magyar Vállalkozásfejlesztési Alapítvány.

Esping-Anderson, Gøsta
1990   The Three Worlds of Welfare Capitalism. Cambridge, MA: Polity Press.

Farkas, E. János and Ágnes Vajda
1992   Housing. In Social Report 1990. R. Andorka with T. Kolosi and Gy. Vukovich, eds. Pp. 91–113. Budapest: TÁRKI.

Frey, Mária
1996   A nők helyzete a munkahelyen és a háztartásban [Women's Situation in the Workplace and in the Household]. In Foglalkoztatás, jövedelmi viszonyok, munkakörülmények [Employment, Income, Working Conditions]. F. Munkácsy, ed. Pp. 11–89. Budapest: Struktúra-Munkaügy Kiadó.

1997   Nők a munkaerőpiacon [Women in the Labor Market]. In Szerepváltozások: Jelentés a nők helyzetéről, 1997 [Changing Roles: Report on the Situation of Women, 1997]. Katalin Lévai and István György Tóth, eds. Pp. 13–34. Budapest: TÁRKI-Munkaügyi Minisztérium.

Horváth, Ágota and Katalin Lévai
1996   Szociális munkások és szociális ügyintézők: egy foglalkozási csoport leírása [Social Workers and Assistants: Description of an Occupational Group]. Budapest: Aktív Társadalom Alapítvány.

Horváth, Ágota with Katalin Pik and Katalin Tardos
1992   Szociálpolitikai rendszerváltás [Systemic Change in Social Policy]. Budapest: Max Weber Alapítvány-MTA Szociológiai Intézet.

Hrubos, Ildikó
1994   A férfiak és nők iskolai végzettsége és szakképzettsége [Men's and Women's Levels of Schooling and Qualification]. In Férfiuralom [Male Domination]. M. Hadas, ed. Pp. 196–209. Budapest: Replika Kör.

Kemény, István
1991   Közelről s távolból. Válogatott tanulmányok [From Close Up and from a Distance: Collected Writings]. Budapest: Gondolat.

Kenedi, János
1981   Do It Yourself: Hungary's Hidden Economy. London: Pluto Press.

Kuti, Éva
1996   Az önkéntes munka terjedelme és irányai [The Magnitude and the Direction of Voluntary Work]. Unpublished manuscript.

Laky, Teréz
1995a   A munkaerőpiac keresletét és kínálatát alakító folyamatok [Main Trends in Labor Demand and Supply]. Budapest: Munkaügyi Kutatóintézet.

1995b   A magángazdaság kialakulása és a foglalkoztatottság [The Formation of the Private Economy and Its Impact on Employment]. Közgazdasági Szemle 7–8:687–707.

1996   A munkaerőpiac keresletét és kínálatát alakító folyamatok [Main Trends in
        Labor Demand and Supply]. Budapest: Munkaügyi Kutatóintézet.
1997   A munkaerőpiac keresletét és kínálatát alakító folyamatok [Main Trends in
        Labor Demand and Supply]. Budapest: Munkaügyi Kutatóintézet.
Levendel, László
1987   Az alkoholbetegek gyógykezelése és gondozása [Cure and Care for Alcoholics].
        Budapest: Akadémiai Kiadó.
Lippai, Sándor
1996   Itt laktunk, a hatoson [Here We Lived, on Row 6]. *In* Az elmesélt idő [Narrated
        Times]. Ágota Horváth, ed. Pp. 225–255. Budapest: Max Weber Alapítvány-
        MTA Szociológiai Intézet, Kávé Kiadó.
Nagy, Beáta
1997   Karrier női módra [Careers in Female Style]. *In* Szerepváltozások: Jelentés a
        nők helyzetéről, 1997 [Changing Roles: Report on the Situation of Women,
        1997]. Katalin Lévai and István György Tóth, ed. Pp. 35–52. Budapest:
        TÁRKI-Munkaügyi Minisztérium.
Neményi, Mária
1994   Miért nincs Magyarországon nőmozgalom? [Why Is There No Feminist Move-
        ment in Hungary?]. *In* Férfiuralom [Male Domination]. M. Hadas, ed. Pp.
        235–246. Budapest: Replika Kör.
Oakley, Ann
1974   The Sociology of Housework. Bath: Martin Robertson.
Pahl, R. E.
1984   Divisions of Labour. Oxford: Basil Blackwell.
Pető, András
1997   Ránk van írva a C betû ["C" is Stamped on Us]. Heti Világgazdaság
        52–53:45–47.
Sík, Endre and István György Tóth
1997   Az ajtók záródnak?! [Do the Doors Close?!]. *In* MHP Műhelytanulmányok
        8. Endre Sík and István György Tóth, eds. Budapest: TÁRKI-BKE Szocio-
        lógia Tanszék.
Spéder, Zsolt
1992   Az egyének és háztartások munkaszférában való részvétele [Participation of
        Individuals and Households in Work]. *In* MHP Műhelytanulmányok 1. Endre
        Sík and István György Tóth, eds. Budapest: TÁRKI-BKE Szociológia Tanszék.
Szalai, Júlia
1991   Some Aspects of the Changing Situation of Women in Hungary. SIGNS
        17(1):152–171.
Szalai, Júlia and Éva Orosz
1992   Social Policy in Hungary. *In* The New Eastern Europe. B. Deacon et al., eds.
        Pp. 144–167. London: Sage.
Timár, János
1994   A foglalkoztatás és a munkanélküliség sajátosságai a posztszocialista országok-
        ban [Characteristics of Employment and Unemployment in Post-Socialist
        Countries]. Közgazdasági Szemle 7–8:633–647.
Vági, Gábor
1985   Az otthoni munka és a szolgáltatások kapcsolata—fejlődési tendenciák [The
        Relationship between Housework and Services: Trends of Development]. *In*
        Nők és férfiak: hiedelmek és tények [Women and Men: Beliefs and Facts].
        Katalin Koncz, ed. Pp. 213–238. Budapest: MNOT-Kossuth Kiadó.

Vajda, Ágnes
    1996   Munkavégzés a szervezett munkaerőpiacon kívül az 1980–90-es években [Work
            Outside the Organized Labor Market in the 1980s and 1990s]. Unpub-
            lished manuscript.
Ványai, Judit and Erzsébet Viszt
    1995   A szolgáltatások növekvő szerepe [The Growing Role of the Services]. Közgaz-
            dasági Szemle 7–8:777–787.
Vekerdy, Lászlo
    1984   Óvodák [Kindergartens]. Valóság 11:28–41.

CHAPTER 8

Women's Sexuality and Reproductive Behavior in Post-Ceaușescu Romania: A Psychological Approach

ADRIANA BĂBAN

THE COLLAPSE OF THE Ceaușescu regime brought to worldwide attention the dramatic consequences of that regime's highly politicized and repressive reproductive policies. State control of women's bodies led to the common practice of using illegal abortion to regulate fertility and resulted in a high maternal death rate, an infant AIDS epidemic, the overcrowding of orphanages with abandoned children, and, after the revolution of 1989, international trafficking in babies through adoption (see Kligman 1992, 1998). The cynical folly of the regime's reproductive policies—instituted, in part, for nationalist purposes—becomes apparent when understood in terms of the dire conditions of everyday life, especially during the 1980s. The regime bestowed upon its citizens chronic shortages of basic living necessities, including heat, electricity, hot water, medicine, and medical supplies. As one member of Les Medicins du Monde remarked in 1990, "Kafka is nothing compared to Romania" (cited in Kligman 1991:152).

The Ceaușescu regime's pro-natalist policies affected all adult citizens and, in particular, those over the age of 25. So pervasive was its intrusion into the intimate lives and privacy of Romania's citizens that the first post-Ceaușescu government, on the very day that it assumed power, revoked all prohibitions against abortion and contraception. This political act represented the "legal liberation" of male and female sexuality, both of which had been significantly, if differentially, influenced by the Ceaușescu policies. Have women and men similarly experienced the legal liberation of sexuality and reproduction? Under Ceaușescu, women's sexual and reproductive behavior, in particular, was explicitly misappropriated for political purposes. In this chapter, I focus on the legacies of these harsh reproductive policies, especially with respect to the intimate lives of women. In part, my goal is to explore, from a social-psychological perspective, women's attitudes and beliefs about sexuality and reproduction. I also discuss the effects of the current societal transition in Romania on reproductive decisions and practices.

To locate the discussion of sexuality and reproduction in sociopolitical and economic context, I first examine gender relations in Romania and review the reproductive policies of the Ceaușescu regime and their consequences then and now. In the following two sections, I present the results of my research regarding beliefs and attitudes about (1) reproduction and (2) sexuality and the body. The extended project, which relied on both qualitative and quantitative methods, included in-depth individual and semi-structured group interviews of women representing different ages and socioeconomic, marital, and professional statuses; analysis of statistical data and surveys; and analysis of mass media treatment of gender, sexuality, and reproductive issues.

GENDER AND REPRODUCTIVE RELATIONS: CONTINUITY AND CHANGE

Before World War II, Romania was largely an agrarian society with a strong peasant culture. Traditional patriarchal values defined gender roles and relations that endured throughout the socialist era and, to an extent, into the present (Kligman 1988; Hausleitner 1993). In the socialist period, ideological doctrine formally promoted women's equality, which was to be achieved by abolishing private property and providing productive employment for women. In part, these changes were meant to bring women into the public sphere and to secure their economic independence. But, as elsewhere in the Soviet Bloc, "women's emancipation" was undermined by the organization of everyday life during the communist period. Despite an egalitarian rhetoric, the paternalist nature of communist rule reinforced patriarchal attitudes and practices. The paternalist state's "benevolence" fostered dependency among its citizens, thus reproducing and extending the more customary dependency relations of the patriarchal family (see Harsanyi 1993; Verdery 1994; Kligman 1998).

All socialist states instituted pro-natalist policies as a means to ensure reproduction of the labor force; however, under Ceauşescu, the maximization of women's reproductive capacities became the political objective of legislation. In consequence, the double burden of productive work and housework, which itself precluded gender equality, was transformed into a triple burden for Romanian women who, by force of law, were expected to reproduce to meet the demographic "needs" of the state. Besides the conditions of scarcity mentioned earlier, women and their families had to contend with low wages, inadequate childcare facilities (both qualitatively and quantitatively), the absence of modern time-saving household devices and public services, and increasing poverty.

Romania has long been an extreme case in the field of population studies. During the entire period of communist rule, Romania's demographic and related abortion policies were overdetermined by ideological interests. Access to abortion changed as policies shifted from liberalization to strict interdiction, with each trend strongly influencing women's behavior and attitudes toward sexuality, reproduction, and their bodies. For purposes of this study, a cursory review of the shifts in reproductive legislation is in order.[1]

---

[1] For a comprehensive analysis of reproductive politics in Ceauşescu's Romania, see Kligman 1998.

The newly installed communist government banned abortion in 1948, allegedly to facilitate women's entry into the labor force. Rural overpopulation and migration from rural to urban areas provided human resources to meet the demands of heavy industrialization. Declining birthrates had not yet become a focus of governmental policy. In 1957, following the Soviet Union's lead, abortion on request was again legalized in Romania, seemingly out of concern for women's health. At that time, Romania's law was the most liberal in Europe (David and McIntyre 1981). Throughout the ensuing decade, abortion was widely available at low cost. Abortion quickly acquired social legitimacy and became a primary method of birth control. The government did not promote contraceptive education; most couples practiced coitus interruptus or equally inefficient methods. Combined, these factors each contributed to what has been characterized as Romania's "abortion tradition" (David 1992). By 1965, official statistics indicated that for every delivery there were four abortions, the highest rate reported by any country up to that time (Berelson 1979). The birthrate had declined from 22.6 live births per 1,000 women in 1957 to 14.6 per 1,000 by 1965.

In that year, Nicolae Ceauşescu, who succeeded the deceased Gheorghe Gheorghiu-Dej as Secretary General of the Communist Party, decreed population growth to be a state imperative. Ceauşescu's pro-natalist campaign began in 1966 and was vigorously pursued throughout the remaining twenty-three years of his increasingly dictatorial rule—that is, until his overthrow in December 1989. Thus, in October 1966, with no prior warning, legal abortion was restricted to women over 45 and women who had delivered and had in their care four or more children. "Therapeutic abortion" was allowed only if pregnancy endangered a woman's life and no other means could be taken, if congenital risks were high, or if the pregnancy had resulted from rape. At the same time, contraceptive imports were halted, thus making them available only on the black market at exorbitant prices. Medical studies "publicized" the negative effects of modern (Western) contraceptives. State-coordinated surveillance was used to uncover and destroy clandestine abortion networks. Abortion providers (medical and non-medical) were subject to imprisonment, as were women found to have had an illegal abortion—whether it was performed by one of these providers or self-induced.

Over the years, new restrictive measures were added to the anti-abortion legislation. Ceauşescu proclaimed that "the fetus is the socialist property of the whole society." Monthly taxes were imposed on childless couples and unmarried persons over the age of 25, regardless of sex. By the 1980s, having four children was no longer sufficient grounds to petition for an abortion; to qualify, a woman had to have five living children under the age of 18. At state enterprises, compulsory gynecological exams were performed annually—or more often, if possible—to test the reproductive health of the nation's women. The actual intent of these exams was to determine if a woman of childbearing age was pregnant. Once a pregnancy was officially registered, a woman was unable to rid herself of it without considerable risk. The entire repressive apparatus of the state—the militia, secret police, police informers, and prosecutors—was enlisted to enforce this pro-natalist policy. Because hospitals were state enterprises, medical procedures and personnel were watched closely to ensure compliance with the law. Physicians' salaries were also linked to the monthly fulfillment of state-dictated birth quotas.[2]

All the while, official rhetoric celebrated the virtues of motherhood and "the family," despite the increasing degradation of daily life.[3] The state "resolved" the widening discrepancy between the political representation of life under socialism and its citizens' experience thereof through the manipulation and falsification of statistics and "scientific" reports.[4] The consequences of the Ceauşescu regime's irresponsible demographic politics, which ideologized reproduction in terms of the "nation's future vitality," have been well documented by others (see, for example, Kligman 1991, 1992, 1994, 1998; Johnson et al. 1993, 1995; Băban and David 1994). Not least among the regime's "achievements" was the highest recorded infant and maternal mortality rates in Europe (David 1990).

As noted earlier, one of the first official acts of the post-Ceauşescu provisional government was to abolish the restrictive reproductive legislation. It authorized the production, sale, and import of modern contraceptives and legalized first-trimester abortion, on request, if performed by an obstetrician-gynecologist in a hospital, clinic, or private office. For women with no income or with four or more children, the procedure would be free. Otherwise, women must pay for the procedure, the cost of which has increased several times since December 1989. Recently, the price was raised to approximately 12 percent of an average monthly salary. (As of March 1997, an abortion cost 60,000 lei; the average salary was 507,000 lei.) These increases were designed to discourage women from using abortion as a method of fertility control. There is justified concern, however, that the rising cost of abortion compels poor women to undergo this procedure in unsafe conditions; the tragic consequences of this are only too well known in Romania. Indeed, Romania's maternal mortality rate still ranks among the highest in Europe, despite a marked decline since 1989 (see Appendix 8.1).

Since 1990, a number of international organizations have worked collaboratively with the Romanian Ministry of Health and also with newly formed nongovernmental organizations (NGOs)—such as the Society for Education in Contraception and Sexuality (SECS)—to promote immediate and long-term reproductive health goals. With technical and financial assistance, a family planning network has been established and a national strategy designed. The aim is not only to decrease the number of abortions but also to make reproductive health a basic component of the primary health care system and to educate the population about contraception.

[2] For a more detailed discussion of the effects of pro-natalist policies on physicians and medical practice, see, for example, Hord et al. 1991; Kligman 1998.

[3] Mirroring Stalin's practices, the state recognized "heroes of socialist labor." Mothers who had given birth to ten or more children were awarded "heroine medals"; see Kligman 1992, 1998.

[4] For example, to lower infant mortality statistics, it has been reported that newborns were often not registered until up to fifteen days after birth to determine their viability. In many cases, negotiations between doctor and mother resulted in a declaration of stillbirth.

The challenges are manifold. There still is a wide gap between the objectives of family planning programs and effective implementation by families and sexually active persons. The number of family planning clinics is inadequate. As of December 1996, there were some 230 government-sponsored clinics nationwide;[5] SECS had established eleven clinics. The absence of clinics in rural areas, and the poor access to affordable contraceptives, deprives women of modern contraceptive options. (For some, the black market remains an important if unreliable source.) Despite international media attention to Romania's reproductive health problems, Romania's own media (potentially an effective educational tool) has demonstrated a limited interest in these issues, focusing instead on the country's political and economic problems.[6] Until the November 1996 elections, the Ministry of Health also failed to make reproductive health a priority item. At present, budgetary constraints still pose major barriers to effective health policies.

Although Romania's women have been formally "liberated" from Ceauşescu's oppressive reproductive legislation, many feel that their daily burdens not only remain, but have been aggravated by the conditions of life in today's Romania. As elsewhere, the transition has fostered a renewed public emphasis on traditional values, family life, and religion, leading to what has been called "retraditionaliza- tion" (Kligman 1994). Once again, a woman's place is said to be in the home, where she is responsible for housework and for taking care of her husband and children. After years of exhausting six-day work weeks, plus the occasional Sunday given to "patriotic work," many women are eager to return to the role of home- maker. Yet the rising cost of living demands that women join the wage labor force. According to a 1994 national survey, 87 percent of women worked to earn an income; only 10 percent cited career fulfilment as their reason for working (România/PNUD 1994). Moreover, most of the women interviewed for this project noted that economic circumstances have forced them to take second and third jobs, often on the black market.

Despite anti-discrimination clauses in the new constitution, guarantees of equal opportunity and equal pay for equal work are only rhetorical. Job advertise- ments explicitly seek young, attractive, unmarried, and childless women, thereby excluding potentially qualified employees on the basis of age, physical appearance, marital, and maternal criteria. Unemployment, unknown during the socialist period, also presents new hardships, especially for women. Although women represent 45 percent of the total number of employed persons, their unemploy- ment rate is 2.5 times higher than that of men; for women under 25, the unemployment rate is three times higher. Women are laid off more frequently than men, and they enter the labor force at a lower level, even if their qualifications are higher and their abilities equal (Earle 1994). Moreover, women are not recognized as legitimate "heads of the family," although this patriarchal bias flies

[5] Whether or not government-sponsored clinics are fully functioning is unknown.

[6] Some claim that it is because of international attention to these issues that the Romanian media eschews involvement. It is a poor excuse.

in the face of daily life. Women and children have been abandoned by husbands and fathers, too many of whom are alcoholics.[7] In such cases, women are necessarily the sole provider in the family. Adding to this new set of obstacles, many private firms, and even the older state enterprises, prefer not to hire women because of the costs associated with maternity leave and the burden caused by budgetary cuts in social welfare programs.

Other forms of gender discrimination also contribute to women's marginalization. On average, a woman's salary is 11 percent lower than a man's (România 1995; see also Verdeş 1995). Women continue to be employed in occupations poorly suited to their educational level or in low-paying, "feminized" fields such as education, culture, healthcare, and the service sector. Even in these areas, senior positions are held by men.[8] Women's participation in national politics has dropped sharply from 34 percent in 1987 to 5 percent in 1996, meaning that decisions affecting women's lives are made almost exclusively by men.[9] It is customarily believed that men are more suited to political activity than are women, although no data exist to confirm what appears to be a widely held prejudice.[10] Also, many women believe that improvement in their own circumstances will depend upon improvement in Romania's economy. That women's lives may be affected by the gendering of the transition, which differentially shapes male and female opportunities, is not—thus far—a consideration.[11] In this respect, Romanian women themselves are accomplices in perpetuating gender stereotypes that often are disadvantageous to their interests.

BELIEFS AND ATTITUDES ABOUT REPRODUCTION

In post-Ceauşescu Romania, the liberalization of abortion improved women's health, as well as their reproductive rights, by making safe abortion once again available. Maternal deaths from abortion declined dramatically from 545 in 1989 to 181 in 1990, and to 59 in 1995 (see Appendix 8.1). Nonetheless, health planners determined to create an effective family planning program and to transform an "abortion tradition" into a "contraceptive tradition" face a difficult challenge: They must formulate and implement strategies in a climate of economic and political instability (as noted earlier), and they must overcome both healthcare

[7] Abandonment does not necessarily entail divorce. Some fathers simply disappear in order to avoid support payments. However, reliable data on this phenomenon are not available.

[8] In education, women make up 72 percent of primary and secondary school teachers, whereas they constitute only 29 percent of university faculty (România 1993).

[9] In part, women's low involvement in politics today may be a response to their coerced and manipulated participation during the communist era.

[10] Editors' note: This belief is held elsewhere as well. See the chapter by Fuszara in this volume.

[11] It is no wonder that feminist discourse is treated ironically by both men and women. Although unfavorable economic and social measures are open to contestation, the very political discourse that completely ignores women's concerns is not. Feminism is considered to be a Western "trifle" that has no place in Romania. For many women, "feminism" is viewed pejoratively, equated with lack of femininity and selfishness.

providers' and the public's resistance to modern contraception. To better understand the difficulties involved in changing family planning practices and addressing women's reproductive health,[12] I will discuss women's attitudes and beliefs
about methods of fertility regulation, especially abortion (see Appendix 8.2 for
a discussion of interview and study group methods).

Horrors of the Past

Despite the increasingly coercive anti-abortion politics of the Ceauşescu regime,
abortion—obtained by whatever means possible—remained the primary method
for regulating fertility.[13] One woman, an unskilled worker who was married and
a mother of three, recalled:

> As a woman, I had to learn not only to cook, to sew, and to raise my children, but
> also how to induce an abortion. I tried everything that I was told to do. It did not
> matter how much I suffered. I always started with hot baths and lifting weights. I used
> to drink yeast; once I got rid of a pregnancy by drinking photochemical substances. I
> swallowed quinine several times and in huge quantities, but I never succeeded to abort
> this way. However, I couldn't hear for a couple of days. I remember that one of my
> neighbors, who worked for a vet, once gave me oxytocin, an injection they used for
> cows in a similar situation, and she told me that I could abort using it. . . . I had no
> one to help me make the injection. So, I tried to learn it myself, and I used a potato
> for it. When I grew more skillful, I did it myself. It's hard to believe what somebody
> can do when she is desperate. Most of the time, I aborted with the uterine sound,
> which I [would] introduce myself. I went with it inside me to my place of work, to
> go shopping, and to do housework until I started to bleed. A couple of times I thought
> I'd die.

Another young woman, an engineering student, reminisced:

> I expected only simple bleeding to occur when I aborted a baby in my bathroom! I
> was scared to death because it was not what I had expected. I did not know what to
> do with the baby. I simply did not think of throwing it away. So I wrapped it in a
> napkin, called my boyfriend, and asked him to bury it somewhere. He was shocked.

Some women managed to find a gynecologist who would perform—illegally,
and in great secrecy—an abortion using curettage. As one chemist, a mother of
two, recounted, "A doctor agreed, through a go-between, to perform an abortion
on condition that I went at night to a house unknown to me with a scarf tied
around my eyes so as not to recognize him later on."
Fear was the most common feature of this clandestine culture of abortion,
and it affected all persons associated with the arrangement and performance of

---

[12] The research methods used to produce the data on which much of this section is based are
discussed in Appendix 8.2. Also, it is beyond the scope of this chapter to address the difficulties
entailed in changing men's attitudes and beliefs about reproductive health and contraceptive methods.

[13] The information in this section is drawn from previous research. See Băban and David 1994;
also Kligman 1998.

an abortion. Women talked bitterly about the lack of dignity associated with illegal abortion and the dreadful conditions under which they were usually performed. They also spoke of overwhelming terror, especially the fear that they might be caught by the police while the procedure was in progress. A married typist, who already had one child, commented, "While I was lying on a kitchen table for the abortion, I thought I heard a knock at the door and a loud shout 'Open up, Police!' I expected to be arrested."

Compounding the danger inherent in these procedures, women were terrified to seek medical assistance if post-abortion complications arose. Sometimes, children witnessed their mother's post-abortion suffering and, despite their evident fright, tried to help. A married, working woman recalled:

> I felt very sick, trembling all over my body. I had terrible pains and fever and I was bleeding. My husband was at work and my children, 3 and 4 years old, fetched me water and helped me change the bed sheets soaked with blood. They were crying as they caressed my head.

Whatever their own trauma, women knew that hospitalization for what was labeled a "spontaneous abortion" required notification of both the police and the prosecutor's office and was followed by an official inquiry. As one respondent noted, "I knew that if I went to a hospital, doctors could not medically assist me until I denounced the person who had done the abortion."

Another kind of fear resulted from the mandatory gynecological examinations to which women workers were subjected. Women were frightened that an over-zealous doctor might discover a pregnancy. One woman reported:

> In our factory, a female Party Secretary drew up lists of women under 45 years of age. She used to threaten us with dismissal if we were not present for the regular gynecological examination. However, if I suspected I was pregnant I did not show up even at the risk of losing my job. We [women] felt as though we were like breeding cattle.

The constant struggle against unwanted pregnancies and the stress associated with clandestine abortions prompted some women to recoil at the thought of their womanhood and femininity. One technician said, "I was the happiest woman in the world when I reached age 45. I realized that from then on I would have access to a legal abortion." Or, as a woman of 34 stated, "I wished I had [reached] menopause and finished with that dreaded monthly fear." Another added, "When I realized how unreliable our methods of contraception were and that I was pregnant again, I often thought I would be better off going for a surgical operation, removing my uterus, ovaries, tubes, everything."

Women spoke of their reproductive experiences as having robbed them of their youth. One said, "It is a great pity that we were tortured and we lost so many years, the best years of our lives! Nobody can ever give us back what we have lost. But what else was there for us to do?!" A mother of two girls expressed similar feelings, "I would be very unhappy if I knew that my two daughters would have to face all those ordeals I and other women experienced. It would be very unfair to them and to all young women."

Legal Abortion: A "Gift" of Democracy

Today, in post-Ceaușescu Romania, many women consider the legalization of abortion to be their "reward" for having endured the suffering and humiliation caused by the regime's draconian pro-natalist policies. "We have suffered enough for several generations. Nobody can possibly realize what we really lived through unless one experiences the same humiliation and violence that we did," said a 48-year-old woman with a university degree. Almost all of the women interviewed applauded the liberalization of abortion. "Today, young women may at least enjoy their lives in a way that we really could not; we don't want them to live the way we did, carrying the calendar and douche in our handbags and being scared every month. Perhaps they will live better lives by having as many children as they want, when they want, and with whom they want to have them," observed a 40-year-old married shopkeeper.

Whereas illegal abortion was considered to have been their harsh fate, many women now view legal abortion as their right. "Abortion is the only good thing that democracy has brought us. Men have gained the right to be involved in politics and business; we have gained the right to abort! What else have we gained with the change to democracy . . . ? Food and things we cannot afford to buy?!" exclaimed a 31-year-old with only a basic education. "If I got rid of a pregnancy several times through abortion when it was illegal, why shouldn't I do the same now that abortion is legal?" asked a married factory worker with two children, in the hospital for her fourth abortion in two years. Indeed, many women expressed their strong will to terminate any unwanted pregnancy, irrespective of the law. "Nobody and nothing could ever stop me from taking the decision not to keep an unwanted pregnancy," a 33-year-old married factory worker stated emphatically. A kindergarten teacher, herself the mother of three, reflected somewhat more circumspectly,

> I know that abortion is not healthy. But if it happens to you, it is important to know that you can do it without the fear of risking your life, as it was before. I couldn't afford, either before or after 1989, to go to the hairdresser's or the manicurist's, or to buy myself something just for pleasure. At least I can now afford to have an abortion without fearing that my children will become orphans.

According to the 1993 Romanian Reproductive Health Survey, at least two-thirds of every segment of the population believes that there should be no restrictions on abortion and that women should have the right to make decisions about their pregnancies, including abortion (Șerbanescu et al. 1995; the survey was conducted among a nationally representative sample). Once abortion was legalized, clinics were literally inundated with patients. In the summer of 1990, doctors claimed they were performing as many as thirty abortions per day. Bucharest's main hospitals each noted that seventy to one hundred abortions were performed daily (Kligman 1992). More than 992,250 legal abortions were recorded in 1990, a number that declined to 585,840 in 1995 when the abortion ratio stood at 2,124 per 1,000 live births (Ministry of Health 1995; see Appendix

8.1). The figures reported by the Ministry of Health must be interpreted with caution, however, particularly in view of the establishment of private medical practice in mid-1991. It is more likely that the national ratio was closer to 3:1; in Bucharest the ratio in 1994 was believed to have been double the national figure, or 6:1 (Şerbanescu et al. 1995). Abortion rates have exceeded the levels reached in the early 1960s.[14]

For the majority of Romanian women, abortion is viewed as a widely available, safe, inexpensive, and socially acceptable method of family planning. Hence, it is not surprising that the number of repeat abortions remains very high. (One report estimated that during the years of the Ceauşescu regime, Romanian women had, on average, at least five abortions by the age of 40; see the *Guardian* 1990, cited in Hord et al. 1991.) In 1992, repeat abortions accounted for 60 percent of all abortions; among these, 13 percent had been preceded by four or more legal abortions. In random street interviews, most of the women who were stopped and asked about family planning listed abortion as their preferred method of fertility control (Hord et al. 1991). They did not know what contraception meant. To be sure, contraceptive education and counseling are sorely lacking in Romania. Yet, besides educating women and men about birth control alternatives, dependable contraceptives must be made available, accessible, and affordable.

The Decision to Abort: A Response to the Conditions of Everyday Life

In the post-Ceauşescu period, the majority of pregnancies have ended in abortion. In 1990, for example, according to data from the National Center for Statistics, there were 314,700 live births and 992,300 abortions. Since 1989, the conditions of everyday life have grown more uncertain and influence decisions regarding marriage and family size. Women and their families must contend with unemployment and inadequate housing, among other things. To this must be added women's fear of losing their job because of a pregnancy.[15] Between 1990 and 1994, the average salary decreased 52 percent compared to that of 1989.[16] In 1994, 90 percent of families with three children and 58 percent of families with two children lived below the poverty line (Zamfir 1995). State-guaranteed benefits to protect women, families, and children have been drastically cut. In 1994, the state budget for children was 23 percent of the amount allocated in 1989; social assistance for mothers with several children reached only 3 percent of its 1989 value. Also, the number of marriages has declined while the divorce rate appears

---

[14] In 1960, there were 2,186 abortions per 1,000 live births; in 1965, there were 3,997 abortions per 1,000 live births. See Appendix 8.1.

[15] In a survey of 2,116 women in 1993, 67 percent responded that housing problems were a primary reason to limit the size of their families; 20 percent cited socioeconomic reasons; 4 percent partner-related reasons; and 4 percent medical reasons. See Şerbanescu et al. 1995.

[16] It must be kept in mind that buying power decreased while inflation increased continuously.

to be rising.[17] As elsewhere in the region, death and morbidity rates have increased, and life expectancy is among the lowest in Europe. (For example, in 1996, the death rate in Romania was 11.6 per 1,000; general life expectancy was 69 years for men and 73.4 years for women; see Ghețau 1994a.) These figures are all indications of the widespread poverty and prohibitive socioeconomic circum- stances that contribute to women's and family's rational choices about having children.

As in the days of the former regime but for different reasons, women today consider it better to abort than to have to abandon a child they cannot support.[18] A 29-year-old shopkeeper queried:

> How come the members of the Parliament, who were given two or three houses, do not have children? Why is it always us who are expected to produce children even though we live in box-like flats, and are just happy that we own them? We are four in our family and we live in two rooms. What should I say to my mother who is living with us, "Well, you have lived enough; we need your bed because we want to have a second child!" A second child would be a luxury we cannot afford.

A married teacher, the mother of two, added:

> I know that the newspapers report that few women have as many abortions as we do. But is there any place in Europe where people live in such hard conditions as in Romania? In fact, we are not really living, but dragging on with our miserable existence day in and day out, from one salary to the next.

Ethical concerns have seldom informed women's abortion decisions. Only a very few women spoke of abortion as killing a baby. Although religion has reemerged in public life, its influence upon women's reproductive choices appears to be insignificant. The church's limited impact is not surprising after forty-five years of communism. "I never thought I did anything wrong when aborting. I did what I should have done for my family. I was confident God would understand what I was doing and I was not afraid of his curse," commented one housewife. Women believe that abortion offers them a means to protect and secure their already struggling families, and, regardless of any risk to their own health and well-being, they accept abortion as a form of sacrifice and devotion. A 26-year- old married woman, who worked as a factory lab assistant and was scheduled for an abortion at the local clinic, explained:

> It deeply hurts me when we are asked why we don't have any more children. We want another one very much, but how could we raise another when as it is, we live in a one

---

[17] The number of marriages decreased from 9.2 per 1,000 population in 1977 to 7.9 in 1993, while the divorce rate has increased from 1.19 per 1,000 population in 1977 to 1.60 in 1991 (România/ PNUD 1994).

[18] Referring to the Ceaușescu regime, Kligman observed, "It is a luxury to invoke moral arguments about abortion when daily life made it ethically questionable to raise more children" (Kligman 1991:154).

room apartment and my husband is unemployed? I only earn enough to put food on the table. It is easy to have an abortion when you do not want another child. But when you want one yet know that having it will jeopardize the living conditions of the child you already have, then, well, you have an abortion. You can imagine what I feel, but I know that there is no other solution for the moment, perhaps in the future.

In view of the precarious conditions of daily life in Romania, family size is likely to remain small for the foreseeable future, which means, at most, one or two children per family. Barring an effective campaign to educate people about contraception, abortion is likely to remain the most widespread method of regulating fertility.

Reproductive and Contraceptive Responsibility

Although many women choose to have only one or two children, they nonetheless consider their major role to be maternal. "The woman's role is first and foremost to be a mother and wife. It is useless to fulfill yourself as a professional; if you are unaccomplished as a mother and wife you are not accomplished as a woman," said a university-educated woman, then age 46. "To reject having children is a refusal of nature's laws. Only a selfish woman can say that she doesn't want children. Perhaps she is unable to have children and, out of shame, she says she doesn't want them," asserted a married teacher who was the mother of one child. Women consider children to be the main achievement of their lives and a source of protection for their marriages. "In many cases men leave the women with whom they don't have any children for those willing to have a child. It is through children that men are tied to their wives and homes," commented a 28-year-old high school graduate.

Abortion, like birth, is viewed by most women as a purely female experience. "Birth and abortion have always been hard experiences for women just like the army has always been for men," said a 37-year-old female engineer. Two women from the discussion groups talked bitterly about how they associated reproductive problems with personal failure. They felt their self-images took a beating and that they experienced more anxiety about their sexuality. Many women said that men were uninterested in their concerns about birth control, whether that meant abortion or contraception. "I always talked to my husband about abortion. But what could he do to help me?! When it comes down to it I am risking my health, it is I who is going to suffer, so I bear my grief alone. A man is not ever able to truly understand what a woman feels in those moments," an office clerk pointed out. Other women reported that unwanted pregnancies became a source of quarrels with their husbands. "All you know is how to make children," one husband reproached his wife. Another woman remembered, "When I told my husband I was pregnant he replied that it was impossible for it to be his child, because he had always protected me from pregnancy" (Băban and David 1996).

Yet many women, particularly those who are middle-aged, expressed reluctance to use modern methods of contraception. "It is not convenient for me to take contraceptive pills or to use an IUD. After having taken risks twice with illegal abortion, do I also have to face the risk of cancer resulting from the pill?" queried a married office clerk, age 39.[19] "But," she continued, "it would be easier and more pleasant for men if women use contraceptives."

Apart from the fear of side effects, women mentioned their partner's resistance as a major factor in their decision not to use contraception. "My husband doesn't allow me to have an IUD inserted because he said that we have managed by ourselves until now, and so we will in the future," said a high school educated mother of three who had already had three illegal and five legal abortions. Middle-aged men are considered less cooperative in trying to prevent unwanted pregnancies. "Condoms diminish the pleasure," "withdrawal causes nervousness," "vasectomy is an 'attack' on manliness," or "God made men to make love in a natural way!" were but some of the opinions expressed by women's husbands, opinions that reveal the persistence of basic patriarchal attitudes among men.

Data from the 1993 Romanian Reproductive Health Survey (Şerbanescu et al. 1995) shows that, among women of childbearing age living with a partner, only 57 percent use contraception; of these, only 14 percent use modern methods, while 43 percent rely on traditional methods. When respondents were asked about their most recent pregnancy, 34 percent said that it was planned; 12 percent said it was untimely, and 51 percent reported that it was unwanted. Educational level was not strongly correlated with family planning practices. Despite their strong desire to prevent unwanted pregnancies, four out of five women did not want to change their (traditional) method of birth control. Reasons for this were varied and generally reflected misinformation regarding contraception. Many women believe that modern contraceptives are harmful and might increase the risks of cancer, liver, and heart disease or cause them to gain weight, grow body hair, or suffer from heightened anxiety.

Following years of propaganda, such misconceptions are shared by healthcare professionals, who remain reluctant to accept and promote modern methods.[20] This is due primarily to lack of training in family planning and limited access to updated medical literature, but also to the fact that it is more lucrative to perform an abortion than to dispense contraceptives or counsel women about their use (Johnson et al. 1992:7).[21] It should be noted that contraceptives are costly and are not covered by health insurance. Many women, especially those who are unemployed or have several children, cannot afford them. In the current context of economic instability, an occasional abortion is cheaper.

---

[19] The death rate from cervical cancer is thought to be the highest in Europe and is three times the European average. One reason may be that 69.1 percent of women in Romania have never had cervical screening. See Şerbanescu et al. 1995.

[20] One-fourth of the women surveyed who use traditional methods of fertility control claim that their doctors recommended that they do so. Adolescents also lack knowledge about contraception, as is discussed in the next section.

[21] Seventy-four percent of gynecologists admitted abortion is a source of additional income. They estimated that 60 percent of their clients offer them gifts. They also noted that they can perform four or five abortions in the time it takes to properly counsel women on contraception.

To be sure, there is great need to educate both adolescents and adults about reproductive health and family planning. There is evidence that modern methods of contraception are slowly gaining acceptance. A recent study revealed that, in 1990, less than 1 percent of women of reproductive age used modern contraceptives; by 1992, this number had increased to approximately 5 percent, and by 1993 it had grown to 14 percent (Hopulele-Petri and Graaf 1992). This data confirms that Romania's "abortion tradition" can be transformed through education and an effort to make modern contraceptives available and accessible. It is possible to create a culture of contraception if the will exists to do so.

Demographic Trends and Nationalist Fears

The legacies of the old regime's draconian reproductive policies silenced critical discussion about abortion and population policy in the immediate post-Ceauşescu years. That silence is now coming to an end. Debates about limiting access to abortion have begun to appear in public discourse. Nationalists exhort women's responsibilities to the Romanian nation. In what has become their call to action in the face of "demographic catastrophe," they charge that "to endanger the future of Romanian society by claiming precarious economic conditions is to betray your country. . . . To remain passive and not react against the millions of annual abortions is to consent to your people's extinction" (Echinox 1995).

Articles, the very titles of which reflect fear of "national death" (e.g., "Birth Rate: The Future at Stake," "A Family without Children Is Like a Tree without Fruit," and "Why Do We Slaughter Our Babies?"), have been published in the women's magazines *Doina* and *Femeia moderna* [Modern Woman].[22] In some articles, women who choose not to have children, or to have small families, are indicted as traitors to the nation: "There mustn't be any war in Romania; the Romanian woman brings death to millions of lives," or "What will the population of this country be in ten or fifteen years? Who will defend this country in the future, this country in which we were born and upon which, over the centuries, others have made claims?" (*Doina* 1992).

Anxiety about Romania's demographic future is aggravated by what is presumed to be a higher birthrate among the Roma or Gypsies, Ukrainians, and neo-Protestant believers. In group discussions, women, regardless of their educational level, worried that high fertility among Gypsies might pose a serious problem for the nation's ethnic composition. It is estimated that Gypsies comprise 3.6 percent of the population. Over the decades, their numbers have grown steadily from 64,197 in 1966 (0.3 percent of the total population) to 227,398 in 1977 (1.1 percent), to 401,087 in 1992 (1.8 percent)[23] (Mureşan 1996).

Specialists characterize the present demographic situation as exceptional in peacetime (Ghețau 1994b). Between 1989 and 1995, the birthrate declined from 16.0 to 10.4 live births per 1,000 women, as had the total fertility rate (from

---

[22] These titles are reminiscent of those that filled Ceauşescu-era propaganda. See Kligman 1998.

[23] Estimates vary widely depending on who makes them. The figures are more representative of the issue under discussion than they are reliable with respect to the Gypsy population or number of births.

2.19 children per woman to 1.34). At the same time, both maternal and infant mortality rates remained high in 1995.[24] The emigration rate has also increased. By 1992, with a slowly aging population, Romania had reached, for the first time in this century, a negative population replacement level (Comisia Naţională de Statistică 1995). Despite vivid memories of the previous regime, some demographers have called for a demographic policy with clearly defined options and objectives. One prominent specialist asserted that policymakers' demographic inertia "will have merciless consequences which will be almost impossible to amend" (Trebici 1994).

Once again, nationalists and some demographers blame the declining birthrate on unrestricted access to abortion, even though the number of reported abortions (like the number of births) has decreased.[25] In the absence of effective socioeconomic measures to support families with children, and without a concerted effort to promote modern methods of contraception, abortion will continue to be women's fertility control option of choice to make everyday life liveable.

Beliefs and Attitudes about Sexuality and the Body

In addition to the statistically measurable effects of twenty-three years of Ceauşescu's intrusive reproductive policies, there are other legacies that are both pervasive and more subtle. The previously discussed fear of unwanted pregnancy and illegal abortion placed tremendous burdens on the intimate sexual relations of men and women, aspects of which will be explored in this section.

Communicating about Sexuality

Through a combination of traditional cultural attitudes, communist ideology, and a hypocritical morality, sexuality has not been part of public discourse in Romania. Considered vulgar and associated primarily with procreation, sexuality was at best an "absent presence." Under communist rule, even beauty and desire were proclaimed indecent and harmful. As a result of this puritan-like ethic, the nude body disappeared from paintings, decolletage from TV, and love scenes from movies. Eroticism among married couples was replaced by the glorification of the "woman-mother" and a communist cult of maternity. Adolescent sex education, called "sanitary education," was reduced to instruction in hygiene and physiology. Boys and girls attended separate classes, adding to the confusion and secrecy surrounding sexuality. Youth-oriented publications eschewed the topic of sexuality altogether.

Despite an explosion of pornography in post-Ceauşescu Romania, intimate and open discussion of sexuality remains relatively taboo at home and elsewhere.

---

[24] Regarding maternal mortality rates, in 1989, there were 169.6 maternal deaths per 100,000 live births; in 1995, 47.8 per 100,000. The infant mortality rate in 1989 was 26.9 deaths per 100,000 live births; in 1995, 21.2 per 100,000.

[25] The Orthodox Church has recently added its voice to the limited discussions on abortion, accusing gynecologists who perform abortions of being accomplices to a crime. See Zubaşcu 1997.

Many adolescents do not engage in dialogue with their mothers about sexuality because of embarrassment, prudery, or fear of being punished. "I wouldn't even dream of discussing sexuality with my mother. She behaves as if sexuality does not exist, and as if she only made love once in her life, when I was conceived," noted one 16-year-old girl. "The sexual education that my parents are giving me consists of a survey of prohibitions and threats and checking my handbag for contraceptives," commented another young woman in her last year of high school.

In focus group discussions, some mothers thought sexual education should be taught at school, especially because they themselves do not feel prepared to do it. "I can't provide sex education to my children as I simply don't know how to. I am convinced that today's children already know more than we do," said a school secretary. "I would be happy if I knew that school provides my girls with sex education, because I feel embarrassed to talk openly about such problems," revealed another woman, an accountant. Other women dismissed the need for discussion. "Everybody knows what is taking place between a man and a woman in the bedroom. I don't understand why films [and] magazines so explicitly depict these things. Where is the mystery? What happens to intimacy if everything is openly displayed? There must be some decency for that matter!" said a 43-year-old teacher, herself the mother of one child.

According to data from the 1993 Reproductive Health Survey, 757 young people ages 16–25 affirmed the almost total absence of communication between parents and children on sexual themes. Among the respondents, 36 percent claimed to have obtained information about sexuality from magazines and journals, 24 percent from friends, and 11 percent from books. Among these young people, 59 percent considered themselves to be ignorant or superficially knowledgeable about sexuality (Liiceanu 1994). As an example, one-third of the respondents did not know that a woman can become pregnant from first intercourse (Şerbanescu et al. 1995).

Still, the Ministry of Education hesitates to introduce sex education into the high school curriculum. The belief prevails in Romania, as elsewhere, that talking about sexuality encourages young people to become sexually active. Some NGOs, such as SECS and the Soros Foundation, have initiated programs with pupils and teachers in urban schools; these do not exist, however, in small towns and rural areas.

Premarital Sex

Contemporary adult women were raised with traditional values regarding virginal "purity"; premarital sex was usually thought to be immoral or a sin against God. When these women in turn became mothers, they emphasized to their own daughters the virtue of virginity as the "most valuable gift a woman can offer to her husband." Some women view the loss of virginity as a woman's "loss of honor and innocence." A kindergarten teacher said, "I am aware that virginity is not exactly the source of a happy marriage, but as the mother of two girls, I honestly hope they will offer themselves only to their husbands." A university student, originally from the countryside, noted, "My mother keeps on repeating, you have nothing else but your brains, your diligence and your innocence. Don't spoil the sacrament of your marriage or else you have studied in vain." While less educated young women or those living in rural areas tend to accept their mothers' opinions, university students who participated in the focus groups considered their parents' attitudes outdated. Nonetheless, these same young women acknowledge that their male peers are "liberal in a relationship with a girlfriend, but they become traditional when it comes to marriage."

Parental attitudes regarding premarital sex differ for sons and daughters. On the one hand, "It is necessary and useful for boys because it helps them gain experience so that they won't be entrapped by the first woman they meet." But, as explained by one mother of two girls, "Premarital sex entails some risks for a young woman. She gets deeply involved; the failure of a relationship usually scars her experience for life as a woman, mother, and wife." This form of gendered hypocrisy in parent–daughter relationships is evidenced by the number of parents who request to have their daughters' virginity checked. At the Institute of Legal Medicine in Cluj-Napoca, some 300 requests are recorded annually.

The strength of tradition dictates that women abstain from sex before marriage. Of 1,641 adolescents between the ages of 15 and 19 surveyed in the 1993 Reproductive Health Survey, 84 percent reported that they had never had sexual intercourse. Also, 63 percent in a sample of 4,858 women declared that a woman should be a virgin when she marries, although 22 percent admitted to having had premarital sex. Of these women, one-half grew up in urban areas and 30 percent were university educated. In terms of ethnic background, 21 percent were Romanian, 31 percent Hungarian, and 48 percent Gypsies (see Şerbanescu et al. 1995). The same slight difference in the sexual behavior of Romanian and Hungarian women was also found in other research done in Transylvania[26] (Baican and Pah 1995).

According to the National Reproductive Health Survey, the median age of first intercourse for all Romanian women is 20.2 years—only 2.4 months lower than the median age of marriage (20.4 years). However, when only women ages 20–24 were sampled, there was a six-month difference between the median age of first intercourse and marriage—a fact that may signal a transition away from traditional norms of female sexual behavior.

Sexuality in Marriage

Growing up with misconceptions about sexuality does not prepare women to cope with sexual relations and intimacy. As one woman commented, "Before you married, you were not allowed to do anything. Everything forbidden you had to do after marriage." Moreover, within the context of patriarchal values, gender communication is codified. Partners do not generally talk about their

---

[26] How culture shapes behavior is eloquently seen in the sharp contrast between the percentage of Romanian women who have reported premarital sex (22 percent) compared with women from the Czech Republic (99 percent). See Goldberg et al. 1995.

sexual preferences and pleasures. "There is nothing to say about sex in the daylight. It's something that happens in the bedroom," remarked a 49-year-old office clerk (David and Băban 1996).

The fear that sexual relations fostered among women during the Ceauşescu regime profoundly impaired their intimate lives, about which many of the women interviewed expressed frustration, regret, and sadness. "What a pity! But what else was there for us to do?" The unavailability of reliable contraceptives or legal abortion meant that most couples depended on withdrawal, rhythm, douching, or abstinence. Women lived in terror of unwanted pregnancies. Some recalled their anxiety about sex after an abortion, "After abortion, I thought I could no longer make love. I looked at my husband as an enemy," or "It was enough only to see my husband enter the bedroom and I already felt I was pregnant" (Băban and David 1994). Indeed, some women preferred abstinence to protect themselves against monthly anxiety and unwanted pregnancies. One 33-year-old homemaker said, "Sexual life is less important for me. Sexuality is a male thing. Men initiate it when they need it, and women have to provide it." Some women perceive unwanted pregnancy as women's fate, against which they feel helpless and power-less. Others try to avoid the constant struggle with their bodies and their partners by downplaying their femininity. Today, many women resent their partner's refusal to let them control their own fertility through modern contraception. These women also resent their dependency on their partners.

Household arrangements pose another barrier that makes it difficult for couples to achieve mutually satisfying relationships. Most continue to live in small apart-ments together with one spouse's parents. Many women mentioned lack of adequate housing as a drawback to marriage and sexual relations. Exhaustion from the daily burdens of work and family obligations also affect sexual relations. "What pleasure can I have in making love if, in the evening after a day's work, he tells me, 'I'm going to bed so hurry with the dishes since I am waiting!'?" asked a 33-year-old factory worker. Many married women complained of overwork as a result of days that run from 5:00 A.M. until midnight. Housework is not customarily shared. According to a 1994 national survey (n = 612), 75 percent of those sampled considered cooking to be women's work, 78 percent claimed that women did the washing and ironing, and 50 percent reported that women cleaned the house (România/PNUD 1994).

Regarding sexual intimacy, women tend to agree about the female role: A woman is expected to be sensitive, passive, and faithful and to pretend to enjoy sex. "It is not good to refuse your husband when he wants to make love, because if you do, he may look elsewhere for what you're refusing him. Or he will accuse you of having somebody else as the reason for not wanting sex. For the sake of household harmony, it is better to give in whether you want to or not," said a married engineer of 29. Most women believe that men are more interested in and ready for sex than they are, that men should take the initiative in lovemaking, and that satisfaction of men's sexual pleasures takes precedence over their own. In a survey of 600 women, 54 percent responded that they do not, or very seldom, experience pleasure from their sexual life (Baican and Pah 1995).

At the same time, traditional mores persist, including a double standard that grants men more "sexual rights" than women. "If the stability of my family is not affected, I'm not really bothered by his fooling around; he is free to do it as long as I do not know!" commented a 36-year-old nurse. A married factory worker who has two children added, "Even if they fool around, they always come back home. Men wish to have sex in other 'ways,' and they cannot ask this of their wives." Many women believe in the importance of compromise. "Women who are patient and wise enough to understand that this is man-like will not be alone when they grow old. What do you get otherwise? After he's made you suffer so much, if you get a divorce it's you again who will suffer even more!" said a married 46-year-old physicist. A teacher, 40 years old and also married, observed, "Nature has made the woman monogamous while man is polygamous. This can be seen in language as well. A man with many sexual experiences is called a philanderer, a euphemistic word, but for a woman, the denotation [whore] is very nasty." Another married woman, a 53-year-old chemist, explained, "Men are unfaithful because they need permanent confirmation of their maleness. Wooing is routine for them. It is only age that puts a bridle on them. And yet, they keep on trying because they fear old age and they want to be convinced of 'still being good for something.'" A 49-year-old divorced teacher said, "A man who does not sleep with other women becomes impotent after five years." Extramarital sex is sometimes recommended by doctors for treatment of male sexual disorders.

To the extent that sexuality is treated in the contemporary media, it is strongly influenced by stereotypical patriarchal attitudes. In the advice column of women's magazines, women are admonished in moralizing tones to ignore their husband's infidelities because the alternatives are worse: If she loses him, it will be almost impossible for her to manage alone. A wife who won't respond to her husband's erotic fantasies is told that it is necessary for her to satisfy her husband's desires. Women are held responsible for their husbands' behavior and problems. A psychologist responded to a woman who had written about her husband's reticence, "Isn't it the case that you have suffocated him with your greedy appetite and have brought him to this state?" (*Femeia Moderna* 1996).

The Nature of Men

Many women think not only that men's sexuality is different from their own, but also that men and women are fundamentally different. Especially because of the fear associated with pregnancy during the Ceauşescu regime, girls were taught by their mothers to fear boys, who were often represented as an "enemy," with different goals and interests (Băban and David 1994). Among the warnings that daughters received from their mothers were, "Keep away from boys; they are shrewd and try to cheat girls" and "Boys can ruin your future reputation."

Ambivalent and even hostile views about the opposite sex are widespread among women. A young university student exclaimed, "Man is not another gender. He is another species!" A divorced 40-year-old factory worker noted,

"From my experience I can tell you that man is a ferocious animal who, after having taken your vitality, destroys your life as well." A married factory worker, age 47, added, "It is enough to utter the word 'man' and you've already said everything. All men are the same. But they are a necessary evil; as the proverb says—it is hard to live with evil but it is even harder without it." Another factory worker elaborated, "Good or bad as he is, I have a husband of my own and wherever I go I am a married woman and not a single or a divorced one." Some women believe that duplicity helps to keep the balance in a marriage. "You must never tell a man what you really think about him. You must flatter a man and then you'll get what you want from him," said a 26-year-old engineer. In domestic life, men are considered to be helpless persons, no matter how important the decisions they make at their jobs. As a married economist and mother of two pointed out, "You cannot trust men to take care of the children or of the house because they are not able to take care of themselves; if you do not change their shirts, they wear them dirty and people blame you instead."

Signs of change have nonetheless begun to appear. Discussions with teenagers and university students indicate that today's young women do not agree with traditional gender roles. Young men, however, hope to preserve relations between the sexes as they are.

The Social Status of Marriage

From the results of group discussions, it is clear that many women consider marriage and maternity as the source of meaning for their lives. What some social psychologists refer to as "the partnership model" is not accepted because it is thought to jeopardize a woman's reputation. Celibacy results from a man's rejection rather than a woman's choice. According to those interviewed, a divorced woman is considered to be vulnerable because she no longer enjoys married status. As one divorced 31-year-old technician commented, "As a divorced woman you are judged, condemned, and pitied." This traditional view is also reflected in the comment of a 42-year-old, "Women get married and give birth to children because that's the way they are." The cult of marriage and motherhood explains why 21 percent of women marry before the age of 19, the highest percentage in Europe; the mean age for marriage is 22 for women and 25 for men (see Neder 1994).

It seems to be paradoxical that so many women highly value marriage and maternity yet consistently report low marital satisfaction. The mentality of a traditional woman who must compromise or sacrifice herself was vividly described by a female factory worker: "Once you've accepted to bear the yoke, you have to pull it." Women will tolerate alcoholism and adultery, for instance, as long as their husband provides for the family. One worker, married with three children, said, "It is better for your husband to be a womanizer, as my husband is, than an alcoholic." A kindergarten teacher, age 41, said, "I married to stay married and not to divorce. Why should I leave him? What's not good for me will be good enough for someone else. Family and children are everything to me and I can put up with a lot for their sake. I don't want to be judged later by my own children because I left them without a father. What good did women's emancipation do in Western countries? It only brought about divorces and abandoned, unhappy children."[27]

Women's opinions about marriage and their role in it are reflected in and shaped by the images published in women's magazines. Generally, a woman is supposed to be responsible, tolerant, and strong, able to shoulder the burden of her marriage. A psychologist once "counseled" a woman for having confronted her adulterous husband, who subsequently left her, "A more diplomatic and patient behavior could have prevented separation. If you had forgiven him, he would have understood where there is more need for him" (*Femeia Moderna* 1996). Titles such as "The Price of Success" underscore that a woman's happiness depends on having a man. Practical advice is offered about "How to Keep your Husband" or "How to Catch a Man." The "Ten Commandments of the Perfect Woman" teach a woman to adapt to her husband's tastes. When all else fails, women are instructed to rely on the imaginary and are given tips in articles such as "Methods for Seeing Life in Rosy Colors."

But, for many women, life is anything but rosy. Not only are their lives shaped by a patriarchal ethos, which defines violence against women as a husband's right and a woman's due, but they also suffer the consequences of violence perpetrated by the former regime. The socialist state used violence as a tool of repression, and whether it was physical or psychological, Romanians learned that violence is a tool to get what you want. Not surprisingly, domestic violence is common; men and women alike understand it to be a part of private life. A married technician explained, "As a woman you must get used to the evil and to the good because this is woman's fate."

Domestic violence seems to be a means of conflict resolution whenever male authority is not respected. A woman engineer, routinely battered by her husband, declared, "My intellectual superiority is matched by my husband's physical superiority." A woman's refusal to fulfill her wifely duties in the kitchen or in the bedroom may also provoke a "frustrated" husband to violence. Some women accept sex by force, hoping to avoid an escalation of conflict. One factory worker confessed, "If I refuse him, he becomes more violent and he may attack the children as well; if I consent, he falls asleep afterwards, and there is peace in the house." Legally, women may complain to the police, yet very few actually do. Some fear renewed aggression from their husbands. Moreover, the police do not generally intervene in cases of domestic violence. Indeed, they often fail to intervene in cases of family homicide, which seem to be on the rise.

Domestic violence is the principal cause of divorce in Romania. Alcoholism ranks second (Neder 1994), and women blame this as a primary cause of domestic violence. In many cases, petitions for divorce are withdrawn, even after a case has gone to trial. Many women do not feel the law protects them, especially

---

[27] Editors' note: Ironically, abandoned children were among the consequences of Romania's reproductive policies.

when the battering husband is awarded one room in their two- or three-room apartment as part of the settlement. "I want to terminate this nightmare but there is no way to do it short of a miracle!" commented one mother of two, a woman unemployed and resigned to her fate.

There are no hotlines or shelters in Romania, which means that women and children have no place to seek outside help. According to the women interviewed, the only solution for a battered woman and her children is escape to a neighbor's. There are no statistical data about the pervasiveness of domestic violence, yet sociodemographic studies of abused women suggest that such violence is wide-spread among all social groups in Romania (see Minnesota Advocates for Human Rights 1995). Except for occasional media interest in sensationalist aspects of a case, there is general indifference to domestic violence as a topic for public debate.

Body Practices: Use and Abuse

Ceauşescu's reproductive policies subjected Romania's citizens to state violence against their bodies. Women's bodies, in particular, were transformed into instruments in the service of the nation. As a result of pro-natalist policies in general, and of illegal abortions in particular, women were alienated from their own bodies. "I hated my ovaries, my uterus, the whole of my body which harbored potential danger every month," said a married factory worker, 39 years old.

Women's sense of self-sacrifice has fostered an attitude that care of one's body is pointless after marriage, and certainly after childbearing. Attention to one's body was important only to find a partner and build a family. "I used to be beautiful as a young woman but when I started real life I had to forget about beauty. Working hard at home and at the office is now my duty, not putting on cold cream and perfumes," said a married woman of 41 who works as an office clerk. However, husbands themselves often discourage their wives from tending to their appearance. "Getting in shape may be interpreted as looking for a partner," added another office clerk. "Your body must serve you and it must not be celebrated. You only do that when you want to change it into an ornament and that is not my case," commented a 40-year-old married teacher.

Physical and mental exhaustion are mentioned by many women as obstacles to taking care of their own bodies. Indeed, women will see a doctor only if they are seriously ill or after an abortion. It is not customary to maintain either one's appearance or general health. Engaging in sports or other forms of exercise to stay fit seemed preposterous to many working women. "Don't I practice enough sports in my factory and my kitchen?" asked one. "Small indulgences" like buying self-care products (e.g., cosmetics, creams) go hand-in-hand with feelings of guilt. The 40-year-old woman mentioned earlier thinks of herself as old and tired and is resigned to her fate. Another woman said, "The body is the expression of one's soul." A grown woman's energy should be used to help her daughters be attractive to men so that they can end up with a good marriage. "The mirror does not exist for me anymore; my time has gone. . . . It is my daughter's turn now. You can see how men are today; if you look good you will find a well-off husband," pointed out a teacher, age 43.

The fetishized bodies of Western supermodels, which appear in some of the more liberal journals targeted to women, are designed to counterbalance the communist images of sexless women lacking in any female identity. These journals also present the female body as a source of power and financial improvement (Nicolaescu 1996). Pornographic display of the human body, and especially of women's bodies, is considered by many to be "emancipatory," freeing society from the yoke of hypocritical communist sexual mores. Given the absence of sex education, one radio program even suggested that there is educational merit in pornography!

For young, academic women in a society where daily life is a struggle for survival, "looking good" and spending money and time on one's body has come to symbolize being a "winner." In the new Romania, the self-conscious use of one's "beauty" (and body) has become a strategy to acquire a good job and new social identity (Svendsen 1996). But young women also believe that sexual harassment has increased in the new employer–employee relationship.[28] As one woman observed, "To be a secretary today means to offer the most different favors." Out of 600 women interviewed, only 49 percent believed that a woman must not accept sexual advances in exchange for material or professional advantages; 40 percent responded, "I don't know," and 11 percent, "Yes, they can" (Baican and Pah 1995). The law does not protect Romanian women from sexual harassment.

In the face of rising unemployment, some women have quickly learned that their bodies provide a good source of income. "With two clients a night one can earn more than with an average monthly salary," stated one prostitute. Teenagers, women with children, and street children (mostly boys) find clients on street corners, in improvised brothels, in parking lots, in railway stations, or in hotels. Since 1990, there has also been an exodus of Romanian sex workers to Turkey, Germany, Hungary, and other destinations further west. Forced prostitution may be found underneath the facade of agencies offering matrimonial services. However, due to the rapid expansion of the sex trade, police rarely intervene in prostitution-related cases unless some other offense is involved.[29]

There is increasing support from government officials and the public media to legalize prostitution. Legalization is seen as a potentially efficient means to discourage rape, to contain sexually transmitted diseases (STDs, or LUES in Romanian), and to provide men with an institutionalized outlet for their sexual urges. One married woman, a 45-year-old teacher, said, "It will be a way to lower the number of divorces. Whenever a man needs sexual experiences, instead of looking for a lover, he can chose to go to a brothel and he will come home serene afterwards." Another woman expressed a similar opinion, "Legalizing brothels implies, beyond other prophylactic measures, that young people (and not only!) will be able to relieve their sexual energies legally and hygienically." New cases of sexually transmitted diseases have increased threefold from 8.6 per

---

[28] Anecdotal information suggests that women's careers advanced this way during the communist era as well.

[29] Prostitution and the sex trade are highly lucrative; payoffs to police are presumed, although unsubstantiated. This prostitute's comment appears to be typical.

100,000 population in 1987 to 25.6 in 1992. According to Ministry of Health estimates, STDs are on the rise: from 26.5 (per 100,000) in 1993 to 29.1 in 1994, 36 in 1995, and 37 in 1996. In port cities such as Constanța and in Bucharest, approximately 48 of every 100,000 people contract a sexually transmitted disease (Ministry of Health 1995). It is presumed that many infected persons remain unidentified, including adults who are HIV positive or have full-blown AIDS. The true incidence of HIV and AIDS is not known. Unfortunately, the lack of concern about AIDS is widespread. Interviews with prostitutes make clear that they are among those who are uninterested in, yet most likely to be affected by, AIDS. "I have heard about AIDS, but I don't have AIDS. Clients want unprotected sex. And as for me, when I have sex I think about money and not about AIDS," was the response of one of the prostitutes interviewed.[30]

Reports of rape have also increased over the last few years (a 50 percent increase was registered in 1991 compared to 1990). It must be noted, however, that statistics on rape are often unreliable. For example, sociologists consider that the fear and shame of social stigma discourage many women from reporting that they have been raped. And, as elsewhere, it is usually the victim's morality, so-called "provocative behavior," and appearance that are interrogated. Like so many issues in Romania associated with the body and sexuality, rape remains shrouded in silence. Public discussion is necessary, as is a change in the law. The punishment for rape is evidently too lenient; many rapists are recidivists.

The legacies of the Ceaușescu era will endure for many years to come. The social atomization frequently referred to in the literature about socialist states is more than rhetorical flourish. It is not just society that must be reconstituted; an individual's body must be respected as the embodiment of an integrated self.

CONCLUSION

The Ceaușescu regime's repressive pro-natalist policies were not effective. To the contrary, the failure to provide modern contraceptives and the banning of abortion proved to be sinister political decisions that worked against the nation and its citizens. By denying women the right and means to control their fertility, the state produced the highest maternal and infant mortality rates in Europe, not to mention a generation of unwanted children. And despite the positive changes in reproductive health and family planning that have occurred since 1989—notably the liberalization of abortion—women remain deeply affected by a living memory of traumas that they associate with sexuality and illegal abortion.

For Romanian women, the fall of the communist regime liberated their bodies from the coercion of an autocratic state and returned to them control over their fertility and, indeed, their lives. Within this context, they believed that access to legal abortion was an essential freedom made possible by the new democracy. Now legal, abortion remains the preferred method of fertility control. Yet abor-

---

[30] See Kligman 1996 on prostitution and the sex trade in Central and East Europe.

tion also presents potential dangers to women's health. Having gained control over their bodies, women must now assume responsibility for their own health and well-being. In Romania, too many women conflate "legal abortion" with "democracy" and democratic practice. However, as Kligman has cautioned, democracy entails not only the legal protection of this right, but also protection from its abuse (Kligman 1991:155). In view of the conditions of daily life as well as the general beliefs and attitudes about sexuality and reproduction discussed in this chapter, Romania's "abortion tradition" will endure unless contraceptive education and practice are instituted among the population in ways already noted. The negative legacies of distrust, suspicion, and lack of cooperation—which still prevail—do not make this task any easier for educators, health providers, policy makers, or sexually active citizens.

Current economic uncertainty, combined with the patriarchal organization of gender relations (exacerbated by years of rule by a paternalist state), make it difficult to translate newly gained legal rights into equal opportunities and responsibilities for men and women alike. This study has made clear that women today juggle two identities: At work, women are expected to act according to male-defined norms of competitive behavior; at home, women are expected to be obedient, loving, and self-sacrificing, always ready and willing to serve the needs of others.

As Gal has argued, "women's experiences of the economic and political changes are different from those of men; the implications for women's lives are often more damaging" (Gal 1994:254). The marginalization of women and women's issues deprives many women of equality with men not only in the public sphere, but also in the expression of their sexuality and in the exercise of their human right to reproductive health. Women still pay a high price for the gap between discourse and reality. Without attention focused on their basic needs, women and children are vulnerable, and they remain hostage to the indifference of political actors.[31]

To be sure, transforming the damage done by Ceauşescu's rule, on the one hand, and institutionalizing democratic practices, on the other, will require energy, commitment, trial and error, and time. Regarding women's positions in both the private and public spheres, much remains to be done in Romania. Women themselves must be among the main actors in this process. To date, they are not.

BIBLIOGRAPHY

Băban, Adriana and Henry P. David
    1994   Voices of Romanian Women: Perceptions of Sexuality, Reproductive Behavior and Partner Relations During the Ceauşescu Era. Bethesda, MD: Transnational Family Research Institute.

---

[31] Editors' note: This would suggest the need for women to become politically mobilized. See also the chapter by Grunberg in this volume.

1996   Voices of Romanian Women: Perceptions of Sexuality, Reproductive Behavior and Partner Relations during the Ceauşescu Era. *In* Learning about Sexuality: A Practical Beginning. Sonya Zeidenstein and Kirsten Moore, eds. Pp. 19–32. New York: The Population Council.

Baican, Eugen and Iulian Pah
1995   Determinaţii Psiho-sociale ale Natalităţii, Contracepţiei şi Avortului în Municipiul Cluj-Napoca. *In* Asistenţă Sociala ca Activitate de Mediere în Societate. Maria Roth and Livia Popescu, eds. Pp. 164–170. Cluj: University of Cluj-Napoca.

Berelson, Bernard
1979   Romania's 1966 Anti-Abortion Decree: The Demographic Experience of the First Decade. Population Studies 33:209–222.

Comisia Naţională de Statistică
1994   Anuarul Statistic al României [Romanian Statistical Yearbook]. Bucharest: Comisia Naţională de Statistică.
1995   Anuarul Statistic al României [Romanian Statistical Yearbook]. Bucharest: Comisia Naţională de Statistică.

David, Henry P.
1990   Ceauşescu's Psychological Legacy: A Generation of Unwanted Children. Psychology International 2:1–7.
1992   Abortion in Europe, 1920–1991: A Public Health Perspective. Studies in Family Planning 23:1–22.

David, Henry P. and Adriana Băban
1996   Women's Health and Reproductive Rights: Romanian Experience. European Journal of Patient Education and Counseling 28:235–245.

David, Henry P. and Robert J. McIntyre
1981   Reproductive Behavior: Central and Eastern European Experience. New York: Springer.

Earle, John E.
1994   Unemployment and Policies in Romania. Sfera Politicii 13:14–15.

Echinox
1995   Atitudine-Apel. 3(5):2.

Gal, Susan
1994   Gender in the Post-Socialist Transition: The Abortion Debate in Hungary. East European Politics and Societies 8(2):256–287.

Gheţau, Vasile
1994a   De la Prognoză la Politică Demografică. Sociologia Românească 4:549–564.
1994b   Tranziţia şi Impactul său Demografic. Revista de Cercetări Sociale 1:38–42.

Goldberg, H., P. Velebil, Z. Stembera, I. Tomek, and J. Kraus
1995   The Czech Republic Reproductive Health Survey, 1993. Prague: Czech Statistical Office.

Harsanyi, Doina Pasca
1993   Women in Romania. *In* Gender Politics and Post-Communism. Nanette Funk and Magda Mueller, eds. Pp. 39–52. New York: Routledge.

Hausleitner, Mariana
1993   Women in Romania: Before and after the Collapse. *In* Gender Politics and Post-Communism. Nanette Funk and Magda Mueller, eds. pp. 53–61. New York: Routledge.

Hopulele-Petri, I. and P. Graaf
  1992   Current Contraceptive Use in Romania. Planned Parenthood in Europe
          21(2):20–22.
Hord, Charlotte with Henry P. David, France Donnay and Merrill Wolf
  1991   Reproductive Health in Romania: Reversing the Ceauşescu Legacy. Studies
          in Family Planning 22:231–240.
Johnson, Broke R. with Mihai Horga and Laureantia Andronache
  1992a   Knowledge, Experience and Perceptions of Contraception and Abortion in
          Romania. Annual Meeting of the American Public Health Association, Wash-
          ington, DC, 1992.
  1992b   Women's Perspectives on Abortion in Romania. Social Science and Medi-
          cine 42:521–530.
  1993   Contraception and Abortion in Romania. Lancet 341:875–878.
Kligman, Gail
  1988   The Wedding of the Dead: Ritual, Poetics, and Popular Culture in Transylva-
          nia. Berkeley: University of California Press.
  1991   Women and Reproductive Legislation in Romania: Implications for the Transi-
          tion. *In* Dilemmas of Transition in the Soviet Union and Eastern Europe. G.
          Breslauer, ed. Pp. 141–166. Berkeley: University of California Press.
  1992   The Politics of Reproduction in Ceauşescu's Romania: A Case Study in Politi-
          cal Culture. East European Politics and Societies 6(3):364–418.
  1994   The Social Legacy of Communism: Women, Children and the Feminization
          of Poverty. *In* The Social Legacy of Communism. J. R. Millar and Sharon
          Wolchik, eds. Pp. 252–270. Woodrow Wilson Center series. New York: Cam-
          bridge University Press.
  1996   Women and the Negotiation of Identity in Post-Communist Eastern Europe.
          In Identities in Transition: Eastern Europe and Russia after the Collapse of
          Communism. V. Bonnell, ed. Pp. 68–91. Berkeley, CA: International and Area
          Studies, Research Series no. 93.
  1998   The Politics of Duplicity: Controlling Reproduction in Ceauşescu's Romania.
          Berkeley: University of California Press.
Liiceanu, Aurora
  1994   Adolescence in Romania: Developing Future Orientation in a Changing World.
          Bucharest: Society for Education in Contraception and Sexuality.
Ministry of Health
  1995   Official Bulletin. Bucharest: Romanian Ministry of Health.
Minnesota Advocates for Human Rights
  1995   Lifting the Last Curtain: A Report on Domestic Violence in Romania. Minne-
          apolis: Minnesota Advocates for Human Rights.
Mureşan, C.
  1996   L'évolution demographique en Roumanie: tendences passées (1948–1994) et
          Perspectives d'avenir (1995–2030). Population 4–5:813–44.
Neder, Maria
  1994   Women in Post-Communist Romania. *In* Gains and Losses: Women in Transi-
          tion in Eastern and Central Europe. L. C. Barrows and L. Grunberg, eds.
          Pp. 42–51. Bucharest: CEPES-UNESCO, European Network for Women's
          Studies.

Nicolaescu, Mădălina
   1996   The Representation of Female Bodies in Romanian Journals for Women. Canadian Women's Studies 16:32–34.
   1995   Raportul Comitetului Român pentru Conferința Mondială Privind Condiția Femeii. Bucharest.
România/PNUD
   1994   Participarea femeilor la dezvoltare: statistici la zi privind femeile. Buletin Informativ 2:5.
Șerbanescu, Florina with Leo Morris, A. Stănescu and C. Cruceanu
   1995   Romanian Reproductive Health Survey, 1993. Bucharest: Institute for the Care of Mother and Child, in Cooperation with the Romanian Ministry of Health and the Centers for Disease Control, Division of Reproductive Health.
Svendsen, M. N.
   1996   The Post-Communist Body: Beauty and Aerobics in Romania. The Anthropology of East Europe Review 19(1):8–14.
Trebici, Vasile
   1994   Este Necesar o Politică Demografică în România? Revista de Cercetări Sociale 2:47–48.
Verdery, Katherine
   1994   From Parent-State to Family Patriarchs: Gender and Nation in Contemporary Eastern Europe. East European Politics and Societies 8:225–255.
Verdeş, D.
   1995   Egalitatea Între Sexe? Dilema 150 (November 24–30).
Zamfir, Gheorghe
   1995   Social Security Policy. Journal of Social Research 1:156–172.
Zubaşcu, I.
   1997   Întro Pastorală Citită în Toate Bisericile din România: Sfântul Sinod Acuză Ginecologii care fac Avorturi de Complicitate la Crimă. România Liberă (June 7).

APPENDIX 8.1

Birth, Abortion, Maternal and Infant Mortality Rates and Ratios: Romania 1955–1996

	Live Births	Birth Rate	Total Registered Abortions	Abortion Ratio[a]	Total Maternal Deaths	Maternal Mortality Rate[b]	Maternal Deaths From Abortion	Abortion Related Maternal Mortality Rate[a]	% of Maternal Deaths Due to Abortion	Infant Mortality Rate[b]	Total Fertility
1955	442,900	25.6								78.2	3.09
1957[c]	407,800	22.9								80.9	2.73
1960	352,200	19.1	769,800	2,186	298	84.6	96	27.2	32	74.6	2.36
1965	278,400	14.6	1,112,700	3,997	237	85.1	47	16.9	20	44.1	1.91
1966[d]	273,700	14.3	973,400	3,556	235	85.9	64	23.4	27	46.6	1.90
1970	427,000	21.1	292,400	685	497	116.4	315	73.8	63	49.4	2.98
1975	418,200	19.7	359,400	859	516	123.4	385	92.1	75	34.7	2.62
1980	398,900	18.0	413,100	1,036	527	132.1	441	110.6	84	29.3	2.45
1985[e]	358,800	15.8	302,800	844	493	137.4	425	118.4	86	25.6	2.26
1986	376,900	16.5	184,000	488	571	151.5	488	129.5	86	23.2	2.40
1987	382,200	16.7	182,400	476	575	150.0	491	128.1	85	28.9	2.39
1988	380,000	16.5	185,400	488	591	155.5	524	137.9	89	25.4	2.32
1989	369,500	16.0	193,100	523	627	169.6	545	147.4	87	26.9	2.20
1990[f]	314,700	13.6	992,300[g]	3,153	263	83.5	181	57.5	69	26.9	1.83
1991	275,300	11.9	866,800	3,149	183	66.5	114	41.4	62	22.7	1.56
1992	260,400	11.4	691,900	2,657	157	60.3	100	38.4	64	23.3	1.51
1993	250,000	10.9	585,800	2,343	133	53.2	86	34.3	65	23.3	1.44
1994	246,700	10.9	530,200	2,149	149	60.4	94	38.1	63	23.9	1.41
1995	236,640	10.4	502,840	2,124	113	47.8	59	24.9	52	21.2	1.34
1996	231,348	10.2	456,221	1,972	95	41.1	51	22	54	22.3	1.30

Sources: Compiled from annual reports published by the National Center for Statistics (Bucharest: Comisia Naţională de Statistică) and by the Romanian Ministry of Health.

[a] Per 1,000 live births.
[b] Per 100,000 live births
[c] Abortion on request was legalized in September 1957.
[d] Access to abortion was restricted in September 1966.
[e] Access to abortion was further restricted in December 1985.
[f] Abortion was again legalized in December 1989.
[g] Includes legal abortions and women admitted to hospitals for follow-up care or for treatment of complications from spontaneous or illegally induced abortions.

APPENDIX 8.2

METHODOLOGY AND STUDY GROUPS

The data for this study were collected between October 1995 and February 1996. The researcher led eight focus groups and conducted twenty-four in-depth, individual interviews. Women were asked to participate on a voluntary basis, with the aim of discussing their beliefs and attitudes about sexuality, reproductive behavior and policies, gender roles, and other practices related to the body. They were offered 5,000 lei in compensation for their participation. So that subjects would represent the specified criteria of age, education, marital status, occupation, and ethnicity, women were recruited from different social/professional institutions: two schools, one factory, one university, one outpatient clinic, and the Institute of Legal Medicine. In addition, five prostitutes were contacted through the owner of a night club.

Each focus group included 8–12 participants, making up a total of 83; there were two groups in each of the following age categories: 15–19, 20–29, 30–39, and 40 and above. Demographically, the 107 participants can be characterized as follows:

Marital status: 45 unmarried; 49 married, 7 divorced, 4 divorced and remarried, and 2 cohabiting

Number of children: 39 with no children, 31 with one child, 32 with two children, 4 with three children, and 1 with four children

Educational level: 11 had a basic education, 65 had secondary education, and 31 had university degrees

Religious affiliation: 68 were Orthodox Christians, 23 were Greek Catholics, 10 were Protestants, 3 declared other religions, and 3 declared no religion

Ethnicity: 31 were ethnic Hungarians; 76, ethnic Romanians.

Occupation: 22 factory workers, 10 office clerks, 7 technicians, 9 teachers, 4 kindergarten teachers, 4 engineers, 2 chemists, 1 physicist, 1 economist, 1 housekeeper, 1 nurse, 1 janitor, 1 superintendent, 1 migrant laborer, 5 prostitutes, 24 high school students, 12 university students, 1 unemployed

The same semi-structured interview was used in all groups, and the questions reflected the objectives of the study. Some topics received greater emphasis partially in accordance with the age or experience of the participants. Group discussions lasted from two to three hours, depending in part on how talkative the participants were. The topics of the semi-structured interview were:

sex education and knowledge (including AIDS transmission and prevention)
male and female sexuality
reasons for getting or not getting married
the ideal and desired number of children
the concept of family planning and contraception
attitudes on abortion
attitudes about family decision making and role sharing
opinions about women's emancipation and role conflict
opinions about past and present reproductive policies
attitudes toward pornography and prostitution
attitudes toward the body, for example, care versus ignorance and neglect

Individual in-depth interviews focused on women's sexual and reproductive life histories, the quality of partner relationships, and traumatic experiences such as domestic violence and abortion.

Additional information gathered in interviews with prostitutes included:

sociodemographic and educational profiles
family background
age and circumstance of sexual debut
perception of sexuality
decision to become a prostitute
ways of practicing prostitution (alone, inside a network, places, customers, payment, risks)
perception of prostitution
opinions about legalization of prostitution
problems with the police and District Attorney's office
present and future life expectations.

To supplement this data, which were gathered between 1995 and 1996, I have also drawn from fifty women's case histories collected between 1992 and 1993 and used in a study that I undertook with Henry David (see Băban and David 1994, 1996).

PART THREE

Arenas of Political Action:

Struggles for Representation

CHAPTER 9

New Gender Relations in Poland in the 1990s

MAŁGORZATA FUSZARA

> Our demands are far from ideal. They are very modest and moderate. If our requests concerning women's participation in government, civil service, representative bodies, etc. became law, then it would be naive to think that on the basis of rights women could become really equal in the area of administration. Old prejudices, the pursuit of egoistic interests of representatives of the privileged sex, as well as other obstacles, will hamper not only the goal of full equality and equity, but even an approximation of such a situation, especially in the beginning. In practice, rights will be acquired only by fairly few women, only the exceptionally prominent ones, far more brave and prominent than the men with whom they compete for membership in Parliament or for political office. All other women will be pushed aside by men who are less brave, less talented and who have contributed less, even by those whose only merit is the fact that they are men.
> —*Leon Petrażycki,* On the Rights of Women, *1919*

THESE REMARKS, made by a prominent Polish professor of sociology and law, were prescient at the turn of the century and remind us today that the process of transforming gender relations in the public sphere has been long and slow. Petrażycki's words are echoed by many contemporary women who, having reached high positions, note that a woman must be twice as gifted as a man in order to attain the same position. Still, while Petrażycki anticipated that true gender equality would require considerable time to achieve, he did not foresee that the road to equality would meander so much, nor that there would come periods when all prior achievements would be questioned. Yet so it is in East Central Europe today, as women's status is once again being redefined in consequence of economic and political transformation.[1]

The political changes that occurred in 1989 prompted public discussion in Poland about women's status, gender relations, and equal opportunity—the latter constituting part of a broader debate about the extension of rights and opportunities to various persons and groups in post-communist society. Freedom

---

[1] The manner in which women's roles change appears to be similar in many if not all of the region's countries even though in each instance there are context specific distinctive features.

of speech, together with the right to form political parties and nongovernmental organizations (NGOs)—assured for the first time since World War II—facilitated intensive discussions about individual liberty, civil society, and the role of the state, including the extent to which government can, or should, be involved in safeguarding rights and assisting vulnerable groups. These debates and discussions will be decisive for gender relations in Poland and for the professional and political opportunities available to women. Yet women's actual circumstances have not necessarily been central to these debates and discussions.

This chapter will discuss women's political representation and presence in various public arenas in post-communist Poland. Researchers have noted that women in eastern Europe are losing privileges and social benefits, especially those that, under communism, allowed them to combine paid work and childcare.[2] Scholars in the East and West alike are concerned that women are being pushed out of the public sphere and into their homes and that their increasingly "private" roles are being redefined not according to their own interests and ambitions, but in response to the "needs" of their families and others. While these arguments are clearly relevant to women's situation, they are too simplistic by themselves to describe the state of gender relations in contemporary Poland.

The first part of this chapter presents a brief overview of women's position in areas that significantly affect social mobility and opportunity, namely, education and paid professions. These two factors seem to contribute most to women's independence, which in turn appears to be correlated with women's political participation and influence. In Poland, higher education is a necessary condition for political activity, especially for women. While a man can attain high office without holding a university degree, a woman cannot. For example, after the 1993 parliamentary elections, 92 percent of the female representatives, compared to 78 percent of the male representatives, were college graduates. This pattern suggests the contradictory nature of women's changing experience in Poland: While women have continued to improve their educational opportunities, their income and participation in the labor force have declined significantly in the past decade.

The second part of the chapter will assess women's participation in various aspects of Polish political life since 1989. According to data from recent opinion polls, there are large numbers of women in Poland who favor and would especially trust female candidates. Polish women are also inclined to advance issues of particular concern to them as women. In addition, the evidence shows that women have sufficient education and public sphere experience to be able to contribute to political decisions. I argue that the poor representation of women and women's issues in Polish political life is a result of men's dominance in party politics. Thus far, men have ignored the importance of women's vote and have not allowed female candidates to represent women's real concerns.

---

[2] See Baalsrud 1992; Rosenberg 1991:129–151; Heitlinger 1993; and Einhorn 1993. In Poland between 1989 and 1994, the number of nursery schools decreased by 59 percent; the number of kindergartens decreased by 25 percent (see Kowalska 1996:56).

At this point, a word of caution is in order. The meaning of the term "political," as well as the distinction between "public" and "private," is currently the focus of heated debate, analysis, and redefinition. In the past few years, organizations have emerged that have profoundly changed the boundaries of politics in eastern Europe. Many NGOs, for example, have enormous influence in shaping post-communist society, particularly by influencing the choices that are made in the most important public arenas. Yet the redefinition of what is "public" and "political" often obscures the means by which women exert influence or participate in politics. To be sure, women frequently exercise their influence differently or in different spheres than men do. It is also true that women in many countries do not enter institutionalized politics (through political parties, for example) as willingly or as frequently as men do. This does not mean that women do not exert real political influence through other types of activities or organizations, such as through NGOs. Still, optimism about women's participation in politics should be tempered by the reality that most decisions that affect women, and that shape women's situation and opportunities, continue to be made in traditionally defined, male-dominated political bodies, such as Parliament and government. Indeed, the clear decline in women's participation in traditional political arenas has undermined women's influence on the decisions and regulations that directly affect women's scope of freedom and ability to shape their own lives and actions. As a consequence, at least in the early period of transition, the needs and aspirations specific to women are not being realized to the extent that they are for men. Thus, it is crucial to study the mechanisms of inclusion and exclusion, which affect not only women's participation in politics but also the opportunities thereby available to them.

It is important to note that, in this period of political transformation, sociological research is fraught with difficulties. Before 1989, data on women were not systematically studied and analyzed. Under state socialism, a priori assumptions of equal opportunity for women prevailed over informed analysis, and it is only recently that the gender inequalities of the communist period have been brought to light. Today it is possible to conduct less biased research on women's lives under communism, especially when looking at inequities such as the wage gap and the authority gap. Gradually, the myths and slogans of communist gender equality are being replaced by a more sophisticated analysis of social reality. Nonetheless, the large number of unknown factors necessarily hampers comparisons of women's situations before and after 1989. For example, no longitudinal data are available regarding women's changing perceptions of their situation or their understanding of their rights and how to defend them. Research of this kind was simply not conducted.

But problems emerge even when comparisons are made on the basis of data regarding "objective" conditions. For example, information about women's participation in politics is available. While this might suggest that a comparison could be made, how does one examine women's political participation at a time when elections were not free and competition between candidates did not exist? How can this be compared with women's participation in a democratic system, which implies free elections and election campaigns, competition between party programs, and open conflict among various interest groups? How is participation measured in countries where national assemblies were mere facades of parliaments and were dominated by a single party? How is this compared to a situation in which Parliament has regained its power and function yet operates amidst widespread uncertainty concerning its proper role? How does one compare opportunities in an environment of guaranteed employment, centrally defined wages, and guaranteed maternity leave and family support with opportunities in a tight labor market characterized by high unemployment, harsh competition, and limited concern for the plight of vulnerable groups (such as women with young children)?

With these shortcomings in mind, I now turn to women's position in contemporary Poland. Specifically, I assess the ways in which gender relations are being transformed and look at how and to what extent women shape the conditions, regulations, and principles that define their position in the public sphere. To begin, I examine women's participation in educational institutions. As noted earlier, educational degrees are the most important resources for participation in the public sphere, without which a woman's chances for directly influencing political decisions are minimal.

EDUCATIONAL AND EMPLOYMENT OPPORTUNITIES

Women and Education

One area in which researchers feared an increase in gender inequality and a decline in opportunities for women is the field of higher education. Specifically, many argue that women are potentially at a disadvantage as schools (from elementary school to universities) are privatized and tuition is charged. If a family can pay tuition for only one child and must choose between educating a son or daughter, they may favor the male child.

I evaluate this claim and examine some of the trends in women's education—particularly higher education—using data from a survey conducted for this project,[3] as well as opinion polls and aggregate statistics. To briefly summarize the findings: Women, and especially younger women, have a distinct educational advantage over their male peers. Indeed, many of the fears concerning the effect of private schooling on gender equality appear to be unjustified. A large percentage of Poles desire higher education for their children and, in fact, more people would accept a lower education for their sons than for their daughters.[4] Moreover,

---

[3] A national random sample of 1,219 Polish residents, each of whom was raising at least one child under the age of 19, was conducted by the Social Opinion Research Center (CEBOS) on September 10–12, 1994.

[4] Research was conducted in 1995 by Małgorzata Fuszara and Beata Łaciak at post–high school private schools in Warsaw (data on 22 out of 28 schools) and at private institutions of higher learning throughout Poland (data on 49 of 78 registered schools). Not all schools were in operation, which accounts for much of the missing data.

women place a higher value on education than men do, and women continue to outpace men in seeking higher education.

These opinions seem to be reflected in the real behaviors of men and women in recent years. Table 9.1 shows that, in the population under 60 years of age, women are more likely than men to hold a high school degree. There also are more women than men among high school students (see Table 9.2), and it is this population that goes on to higher education. However, one cannot conclude that Polish women are, overall, better educated than Polish men because women are more likely than men to have only elementary education or less, especially in the older age groups.

There also are marked differences in the level of schooling across age groups in the population. The oldest group, of course, is the most poorly educated, with only a small proportion of people having earned a university degree; gender inequality in favor of men is most pronounced here. In the case of the younger generation, however, the situation is the opposite (see Table 9.1). While among the 60- to 64-year-old group (those born before World War II), only 13 percent of women graduated from high school; among the youngest cohorts 42 percent had. Thus the proportion of high school educated women is over four times higher in the younger than in the older cohorts, while the corresponding factor among men is less than two, an increase from 16 percent to 23 percent.

TABLE 9.1
Educational Level of Men and Women in Poland, by Age, in 1988 (Percentages)

	18–24	25–29	30–44	45–59	60–64	65+	All
Higher education (university)							
Men	1	7	10	10	7	5	8
Women	1	9	10	7	3	2	6
High School							
Men	23	28	25	19	16	12	22
Women	42	47	39	23	13	10	31
Vocational school							
Men	50	50	40	22	12	9	34
Women	33	30	23	8	4	3	17
Elementary school							
Men	25	14	23	44	53	53	32
Women	23	13	26	55	63	57	38
Incomplete elementary							
Men	1	1	1	4	11	22	4
Women	1	1	1	7	16	29	8
n (in thousands)							
Men	1,777	1,442	4,432	2,812	784	1,396	12,643
Women	1,632	1,399	4,396	3,030	1,003	2,293	13,753

Source: Polish Census, 1988.

We can observe a similar process among the small group (7.7 percent of Poles 25 years or older) with a university or college education. Again, there is a significant difference between those who are older and those who are younger than 45. In the younger group, women are as likely, or more likely, than men to hold a college degree; in the older group, men dominate the college graduate population (see Table 9.1).

If we look at the proportion of women among university students, we find that women reached equity around the 1980s; at this time, they constituted 51 percent of the university student population, which is roughly proportionate to their representation in the whole population. In 1980 women constituted 49 percent of the university-age population between ages 18 and 24; men constituted 51 percent.[5] In some years, the proportion of female students exceeded the proportion of women in the general population (for example, in 1984 women constituted 55.5 percent of students).[6] Currently, women are slightly overrepresented; they still constitute 51 percent of the population, but 53 percent of students (see Table 9.2 for the 1994–1995 academic year).

Importantly, there are differences in the majors selected by men and women. Despite important social changes and the fact that women are strongly encouraged to choose majors that are "male-typed," there remains a traditional division between women and men's chosen fields of study. As was the case before World War II, women constitute the majority of students in the humanities. They are less likely to be candidates for degrees in engineering and technical sciences. In the 1930s, women constituted only 7 percent of the students in these majors; by 1992, their proportion had increased only to 19 percent (Fuszara and Grudzińska 1994:139–148).

If the trends in the gender distribution of education continue, women in the labor force will soon be more educated than men. Although the future of higher education cannot be easily predicted, there are reasons to expect change. In the near future, university enrollment is likely to be influenced by two contrary tendencies. The first is the significant increase in the number of students enrolled in universities since 1989. Admissions ceilings imposed by the Ministry of Education during the communist era have been lifted, and democratization has opened the gates of the universities. Today, admission is based on entrance exams and university-determined limits. The latter are currently higher than those set by the communist regime, thus enabling more young people to matriculate. However, the introduction of tuition at universities constitutes a new financial burden. (The exact arrangement or amount remains to be decided.) This could prove to be an obstacle for some students.[7]

[5] See Central Statistical Office 1981.

[6] The participation of women in higher education has a long tradition in Poland, extending back to pre–World War II years. From 1935 to 1956, women on average constituted 27 percent of students, with record numbers at certain universities. For example, 40 percent of all students at Warsaw University were women, an exceptionally high figure.

[7] In general, Poland is expected to be similar to other European countries in terms of the proportion of people in the general population with higher education.

TABLE 9.2
Gender Distribution of Students in Selected Schools in Poland,
1994–1995 Academic Year (Percentages)

	Elementary	Basic Vocational	Vocational High School	General High School	Post-Secondary Education
Females	48.5	35.7	48.0	69.2	53.3
Males	51.1	64.3	52.0	30.8	46.7
n (in thousands)	5,195	719	811	648	583

Source: Education in Poland in Academic Year 1994–1995 (Warsaw: Central Statistical Office, 1995).

The data do not confirm the fear of growing gender inequality due to the appearance of a cost barrier at private schools. While women constitute 51 percent of students at public schools, this figure is 55 percent at nonpublic institutions. Our research shows that the percentage of women among students is not dependent on the cost of tuition.[8] Many women attend schools with both very high and low educational fees. Gender segregation by majors is observable, however, in private schools; women dominate in fields such as pedagogy and the humanities, while men are more likely to earn degrees in potentially more lucrative fields such as computer science or management.

Other interesting processes are occurring at the high school level. Although girls constitute a relatively small percentage of students at public vocational schools (36 percent), they represent 69 percent of students in private schools. This suggests that the education offered by private, in contrast to public, vocational schools is attractive to women and gives them an opportunity to learn a valuable skill such as accounting, tourism, hotel management, or cosmetology. Public vocational schools provide training mainly in areas such as electronics and auto mechanics.

It is interesting that the opposite tendency holds true for general high schools, where girls constitute the majority. In this area, private schools have become more attractive for boys; girls constitute 70 percent of public high school students and only 56 percent of private high school students. One possible explanation may be that girls do better at primary schools and may pass the entrance exams to public high schools with better grades. Not all private high schools require entrance exams. Private schools also accept pupils who passed the public school entrance exams but were not accepted due to space limitations.

These data suggest both encouraging and discouraging developments. On the negative side, gender segregation in the choice of educational tracks has not diminished in recent years; women are still more likely than men to choose majors that lead to low-paying jobs. On the positive side, however, there is a large and increasing number of women achieving higher levels of education. And, despite expectations to the contrary, the introduction of tuition in some schools

---

[8] See note 4 regarding the source of data.

does not seem to have affected their level of participation. It is also encouraging that a high percentage of parents (especially women) value schooling and feel that their children, especially their daughters, should be educated.

Higher education is clearly a necessary prerequisite for political activity in Poland, and this is particularly true for women. Notably, after the 1991 elections, 89 percent of female representatives had an advanced degree, compared to 76 percent of male representatives. Two years later, 92 percent of women elected to Parliament had college degrees, compared to only 78 percent among their male peers. Clearly, without attaining a higher education, women's chances of participating in political decision making are minimal. A second, similarly important factor determining women's success in politics is their experience in the paid labor force, to which I now turn.

Women and Work

The change from a centrally planned economy to a market economy has caused a significant reduction in the size of Poland's labor force; the employment level has declined among both men and women. Even though women made up the majority of unemployed persons in 1994, they still constituted 46 percent of the labor force, a proportion that has not changed significantly since the 1980s. (For example, in 1985 women made up 45 percent of the labor force.)[9]

In 1997, gender differences in the level of economic activity have become most marked in two age groups: those between 20 and 34 years of age and those 50 years or older (see Table 9.3). Similar differences were observed in 1995 (see Kowalska 1996). In the first group the differences are especially noteworthy, as they indicate that women continue to bear the majority of the burden related to childcare and find it difficult to combine paid work with work performed at home when the children are young.[10] The difference concerning the latter group, 50 years old and older, is primarily due to the lower retirement age for women.[11]

[9] In the 1980s, many women in Poland took paid or unpaid educational leave in order to take care of their children. While on leave, they were not considered part of the active labor force although they were guaranteed a position upon return to the labor force. After 1989, women on leave were among the first workers to be dismissed from their jobs. Also, in the 1980s, some women opted for early retirement at age 55. As a result, in the late 1980s, women's employment activity was lower than in the 1970s (e.g., in 1988, it was 1.7 percent lower than in 1978 and 5 percent lower than in 1970).

[10] Unfortunately, this data and that of the 1980s cannot be compared. Current data are collected according to the BAEL scheme, that is, the Badania Aktywności Ekonomicznej Ludności [Survey on Economic Activity of the Population], which was introduced in 1992 to meet International Labor Organization (ILO) criteria. Before 1989, data were collected differently, hence the difficulty in making a meaningful comparison.

[11] The retirement age for women is 60; for men, 65. There are proposals to raise women's age limit to 65. It should be noted that women are not unanimous in their views on this issue. Highly educated women often resist being "sent home" earlier and try, sometimes successfully, to use the existing procedures to enforce their right to nondiscriminatory treatment in the labor force. However, many women have also objected strongly to the proposed law providing for equal retirement age for both men and women, that is, to an increase in women's retirement age. With respect to these rights, I believe women's preferences differ depending on factors other than their gender, namely, their level

TABLE 9.3
Economic Activity of the Population Aged 15 and Over by Age in
Poland, May 1997 (Percentages)

	Male Activity Rate	*Female Activity Rate*
15–17 years	4.3	1.8
18–19 years	21.0	12.5
20–24 years	69.6	55.7
25–29 years	92.6	69.3
30–34 years	94.7	76.3
35–39 years	93.0	82.0
40–44 years	91.9	83.0
45–49 years	85.4	78.4
50–54 years	77.1	62.7
55–59 years	58.1	37.9
60–64 years	36.0	21.1
65 years and over	15.5	8.0
All economically active (%)	66.0	50.2
All economically active (in thousands)	9,275	7,785

Source: Labor Force Survey in Poland. (Warsaw: Central Statistical Office, 1997).

Women ages 35–49 display the strongest attachment to the labor force. Among this group, women's rate of participation in the labor force ranges between 78 and 83 percent, close to the rate of participation for men.

During the communist era, the wage gap between men and women was a taboo topic. Recently, however, Domański (1992) showed that this gap was quite significant, reaching as high as 30 percent. In the past few years, the wage gap in the public sector, which employs a large number of women, widened further. While in 1991 the difference amounted to 22 percent, in 1993 it reached 26 percent. At the same time, differences in remuneration in the private sector are decreasing—from 23 percent in 1991 to 18 percent in 1994 (see Kowalska 1996). It must be stressed, however, that the latter data concern salaries and not total revenue, which may exceed salary earnings as a result of extra work, especially undertaken in the so-called gray economy. Research indicates that women are less likely than men to hold unregistered jobs. In 1994, they accounted for only 36 percent of the total number of persons in such jobs.[12]

One reason for the gender gap in pay is that women usually hold positions at lower rungs of the occupational hierarchy. A good example of this is the gendered

---

of education or professional position. It would seem that the best solution would be to introduce a flexible retirement age as recommended by the European Council. Such a solution would permit employees to choose when they retire. However, this option is not being discussed in Poland.

[12] The nature of unregistered jobs differs depending on the education and age of women. In the youngest and the oldest age groups, especially among poorly educated women, this is most often the only type of job performed by women who cannot find employment elsewhere. For highly qualified women, unregistered unemployment constitutes an extra source of income over and above their regular salaries.

"authority" gap within the educational system. A large percentage of women are found among elementary school teachers; at this level, the number of women employed exceeds the number of men. A somewhat smaller number of women teach at the high school level, and we found the fewest women employed by universities, where men clearly dominate. Table 9.4 shows that only 17 percent of all full professors, but 43 percent of all assistant professors, are women in public universities. The gender gap is even larger in private schools, where academic rank is more closely associated with an increase in pay. Overall, women are less likely to teach in private schools (25 percent, compared to 37 percent in state-owned schools) and the differences in rank are reproduced here as well.

Unemployment and a general reduction in the availability of paid work hit the Polish population hard after 1989. It seems that education is one of the best indicators of a person's success in the tightening labor market. According to the 1995 Survey on Economic Activity, women with a high school or university education were as likely, or more likely, to be economically active as men with the same educational background (Kowalska 1996). Women tended to be less active than men in the labor market only among those groups with an elementary education or vocational training. By May 1997, the largest gender differential still appears among the least educated groups, where women display a low, constantly decreasing level of economic activity (see Table 9.5). What is notable, however, is that the relative change in women's economic activity is most significant among those with a post-secondary or university education; while educated women were on par with men in 1995, they were less likely than their male counterparts to be economically active in 1997.

Overall, it is safe to argue that women in Poland were harder hit by unemployment than were men. In June 1995, women accounted for 54.8 percent of the unemployed; in June 1997, 61.2 percent (see Table 9.6). Issues of major concern

TABLE 9.4

Proportion of Women Academics by Position in Public and Private Schools in Poland, 1994–1995

	State Schools		Private Schools	
	Percent women	*Number of women*	*Percent women*	*Number of women*
Full professor	17	1,748	14.2	91
Docent	15	124	14	12
Adjunct (with Ph.D.)	33	7,774	21	87
Assistant	43	7,791	27	81
Other (lecturer, etc.)	52	6,653	52	202
All professors	37	24,090	25	473

Note: Positions are arranged from high to low status in the academic hierarchy.

Source: Higher Education in Poland in Academic Year 1994–1995. (Warsaw: Central Statistical Office, 1995).

TABLE 9.5
Economic Activity of the Population Aged 15 and Over by Level of
Education in Poland, May 1997

	Male Activity Rate	Female Activity Rate
University	83.1	80.9
Post-secondary	80.5	79.2
Vocational secondary	77.8	69.9
Secondary	53.0	49.3
Vocational	81.7	65.6
Primary and incomplete primary	39.1	25.5
All economically active (%)	66.0	50.2
All economically active (in thousands)	9,275	7,785

Source: Labor Force Survey in Poland. (Warsaw: Central Statistical Office, 1997).

include the facts that more women than men are unemployed for long periods
of time and that the demand for female employees is far lower than for male
employees. In 1992, there were twice as many women as men for each job
opening. The discrimination women face in the labor market starts with job
advertisements. Women are sought for auxiliary positions, especially as secretary
or assistant to the manager, while positions offered to men require independence
and involve substantial responsibility. Polish law does not directly ban such
practices, which are widely followed by local employers and also by foreign
employers from countries in which such practices are illegal.

The effect of education on men's and women's risk for unemployment differs.
Unemployed women in Poland are better educated than unemployed men. It
would seem that a degree protects men from unemployment more than it protects
women. In 1997, among unemployed men, 1 percent had completed university

TABLE 9.6
Registered Unemployment in Poland

	Males	Females
December 1990 (%)	49.1	50.9
December 1991 (%)	47.4	52.6
December 1992 (%)	46.6	53.4
December 1993 (%)	47.8	52.2
December 1994 (%)	47.3	52.7
December 1995 (%)	44.9	55.1
December 1996 (%)	41.7	58.3
June 1997 (%)	38.8	61.2
n (in thousands, June 1997)	790.5	1249.4

Source: Registered Unemployment in Poland, First and Second Quarter 1997.
(Warsaw: Central Statistical Office, 1997).

and 16.2 percent had only a secondary education. (According to census data, this reflected 8 percent and 22 percent, respectively, of the entire male population.) Among unemployed women, 1.4 percent had a university education and 34.2 percent had a secondary education (corresponding to 6 percent and 31 percent, respectively, of the entire female population).

Sexual harassment constitutes another phenomenon related to women's participation in the public sphere. This topic has not been widely discussed in Poland. Only recently has the media begun to address the issue, publishing accounts of women defending their rights in such situations. A mini-survey conducted among 30 women from various backgrounds (office employees, doctors, nurses, and students) indicated that a majority (18) has dealt with this problem. Women most frequently reported being touched, grappled, and patted (10); they also reported invitations to sexual intercourse (7); repeated invitations for dates (5); or comments on their looks (4). Some were targets of verbal harassment and embarrassing gestures (4); they reported that the excessive, overbearing presence of their harasser continued despite their protests (3), as did lengthy, intimate discussions of relations between the sexes (1). The fact that a very large proportion of women (as many as 7 out of 30) had experienced the most brutal form of sexual harassment—invitations to sexual intercourse, leading even to attempted rape—is very striking. Generally, harassment was repeated several times. In but two instances did such behavior occur only once. In three instances, women mentioned threats intended to intimidate them and prevent them from filing a complaint.

Most women experienced nervousness and irritation (15), disgust and anger (12), and helplessness (11) in these situations. Respondents mentioned emotional problems, but said they were keeping their feelings to themselves for fear of losing their jobs. The women were also anxious about other people's reaction. Eleven of the eighteen women stated that they had to leave their jobs as a result of sexual harassment, while their tormentor did not face any consequences for his actions. These women were of the opinion that the victim stood no chance of fighting such behavior, and the anticipated reaction of others led them to abandon their work without filing a complaint. This situation may, however, be changing. Some Western employers, following similar practices in their home countries, have begun to inform their employees that sexual harassment is not allowed in a place of work. At least one precedent has been established; in a case recently taken up in Warsaw, a victim of sexual harassment was awarded substantial compensation (see Bieńczycka 1996). The support of an independent women's organization (Centrum Prawa Kobiet) was extremely effective here. The emergence of women's NGOs and their growing influence, not only in helping women to defend their rights but also in shaping a new gender contract in Poland, is discussed below.

I have described two factors—educational level and experience in the paid labor force—that are important for creating the conditions for women to actively engage in and influence political decisions in Poland. I have argued that while women's progress is uninterrupted in the field of education, women face severe discrimination and inequities in the labor force. Whether or not women can successfully enter the public sphere and what opinions and demands they bring to the Polish political arena are the topics to which I now turn.

WOMEN AND POLITICS

Women's Participation in Government

Countries in which women's participation in government is low are often described as "incomplete democracies" (see Haavio-Mannila 1985). This concept fits the present situation of post-communist countries, including Poland. In many, but not all, respects, Poland already is a democratic nation. For example, personal liberty, freedom of the press, and freedom of expression are guaranteed, as are equal rights, including equal electoral rights. However, Poland is not a "complete democracy." Although there are no legal obstacles preventing participation, a number of barriers exist that exclude large social groups from having real influence on politics and on government. Notably, Poland's democracy falls short in terms of women's access to real power.

Let us begin to evaluate women's participation in politics by reviewing data on the proportion of women in Parliament since World War II (see Table 9.7). Women's representation in Parliament was highest between 1980 and 1985, when 23 percent of MPs were women. It should be emphasized that, contrary to popular belief, Poland had no quota rule to guarantee women a defined number of places in Parliament. The appointment (rather than real election) of candidates was done on the basis of a certain "key," and the composition of members of Parliament (MPs) was drafted to allow various social groups some degree of "representation." Moreover, while the Polish United Workers' Party (PZPR) supported women's presence in Parliament, it did not usually include women at the top of state and party hierarchies, except for a token woman or two selected to bear witness to the party's professed commitment to gender equality. To be

TABLE 9.7
Proportion of Women among MPs in Poland after World War II

	Women among MPs (Percentage)		Women among MPs (Percentage)
1952–1956	17	1980–1985	23
1956–1961	4	1985–1989	20
1961–1965	13	1989–1991	13
1965–1969	12	1991–1993	10
1969–1972	13	1993–1997	13
1972–1976	16	1997–	13
1976–1980	20		

Source: Statistical Yearbook 1997. (Warsaw: Central Statistical Office, 1997).

sure, the system in Poland did not share the kind of open quota system known to many modern parties of Western Europe.[13]

As Table 9.7 illustrates, women's representation in Parliament reached its lowest level (4 percent) in the period 1956–1961, during the second term of the People's Republic of Poland (Polska Rzeczpospolita Ludowa [PRL], in Polish). What is particularly noteworthy about this table is that women's participation in the communist "Parliament" fell precisely in those years when the Polish people had hopes of achieving a parliamentary democracy—that is, in the aftermath of 1956 (a time commonly referred to as the "thaw"). To reiterate, women representatives, at that time, constituted a record low proportion of MPs: 4 percent.[14] Similarly, women's participation dropped markedly—from 20 to 10 percent—after the first free elections in 1989. It increased slightly (to 13 percent) following the 1993 elections.

Women's presence in Parliament appears to be significantly lower when Parliament acquires real power. Related trends have been observed in other post-communist European countries. In all these nations, the proportion of women in Parliament dropped drastically after 1989. (This nonetheless does not translate into a dramatic decrease in political power because women's share in offices with real authority has always been very low.) The drop in women's share of parliamentary seats did not result from any top-down decision or legal provision but, rather, from a combination of principles contained in electoral regulations and from individual party decisions. Hence, earlier efforts to increase women's representation in Parliament are being reversed in Poland. This tendency is the exact opposite of what is seen in Western Europe, where women's representation in Parliament has been on the rise and, in some cases, has even exceeded 30 percent.[15]

What explains the distinct decline in women's participation in the parliaments of post-communist nations? There is some indication that at least part of the

---

[13] There are no official estimates of the proportion of male and female candidates on lists, on government committees, or in Parliament. During the communist period, party officials created the candidate list in the form of one candidate for one place. No predetermined rules guided who was placed on the list; there was no quota rule in effect in Poland. Determining lists in this way also clearly determined how many women were on them. The percentage of women in the communist "Parliament" changed significantly over time (see Table 9.7). The system had nothing in common, for example, with the present Belgian Electoral Law form 29 VII, 1994, which prohibits lists of candidates with one sex exceeding two-thirds representation, or Section 4 of the Finnish Equality Act, which designates that the minimum percentage of women and men on government committees, advisory boards, and other corresponding bodies will be 40.

[14] October 1956 represented the climax of changes in Poland related to the collapse of Stalinist rule. The Poznań workers' demonstrations in June had been ended by government force and violence. This show of power served as the catalyst for open criticism of the ruling system and especially of the actions of the secret police. Many political prisoners were released, and Władysław Gomułka, himself a former prisoner, was elected to the position of first secretary of the PZPR. This period immediately following 1956 has been called the "thaw" because of the increase of civil liberties, a revival of various societies, and the modernization of political, cultural, and economic systems.

[15] For example: Norway, 39.4 percent; Finland, 33.5 percent; Sweden, 40.4 percent; Denmark, 33 percent; Netherlands, 31.3 percent. See Inter-Parliamentary Union 1995.

TABLE 9.8

Men's and Women's Opinions about the Importance of Gender in a
Political Candidate, Poland 1993

	Percent of Respondents Who Claimed That Gender:							
	Is an Advantage		Is a Disadvantage		Makes No Difference		No Response	
	Women	Men	Women	Men	Women	Men	Women	Men
Female candidate	39.2	27.6	4.0	6.8	54.0	62.9	2.8	2.7
Male candidate	30.1	33.6	2.1	1.0	64.8	62.7	3.0	2.7

Source: Survey conducted by the Public Opinion Research Center (OBOP) on December 10, 1993, on a representative sample of 1,087 adult Poles: 591 women and 496 men.

reason is a general lack of trust in women politicians. In one survey conducted by the Social Opinion Research Center (CEBOS), as many as 70 percent of respondents agreed with the statement that "men know what politics are about better than women do." Among female voters, approximately 25 percent claimed that they preferred male candidates, compared to the 19 percent who favored female politicians.[16]

Other surveys, however, present a different picture. In this section I rely on opinion polls, together with an analysis of party programs and televised election campaigns, to argue that there is a sizeable group of people in Poland who support, and even prefer, female candidates and would trust them in particular to represent issues relevant to women. However, the voice of this segment of the electorate is not yet being heard, which makes it difficult for women to get elected.

A survey conducted before the parliamentary elections indicates that women, more so than men, are willing to vote for other women and are more likely to recognize their role in government.[17] In this opinion poll, respondents were presented with sixty-two characteristics and were asked to evaluate the importance of each in terms of their final choice. Gender differences emerged in only two items: the candidate's sex and the candidate's religious beliefs (see Tables 9.8 and 9.9). Significantly more women than men claimed that the fact that the candidate was a woman was an advantage: Almost 40 percent of women, compared to 28 percent of men, considered this a plus, while the majority of the population claimed it made no difference. A significantly smaller difference appeared when respondents were asked about male candidates. In this case, an even higher proportion of voters, both men and women, said that being male is "neither an advantage nor a disadvantage" (see Table 9.8). Thus, despite earlier indications that women consider men more knowledgeable about politics and despite claims from approximately 25 percent of women respondents that they probably would

[16] Based on a CEBOS (Social Opinion Research Center) survey conducted August 7–19, 1993, on a representative sample of 1,087 adult women.

[17] See research conducted by the Public Opinion Research Center (OBOP) on December 10, 1993, on a representative sample of 1,087 adult Poles.

TABLE 9.9
Opinions Expressed by Men and Women about the Importance of a
Political Candidate's Church Affiliation, Poland 1993

		Candidate is a Devout Catholic	Candidate is Supported by the Church
Claim it is an advantage (%)	*Women*	29.9	36.1
	Men	23.1	26.5
Claim that it makes no difference (%)	*Women*	39.4	43.3
	Men	39.7	47.0
Claim it is a disadvantage (%)	*Women*	26.3	16.7
	Men	33.5	23.6
No response (%)	*Women*	4.4	3.9
	Men	3.7	2.9

Source: Survey conducted by the Public Opinion Research Center (OBOP) on December 10, 1993, of a representative sample of 1,087 adult Poles: 591 women and 496 men.

vote for a man, this survey indicates that a large group of women sees an advantage in a "woman candidate."[18]

Women's support for female candidates was also confirmed by research conducted before the 1995 presidential elections. In these elections, one female candidate, Hanna Gronkiewicz-Waltz, President of the National Bank of Poland, ran along with a number of men. Pre-election polls indicated that she was more popular among women than among men throughout the campaign period. Although the election, in the end, was between two male candidates, more women than men voted for the single female candidate.[19]

Not only are women more likely than men to vote for women candidates, they are also more likely to view female politicians as the best representatives of their own problems. In the survey under discussion, respondents were asked to decide if men and women are equally successful at solving women's problems or whether the presence of a significant number of female government members is necessary for the best representation of women's issues. We can observe a significant gender difference in response to these questions. As shown in Table 9.10, about half of all women, but two-thirds of all men, believe that men are just as qualified as women to solve issues most relevant for women. Less than one-third of men, but almost half of all women, agreed that women's issues are best represented by women in political office.

[18] In addition, 30 percent of women but only 23 percent of men said that being a devout Catholic was a plus for a candidate when they made their choices. See Table 9.9.
[19] In a representative sample of 1,150 adult Polish residents conducted by the Social Opinion Research Center (CEBOS) on September 1–4, 1995, 13 percent of men and 19 percent of women declared that they intended to vote for Hanna Gronkiewicz-Waltz; in a representative sample of 1,126 person conducted October 6–9, 1995, 10 percent of men and 15 percent of women declared they would vote for her. On election day, 2.2 percent of men and 3.9 percent of women actually voted for her.

TABLE 9.10
Opinions about Women Politicians Working on Problems Important for
Women in Poland, 1993

	Women Who Agree (%)	Men Who Agree (%)	All (%)
1. The gender of top level politicians is NOT important because men can deal with problems that are important for women	49.7	66.9	57.7
2. Problems important for women are treated seriously and settled favorably for women only when there is a large number of women in high government positions	47.2	29.3	38.9
No response	3.1	3.8	3.4

Source: Survey conducted by the Public Opinion Research Center (OBOP) at my order on
October 18–19, 1993, of a representative sample of 1,073 adult Poles: 574 women, and 499 men.

When campaign managers and party politicians are reluctant to nominate
women as candidates for political office, they seem to disregard the expressed
desires of at least part of the electorate for more gender balanced political
leadership. We asked respondents what percentage of Parliament and local government should be constituted by women MP's (see Tables 9.11 and 9.12).[20] As
expected, more women than men claimed they would prefer at least 30 percent
representation by women in Parliament. Almost a third of all women, but only
17 percent of all men, said this would be desirable. What is most noteworthy,
however, is that approximately 60 percent of the entire population—men and
women—would like to see women's representation in Parliament higher than
the current 10 percent. This indicates that the present situation does not meet
the expectation of a large group of Polish citizens.

A similar, although weaker, relationship between gender and preferences for
women's level of participation in government was revealed in respondents' answers
to the same set of questions concerning women in local government. Again,
more men favored the lowest level of women's participation (10 percent), while
women more often than men favored a level of 30 percent or more for women's
participation in local government (see Table 9.12).

The respondents' justifications for their opinions were also very interesting.
Those in favor of increasing the number of women in government most frequently
reasoned that women should represent and decide about the issues most pressing
for other women. A somewhat smaller number of respondents argued that women
have certain unique "practical" skills and predispositions, such as thriftiness, a
better orientation in everyday life, and better decision-making ability. There was

[20] This research was conducted by the Public Opinion Research Center (OBOP) on October
18–19, 1993, on a representative sample of 1,073 adult Polish residents.

TABLE 9.11

Opinions Regarding Women's Participation in Parliament
(Percentages)—Responses to the Question: What Percentage Should
Women's Representation be in Parliament?

	Women	*Men*	*All*
10% or less	23.3	33.7	28.2
11–30%	34.3	36.1	35.2
31–50%	27.0	14.8	21.4
51% or more	4.4	2.2	3.4
No response	11.0	13.2	11.8

Source: Survey conducted by the Public Opinion Research Center (OBOP) at
my order on October 18–19, 1993, of a representative sample of 1,073 adult Poles:
574 women and 499 men.

TABLE 9.12

Opinions Regarding Women's Participation in Local Government
(Percentages)—Responses to the Question: What Percentage Should
Women's Representation Be in Local Government?

	Women	*Men*	*All*
10% or less	25.1	30.3	27.5
11–30%	33.8	34.5	34.1
31–50%	25.6	16.2	21.2
51% or more	3.5	2.0	2.8
No response	12.0	17.0	15.1

Source: Survey conducted by the Public Opinion Research Center (OBOP) at
my order on October 18–19, 1993, of a representative sample of 1,073 adult Poles:
574 women and 499 men.

also a relatively large group of people who believed that increased representation
of women was required by the principle of equal opportunities and equal rights,
for example, and that there should be a more equitable distribution of positions
of power. Another group of respondents stressed that women have different values
than men: They are more subtle and have a better sense of justice, they are more
empathetic and understanding, and they are more willing to compromise.

Among those opposed to increasing women's participation in government,
most persons simply stated that men should govern and that women are not
competent to do so. Others advocated a traditional division of roles allowing
women to make decisions in matters of the home only. Others emphasized
decisiveness, a "strong hand," and better decision making among men.[21] Thus
far I have argued that there are large groups of Polish women who are sufficiently
qualified to participate in politics. In addition, a significant part of the population
would like to see more women in public office, and women themselves would

[21] None of these justifications went beyond the usual stereotypes. Interestingly, certain characteristics such as good decision making were attributed to both men and women. Some respondents
claimed that women have good common sense while others denied it.

entrust female politicians particularly to represent their interests. Why is it then that women constitute hardly more than 10 percent of MPs, and their proportion in government is even lower? The analysis of party programs and televised election campaigns will shed some light on this question in the next section.

Women and Women's Issues in Party Programs and the Media

I argue that one of the reasons for women's low representation in politics is the male bias that campaign managers and party politicians themselves express through their political programs and campaign management practices. These influential figures play an important role in limiting the scope of women's issues that appear on the agenda and in restricting the number of female candidates nominated for office. In this part of the chapter I analyze the written programs of political parties and the pre-election television programs broadcast and recorded 1993.[22] In general, neither the brochures and information booklets nor the television programs dedicated much time and attention to women's problems and female candidates. In terms of the parties' position on women's issues, we can classify them in three groups.

The first group includes parties whose pre-election materials contained no references whatsoever to women's issues. Unfortunately, such parties constituted the decisive majority. This group included right-wing and moderate parties, a trade union, and a party created by the president's initiative. Thus, among the materials presented by Unia Demokratyczna [Democratic Union], Kongres Liberalno-Demokratyczny [Liberal Democratic Congress], NSZZ Solidarność [Independent Self-Governed Trade Union, Solidarity], PSL [the Polish Peasants' Party], BBWR [Non-Party Reform Support Block], and several other parties and coalitions, issues of concern to women were not mentioned.

The second group includes parties that mentioned women and specific problems they face, but only in the context of women's traditional roles in the family and in agriculture. In these parties' programs, women did not exist as autonomous individuals with their own needs and interests. An example here is the literature of Porozumienie Centrum–Zjednoczenie Polskie [The Center–Polish Alliance Agreement], which addressed women's situations in the context of family policy. This coalition was in favor of extending maternity leave and equalizing the monetary value of educational leave and unemployment benefits. They also proposed extending the educational leave to all mothers of small children. Not only did these programs fail to address problems faced by most women, but they also suggested, by proposing an increase in benefits and part-time employment, an emphasis on women's obligations toward children rather than the shared obligations of both parents.

[22] I analyzed programs written especially for the 1993 elections by all fourteen committees that registered national candidate lists as well as the written programs of the parties that formed these committees (twenty-seven). (Some of the committees were constituted by more than one party.) I also analyzed all fifteen hours of pre-election TV programs.

The third, smallest group of parties, which included the SLD [Democratic-Left Alliance] and the Unia Pracy [Labor Party], did consider women's problems in their printed materials. Their programs opposed discrimination against women and supported the liberalization of abortion regulations, measures to protect against the feminization of poverty and to counteract high unemployment among women, and the creation of a safety net that would provide assistance to mothers and children, especially single mothers.

Not only were women ignored in the printed literature of most political parties, but women's issues rarely appeared in the televised messages aired during the campaign. The issues that were raised by the third group (which represented more left-wing parties) practically disappeared from these programs. The majority parties did not mention women's problems at all during their television programs, even if they included women on their party list.[23]

Issues such as abortion, discrimination in the labor market, and women's representation in politics and decision making were not addressed at all in television programs. Statements usually implied that women's problems were connected to their traditional role in the family and home and to women's "calling" as mothers and homemakers. A television program of this type was prepared by the right-wing party Samoobrona [Self-Defense], in which a man spoke about the "cross" carried by Polish women, the cross being childcare and household labor. A woman's work in the home, performed without the help of a man, was thus characterized as a woman's cross to bear alone. Samoobrona did not explain why this is so, but assumed it to be obvious. One of the party's female candidates spoke in a similar manner about women's battle for survival, about the closing of daycare centers and preschools, and about the necessity for mothers to care for their children.

An analogous statement was made by a male candidate of the Confederation of Independent Poland (KPN) when presenting his party's stand on women's issues. He claimed that women were forced to work out of economic necessity because men were not able to support their families and because family benefits were too low. Such statements describe as ideal a situation in which only men engage in paid work and can earn a family wage, while women stay at home, have no professional aspirations, and are content to serve their families.

When female candidates—of various parties—appeared in political forums, they mainly addressed issues such as healthcare, social security, retirement, unemployment, poverty, education, the situation of children, and public safety. While

[23] Within the fifteen-day period before the end of the election campaign (e.g., twenty-four hours prior to voting), public television (Polish Television) and radio (Polish Radio) broadcast election programs prepared by election committees for free. In national broadcasts only those committees that had registered national candidate lists had the right to free programming; in regional broadcasts, those committees that had registered a list in at least one constituency. At the national level, total free broadcast time was fifteen hours divided equally between all entitled organizations. The sequence of broadcasts was devised daily. Each election committee could also order paid broadcasts whose total time could not exceed 15 percent of the total time granted for free broadcasting (see the May 28, 1993, Electoral Law of the Republic of Poland).

these are crucial issues, it is worth remarking that women rarely had clear positions on issues concerning the governmental system, the constitution, economic reform, and related matters. Statements by female politicians took up the themes of daily life, particularly the care of children, husbands, and the elderly. Only two women, former Prime Minister Suchocka and Ziołkowska, one of the leaders of the Work Union, were presented in another context; they were shown primarily at large meetings, being applauded by a crowd of potential voters.

Female candidates themselves say that they were not given the option to choose the way in which they were represented in campaign programs. Women candidates complained that men designed the party campaigns and typically decided what problems female candidates would discuss in the televised programs. Not surprisingly, these were the issues deemed to be appropriate, or "traditional," for female candidates.[24]

The way in which individual parties represented women was indicative of the party's general orientation toward women's issues. For example, the Liberal Democratic Congress most frequently pictured women in modern offices, thus suggesting professionalism and promoting an image of the female candidates at work. At the other end of the spectrum, the KKW "Ojczyzna" [Catholic Electoral Coalition "Fatherland"] presented the following images: Children are playing happily at a picnic, riding bicycles, and roasting potatoes at a campfire. Dusk falls and the children return home. As a curtain opens, a woman appears in the window waiting for them (probably their mother). There is no father in this mini-film. A female candidate of the Koalicja dla Rzeczpospolitej [Coalition for the Republic] also spoke of the lack of safety in the streets and her anxiety while waiting for her children to return home.

As these examples illustrate, there is a discrepancy between many women's expectations of female candidates and the manner in which women are represented in election campaigns and party programs. According to the public opinion research cited here, women expect solutions to problems that are important for them, and they place their hopes in female MPs. Yet in most of the party programs and during the campaign, only some of these issues were addressed. Women—female candidates included—were seen merely as "natural" homemakers rearing children, caring for others, and managing the day-to-day activities of the household.

Women as a Potential Voting Block

Judging from the returns of the 1993 parliamentary elections, it is in policy makers' interest to take women's opinions and interests more seriously. According to election polls, women were more likely to vote for the parties with more female representatives. If effectively mobilized, women's votes, roughly half of the electorate, could be decisive for an electoral victory. In fact, there are clear

[24]This information was collected through personal interviews I conducted with three female candidates representing different parties.

signs that women constitute a potentially strong voting block, yet because issues of particular concern to women have been kept off party agendas, women's electoral power is still largely untapped.

There was wide variation in the number of women each party nominated and sent to Parliament, although there is only a weak correlation between this and the frequency of women's presence in party programs. For example, left-wing parties did not send the highest number of women to Parliament: Only 13 percent of the candidates on party lists and 17 percent of the actual MPs of the Democratic-Left Alliance are women. The Democratic Union included the largest number of female candidates on its lists (18 percent), and ended up with the highest proportion of female MPs (22 percent). Yet, as we saw earlier, the Democratic Union made no mention of gender-related issues in its party program.

What is important to note in these two instances, and in the case of several other parties, is that the proportion of women on party lists is usually lower than their actual proportion in Parliament. This supports the earlier finding that policy makers display a stronger male bias than the population does; more women were elected in individual precincts through direct elections than from party lists. It seems that the Polish electorate is more prepared to send women to Parliament than top level party politicians would like to acknowledge.

Nevertheless, women seem to have chosen parties with the highest number of female representatives over those that had only a few or no women nominated, 66 percent of Democratic Union voters were women, 62 percent of the Labor Party's [Unia Pracy] supporters were women, and 53 percent of the Democratic-Left Alliance's supporters were women.[25]

An exception to this argument can be found in the case of parties that had a strong relationship with the Catholic Church. Women voted for these parties in higher numbers than men, even though they did not bring female representatives into the Parliament (e.g., Fatherland, The Center–Polish Alliance Agreement). Men, on the other hand, constituted the majority of those voting for groups that did not send any women into Parliament at all (Non-Party Reform Support Block) or sent only a very small number of women (Confederation of Independent Poland). Thus, although many women claimed in public opinion research that men had a better knowledge of politics and that they planned to vote for a male candidate, the parties that paid attention to women's problems in their programs and those that had more female candidates were successful in the elections to a large degree because of the votes cast by women.

It is important to point out a contradiction here. On the one hand, I have identified a significant group of women who claim to favor pro-women policies and who would like to see better representation of women in Parliament. Although some of these women cast their ballots for parties with a high number

[25] According to a survey conducted by the Public Opinion Research Center (OBOP) on November 10, 1993, 36 percent of men and 38.3 percent of women (among a representative sample of 491 adult men and 588 women; n = 1079) claimed that they would not vote in 1993. It must also be considered that in reality, more people do not vote than those who actually state they will not.

of female candidates, the majority still voted for male candidates. As I argued in the previous two sections, the reason for this discrepancy is that neither the parties' solutions to women's problems nor the female candidates put forward on party lists appeal widely to Polish women. It is still men who formulate women's problems, who choose the candidates, and who project stereotypical images of women candidates as wonderful homemakers. In part, this is because there are not sufficient numbers of powerful women in positions of authority. The majority of women voters dislike both the homemaker stereotype and the disregard for women's issues. Hence, most women still do not vote for female candidates despite an expressed desire that women represent and solve their problems because there are no candidates who meet their substantive expectations.

Outside Party Politics

Even though women have relatively little power in influencing party politics within formal political organizations, there are alternative means through which women's voices may be heard. Since 1989, women in Parliament have been trying to form a group that would bring together women from different political parties to address problems of particular concern for women. In 1991, the Parliamentary Women's Group was created and included two-thirds of female representatives; after the 1991 elections, however, only one-third of the female MPs belonged to the group. Their numbers increased again in the last Parliament elected in 1993; now 52 of the 62 elected female representatives are members (Siemieńska 1993). One of the group's recent initiatives was to present a draft of the Act Concerning the Equal Status of Men and Women, which would allow for better legal protection of the principle of equality.

Lobbying groups have also been created outside Parliament. Before the 1994 local elections, the group Kobiety Też [Women Too] invited candidates and local reporters to special training sessions in an effort to forge an alliance among female candidates and to help them avoid the mistakes of the past. They were quite successful, as evidenced by the increase in women's participation in local government after the 1994 elections. Kobiety Też is now preparing for future parliamentary elections.

Women Too is one among a large number of diverse women's organizations that are emerging in contemporary Poland. These groups provide a nontraditional, noninstitutionalized arena for women's political activity. The *Directory of Women's Organizations and Initiatives in Poland*, published in 1995, describes more than seventy such organizations and initiatives. They include feminist movements, professional and church organizations, party factions, university groups, and Polish divisions of international associations. Some groups were founded primarily to assist women entrepreneurs, for example, the Federation of Business and Professional Women Clubs, the International Forum for Women, and the Women Now Association. Others assist families, single mothers, or battered women. These groups include the Association for Battered Wives, the Association for Women and their Families, the Parabola Foundation, Help for Single Mothers Foundation, and the Catholic Association of Single Mothers.[26] There are a number of organizations fighting for women's rights and abortion rights, and still others promote women's participation in politics or draw attention to the problem of violence against women. Polish women's organizations display a variety of organizational structures. Some groups, such as Parlamentarna Grupa Kobiet or Oliborskie Centrum Kobiet, have strongly formalized hierarchies and pursue activities according to specific objectives, methods, and a strict division of authority. Other groups, such as Nieformalna Grupa Na Rzecz Pekinu, have a flexible structure and engage in more spontaneous, less conventional political activities.

While these organizations are diverse, they share at least one common feature. In the entire post-communist region, women's groups and individual activists are reluctant to be identified as feminists. Under communist rule the term "feminism" was ridiculed and associated with irrational and meaningless political activity. The consequences of this propaganda are still observable in Poland, as well as in other post-communist states. For instance, journalists who invite representatives of women's groups to participate in television or radio programs always stress that they are not feminists and that the program has nothing to do with feminism. When asked to specify what it is that they are so busy distancing themselves from, they usually cannot give an answer. Most people reject the term feminism without having a good understanding of the term.[27]

CONCLUSION

Changes in women's situations, which have occurred in response to the transformation of Poland's political and economic system, should not be evaluated in a superficial or one-dimensional manner. Many women are surprised that in post-communist Poland, even the principle of equality has been questioned, and some parties have openly advocated a return to traditional gender roles and the division of masculine and feminine spheres. However, it should be remembered that the

---

[26] In Polish, these are the Federacja Klubów Kobiet Aktywnych Zawodowo, Międzynarodowe Forum Kobiet, Stowarzyszenie Teraz Kobieta, Stowarzyszenie Bitych Żon, Stowarzyszenie na Rzecz Kobiet i Ich Rodzin, Fundacja Parabola, Fundacja Pomocy Samotnej Matce, and Katolickie Stowarzyszenie Samotnych Matek.

[27] In March 1996 I conducted a survey (using a representative sample of 1,158 adults, including 547 men and 611 women) to explore what the population knows about feminism. Respondents were asked: "If a member of your family or a friend asked you what 'feminism' meant, how would you explain your understanding of this term?" The research confirmed my expectations: Fifty-six percent of respondents could not answer the question at all. Of the remaining group, some mentioned equal rights (12.4 percent) or women fighting for their rights (11.2 percent); others (6 percent) said that feminism meant political action, striving for or defending women's rights and women's interests. Other respondents claimed that feminism was identical to women's organizations (8.2 percent), and a small number (5.4 percent) explained feminism in terms of women's freedom, liberation, or independence.

attempt to return to old stereotypes is not universal, nor does it appear with equal force in all areas of life. Data presented here demonstrate that, contrary to expectations, the introduction of tuition in schools does not prevent parents from sending their daughters to school. The opposite in fact holds true: The proportion of women in higher education is increasing, and parents' aspirations regarding their children's education remain high—even higher for daughters than for sons. Nevertheless, there is still a weak relationship between education and income, and many professions that require high qualifications are poorly paid (physicians, for example).

Women face more serious threats in their professional life. High unemployment opens the possibility that vulnerable groups, such as women, will be pushed out of the labor market. A variety of popular arguments bode poorly in this regard. Among them is the right-wing ideology that claims that women should devote themselves to their families and homes. Another is the claim that administrative workers (who are mainly women) are redundant or expendable. Yet another is the argument that women are less valuable to employers because they must divide their energies between work and their family and household duties. These arguments weaken women's economic position while simultaneously strengthening men's position, and it is men who make the overwhelming majority of political and economic decisions.

Importantly, men have successfully ignored women's issues and have excluded women candidates from political party lists. My research indicates that this is quite contrary to the voting preferences of most women (and some men as well). Indeed, many would like to see a more gender balanced distribution of political power and position and would trust female politicians to represent women's best interests. Moreover, parties would likely gain votes and political power if they took into account women's political preferences.

Women's participation in institutionalized politics is of particular importance during the transition period. It should be remembered that in post-communist societies, the public sphere has opened up and formal political institutions are regaining importance; political parties, government, and Parliament now have real power. Because of this institutional shift, it is hard to evaluate whether or not women's actual political influence has declined. What is clear is that their representation is far from equal in the post-1989 "democratic" regimes.

It has been demonstrated elsewhere that one way to effectively improve women's representation in decision-making bodies is to implement a quota system. In Poland, discussion of this possibility is sorely needed—although it must be free of the kinds of demagogic arguments that associate quotas with the former regime. The fact that the Labor Party recently introduced a quota system (the first of its kind) for its party leadership is promising.

One of the most important changes in recent years has been the emergence of lobby groups, social movements, and NGOs. In today's political environment, these groups have the greatest potential to promote women's interests in Poland. For example, the Office for Family and Women's Issues, a government bureau, sponsored a grant competition for nongovernmental women's organizations. By providing necessary financial support for research, information, and training, such grants would facilitate the continued functioning of women's organizations, and thereby offer women a better chance for representation in politics. Whether such representation is accomplished through traditional or new political institutions, this is an important goal to achieve in order to complete the still "incomplete" democracy of post-communist Poland.

BIBLIOGRAPHY

Baalsrud, Elle Sofie
    1992   Free and Equal? Female Voices from Central and Eastern Europe. Norwegian Equal Status Council.
Bieńczycka, Sławomira
    1996   Łatwy łup [Easy Prey] Super-Express (June 24).
Central Statistical Office
    1981   Polish Statistical Yearbook. Warsaw: Główny Urząd Statystyczny.
Dahlerup, Drude
    1986   Is the New Women's Movement Dead? Decline or Change of the Danish Movement in the New Women's Movement. *In* The New Women's Movement: Feminism and Political Power in Europe and the United States. Drude Dahlerup, ed. Pp. 217–244. Beverly Hills, CA: Sage.
Domański, Henryk
    1992   Zadowolony niewolnik? [Happy Slave?] Warsaw: Polish Academy of Sciences.
Einhorn, Barbara
    1993   Cinderella Goes to Market. London: Verso.
Fuszara, Małgorzata
    1991   Will the Abortion Issue Give Birth to Feminism in Poland? *In* Women's Issues in Social Policy. Mavis Maclean and Dulcie Groves, eds. Pp. 205–228. New York: Routledge.
    1993   Kobiety, mężczyźni i etos klas średnich [Women, Men and the Ethos of the Middle Class] *In* Biznes i klasy średnie [Business and the Middle Class]. Jacek Kurczewski and Jakubowska-Branicka, eds. Pp. 185–204. Warsaw: University of Warsaw Press.
    1997   Women's Movements in Poland. *In* Transitions, Environments, Translations and Feminism in International Politics. Joan Scott, Cora Kaplan, and Debra Keates, eds. Pp. 128–142. New York: Routledge.
Fuszara, Małgorzata and Beata Grudzińska
    1994   Women in Polish Academe. *In* World Yearbook of Education 1994. Susan S. Lee, with Lynda Malik and Duncan Harris, eds. Pp. 139–148. London: Kogan Page.
Haavio-Mannila, Elina
    1985   Unfinished Democracy. New York: Pergamon Press.
Heitlinger, Alena
    1993   Impact of the Transition from Communism on the Status of Women in the Czech and Slovak Republics. *In* Gender Politics and Post-Communism. Nanette Funk and Magda Mueller, eds. Pp. 95–108. New York: Routledge.
Inter-Parliamentary Union
    1995   Women in Parliament. Geneva: The Inter-Parliamentary Union.

Kowalska, Anna
  1996   Aktywność ekonomiczna kobiet i ich pozycja na rynku pracy [Women's Economic Activity and Position in the Job Market] Warsaw: Central Statistical Office.
Offe, Claus
  1985   New Social Movements: Challenging Boundaries of Institutional Politics. Social Research 52(Winter):817–867.
Pakulski, Jan
  1991   Social Movements: The Politics of Moral Protest. Melbourne: Longman Cheshire.
Rosenberg, Dorothy J.
  1991   Shock Therapy: G.D.R. Women in Transition from Socialist Welfare State to a Social Market Economy. SIGNS 17(1):129–151.
Siemieńska, Renata
  1993   Wybieranie i głosujące: kobiety w wyborach parlamentarnych III rzeczpospolitej [Election and Voting: Women in the Parliamentary Elections of the III Republic of Poland]. *In* Kobiety: dawne i nowe role [Women: Former and New Roles]. Renata Siemieńska, ed. Pp. 27–44. Warsaw: European Council Information and Documentation Center.
Skjeie, Ilege
  1987   The Feminization of Power: Norway's Political Experiment (1986–   ). Oslo: Institute for Social Research.

CHAPTER 10

New Parliament, Old Discourse?
The Parental Leave Debate in Hungary

JOANNA GOVEN

CIVIL SOCIETY, that allegedly crucial actor in the 1989 "revolutions," remains relatively undeveloped in Hungary. Political parties dominate the Hungarian public sphere, effectively making Parliament "the only scene of the political drama" (Ägh 1993: 242). As a result, Parliament itself plays an unusually important role in the development of political discourse in Hungary. One could argue that the parties' elite nature and poorly developed connections to any grassroots constituency devalues the importance or relevance of this discourse. Nonetheless, decisions made by Parliament today will have long-lasting consequences; new policies, as well as the rationale behind them and their structural and ideological effects, will set the context for any future civil society activity.

The weakness or absence of feminist ideas and movements has been noted repeatedly in the post-1989 literature on Eastern Europe. In light of a relatively undeveloped civil society, it is hardly surprising that no significant feminist movement has emerged on the Hungarian political scene. But what role does gender play in Hungarian political discourse? Conspicuously absent from this discourse is the notion of "women's rights." But if women's rights are not yet part of the political lexicon, in what terms *are* policy decisions that impinge particularly upon women's lives discussed?

This chapter examines a recent parliamentary debate on parental leave to illuminate the interrelated construction of gender, social policy, and post-socialist political identity in Hungary. By political identity I mean, first, the posturing by political parties, in relation to one another, that sets the boundaries of the political field, and, second, the developing bases of political membership, which is to say, the reconstruction of citizenship. Significantly, this latter form of political identity is being forged in a socioeconomic environment in which recent gains in formal political rights have, for many, been accompanied by the loss of resources necessary to exercise those rights. Social policy formulation can be seen as a process by which political membership is differentiated, as those in different social structural locations are assigned different sets of rights and obligations, entitlements, and dispensations.[1]

I locate this discussion at the intersection of the state-socialist legacy of political discourse, the general economic pressures of the post-socialist period, and the

---

[1] It can also be a process whereby such differentiation is resisted.

specific recommendations of the World Bank for social policy "restructuring." I argue that the discursive tradition has significantly shaped the ways in which international influence and economic pressures are translated into policy. This does not mean that political discourse is static. As the discursive tradition interacts with current political and economic exigencies, new discursive categories emerge, which then organize new patterns of gendered political identity.

PARLIAMENTARY POLITICS AND THE DISCURSIVE LEGACY

Much recent parliamentary debate recalls the more constrained "debate" that took place in the press during the 1980s. This is not surprising, given the movement of anti-communist "dissidents" into positions of formal political power. To a large extent, Hungary's current political parties echo the positions taken by former critics of the communist regime—the major exception being the Socialist Party, which reflects the (more or less) revised position of the old ruling party. This is particularly true with regard to gender-defining issues. As many have noted, there was no "gender revolution" in 1989 except, perhaps, a "silent revolution" (Watson 1993) that quietly consolidated male power. There has been no radical change in gender politics. On the contrary, current political discourse shows remarkable continuity with the gender discourse of the last decade.

In the 1980s, women—or so-called "emancipated women"—were publicly attacked as deviant and destructive. As Ferge (1983) describes it, the female ideal was the "good wife-mother-caregiver," whose most important characteristic was her willingness to sacrifice herself for her family. "Emancipated women" were attacked for deviating from this norm, thereby endangering the Hungarian people. These attacks took several forms, each associated with a different political current.

The "dissident" opposition embraced a form of liberalism, based on individual rights, which they associated with bourgeois culture generally.[2] Their "anti-politics" celebrated private life for its autonomy from the state; this was the realm in which aspects of bourgeois culture could be reconstituted.[3] The emphasis on individual rights coexisted with a highly gendered division of labor, which assigned women the role of maintaining a domestic space in which men could conduct their "anti-political" activity. This division of labor was regarded as both rational and natural.

There was no room here to challenge women's domestic role or agitate for their rights. The enemy was the communist state, and Western feminism (misguided, in any case) was a luxury that could only undermine opposition to the state. Women's most constructive role was to enhance (through their labor, nurturing,

---

[2] For an expanded discussion of "civic anti-feminism," see Goven 1993a, especially chapter 5.

[3] "Anti-politics" refers to a disengagement with what is traditionally state-linked political activity in favor of private life and the reconstitution of civil society. Ideally, it was the practice of acting outside the state as if one lived in a democracy; private "civil society" was a substitute for democratic politics.

and submissiveness) what the state strove to eliminate: male autonomy in an expanded private sphere—a substitute, and possibly a rehearsal, for a "redemocratized" public sphere. In this framework, "emancipated women" were not just unnatural; they undermined the possibility of Hungarian democracy.

The nationalist, or "populist," opposition also attacked emancipated women as unnatural.[4] Their argument, however, was not about threats to bourgeois democratic development, but about threats to the nation. Populists conceived of the nation as a kind of family. Comprised of people whose physical and cultural inheritance purportedly marked them as Hungarian, the "nation" expressed a natural longing to live in a community "of their own kind." Communist emancipation, they charged, had turned women against motherhood. By refusing to reproduce and failing to adequately nurture the children they did have, emancipated women were destroying the nation. "National losses," represented by abortions and avoided pregnancies, were equated with the devastation of historical military defeats.

A third strand of anti-feminist discourse might be called "scientific anti-feminism."[5] While both populist and liberal discourse are associated with opposition to the Communist Party-state, scientific anti-feminism has some association with the Party-state itself. During the 1980s, mainstream popular and academic journals published a variety of arguments by social scientists claiming that women's emancipation—particularly full-time employment outside the home—was "irrational" (meaning expensive) and destructive to society. Various social pathologies, as well as the high divorce rate, were attributed to women's full-time employment and consequent inadequate mothering (see, for example, Munkácsy 1986; Molnárné 1986; Czeizel 1985; Csaba 1985; Buda 1985).

At a time when Hungary faced worsening economic conditions and burgeoning debt levels, the implication that women should spend more time at home suited a government that already was trying to retreat from a policy of full employment and was seeking ways to reduce social spending without inciting a political backlash (or a further drop in the birthrate). Of course, poor economic conditions have intensified since the mid-1980s.

When the government agreed to engage in Roundtable discussions in 1989, it created a strong impetus for party formation, since all opposition parties could claim the right to representation. Broadly speaking, one could say that the "liberal dissidents" formed what came to be called the liberal parties—the Free Democrats [Szabad Demokraták Szövetsége] and the Young Democrats [Fiatal Demokraták Szövetsége]; the "populist" opposition formed what came to be called the Christian nationalist parties—the Hungarian Democratic Forum [Magyar Demokrata Fórum], the Independent Smallholders Party [Független Kisgazdapárt], and the Christian Democratic People's Party [Kereszténydemokrata Néppárt].[6] The

---

[4] For an expanded discussion of "ethnic anti-feminism," see Goven 1993a, chapters 3–5.

[5] For discussions of what I am calling "scientific anti-feminism," see Ferge 1987; Goven 1993a, chapter 5; Gal 1994.

[6] There has since been some splintering within these parties, but they remain the major parliamentary players.

Hungarian Socialist Workers' Party reconstituted itself as the Hungarian Socialist Party [Magyar Szocialista Párt].

During the 1990 election campaign and the years of the first government, members of the Christian nationalist parties openly called for women to return to the home. The liberal parties, while fashioning a liberal discourse of rights, showed no interest in *women's* rights. The Socialist Party defended women's rights, albeit not vigorously, yet it remained a marginal political force in the early transition years. Indeed, the Hungarian political scene was notable at that time for the absence of parties on the left (Szelényi and Szelényi 1991). The Socialist Party was unpopular, and the Social Democratic Party, as well as the "hardline" splinter of the Hungarian Socialist Workers' Party, fell short of the percentage threshold required for representation in Parliament. However, the 1994 parliamentary elections produced a stunning victory for the Socialist Party, which, although it had an absolute majority, formed a coalition with the Free Democrats.

ECONOMIC RESTRUCTURING AND SOCIAL POLICY

The transition from state-socialism to "democratic capitalism" involves, as Offe (1993:682) noted, "giant fiscal crises". These crises differ significantly from the Western pattern according to which expenditures outpace revenue; in Eastern Europe, revenue declines faster than expenditures (Campbell, cited in Offe 1993:682–683). Deepening the crisis is the fact that falling revenues are accompanied by increased need, a result, among other things, of widespread unemployment and the rising cost of basic goods and services. Enterprises cut back on employee services; underfunded local authorities close daycare centers; inflation and unemployment, characteristic transition phenomena, increase people's dependence on state subsidies. Thus the demand for social programs, in particular, grows while the state's financial resources shrink (Gedeon 1995:454). In Hungary during the initial post-socialist period, the result was a large and increasing budget deficit (Gedeon 1995:434).

The restructuring programs insisted upon by the Bretton Woods agencies require shrinking of the state in general and reduction of public debt in particular. Hungary's growing deficits have only intensified the pressure. A significant proportion of government spending has long been directed to social programs; the World Bank and the International Monetary Fund (IMF) have called for a radical "restructuring" of state entitlement policies.

The first "transition" government, a coalition led by the Democratic Forum from 1990 to 1994, was, according to Gedeon, "inclined to postpone the comprehensive reform of social policy," fearing the electoral consequences of cutting social services and benefit payments in the midst of a serious recession (Gedeon 1995:433). Gedeon argues that the government was hoping for an upsurge in the economy, which might have made the cuts more palatable (Gedeon 1995:433–434). Officially, the government committed itself to maintaining social security;

it also developed plans for social policy reform that were generally in accordance with World Bank/IMF recommendations. However, these plans were largely unimplemented. Restrictions in spending were achieved largely through inflation and devolution of responsibility.[7] Inflation caused a serious decline in the real value of pensions and family allowances. Responsibility for social assistance programs was transferred to local government, but the funds necessary to administer them did not follow[8] (Gedeon 1995:442–452 and note 47; see also Bird et al. 1995:88). The government emphasized self-help, the role of voluntary organizations, and (especially) the central role of the family in providing for social welfare. Despite increasing pressures, the Forum-led government delayed major structural reforms, effectively leaving them for its successor to address.

The Socialist-led government, facing a large and growing budget deficit and intensified pressure from the World Bank and IMF, embarked upon a restructuring program that targeted the various parental leave policies upon which Hungarian women have relied since the late 1960s.

The World Bank and Parental Leave

A policy of extended paid parental leave has been in place in Hungary since 1967, when a flat-rate allowance (hereafter FRA) was introduced.[9] At that time, the FRA was equal to about 40 percent of the average female wage; after 1978 it lost considerable value due to inflation (Horváth Sándorné 1986:29). The FRA began paying benefits after a woman's six-month, fully paid maternity leave expired; it provided paid leave from work until the child's third birthday.[10] The mother had to have been employed full-time for twelve of the eighteen months preceding the birth. Officially, she would be on unpaid leave, and her employer was required to reemploy her in the same or a similar job when she returned.

In 1985, in response to concerns over the small size of middle-class families, a second type of allowance was introduced. This earnings-proportional allowance (hereafter EPA[11]) would pay the mother up to 75 percent of her average recent earnings, from the expiration of her maternity leave until the child's second birthday. She could then opt to take the FRA until the child's third birthday.[12] The EPA, it was hoped, would attract relatively well-paid women to motherhood.

[7] Social spending as a proportion of the state budget grew from 38 to 54 percent between 1985 and 1992 (Gedeon 1995:454).

[8] The cost of providing pensions—a major state expenditure—was also reduced by changing the formula for calculating benefits (Gedeon 1995:443).

[9] This allowance is known in Hungarian as the *gyermekgondozási segély*, or GYES.

[10] From 1982, eligibility for FRA was extended to include married fathers after the child's first birthday; single fathers were already eligible.

[11] This is the allowance known in Hungarian as the *gyermekgondozási díj*, or GYED.

[12] Fathers were eligible for EPA only after the child's first birthday. For a more complete discussion of both allowances see Horváth Sándorné 1986.

In 1993, the Forum-led government introduced a third allowance, the child-raising benefit,[13] which paid the equivalent of a basic pension to a mother—or, in exceptional cases, a father—who had three or more children at home, the youngest of whom was between the ages of 3 and 8. (This policy, enacted by a government that explicitly supported "full-time motherhood," effectively extended parental—or rather, maternal—leave until the child's eighth birthday.)

In a 1992 report on Hungarian social policy reform, the World Bank evaluated parental leave and the six-month maternity benefit as follows:

> Maternity and child care benefits . . . represent a significant and costly item in the State budget. In view of the present budgetary difficulties, this alone provides sufficient reason for an appraisal of the present system. The change to a market economy provides a second reason; the present arrangements are unlikely to be compatible with the development of a large private sector. (1992:79)

The Bank recommended that the six-month maternity leave be shortened (although they did not specify by how much) and that the rate at which it is paid be cut from 100 percent of previous earnings to no more than 80 percent. They further recommended that all paid parental leave (and, with an eye toward future legislation aimed at private employers, unpaid leave as well) should not exceed two years. In addition, they argued that the earnings-proportional allowance should be abolished and all parental leave be paid at a flat rate (World Bank 1992:81–85).

The authors of the report suggest several reasons for abolishing the EPA. First, they claim, the "child welfare rationale" behind the policy "calls for income support that is the same for all children" (World Bank 1992:82). That is, it is the child(ren) rather than the parent who is entitled to the payment, and there is thus no reason for the payment to be proportional to the parent's earnings. Second, such changes would alter the incentives for women in a way that the World Bank regarded as favorable. The shift to a single flat-rate leave policy "decreases the incentive for the presumably more productive, higher earning women to stay out of the labor force" (World Bank 1992:82). Parental leave, they said, is sometimes justified on grounds that it is an effective means for "raising the labor force participation of married women, and encouraging women to enter careers requiring a substantial period of training" (World Bank 1992:80). But they questioned whether the current length of leave and level of earnings replacement were necessary to provide that incentive. After all, they noted, it is the "more highly educated women" who are reportedly returning to work sooner than others—that is, before their leave expires—in order to protect their careers from the detrimental effects of a protracted absence. The World Bank appears to be claiming that its recommendations would be particularly beneficial for women, citing criticisms by West European "feminist movements" of "very extended maternity leave" on grounds that it encourages women to stay away from work "too long" (World Bank 1992:80–81).

---

[13] This is known in Hungarian as the GYET.

Furthermore, the Bank argued, it is doubtful that private employers would be willing to guarantee job rights for three years; moreover, employers might be reluctant to hire—or eager to terminate—female employees if they are required to guarantee a three-year leave (World Bank 1992:83). Others allege that parental leave helps to cushion, or disguise, female unemployment. But, the World Bank says, it is less efficient to encourage the withdrawal of "younger and relatively well-educated women" from the labor force than to provide unemployment benefits for those (presumably older and less well educated) women "who are 'selected out' of the workforce by the process of restructuring" (World Bank 1992:81). In addition, "the government cannot expect to pay high enough compensation to make it financially attractive for many women to forego their full-time labor for full-time child care" (World Bank 1992:81).

And, of course, they argue that the proposed changes would save the state money. In 1989, the average EPA payment was 4,340 forint while the FRA paid 2,660 forint;[14] the replacement of EPA by FRA would have saved about 3.2 billion forint, according to 1989 figures—nearly 30 percent of the total. Presumably, the lower rate of pay would encourage women to return to work earlier, thus saving more money (World Bank 1992:82). In addition, by limiting the FRA to two years per child, the state would save approximately 20 percent of parental leave costs (or 2 billion forints, according to 1989 figures) (World Bank 1992:83).

The Bank suggested that the cost of "a short initial period of maternity leave, say one month" be born by the employer (World Bank 1992:82). But they also suggested that an employer-provided benefit might depend on the length of continuous employment with the particular employer and that this "could have implications for eligibility" (World Bank 1992:83). It is unclear whether the government would provide for those rendered ineligible or if these women would instead fall out of the system, thus saving public money.

The Bank went on to argue for continued, even increased, state funding for development of the nursery or creche system, the responsibility for which has in fact been in the hands of local government (and the private sector) since 1990. It suggested that some of the savings gained from restructuring parental leave could be used for this purpose, through the distribution of specially designated state grants to local government for the maintenance of creches. The creche system, it argued, should employ a differentiated fee structure (based on ability to pay); additionally, the Bank recommended that the state encourage private provision through tax incentives for both providers and users of private childcare centers[15] (World Bank 1992:84–85).

---

[14] The "minimum subsistence line" was drawn at 3,840 forint per capita per month for 1989 (World Bank 1992:145).

[15] The responsibility for creches was shifted in 1989 away from central government (the Ministry of Social Welfare) to local governments, which have in turn shut many of them down to save money. Adamik reported in 1994 that there already were counties with no functioning creches (Adamik 1994). The Forum-led government, which preferred "full-time motherhood," was hostile to the creche system and discouraged it through neglect. The Socialist government did not reverse this trend.

In its 1995 report on Hungary, the World Bank approached the issue of parental leave from the perspective of the "dramatic rise in the dependency ratio for the working age population" between 1990 and 1994 (from an employed/dependent ratio of nearly 4:1 in 1990 to one of 1.5:1 in 1994) (World Bank 1995:43). This reflects growing unemployment (there was a net loss of about 1.4 million jobs between 1990 and 1994) and rising numbers of working-age pensioners (whether through early retirement or disability) and working-age students, as well as "women on paid childcare leave" (World Bank 1995:43). To "get people back to work," the World Bank suggests rearranging incentives to make "working more attractive and being dependent on welfare less attractive" as well as "policies to make the unemployed more employable" (World Bank 1995:44).

But Hungary, says the World Bank, "has a particular reform challenge that differs from most OECD countries": One-tenth of the working-age population is on paid childcare leave or disability and early retirement pensions (World Bank 1995:45). Since these benefits tend to be more expensive for the state than the unemployment benefit (EPA is specifically cited as paying more than the unemployment benefit), the World Bank recommends that measures be taken to encourage people "to reverse past decisions to withdraw from the labor force" and to discourage such decisions in the future (1995:45). The "preferred approach" for all paid parental leave programs, according to the World Bank, is to abolish them: "They [are] no longer appropriate as instruments to encourage women to participate in the labor market, and ... if women choose to take extended maternity leave it should not be at the cost of the budget." Instead, steps should be taken "to encourage the provision of creche and nursery care" and to provide "more efficient and better targeted poverty prevention/poverty alleviation programs." An alternative, "transitional" measure would be the option of a flat-rate, paid leave with a two-year maximum benefit (World Bank 1995:45–46).

On the one hand, the World Bank treats parental leave policies as maternity leave policies. While this ignores the "progressive" letter of the law with respect to FRA and EPA, it recognizes social reality in Hungary, where the use of FRA and EPA by men is a rare exception. (Perhaps male unemployment would have been a catalyst to change this; it still may be, with the new law permitting either parent to take leave, regardless of prior employment.) On the other hand, it generally treats women as employees, that is, as economic assets more or less valuable ("the high labor force participation rate amongst married women in Hungary should be seen as an economic asset not held by many developed countries"; World Bank 1992:80). Because young, well-educated women are more "valuable," older women will be "selected out" of the workforce; thus the attention given to the creche system. (Presumably state support is seen as "transitional," with the eventual goal being privatization of the creche system and a shift to unpaid leave.)

The World Bank authors acknowledged the pro-natalist grounds for parental leave policy, but argued that it has been ineffective in this regard, echoing Hungarian studies of the 1980s that indicated that natalist policies tend to affect the timing rather than the number of births). In their discussion of the family allowance program,[16] they argued for a differentiated system targeting low-income recipients (World Bank 1992:70–77; 1995:52–56). In particular, they argued for more "supportive" treatment of single-parent families. Interestingly, and unlike the discussion of parental leave policy, the World Bank refers to single parents rather than single mothers, although the majority of single-parent families are headed by women. They note that "single parents with three children receive the same total child support as families with both parents present," which "does not seem a sensible arrangement" (World Bank 1992:71). At the same time, they recommend that any form of family allowance, whether through tax credits or benefit payments, be directed toward the mother "to better ensure that the benefit is spent for the child regardless of income sharing between the parents" (World Bank 1992:77). Thus women are regarded as employees and economic assets (producers and taxpayers) rather than "dependents," but they are also the preferred parents—the presumed nurturer and proper conduit for channeling resources toward children. Again, this may be acknowledging unfortunate reality; that is, women may actually be more likely to spend the money on their children, and such a policy may be necessary indeed to protect children's welfare. But it also contributes to the reproduction and legitimation of this difference, particularly when, in public discourse at least, it increasingly appears that women's only legitimate identity is "mother."

The Parental Leave Debate

On February 23, 1996, a proposal to modify Hungary's parental leave policy, and several other social programs, was put before Parliament. Proposed changes included abolition of the EPA; the flat rate FRA was to remain, but become means-tested. Recognizing the increased frequency of involuntary unemployment, the requirement that beneficiaries be previously employed was removed.[17] In

---

[16] This was another form of cash benefit paid to families with children. It was universal at the time the World Bank report was written. Payments per child increased with the second and third child of two-parent families and decreased with the fourth child; in the case of single-parent families, the initially larger per child payment increased with the second child, but fell back again with the third, resulting in two-parent families with three children receiving the same amount as one-parent families with three children. Inevitably, this sent clear signals about the desirability of single-parent families, and also perhaps about the value of children raised by single mothers. The family allowance program is now a means-tested benefit; the shift to means testing was part of the same 1995 legislative "package" that included the reform of parental leave policy.

[17] This was the government's second attempt to reform parental leave policy. The first attempt, part of the "economic stabilization" legislation introduced in March 1995, was partially invalidated by the Constitutional Court. This legislation was promulgated on June 15, 1995, and was to take effect on July 1, 1995. The Court took exception to the suddenness of the change. The Court's decision emphasized the importance of the security of the public regarding laws and their rights under the laws. It ruled that sudden changes could not be made in a system of social provisioning that had been regarded as reliable and that played a significant role in family income. The law must,

effect, the FRA would no longer be a parental leave program at all, but a provision for full-time, paid motherhood/parenthood. It would retain a measure of the previous government's pro-natalist policy by granting automatic (non-means-tested) entitlement to families with three or more children. According to the government, this was justified on pro-natalist grounds, but also because large families are more likely to be poor. Single parents would still have to pass the means test (although their families, also, are likely to be poor), although the income threshold was raised (23,400 forint per capita per month for single-parent families, versus 19,500 forint for two-parent families).[18] The amount of the FRA payment would not vary.

On February 28, Parliament held a day-long debate about the government's family policy, in which the proposed measures were discussed at length. The following discussion is based on that and subsequent debates that took place March 12, 19, and 25 and April 2 and 9, 1996.

Although parental leave, in fact, is used almost exclusively by women and was discussed in terms of "maternity leave," policy changes were not portrayed as a matter of concern to women wanting to maintain both a career and family. Women were discussed as mothers only; their needs and rights included the right to stay at home if they wish and to have, as stay-at-home mothers, appropriate social recognition. These notions had broad agreement. Disagreements hinged on other issues; for example, should social policies aim to provide "equal opportunity" for all children, and thus help "needy" families? Or should they be part of a demographic policy that seeks to "save the nation" by reversing population decline? Should the relevant distinctions be drawn according to class (e.g., between needy and nonneedy families) or ethnicity (e.g., between ethnic Hungarian and ethnic Roma families)?

This last question, of course, was not explicitly posed. By addressing the "needy," the Socialist government could talk about class without actually using the term (although it has long been customary to use terms like "certain social strata" when discussing Roma and "middle-stratum" or "middle-class" when the intention is to designate "ethnic Hungarian.") For the Socialists, class is a troubling issue for several reasons. First, like "women's emancipation," it recalls the official ideology of state-socialism, from which they would prefer to distance themselves. Second, to speak of class is to explicitly acknowledge the development

---

it said, be amended to allow the population greater time to prepare for the changes. Citing articles 15, 16, 66, and 67 (1) of the Constitution, the Court also reminded the government that it had an obligation to protect mothers, children, and the family; economic reasons alone could not justify changes in policy that harmed the interests of those groups. The Court also argued that the state had an obligation to protect human life, and under the prevailing law that was taken to begin at the moment of conception. The state, it wrote, is also obliged to protect the mother's right to self-determination; it is thus required to protect and support the mother before and after the birth of a child, as well as to support the child (see June 30 Constitutional Court Decision 43, 1995). The government then reformulated the changes, altering the timing of their introduction as well as some of their content.

[18] The "minimum subsistence line" at this time would have been approximately 14,000 forint per capita per month. (This figure comes from Haney 1996:17.)

of class conflict in the new Hungary. While social inequality and class stratification may be welcome to upwardly mobile neoliberals, these developments are problematic for the Socialists, who are trying to hold onto working-class support without deliberately styling themselves as a class-based party.[19] If they address the needs of a particular class, they would be tacitly acknowledging that their policies, rather than ameliorate class divisions, have produced or exacerbated them. This dilemma, combined with state-socialist overtones of "women's emancipation" and the effects of the discursive legacy discussed earlier, contributes to the tendency to interpret "need" in terms of the individual or the family; the role of structural inequality in the determination of need is discursively obscured.

"Need" versus "Nation"

The Minister of Social Welfare, Socialist Party member György Szabó, presented the government's case. Given the difficult economic environment and limited state resources, he argued, the state should focus on guaranteeing that "the basic needs of the neediest families" are met.

> Since the child and the family are social values, these values must figure in our social responsibilities. And the goal and direction of such social responsibility must always be that through assistance we minimize inequalities of opportunity, so it should not be the case that a child must necessarily inherit the social status of its parents.... With the dramatic drop in employment levels, we would have to take an unbearably large amount from those still working in order to maintain the system unchanged.... If we accept that the goal of family assistance is to ensure the equal opportunity of children, and if the current level of support places too great a burden through taxation, then the policy of decreasing inequalities requires an internal reorganization [of the family support system]. (Parliamentary debate, February 28, 1996)[20]

According to fellow Socialist Pál Filló, "social justice" requires that "support must be given to those who need it, to those for whom this amount of money will make a significant contribution to child-rearing expenses" (Parliamentary debate, March 12, 1996).[21]

The opposition's answer to the government position was that "need" is not the appropriate principle for family policy, since the family constitutes the foundation of the nation (that is, the needs of the nation should take precedence over the needs of [some] individuals). Family policy should aim to encourage (1) more children and (2) the right *sort* of children.

---

[19] As Kovács notes in this volume, there is no working-class or labor party in Hungary.

[20] All citations are to transcripts of parliamentary debates (*Országgyűlési jegyzőkönyvek*, in Hungarian), available at http://www.mkogy.hu/naplo.

[21] The government claims that dropping the employment requirement would result in coverage for an additional 30,000 families, while an increase in the level of FRA payments would result in a higher benefit for 120,000 families. Means testing, it is argued, can be expected to result in the exclusion of 7–20 percent of families (see György Szabó and Lajos Koleszár in the March 12, 1996, debate).

Christian-Nationalist MPs used the arguments and tropes of populism, which already had found a place in the post-socialist abortion debate of the early 1990s (Gal 1994). They warned of tragic population losses and of threats to the nation's very survival through decline and dysgenic development. According to Terézia Császár Szilágyi of the Christian Democratic People's Party:

> The government has taken another decisive step in its own negative population policy. It does all of this in the millenarian year, while the population of the nation declines disastrously and the birthrate reaches a low point never before seen in our history (Parliamentary debate, March 12, 1996).

Sándor Györiványi of the Smallholders Party denounced the "anti-child agitation" carried out under state-socialism, including in his attack both "sociologists working in the spirit of Engels and Kautsky" and "liberalistic and vulgar-materialist predictions, according to which the family must disappear." According to Györiványi, this has had destructive consequences, "the most visible of which is the decline in the number of children." He contrasted Hungary's population decline to the [alleged] rapid growth rate in Romania and Slovakia, as well as in Bulgaria, Poland, and South Korea (Parliamentary debate, February 28, 1996).

The speech most suggestive of traditional populist rhetoric came from Zoltán Pokorni of the Young Democrats, originally the ultra-(neo)liberal party of anti-communist youth. Pokorni cited well-known populist writers of the interwar period who lamented the "race suicide" allegedly resulting from low birthrates; he used these writings to argue that Hungary faces a worse situation than other (Western) countries because population decline is more long-standing in Hungary. "We lose a city every year. In ten years we lost 330,000 citizens in this country; that is the size of Somogy or Heves county" (Parliamentary debate, February 28, 1996). He further linked this to the fate of Hungarians abroad:

> We must recognize that if our population decline continues, then the adults among the Hungarian minority populations abroad who can respond to labor market demands will appear on the Hungarian labor market. What does this mean? It means that the skilled workers and the educated will emigrate from those territories. This presents us with the picture of the assimilation of Slovakian and Croatian Hungariandom within a generation and the tragic collapse of Transylvanian Hungariandom. (Parliamentary debate, February 28, 1996)

Pokorni appears to be arguing here that the more skilled and educated form the bulwark—and are, perhaps, the only "proper" representatives—of the Hungarian minority communities. Their removal (he seems to think, contrary to observed tendencies, that *their* assimilation is unlikely) would result in the assimilation and ultimate collapse of the remaining Hungarian communities.

Pokorni echoes and updates the anti-consumer rhetoric of the populists, attacking the type of "future-robbing behavior" evident, he believes, since 1957. "If a community, the society of the present, refrains from childbearing and child rearing in order to have an easier life, that community consumes its own future" (Parliamentary debate, February 28, 1996).

The problem posed is not simply that the population will decline, but that it will become "distorted." Császár Szilágyi charged that, as a result of the government's "negative population policy,"

> [It] is very likely that, once again, and to an even greater degree, we will see undesirable differences in the average number of children of different strata, which the introduction of EPA was able to ameliorate to some degree. (Parliamentary debate, March 12, 1996)

The fact that the FRA would no longer be tied to employment, she claimed, "makes it possible for certain groups in the population to make a living by having a string of children, with all the undesirable social consequences that go with that" (Parliamentary debate, March 12, 1996). She argued that it is wrong to use the same policy "tools" for everyone. Some families should receive a monetary benefit, while others should receive only in-kind aid. And some should be compensated, proportionately, for the income they give up by leaving a job to look after children, since "being without income due to childbearing and child rearing is not a case of it being their own fault" (Parliamentary debate, February 28, 1996).

The Young Democrats joined in this line of attack, harmonizing it with their original liberalism by speaking favorably about the "middle class," autonomy (from the state), and "individual responsibility," while assailing the alleged dependence of the needy on a paternalistic, oppressive state. According to Pokorni:

> The problem is not that anyone wishes to reform the obsolete, badly structured benefit system that reproduces the mechanisms of the paternalistic state, and reproduces rather than minimizes disadvantages. The problem is that the Horn government has only managed the dismantling phase, and cannot create a new system that corresponds to a civil/bourgeois[22] system that gives equal priority to individual responsibility and to need. (Parliamentary debate, February 28, 1996)

Gabriella Selmeczi, also of the Young Democrats, makes a similar argument on behalf of those excluded through means-testing:

> Unfortunately one of the first policy measures the Socialist-Free Democrat Coalition has succeeded in putting together excludes from the sphere of supportive activities those who have time and money to put into child-rearing. (Parliamentary debate, March 12, 1996)

Selmeczi appears to be arguing that the people classified as most deserving of state support are those who need it least. Distinguishing between "deserve" and "need" is, of course, a familiar practice in the history of the Western welfare state (or, for that matter, in state-socialist "welfare" schemes in which benefits were tied to state employment—that is, given in recognition of one's contribution to society). Underlying much of the opposition discourse is the implication that

---

[22] The Hungarian word is *polgári,* which combines the meaning of bourgeois and citoyen.

the "needy" are lazy and immoral, and therefore undeserving. Channeling benefits to such people, it is argued, perpetuates their immorality ("reproducing" it in both senses) and the paternalist/dependency pattern of state-socialism.

This, of course, mirrors the neoliberal discourse of many Western capitalist countries, where the contention is that state cuts in welfare programs will "enable" the population to get "beyond dependency."[23] As earlier discussed, international agencies such as the World Bank and the IMF have eagerly insinuated the neoliberal approach into Hungarian political discourse. Not surprisingly, as Gedeon notes, "economic exigencies" were pushing the Socialists toward a "residual" welfare state model, characterized by minimal public provision of means-tested benefits (Gedeon 1995).[24] This style of social welfare provision (particularly in contrast to a universal model based on citizenship) tends to stigmatize the beneficiaries, whose situation is deemed to be the result of moral failure or a basic character fault; it also leads to programs that are particularly vulnerable to political attack (see, for example, Gordon 1990; Fraser 1989, especially chaps. 7–8; Przeworski et al. 1995:79; Ware and Goodin 1990). For potential beneficiaries, it does not bode well that the discourse of Hungary's opposition parties already distinguishes between the "failures" (who, at best, might deserve in-kind aid from a paternalistic state) and the "contributors" (to whom assistance represents monetary compensation for a service to society and for whom paternalistic supervision is unnecessary). Significantly, this distinction carries the markers "Roma" and "Hungarian"; the moralization of class formation is thus intensified by the discourse of ethnic nationalism.[25]

Valuing Motherhood

Perhaps not surprising in a political debate, virtually all the participants portrayed themselves as defenders of mothers and families. More interestingly, government and opposition MPs alike raised the question of how a market system recognizes or compensates motherhood. Several government MPs, specifically Judit Csehák of the Socialist Party (Social Welfare Minister in the pre-transition government) and Gabriella Béki and György Szigeti, both of the Free Democrats, raised objections to the fact that not everyone on FRA would be credited with time toward their retirement pension. Under the proposed legislation, only those who met the employment criterion for six-month maternity leave (now set at nine months' employment during the previous two years) would be credited; those

[23] As a recent neoliberal inspired conference on welfare in New Zealand was entitled.

[24] The United States is typically taken to be the exemplar of this model. Yet it should be noted that stigmatizing means-tested benefits is only one channel of what has been called a "two-channel welfare state" (Nelson 1990); the second channel consists of social insurance programs (such as Social Security and Medicare) that are contributory, seen as "earned," and thus not stigmatizing. The two channels are, of course, gendered, institutionalizing the "dependent woman" and the "working man."

[25] Note the construction of U.S. welfare policies has been shaped by concerns over "race suicide" (among the politically dominant population) and the moral failings of other "races" (including, of course, immigrant Hungarians). On this, see especially Mink 1990.

who were newly eligible for FRA but did not have the required employment history would receive no credit toward their pension. Csehák argued that most of the unemployed suffered not from a lack of inclination, but from a lack of opportunity, to work. Such people are among the most needy, and would be unnecessarily penalized if denied a portion of their future pension benefit. Szigeti's argument was based not only on the principle of equal treatment, but on "valuing" motherhood:

> Approximately thirty to forty thousand mothers will not have FRA time recognized for pension purposes; the rest will. This will surely cause tensions, and here we must consider not only the present proposal, but also with regard to pension reform, how much do we value mothers, and how do we evaluate time spent raising children in terms of pension time? (Parliamentary debate, March 12, 1996)

Terézia Császár Szilágyi, of the Christian Democratic People's Party, argued that care of the next generation cannot be left to a market that neither recognizes nor rewards child rearing. Géza Gyimothy, of the Independent Smallholders Party, argued that:

> the state's primary redistributive task must be to compensate families as much as possible for their material disadvantages arising from the fact that some work—particularly child rearing—is not recognized by the market. (Parliamentary debate, March 12, 1996)

The draft law was amended to allow anyone receiving FRA benefits to accrue time credit toward a retirement pension. Thus, not only would mothers be paid by the state for rearing children, but their efforts would be formally recognized as full-time employment! Of course, all this happened at a time when public pensions had already begun to lose value; in ten or twenty years, it is quite possible that pensions will not exist at all. Still, it is worth noting that a goal close to the hearts of some Western feminists—that is, putting a symbolic and monetary value on "traditional women's work"—was won despite this relatively inhospitable setting.[26] Or perhaps it was won because of it.

It is also worth noting how seldom extra-domestic childcare was mentioned. Several opposition MPs, while attacking the government for excluding those who are better off, mentioned in passing the scarce access to creches ("Where are they to put their children when so many creches have been closed?"). But since the previous government deliberately underfunded them, one is inclined to regard this as a case of throwing all available stones at the political opponent, rather than see it as an indication of support for public daycare. Erzsébet Pusztai of the Democratic Forum, for example, said that many women would neither have a creche available to them nor be able to afford it, but she then followed

---

[26] This would not be the first time that women were awarded some form of state support by those, unsympathetic with the goals of a "women's movement," concerned to bolster women's accepted social roles, particularly motherhood. This is one important pattern in the history of Western welfare states. Securing material benefits for (some) women by "maternalist" middle-class female social reformers, who exalted women for their mothering "virtues" but also sought to extend those virtues to the public sphere, is another. For a review of recent scholarship on the role of "maternalist" politics in the development of the U.S. welfare state, see Kornbluh 1996.

with the assertion that a "healthy upbringing" requires that the mother stay at home (Parliamentary debate, March 25, 1996).

The lack of attention given to creches also suggests the importance of the "rights talk" that animates this debate.[27] Among the many "rights" cited were children's rights to equal opportunity and to a stay-at-home mother, the right of stay-at-home mothers to social recognition, the right of previously unemployed stay-at-home mothers to equal treatment under the pension regulations, and a fetus's right to life.[28] The right of mothers to choose to work, or the right of children of working mothers to appropriate childcare, was not mentioned.

Instead, both sides championed a mother's "right to choose" to stay home. Opposition MP Mrs. József Torgyán[29] (Smallholders Party) called for a change in tax policy that would enable, or encourage, women to leave the workforce when they have children. She argued that this would help to alleviate unemployment, and she further cautioned against the deleterious effects of a declining middle-class birthrate on the fate of the nation (Parliamentary debates, February 28, 1996). Socialist MP Mrs. István Timár also favored policies that would enable women to stay home and care for their children. She argued that life for working women with families had become even more difficult, particularly given the loss of such services as childcare and cheap laundries and the sudden need to shop around for lower prices. If there are insufficient public funds to pay for full-time motherhood, she argued, tax credits should be given to those families in which the mother stays home. This would reduce unemployment and improve the mental and emotional health of both children and adults. More home-based and part-time work should be made available for women if they cannot leave the world of paid work entirely (Parliamentary debate, February 28, 1996).

Far from articulating a discourse of women's rights, such arguments actively reinforce the prevailing conception of gender roles and the "natural division of labor" within the family. Although the Free Democrats are committed to individual rights, this does not translate into protecting the rights of autonomous women. In view of both the gendered history of the liberal "individual" (see Pateman 1987) and the discursive legacy discussed earlier, it's not surprising that the Free Democrats would regard men as the standard bearers of individualism and women as dependent upon them. Free Democrat MP Mrs. Rudolf Szabó argued that men's unemployment had created gender role reversals in the home. She argued that men's dependence on their wives had been destructive to the family and that emphasis should therefore be placed on getting fathers back to work[30] (Parliamentary debate, February 28, 1996).

---

[27] On the notion of "rights talk," see Fraser 1989:164ff.

[28] László Surján, Christian Democrat MP and former Minister of Social Welfare, argued in the debate that the government's redesign of various pregnancy and parenthood benefits violated the fetus's right to life.

[29] I use this form of address because this MP, like the two that follow, has herself chosen to be known by her husband's name (that is, József Torgyán).

[30] The point I am making here is not that efforts should not be made to enable unemployed men to get back into the workforce; rather, it is to draw attention to the degree to which the appropriateness of "dependency" is seen to vary with gender.

Conclusion

In the debate over family leave policy, the absence of a women's rights discourse is notable but not surprising. It is notable because a discourse of rights for other categories of citizens—fetuses, mothers, and children, for example—was quite clearly present. It is also notable in light of the political ideal after which the post-socialist state is said to be fashioning itself; that ideal is the liberal democratic Rechtsstaat, in which government is controlled and limited by the rule of law, citizens' rights are protected, and civil society flourishes. Indeed, Article 66 of the Hungarian Constitution affirms the "equal rights" of men and women, and the Constitutional Court (whose job it is to ensure that government laws do not violate citizens' rights) rejected the first version of the legislation discussed. The Court cited both state obligations and the rights of citizens (including "a mother's right to self-determination"; see note 17). Furthermore, two of the parliamentary parties, one in government (the Free Democrats) and one outside government (the Young Democrats), quite deliberately and self-consciously positioned themselves in the liberal rights tradition. Nonetheless, the absence of a discourse of women's rights is unsurprising given the hostility exhibited toward feminism by all of the major political players (including the Free Democrats and Young Democrats); it is a reminder of the taxonomical power of the discursive tradition.

The very absence of "women's rights" can be seen to have shaped the debate. Most obviously, it allowed Parliament to discuss public assistance to families and children without ever focusing on the need for extra-domestic childcare. To be sure, present policies have been shaped by the past, and family leave is no exception. While it is difficult to imagine the *introduction* of a paid parenthood scheme today, such an outcome simply reflects a revision of the old system. One might expect a similar effort to revise childcare laws. Hungary's transition government inherited a childcare provision, the loss of which is clearly making life difficult for many. Moreover, expanding publicly provided childcare as a concomitant of parental leave reform was a task recommended by the fiscally conservative World Bank. Yet, apart from maternal responsibility, childcare scarcely figured in the debate.

This suggests two further points. The first concerns the degree and type of influence exerted by international financial institutions on the political sphere. The parental leave debate indicates that these institutions have not "captured" the discourse of policy formulation. While they undoubtedly exert some pressure toward policy reform, they must contend with the discursive legacy of Hungarian politics that shapes both the interpretation of policy and the course of political bargaining. It may not be coincidental, however, that the Hungarian government, in this case, is "erring" on the side of more rather than less neoliberalism.[31] Gedeon predicts a continuation of this pattern, arguing that "economic exigencies may

[31] That is, in not directing some of the savings toward publicly supported childcare centers, the government is being more liberal than the World Bank; but if I am correct in surmising that the World Bank intends for public benefits to eventually be phased out, the government's neoliberalism will remain in "surplus" (at least on this question) only for the short term.

well force the government to opt for radical reforms that in certain respects may match or even partly overshoot the former propositions of the IMF and World Bank" (Gedeon 1995:457).

A second point suggested by the lack of attention to extra-domestic childcare is the political nature of the process by which "needs" are recognized and interpreted. Nancy Fraser has argued for a focus on the politics of the *interpretation of needs* (1989, especially chaps. 7–8). This approach directs attention to the process of *identifying* need, rather than simply to the question of whether or not a (prede-fined) need can or will be met. It reminds us that a "need" must be allowed to emerge in public debate and that the terms in which it is eventually discussed will shape the range of "appropriate" options available to address it. In this case, the need for mothers to stay home with their children was recognized (although this was not necessarily regarded as a *mother's* need); the need (of both mothers and children) for access to extra-domestic childcare was not. Intertwined in this discussion was recognition of men's—but not women's—need for (and right to?) autonomy; the nation's need for middle-class children; middle-class families' need for (and right to) compensation and autonomy (e.g., non-means-tested benefits, paid in cash, with neither restriction nor supervision over how such benefits were spent); and "other" families' need for supervision and discipline (e.g., the suggested provision of in-kind benefits for certain families).[32]

Finally, although "women's rights" were absent from the debate, so too was explicit anti-feminism. While much of the debate recalled the anti-feminist tracts popular in Hungary from the 1960s through the 1980s, there was no direct reference to or vilification of "emancipated women." I have argued elsewhere that "emancipated women" were portrayed and demonized as allies or agents of an intrusive state who had traded away their nurturing role to a state that abused it (Goven 1993a, b; see also Verdery 1994). Perhaps with the demise of the old regime and with an electorate that now suffers more from the state's withdrawal than from its intrusion into their lives, that argument has lost its political attract-ion. The image of a "good wife-mother-caregiver," however, remains; apparently there is no other way to talk about women in a parliamentary context. The anti-feminism of the 1980s left as its legacy the truncated discourse of the 1990s.

I will end by confessing that it is not entirely true that a discussion of "women's

---

[32] Is recognizing need the same as identifying a target group as "needy?" Does the transformation of the "mothers' allowance" into a means-tested benefit indicate that those receiving it will be stigmatized? This may depend on where the threshold is placed: Is a "privileged minority" excluded from a widely shared benefit, or is a "needy" minority being subsidized by the hard-working majority? In their examination of the social policy question in "transition" societies, Przeworski et al. weigh the expense of universal policies against the political vulnerability of means-tested policies, place them in the context of the socioeconomic requirements for effective exercise of political rights, and recommend "policies that go a long way toward but stop short of universalism" (1995:79). As we have seen, the government estimates that 7–20 percent of families will be excluded from the means-tested childcare allowance. Haney (1997) argues that the shift, beginning in the 1980s, from other family support programs to means testing has already produced such stigmatization on the part of social workers and other benefits administrators; she expects the change in the childcare allowance to reinforce this. It seems highly unlikely, in view of the nature and distribution of existing discursive and other political resources, as well as the international economic and ideological policy environment, that the government will commit itself to making the childcare allowance a near universal benefit.

rights" was absent from the parental leave debate. In his concluding remarks on February 28, after a day-long debate, Social Welfare Minister Szabó noted that monetary incentives to increase the birthrate have not generally been successful, tending to affect the timing rather than the number of births. Among developed countries, he said, the birthrate is highest where there is a strong women's movement, because it is then possible to combine individual achievement with family life. This singular observation went unheeded (even by Szabó himself) in the debates that followed. It was, perhaps, too far removed from the prevailing discourse(s) to be meaningful or effective.

BIBLIOGRAPHY

Adamik, Mária
   1994   Hungarian Social Policy from the Perspective of Gender Relationships. Unpublished manuscript.
Àgh, Attila
   1993   The "Comparative Revolution" and the Transition in Central and Southern Europe. Journal of Theoretical Politics 5:231–252.
Bird, Richard M. with Christine I. Wallich and Gábor Péteri
   1995   Financing Local Government in Hungary. In Decentralization of the Socialist State: Intergovernmental Finance in Transition Economies. Richard Bird with Christine Wallich and Robert Ebel, eds. Pp. 69–116. Washington, DC: The World Bank.
Buda, Béla
   1985   Női Szocializáció, Női Identitás. In Nők és Férfiak: Hiedelmek, Tények. Katalin Koncz, ed. Pp. 93–110. Budapest: MNOT/Kossuth.
Csaba, György
   1985   A Nők Biologikuma és Társadalmi Szerepvállalása közötti Ütközések és azok Következményei. In Nők és Férfiak: Hiedelmek, Tények. Katalin Koncz, ed. Pp. 51–67. Budapest: MNOT/Kossuth.
Czeizel, Endre
   1985   A Nők Biológiai 'Természete' és Társadalmi Lehetőségei. In Nők és Férfiak: Hiedelmek, Tények. Katalin Koncz, ed. Pp. 21–50. Budapest: MNOT/Kossuth.
Ferge, Zsuzsa
   1983   Változik-e Manapság a Nők Helyzete? In Tanulmányok a Női Munkárol. Árpád Olajos, ed. Budapest: MNOT/Kossuth.
   1987   Kell-e Magyarországon Feminizmus? Ifjusági Szemle 7(2):3–8.
Fraser, Nancy
   1989   Unruly Practices: Power, Discourse and Gender in Contemporary Social Theory. Minneapolis: University of Minnesota Press.
Gal, Susan
   1994   Gender in the Post-Socialist Transition: The Abortion Debate in Hungary. East European Politics and Societies 8(2):256–287.
Gedeon, Péter
   1995   Hungary: Social Policy in Transition. East European Politics and Societies 9(3):433–458.

Gordon, Linda
1990   Women, the State, and Welfare. Madison: University of Wisconsin Press.
Goven, Joanna
1993a   The Gendered Foundations of Hungarian Socialism: State, Society, and the Anti-Politics of Anti-Feminism, 1948–1990. Ph.D thesis, University of California.
1993b   Gender Politics in Hungary: Autonomy and Antifeminism. *In* Gender Politics and Post-Communism: Reflections from Eastern Europe and the Former Soviet Union. Nanette Funk and Magda Mueller, eds. Pp. 224–240. New York: Routledge.
Haney, Lynne
1997   "But We Are Still Mothers:" Gender, the State and the Materialization of Need in Post-Communist Hungary. Social Politics 4(2):208–244.
Horváth Sándorné, Erika
1986   A Gyestől a Gyedig. Budapest: MNOT/Kossuth.
Kornbluh, Felicia A.
1996   The New Literature on Gender and the Welfare State: The U.S. Case. Feminist Studies 22(1):171–197.
Mink, Gwendolyn
1990   The Lady and the Tramp: Gender, Race, and the Origins of the American Welfare State. *In* Women, the State, and Welfare. Linda Gordon, ed. Pp. 92–122. Madison: University of Wisconsin Press.
Molnárné, Júlia Venyige
1986   Nők a Változó Társadalmi Munkamegosztásban. Társadalmi Szemle 41:43–52.
Munkácsy, Ferenc
1986   A Nők Gazdasági Aktivitása és a Termékenység. Közgazdasági Szemle 33:1456–1462.
Nelson, Barbara
1990   The Origins of the Two-Channel Welfare State: Workmen's Compensation and Mothers' Aid. *In* Women, the State, and Welfare. Linda Gordon, ed. Pp. 123–151. Madison: University of Wisconsin Press.
Offe, Claus
1993   The Politics of Social Policy in East European Transitions: Antecedents, Agents, and Agenda of Reform. Social Research 60:649–684.
Parliament of Hungary
1996   Országgyülési Jegyzőkönyvek [Transcripts of parliamentary sessions], February 28, 1996; March 12, 19, and 25, 1996; and April 9, 1996. Electronic document. http://www.mkogy.hu/naplo; http://www.ned.org.
Pateman, Carol
1987   The Sexual Contract. Palo Alto: Stanford University Press.
Przeworski, Adam et al.
1995   Sustainable Democracy. New York: Cambridge University Press.
Szelényi, Iván and Szonja Szelényi
1991   The Vacuum in Hungarian Politics: Classes and Parties. New Left Review 187:121–137.
Verdery, Katherine
1994   From Parent-State to Family Patriarchs: Gender and Nation in Contemporary Eastern Europe. East European Politics and Societies 8:225–255.

Ware, Alan and Robert E. Goodin
   1990   Introduction. *In* Needs and Welfare. Alan Ware and Robert E. Goodin, eds.
              London: Sage.
Watson, Peggy
   1993   Eastern Europe's Silent Revolution: Gender. Sociology 27:471–487.
World Bank
   1992   Hungary: Reform of Social Policy and Expenditures. Washington, DC: The
              World Bank.
   1995   Hungary: Structural Reforms for Sustainable Growth. Washington, DC: The
              World Bank.

CHAPTER 11

Women's NGOs in Romania

LAURA GRUNBERG

> Particularly after 1989, most of the men that I have had the opportunity
> to discuss the problem with endorse the emancipation of women . . .
> within given parameters, in the social, civil, and political life—except for
> their own wives and daughters.
> *National Liberal Party member*

PRIOR TO 1989, women and other minorities were represented in the Romanian
government according to the predefined ratios of a quota system. In 1987, for
example, 34 percent of the Grand National Assembly and 11.6 percent of government ministers were women. In 1989, at the very moment when the exercise of
power acquired substantive meaning, women disappeared from the political scene.
Between 1992 and 1996, women made up only 3.4 percent of Parliament, and
no woman has held a ministerial post since 1989.[1] After the 1996 local elections,
only 2.75 percent of the 2,954 elected mayors, 6.11 percent of the 39,831 elected
local representatives, and 5.47 percent of the 1,718 elected county representatives
were women (Comisia Naţională de Statistică 1996). Although women comprise
a significant share of the total active population—43.8 percent as of May 1996—
their access to and participation in the formulation and implementation of social
and economic policy and their role in decision making are hardly representative.
Only 24.5 percent of the total number of working women held positions either
in legislative and executive bodies or as high-ranking civil servants or officers of
socioeconomic and political institutions (National Commission for Statistics
1996 [English translation]).[2]

Yet the national government is no longer the only legitimate forum for public
and political action, and women now actively participate in civil society. While
any parliamentary or government session clearly illustrates the monopoly men
hold over the standards, speed, and priorities of transition, any meeting of civil
society representatives suggests at least the potential for a gender partnership in

---

[1] One month prior to the 1996 presidential elections, one woman was appointed (though she was
not renamed after the elections) Minister of Public Health, and three women were appointed
Secretaries of State. After the elections, only one woman was appointed Secretary of State, for
the handicapped.

[2] The reasons for this lack of visibility are multiple and are characteristic of the new society rather
than a manifestation of the frequently invoked "Elena Ceauşescu Syndrome."

finding viable solutions to transition crises. Even with a fragile gender contract at the level of civil society, women have failed to realize their potential as political and public players. Women's involvement in local politics and civil society reflects a striking ambivalence, especially with respect to women's issues. Many women are active in nongovernmental organizations (NGOs) that do not address women's issues, and many Romanian women are either disinterested in or uninformed about feminism per se. All too often, women's groups respond to and reflect the demands and interests of foreign funders, thus transferring, but not internalizing, Western gendered discourses into the Romanian context. It is frequently unclear whom the beneficiaries of these programs are meant to be. At the same time, the rhetorical style and organizational structure of some women's NGOs reproduce former communist patterns of communication and organization. Nonetheless, following the legacy of a regime that systematically denied its citizens access to the rights and privileges of civil society, women's efforts to learn the art of association are indicative of the confusing process of transformation in Romania today (Kligman 1990:420).

This chapter evaluates Romanian women's participation in civil society by focusing on the role and impact of women's organizations. Data about women's NGOs, their programs, and their representatives were collected over a period of eight months in 1995–1996 and include questionnaire responses,[3] semi-structured interviews with women NGO leaders,[4] and participant observation at a number of NGO events. The information upon which this study is based[5] includes the formal discourse and stated objectives of women's NGOs compared to their concrete achievements; women's personal reasons for becoming involved in an NGO; the effects of competition for limited resources as well as competition between women of different generations; the public image of women's organizations; and their overall place within the civil society movement.

From this data, the chapter offers a critical assessment of civil society in post-Ceaușescu Romania and of women's role in the NGO movement; of the creation

[3] The five-page questionnaire included four parts: personal data, general information about organizational structure, activities, and a personal assessment of women's situations in Romania (such as economic opportunities, political representation, women's rights, women's role in the family and in ethnic conflicts, etc.). The questionnaire was sent in September 1995 to all fifty organizations included in the database of the UNDP/WID Programme (see Appendix 11.1) and was resent in February 1996 to those groups that had not yet responded. In the end, twenty-nine women among the leadership of Romania's women's organizations completed and returned the questionnaire, representing 58 percent of the NGO's queried. Of these, five were from outside Bucharest.

[4] Between September 1995 and May 1996, I interviewed six women who were prominent NGO leaders. Two were leaders of national organizations, two were presidents of professional NGOs, one was the coordinator of the Şanse Egale [Equal Opportunity] Department of the National Council of Free Trade Unions-Frăția (CNSLR), and one was the leader of a women's religious organization. The interviews were semi-structured and lasted one to one and a one-half hours each. Interviews were conducted in the subject's office or at my house. Being an "insider" (a member of a women's organization) proved to be more of a handicap than an asset; my own partisanship (personal dislikes and affinities) and the lack of "glasnost" from individuals competing for the same resources was problematic.

[5] Data was primarily collected for women's NGOs, although some information was gathered from NGOs that deal with human rights, environmental, or educational issues. Unless otherwise noted, all quotations are drawn from personal interviews or questionnaire responses.

of a women's movement in Romania and the difficulties associated with foreign (specifically Western) assistance; and of the general impact of women's NGOs and feminism on Romanian society. As will be discussed in the following sections, Romania's nascent women's movement was marginalized before it could be firmly established.[6] In the broader context of civil society initiatives, the women's movement is being symbolically crippled. Significantly, Romanian women's NGOs contribute to their own marginalization because they lack open dialogue with the very women they purport to represent. These groups tend to take a superficial approach when identifying program objectives and target populations, and their ineffective public rhetoric neither corrects the perception that they mimic foreign models nor attracts support for their causes. Moreover, the mass media and the population in general tend to ignore or trivialize the women's movement. As Romanians reconstitute their political culture, this failure to get a message across disadvantages everyone.

From Multilaterally Developed Socialist Society to Civil Society

Before 1989, there was one political party in Romania. By 1992, there were roughly two hundred. On the eve of the 1996 presidential and parliamentary elections, fifty-one parties and sixteen presidential candidates were officially registered. Since the fall of the Ceauşescu regime, institutions considered necessary for democracy (e.g., parliament, political parties, civic organizations) have emerged. Yet despite the trappings of democratic procedure, there has been—at least up until the November 1996 elections—an all too evident lack of political will.[7] A new constitution was written and approved in 1991 but remains problematic (see Focşeneanu 1992; Varlam 1993; Pietraru 1997). Parliament has delayed in its task of enacting laws to safeguard democratic rights and facilitate privatization. As a result, Romania's legal code is a mixture of new laws similar in content to (West) European standards and remnants from the communist and inter-war periods.[8] The justice system has yet to become fully independent. The post-1989 governments under the rule of President Ion Iliescu failed to display consistent managerial competence. Confusion about and dissatisfaction with the speed and effectiveness of reform has intensified distrust of public institutions. Parliament,

[6] I prefer to use an inclusive rather than exclusive definition of the women's movement that incorporates national, regional, and international groups that are service- and education-oriented; trade unions; professional associations; foundations; business organizations; and youth and research groups active in the field of women's issues.

[7] The full collapse of the totalitarian regime was a prolonged process, as suggested by the political response to several diverse, collective actions that occurred in 1990. Examples of public unrest include the ethnic conflict in Tǎrgu Mureş, the University Square demonstrations, and the miners' rampage through Bucharest. See, for example, Verdery and Kligman 1992, among others. These events played a crucial role in the restructuring of the new political field.

[8] Among them, see the law on the operation of nonprofit associations and organizations, dated 1924, which impedes the formation of NGOs. A project to modify this law is still pending debate in The Chamber of Deputies.

political parties, private businesses, and civic organizations are still regarded with suspicion. In poll after poll, the army and the church—institutions that represent authority and stability—have the highest credibility. It is important to note, however, that the democratic opposition's victory in the November 1996 elections offers, at least for the moment, a viable alternative; the new government's anti-corruption campaign has given some credence to its democratic aspirations.

Nonetheless, Romania's political culture remains tarnished by deeply internalized totalitarian prejudices and predispositions; changing such lingering mentalities will be a slow and arduous process. During the communist era, Party-controlled mass organizations, including youth, women, and children's organizations and unions and professional associations, were examples of "form without content."[9] Official propaganda characterized these groups as being devoted to the (demagogically defined) public good; feigning mass participation, the Party pointed to them as evidence of the superior socialist democracy that was being constructed.[10] Terms such as "democracy" or "human rights" were stripped of their historical meaning and ideologically recast to suit the interests of the regime. Even a cursory reading of party documents, secondary school and university texts, or newspaper articles will show that the notion of civil society utterly vanished from theoretical and colloquial use.

Many Romanians refuse to acknowledge that they are now involved in politics or political acts. They have a long tradition, in fact, of treating politics as something apart from society, even shameful. More than 80 percent of the population today, born after World War II, has no familiarity with democratic institutions and practices, market economies, or civil society. Moreover, Ceauşescu's neo-Stalinist regime was, by the late 1980s, notorious for its ideological commitment to a highly centralized economy and polity. It was only after the 1989 revolution that Romanian intellectuals invoked the anti-political reinterpretation of civil society that inspired other Central European intellectuals in the 1980s.[11] Even so, in January 1990, prominent intellectuals, as well as members of trade unions and NGOs, publicly insisted that "we are not parties, and we are not engaged in politics." These claims were intended both to underscore their good intentions and to dissociate themselves from the struggle for (and taint of) power (Kligman 1990).

However, adopting a politics of anti-politics is not appropriate for post-1989 circumstances (Pavel 1996). Despite the rhetorical legitimacy given to democracy, many Romanians still find it hard to accept that working for an NGO is itself a political act that entails mediation between the state and its citizens. Women in particular, although they are redefining the politics of reproduction, social welfare, and education, resist the notion that their activities are political. Some leaders of women's organizations acknowledge this reticence. For example, when

[9] This term was introduced by Titu Maiorescu regarding the "formal" institutional, but not societal, changes produced by the revolution of 1848. See Maiorescu 1868.
[10] This superior democracy was officially labeled "original democracy."
[11] The works of Havel, Konrad, and Michnik come immediately to mind. Tismăneanu 1992 presents an overview.

a 50-year-old researcher in engineering science was asked, "What is it that you are unhappy with in connection with the women's movement in Romania?," she replied, "I am unhappy with the failure to identify the real problems, with the incoherent means of action, and with the lack of understanding that the solution is in the political sphere."

Despite the obstacles presented by communist era mentalities and behaviors, Romania's political culture has become more flexible as a result of the infusion of Western models. The institutions of civil society have burgeoned and are beginning to tackle a wide range of issues. According to the Romanian Ministry of Justice, 6,961 associations and foundations were registered between 1990 and 1994. The Catalogue of Non-Governmental Organizations in Romania, edited in 1994 by the Soros Foundation, identified 1,034 NGOs, more than 500 of which had begun operating in 1990. Roughly four million people, 55 percent men and 46 percent women, were then estimated to be active in an NGO. More than 11 percent of these organizations were engaged in human rights, and approximately twenty-five groups were devoted to women's issues (Soros Foundation for an Open Society 1994).

These figures illustrate the difficulty in determining the actual number of NGOs currently operating in Romania; it is equally if not more difficult to characterize their membership in terms of sex, age, or education. In 1996 the Foundation for the Development of Civil Society (FDSC), a component of the European Union's PHARE program, started a database of what was estimated to be 12,000 NGOs in Romania. The latest catalogue, published in early 1997 with a series of studies on Romania's nonprofit sector, lists 3,050 NGOs (Foundation for the Development of Civil Society [FDSC] 1997). An Inter-Ministerial Working Group for Supporting Civil Society (GLIM) was also established as a consultative body subordinate to the Council for Coordination, Strategy, and Economic Reform. In collaboration with experts from PHARE's Public Administration Reform Program,[12] the Working Group will issue an annual NGO report outlining the historical and legislative framework of Romanian civil society and providing an up-to-date statistical and descriptive review of NGOs in the country.

It is estimated that approximately one-half of Romania's 12,000-strong NGO membership are women, many of whom are the founders or leaders of their respective associations. The UNDP's Women in Development Program (UNDP/WID)[13] has identified fifty organizations that are actively involved in women's issues. (According to data collected for this study, the actual number is closer to sixty; see Appendix 11.1.) While this may seem a reasonable or even high number,

---

[12] PHARE (Poland-Hungary Aid for Restructuring the Economy) is a European Union assistance program operating throughout Central and Eastern Europe.

[13] UNDP/WID was established at the beginning of 1994 by the UNDP together with the Ministry of Labor and Social Protection. Its mandate is to bring women's issues to the attention of decision makers and the public; to gather relevant information about the situation of women and women's NGO activities; to promote strategies that offer equal opportunities to women and men; and to initiate programs that create jobs for women.

these figures must be contextualized. To illustrate, approximately sixty NGOs have been established among the Roma or Gypsy community, whose total population is estimated at 400,000; there are, by contrast, approximately twelve million women in Romania (National Commission for Statistics 1996). From this perspective, women's organizations are not overrepresented.[14]

In view of the enduring effects of communism, it comes as no surprise that NGOs typically exhibit an ambivalent attitude toward the state (Racioppi and See 1995). In its turn, the state manifests similar reservations toward NGOs. Until recently, the establishment of an NGO was contingent on the approval of a corresponding government ministry. While only a formality, the necessity for such approval reflects the government's ongoing concern about NGO autonomy. According to a law that dates back to 1924 (see note 8), NGOs are treated as a commercial business and are subjected to an endless series of bureaucratic hurdles. Far from facilitating the institutions of civil society, the Romanian tax system actually strips NGOs of significant resources.

To recognize the distinctive features of Romanian women's NGOs, it is helpful to assess their activities in terms of the framework developed by the Center for Political Studies and Comparative Analyses. According to a Center study, NGOs vary according to three basic types, each distinguished by the domain in which it is active. For example, *institutionally oriented* NGOs might focus on government policies, election processes, and civil and political behavior; *community-oriented* NGOs might focus on culture, art, education, ethnic relations, and religion; and *everyday-oriented* NGOs might focus on ecology, the media, healthcare, social protection, and leisure (Şandor 1995:9). As will be discussed below, the programs carried out by women's groups in Romania tend to be concentrated at the everyday and, to a lesser degree, community level.

CREATING A WOMEN'S MOVEMENT IN POST-COMMUNIST ROMANIA

For more than forty years, women and men endured the ordeal of living in a "multilaterally developed socialist society" in which everyone was officially equal.[15] In reality, Romanians were equally alienated, impoverished, and indoctrinated. Individuality was effectively destroyed. The homogenization policy of the Ceauşescu era was devised to mask the differences between social categories and the real discrepancies in people's living situations (Kligman 1992:368). Officially, unemployment did not exist and social benefits were distributed to all. In practice, women were victims of veiled unemployment and wage discrimination. They were also guinea pigs for a pro-natalist policy that brought worldwide notoriety to Romania after the fall of the regime (Kligman 1992, 1998). Despite these

---

[14] As of July 1995, the population of Romania was 22,681,000, 49 percent of which was male and 51 percent female; 1.8 percent of the total population is estimated to be Roma (Comisia Naţională de Statistică 1996:82).

[15] The term "multilaterally developed socialist society" was first introduced by Ceauşescu at the Tenth Party Congress in 1969.

circumstances, women did not view their situation in gendered terms; instead, gender distinctions were blurred by the human solidarity felt vis-à-vis the totalizing oppression of the regime. Because gender-based constraints were perceived as neither legitimate nor as a primary concern in their lives, no serious political or intellectual movement could be mobilized around "women's oppression" during communism (Šiklova 1993).

What has been widely described as "the victory of socialism over the Romanian people" has been followed by the victory of "original democracy" over the Romanian people, translated into the political, economic, and social crises of transition. Women, in particular, have experienced these crises in terms of increasing unemployment and the feminization of poverty, the inadequacy or even lack of social protection and assistance, violence, and a continuation of totalitarian or patriarchal mentalities. Even so, the gender awareness necessary for a coherent women's movement to emerge has not surfaced. After more than forty years of communist-style emancipation, feminist discourse does not naturally resonate among Romania's women.[16]

The budding women's movement in Romania has not grown from the kind of social discontent that typically motivates people to join a political or social movement, nor from any charismatic popularization of feminist ideology or leadership.[17] Women's issues have not figured among other priority social concerns such as unemployment, human rights, the environment, public health, or the situation of street children, all of which have been on the agendas of post-1989 governments. Neither are women's issues considered pressing by NGOs or the general population. Indeed, the activities of women's NGOs are rarely driven by the needs and concerns of Romanian women. To date, and despite several propitious opportunities, no "precipitating factor" has provoked a common effort to improve women's position in Romania.[18]

Nonetheless, a women's movement is being institutionally formalized. The years 1991 and 1992 were marked by heightened activity among Romanian NGOs organizing to address women's issues. Approximately forty such organizations existed by early 1993. What motivated women's involvement in these NGOs? "The need for change" might be characterized as the leitmotif response among women surveyed for this study (see Table 11.1). In part, consensus on this issue reflects an ingrained rhetorical response, echoing the wooden language of the communists who subordinated individual interests to the collective and

---

[16] Editors' note: The conflation of women's organizations with feminism, about which negative sentiment and disinformation are high, presently contributes to the difficulties of organizing on behalf of women's issues.

[17] As presented in sociology handbooks, these two phases typically precede the formalization of a social movement. See, for example, Dodgen and Rapp 1993:406.

[18] For example, women might have rallied around any of the following: In 1992, Smaranda Enache, a former dissident and founding member of the Civic Alliance Party and current leader of the Pro Europe League, was not included on the electoral list of her own party. There is also, the "Maria" case, widely aired by the media, about a woman who prostituted herself to feed her seven children; another case is of the Romanian mother who sued the Ministry of Health (and eventually lost) on grounds that her child was infected with HIV while hospitalized in a state hospital.

TABLE 11.1
Reasons for Women's Involvement in an NGO

Reason for Involvement	Number of Times Cited	First Place	Second Place	Third and Fourth Place
Desire for change	26	22	2	2
Concern for women	20	15	2	3
Confidence in NGO role	18	5	7	6
Love of country/patriotism	3	2		1
A changed image of the country	1	1		
Personal experience	2	2		
By chance	1			1
Other	2	1		1

spoke of all things "for the benefit of the country and the people." Other reasons given for participating in an NGO were "love of country" and the desire "to change Romania's image in the world." Some respondents went so far as to criticize the questionnaire, asking why the "key question, patriotism" had been omitted. It should be noted that, after the turmoil of 1989, "patriotism" was expropriated by advocates of a new xenophobic discourse, and has since implicitly referred to post-communist demagogic nationalism[19] (Pleşu 1996).

Although small in number, a few women cited personal experience or opportunity as the primary factor motivating their participation in an NGO. For example, one woman noted that, "It is men's insensitivity that prompted me into this activity." A leader of a women's political organization confessed in an interview that, "A few months after my husband died, the President of the Party—a good friend of my husband's—came to me and said, 'I'll trust you with the women's organization; you'll have to work, [but] I have confidence in you.'" In general, however, most women did not formulate their response in terms of self-interest or opportunity.[20] Most women, accustomed to caring for others before themselves, found it difficult to escape a collectivist legacy that had simply reinforced patriarchal cultural practices.[21] Indicative of this type of reasoning was the response, "I did not think of myself; I thought of my children."

Despite their enthusiasm, the leaders of Romania's post-communist women's movement lack the organizational training and infrastructural resources necessary to get their message across. Indeed, since 1989, NGOs in general and women's NGOs in particular have been promoted and supported primarily by foreign organizations eager to supply consultants, financing, equipment, and basic "know

[19] In many questionnaires, not only were such reasons listed first, but they were underlined, encircled, specially marked, and repeated during the interview to emphasize the importance of working for the nation.

[20] After forty plus years of living under communism, this is not surprising. The collective interests of "the workers," "the people," and "the nation" were dominant rather than those of the individual.

[21] Regarding "traditional" gender relations, see Kligman 1988.

how"[22] (see Table 11.2). American donors, for example, view NGOs as "the connective tissue of democratic political culture—an intrinsically positive objective" (Wedel 1994:323). In 1995, 56 percent of NGO financing came from foreign governmental and nongovernmental organizations (Constantinescu 1997).

Most NGOs do not depend exclusively on foreign financing, although few are self-sustaining (sustainability is a major goal of democracy assistance). National organizations have been more successful in obtaining Romanian funding, while small professional associations have demonstrated the greatest interest in (and need for) external support. Those NGOs that received foreign financing from the outset have managed to survive and remain active. However, only four out of the twenty-nine women's organizations reported having permanent financing, foreign or domestic, indicating the precarious condition under which most of them operate. Inadequate financing results in part from the failure of many NGOs (at least half) to publicize their activities in bulletins, leaflets, posters, or other informational materials. Some organizations depend on monthly contributions, which often become a means of survival rather than a source of long-term financing. Funds typically are used to purchase equipment, cover the cost of organizing seminars, and pay the salaries of NGO personnel. With respect to wages, however, most of the women's groups surveyed (twenty-one out of twenty-nine) maintain that they operate on a strictly volunteer basis, except for the services of a salaried accountant.

Foreign funders represent varied interests ranging from the Mormon Church to the United States Agency for International Development (USAID) or the British and Danish Embassies.[23] In recent years, the European Union has

TABLE 11.2
Types of Financing for Women's NGOs

Types of Financing	Number of Positive Answers
Temporary external financing	11
Permanent external financing	4
Temporary internal financing	6
Permanent internal financing	2
Temporary external/internal financing	10
Self-Financing (e.g., through monthly contributions or lucrative activities)	7
No financing	3

[22] Since World War II, many Romanians have continued to hope that the Americans would come and save them. Immediately after the war, it was customary to hear, "Are you watching the skies to see if the Americans are coming?" Finally, after the revolution of 1989, the Americans, along with others, have arrived in Romania.

[23] For example, the Netherlands has supported the strengthening of human rights in Romania by financing important organizations such as the Helsinki Committee and the Romanian Independent

allocated large sums of money to women's NGOs. Out of forty-eight applications in 1996, twenty-two were funded by the PHARE Lien Program and thirteen by the PHARE Program for Democracy, representing a grant total of 201,809 and 129,044 ecu, respectively. In the same year, the Soros Foundation allocated U.S. $20,000 to women's organizations (for equipment and general funds, scholarships, etc.) plus an additional $10,000 to programs that would foster women's entrepreneurial skills. Romania was the only country in the region to which USAID awarded funds for family planning programs. Over a five-year period, the Center for Development and Population Activities (CEDPA) gave a total of $5 million to the Society for Contraceptive and Sexual Education (SECS), Tineri pentru Tineri [Youth for Youth], and Vrancea (a family planning movement). The British Know-How Fund and World Learning also invested in the nonprofit sector, awarding several grants to women's organizations. The United Nations Development Program (UNDP) contributed $85,000 in 1996 to projects for the advancement of women. Between July 1996 and May 1997, the Foundation for the Development of Civil Society (FDSC) distributed 1,400,000 ecu among 215 NGOs. Of these, seven were women's NGOs that received sums ranging from 3,000 to 20,000 ecu (FDSC 1997). Other Western organizations, including the Network of East-West Women (NEWW), have supported specific programs carried out by Romanian women's NGOs.

Yet foreign assistance has been a double-edged sword and has generated disappointment on both sides. In large measure, this is a result of the different sociocultural and political contexts in which NGOs have emerged in Eastern Europe (Wedel 1992:131–138; Carothers 1996). According to Sampson's astute observation, the mechanisms by which "the West-East inequality came to be called partnership" have played an important role in this and include imported development models (the very jargon of which is often difficult to translate into Romanian, for instance, implementation, sustainability, assessment); the rituals of training workshops, roundtables, and seminars; fundraising and the ceremonial tasks of filling out PHARE application forms; being interviewed for Soros fellowships; or writing letters of intent to World Learning (see Sampson 1996).

The phenomenon of idealizing the benefactor has led to some resentment of Western specialists who travel from what are assumed to be lush offices in their home institutions to the improvised offices of the recipient NGOs. "They'll all give you money to organize a seminar, especially if you invite one of their very well-paid experts. . . . [And] who is willing to come to Romania or Albania anyway? . . . Most likely those starting their careers," commented one leader of a national organization, a 40-year-old engineer. Or as a member of another national organization noted, "They are so bureaucratic. . . . What's the use of all those assessment reports, when out of politeness they automatically say that everything's great anyway?" A 35-year-old teacher and professional NGO leader scoffed, "These American ladies think we have just come fallen out of the

---

Society for Human Rights (SIRDO). The United States, Canada, and Japan have invested heavily in environmental NGOs, providing support to roughly 128 organizations.

trees. . . . [Our] women are highly educated [*sic*]." During an informal discussion, a government expert remarked cynically, "[If you] say that you want to contribute to the integration of the Gypsy community, you are likely to find assistance more easily. . . . [By] helping you be democratic and nondiscriminating, they are actually protecting themselves."

The "colonialist" comportment attributed to some Western experts has also become a topic on Internet discussion lists to which Easterners now have access. Recently, an East European lecturer, formerly with the Civic Education Project, declared, "I believe a great many Western 'advisers' in fact parachute into a country believing they have the right recipe to solve its problems in a particular sphere, while paying little attention to the details of the situation really existing on the ground." Such negative assessments notwithstanding, women's NGOs, even the few that are self-sustaining, continue to seek assistance from Western groups rather than cooperate with sister organizations in Romania.

The countries most active in exporting a women's movement are the United States, Germany, the United Kingdom, Ireland, and France. Romanian women's NGOs, in their search for foreign funding, have learned that the "magical power of words" can make the difference in receiving a grant. Thus, the women involved with these groups are suddenly fluent in the language of "women's empowerment" and the "gender dimension of the transition," even though such phrases previously rang hollow and were negatively associated with the regime's version of women's emancipation. In the current context, women are prompted to use another "wooden language" (albeit of Western origin) to achieve their objectives. A sense of pragmatism is at play here, combined with a kind of cultural arrogance, particularly evident among the women leaders interviewed. "As a matter of fact, we write what they want us to write, and then we go ahead and do what we want," one young NGO leader explained when describing the difficulty of raising money to pay the office rent.[24] "When submitting a budget for a proposed project, you request 10 percent of the funds for 'administrative expenses.' From two or three projects you can amass the [rent] money. It sounds absurd, but what do you do if nobody gives you money explicitly for the rent?"

Thus, relations between donors and recipients entail duplicitous posturing that has been generated, in part, by the priorities and bureaucratic requirements of donor organizations, the inflexibility of national laws, and the rebirth of an entrepreneurial spirit among Romanians, both male and female.

ROMANIAN WOMEN'S NGOs: CHARACTERISTIC FEATURES

The women's movement in Romania includes a wide range of institutions operating at local, national, and international levels and is comprised of professional and charitable organizations, as well as groups affiliated with trade unions,

---

[24] Office space is an acute problem. One out of five women's organizations lacks space. Certain donor constraints create problems for the donor and beneficiary alike. For example, SECS was the

political parties, and religious institutions (see Appendix 11.1). Women's NGOs tend to be small; particularly among local or professional organizations, active membership averages between twenty and thirty people. According to the questionnaire data, women active in these groups tend to be middle-aged, well educated, and married with one or two children; the average age of women NGO leaders is 40, and approximately 30 percent are divorced or single. While older women are more prominent in national organizations, younger women tend to be concentrated in local or professional groups. Approximately 80 percent are university graduates. Professionally, members of the women's movement are architects, physicians, lawyers, engineers, economists, and teachers, to name a few.

Some national and international organizations appear to have reconstituted the structure and mentality of the now defunct communist era National Union of Women. In contrast to most women's NGOs, these organizations have clearly defined structures and a large member base, ranging in size from 1,000 to 26,000 people. They set out a broad agenda and claim to represent all the women and NGOs in Romania. For example, in 1993, a Women's National Forum was established under the auspices of a national organization representing itself as the coordinator of the women's movement. In 1996, the Council for Social Dialogue Among Women's NGOs was formed and, according to its charter, constitutes a "forum that truly expresses the aspirations of the women's movement in Romania." Of the women who do identify themselves as feminists or members of the women's movement, few wield much influence because of their connections to the former regime.

Although most women's organizations invoke "women's rights," this term as understood and practiced in the West has proven difficult to introduce into the Romanian context. Indeed, whether in reference to women's rights or human rights in general, the Western "rights" discourse is not yet meaningful (Pasti et al. 1997).[25] Romania's collectivist culture—a legacy of communism under which laws and rights were applied to groups or categories of persons (e.g., workers)—differs from the individualistic cultures of the West. Moreover, Romanians have been socialized to focus on their duties to the state rather than on their individual rights. It is a peculiar paradox that, in 1996, the Ministry of Labor and Social Protection established the Department of Women's Rights and Family Policy when, to be sure, there has been no practical recognition of either the meaning or legitimacy of "women's rights."

While women's organizations readily affirm the importance of women's rights, this generally remains at the level of discursive abstraction. Indeed, only three of the twenty-nine organizations studied between September 1995 and March 1996 initiated any concrete activities on behalf of women's rights. When asked if women in Romania have lost any rights, 27 respondents answered yes, citing

---

first organization to receive support for family planning but, over a four-year period, they spent significant funds just to cover exorbitant rents. They were forced to move seven times due to the effects of inflation on property values, rents, and so on.

[25] Whether "rights" should be understood according to Western tenets is another matter and is beyond the scope of the present discussion.

such things as the loss of "the right to be appreciated" (1); "the right to be elected to an institution's governing board or to the country's government" (1); "the right to a decent living standard" (2); or even "the right to go to a seaside resort"(1). Only 10 women responded affirmatively when asked, "Have women in Romania gained any rights after 1989?" Most emphasized "the right to have an abortion" (7). "Freedom of speech" was mentioned four times, "the right to association" was mentioned twice and, ironically, "the right to speak without being listened to" was also mentioned. As one union leader observed, "Women have gained no liberty; their life has become more complicated; they have fostered a nostalgia for cheap vacations at the seaside or of kindergartens located in the vicinity of the factories where they work."

To the question, "Have you encountered concrete cases of the infringement of women's rights?" 25 respondents answered yes, some claiming "innumerable" (2) and "ongoing cases" (2). When asked to give specific examples, 9 women mentioned rape, sexual harassment, employment discrimination, or obligatory support for the ruling party as a condition of attaining unemployment benefits. Some commented on "the disregard of women's important role in the church" or "the malevolent intention of leaders to stop the development of civil society."

Respondents to the questionnaire found it easier to identify biases and stereotypes regarding women's involvement in social, political, and professional life. Most considered a certain mentality about women rather than their rights per se to be the problem. To quote a prominent representative of the National Liberal Party, "Young lady, you seem to think with your glands. Yes, we have primarily men, from the local mayors to representatives up to the parliamentarians, from business owners—who hire only uneducated but good-looking young girls—to taxi drivers." He then added that it is important to recognize men's duplicity in the face of possible partnerships with women in public life; "I have very many examples. Particularly after 1989, most of the men that I have had the opportunity to discuss the problem with endorse the emancipation of women and are in favor of their emancipation within given parameters in social, civil, and political life—except when it comes to their own wives and daughters." The issue of women's emancipation is generally acknowledged by Romanian men, who may even display tolerance and good will toward women's efforts to achieve this goal. However, emancipation of the women closest to them is another matter and engenders stronger reservations. Sharing public responsibilities with these women would also entail sharing in their private lives, which still seems unnatural to Romania's men.

When assessed in terms of the NGO framework elaborated here, a distinctive feature of the Romanian women's movement is its lack of a clearly defined objective or set of priorities. In many women's organizations, the domain of activity is unclear, although education and public health, especially reproductive health, are well-represented at all three levels (see Appendix 11.1). The Society for Contraceptive and Sexual Education has already opened eleven family planning centers in Romania's larger towns. Tineri pentru Tineri has developed training sessions on sexual education in more than ten high schools in Bucharest and produced manuals on this issue.[26] National organizations like the Inter-Balkan League and the Women's Confederation of Romania have trained medical practitioners and social workers in contraceptive education and have provided equipment to hospitals and polyclinics. Some groups, by organizing successful television appeals, have raised enough funds to set up school counseling centers and to underwrite the cost of mass-media campaigns promoting contraception.

At the institutional level, women's organizations are significantly less active than other types of NGOs. Generally speaking, civil society discourse in this domain is anti-state, and is also elaborated by men, often as a means for them to launch their political careers. Although women participating in NGOs have frequently been at odds with men, they have been less visibly so with the state. At least until the November 1996 elections, women's seemingly uncritical attitude toward the state weakened their influence and prestige. Moreover, the fact that women have been engaged in a dialogue among themselves instead of with those in power has contributed to their marginalization.[27]

At the community level, many women's NGOs focus their activities on the family. They may assist poor families, for example, particularly those with many children or with children suffering from AIDS.[28] Typically, Romanian women identify themselves in terms of family rather than gender, and they do not customarily view family and gender interests together. Many women are also involved in the women's religious movement, which is well defined and has a considerable following. In response to an initiative taken by the World Council of Churches, several denominations that lend financial support to NGOs formed the Inter-Church AID Department in Romania (AIDrom). Inter-Church AID has established an ecumenical platform for dialogue and promotes programs on religious education, as well as social and environmental projects. The Ecumenical Forum of Women in Romania, which is linked to the Catholic, Protestant, Reformed, Unitarian, and Orthodox Churches, is also active.[29] Women's NGOs

[26] Regarding SECS and other NGOs activities in the field of reproductive health, family planning, and contraceptive education, see Adriana Băban's chapter in this volume.

[27] There have been noteworthy exceptions. The Women's Department of the National Council of Free Trade Unions in Romania-Frăția (CNSLR) initiated a tri-party dialogue (government-union-private enterprise), which was to negotiate the participation of NGOs as well. This initiative was part of an ILO/PHARE project. As per Government Decision no. 349/20 July 1993, the Tri-Party Secretariat was established as a nonpolitical and nonprofit body to facilitate social dialogue. However, this project still exists only on paper. The initiative of Grup 222 [Group 222] is also noteworthy, despite its failure.

The Equal Opportunity Department, Șanse Egale, of the National Council of Free Trade Unions and some party organizations are active and often more efficient in promoting women's interests because of their links with grassroots constituencies. Collaboration between women's NGOs and women's organizations inside the parties or unions is still difficult.

[28] There are other NGOs with programs directed to the family. For example, the Asociația Familia Regăsita works to reintegrate abandoned children into their families; another group helps reintegrate women released from prison back into their families.

[29] The Forum is not officially registered because the Orthodox Church has so far failed to sign a written agreement.

with a religious orientation have focused on educational programs, specifically promoting Christian family values.

Some issues, such as domestic violence, are addressed mainly by women's organizations and pertain to all three domains of NGO activity. Violence aimed at women and children is common in Romania and is among the concerns of international NGOs. Thus far, however, Romanian legislators and society at large have failed to take the problem seriously. A 1995 report on Romania, prepared by the Minnesota Advocates for Human Rights, was the subject of intense discussion at the Fourth World Conference on Women in Beijing; in Romania, the report was either criticized or ignored. To begin to address this issue in Romania, domestic violence must first be recognized as a social problem. The persistence of attitudes such as "dirty laundry is done in the family" or "garbage is not swept over the threshold" constitutes a barrier to bringing domestic violence out of the private sphere and into the realm of public consciousness. To this end, some women's NGOs and the government have begun to focus attention on this issue by undertaking empirical studies and developing programs for the victims of domestic violence.[30] Increasingly, the problem is a subject of grant proposals, conferences, and seminars. To be sure, civic education programs and media presentations about domestic violence could contribute importantly to raising public awareness of the multiple aspects and consequences of such behavior, but, at present, such programs are nonexistent. While legislation punishing domestic violence is necessary, it will not be forthcoming without social mobilization, meaning the prospects for legal recourse remain limited. No formal lobby presently exists on behalf of the country's women.

The lack of effective social mobilization around and institutionalization of women's issues underscores the problem of "form without content," that is to say, the prevalence of institutions that have formal bureaucratic structures (such as a governing board) but lack a positive performance record. For example, the Department of Women's Rights and Family Policy, a State Secretariat within the Ministry of Labor, was created in May 1996 to develop strategies for improving the status of women, families, and children in Romania. The impetus behind this move was a meeting between several women's groups—reputedly acting on behalf of all women's NGOs—and then President Ion Iliescu. Eighty percent of the questionnaire respondents for this study and all of the women interviewed questioned the efficacy of this department and noted that it serves agendas other

[30] See, for example, the program Stop Domestic Violence carried out by the Romanian Independent Society for Human Rights (SIRDO). The Democratic Party's Head Office in Bucharest's District 2 initiated a program, The Open Window, consisting of weekly counseling hours for abused women. The Ministry of Social Protection has opened the first shelter for abused women in Bucharest. Also, there are motions to modify the Penal Code to increase sentences for committing domestic violence. In Sibiu and Timişoara there are efforts to open a hotline and shelters for women and children. The Faculty of Social Work, reopened after 1989, offers courses in social assistance for women. A PHARE Program of the Association of Women Journalists in Romania (Ariadna), in collaboration with the Bucharest Police Department and SIRDO, is designed to draw public attention and to involve the media in fighting this phenomenon.

than that for which it was established. Some considered it to be profoundly nonfeminist because it defines women as an entitlement category, like the disabled or street children, eligible for special governmental programs. Others described it as an effort to reinstitutionalize "women and children" as a single entity, noting that the "natural affinity" presumed to exist between them runs counter to the formation of a new gender contract in post-communist Romania. Still others saw the new institution as one more bureaucratic means to obscure their real problems and interests, while serving the self-interested attempts by certain individuals to acquire coveted government positions. Whatever its problems and deficiencies, the department exists and is led by a woman. Many similar "forms without content" continue to emerge, each claiming to be a force of change.[31]

Yet such institutions invariably fail. Group 222, for example, was formed to put as many women as possible on the 1996 election lists (222 is approximately one-half the number of seats in Parliament). Group 222 supported women in politics and promoted a kind of gender solidarity. It was well funded and publicized in the media, and the initiative generated great enthusiasm; in 1995, over 200 people—mostly women—signed petitions of support. Group 222 purposefully declared itself to be informal in character rather than an institutional endeavor. Yet this informality detracted from Group 222's ability to communicate a clear message and to foster dialogue among the various parties. The few parties that were receptive to female candidates were accused of engaging in electoral propaganda.[32] Selection and promotion of women candidates by Group 222 and those associated with it never materialized.

The general absence of positive role models for women leaders—in politics, history, or the media—combined with the linguistic bias of a Constitution in which the president is referred to in the masculine form were and remain cultural factors that shape(d) perceptions and actions. Ninety percent of the respondents answered negatively when asked, "Do you have a positive role model for a woman leader?" Among the few who said yes, only Margaret Thatcher was named. When asked, "Would you support a woman candidate for President simply because she is a woman?" the answer was a resounding 100 percent "no." While this may be taken as a sign of political maturity, it may also point to the lack of solidarity among women. As previously mentioned, women have been unwilling to lobby for their interests even though social mobilization of this sort is a necessary feature of civic involvement.

In short, women's organizations are promoting neither gender consciousness nor public discussion of women's contributions, despite the fact that some women speak of "a feminine solution in all fields," to use the words of one 40-year-old Romanian teacher. Nor are women's organizations actively engaged in other

[31] In 1997 a new Department of Equal Opportunities, financially supported by UNDP, was to be established within the Ministry of Social Protection.

[32] The Democratic Union of Hungarians in Romania (UDMR), an ethnic party that itself has generated significant debate, was the first to sense the pragmatic value of winning women's votes. Center-right-wing parties in the Democratic Convention were more reluctant, while extremist parties avoided the issue altogether.

community level projects, for example, in the arts or culture. Romania has no association of women artists. Women in these fields are reluctant to label their work "feminist." Prominent figures like Ana Blandiana, Mariana Celac, Gabriela Adameşteanu, and others have been quite open in declaring their reservations about the women's movement in general and about feminism in particular. These women prefer to participate in other civil society movements, like the Grup pentru Dialog Social [Group for Social Dialogue].[33] Indeed, many women do not identify themselves as feminists, but are active in NGOs devoted to human rights, the environment, and urban problems. As a rule, women's NGOs do not focus on these issues.

Feminism and Women's Activism—for Whom?

At present, women's issues and feminism are largely perceived to be Western concerns that are inappropriate to the Romanian context. In general, Romanians will accept whatever they must to be accepted into NATO or the European Union.[34] This does not hold true, however, for women's issues, and especially feminism, toward which there is widespread hostility. Even within women's NGOs, seventeen out of twenty-nine women interviewed do not identify themselves as feminists. One 42-year-old doctor, herself a leader of a professional NGO, remarked, "I am not at all a feminist. . . . I believe women fulfill themselves through their families, children, and husbands, but they do need help." A 38-year-old lawyer said, "I am not a feminist. The man–woman relationship is a complementary one. I believe in equal opportunities for all and in mutual respect." Another doctor, 45 years old and active in a women's group commented, "The masculine gender is a 'partner' in a woman's achievements, and actually in all aspects of life." Those women who consider themselves feminists said they do so because they "love women and are concerned about their moral and spiritual condition after 1989," because "women stand for the future," or "because it is only by getting out of the kitchen that we will really find out who we are and what we want." Some women confessed a sense of ambivalence, evident in the following remark, "I really do not know. Anyhow, I'd rather not be called that."

Thus, when asked, "Can we speak of a feminist and/or women's movement in Romania?" 90 percent said there is only a women's movement. Three answers were contradictory, for example, "The objectives of a feminist organization are different. They want special rights, while we want equal rights," noted a 50-

---

[33] It should be noted that the Group for Social Dialogue itself lacks any real dialogue with the civil society it allegedly represents. With respect to the women mentioned, Ana Blandiana is a highly regarded poetess and president of Civic Alliance; Mariana Celac is a noted architect and prominent member of the Group for Social Dialogue; Gabriela Adameşteanu is a well-known writer and Editor-in-Chief of the weekly 22.

[34] For example, Romania responded to pressure by revising article 200 of the Penal Code to decriminalize homosexuality and by adopting EC Recommendation 1201 regarding local autonomy. The latter was a point of contention in the bilateral agreement between Romania and Hungary.

year-old leader of a political organization. Another stated, "We are not a feminist organization because there shouldn't be fighting between the sexes." A 38-year-old architect and member of a professional organization pointed out that, "Most of the organizations do not publicly claim to be feminist. There is no trace of tolerance in our society for such a movement." Indeed, the only organization with the word feminist in its name, the Society for Feminist Analysis (ANA), is considered elitist. Another group, Gender, is often belittled for its cosmopolitanism; since there is no Romanian equivalent of the word gender, its very name signifies something foreign.

The rejection of feminism can be attributed to various factors, including hints of nationalism and elitism. As noted earlier, issues concerning the Motherland are, for many Romanians, more important than personal concerns. Also, the perception that feminism is a dangerous Western import has been reinforced by the rhetoric used by women's NGOs.[35] More often than not, talk about women's needs and how to meet such needs in the context of transition mirrors a Western discourse that is subject to minimal modification by Romanian women. Feminism also tends to be associated with a brand of left-wing politics that is no longer fashionable among intellectuals. Moreover, there is a certain vanity among educated women who believe in gender equality and do not perceive themselves to be discriminated against because of their sex. To be sure, there is a great deal of uncertainty and even disapproval of feminism in Romania today. Yet in view of the fact that most women lack knowledge about feminism, it would be inaccurate to label them anti-feminist.

In terms of civil society initiatives, it might be said that women's NGOs are busy helping women but not emancipating them. A premium is placed on meeting practical needs rather than strategically addressing the broader issue of gender relations. Although NGO leaders are effectively engaged in efforts to assist women within the existing framework of gender roles, they are not redefining the division of responsibility between women and men (Moser 1993:196–211). One Irish expert remarked at a training course on gender, "It is one thing to want changing tables for babies in as many women's rooms as possible in Romania; it's quite another to want the same thing in men's rooms." Among those present at the meeting were members of trade unions and NGOs, including the Society for Feminist Analysis, Gender, the Girl Scouts Association, and the Pro Europe League. These women were highly "gender conscious" and seemed to have understood the gist of the trainer's comment, yet no one could offer a related example. It remains difficult even for gender-conscious women in Romania to translate Western strategies into everyday concepts and contexts. With respect to placing changing tables in public buildings, such an idea as part of a set of gender strategies seems a luxury. A more appropriate form of "Westernization" may simply be improved hygiene in public facilities.

The issue of gender consciousness notwithstanding, it is clearly problematic to import models for women's empowerment in a political economy in transition. Attempts by Romanian women to formulate a self-referential discourse about

---

[35] For the relationship between feminism and nationalism, see Miroiu 1995a, b.

women's interests has failed, in part, because of the crude appropriation of Western concepts noted throughout this chapter, as if the East-West dialogue were predicated on a simple matter of linguistics.[36] It is one thing to introduce Western ideas about women and feminism; it is quite another to "implement" them given the complex dynamics of transition. Moreover, as captured in the following caustic remark, Western strategies are often viewed as the self-indulgent activities of women with nothing better to do: "Even though the country is in flames, the old bag is doing her hair." Some accuse feminists of engaging in a "sophisticated language" that is too abstract for the needs of daily life. "What good is it to be in all those organizations for broads?" queried a female doctor, who lives in an area of rural Transylvania where newspapers arrive several days late and there is no access to private television. Esoteric seminars in Bucharest on women's empowerment or, for that matter, on the mayoral campaign, simply do not resonate with the lives and needs of rural women.

It is important here to note that women's NGOs are primarily an urban phenomenon. Approximately 80 percent of women's organizations are active in Bucharest, which is also where funders have their offices. These NGOs readily speak in the name of all Romanian women, forgetting that many of their sisters live elsewhere and in very different circumstances. Except for national organizations with branches in rural areas (many of which exist on paper only), there are only ten NGOs operating in towns outside Bucharest, including Iaşi, Tărgu Mureş, Braşov, Focşani, Suceava, Craiova, and Oradea. The Women's Association of Tărgu Frumos in Moldova, a region in the northeast of Romania, is the only NGO in a rural locale.

Of Romania's total population, 12.5 million inhabitants, or 54.9 percent, live in rural areas (National Commission for Statistics 1996). Rural women are not represented by nor do they benefit from the possible advantages that may result from NGO activities. This has contributed to rising tensions and frustrations among women, as well as to instrumental opportunism on the part of some NGOs that receive funds designated for projects in other regions of the country. For example, foreign donors may be told, for strategic funding purposes, that a seminar or course on women's rights will be organized for women outside Bucharest; such an event, however, is never held or, if it is, may be quickly improvised. The funds are accounted for nonetheless.

The cross-continental misunderstandings that have grown out of different languages and meanings have been reproduced in Romania between women's NGOs and the general population. "Equality," for example, now means something different to NGO activists than it does to many women in the general population. The latter tend to want equality based on the recognition of difference; women's NGOs, on the other hand, speak more of the need for equal treatment. Outside the women's movement, women are more likely to demand

---

[36] To illustrate, a professional NGO organized a seminar on gender at Sinaia, a resort town. Use of the term "positive discrimination" triggered debate not only about its meaning, but also about the "McDonaldization" of Romanian culture. "What do you mean by positive discrimination . . . ladies, let's openly call it support, favoritism, assistance. . . . We have given up our own language, our own brains," a 40-year-old journalist irately remarked.

dignified domesticity than individual equality. Such differences are well illustrated by the split regarding the retirement age for women.[37] A majority of less educated women do not regard early retirement as a form of discrimination, as do more highly educated women whose professional interests and opportunities will be affected by state-mandated early retirement.

Parental leave is another issue that has provoked disagreement among women and points to the increasing social differentiation of gender issues in post-communist Romania. Many representatives of women's NGOs have spoken (again, in the name of all Romanian women) about the need for parental leave legislation. However, the leader of the Equal Opportunities Department of the National Council of Free Trade Unions-Frația (CNSLR), an organization that enjoys authentic grassroots support, countered that popular reaction to this proposal is decidedly negative. In June 1995, the Council organized a debate on parental leave in a large Bucharest factory that employs mainly women; the session was moderated by Belgian experts. Taking the floor, one participant said, "To us it would be foolish. . . . Those who would like their husbands to stay home, raise your hand!" Not one hand among the hundred women present was raised. Many women view parental leave as a policy that would complicate their lives and force them to take care of both their children and their husbands. Yet whatever the difference in public opinion on this matter, parental leave was passed into law in 1997 as part of the government's effort to bring Romania in line with European standards. It warrants mention that television announcers explained the law as "maternity leave which may be taken by the father!"

Clearly, there is a communication gap between the large majority of women and those who are active in women's NGOs. Again, the latter echo a Western feminist discourse of equal treatment that, although it may sound attractive abroad, loses its audience at home.[38] After seven years, women's NGOs still have trouble getting their messages across. Many self-professed representatives of Romanian women are out of touch with their constituencies; they really do not know to whom they are "speaking" or whom they represent. In response to the open-ended question, "What do women's NGOs in Romania lack?," most women said, "To know what we want," "To have clear objectives," or "To be clearer." The lack of funding and of credibility took second and third place, respectively.

These problems do not facilitate effective prioritizing of women's different needs and interests. As a result, NGO objectives are blurred. Three of the organizations studied have not even defined their objectives. One listed "civil society" as its primary objective. Others emphasized improvement of public health (2), welfare (1), woman's image in our society (2), women's living standards

---

[37] In Romania, retirement age for women is 55. The proposed Law on Social Insurance and Pensions not yet passed by Parliament increases women's retirement age to 62; men's, to 65. There are also proposals to raise the age limit to 65 years for both sexes, which is the OECD age level. It should be noted that the average life expectancy is 69.

[38] Criticism that the Western women's movement is oriented to "white middle-class women" has also been directed at the nascent movement in Romania, which, at present, is an elite movement that lacks a grassroots following.

TABLE 11.3
To Whom Do Women's NGOs Speak?

Target Group as Indicated by NGOs	Number of Answers
Women	14
Young people	3
Unemployed, young female graduates	2
The disadvantaged and sick	2
Romanians in general	1
Women, teenage girls, the third age group	1
Union members	1
Girls between age 7 and 18	1

Note: Two "No" replies indicate that the question was not properly understood.

(4), or women's and children's living conditions (5). Some NGOs claim their objective is to promote women's rights (6) or women's access to and advancement in politics or the professions (4). Content analyses of NGO catalogues or organizational charters and by-laws also reveal a lack of clearly defined aims. The leaflet of one local women's group listed among its objectives "the political participation of women," "education and culture," "the image of women," "studies on women," "woman's rights" (singular), "assisting needy children" and "the elderly."[39] Another organization represented in this study defined its objectives as "defending social and economic rights, the improvement of the image of women in our society, the generation of laws supporting the single-parent family, pre-maternity leave, children's rights, education on public health and family planning." The scope of this NGO's activities was apparently delimited by the space available on the form.

As this discussion suggests, it is still premature to claim that Romania's women are the primary beneficiaries of NGO initiatives. Instead, the benefits currently gained from women's NGOs are more constitutive than substantive. As one NGO leader remarked, "democracy wins;" that is, democracy is served by the burgeoning of women's NGOs. Questionnaire responses mirrored this sentiment (see Table 11.3). Although in the abstract this may be true, the gap between women's expectations and the actual accomplishments of women's NGOs is clear.

WOMEN'S NGOS: THE "OTHER" WITHIN
ROMANIA'S CIVIL SOCIETY MOVEMENT

In today's Romania, against a background of deeply entrenched social polarization that virtually precludes dialogue among the myriad of groups in society and in the absence of a clear gender consciousness, the possibilities for promoting gender-specific issues are limited. It is important here to note the relationship

---

[39] In the questionnaire responses, there was a correlation in only two instances between the stated aims of the NGO and its declared target group.

between "human rights" and "women's rights" in Romania today. While many NGOs are active in the field of human rights, "women's rights" have been virtually silenced in the public sphere. It is more customary—even among women themselves—to speak about the rights of homosexuals, Roma or Gypsies, the Hungarian minority, or street children than about the rights of women. Indeed, the Roma community has become increasingly adept in defending its interests; the Democratic Union of Hungarians in Romania (UDMR) has a strong voice in the government; the younger generations have more easily identified common concerns, namely sexual issues (including family planning) and job opportunities. Human rights organizations, such as the Helsinki Committee Association for Defending Human Rights in Romania (APADOR-CH) or the League for Defending Human Rights (LADO), have marginalized the issue of women's rights, while the prestigious Pro-Europe League, which sponsors interethnic and intercultural educational programs, does not consider gender to be a significant variable in ethnic conflict. Some NGOs, like the Helsinki Committee, view all human rights as universal and therefore do not recognize rights that can be attributed only to women. Among all of these groups, there is a basic antipathy toward women's rights as distinctive. Not one of these organizations participate in explicitly feminist activities, nor do they use the term "women's rights."

Women's NGOs must learn from other interest groups to organize around issues for which sufficient consensus exists. Unlike the afore-mentioned "successes" of the Roma, Hungarians, and youth, women have seemingly failed to find a common platform of interests and strategies, not to mention a common language. In consequence thereof, women's NGOs hold little status within Romania's civil society movement; this is quite clear from their lack of representation at the Forum of Non-Governmental Organizations in Romania and from the media's attitude toward them.

The annual forum, organized with the generous support of international donors, was designed to mobilize and consolidate Romania's civil society movement; each meeting was well attended. Unfortunately, women's NGOs were repeatedly marginalized. At the first conference in 1994, only two out of forty NGOs were women's groups. The second meeting, held in Braşov, brought more than sixty-five NGOs together with international organizations, representatives from the U.S. House of Representatives and Senate, and officials of the Romanian government. NGO representatives were selected and grouped according to six fields of activity: civic, economic development, human rights, mass media, environmental protection, and youth. More than half of the conference participants were women—clear evidence of women's involvement in civic life. However, only three women's organizations participated: the National Association of Women with University Degrees, the Women's League of Braşov, and the Girl Scouts Association, which specializes in youth programs. The first group had not been invited and its representatives paid their own way.[40]

---

[40] I was unable to learn the criteria by which invitations were issued, but overheard informal talk among the organizers that "women's organizations are weak, too feminist, and less representative."

Although the event had no specific theme, not fewer than eighteen environmental organizations attended, constituting half of all organizations present.[41] To be sure, environmental issues are extremely important in Romania. But there are other pressing matters that merit similar attention, such as unemployment (10.6 percent of women and 7.5 percent of men were unemployed in 1995),[42] sexual education and family planning (particularly in rural areas), and social assistance.

The third NGO forum took place in Bucharest in 1996; ninety-six local NGOs and seventeen financial organizations (both local and foreign) participated, as did Romanian and international observers. Government officials, parliamentary representatives, and eight NGOs from the Republic of Moldova were also present. Culture and society was added to the previous list of six fields. According to the organizers, the CENTRAS database (Centre for NGO Assistance) was used to prepare the invitation list, as were suggestions put forward by authors of the NGO "white books."[43] Excluding the Pro-Europe League of Târgu Mureş, which was inaccurately listed as a women's organization, women's NGOs were better represented than at the previous meetings. Three Romanian NGOs— Equal Opportunities for Women from Iaşi (included in the economic section), the Society for Contraceptive and Sexual Education (included in the civic section), and the National Association of Women with University Degrees—participated together with international women's associations and the Organization of Women Diplomats (which provided conference funding). None of the other fifty-plus women's organizations were invited, and none participated in the human rights, society, or mass media sections. When analyzing the participant lists, the conference themes, and the resolutions adopted at all three fora, one cannot fail to conclude that women's NGOs and women's issues were marginalized and ignored—again, despite the fact that women constitute more than half of both the Romanian population and the country's active NGO membership.[44]

The marginalization of women's NGOs and women's issues is widespread in the public sphere. While a full analysis of the media's treatment of gender issues is beyond the scope of this chapter, a cursory discussion is nonetheless in order.[45] In general, the Romanian media does not cover NGO activities and is rather hostile to civil society organizations. A lengthy article published in 1996 in the

[41] Not surprisingly, one of the three final resolutions addressed modification of the Penal Code with regard to forest preservation in Romania. The other two resolutions dealt with the operation of associations and foundations and free access to information.

[42] See the National Commission for Statistics 1996 and United Nations Development Program & Women in Development (UNDP/WID) 1995.

[43] These books provide general information on NGOs and were compiled by a team of ten authors, two of whom were women. Neither of them belonged to a women's NGO.

[44] The Fourth Annual Forum was held in June 1997. This time, the list of workshop sections was expanded to ten and included gender. Because "gender" was listed in English and not translated, it was confusing for all participants, including representatives of women's NGOs.

[45] Due to space constraints, discussion of the so-called women's reviews (*The Woman, The Women's Magazine, Women's World, My Family*, etc.) have been excluded from this summary.

TABLE 11.4
Assessment by Women's NGOs of Government and Media Reaction to
Their Message

Institution	Very Good	Good	Satisfactory	Not Satisfactory
Newspapers	1	1	8	19
Radio	3	2	12	12
Public TV	0	1	7	21
Private TV	3	1	11	14
Government	0	2	4	23
Ministries	0	4	12	13

newspaper *Adevărul* questioned the merits of the twenty-seven projects funded by PHARE, implying that some were makeshift or phantom operations.[46]

Women's organizations are almost never acknowledged or taken seriously by the media. The print media is most problematic, with radio and television coverage being somewhat less dismissive (see Table 11.4). Although reporters are invited to participate at events sponsored by women's NGOs, they rarely attend. On March 8th, International Women's Day, the media will customarily pay lip service to women's issues. Otherwise, they cover mundane gossip regarding women's personal lives instead of substantive concerns,[47] leaving the impression that women's NGOs are characterized by clannishness and amateurishness. Overt disregard for the legitimacy of women's NGOs or women's issues is typical. In *România Libera,* one of the most widely read newspapers in post-Ceauşescu Romania,[48] feminism was represented as "one of the contemporary world's follies" (July 6, 1996). When an international summer seminar on "women's equality with men in Eastern Europe" was held at the Babeş-Bolyai University of Cluj-Napoca in July 1996, the local independent television station reported on the "Lesbian and Gay Congress in Cluj." None of the first four issues of *Info ONG,* an NGO information bulletin published by CENTRAS, listed any of Romania's women's organizations, although the bulletin claims to cover the gamut of newly established NGOs. It should be noted, however, that women's NGOs have become more visible in recent issues. Also, and despite the generally poor coverage of women's issues, there are a number of cultural reviews that have allotted space, on occasion, to feminist concerns.[49]

[46] *Adevărul*, April 23, 1996. "Fondurile Phare-înghiţite de organizaţii fantome care vînează cai verzi pe pereţi" [PHARE Funds Swallowed up by Phantom Organizations Hunting Green Horses on the Walls]. The information on which this article was based was gathered from telephone calls made by the editor, coincidentally a woman.

[47] See, for example, *Evenimentul Zilei,* No. 158, August 1996. Of course, clannishness and amateurishness are accusations hurled at the government and the opposition alike.

[48] This was an opposition newspaper until the November 1996 elections, when "its" candidates wrested power from the Iliescu government.

[49] For example: *22,* no. 87, 1994; *Dilema,* no. 150, November 1995; no. 220, April 1997; no. 226, May 1997. The political monthly *Sfera politicii* published articles on women and feminism in nos.

CONCLUSION

The data analyzed for this study suggest that the women's movement in post-communist Romania is relatively weak.[50] Various factors have contributed to this, not least of which is the ambivalence expressed by women themselves about women's NGOs in general, and about feminism in particular. The absence of gender consciousness, combined with lack of knowledge about the objectives of women's NGOs and, relatedly, feminism, is inadvertently reinforced by the lack of communication among women's NGOs, and between them and other civil society organizations and the majority of women in Romania. In short, the women's movement in Romania plays an important role in its own marginalization. Some women active in the women's movement reproduce modes of thinking and interacting reminiscent of the communist past; others, having appropriated what might be called "transition speak," use jargon that is meaningless in the context of daily life in Romania. What is perceived as the elitism of the women's movement is often manifest in the attitudes of NGO leaders toward the women they claim to represent. In consequence, the women's movement has been ineffective in engaging either women or society at large in constructive dialogue.

The political and cultural traditions in which gender relations are embedded also contribute to the marginalization of women's issues and the women's movement. The diversity of women's voices are not heard, even by women active in civil society. A widespread misconception that women's emancipation constitutes a threat to family harmony only encourages the trivialization of women's concerns. Like the army and the church, the family is highly valued as a site of stability, especially amidst the uncertainty provoked by the post-communist transition.

Women represent a genuine force in civil society whose potential has not yet been adequately recognized or realized. In Romania, the women's movement is evolving within the topsy-turvy context of transition. For the time being at least, the women's movement exists in a Wonderland where everything is upside down. Until 1992, during the first stage of post-communist transition, women's issues were not considered among the list of pressing priorities. But now that the initial euphoria of "anticipatory reformism" (that is, a positive approach to democracy and a market economy) has given way to "reaction reformism" (that is, individual and collective attempts to counteract the negative effects of reform; see Sandu 1996), there is both room and need for women's voices to be heard. Women's NGOs must now address the uncertainties of transition and work to rebuild Romanian civil society—for men, women, and children. To do so, women's NGOs must learn to communicate their objectives in the spirit of civil society,

3/4, 1994 and no. 47, 1997. The cultural review *Secolul XX* dedicated an entire issue to feminism (no. 7-8-9, 1996). Several books on feminism have also been published recently, including Miroiu 1995a, b; Miroiu 1996; Grunberg and Miroiu 1997a, b.

[50] Of course, this may also be the result of sample bias. The most effective voices in the women's movement may not have been those represented in this study.

the very ideal of which is to seek mutual respect and cooperation in the realization of common interests.

BIBLIOGRAPHY

Carothers, Thomas
    1996   Assessing Democracy Assistance: The Case of Romania. Washington, DC: Carnegie Endowment for International Peace.
Comisia Naţională de Statistică
    1996   Anuarul Statistic al României [Romanian Statistical Yearbook]. Bucharest: Comisia Naţională de Statistică.
Constantinescu, Ştefan
    1997   The Dimensions of the NGO Sector in Romania. FDSC: Studii şi cercetări asupra sectorului nonprofit 3(Iunie):3.
Dodgen, Lynda I. and Adrian M. Rapp
    1993   Looking through the Window of Sociology. Dubuque, IA: Kendall/Hunt.
Focşeneanu, E.
    1992   Istoria constituţională a României. Bucharest: Humanitas.
Foundation for the Development of Civil Society
    1997   Catalogul Organizaţiilor Neguvernamentale din România. Bucharest: Foundation for the Development of Civil Society.
Gal, Susan
    1994   Gender in the Post-Socialist Transition: The Abortion Debate in Hungary. East European Politics and Societies 8(2):256–287.
Grunberg, Laura and Mihaela Miroiu
    1997a   Gender and Education. Bucharest: Smartprint.
    1997b   Gender and Society: An Introductory Guide to Gender Issues. Bucharest: Alternative.
Grupul pentru Dialog Social
    1993   Raport asupra evenimentelor din 13–15 iunie 1990. Bucharest: Grupul pentru Dialog Social şi Asociaţia pentru Apărarea Drepturilor Omului dîn România.
Kligman, Gail
    1988   The Wedding of the Dead: Ritual, Poetics, and Popular Culture in Transylvania. Berkeley: University of California Press.
    1990   Reclaiming the Public: A Reflection on Creating Civil Society in Romania. East European Politics and Societies 4(3):393–438.
    1992   The Politics of Reproduction in Ceauşescu's Romania: A Case Study in Political Culture. East European Politics and Societies 6(3):364–418.
    1995   Political Demography: The Banning of Abortion in Ceauşescu's Romania. *In* Conceiving the New World Order: The Global Politics of Reproduction. Faye Ginsburg and Rayna Rapp, eds. Pp. 234–255. Berkeley: University of California Press.
    1998   The Politics of Duplicity: Controlling Reproduction in Ceauşescu's Romania. Berkeley: University of California Press.
Maiorescu, Titu
    1868   În contra direcţiei de Astăzi în Cultura Română. Revista Convorbiri Literare.
Minnesota Advocates for Human Rights
    1995   Lifting the Last Curtain: A Report on Domestic Violence in Romania. Minneapolis: Minnesota Advocates for Human Rights.

Miroiu, Mihaela
  1995a   Gender Identity and Self Sacrifice. Gender and Culture Workshop on Feminism and Nationalism, 1995. Essex University.
  1995b   Gândul umbreii: abordări feministe in filosofia contemporană [In the Shadow of Reason: Feminist Approaches to Contemporary Philosophy]. Bucharest: Alternative.
  1996   Convenio: On Nature, Women and Morality. Bucharest: Alternative.
Moser, Caroline O. N.
  1993   Gender Planning and Development: Theory, Practice and Training. New York: Routledge.
Pasti, V. with Mihaela Miroiu and C. Codiţă, ed.
  1997   România-Stare de Fapt. Vol. 1: Societatea. Bucharest: Nemira.
Pavel, Dan
  1996   Societatea contra statului: în ajutorul acestuia. Dilema 175.
Pietraru, D.
  1997   The Constitution of Romania: The Stolen Constitution. Ph.D. Dissertation. New School for Social Research.
Pleşu, Andrei
  1996   De Vorbă cu Adam Michnik. Dilema 190:3.
Răboacă, G. and A. Popescu
  1994   The Condition of Women in Romania (1980–1994): A National Report. Bucharest: National Committee for the World Conference on Women.
Racioppi, Linda and Katherine O'Sullivan See
  1995   Organizing Women Before and After the Fall: Women's Politics in the Soviet Union and Post-Soviet Russia. Signs 20(4):819–848.
Sampson, Steven
  1996   The Social Life of Projects: Bringing Civil Society to Albania. *In* Civil Society: Challenging Western Models. C. Hann, ed. Pp. 121–142. New York: Routledge.
Sandor, Dorel
  1996   Dinamica sectorului neguvernamental în România. *In* Dezvoltarea societăţii civile. Alexandru R. Săvulescu, ed. Pp. 8–15. Bucharest: Fundaţia Internaţională pentru Sisteme Electorale.
Sandu, Dumitru
  1996   Încrederea ca resursă a tranzitiei postcomuniste. Sfera Politicii 38(23).
Šiklova, Jirina
  1993   Feminism and Citizenship. Ankara, Turkey: Third HCA Assembly.
SOROS Foundation for an Open Society
  1994   Catalogul Organizaţiilor neguvernamentale din România. Bucharest: Fundaţia SOROS pentru o Societate Deschisă [SOROS Foundation for an Open Society].
Strickland-Šmekalova, Jirina
  1995   Revival? Gender Studies in the "Other" Europe. Signs 20(4):1000–1006.
Tismăneanu, Vladimir
  1992   Reinventing Politics: Eastern Europe from Stalin to Havel. New York: The Free Press.
United Nations Development Program/Women in Development
  1996   Catalogue of NGOs Active in Women's Issues. Bucharest: UNDP/WID.

Varlam, I.
  1993   Noua constituție a României. Bucharest: Evenimentul.
Verdery, Katherine and Gail Kligman
  1992   Romania after Ceaușescu: Post-Communist Communism? *In* Eastern Europe
          in Revolution. Ivo Banac, ed. Pp. 117–147. Ithaca, NY: Cornell University
          Press.
Wedel, Janine R.
  1992   The Unintended Consequences of Western Aid to Post Communist Europe.
          Telos 92:131.
  1994   U.S. Aid to Central and Eastern Europe, 1990–1994: An Analysis of Aid
          Models and Responses. *In* East-Central European Economies in Transition:
          Study Papers Submitted to the Joint Economic Committee of the United States
          Congress. Pp. 299–335. Washington, DC: U.S. Government Printing Office.

APPENDIX 11.1:
Romanian NGOs Active in the Field of Women's Issues

Name of NGO	*Location*	*Keywords*
Association of Women Journalists and Artists of Romania (ARIADNA)	Bucharest	Women and mass media
Association "Saint Stelian"	Bucharest	Charity
Association of Gypsy Women of Romania	Bucharest	Gypsy women
Association of Judges in Romania	Bucharest	Women's rights
Association of Optimist Women	Bucharest	Women
Association of Women with a Juridical Career in Romania	Bucharest	Women's rights
Association of Women in Romania	Bucharest	Women
Association of Women Managers	Bucharest	Women and economy
Association of Women with Special Problems	Bucharest	Women at risk
Association of Young Mothers: St. Nicholas	Bucharest	Charity
Association of Women Inventors	Bucharest	Women and science
Catholic Organization in Romania, Branch of Catholic Women	HQ Braşov	Women and church
Center for Development and Population Activities (CEDPA)	Bucharest	Women and health
Civil Action Foundation, Centre for Women in Civil Society	Bucharest	Women and politics
Committee of Women for Defense and Protection	Bucharest	Women's rights and health
CRED Foundation, Bucharest	Bucharest	Women and information
Democratic League of Women Students in Romania	Bucharest	Young women and democracy
Dignity Society of Women	Constanţa	Women
Ecumenic Forum of Women in Romania	Tărgu Mureş (HQ)	Women and ecumenism
Equal Opportunity Department of the Confederation of Free Trade Unions— CNSLR	Bucharest Fraţia (HQ)	Women and education, women and economic rights
Equal Opportunities for Women Foundation	Iaşi	Women and entrepreneurial skills
Family Planning Movement	Vrancea	Reproductive health
Femina Club	Ploieşti	Social and cultural activities
GENDER	Bucharest	Family planning
Girl Scouts Association of Romania	Bucharest	Girls and education
International Soroptimist Club	Craiova	Women and the soroptimist spirit
"Ladies First" Foundation	Odorheiu Secuiesc	Women
League for Social Integration of the Unemployed in Romania	Bucharest	Women and unemployment
League for Women's Dignity	Oradea	Women
Municipal Committee of Women	Bucharest	Women and health, women's rights
National Association of Medical Women	Bucharest	Women and health
National Association of Women with University Degrees	Bucharest	Women

APPENDIX 11.1: *(cont.)*

Name of NGO	Location	Keywords
National Council of Women from Romania (CNFR)	Bucharest	Women
National Federation of Women from Romania	Bucharest	Women
National Federation of Business Women's Clubs in Romania	Suceava	Women and business
National League of Women	Bucharest	Women
National League of Women from the 1989 Revolution	Bucharest	Women
National Organization of Women of the Democratic Party	Bucharest	Women in politics
National Society of Romanian Orthodox Women	Bucharest	Women and church
Organization of Women from Târgu Frumos	Târgu Frumos	Rural women
Pro-Europa League, Women's Department	Târgu Mureş	Women and intercultural education
Regional Association of Women	Regional	Humanitarian activities, professional requalification
Romanian Abolitionist Society	Bucharest	Women's rights
Romanian Association for the Development of Palliative Care	Bucharest	Elderly women
Romanian Association for Women's Rights	Bucharest	Women's rights
Romanian Centre for Information and Documentation for Young People	Bucharest	Women and information
Romanian Independent Society for Human Rights (SIRDO)	Bucharest	Violence against women, women's rights
Romanian Institute for Human Rights (IRDO)	Bucharest	Women's rights
Society for Contraceptive and Sexual Education (SECS)	Bucharest	Reproductive health
Solidarity of Women in Romania	Bucharest	Women
Society for Women's Inter-Balkan Cooperation in Romania	Bucharest	Charity, women and health
Society for Feminist Analyses (ANA)	Bucharest	Women and education
Women's Organization of the Social Democratic Party	Bucharest	Women and politics
Women's Organization of the National Peasant's Party	Bucharest	Women and politics
Women's Organization from Bihor	Oradea	Women
Women's League from Braşov	Braşov	Women

Source: UNDP/WID Catalogue, 1997.

Note: The UNDP/WID list contains names of some organizations that I have heard of during my research. The keywords provide information about the primary, but not exclusive, area of interest within each organization. In my classification, "women" as a keyword means that the organization's area of activity is too general or that I do not have information.

Women's Problems, Women's Discourses in Bulgaria

KRASSIMIRA DASKALOVA

DISCUSSIONS ABOUT WOMEN AND their role in society have pervaded the public debates and newly emerging mass media of the post-1989 era in Bulgaria, as in other countries of the region. Simultaneously, women's organizations of varying size and influence have proliferated. My aim in this chapter is to map the different images of women and assumptions about gender difference that are now important features of public life and to describe how, in the midst of all these images, women's organizations formulate and pursue their goals. What obstacles do they encounter? How does the institutional structure of women's organizations shape or constrain the discourse of these groups? How are their ways of imagining women's problems related to earlier discourses of communism and to the current political ideas and institutions with which they must compete and interact? I assume that discourses are important to analyze because the terms of public debate set crucial constraints on what can be imagined, what can be publicly claimed, and thus, what can actually be done in the areas of social policy, legal reform, and other political action concerning women in Bulgaria. I also assume that, to understand the significance of any one discourse, it is necessary to examine the social and cultural context in and against which it is formulated, as well as the historical precedents on which it is built. Therefore, this chapter tries to sketch in rough outline the field of discussion about women in order to locate the discourses of women's organizations.

Many institutional and individual actors engage in discussions about women or in discussions in which women emerge as the "object" of interest.[1] These discussions take place among men and women scholars, political party leaders, activists in women's organizations, politicians—speaking in Parliament or at informal events and celebrations, editors and contributors to women's journals and magazines, and television and radio commentators. The ideas I focus on here reflect a broad range of opinion in Bulgaria and can be classified as: (1) ordinary images of "femininity;" (2) nationalist arguments; (3) scholarly discourse, especially in the fields of medicine, demography, and sociology; and

[1] The notion of discourse is rather vague and is defined differently by various authors and traditions. In this presentation I simply have in mind bodies of statements (written or oral) in which women are the topic or central "object." In my opinion, what justifies the use of the term here is the idea that words, far from innocuous, are connected with power practices. To say the least, they are symptomatic and expressive of modes of thinking, which they propagate, reinforce, and automate. For a discussion of similar types of discourses, see Gal 1994.

(4) maternalist arguments about social welfare. These are heuristic categories, meant to organize analysis. In any one body of materials, we may find arguments, images, projections, or value-laden words typical of several categories. Rather than conduct an exhaustive, systematic investigation into various forms of gender discourse, I have focused this analysis on a selective reading of media that reproduce certain "ways of talking" and on an examination of interviews with women active in Bulgarian public life. I have also allowed my own impressions as a "participant-observer" in Bulgarian society since 1989 to inform my conclusions.

The seventy women I interviewed included leaders of women's organizations— both old and new, women activists, and women in Parliament. The interviews were of an unstructured type, but they included standard questions about the situation of women in post-communist Bulgaria. Each interviewee was asked to arrange several issues in priority order; to express her understanding of "women's rights," "emancipation," and "feminism"; and to assess the degree of emancipation achieved by Bulgarian women and the changes since communism.[2] My discussion draws upon these interviews, within the context of Bulgaria's women's movement in general. Particularly important, I argue, are the contradictions and ironies evident in attempts by women's groups to navigate between "rights" talk, maternalist and welfarist notions, and forms of discourse about "emancipation" that were standard in the communist era.

The changing set of opportunities and constraints upon women's activism in Bulgaria can only be understood against the broad background of women's material circumstances after communism, which constitute the problems that these organizations try to evaluate and to which they propose solutions. I try to piece together a broad picture of the situation facing Bulgarian women, cautiously relying on a range of international and national statistical sources. This chapter is accordingly divided into three sections. In the first section I briefly outline the conditions of employment, reproduction, and social welfare currently in force, attending to how these differ (if they do) from the previous era. In the second section, I characterize the various discourses just listed, particularly in terms of how they conceptualize women's circumstances, what they consider important or problematic, and what they consider worth changing. Using this as context and background, I then examine a range of women's organizations and activists, illustrating the relationship between their ideas and other discourses and high-lighting the dilemmas and contradictions of their positions.

BACKGROUND: WOMEN'S SOCIAL CIRCUMSTANCES

In Bulgaria, the transition from communism has led to mass impoverishment. Although statistics as well as definitions of what constitutes a minimum standard

---

[2] Questions were also asked about the situation of women in the family. The interviews ranged between one-half hour and one hour, and each session was recorded, transcribed, and then studied for attitudes expressed through speech.

of living are in dispute, various estimates place about four-fifths of the population below such a minimum and about two-thirds below the level of basic subsistence. Economic inequalities have increased dramatically.[3] Families with several children or with members who are unemployed, disabled, or retired are in the worst condition. Housing has long been a problem; indeed, it was one of the blatant failures of the communist regime.[4] Now, public services in the cities also have deteriorated and, at the same time, have become very expensive. This is true of transportation, mail, and telephone services. The monthly sum paid for central heating approaches that of an average pension, reflecting a cost increase generally explained by the fact that the government treats such fees as a means of raising emergency revenue. Occasionally, there are even irregularities in the basic supply of electricity and water.[5]

The general deterioration in living conditions affects women most, and is reflected in the increased amount of time women spend on housework and childcare.[6] Poor kitchen equipment and the absence (or prohibitive cost) of processed foods also influences the way Bulgarian women make use of their time. Although the division of labor between men and women and the strength of patriarchy varies from family to family, it is within this kind of domestic setting that male authority is exercised.

In addition to performing household work, almost half of Bulgarian women in 1992 were also employed outside the home.[7] Since 1989, conditions of paid

[3] According to one study, 10 percent of the poorest households have 3 percent of the GNP, while 10 percent of the richest households have 25 percent of the GNP (Dakova 1995).

[4] Sixty-three percent of the urban population and 43 percent of the village population live in overcrowded homes, defined as a space in which the number of people is greater than the number of rooms. (It is important to note that all rooms, including kitchens, are counted.) According to data from the National Statistical Institute, the average childless family has 1.44 rooms per person; families with one child average 1 room per person; those with two children average 0.74 rooms per person; and those with three children, 0.69 rooms (Genov 1995:19).

[5] While irregularities in the supply of electricity have occurred in Bulgaria since 1984, the years 1993 and 1994 were notorious for water shortages in Sofia, the capital city, and for the subsequent introduction of a water rationing regime to meet the most basic domestic needs. Shortage of water in several smaller cities is chronic.

[6] Conducted at the beginning of the 1980s, research on the "use of time" demonstrated that Bulgarian women spent more hours on domestic work than they had 20 years earlier. In the beginning of the 1990s, women spent three times more time in domestic work than did men (Dinkova 1985:19–20, 23–25; Vangelova and Kuncheva 1991:24–34; Nikleva 1990:6–7; Popova 1992:14–15). Moreover, according to U.N. statistics, the domestic obligations of Bulgarian women had increased over time (the opposite of the situation for women in the Czech and Slovak Republics, Hungary, the USSR, and Poland). For example, in 1965, Bulgarian women spent 28.6 hours per week on household chores and childcare (compared to 12.5 hours for men); in 1988, they spent 33.7 hours (compared with 15.5 hours for men) (United Nations 1991:101).

[7] According to a report of the United Nations Development Program (UNDP), Bulgaria ranked very high in the rate of women's employment, which, in 1992, was 47 percent. The same index registered 41 percent for American women, 39 percent for German women, and 36 percent for Swiss women. According to the same report, the ratio of unemployed men to women in Bulgaria was 109:100 in 1992, while the same ratio in the European Union was 152:100 (Dakova 1995). However, one should not make too much of this favorable comparison with affluent countries. Women's

labor have deteriorated greatly, and since mass privatization began in 1996, unemployment has been on the rise. While this affected women more than men at the beginning of the transition, the disparity soon diminished.[8] Nevertheless, there are important and enduring differences between the opportunities for men and women in the present crisis. Women are less likely to find jobs in the private sector, which tend to pay better.[9] As a rule, women who work in a family business receive no direct wages and have little say in decision making. Beyond these broad generalities, the extended crisis of post-communism has differentially affected various professions and regions. For example, a large number of women with technical engineering skills were dismissed during the widespread personnel cuts that began in the early 1990s;[10] some eventually started small retail businesses, often selling goods in open-air stalls.[11] Likewise, the situation of women engaged in tobacco cultivation worsened as a result of the dramatic drop in the price of state-purchased crops; as men were deprived of tobacco income and forced to migrate to the cities, women were left alone to cope with the household.[12]

Discrimination against women in the labor market appears in several forms and is frequently a continuation of patterns established in the communist period. On the whole, young women have fewer chances than young men to work in a profession for which they are educationally qualified.[13] When reviewing job applicants, employers show an explicit preference for hiring men.[14] In part, this

---

employment under state socialism had a very different meaning than it had in the West, namely, the mobilization of the entire labor force to realize the communist ideal. Western women's employment, on the other hand, was indicative of women's emancipation from the domestic sphere. Currently, a minimum level of subsistence is better assured by employment in Eastern Europe generally than it is by the western welfare system, although this says little about gender equality. In short, the "meaning" of employment is quite different across countries.

[8] In the beginning of the 1990s women constituted between 63 percent (June 1990) and 68 percent (October 1990) of the unemployed, but the difference grew less significant (52.2 percent in April 1992). See Ilieva and Mikhova 1992:60–62. For data on unemployment, see the National Statistical Institute 1994:28, 1995:68, 1996. There are good reasons to suppose that not all of the unemployed register at the unemployment office; thus official figures are probably lower than actual unemployment. There are no valid reasons to suppose, however, that women more often fail to register than men.

[9] According to data from the National Statistical Institute, private firms employed 336,400 persons in September 1993, of whom 188,300 were men and 148,100 were women. In October 1994, the total figure was 461,600, of whom 271,200 were men and 190,400 were women. See the National Statistical Institute 1994:28.

[10] In 1992 unemployed women with engineering-technical education constituted more than 50 percent of all unemployed women with higher education. See Ilieva and Mikhova 1992:62.

[11] According to interviews with the author, some felt themselves to be victims of the transition, while others were proud of having successfully coped with the situation.

[12] This affected the tobacco regions of the Rhodopes in southwestern Bulgaria, where much, although not all, of the population belongs to the Turkish minority (author interview with Giulbie Redzhep).

[13] In the beginning of the 1990s, about 57 percent of young men and 63 percent of women in the same age group worked at a level below their educational qualifications (Dinkova 1990:5–10).

[14] According to one survey, 54 percent among employers at various state industrial enterprises expressed a preference for men to fill management and expert jobs, compared to 25 percent who expressed a preference for hiring women. In hiring specialists, 59 percent noted a preference for

is made possible because Bulgarian labor laws include no provisions against gender discrimination, and society in general is not sensitive to this issue.[15] Old stereotypes about "male" and "female" professions also persist, leading to differential treatment in employing men versus women. In general, women are pushed toward occupations that involve manual, monotonous, and undesirable work. Furthermore, women tend to hold positions lower in the hierarchy or positions that offer few opportunities for advancement (*Pazar na truda* 1993:218). Despite the communist regime's self-congratulatory assertions about gender equality and equal employment opportunities, these patterns are well documented for the communist period.[16] The "transition" has only made the situation more manifest, as people have been allowed to speak openly about it.

Discrimination against women also shows up in average wage levels. As indicated by research done at the National Statistical Institute covering the period 1992–1994, a gender gap existed in most professions with respect to remuneration for labor, and women were heavily overrepresented in sectors with low salaries. Work in education and medical care, for example, is generally low-paid, and these constitute the most "feminized" professions.[17] The gender gap in remuneration is also due to women's lower position in the various professional hierarchies. Thus the highest salaries in industry and business, which in general are paid to managers, go to men who predominate in these positions;[18] the same applies to skilled workers.[19] Civil servants also receive very low incomes, and this in turn has led to the feminization of the lowest administrative positions. There is even some

---

men while only 3 percent noted a preference for women (*Pazar na truda* 1993:226). Preferences for hiring women under age 35, especially in private firms, is another manifestation of discrimination.

[15] On the contrary, opinion seems to credit the employer with complete freedom in this respect. Characteristically, in interviews with the author, some female MPs were quick to agree that the employer has "the right of opinion" in choosing the specialists she needs.

[16] State socialism was notorious for the "feminization" of certain routine and low-paid professions. These included the textile, leather, and shoe industries and the clothing industry, where women represented 70–75 percent of the employed. Women were, and still are, heavily overrepresented in the fields of healthcare and education and among low-level professionals such as accountants and librarians.

[17] Characteristically, the transition opened up some positions for women on the bench. The low remuneration of these jobs—paid as a state salary—made them unattractive to men, who often shifted into more lucrative jobs as attorneys.

[18] The practice of lumping together categories in the Bulgarian statistical yearbooks makes it difficult to establish the exact ratio between men and women in managerial positions. One can read in the *Statistical Yearbook* for 1991 that women in managerial positions accounted for 30 percent of all persons in such positions. According to the last Bulgarian census, in which another criterion was used, women accounted for 41 percent of the "managers of economic units: enterprises, stock-holder companies, organizations, firms" (Kotseva and Todorova 1994:28). Contrary to official data, some sociological studies (from the end of the 1980s and the beginning of the 1990s) reveal a much smaller presence of women in management; according to a 1985 survey, women comprised 17.1 percent of the managers-in-chief of large enterprises and 10.8 percent of the managers-in-chief of small enterprises; another study (on problems of ecology) found only 36 women (i.e., 6 percent) among 600 directors of industrial enterprises (Kotseva and Todorova 1994:29).

[19] Skill definitions themselves are saturated by sexual bias; thus the fact that a certain kind of work is performed by women may mark it as unskilled (Phillips and Taylor 1996:317–330).

evidence of a wage differential between women and men performing the same kind of job.[20]

Still other reasons justify speaking about the "feminization of poverty" in Bulgaria. Divorced women with children are in an especially disadvantageous position because the assistance they receive from their ex-husbands for raising the children is negligible. Ironically, some of the protective regulations of the communist welfare system have, in the new environment, turned from benefits into negative sanctions. Restrictions in employing women for certain jobs (considered physically inappropriate) are actually reducing women's opportunities, while retirement at age 55 (five years earlier than the retirement age for men), coupled with women's longer life expectancy, condemns older women on meager state pensions to poverty[21] (Hassan and Peters 1995:29–30).

Current labor conditions affect women more harshly in yet another sense. Given the present economic crisis, the scarcity of employment opportunities, general disorder, and the difficulties in making people adhere to the law, it is not surprising that women are especially vulnerable to sexual harassment.[22] Pressure of this sort may be exerted as a condition for being offered a job (especially by a private firm) or under threat of being fired. Although information on this subject is scanty for obvious reasons, there is sufficient anecdotal data available to suggest the general climate (see Georgieva 1994:14).

Broadly speaking, it is within a context of diminishing job opportunities, lack of job security, and women's special vulnerability in a male-dominated work environment that women, including activists in women's organizations, sometimes express disappointment with "professional work" and a desire to "return to the family" (Petrova 1993:22–30).[23] But I would argue, on the contrary, that

---

[20] Thus among managers, men earned approximately 20 percent more than women; among skilled workers the difference was 11 percent in favor of men; among civil servants, it was 5 percent in favor of men (*Pazar na truda* 1993:230). According to a UNDP report, the difference between the remuneration of men and women is smaller in Bulgaria (where women's salary is 74% of men's) than in the U.S. (where it is 59% of men's), but larger than in the European Union (where it is 80 or 85% of men's) (Dakova 1995).

[21] While the first restriction (as to the type of work women can perform) is not often adhered to, the retirement age is quite strictly observed, since there are so many younger unemployed people. There is some awareness on the part of state authorities about the disadvantages of early retirement, but still nothing has been done to change this state of affairs.

[22] There is no provision against sexual aggression of this sort in the present Bulgarian legislation. The Democratic Union of Women has recently undertaken some initiatives to prompt the executive branch of government into action on this problem (characteristically, the executive, not the legislature, was contacted). In general, police and court procedures connected with all types of violence upon women are so humiliating that one may suppose that most victims of sexual violence prefer not to report their experiences to the police.

[23] Data from an opinion survey conducted in 1991 by the Institute for Trade Union and Social Science Research do not yield conclusive results. Of the 1,600 women respondents who were asked if Bulgarian women should work, 25 percent answered "yes, if they want to"; 31.5 percent answered "yes, after their children grow up"; 23.3 percent answered "yes, but part-time"; 8.6 percent answered "yes, if they are not married"; 3 percent answered "yes, from time to time"; 6.2 percent

low wages and job insecurity put more pressure on women to seek employment in order to support themselves and their families. The desire to remain at home betrays a nostalgia for security and actually amounts to a sort of utopian escape from uncertainty and growing stress. But it is hardly envisioned as a realistic solution, even by those who cherish it.[24]

Certainly it would be wrong to take such opinions at face value and call this a "retraditionalization" of Bulgarian life. First, it is unclear to what extent Bulgarian society under communism really departed from traditional gender notions, roles, and practices, so that one may now speak about a *return* to tradition. In fact, as several researchers have pointed out, the socialist "emancipation" of women only scratched the surface of gender relations, especially within the family.[25] The massive, post-war influx of women into the labor force, motivated by the need for workers in the "construction" of socialism (and of socialist industrialization in particular), did not seriously question the power asymmetry and division of labor within the family. Although women did work alongside men before the war,[26] in the communist period, more than ever before, the burden of paid work was simply added to the burden of domestic work, while earlier behavioral and normative stereotypes persisted.[27] Since such "traditionalism" was never replaced, it seems to me that "retraditionalization" is a false danger. It is true, however, that current financial and job insecurity—felt by women and by families in general—is conducive to women's increased dependence on men in the family context.[28]

Turning now from questions of employment, I will briefly consider women's situation with respect to reproduction. The general overview needed here is most

---

answered "no"; and 2.4 percent did not answer. These data have been interpreted by some Bulgarian scholars (Kostova 1993:103) as indicative of a strong motivation to work. I think that the tendency to make work conditional (upon motherhood and family) is even more significant.

[24] In fact, the danger comes not from a willful retreat to the domestic sphere but from the lack of employment opportunities resulting from the delay of reforms during the post-communist transition. See the research by Rose 1992:53.

[25] More than 25 years ago, Hilda Scott answered the question, "Does socialism liberate women?" in the negative (Scott 1975). For a discussion of the manipulation of Bulgarian women under the cover of emancipation under the communist regime, see Reeves-Ellington 1996a, b. For a discussion of the actual suppression of women in Russia, see Voronina 1994:37–38.

[26] As Maria Todorova rightly points out, before communist rule the vast majority of Bulgarian women (then peasants) did work alongside the men in the fields as well, besides doing the household work (Todorova 1993:31–32).

[27] As pointed out by historians of women, employment of women does not change substantially the traditional gender attitudes and roles within the family. About the impact of industrialization in England and France upon the status of working women, see Tilly and Scott 1987. Women's waged labor is, of course, not an invention of state socialism; it only introduced it more dramatically by way of state policies and on a much larger scale.

[28] The incidence of domestic violence notwithstanding, the family is still treated a priori in terms of accord and common interests. This blocks the way to inquiry into domestic forms of domination and violence and, still more significantly, to police intervention in such cases. Thus, for instance, cases of domestic violence were reported in the press, but only where the violence ended with murder (Tsitselkov 1994:2–4).

easily constructed by considering demographic statistics. While it is obvious that such information does not correspond to women's actual reproductive experience, it provides a useful glimpse of the circumstances within which women have had to construct their lives.

Bulgaria's demographic situation evokes despair among population experts and is a source of apocalyptic visions for nationalists, as we will see below. A currently negative population growth rate reflects the conjunction of several unfavorable, ongoing tendencies: a drop in both the birthrate and the marriage rate, a rise in the death rate as a consequence of the aging of the nation, an increase in infant mortality as a result of deteriorating living conditions, and the exodus of (mainly) younger people from the country.[29] At the time of the 1992 census, Bulgaria's population was 8,484,900—a substantial drop from the almost nine million registered in the 1980s. In the last three years, the population has decreased still further and, according to recent data from the National Statistical Institute, it dropped to 8,384,000 toward the end of 1995.[30] Relatedly, for the last few years, life expectancy has been 67.2 years for men and 74.8 years for women, rather short by Western standards (National Statistical Institute 1995:28; World Development Report 1992:281). Infant mortality in particular increased from 14.8 per 1,000 births in 1989 to 16.3 in 1994. Among the factors causing it to rise are premature births, insufficient fetal nourishment, and infectious diseases (Dakova 1995:59).[31] Maternal mortality also increased from 18.7 per 100,000 live births in 1989 to 20.0 in 1993, reaching one of the highest levels in Europe.[32]

---

[29] The population decreased by about 600,000 persons as a result of the great emigration wave in the end of the 1980s and the beginning of the 1990s. It has been pointed out that in all six wars waged by Bulgaria in the last one hundred years, the losses amounted to 338,000 persons; emigration from Bulgaria was 410,000 (and more than offset by the influx of people). The main reason for the unprecedented current emigration lies in the deep economic crisis and extremely high unemployment (Minkov 1991:4–5).

[30] The growth rate of the Bulgarian population has been negative for a number of years: It decreased from −2.2 per 1,000 in 1992 to −5.1 at the end of 1995. This results from a drop in the birth rate from 10.4 percent in 1992 to 8.6 percent in 1995 (an extremely low value for an European state) due to the diminishing and aging of the "fertile group" combined with an increased mortality rate (11.1 per 1,000 in 1980; 11.9 in 1989; 12.6 in 1992; 13.3 in 1994) due to the great number of people in the upper age brackets and the worsening of health parameters resulting from deterioration of living conditions (Genov 1995).

[31] On the negative effects of the Chernobyl catastrophe, which had been officially denied by the Bulgarian authorities at the time, thus leaving the population exposed to its full consequences, see Popova 1990:3.

[32] The same index for Denmark in 1990 was 1.6; for Great Britain, 8.1; for Portugal, 10.3; for Poland, 12.8 (Genov 1995:8). This index is several times higher for women over the age of 30, meaning an additional risk for women who postpone having children. If the data stemming from a comprehensive medical study are correct (and insofar as earlier data are correct), the incidence of a number of diseases has risen dramatically among women. Among the specifically women's diseases, breast cancer has increased greatly. The cases of neurosis and depression among women and the consumption of tranquilizers and narcotics are reportedly on the rise, not without connection with the increased stress of living in insecurity under post-communist conditions. The grave economic crisis and the lowering of living standards resulted in a marked increase in poverty and in diseases

No doubt prompted by dismal demographic prospects, the communist regime pursued active pro-natalist policies in the 1980s, with predictable effects on women's lives. These policies included restrictions on abortion,[33] on the one hand, and incentives or "encouragement" for giving birth, on the other.[34] While these measures may have increased the birth rate initially, their efficacy declined in the 1980s.[35] On the wave of liberalizing change in general, a new, liberalized abortion law was adopted in 1990 without much debate in Parliament.[36] The law made abortion available (for a certain fee) to all women in the initial three months of pregnancy (and, later, for medical reasons), independent of family status and of whether or not they already have children. Unlike the former communist law, the new law does not require the consent of the husband. When the law was first promulgated, there was an initial spurt in the rate of abortion, but then the numbers began to decrease. This is partly due to the availability of contraceptives and to the growing sexual culture of the population. Yet, abortion figures have remained extremely high, for a time higher than the number of

resulting from malnutrition (especially tuberculosis), although this affects men and women in the same way.

[33] During the first three months of pregnancy, abortion was available to unmarried women (after passing through humiliating medical committees) and to married women with two children and more (or where medical reasons made abortion necessary). One should also bear in mind that the relative unavailability of contraceptives on the market made abortion often the only way to get free of undesired pregnancy; thus, many women risked their lives in the rather uncertain conditions of illegal abortion. According to data quoted by Dr. Nikolai Golemanov, 90 percent of the deaths caused by abortion between 1964 and 1990 resulted from illegal abortion (Golemanov 1991:7–12).

[34] Encouragement for having (more) children followed a comprehensive plan. This included measures such as long maternal leaves (paid during the two years after giving birth, then, upon request of the mother, a third year of unpaid leave); comparatively easily granted absences from work for "domestic reasons"; special advantages for student-mothers; a monthly bonus for every child; certain support for single mothers and families in need; free medicines for children; long-term loans available to young families under very favorable conditions for buying a home (part of the loan being annulled upon giving birth to a second child, and another part after a third child); earlier retirement age for women (at 55, then a privilege); an increase in state funds for public daycare centers and kindergartens; orders that enterprises and organizations were to extend social services for their employees, and so on (Ilieva 1989:22; Dinkova 1985:10–16). Yet however nice these social benefits sound, one has to bear in mind the generally low standard of living in Bulgaria (irrespective of maternal support). Given the very limited resources at the state's disposal, some of these measures simply could not have been implemented. For example, even if one had the money, it was not possible to buy an apartment because only a very restricted number were available; these were centrally distributed, allegedly "according to need," but most often by virtue of a bribe or those all-important "connections." Still, some benefits were real and effective.

[35] About the effectiveness of the pro-natalist policies, see Filipova 1993:40–51. According to the author, the demographic policies resulted in 20 percent increase in the birthrate until the end of the 1970s, but the effect declined from the beginning of the 1980s. According to Robert McIntyre, the abortion legislation had a relatively small effect on aggregate fertility in Bulgaria because fertility control already existed in Bulgarian families (McIntyre 1980:147–170).

[36] In any case, there was in post-communist Bulgaria nothing like the anti-abortion reaction of the Catholic church in Poland or the sharp (and moralizing) pro-life versus pro-choice debate in the United States. There was little opposition to the law, given the weakness of the Orthodox church at that time and the support for it by the anti-communists in power. Clearly, the concerns and priorities of Western feminists cannot be simply projected upon the Bulgarian situation.

births.[37] The Ministry of Health and some women's organizations have undertaken initiatives to popularize contraceptives and to improve the sexual education of the younger generations in particular. International and Bulgarian nongovernmental organizations (NGOs) have also made efforts recently to promote family planning. Still, data about sexually transmitted diseases (Bozhanova 1991:12–14; Tsurkova 1992a:35–36; 1992b:16–18) as well as the high number of abortions and early pregnancies attest to a neglect of safety norms of sexual behavior.

Also related to sexual and reproductive issues is prostitution, which is widely practiced. A taboo topic concealed by the former communist regimes, it became, after communism, publicly visible and much more common. Among the documented trends are a growth in the number of prostitutes and of places for practicing prostitution, including international highways; an influx of educated women, particularly with knowledge of foreign languages (Noninska 1990:24–25); higher levels of organization (and the frequent presence of pimps); the prostitution of very young girls—12–13 years old, for example (Zagorova 1992:8–9, 22; Kostadinova 1993:32–33); and the existence of legal channels for recruiting prostitutes, especially through the advertisement of jobs (or training courses) for dancers, models, and "Miss So and So" competitions. There is also documentation of the organized export of Bulgarian prostitutes and of "hiring" practices that take place under the cover of impresario and tourist agencies (Mikhailova 1992:20–21; Filipova 1993:19).[38] Other studies suggest that, as elsewhere in the world, prostitution is seldom a question of voluntary choice: It often starts with violence and rape; it is, in many cases, an alternative to hunger (sad examples of women falling victim to striking social injustice); it creates risks of diseases (AIDS, among others); and women are severely exploited by pimps and those associated with the criminal world (Radev 1993:25–27).

In addition to household labor, waged work, and the conditions of reproduction we have reviewed, it is also important to consider what has happened in the last decade to the social safety net of the communist period, especially its pro-natalist aspects. The breakdown of these benefits is due in part to the requirements and suggestions of international organizations like the International Monetary Fund (IMF), but the Bulgarian government has also used such agencies as a convenient pretext for curtailing social assistance. Although the new Labor Code, in force since December 1992, kept paid maternity leave at two years,[39] many benefits

[37] Thus there were 132,021 abortions in 1989; 138,405 in 1991; 132,891 in 1992; 107,416 in 1993; 98,478 in 1994; and 97,399 in 1995. There were, in 1995, only 72,500 births (National Statistical Institute 1993:229; 1995:42).

[38] A study of the Council for Criminological Studies to the Office of the Attorney General provides information about increasing prostitution since 1989. One may point to scandalous revelations in the Bulgarian press about the connections between the Bulgarian entertainment agency Zlatniiat Orfei and the Italian agency Golden Star for export of "ballerinas" and singers "with consumption" (*Obshtestvo i pravo* 1992 a, b).

[39] The maternity leave is divided into three parts, full salary is paid for some time before and after giving birth (120 days for a first child, 150 days for a second child, 180 days for a third child), and then the minimal salary is paid for the remaining period, in the event that the mother chooses not to resume work. According to the law the father may substitute for the mother in taking care of the child (Pazar na truda, 1993:34–37, 70–73). In fact, since the minimum salary is so low and,

(such as loans) were simply abandoned, while others were reduced by inflation to practically nil. State support for mothers, lagging far behind the costs of raising a child, has been reduced to the point of insignificance, so that it actually plays the role of a negative sanction.[40] In order to have children, Bulgarian women need support from elsewhere, mainly from their husbands. This makes single mothers particularly vulnerable, especially since they are also more likely to be unemployed (Ivanova 1992:26). These conditions explain much better Bulgaria's currently low birthrate and high abortion rate than does the supposed ideal of the two-child family (Atanasov 1985:43–72).

The loss of a social safety net has particularly grave consequences for Bulgarian Roma or Gypsies, who are an especially threatened population. They are over-represented among the unemployed, in part because of their generally low education and lack of professional training, but also because of cultural biases against them. For a Gypsy mother, bearing children often remains the only legal way to acquire the cash necessary for mere survival. Small though this income is, having children is often treated in this milieu in a purely instrumental manner and without much consideration. It is hardly a surprise that most of the deserted children, left in state care, come from this sadly neglected ethnic group.

To complete the picture of Bulgaria's current social welfare system, other discontinued benefits should be mentioned. Free medicines for children below a certain age have been canceled, allegedly to prevent misuse and squander.[41] Also, public expenditures on childcare (for daycare centers, kindergartens, and orphanages) are kept at a level far behind inflation, while the corresponding fees at these facilities have increased several-fold, quite proportionate with inflation. What is more, services at these facilities have deteriorated, partly due to insufficient subsidies, but also due to a lack of motivation on the part of underpaid personnel.

All in all, one can say that the collapse of Bulgaria's social welfare system, and especially of the pro-natalist policies that concern us here, has, as it has in most former socialist countries, effectively dissuaded women from having children. A society in deep economic crisis cannot, of course, maintain a broad social welfare system. But in this case, the benefits that remain are no longer distributed to an economically homogeneous population, but to an increasingly stratified one. Thus badly targeted, the current social benefits actually favor those who are better off.[42]

---

absent other resources, does not provide adequately for basic support, most mothers choose to resume work as early as they can.

[40] According to data from the National Statistical Institute, the average annual index of consumer prices (1990 as a base = 100) was 438.5 in 1991; 786.6 in 1992; 1227.5 in 1993; and 2296.3 in 1994 (National Statistical Institute 1995:80).

[41] It seems true that much stealing was taking place behind the cover of this provision and it is hard to envision how this could be prevented, given the ineffectiveness of law enforcement and the general chaos accompanying the transition. But the cancellation of free medicines hit poor families badly, without compensating them in another way. The authorities took easy advantage of an opportunity to cut a social expenditure from the budget, not caring for the consequences.

[42] The pressing need to change the existing social safety net in Bulgaria, especially the system of child allowances, so that allowances may go only to families with minimal incomes, is underscored

DISCOURSES ABOUT WOMEN

Against this backdrop of social conditions in which women have lived since 1989, it is instructive to examine the different lines of argument through which these problems are publicly discussed and understood in Bulgaria.

Ideals of Femininity

The "feminine" woman is perhaps the most common and widespread image of women in Bulgarian society at large. She basically ignores the difficulties outlined here, and focuses on matters of beauty and domestic skill; she is sometimes presented in connection with, and sometimes opposed to, entrepreneurial efforts to make money. Magazines and newspapers that reproduce this type of discourse include *Zhenata Dnes* [Woman Today], *Vestnik za Zhenata* [A Newspaper for Women]; *"Super Market": Daidzhest za Semeistvoto i Biznesa* [Supermarket: A Digest for Family and Business]; *Vsichko za Vseki: Sedmichnik za Semeistvoto, Traditsii, Biznes, Otmora* [Everything for Everybody: A Weekly about Family, Traditions, Business, Recreation]; *Nie, Zhenite* [We, the Women]; and *Zhena* [Woman]. The subtitle of this last magazine is telling: "16 super pages about home, love and business." Another magazine with a similarly revealing title is *Khubava zhena* [Beautiful Woman]. These magazines began to appear in 1984 with the introduction of Soviet perestroika, but it was after 1989, following commercialization of the press, that a real explosion of such magazines occurred.

To varying degrees, these publications copy Western women's magazines, and it is from them that most of the photos and models are taken. Increasingly, however, images are drawn from the domestic scene, as it becomes apparent that the preferences and opinions of (or just gossip about) native "stars," including singers, fashion models, actresses, and "high society" women, have a marked impact on the Bulgarian audience. The messages in these magazines vary widely. Some images advertise consumer goods such as furnishings, clothes, accessories, or the accoutrements of a particular lifestyle. Others play on emotions, from romantic love to eroticism. Still others focus on self-care, especially in terms of promoting self-assurance and attractiveness to others. Of special interest for the present study are those images included in the last group.

Publications of this sort include within their purview tips and fashions for looking desirable. They abound in beauty advice, offering recommendations for clothing and behavioral styles and tips for improving one's body image, including information about various diets, sports and exercise (indoor "female" sports such as aerobics or yoga seem to be particular favorites), and medical procedures, especially the so-called "cosmetic surgery" of breast enhancement or removal of

in research for the World Bank (Hassan and Peters 1995:22–31). According to this report, under the current system child benefits are particularly poorly targeted with less than 20 percent accruing to low-income households (p. 27). Public spending on child allowances actually favors the well-off. On the marginal situation of older women, see Rose 1992, esp. p. 43.

wrinkles (Simeonova 1995:16–17). One message conveyed is that beauty is a woman's most valuable asset, and every woman should try to make herself sexually attractive to men. A typical title exhorts women to "Be more feminine and less business-like!" Femininity is thus presented as a woman's essence and predestination, her ultimate source of self-fulfillment.

But the magazines also emphasize certain skills. They contain recipes, commercials for household and kitchen appliances, and fashion features of the "do-it-yourself" variety. While they appear to serve preexisting interests and needs, they actually contribute to the formation, and encourage the cultivation, of an array of traditional domestic skills. By advertising activities and objects in which "every" woman should interest herself, writings of this sort posit standards and ideals of womanhood. In the end, the "feminine mystique" comes very close to the image of "a happy housewife heroine" (for a familiar U.S. version, see Friedan 1963). If we examine the range of skills encouraged and what they are meant to achieve, the "perfect" woman emerges as an obedient and self-negating creature, existing through her children and her husband.

While these magazines do not make overtly moralizing claims, they open the way to moral evaluations of female "virtues." In fact, they are most effective when they appear not to have obvious moralizing overtones. Women's appearance, skills, motivations, behavioral styles, and notions about what constitutes the female world, its ambiance, sensibilities, and culture are transmitted via otherwise unobtrusive statements and images. They do not convey their messages directly, but simply assume that, for women, there are certain "right" things to do and correct ways to behave. As women (and men) read and hear such talk, they internalize these representations and evaluations to the point that they become ingrained in the body as "habitus" (Bourdieu 1977). The peculiar thing about this sort of discourse is that women themselves willingly partake in an ideology of "femininity," and thus become complicitous in their own subjugation. It is an illustration of precisely this paradox that most of the magazines that cultivate femininity in this sense and promote domestic virtues are run by women's organizations.[43]

It is important to note that, although the appearance of these magazines coincided with the end of communism and although communist-era media was

[43] *Zhenata dnes* is a continuation of the publication of the old communist women's union. Since 1989 there have also appeared several dozen pornographic newspapers and magazines, including local productions such as *Pregled sex-show, Az i Ti, Adam i Eva, Mirazh, Eros,* etc., as well as imported ones such as *Playboy* and *Eve*. These bear mentioning along with the purveyors of "femininity" because both are premised, in different ways, on an objectification of womanhood. It is part of the irony of the current Bulgarian scene that the son of a former minister of culture (Elka Konstantinova) published a pornographic magazine while his mother was still in office. Despite legal prohibitions, pornography journals and magazines are being sold right in the most public spaces, for instance, in the center of Sofia, around Sofia University and the National Library, and even near the National Assembly, thereby mocking the efficacy of that body's legislating activity. While pornography is a universal modern phenomenon, it seems to me that its warm reception in present-day Bulgarian society is due in part to the fact that it reinforces fundamental notions of women's inferiority that were present before, during, and after the communist period.

neither as slick nor as sophisticated looking as these publications, communism itself was not averse to these same notions of femininity. The manlike, sexually neutral images of women workers and peasants depicted in the art of socialist realism were long gone by 1989. In any case, it is not clear how effectively such images had suppressed historically embedded notions of femininity, even during their heyday in the 1950s. The vast dissemination of women's "beauty magazines" since 1989 must be taken simply as a quantitative increase in an already existing phenomenon. Of course, it is only now that consumerism (as an ideology rather than an actual practice) is openly advertised and ascendant in Bulgarian society.

Nationalist Voices

Nationalist discourse has a long tradition and a secure niche in the Bulgarian public space. Women are treated by extreme nationalists in arch-patriarchal terms, and in such an undisguisedly militant manner, that one wonders about the state of mind (and the epoch) in which this discourse is produced. In Bulgarian nationalist writings, as elsewhere, women are considered first as mothers who bear children, perform domestic work, and obey their husbands in all matters that fall outside their own tightly circumscribed sphere. Premised on the absolute priority of the community (family, ethnic community, nation) over the individual, nationalism defines the motherly function as a duty and obligation to the nation; it has no use for the idea of individual rights. As has often been noted, nationalist discourse employs gendered categories such as the fatherland, motherland, and brotherhood of a people. Nationalists present themselves as the guardians of "tradition," and indeed are the most ardent advocates of "traditional values and virtues." This means, of course, the sanctification of traditional female roles and of male patriarchal authority. The following text, taken from the program of the Obshto Bŭlgarski Sŭiuz [All-Bulgarian Union], an obscure ultra-nationalist party, speaks for itself:

> According to our party, the Bulgarian woman must of her own will and in her best interest renounce the "achievements" of the ill-conceived Bulgarian "emancipation." The Bulgarian woman must be wife, mother and housewife, as life has created her and predestined her to be, to give birth to children, rear them and instruct them and assist them in their studies. . . . The Bulgarian woman must once and forever and by means of law be freed from the heavy burden of work in shifts. She must, after becoming wife, work reduced working hours, and after becoming mother, be entitled to at least ten years' maternal leave after giving birth to her last child. (*Pressluzhba Kurier* 1990a:10–11; see similar statements in *Pressluzhba Kurier* 1991h:14)

According to nationalist discourse, this is the "right" and "healthy" order of things; it is presented as the return to a sound tradition, following an alleged deviation brought about by the communist "emancipation" of women.

The nationalist parties, insignificant and obscure though they currently are, favor strong pro-natalist policies. Moreover, they know no limits when it comes to making electoral promises of benefits to mothers and children, as long as such benefits fall within a "regulated policy of conscientious parenthood" (*Pressluzhba Kurier* 1991e:5–6; 1991g:10). They foretell the "dying out" of the Bulgarian nation, unless urgent measures are taken to restore the traditional family. To cite a statement made in all earnestness, they recommend "the spirit of Christian virtues, where the man has the self-confidence of a master of the home, and the woman is happy with being a mother" (*Pressluzhba Kurier* 1990c:2; 1990d:8–9). According to the Christian Radical Democratic Party, if this spirit were followed, public childcare would be unnecessary because mothers would take care of their children themselves; only orphanages would remain, and these would be entrusted to the Church (*Pressluzhba Kurier* 1991c:2–3).

It must be noted that apprehensions about high reproduction rates among minorities (especially Turks and Gypsies) create special problems for pro-natalist nationalists in Bulgaria, forcing them to envision ethnically "differentiated solutions" to the population problem. Thus the Christian Radical Party promised benefits and encouragement only to those ethnic groups with low fertility rates: Bulgarians, Armenians, and Jews (*Pressluzhba Kurier* 1990b:17). Clearly, extreme nationalists are concerned with the "death of the nation" as a demographic problem (*Pressluzhba Kurier* 1991a:6; 1991b:2; 1991d:9; 1991f:4; 1991g:10). But they are not the only ones engaged in this kind of discussion; as I will show below, some women's organizations also participate.

Science and Scholarship

Demographic, sociological, and medical scholarship are most likely to touch upon the subject of women in one way or another. As many have noted, what is common to all of these fields is the appeal to the authority of science, which is signaled by the impersonal, presumably objective tone of the discourse, abundant use of technical terms, depersonalization of the object of analysis, and presentation of the author in terms of his or her scientific degree.

As elsewhere, Bulgarian demographers view the population in aggregate terms; hence the more neutral-sounding "population" instead of "people" or "nation" and "cohorts" instead of "generations." They also calculate biological capacities and potential as they would any other resource. Also, like others in the region, Bulgarian demographers voice panic over the extremely negative reproduction statistics discussed earlier. While most Bulgarian demographers are content to present the data on "population movements," which of course are very suggestive in themselves (Balkanski 1993:228–230; Mikhova 1993:47–58), some go beyond the strictly scientific arena to press for emergency reproductive policies aimed at preserving the Bulgarian nation (Ilieva 1991:35–46, esp. 45). This is but a step away from nationalist prophecies of the dying nation; demographers simply describe the situation in the more matter-of-fact, neutral terms of their discipline, and they show more restraint in proposing "cures."

Sociological writing is another important venue for the discussion of women and their problems in Bulgaria. Virtually no difference can be detected in style or substance between sociological writings published during as opposed to after communism. Perhaps this is not surprising, since the individuals who count as scholarly "authorities" have remained the same. Here too, women are viewed with a presumption of objectivity, as if from an elevated vantage point; they are spoken of in impersonal terms, for example, with respect to their "reproduction" or their social and biological "functions." This continues a communist-era tradition of sociological writing on women, the purpose of which was to justify the state's pro-natalist policies by stressing the included welfare provisions—lauded as care for the woman and family. The uninhibited use of the singular ("the Bulgarian woman") when speaking about women's problems is noteworthy for its typifying and essentializing effect and for the patronizing attitude it suggests.[44] With the newly felt need to critically distance themselves from the former regime, some authors have claimed barely perceptible nuances in their position as crucial "differences."[45] Yet mother-centered welfare as a "policy for women" is the basic assumption of all such writings, and arguments are defended by an implicit appeal to governmental authority. Such a pattern is strikingly reminiscent of writing by "scientific" advisors to the former communist regime.

As we shall see below, ideas put forward in this kind of scholarly work are often subscribed to by women's party organizations (Ilieva 1991:35–46; Atanasova 1991:3–6; Terzieva 1991:13–19).[46] What makes this paradoxical and sad is that the "care for the woman" stance is premised upon an essentialist position concerning women's nature and reproductive "function." The fact that such material is usually written by women who, during the communist era, were herded into the feminized occupations of social welfare services and related research endeavors only deepens the irony.

As a final example of scholarship about women, I will briefly consider medicine in the popular press. Physicians, popular healers, and experts in the Eastern arts of healing all offer counsel to women on the treatment of illnesses, on matters of disease prevention and health maintenance, on hygiene, on body care, and on ways to combat the destruction of old age by living a "natural life." Attention is usually focused specifically on women's diseases or on those that affect women more than men. The questions of drug addiction and alcoholism also attract attention. Because such medical writing stresses women's distinctive biology (or physiology) to explain their vulnerability to specific diseases, medical discourses are easily misused for the purpose of naturalizing gender differences and justifying gender inequalities. To take one example, increased alcoholism among Bulgarian

[44] For examples of such writing, see Dinkova 1980, 1985:9–42. As suggested by Denise Riley (1983), not only "woman" but also "women" can be troublesome for feminist analyses. Joan Scott (1996:7) also pointed out that different platforms and policy recommendations offered in the name of "women" in the political process actually contribute to their constitution as immutable natural beings.

[45] For example, the claim that "in opposition" to the "totalitarian" regime and in doctrinal dissent from the socialist "theory" of labor contribution, the author was "even then" in favor of extending social welfare provisions to all mothers, whether employed or not, working or not.

[46] It is worth noting that these (and some other) publications resulted from a conference, "The Woman in the Transition toward Market Economy," organized by the Commission on the Problems of the Woman of the Bulgarian Academy of Science and the Institute of Demography. See in the same style Andreeva 1992:40–47; Ilieva 1993:49–59.

women has been "explained" by the impossibility of reconciling traditional values and roles with new social requirements, alien to the female "biology." An identity crisis supposedly ensues, leading to neurosis and alcoholism (Gerdzhikova 1989:12–13). Members of the medical profession exacerbate the problem when, in writing for newspapers and popular magazines, they freely mix expertise about the nature or causes of certain diseases with the uninhibited expression of ideological opinions and value judgments of all kinds. Although such judgments would never appear so baldly in scientific journals, doctors are sure to sign articles in the popular press using their medical titles.

WOMEN'S ORGANIZATIONS AND THEIR DISCOURSES

Having thus established the background against which various forms of women's activism become intelligible, I now turn to the ways in which assumptions about gender factor into emerging public debates and influence women's efforts to shape the reform agenda. Among the many changes that have unfolded since 1989, it is important to note the particular issues that women's organizations have formulated as problems and to understand how and to what extent their definition of these problems is shaped by the history of Bulgaria's women's movement and by the competing discourses previously discussed.

Women's organizations proliferated after 1989, very much in tune with the burgeoning of political life in Bulgaria generally. By 1995, there were thirty-five women's organizations. I single out certain groups for analysis either because they are notably influential or because I consider them representative of a certain type. Among the most influential groups are women's organizations that exist within, or are closely connected to, political parties, notably the major parliamentary parties. The price of being thus linked, in terms of having to subordinate women's concerns to party interests and party discipline, is high, especially when women enter the National Assembly on party lists. However, this does not seem to bother the women active in these organizations, who consider themselves first and foremost party representatives, entrusted with the task of capturing women's votes for the party by addressing the concerns of a female audience. As my interviews with women Members of Parliament (MPs) revealed, they are, in general, content with their role as representatives of a women's annex to the party. Nevertheless, their link to political parties is not itself the problem. It is, rather, that the scope for autonomous action by such organizations is very limited; their agenda is subject to change upon notice from the party leadership, and it is easily co-opted to serve party propaganda purposes. In principle, parties could promote women's interests as well as any other organization. But in practice, parties readily ignore the actual goals of their "women's section" and simply regard these organizations as conduits for electoral propaganda. At times, this relationship has resulted in outright manipulation. For instance, at the beginning of the transition in 1991, the Communist Party established the Movement of Women and Mothers Against Violence. In this case, "violence" meant anything opposed to communist rule. The "movement" consisted of groups of women shouting around the buildings of the national TV and radio station, clearly mobilized to present what would appear to be grassroots opposition to change.

A prime example of a party-linked organization is the Democratic Union of Women (DUW), the largest of all women's organizations and heir to the official Women's Union (BUW) of the communist period. Although renamed, the organization relies at the local level on the former structures and financial support of the Bulgarian Socialist Party, itself heir to the former Communist Party and currently the strongest political party in Bulgaria. DUW's leader, Emilia Maslarova, entered the first democratically elected National Assembly on the Communist ticket, although she insists on the independence of her organization.

DUW's platform abounds in declarations of good intentions, phrased in general terms and reminiscent of the communists' resounding and hollow style. Notably, the organization undertakes to express the interests and defend the rights of Bulgarian women, children, and the family; to work for the attainment of real equality; and to support women's search for self-fulfillment and spiritual renewal. They voice concern for women's dignity, rights, and freedoms. In addition, DUW campaigns for "economically justifiable" (that is, within the parameters of a market economy) social protections for the Bulgarian family and for women; for women's real participation in all power structures; for the reduction of unemployment and removal of all obstacles to women's professional fulfillment; for state support to new families and families with many children; and for the protection of women against violence (and crimes against the person in particular). As a way to "strengthen the family," DUW also purports to work for "recognition in the laws" of the social utility and significance of parenthood in general, and of motherhood in particular (and of women's domestic work); it also presents itself as a champion of children's rights (Demokratichen sŭiuz na zhenite 1992:2–3).

Another DUW document states that women's contribution to the family budget, in terms of time spent in gainful employment, "substantially limits the time that women can devote to the rearing and the instruction of children," which in turn presents "one of the factors leading to the upsurge of a host of undesirable phenomena, of which the most difficult to overcome are juvenile delinquency, under-age prostitution, drug addiction, the adherence to religious sects that are foreign to our traditions and restrict personal freedoms" (Demokratichen sŭiuz na zhenite 1992:14). Note that it is mothers and their jobs that are held responsible for such problems; the role of fathers and the economic chaos of transition are not even mentioned. The only change here from the old communist line on women's "emancipation" through compulsory wage labor is that instead of explicitly *requiring* women to combine work at home with outside employment, the DUW wants women to choose between the two. Unfortunately, in the current economic circumstances, no one can afford to give up either.

There is a bit of everything in these "catch-all" documents. Some statements are so general as to be meaningless; others are entirely unrealistic and smack of demagoguery. If we look carefully at the platform's substance, it is at best a welfare agenda, aimed at the "protection" of women (and in the same breath, of the family); at worst it is a conservative stance aimed at the preservation of traditional gender roles. The platform also reveals a patronizing attitude toward women, who are viewed from above, as by a condescending and caring agency.[47] The long patriarchal tradition of the Communist Party here hides behind the thin veil of women's activism.

The DUW is important because of its size, its vociferous and manipulative routines, and its links to the strongest (the Socialist) political party in Bulgaria. But other women's organizations are similarly tied to parties and share much of this rhetoric. Other parties that have "women's organizations" (or women's clubs) include the Bŭlgarski Zemedelski Naroden Sŭiuz [Bulgarian Agrarian National Union (BANU)], the Bulgarian Social Democratic Party (the Federation of Women's Clubs), and the Bulgarian Green Party (Women for a Pure Natural Habitat and the National Ecology Club). Bulgaria's largest two trade unions, *Podkrepa* and the KNSB (Confederation of Independent Trade Unions in Bulgaria), also have women's sections attached to them, oriented toward the social protection of unionized women. The public activities of all these organizations are very much dependent on the views and instructions of their respective party leadership. Without question, Parliament itself frequently constitutes a grave obstacle to the wider propagation of their views and the promotion of their initiatives. While intentions and programs are always in good supply, resources remain meager, and organizations—especially local—remain undeveloped, the one exception being the DUW. Accordingly, the activities of these groups are severely handicapped. As the president of the Federation of Women's Clubs revealed in an interview with me, women affiliated with the Social Democrats in particular are convinced that their party is not represented.

The Christian Women's Movement provides a somewhat different example. Through its association with the Bulgarian Socialists, this group currently has several representatives in the National Assembly. Elaborating a curious mixture of nationalism and Christian patriarchalism, the Christian Women's Movement purports to speak on behalf of women for whom "biology is destiny" and "who consider their situation as mothers and wives to be honorable enough, and conceive of it as a supreme fulfillment of their duties as citizens." At the same time, this organization professes to support women's right to chose between "bearing many children and a professional career." Yet because the first alternative, in their view, leads to economic and social inequality between men and women, they favor recognition of "the social utility of the mother's work" and restoration of the traditional family as a means to achieve the "humanization of society" (*Pressluzhba Kurier* 1991i:11–12). At the same time, this Christian organization

---

[47] The notion that provisions for the family are to be provided only when "economically justifiable" is a good example of this. Decoded, this means that the realization will depend upon available financial resources and that it is up to the party in office to decide what is financially feasible (women's claims will be given free rein only while the Socialist Party is in opposition). One might consider this to be only realistic, and perhaps honestly so, were it not masked behind the seemingly "objective" and hence demagogical formula of "economic justifiability."

takes a liberal view on both abortion and pornography, provided they are restricted to "special zones." To quote the optimistic view of its leader, Bulgarian women have always enjoyed a high position within the patriarchal family, and this may well become the basis for creating a "new value system" (author's interview with Elisaveta Milenova).

The links between women's initiatives and the ecological movement provide yet another, somewhat different, example of the relationship between women's activities and national politics. The Bulgarian ecological movement originated in the late 1980s in the town of Russe (which was exposed to heavy air pollution from a Romanian plant across the Danube) as a protest movement and genuine civic initiative. Many women were active in it. In the events immediately preceding and following November 10, 1989 (when the long-term Bulgarian Communist ruler Todor Zhivkov was overthrown in a palace revolt), the ecological movement became politicized with a manifestly anti-communist profile. Subsequent developments led to the glaring but understandable failure of the ecological agenda in Bulgaria, as the anti-communist opposition (which had promoted it) won the October 1991 elections and formed a government. With this victory, the ecological organizations were no longer needed to oppose the communists. Once in power, the anti-communist coalition simply ignored them. No less important is the fact that Bulgaria's present economic crisis makes ecological initiatives seem entirely utopian. The nongovernmental organizations (NGOs) that now parade under the sign of feminist ecology lack grassroots support and attend most directly to acquiring financial support from institutions of the European Union. Some NGOs seem to be organized solely for this purpose (see Daskalova 1997:164).

There also are several women's organizations not affiliated with parties. Perhaps most influential among these is the Bulgarian Women's Association (BWA), which claims to be heir to the large, pre-communist (that is, "bourgeois") Women's Association.[48] With 2,500 members, the BWA is organized on a territorial basis; it has nineteen groups in Sofia and thirty-two groups in other communities around the country.[49] Although not affiliated with any particular political party, the association leans strongly toward the anti-communist or anti-socialist forces.[50] Through its representation in Parliament, the BWA is working to establish a special parliamentary committee entrusted to monitor and protect the constitutional rights of women in Bulgaria. The BWA is perhaps the most socially active among women's organizations, and it is engaged in the widest range of activities, from organizing free retraining courses for unemployed women to providing free legal counseling and medical advice for women. The association initiated a program to assist orphans, who are obliged at the age of 18 to leave the orphanage

---

[48] The issue of property restitution blocks the formal recognition of this organization as heir of the older Women's Association (1901–1944), whose property was actually confiscated by the state after 1944.

[49] Data were supplied by Darlia Vladikova, deputy chairwoman of this organization.

[50] Most of the women MPs of the Union of Democratic Forces, the backbone of the initial anti-communist opposition, are at the same time members of the Bulgarian Women's Association.

and adapt to life "outside." The program envisions, among other things, that these orphans might be trained as social workers. The BWA also actively supports vulnerable young families and members of the Gypsy minority (for instance, by providing milk and baby food); it also has developed an educational program to combat drug addiction. With Dutch financial support, the BWA organized a "Telephones of Confidence" center, which provides free counseling and temporary shelter for women subjected to violence.

As this list of projects suggests, the bulk of the BWA's activities fall within an older tradition of women's charity work. Thus, while making sincere and laudable efforts to help individual women and admirably stretching the very inadequate means at their disposal, this organization nevertheless operates according to traditional and widely held concepts of women's roles and identities. And, while the BWA wants to promote policies and legislation favoring women, they conceive of this in a protectionist, welfarist, and pro-natalist sense. For example, BWA wants to legally recognize women's and mother's work by lowering the retirement age by two years for every child that a woman rears; it seeks a tax reduction for employers who employ mothers with children under 10 or young people from the orphanages; and it advocates remuneration for mothers looking after their children, up to a certain age, thus treating domestic work as equal to employment (Bulgarian Women's Association 1994:1). Significantly, the BWA's program also includes projects that echo the nationalist views discussed earlier, such as introducing religious education into the secondary schools and "solving" the demographic question by raising birthrates. Indeed, they have even authored a document entitled "Foreign Policy and the Attitude of Bulgaria toward Bulgarians Outside the Bulgarian Lands."

The Single Mothers Association, registered in 1991, is representative of women's organizations dedicated to a specific goal, but not tied to national politics. Among this association's approximately three hundred members are single mothers (divorced or unmarried), adoptive mothers, and even some single fathers. Their activities are geared toward solving the problems specific to this group, which they understand to be possible through a combination of social benefits, legal counseling, and financial support for the socially disadvantaged. For example, the association lodged a petition with the presidency to lower the interest rate on housing loans taken by single mothers. Another petition, lodged with Parliament, sought to prolong the retirement age for mothers who give birth at an older age or adopt a child late in life, so that instead of relying on inadequate state pensions, these women might continue working and provide for their children until they come of age (Ivanova 1992).

There are, in addition, various women's organizations constituted along professional lines, such as the Bulgarian Association of Women in Law; Eterna (a businesswomen's club); Zherika—Zheni razvitie kariera, risk i kriza [Women, development and career, risk and crisis]; Women in Science (affiliated with the Union of Scholars in Bulgaria); the Association of Women's Clubs in Business and the Liberal Professions; the Club of Women Inventors; and the Club of

Women in the Information Technologies, among others. All of these groups are centered on the particular professional problems of their women members. While most undertake a limited number of activities aimed specifically at protecting member interests and some do hardly anything at all, others have an established international status. A case in point is the Bulgarian Association of Women in Law, which was established in 1991 and receives financial aid from the European Union. Via the participation of its members in working groups of the National Assembly, this organization assists Parliament in the drafting of bills concerning the rights of women, children, and the family. Its goal is to improve the Bulgarian legislature's record in protecting such rights by bringing new laws into harmony with such international agreements as the UN Convention on Children's Rights.[51]

Among women's professional organizations are several associated with the academy. The Bulgarian Association of University Women (BAUW), established in 1991, restored a pre-communist tradition of university women's organizations. In terms of both its membership and its goals, it has a more intellectual orientation than any of the other groups. Being a member of the International Association of University Women, the BAUW recognizes the goals of that organization, namely to support the personal, professional, and social self-fulfillment of well-educated women. The association is broadly democratic and progressive, although, to quote its leader, "not exactly feminist" (author's interview with Ralitsa Mukharska). On the other hand, there are among its members women who are well read in feminist literature and some who share feminist views of one kind or another. In addition to representing its members, the association is currently engaged in a project to introduce women's studies into the curriculum of several Bulgarian universities.

Another professional women's organization, Women in Science, regards as its central task the creation of more favorable conditions for women's professional development in the sciences. Established in 1993, the organization considers among its priorities support for women's advancement into positions of authority. Leaders of this group feel obliged to stress, however, that promoting women in the sciences will not compromise the criterion of professionalism and the priority of scholarly merit. Instead, they argue, these considerations will actually guarantee higher positions for women in science. One might say that the somewhat defensive position of this organization echoes the stance taken by the Bulgarian women's movement at the turn of the century, when women wanted to prove their worth in professional and public life on male terms, without ever questioning the traditional division of labor between the sexes (see Dzhidrova 1912; Ivanova 1923, 1926).

Finally, a relatively new organization, Zherika, deserves mention. It was established in December 1994 with the ambitious goal of supporting women under stress and in psychological crisis. It assumes that the rapid social change in

---

[51] Thus, in working out the Children's Law, the association consulted the treatment of children's rights and the relations between parents and children in current foreign legislation and practice; it also considered the role of courts in cases of child abuse and the possibility for entrusting the children to alternative custody and other issues (author's interview with Genoveva Tisheva).

Bulgaria adversely affects the lives of women much more than it affects men, the feminization of poverty being just one manifestation of this. Despite the generally inflated style of this group's rhetoric—which is characteristic of all the organizations I have discussed—this group plans to offer its members information services as a way to obtain medical, social, and educational counseling. Its program suggests a somewhat technological approach to women's problems.

Having described a range of women's organizations representative of certain broadly defined types, it is possible to make a number of generalizations. First, it seems futile to try to differentiate between women's organizations on the basis of whose interests they represent. With the exception of the professional organizations, each of them claims to speak for *all* women, and especially for women experiencing some hardship. Given the deterioration of living standards in Bulgaria, this is not remarkable. It is also difficult to differentiate among organizations in terms of the identities of their leadership. There seems to be within all of these groups a preponderance of women with advanced degrees; most were educated in the humanities, although some have trained in the sciences or engineering or work in a profession. In the current context of unemployment and inflation, however, this does not say much about their economic status, which could vary substantially.

Second, most women's organizations have strong links with political parties, which often subordinate women's interests to their own purposes. To be sure, political parties could be instrumental in attaining certain goals, particularly by supporting new legislation. Yet the danger is that women's issues are simply exploited to attract votes and are not taken seriously.[52] As I have indicated in my examples, both communists (for instance, Women and Mothers Against Violence) and anti-communists (the ecological movement, for instance) have manipulated women's groups. In fact, the parties often include in their programs measures for the "social protection" of women, only to forget them when the electoral campaign is over. Moreover, parties in office are extremely reluctant to have women's issues pressed upon them by independent organizations or through citizen initiatives. Rather, it would seem that they set up their own women's section precisely in order to preempt such action and to monopolize the right to speak for women—which ultimately means being able to ignore them.

This linkage between women's groups and political parties is made even more problematic by the sharp political polarization that characterizes Bulgaria in the post-communist era. It subverts any possibility of solidarity among women that would cut across other, supposedly more "basic," political divisions. Thus, even women activists are prone to give priority to the dominant political interpretations of reality and to consider their own aims as secondary and conditional upon other, allegedly more pressing issues. The problem is that there is never an end to "more pressing needs." This was as true of the pre-communist past as it is of

---

[52] Besides, parliamentary party discipline stands in the way of lobbying across parties in favor of issues on which women activist members of different parties otherwise agree. Bulgarian women-activists (and MPs) complained (in interviews) that previously reached agreements would be subverted when it came to actual voting and party lines again predominated.

today's overpoliticized environment. Indeed, throughout the region, "unresolved" national issues and economic exigencies repeatedly take precedence over women's issues, and women willingly subordinate their own needs to those of the national community (for a comparison, see Wolchik 1985:49). In a nationalistic milieu, women acting on their own agenda are reproached for being selfish. And, more often than not, women themselves accept this judgment, thus internalizing the blame for being "unpatriotic." Evidently, women do not often conceive of their problems as part and parcel of the community's most pressing concerns.[53]

Given the polarization of the political parties to which they are linked, many women's organizations seem opposed to each other institutionally, as the parties are opposed politically. Yet, ironically, in the programs they advocate and in the discourses through which they speak, the differences between organizations, especially the large party-linked ones, are in fact slight. Most are overwhelmingly focused on the mother role and on pro-natalism in general; they often espouse an implicit biological essentialism. They share these emphases with nationalist discourses. Indeed, one often hears—from all sides—exalted statements about motherhood and exhortations to protect women so that they can bear and raise children and thus increase the population.[54]

Most importantly, those organizations linked to a political party are all geared toward "welfarist" protections for women and the family. In this they match not only the nationalist but also the communist-era sociological discourses discussed earlier. Their preoccupation with social welfare needs reflects, in part, the collapse of the communist-era welfare system and the current insecurity of daily life. But ironically, because these same conditions have made the state too poor to provide adequate services, the welfarist agenda sounds entirely utopian; when advanced by people in positions of authority, it appears an unashamed exercise in demagoguery.

I have emphasized the way in which the discourse of most women's organizations centers around women's collective interests—that is, on women as a "category" rather than as individuals entitled to basic rights. Indeed, women's claims may be framed either in terms of rights or in terms of entitlements and social benefits. Oddly, there is barely an awareness among the leaders of women's organizations of the differences between these conceptions, let alone of their implications or the underlying philosophies that justify them. The danger in not

---

[53] An attempt to overcome this polarization is the National Women's Forum, a formation that purports to unite and coordinate the efforts of all existing women's organizations in Bulgaria, thus forming a sort of umbrella organization for meeting and discussion. According to its charter, signed in 1994, the forum was conceived as a kind of interest organization to lobby the legislative and executive branches, the church, and various public bodies on behalf of the interests of women on particular issues, while each member organization preserved its own profile and organizational independence. It also provided representation for Bulgarian women at various international conferences and meetings. But in its actual workings, this organization has found that, for the reasons of party politics and the everyday jockeying for power alluded to earlier, unified action has been extremely difficult (Daskalova 1997).

[54] I admit that even "motherly" identities (or the appeal to chivalrous generosity of the "stronger sex") may have strategic use in a "politics of identity" and may serve immediate feminist goals (e.g., protection of women in a crisis), but I doubt that this is meant as "strategy" in the Bulgarian case.

attending to these differences is that viewing women only as potential beneficiaries of a welfare system (whether such a system actually exists or not) may in fact, and even unwittingly, reinforce traditional women's roles and perpetuate inequalities. This is because the "welfare" and "entitlement" idiom itself invites a patronizing, condescending attitude by inviting the treatment of women as "objects" of social protection. An appeal to the liberal idiom of rights, and especially of equal rights, would have a different effect. Nevertheless, my interviews indicate that women activists believe an insistence upon gender differences is more beneficial to women's cause, hence the ubiquity of claims for the "special treatment" of women rather than for equality or individual rights. This preference is exacerbated by the fact that "equality" has been discredited by its long and duplicitous use under socialism.

Indeed, in trying to understand the commitment to social welfare measures in the discourse of mainstream women's groups, it is important to look beyond the present crisis, which offers only a superficial justification for such demands. The centrality of welfare-based programs also suggests ideological links with official, communist-era views about gender. To be sure, all discourses have their own conceptual inertia, and people typically work with what they know and with what is familiar. In the discourses of women activists in Bulgaria, one cannot help but notice the strong influence of socialist ideas (Meyer 1985:13–30). For instance, relatively crude concepts of gender equality prevail. Emancipation is regarded mechanistically as the result of women's employment; that is, it is understood in the same way that one previously conceived of socialist emancipation through work.[55] Similarly, the presence of *individual* women in political bodies, as *representatives* of parties, is vaguely regarded as women collectively entering the political arena. Demands for social welfare also draw upon socialist notions about the ubiquitous responsibility of the state. Importantly, all of these ideological positions were advanced by post-war communist regimes as a way to expunge the pre-war "bourgeois" women's movement in Bulgaria, the roots of which could be traced to a proto-movement for women's education in the mid-nineteenth century (Daskalova 1992). When the communists assumed power, they created a new, socialist women's organization, thus establishing a monopoly over definitions of gender equality based on full employment, social benefits, and parliamentary quotas.[56]

Other legacies of the communist period are evident in the inflated, ill-defined rhetoric of women's programs and in the striking discrepancy between the resources and professed purposes of women's organizations. Even for those groups not tied to political parties, the forms of action envisioned and generally

---

[55] As I have noted, the socialist notion of "women's emancipation" actually amounted to drawing women into the labor force (as "builders of socialism") and demanding public activism (of a strictly prescribed type). However, the communist regime treated women (and men alike) as subjects of quasi-patriarchal state power while leaving domestic patriarchalism untouched.

[56] The positive results for women of the socialist period cannot, however, be gainsaid: Women's education was substantially extended, and women made a more massive entry into some prestigious professions.

implemented are clearly derived from the previous era. Putting issues directly to the authorities, as in petitions addressed to state bureaucracies or the National Assembly, rather than mobilizing support in a broad public campaign, seems to be a habit from the past that puts faith in administrative intervention; in this case, anyway, it is not likely to occur. It is here that the general weakness of civil society in Bulgaria becomes obvious. It is especially evident in the underdevelopment of genuine, voluntary civic groups organized around various causes and in the difficulty, or lack of interest, that women's organizations show in rousing public opinion or social protest. The Bulgarian women's movement is fairly invisible to the public eye; it has not yet managed to present gender issues in a way that would capture popular attention and support for legislative advocacy. This failure results neither from a lack of space for public debate nor from a weakened mass media. Rather, it is due to the fact that public space is now occupied by the discourses of "femininity" and popularized science outlined earlier. At times, particular issues may take center stage. For example, a debate about prostitution was aired on local and private TV in 1995. The tenor of debate reflected a spirit of tolerance and understanding, as participants blamed economic pressures for driving women to prostitution. But the debate ignored the sociological evidence of coercion, deception, and the involvement of children in prostitution.

This climate, sustained in part by women's organizations' dogged support for motherhood, suggests that there is little room to discuss other aspects of women's experience or alternative conceptualizations thereof. Issues of women's identity, professional fulfillment, and the division of labor within the household, as well as problems of domestic violence and everyday forms of gendered humiliation, are thus marginalized in the public discourse. Cultural stereotypes about weak and vulnerable women perpetuate socialized forms of domination. Thus deeply ingrained, patriarchal attitudes, habits, opinions, and judgments are difficult to change, especially if women remain insensitive to, and therefore complicitous in, their own domination. Moreover, male power is expressed through a variety of seemingly minor or innocuous forms of subjugation, the dynamics of which are similar to what Foucault calls the micro-physics of power (Foucault 1975:31–34). These are anything but trivial. Forms of addressing women, sexual jokes or insinuations, and the expression of disparaging opinions or common "wisdom" about "a woman's" qualities and capacities are indicative of power asymmetries, besides being deeply offensive. Because such indignities occur within everyday relationships, they are normalized and become features of women's daily experience. As one activist put it, women (at least the more sensitive) come to live in a state of "monotonous discomfort" (Dakova 1996). Yet, generally speaking, Bulgarian society—many women included—is remarkably insensitive to these forms of micro-violence.

Historically, middle-class women, especially women of letters and those in the liberal professions, addressed some of these concerns (Daskalova 1995). It is noteworthy that the pre-1945 "bourgeois" women's organizations fought for educational equality, voting rights, and access to the professions. Today, women in academic and professional organizations, some of whom explicitly describe their work as a continuation or "restoration" of the pre–World War II women's movement, are again focusing on these issues. But feminist voices are rarely heard in Bulgaria's public space. Occasionally one may see a feminist article published in an intellectual literary or cultural journal, such as *Literaturen Forum, Kultura,* or *Literaturen vestnik* [Literature Newspaper], or in a scholarly journal such as *Glas* [Voice], *Sotsiologicheski pregled* [Sociology Review], *Politicheski izsledvaniia* [Political Research], or *Obshta i prilozhna kulturologiia* [General and Applied Cultural Studies]. These journals not only explore women's roles and identities but also address and critically examine gendered power relations and stereotypes about women in Bulgarian society. They also provide a venue for writing about women in other countries. For example, in a special 1995 issue on feminism and women's history, *Kultura* published interviews with Julia Kristeva and Ida Blom (then president of the International Federation for Research on Women in History). In 1996, Sofia University Press published a volume on women's history. Nonetheless, feminist sensibilities are the exception in Bulgaria. "Feminism" itself is a derogatory word, even among the leaders of women's organizations. Stigmatized during the communist era, it is now perceived as a threat to normal relationships between men and women and as an impingement on "traditional Bulgarian values" of love, marriage, and family. My interviews revealed that, with few exceptions, the leaders of women's organizations emphatically disclaim "feminism" or, to be more precise, some caricature of it.[57]

Conclusions

My aim in this chapter was to provide a socioeconomic and discursive context in which to understand the ways that Bulgarian women's organizations formulate women's problems. I have also argued that it is necessary, as well, to consider the realities of everyday politics in post-communism and the ways in which women's organizations, as organizations, are linked to political parties and thus subject to party antagonisms. These factors constrain both women's choice of issues and the available means of social action. Equally important is the legacy of the communist period. As I have shown, socialist patterns of thinking are embedded in mainstream women's discourses and have a strong, if subtle, influence on what women conceive to be problems and on how they frame potential solutions.

I have also tried to indicate the diversity that exists among women's organizations in Bulgaria today. Although clearly constrained by socioeconomic and historical factors, these groups are not completely encompassed by these factors. Other discourses, and especially more critical ones attending to everyday

---

[57] Vulgar notions commonly associated with feminism are "hate monger" living single ("an old spinster"), or being lesbian. As Nancy Cott writes about the situation in the United States at the beginning of the century, feminism and "militance" are not the same thing, but common parlance linked them.

interactions and subtle power dynamics, are possible; indeed, they are starting
to exist in marginal spaces such as academic circles and intellectual publications.
Furthermore, ties to international women's organizations and to other bodies,
such as the European Union, the United Nations, and international scientific
societies, are a new and intriguing development. As I have suggested, in some
cases such links lead to the formation of empty organizations that try to match
foreign expectations; in other cases they stimulate, fund, and provide a focus for
genuine efforts at local reform. In general, Western-style feminist activism must
await the rise of a strong middle class, the advance of the professions toward
greater autonomy, and a further reflection on women's issues within the academy.
It is in such milieus and social spaces that a more reflexive form of thinking
could develop, one that questions received social and cultural gender identities
and one that could exist alongside the older, maternalist and social protectionist
versions of women's activism.

BIBLIOGRAPHY

Newspapers/Media

Obshtestvo i pravo
  1992a   Koi ima interes ot unishtozhavaneto na "Zlatniia Orfei" 9.
  1992b   Kurazh samotni maiki (6):26.
Pazar na truda
  1993   Pazar na truda i reformata v bŭlgarskata promishlenost. Materiali ot mezhdu-
          narodna konferentsiia, provedena v Sofiia (18–20 mai):226.
Pressluzhba Kurier
  1990a   (May 17) Programa na partiia natsionalen Patriotichen Sŭiuz 97(115):10–11.
  1990b   (May 17) Programa na Khristian-radikalnata partiia 97(115):17.
  1990c   (May 29) Manifest na Khristian-republikanskata partiia 104(122):2.
  1990d   (June 27) Programa na Sŭiuza na demokratichnite partii "Era–3" 125(143):8–9.
  1991a   (January 25) 18(293):6.
  1991b   (April 23) 79(354):2.
  1991c   (May 6) Politicheska programa na Khristian-radikal demokraticheskata par-
          tiia 87:2–3.
  1991d   (June) 110(385):9.
  1991e   (Aug. 8) Politicheska platforma na Bŭlgarskiiat biznes blok 154(429):5–6.
  1991f   (Aug. 9) 155(430):4.
  1991g   (Sept. 5) Programa na Otechestvenata Partiia na Truda 174(449):10.
  1991h   (Sept. 25) Sotsialna programa na Bŭlgarskata demokraticheska partiia
          188(463):14.
  1991i   (Dec. 3) Publication of the Christian Women's Union 237(512):11–12.

Books/General

Andreeva, Dimitrina
  1992   Za sotsialna politika po problemite na zhenata i semeistvoto. Problemi na
          truda (1):40–47.
Atanasov, Atanas
  1985   Niakoi sŭvremenni tendentsii v razhdaemostta u nas. *In* Mladoto semeistvo:
          Rezultati ot sotsiologicheski prouchvaniia. Pp. 43–72. Sofia.

Atanasova, Nikolina
  1991   Neobkhodimost ot nov pogled vŭrkhu problemite na bŭlgarskata zhena v prek-
          hoda kŭm pazarna ikonomika. Problemi na truda 9:3–6.
Balkanski, Doz. P.
  1993   Abortite i planiraneto na semeistvoto. Zdraveopazvane 228–230.
Bourdieu, Pierre
  1977   Outline of a Theory of Practice. Cambridge: Cambridge University Press.
Bozhanova, Kornelia
  1991   Prostitutsiata, spinŭt i bolestite na Venera. Obshtestvo i pravo 5:12–14.
Brown, Wendy
  1995   State of Injury: Power and Freedom in Late Modernity. Princeton, NJ:
          Princeton University Press.
Bulgarian Women's Association
  1994   Our Strength Is in Action. Sofia: Bulgarian Women's Association.
Bŭlgarskata natsionalna demokraticheska partiia
  1990   Platforma na Bŭlgarska natsionalna demokraticheska partiia. Zora 1(14 mai):6.
Chester, Gail and Julienne Dickey
  1988   Feminism and Censorship: The Current Debate. Bridgeport, Dorset, England:
          Prism Press.
Cott, Nancy
  1987   The Grounding of Modern Feminism. New Haven, CT: Yale University Press.
Dakova, Vera
  1995   Bulgaria 1995: The Situation of Women. Sofia: UNDP.
  1996   Interview. Kultura 10(March 8):8.
Daskalova, Krassimira
  1992   Obrazovanie na zhenite i zhenite v obrazovanieto na vŭzrozhdenska Bŭlgariia.
          Sofia: Izdatelstvo na Sofiiskiiat Universitet.
  1994   Za ravni prava na zhenite v Bŭlgariia. Sofia.
  1995   Diskursite po 'zhenskiia vŭpros' i miastoto na zhenite v bŭlgarskoto obshtestvo
          1878–1944. Sofia: Vseobshta konfederatsiia na belgiiskite trudeshti se.
  1997   The Women's Movement in Bulgaria after Communism. In Transitions, Envi-
          ronments, Translations. Joan Scott et al., eds. Pp. 162–175. New York:
          Routledge.
Demokratichen sŭiuz na zhenite
  1992   Platforma na Demokratichen sŭiuz na zhenite. Sofia: Ustav na Demokratichniia
          sŭiuz na zhenite.
Dzhidrova, Maria
  1912   Iskaniiata na bŭlgarkata: Skazka. Sofia: Pechatnitsa "Grazhdanin."
Dinkova, Mariia
  1980   Sotsialen portret na bŭlgarskata zhena. Sofia: Profizdat.
  1985   Tendentsii i problemi vŭv formiraneto na mladoto semeistvo. In Mladoto
          semeistvo: Rezultati ot sotsiologicheski prouchvaniia. Pp. 9–42. Sofia: TsK
          na DKMS.
  1990   Do koga shte sŭshtestvuva "vtoriiat por?" Zhenata dnes 5:5–10.
Dworkin, Andrea and Catherine A. MacKinnon
  1988   Pornography and Civil Rights: A New Day for Women's Equality. Employ-
          ment and Unemployment 3.

Filipov, Dimitŭr
1993   Naprechno-kokhorten analiz na efekta na demografskata politika. Statistika 2:40–51.
Filipova, R.
1993   Zhertvi na sŭdbata, sistemata ili na samite sebe si. Obshtestvo i pravo 4:19.
Foucault, Michel
1975   Surveiller et punir. Paris: Gallimard.
1980   Power/Knowledge: Selected Interviews and Other Writings 1972–1977. Colin Gordon, Leo Marshall, John Mepham, and Kate Soper, transl. New York: Harvester Press.
1984   Le pouvoir comment s'exerce-t-il? *In* Foucault: un parcourts philosophique. Hubert L. Dreyfus and Paul Rabinow, eds. Pp. 308–321. Paris: Gallimard.
Fox-Genovese, Elizabeth
1996   Feminism Is Not the Story of My Life. New York: Doubleday.
Friedan, Betty
1963   The Feminine Mystique. New York: W. W. Norton & Company.
Gal, Susan
1994   Gender in the Post-Socialist Transition: The Abortion Debate in Hungary. East European Politics and Societies 8(2):256–287.
Genov, Nikola
1995   Bŭlgariia 1995: Razvitieto na choveka. Sofia: UNDP.
Georgieva, Petia
1994   Meraklii. Obshtestvo i pravo 4:14.
Gerdzhikova, Dr. Z.
1989   (Dec. 12) Zhenskiiat vŭpros. Otechestvo 23:12–13.
Ginsburg, Faye and Rayna Rapp
1991   The Politics of Reproduction. Annual Review of Anthropology 20:311–343.
Golemanov, Nikolai
1991   Abortŭt i zdravoslovnoto sŭstoianie na zhenite v Bŭlgariia. Problemi na truda 9:7–12.
Hassan, Fareed and R. Kyle Peters
1995   Social Safety Net and the Poor during the Transition: The Case of Bulgaria. Washington, DC: The World Bank.
Ilieva, Nikolina
1989   Zhenata v Narodna Republika Bŭlgariia: Sotsialno-ikonomicheski pridobivki. *In* Spravochnik. Sofia: Profizdat.
1991   Sotsialnata politika za zhenata pri prekhoda kŭm pazarna ikonomika. Problemi na truda 9:35–46.
1993   Zaetost i bezrabotitsa pri zhenite. Naselenie 2:49–59.
Ilieva, Nikolina and Genoveva Mikhova
1992   Zhenite v strukturata na naselenieto na Bŭlgariia. Naselenie 5:60–62.
Ivanova, Dimitrina
1923   Dneshniiat dŭlg na bŭlgarkata: Bŭlgarkata pred sŭbitiiata. Zhenski glas.
1926   Strakhŭt ot feminizma. Zhenski glas, 11 (1 mart).
Ivanova, Lidia
1992   Kurazh samotni maiki [Courage, Single Mothers]. Obshtestvo i pravo 6.
Kligman, Gail
1992   The Politics of Reproduction in Ceauşescu's Romania: A Case Study in Political Culture. East European Politics and Societies 6(3):364–418.

Kostadinova, F.
  1993   Maloletnite prostitutki. Obshtestvo i pravo 7:32–33.
Kostova, Dobrinka
  1993   The Transition to Democracy in Bulgaria: Challenges and Risks for Women. *In* Democratic Reform and the Position of Women in Transitional Economies. Valentine M. Moghadem, ed. Pp. 92–109. Oxford: Clarendon Press.
Kotseva, Tatiana and Irina Todorova
  1994   Bŭlgarkata: Traditsionni predstavi i promeniashti se realnosti. Pernik: Krakra.
MacKinnon, Catherine A.
  1996   Only Words. Cambridge, MA: Harvard University Press.
Mamonova, Tatyana
  1989   Russian Women's Studies: Essays on Sexism in Soviet Culture. New York: Pergamon Press.
McElroy, Wendy
  1995   Women's Right to Pornography. New York: St. Martin's Press.
McIntyre, Robert
  1980   The Bulgarian Anomaly: Demographic Transition and Current Fertility. Southeastern Europe 7(2):147–170.
Meyer, Alfred G.
  1985   Feminism, Socialism, and Nationalism in Eastern Europe. *In* Women, State and Party in Eastern Europe. Sharon L. Wolchik and Alfred G. Meyer, eds. Pp. 13–30. Durham, NC: Duke University Press.
Mikhailova, G.
  1992   Balerini v mesarnitsite na Kipŭr (razkaz na edna ochevidka). Zhenata dnes 12:20–21.
Mikhova, Genoveva
  1993   Reproduktivni i migratsionni naglasi na bezrabotnite zheni. Naselenie 1:47–58.
Minkov, Minko
  1991   Prebroiavane na zagubite: Interviu s Prof. Minko Minkov, Direktor na Instituta po demografiia pri BAN. Zhenata dnes 9:4–5.
Minnesota Advocates for Human Rights
  1996   Domestic Violence in Bulgaria. Minneapolis: Minnesota Advocates for Human Rights.
National Statistical Institute
  1993   Zdraveopazvane. Sofia: Natsionalen Statisticheski Institut.
  1994   Employment and Unemployment. Sofia: National Statistical Institute.
  1995   Statisticheski spravochnik. Statistichesko izdatelstvo i pechatnitsa.
  1996   Statisticheski barometŭr, Vol. 89:(2–3).
Nikleva, Elena
  1990   Bŭlgarkata v ponedelnik. Zhenata dnes 1:6–7.
Noninska, N.
  1990   Drugarkite na noshtta. Obshtestvo i pravo 1:24–25.
Pateman, Carole
  1992   Equality, Difference, Subordination: The Politics of Motherhood and Women's Citizenship. *In* Beyond Equality and Difference: Citizenship, Feminist Politics and Female Subjectivity. Gisela Bock and Susan James, eds. Pp. 17–31. New York: Routledge.

Petrova, Dimitrina
1993   The Winding Road to Emancipation in Bulgaria. *In* Gender Politics and Post-Communism: Reflections from Eastern Europe and the Former Soviet Union. Nanette Funk and Magda Mueller, eds. Pp. 22–30. New York: Routledge.

Phillips, Anne and Barbara Taylor
1996   Sex and Skill: Notes toward a Feminist Economics. *In* Feminism and History. Joan W. Scott, ed. Pp. 317–330. New York: Oxford University Press.

Popova, Diana
1990   Chernobil: chetiri godini po-kŭsno. Zhenata dnes 3:3.
1992   Vchera beshe nedelia. Zhenata dnes 10:14–15.

Radev, Veselin
1993   Prostitutki, gradusi i chenchadzhii sŭzdavat obedinen front. Obshtestvo i pravo 7:25–27.

Reeves-Ellington, Barbara
1996a   A Woman's Place in Bulgaria: Past Perspective, Current Hopes. Presented at the Seventeenth Annual Conference of the National Women's Studies Association, Skidmore College.
1996b   Emancipated or Manipulated? Bulgarian Women's Narratives of Work before and after 1944. Unpublished manuscript.

Riley, Denise
1983   War in the Nursery: Theories of the Child and Mother. London: Virago.
1988   "Am I That Name?" Feminism and the Category of "Women" in History. Minneapolis: University of Minnesota Press.

Rose, Richard
1992   Divisions and Contradictions in Economies in Transition: Household Portfolios in Russia, Bulgaria and Czechoslovakia. Glasgow: University of Strathclyde.

Scott, Hilda
1975   Does Socialism Liberate Women? Experiences from Eastern Europe. Boston: Beacon.

Scott, Joan W.
1996   Introduction. *In* Feminism and History. Joan W. Scott, ed. Pp. 1–13. New York: Oxford University Press.

Simeonova, Lidiia
1995   Estetichnata meditsina. Zhenata dnes 5:16–17.

Terzieva, Vania
1991   Sotsialna tsena na roditelstvoto i maichinstvoto v usloviiata na demografska i ikonomicheska kriza. Problemi na truda 9:13–19.

Tilly, Louise and Joan Scott
1987   Women, Work and Family. New York: Methuen.

Todorova, Maria
1993   The Bulgarian Case: Women's Issues or Feminist Issues? *In* Gender Politics and Post-Communism: Reflections from Eastern Europe and the Former Soviet Union. Nanette Funk and Magda Mueller, eds. Pp. 30–38. New York: Routledge.

Tsitselkov, Ivan
1994   Ubili, za da zhiveiat. Obshtestvo i pravo 7–8:2–4.

Tsurkova, Fani
    1992a   Spin ni nagazva: Nosete si novite prezervativi. Obshtestvo i pravo 10:35–36.
    1992b   Sramnite bolesti izliazokha na megdana. Obshtestvo i pravo 11:16–18.
United Nations
    1991   The World's Women: Trends and Statistics 1970–1990. New York: The United Nations.
Vangelova, Svetla and Stoianka Kuncheva
    1991   Biudzhet na vremeto na bŭlgarskata zhena. Problemi na truda 1:24–34.
Voronina, Olga
    1994   The Mythology of Women's Emancipation in the U.S.S.R. as the Foundation for a Policy of Discrimination. *In* Women in Russia: A New Era in Russian Feminism. Anastasiia Posadskaya, ed. Pp. 37–56. New York: Verso.
Wolchik, Sharon L.
    1985   Introduction. *In* Women, State and Party in Eastern Europe. Sharon L. Wolchik and Alfred G. Meyer, eds. Durham, NC: Duke University Press.
    1993   Women and the Politics of Transition in Central and Eastern Europe. *In* Democratic Reform and the Position of Women in Transitional Economies. Valentine M. Moghadam, ed. Pp. 29–47. Oxford: Clarendon Press.
World Development Report
    1992   1992 World Development Report. New York: Oxford University Press.
World Health Organization
    1994   AIDS: Images of the Epidemic. Geneva: WHO.
Zagorova, L.
    1992   Vmesto da igraiat na kukli, detsa prodavat liubov. Obshtestvo i pravo 3:8–9, 22.

CHAPTER 13

Belgrade's SOS Hotline for Women and Children Victims of Violence: A Report

ZORICA MRŠEVIĆ

IN WHAT IS NOW the former Yugoslavia, the late 1980s were the pre-war years, although none of us living there realized it at the time. In hindsight, the signs of conflict were everywhere: tensions between the governments of the various federal republics led to a series of political crises accompanied by a split within the League of Communists (LCY), demands for more democracy, and the spread of nationalist propaganda. In short, it was a time of men's anger and aggression and of men's expanding power. The pre-war period, as well as wartime itself, was characterized by women's massive retreat into the private sphere following their removal—forced or voluntary—from the public domain. For example, at both the federal and republic levels, fewer and fewer women held seats in Parliament; they made up less than 3 percent after the first free election in 1991. Women's membership in all political parties and trade unions declined, as did their presence in leadership roles in the media and in cultural and scientific life. The 1980s were also a time of economic crisis, and women suffered particularly. Branded as surplus labor, they were often laid off without recourse. Women's expulsion from the labor force was heralded as a return to "good, traditional, national, and family values." As the crisis intensified, women were compelled to return to their homes—after all, "someone" had to struggle for the everyday survival of children and the elderly.

In response to the increasing violence of everyday life, women organized themselves into autonomous women's organizations. Their grassroots methods constituted a form of political action different from that customarily associated with "political action" in Serbia, yet appropriate to these years of radical change (i.e., the late 1980s and early 1990s). The SOS Hotline Belgrade,[1] the first hotline of its kind in Serbia and the third in the former Yugoslavia, emerged

---

Editors' note: This chapter was written during the war in Bosnia and refers to the years between 1990 and 1997. On the hotline, see Mršević and Hughes 1997.

[1] Because no term comparable to the word "hotline" exists in Serbian, it would have been necessary to describe, rather than translate, the concept; any name so derived would be cumbersome and lack clarity. "SOS" is widely known as the international distress signal and, combined with the word "telephone," invokes a strong, clear image. In this chapter, "SOS" used alone refers to the organization SOS Hotline Belgrade for Women and Children Victims of Violence; used in conjunction with "hotline," it refers to the service this organization provides.

from the women's movement, notably from the feminist discussion group Women and Society. Other initiatives followed soon thereafter, among them the Women's Studies Center, Women in Black, the Autonomous Women's Center against Sexual Violence, SOS for Girls (One and Two), and the Law Group.

In response to events leading up to and following Yugoslavia's violent collapse, international attention focused on the use of rape as a weapon of war and on the widespread, often systematic, and collective abuse of women. Much less is known about the violence experienced by women in their everyday lives. In this chapter, I present a "herstory" of the SOS Hotline Belgrade, describing its role in helping women victims of domestic violence. In contrast to the gendered violence of war, this report sheds light on the process by which women organized themselves against what may be viewed as the micro-practices of violence in daily life. The first section addresses questions such as: What is the SOS Hotline? How, why, and when was it created, and by whom? How are its activities organized, and by whom are they supported? Who are the women who volunteer, and who are the ones who call for help? What motivates them? Section two examines cultural and legal aspects of domestic violence in the former Yugoslavia. What is the traditional understanding of gender roles in marriage and the "legitimate" use of violence against women? What types of violence typify domestic violence? I present case summaries to illustrate customary forms of violence and conclude this section with a cursory critique of the politics of domestic violence among feminist groups. Finally, I review the contributions of SOS to the public debate on violence against women. As will become clear, the SOS Hotline was constituted primarily by and for women, too many of whom were and are the victims of gendered violence against them.

HERSTORY OF THE SOS HOTLINE

The SOS Hotline for Women and Children Victims of Violence began operating in Belgrade in March 1990. By then, feminists from Ljubljana (the capital of Slovenia), Zagreb (the capital of Croatia), and Belgrade (the capital of Serbia and of Yugoslavia), had been working together for almost two decades. Their joint efforts to establish SOS hotlines are examples of continuing, if limited, cooperation—despite the war. The first hotline in the Balkan peninsula opened in Zagreb in 1989; a second was established a few months later in Ljubljana. When Belgrade feminists sought approval from city authorities for the allocation of office space and necessary telephone lines, they were strongly backed by feminists in Zagreb. The first training program for Belgrade SOS volunteers was also organized by Zagreb feminists.

Prior to the creation of SOS, the group Women and Society had been the focal point of feminist activity in Belgrade. Most but not all of the women who met to discuss feminist concerns came from socially privileged family backgrounds and tended to be highly educated. They spoke foreign languages and had spent several months or years abroad, usually in the West, engaged in work or study.[2] Some among the women activists were lesbians and had connections with lesbian groups abroad, again primarily in Western countries. Contact with Western feminists and the introduction of "Western" feminism were among the many aspects of daily life that reflected Yugoslavia's political openness at that time. As citizens of the most open of all former socialist countries, Yugoslavs were entitled to hold passports and to travel abroad without restrictions.

Initially, participation in the feminist movement meant attending weekly meetings during nonwork hours.[3] Typically, these events concluded at one of the restaurants frequented by feminists and/or lesbians, for example, Zona, Manjež, or Sunce. After the war began, however, this feminist discussion group was quickly transformed and began taking on a variety of activist projects. No longer was "feminism" something in which women participated for a few hours once or twice a week; the feminist movement came to demand full commitment, which meant entire days of dedicated work. Many women, who had other interests or previous obligations to an employer or family, were unable to accommodate themselves to this new situation. Of the women who remained, the majority were unemployed, unmarried, and childless (although some had adult children).

During the war, feminists from Belgrade and Zagreb met at conferences abroad and lamented the tragedies of the ongoing strife. Although some feminists from Zagreb were sympathetic to the nationalist cause in Croatia, others resisted and maintained their ties with feminists from Belgrade. In Belgrade, those feminists who were also Serb nationalists remained silent about their political sympathies. In general, Belgrade feminists were unaware of the nationalists among them. Throughout the war, feminist organizations continued to function in their respective countries.

Today, Yugoslavia no longer exists; its remnants are presided over by nationalist strongmen. As daily life in Croatia and Serbia has been "normalized," contacts between feminists in Zagreb and Belgrade have become more frequent.[4] At the same time, and partially as a result of increased stability, the tensions between feminists, which previously had been held in check by the war, have surfaced, shaking the foundations of solidarity that underlie their work.

---

[2] Since the mid-1960s, most pupils studied English as a foreign language; even students at the military academies learned English. For many, proficiency in English was a bridge to establishing communication with Westerners.

[3] For example, in 1972, the Student Cultural Center opened and served as a venue for promoting political, philosophical, artistic, and cultural models. It served as the first permanent meeting place for Belgrade feminists.

[4] The great accomplishment that made communication possible was the establishment of ZAMIR (*za mir*, in Serbian, means "for peace"). Zamir is the BBS e-mail system that accommodated all the territories of the former Yugoslavia. This enabled women from Zagreb and Belgrade to communicate during the period of armed conflict and during periods when telephone lines between the two countries did not exist.

SOS: Structure and Operating Principles

SOS is a service provided by and for women. The public nature of SOS's work is meant to call attention to, and change public opinion about, the deeply entrenched societal devaluation, distrust, and humiliation of women. It is a nongovernmental organization (NGO) created on the initiative of women who are unaffiliated with political parties. SOS is not a professional service; therefore, educational credentials are not a factor in the selection of volunteers. Formally nonhierarchical in structure, SOS divides its work among various groups, each of which has its own coordinator. Still, after years of operation, an invisible elite or power center has emerged, although its members have never been officially nominated. Nonetheless, an egalitarian ethos has prevailed among SOS participants since the beginning. This was considered fundamental in order to preclude misunderstandings based on status or social distinction between volunteers and callers and to create an atmosphere of mutual trust and support in which victims of violence could deal with their personal traumas.

SOS began as a telephone hotline service but, over time, expanded the scope of its activities to include necessary outreach interventions such as escorting women to court, to the police, and to clinics. It had become readily apparent that state or "public" institutions do not value women's experience, nor do they take seriously the dangerous circumstances that confront women on a daily basis. SOS's uniqueness derives from its exclusive focus on violence against women and children. SOS is dedicated to exposing the implicit threat of violence—manifest in diverse forms and combinations thereof, including physical, psychological, economic, and sexual violence—and the dramatic and serious consequences of such violence for the lives of its victims.

To this end, SOS has built a network of professional support providers for women in need, among whom are social workers, lawyers, journalists, scientists, researchers, and politicians. This network represents both women's solidarity in action and the positive potential of such collective endeavors. Women hope that their common goals and efforts will contribute to changing both public opinion about violence against women and the broader culture of violence in which such practices are embedded.

SOS publicizes its services by giving interviews with journalists sensitive to women's issues; two volunteers are nominated every two years for the express purpose of handling media issues. The most intensive public relations work involves distributing public announcements and notices each year prior to the annual training session for new volunteers. Despite these publicity efforts, few people realize that the hotline is an independent women's initiative with no connection to official state agencies. Because SOS's telephone number appears in the "Important Numbers" section of both the state and opposition daily newspapers, many people mistakenly assume that the hotline is a special state-regulated and state-financed social service.

When SOS began its work, the city of Belgrade provided office space. Until 1993, SOS operated from a room provided in the Youth House. However, after publishing its 1993 *Antiwar Bulletin*, SOS became the target of harassment in the form of break-ins, confiscation of furniture, and frequent difficulties with their telephone line (see below). That there was no theft underscored the political nature of these "warnings." In the end, SOS was evicted from the building. Fortunately, feminists with private connections to women in powerful positions were able to secure a new home for SOS. Since 1993, SOS has been located in an official building that provides office space for the Public Statistics Office. Felicitously, the SOS office is protected by an armed guard who stands at the building's main entrance twenty-four hours a day.

In the early years, all SOS operating costs (e.g., office supplies, emergency needs) were covered by unsolicited contributions from volunteers. Women collected money amongst themselves when it was necessary to purchase something. Today, SOS is financed, for the most part, by other women's groups, particularly by the Autonomous Women's Center against Sexual Violence. Operating costs remain relatively modest: a monthly telephone bill, a salary for one administrative worker, and attorney fees for its legal counsel.

Financial resources have also been acquired in some unusual ways. At the beginning of the war in 1991 and 1992, certain well-known feminist leaders in Belgrade began to receive envelopes with small sums of money. Friends in Western countries, or women who had met them at past women's conferences, had anticipated the economic crisis that ensued in Belgrade—although the media cannot be said to have accurately informed them of daily living conditions— and felt compelled to help in some way. Because of the war and, in particular, the world trade embargo against Serbia, Belgrade's inhabitants suffered from the cold and hunger; public heating barely functioned, while public transportation was virtually nonexistent. Inflation soared to a peak of 2 billion percent in 1993. Although women beyond the borders of Serbia could not know these details, they did know that their friends needed assistance. The letters were heartwarming; often sent by an unknown but sympathetic woman, they contained small bills in foreign currency (20 or 50 German marks, perhaps) and a note saying, for example, "We are crying with you. . . . This is only a small sum but we haven't more. Use it however you think proper," or, "We pray to God for you, brave women from Belgrade. Take this money as our contribution to SOS."

International solidarity of this sort was countered by the emergence, at the outbreak of the war, of the first conflicts among feminists. Some disagreed with the role played by certain Western countries in the disintegration of Yugoslavia and also with the practice of "uncritically accepting everything from the West." At the same time, Belgrade feminists were invited to participate in many international women's events, to speak about their situation, and to share their experiences with women throughout the world. They also returned home with the first grants for women's groups in Belgrade. The majority of funds came from women donors in Switzerland, Germany, the Netherlands, Austria, Sweden, the United States, Italy, and Spain. These Western feminists supported the anti-nationalist, anti-war, and pacifist stance of Belgrade's feminists.

Responding to Callers and the Community

The SOS office is open daily. Someone is available to answer the telephone hotline during regular office hours, Monday through Friday from 11:00 a.m. to 6:00 p.m., and also during "duty time," evenings from 6:00 p.m. to 10:00 p.m., plus weekends and holidays when SOS volunteers cover the phones. To the extent possible, two trained volunteers are on duty at any given time. SOS support to women victims of violence is predicated on a set of key principles: (1) What a woman says must be trusted completely; (2) no woman is responsible for the violence she has suffered; (3) violence is a social phenomenon and is not the fault of any particular woman; (4) a woman calling SOS must be informed that her problem is not unique, but is shared by myriad other women who suffer abuse "legitimated" by a patriarchal social structure; (5) women must be reminded that all human beings have a right to live free of violence; (6) a woman's autonomy must be respected and encouraged in order for her to move away from dependency and the closed circle of violence; and (7) a woman should be given constructive support rather than instant solutions.

Each day the SOS hotline receives five to ten calls. More than 3,000 calls are recorded per year, the vast majority of which are made by women in trouble (see below). Other calls involve official communications with local and foreign institutions. Some callers inquire about the work of SOS. Still other calls may come from a victim's brother, boyfriend, male colleague, or a neighbor who wants to help. There are also "men's calls," that is, from men whose wives have sought help in leaving their abusive partners. These women's husbands are usually angry and violent, and this is reflected in the menacing messages they phone into SOS: "Fuck you and your relatives and everything valuable to you in the world"; "You fucking lesbians, somebody should kill the lot of you"; "Damn the one who let you organize"; "There's a law for you, just wait and see"; "I know who you are, but you don't know who I am. You'll get yours yet"; "You are simply men-haters, frigid, self-hating bitches. A penis is what all of you wish for, night and day. That's what you all lack, and that's your problem." Enraged male callers may attempt to justify their behavior by rationalizing their actions against women: "If she treated you that way, you'd hit her too"; "She pushes my buttons, she really asked for it"; "I couldn't help myself, I just lost control"; "If she would just listen to me"; "Sorry, but I was blinded by jealousy . . . but, never again!" Calls also come in from unidentified speakers who threaten one or more SOS volunteers and make perverse and/or damaging statements about the volunteer(s).

Among the most annoying and often problematic calls to SOS are the "silent calls." While these may be anonymous crank calls or represent harassment against SOS, silent calls may also alert volunteers to the most serious cases of violence when a victim is unable to speak.

It is noteworthy that the authorities have never displayed an openly negative reaction toward SOS nor have they forbidden its work. Clearly, they cannot ignore the political engagement of SOS members who travel abroad and participate at conferences, discussing topics such as the situation of women in the former

Yugoslavia, violence against women, war crimes, and genocide. Nor can the authorities ignore SOS's presence in the domestic media. In consequence, the authorities have tended to react in one of two ways:

1. They ignore SOS, believing that women's work is of no importance to serious men and that any discussion generated by women is, a priori, unworthy of notice.

2. They employ subversive, covert tactics aimed not only at SOS and other feminist groups in Belgrade, but also at feminist solidarity in general. Their methods include infiltrating SOS with agents, blackmailing current members into collaborating with the authorities, and poisoning the atmosphere by destroying friendships and the feeling of solidarity and kinship within SOS. To this end, they use basic harassment techniques: circulating anonymous letters that range in content from the obscene to the offensive or from the derisive to the threatening; making frequent, anonymous night-time telephone calls; breaking into offices used by women's groups or into the private apartments of their members, although taking nothing; confiscating and/or destroying items from an SOS office or the Women's Center; making libelous attacks in the yellow press; and provoking or exacerbating disagreement and conflict among lesbian feminists. All of these actions sow discord among members and promote an atmosphere of distrust, disappointment, and insecurity. It should be mentioned that the dark hand of the state security service has also been noticed (but not corroborated by any evidence) in other organizations such as political opposition parties, independent trade unions, human rights advocacy groups, and the independent media.

By and large, cooperation between SOS and other institutions has been limited, except where friends of volunteers are called upon or connections based on friendships have been deliberately cultivated. Otherwise, assistance from other institutions depends on the respective institution's leadership or on the goodwill of particular individuals. For example, police officers may prove especially understanding and even helpful. But, more often than not, they reject all suggestions made by SOS. Other professionals inadvertently undermine the activities of SOS. Social workers frequently insist on obtaining the real addresses of battered women who are in hiding; they claim that the law requires this information. However, it is this very secrecy concerning women's whereabouts that often saves lives. Indeed, knowledge of these addresses could give perpetrators of the most violent crimes easy access to their victims. Everywhere—in courts, centers for social work, police stations, and medical institutions—employees, whether women or men, usually display an insensitive approach toward battered women, an approach that is colored by all possible prejudices concerning violence against women and that SOS tries to combat and change.

A Profile of SOS Staff and Volunteers

In addition to data collected through previous research on the social backgrounds and particular problems of the women who have called the hotline for help (see below), SOS maintains its own statistical data on the women who kept the organization alive and functioning during the war years.[5]

SOS Hotline Belgrade places no restrictions on the qualifications of staff and volunteers. The hotline is open to all mature women, and members are required only to complete an annual training program; this training is designed to ensure consistency and professionalism in addressing the needs of women who are victims of violence and also to encourage a sense of organizational cohesion. Since 1995, SOS members have participated in the selection of candidates for the training program and in the selection of volunteers. By the summer of 1996, SOS maintained a list of forty volunteers, ten of whom worked regularly on telephone duty. (And, as noted below, many volunteers contributed their time working at other women's groups, too.) To reiterate, SOS is committed to developing a volunteer corps that reflects the diversity of its callers. For example, more than 12 percent of callers have been victims of sexual violence, while 19 percent of SOS staff are themselves survivors of sexual violence. Despite this ideal, SOS volunteers do not constitute a representative sample of the population. For example, in 1994, the typical volunteer had a university education, was an employed Serbian woman under the age of 35, was unmarried, and had no children. She was not affiliated with any political party. She had not been the victim of serious violence, had spent less than three years at SOS, was on telephone duty once per week, and was also active in the Autonomous Women's Center against Sexual Violence. At the same time, this typical volunteer was neither Roma[6] nor Muslim, nor was she a woman with only primary school education (or less), disabled, a refugee, from a low socioeconomic background, or over the age of 60. Also, 12 percent of SOS volunteers are lesbian, which is a higher percentage than that among the general population.

The SOS volunteer database was compiled on the basis of interviews with women working at any of the three existing SOS hotlines in Belgrade: the SOS Hotline for Women and Children Victims of Violence, the SOS Hotline and the Center for Girls, and the SOS Hotline against Sexual Violence. Because the majority of women interviewed were volunteers at two or at all three hotlines, it is virtually impossible to distinguish those who worked at the SOS Hotline for Women and Children Victims of Violence from those who worked at the other two. Moreover, volunteers at all three hotlines completed a standard training program conducted by the main SOS Hotline for Women and Children Victims of Violence.

To better understand the reasons behind women's participation in SOS, we asked women who had been active since the organization's inception about their motivation for being involved. We conducted twenty-seven interviews, the majority of which took place in an informal setting, that is, between workshops at the International Feminist and Pacifist Summer Camp. This event had been

---

[5] These years probably were the "golden age" of Belgrade's SOS Hotline; never did they have more volunteers than at this time. Nor is it likely that they will in the future, given existing internal tensions in the organization.

[6] "Roma" is preferable to the term "Gypsies," which is considered pejorative.

organized by Women in Black and was held in Novi Sad in early August 1996. Women who did not attend the summer camp were interviewed at other locations, for example, at the SOS office, the Women's Studies Center, or the Autonomous Women's Center. Those interviewed were all asked the same questions regarding their motivations for joining SOS and the feminist movement. Violence against women figured prominently in all cases. In general, the founding members of SOS tended to hold in common the set of reasons excerpted below, while those who joined later usually accorded greater importance to a single factor. Typical motives were to help women victims of violence, to be among and work with other women, to broaden opportunities and enrich life experiences, to earn money,[7] meet lesbians, or some combination of these. The following excerpts were taken from interview responses and exemplify the most salient reasons behind women's participation in the grassroots efforts undertaken by SOS. To preserve the women's anonymity, names are given only as initials. Many women expressed an interest in helping women victims of violence whether or not they themselves had been victims:

K. is a 46-year-old professor at Belgrade University. She spent six years in SOS and often organized the SOS annual training programs for new volunteers.

I wished to help women gain more self-awareness about their position in society, about the violence they suffered, about social discrimination, etc. While in the United States, I had undergone a similar training program for hotline volunteers. That's why I considered myself a likely person to help establish SOS in Belgrade.

M. is a 32-year-old professor of music. She spent one year at SOS and later emigrated to Australia.

Because a friend of mine had invited me, I, out of curiosity, went to a workshop held by a group of women, where we talked about the violence we had experienced. There I explained how I was raped by a boyfriend; it was the first time I had told this story to anyone. I was strongly supported by the other women and this support was a terrific experience in my life. I realized how important it was to have such a group of women in Belgrade, and I joined in their plan to establish an SOS hotline. I wanted to help other women not to feel isolated, to help them understand that Belgrade was not only a city of violent men, where only men have rights.

L. is a 58-year-old divorced woman. Her daughter, a university student, spent two years at SOS and also volunteered at SOS for Girls.

Thanks to the women from SOS and their strong support, I divorced my husband after spending many years as a victim of violence. The women had organized a training program. I wanted to join them and to prepare myself to help other women victims of violence just as I had been helped. I consider my experience in dealing with violence and a violent partner in day-to-day life to be very important in my work with SOS.

[7] In addition to a lawyer, the position of secretary was also paid.

Other women wanted to broaden their training and experience by working with other women:

R. is a 38-year-old teacher who has volunteered with SOS for Girls for two years.

When I returned from the States, I wanted to join a women's group, but doubted whether one existed in Belgrade. I found a new group trying to establish an SOS for girls and I knew that was what I'd been looking for! I decided to join them.

Z. is a 42-year-old scientist from Belgrade. She spent three years with SOS and is active in the Women's Studies Center and Law Group.

Before the war I was not a feminist at all and did not see any real purpose for these women's gatherings. But when the crises began, I felt a need to be surrounded only by women. I have realized how we all share the same sufferings and how the war was only an extension of men's violence, which has persisted because it is condoned and encouraged. I thought I could be useful to women, and I also strongly needed women— their strength, support, and power, their typical women's atmosphere and free women's space—at a time when all around me men were ruling with verbal aggressiveness, nationalism, machismo.

G. is a 35-year-old social worker. She spent six years with SOS and is a member of almost all of the Belgrade feminist groups. She is most active in Women in Black.

Luck brought me to SOS where I've discovered the craziest women in the whole world. That's why I've stayed.

N. is a 22-year-old psychology student. She graduated with a degree in women's studies, spent two years with SOS, and is claiming her right to be "an independent feminist." She volunteers in various groups and participates actively in organizing feminist events.

I always felt different when I compared myself to others around me. But at SOS I didn't have this feeling; there were many different personalities and individuals, yet it didn't matter. No one was discriminated against. This was possible only at SOS and that's why I have stayed with this particular group of women.

Mi. is a 22-year-old philosophy student. She volunteered for two years with SOS for Girls.

I had just passed important exams at my university, and as I had started school one year earlier than my peers, I considered myself to have plenty of free time. I had to do something else, something different. A friend of mine invited me to the Women's Studies Center, where we found an announcement for SOS training. I didn't think that I'd be able to be a real volunteer, but I wanted to join them, mostly because I wanted to learn something completely new in my life, something different from everything else. I have learned more through SOS than in all my years of formal schooling and now consider this to have been the most important experience in my entire life.

T. is a 21-year-old law student. She graduated with a degree in women's studies from Belgrade University and has spent one year with SOS.

> I first discovered the Women's Studies Center together with my friend. We both liked the courses Women's Human Rights and Theory of Violence. As I was nearing the end of my law studies, I considered volunteering at SOS to be good training, good preparation for my professional career.

Ne. is a 29-year-old trade analyst at a government agency. She holds a degree in economics. She spent one year with SOS for Girls; she no longer believes in feminism.

> I chose my major area of study according to the wishes of my parents, not my own. I got a job thanks to my father's connections; it was a boring, administrative job. My parents had always considered this the most proper type of job for a woman because it offered security and a small salary yet carried little responsibility—it allowed for a settled life. Moreover, my parents were about to find me a husband to lend my life yet more definitive order. SOS helped me discover another life. It helped me see that some women can and do dare to live on their own and that women can have an exciting life.

For some volunteers, SOS provided the opportunity to meet other lesbians:

Zo. is a 23-year-old vendor, occasionally unemployed. She spent one year at SOS for Girls and wants to join an SOS for Lesbians, should it be created.

> I'd heard that a women's group, comprised mostly of lesbians, existed in the city, but I personally didn't believe this. In our society? No, this wasn't possible. But then I found them and started participating in their meetings. At first it seemed that all of them were lesbians; later it seemed none of them were. But then that became less important than our tasks and our way of working, which I liked very much.

Li. is a 23-year-old high school graduate. She spent two years with SOS, is also a member of Arkadia, and works at FROG, a women's secondhand shop. She too wants to join SOS for Lesbians if it is ever created.

> According to our nature, we lesbians are not controlled by any men. This distinguishing freedom that we lesbians have is the most important quality we can possess in helping other women to free themselves from men's violence, the cruelest kind of control men exercise over women.

Some women cited a variety of the reasons just listed. S. is a 30-year-old first-generation graduate of the Women's Studies Program in Belgrade. She spent two years at SOS and currently lives in London, where she works as a social worker. She visits Yugoslavia each summer.

> I became a member of a feminist group in 1987 when there was nothing—only plans, projects, ideas. At that time we had organized several public roundtable discussions about violence against women, and we noticed that we needed an SOS hotline. Within this group a subgroup of women interested in establishing SOS formed. As the subgroup consisted mostly of lesbians, I decided to join them. Also, I strongly wanted some

results from our public speeches, something to happen, some real help for women who suffered violence.

The women in SOS represent ordinary women from Belgrade who found themselves living in radically changed times. SOS offered them an opportunity to take part in unusual projects and to realize unexpected achievements. Through their SOS experience, these women have learned that ordinary people can solve complex problems by working together.

SOS Callers: Women Victims of Violence

To begin gathering information about the women who call the SOS Hotline, we asked volunteers to fill out a standard questionnaire, to the extent that this was possible, during their phone conversations with SOS clients. Because volunteers had primary responsibility to help the women they spoke with, it was neither appropriate nor feasible to conduct more systematic research. Sometimes, the women who called cried or remained silent; some were in life-threatening situations, while others had only a short time to ask for help before the perpetrator returned. Questions about the perpetrators of violence were asked less frequently by volunteers due to the SOS policy of encouraging women to focus on their own lives and to find solutions to their problems rather than talk about the aspirations, attitudes, behavior, and tendencies of their abusers. Hence, there is very little in the way of insight into the motivations and characteristics of the perpetrators. Information is thus limited to questionnaire responses and is incomplete. Data were collected over a combined three-year period, between 1991 and 1993, and again in 1994 and 1995. In the 1991–1993 period, SOS has information on 769 cases; for 1994, 401 cases; and for 1995, 252 cases.

The majority of callers were between the ages of 26 and 45. Many were employed, although employment among battered women declined during the periods we examined. Callers tended to have a high school education. Most had children, many of whom had also witnessed domestic violence. The majority of victims still lived with their violent partners. Women cited the need for a place to live, other economic reasons, and fear as their reasons for staying in the violent relationship. In each of the periods we studied, approximately 25 percent of the women who called cited fear as their primary reason, compared to approximately 75 percent who claimed economic reasons. Most women victims of violence wanted to leave their abusive partners because they felt continually menaced.

DOMESTIC VIOLENCE: CULTURAL ATTITUDES AND LEGAL SHORTCOMINGS

"It is a Serbian custom for a husband to beat his wife." These were the actual words of an officer on duty in the Čukarica (a section of Belgrade) police station the night of March 18, 1994. Spoken by a representative of the law, these remarks were made to a woman who had been brutally beaten by her husband throughout an entire night in front of their 2½-year-old child. The woman did not dare ask the officer for his name.[8]

Within a patriarchal cultural framework, women victims are themselves blamed when they are abused by their partners, especially if they make a public complaint. Women are expected, by tradition, to bear their suffering silently and privately. SOS has encountered this pattern repeatedly. To illustrate, during a training session to establish an SOS hotline in Leskovac, SOS asked how village women deal with violent perpetrators. Leskovac is an industrial town in southern Serbia, surrounded by rural areas that maintain traditional ways of living. All of the women agreed that when a young woman marries, her parents warn her "not to think about a divorce," because a divorce is considered to bring shame upon the family. The bride is not supposed to return to her parents' home, even if she is a victim of violence in her husband's home.[9] "This is no longer your home," are the public words offered by parents as they try to convince their daughters to be "good," obedient wives. But in the husband's home, the first words spoken face-to-face (not publicly) between the husband's mother and the bride are usually warnings to the bride not to let her husband beat her. "When (if) he hits you, at the first moment, fight back!" a mother-in-law customarily advises. "If you do not fight back, he will beat you your whole life, and nobody will be able to help you, nothing will stop him. So, however scared you might be, take anything, a pan with hot water, a chair, a kitchen knife, whatever, and hit him as hard as you can if he attacks you! And then scream, run, and we shall help you. We want our grandchildren to be brought up in a peaceful atmosphere."[10]

Laws Pertaining to Physical Violence:
Implications for Cases of Domestic Violence

Long-held cultural assumptions are clearly not on the side of women victims of violence, neither within the realm of private relations nor in public institutions. From the very beginning of SOS's work, it was clear that the majority of women calling SOS were in urgent need of legal advice. Their questions were many and diverse, such as: How can I get a divorce? Who will get the apartment after the divorce? Who will get custody of the children? How does one write a document addressed to a court, public prosecutor's office, or center for social work? What are the duties and services of social work centers? SOS volunteers were unable to fully answer such questions; hence, it was decided to enlist the services of women lawyers. Initially, attorneys provided both legal counseling and representation in court trials. However, for financial and other reasons, they stopped

---

[8] This is a typical entry in the SOS Hotline case records.

[9] Such "traditional" practices are widespread throughout Southeastern Europe. See, for example, Kligman 1988, chapters one and two.

[10] This advice is typical of that given by women—in their mid-40s or older—who are themselves mothers-in-law.

representing SOS clients in court and restricted their services to counseling.[11] Individual counseling sessions are offered in the late afternoon once or twice per week at the Autonomous Women's Center, where spatial arrangements are best suited to this purpose. To be sure, the need for legal aid services far exceeds available resources.

Regarding the prosecution of domestic violence claims, specific legislation on domestic violence is lacking in Serbia, a situation that is, in part, perpetuated by patriarchal prejudices such as those noted earlier. Serbia's Criminal Code contains only a few paragraphs about physical violence, and these are of a very general nature. Most of these legal provisions pertain to violence that takes place in public places such as in street or restaurant fights. Although none specifically addresses domestic violence, the provisions summarized below may be used by lawyers in the prosecution of domestic violence cases. At least in theory, the generality of these provisions enables skilled lawyers to shape a new field of legal practice.

A legal distinction is made between serious and minor injuries. A *serious physical injury* occurs when an individual seriously injures another person and/ or seriously damages the other's health. Legally, serious physical injury includes injuries involving broken bones, loss of a body part, permanent weakening of an important part of the body or of an organ, and injuries that cause permanent deformity or permanent loss of the ability to work. Punishment consists of a prison term of a minimum of six months, and the offense is prosecuted by the public attorney's office. (According to Serbian law, the legal minimum sentence is thirty days. Also, if a maximum sentence is not specified, then it is understood to be twenty years.)

Minor physical injury, on the other hand, is defined as a criminal offense when an individual causes minor injury to another person. Exactly what is included under the term "minor physical injury" is not circumscribed by law; in practice minor physical injuries are those that do not constitute serious physical injuries. Punishment is a maximum prison term of three years. Depending on the means used for inflicting injury, the offense is prosecuted privately or by the public attorney's office in the event that the perpetrator used dangerous weapons, arms, or tools.

Coercion is a criminal offense when an individual uses the power of a serious threat to force another person to do or not do something or to suffer. The punishment for coercion is a fine or a maximum prison term of three years. The offense is prosecuted privately or by the public attorney's office if threats include murder or serious physical injury.

Illegal deprivation of freedom is a criminal offense when an individual illegally takes another person, keeps him or her locked up, or deprives him or her of the

---

[11] Lawyers requested payment in foreign currency and at sums substantially greater than in other sectors. They received these amounts because of SOS's need for their services and the limited number of lawyers prepared to provide them.

freedom of movement. The maximum punishment is a one-year prison term. If a victim loses his or her life, then the prison term is a maximum of fifteen years. The act is prosecuted by the public attorney's office.

Threat to security is a criminal offense when an individual threatens another person's life or bodily integrity or threatens harm to a close relative or friend. Punishment may be a fine or a prison term of up to six months. The act is prosecuted privately unless many persons were threatened, if the public order was disturbed, or if it caused serious (physical or psychological) consequences of various kinds. In such cases, the offense is prosecuted by the public attorney's office.

In all cases involving physical violence for which there is to be a court decision, evidence must be produced in the form of a certificate, issued from a medical institution, stating the nature and number of injuries. SOS has observed that medical practitioners readily sign such papers in cases of street fights or other violent public acts, but that members of the medical profession are reluctant to issue such papers to victims of domestic violence, despite the fact that they are obligated by law to detail bodily injuries. According to law, such a certificate must be prepared whether or not the victim makes a complaint or requests or states a need for medical certification. Some practitioners rationalize their behavior by claiming, "I don't want to mix in private business," or, "I did not see the other side; maybe the other party in this fight is the more seriously injured. By issuing my evidence to only one party, I'll provide her with an unjust advantage." In view of the problems women have obtaining medical certification of their injuries, SOS instructs the women who call to be adamant when asking for medical certification. They are informed that medical institutions are legally obliged to issue certificates to them, regardless of the private reluctance exhibited by some doctors. Moreover, SOS volunteers underscore that in a court proceeding, this medical certification constitutes the only evidence that violence against the woman did, in fact, occur.

Types of Domestic Violence

Domestic violence is inflicted in varying forms. We have categorized the cases into what we consider to be economic, psychological, physical, and sexual abuse. Although these are often present together and are difficult to distinguish, they nevertheless appear to us to constitute distinct kinds of abuse. Economic abuse is assumed to be a basic feature of all cases of domestic violence. Economic abuse covers all means by which women's property, income, and work are subjected to abuse. SOS has found that violent partners generally own all legal rights to familial assets; houses, apartments, and cars, for example, are always in the name of the man. Only rarely are women in a position of authority where they can decide what to do with their income, let alone that of their spouse. Some women receive a limited daily sum from their husbands that is rarely adequate for basic living expenses. As a result, women often take on extra work, though they may do so without the knowledge of their abusive partner. In other instances, a partner may know of, and grant permission for, his wife's efforts to secure additional income, but she is forced to turn all of her earnings over to him. The following are typical examples drawn from the SOS files.

Case File 1. The husband's family is from Bosnia. Some of his cousins escaped from the battlefield and have come to live with them. They are all men. None of them work and none of them want to work. They all wait for her to prepare food, wash and iron their clothes, and clean the house. (There is no washing machine or running water in the house.) No one gives her money. She has to work cleaning neighbors' houses to earn some money. Her family does not know because, if they did, they would take her money away from her or even beat her because of the shame her working brings upon them. *What will people say, seeing that a woman works outside the home? Will they think that the men are unable to provide enough money?* She also tends her small vegetable garden, which these angry men destroy from time to time. They do not work in the garden themselves—that is not men's work.

Case File 2. When this woman's husband died, she continued to live in his apartment. A new man came into her life. They married. The new husband "convinced" her (more or less without her real permission) to sell her apartment and to build a new, bigger house with the money. He invited all of his family to come to this new house. Together, they threw her out and appropriated her pension. She now sleeps in the fields or on the streets. She once came, hungry and dirty, to the Women's Center. Now she is in a shelter, and court proceedings are under way. This woman is in her seventies.

Case File 3. A woman of 40, married thirteen years to an alcoholic husband, is in hiding from him. He had just returned from jail, where he was serving a six-month sentence for acts of public violence, when he beat her and threw her out of the apartment. She called SOS from her aunt's house; she dared not return home because she feared further abuse. She had gone to the Center for Social Work, but it was not open on Saturdays. She had sustained a terrible head injury. She said, "My husband beats me like a blind man, without watching me at all, as if I were a sack." Now she is in hiding because he is trying to find her.

Case File 4. A young woman of 22, after a conflict with her boyfriend, was left alone on the street after midnight; the buses had stopped running. She decided to hitchhike; a middle-aged man stopped and offered her a ride. He used a knife to force her from the car into his apartment, where he raped her. At about 4:00 A.M., she escaped and reported the rape to the police. But she did not know the man's name nor was she sure of his correct address. She remembered the block of buildings where he lived, but not the exact entrance. In the police station the officers did not believe her, nor did they direct her to have a gynecological examination. Even worse, they accused her of drug dealing. She found that no one believed her at all. From SOS, she acquired an attorney who went with her to the police station and clarified the situation. She was not accused of any crime, but neither was the rapist apprehended in any way.

Case File 5. A woman of 29 has been married two years and has a 15-month-old baby. Her husband beats her. Both partners are highly educated. She is the picture of the perfect, successful businesswoman; she is well educated, speaks foreign languages, and is a good mother. Her husband also seems perfect; he is very neat, well dressed, and earns a good income. She says that she cannot understand what happens to him from time to time. He will be decent for two or three months and then, for no apparent reason, he becomes mad and starts to beat her. Afterward he is nice and peaceful, like a cat, and apologizes a thousand times for what happened, promising "never again." She does not have the strength to obtain a divorce. She is satisfied with her job, with her child, and wishes only that "he could behave more normally." She has promised that she will rethink her whole situation. She hates herself because she is not more energetic and ready to break from this. It is difficult for her to admit to herself that her marriage has not been a success; she mostly blames herself for this failure.

Case File 6. A man killed his former wife intentionally; he stabbed her in her breasts and in the back. Although divorced, they continued to live in the same building complex. The murder resulted from a quarrel. When he asked her to whom she was bringing a cup of coffee, she responded sharply, "Fuck you, it's my business whom I bring coffee to." He maintains that everything soured when she found a job. He assumed she only wanted a job so she could have affairs with other men. After their divorce, he asked her to cook for him, to iron, and to wash his clothes. He considered it his right to control her and her life. He was sentenced to a prison term of ten years.

Case File 7. A woman had been living with her domestic partner and her mother. He had been drinking for a few years. On returning from the war, he went completely mad, showing no concern for anyone. He was in illegal possession of a gun and large knife and used both to create chaos in the home. He typically threatened to kill his partner and his partner's mother, together: "You won't stay alive until tomorrow. First I'll kill your mother in front of your eyes, and then you." His partner was consumed by fear and in a complete panic. She had no trust in the police: "They come when everything is over, and it will be too late if he decides to finish us off." One night, he lunged at her mother with a knife. She (his partner) killed him with his gun. SOS presented witnesses in court, and her account of events was accepted. She will be released; her immediate problem is whether his war friends will eventually seek revenge.

SOS Research on Domestic Violence

Domestic violence occurs in diverse forms and among all social strata. An SOS five-year research project serves as the basis for the following summary of domestic violence.[12] It must be emphasized that this summary reflects the experience of SOS Hotline Belgrade and cannot be generalized with respect to all of Serbia. Moreover, SOS files are based on women's own reports, as written by volunteers. The sample included 250 questionnaires from 1991, 317 from 1992, 202 from 1993 (or 769 for the period 1991–1993), 401 from 1994, and 252 from 1995 (n = 1,422). The actual number of calls was much greater than the number represented here, meaning that the survey was not systematically conducted. This is a by-product of the current imperfection in carrying out SOS work and the reluctance of volunteers to complete questionnaires. The general results reveal that, in most instances, the women victims called the SOS Hotline themselves, and the perpetrators of violence were husbands or ex-husbands, although there was an increasing presence of sons among the perpetrators of violence. (This latter is apparently related to the return of young men from the battlefields suffering from war traumas.) Furthermore, psychological and physical violence appear to be the most frequent forms of violence. No case exists involving only one kind of violence; rather, all cases exhibit some combination of physical with sexual violence, sexual violence with murder threats, and psychological violence with all forms of violence. Data suggest that the incidence of sexual violence has not decreased, although there may be a distortion in the data due to the creation of other women's groups, such as the Autonomous Women's Center against Sexual Violence (formed at the end of 1993) and the SOS Hotline and Center for Girls (formed in the spring of 1994), that deal with sexual violence. Hence, many cases of sexual violence may never appear at SOS, implying that the actual number of cases may have increased. Moreover, the number of reported cases is generally assumed to be lower than the actual incidence of abuse.

The majority of victims have suffered violence on a daily basis over a period of years. Violence appears when the couple begins a life together, and particularly violent incidents occur when men begin to use alcohol or have affairs with other women. The majority of women felt humiliated and angered by the violence inflicted against them, but there are also cases in which women seem more angry than humiliated. Women considered the violence to have been irrational from the first manifestation: The most frequent cause cited for an act of violence was "nothing" (observed in almost one-half of all cases). In a steady one-third of all cases during all years observed, alcohol was the direct cause of violence.

In conceptualizing a way out of the violence, many women claimed to have contemplated the initiation of legal proceedings such as divorce. However, most of them did not pursue legal recourse because of the general bias against women who do so. Women typically lacked "connections" at the courts or with other institutions and authorities, meaning that they generally had no real chance of exercising their legally existing rights. In this respect, women are outsiders devoid

---

[12] The following persons took part in the research: during the three-year period 1991–1993, Zorica Mršević and Tanja Đurđev; during 1994 and 1995, a group of students from the Women's Studies Center led by Zorica Mršević: Nataša Milenković, Sunčica Vučaj, Milica Minić, Biljana Maletin, Marija Lukić, and Ljiljana Đorđević.

of social power as well as sociolegal protection. More than two-thirds of the women who called SOS during the first three years (1991–1993) had prior official contact with representatives of institutions that are supposed to deal with violence and protect citizens from it: the police, social services, physicians (including general practitioners, specialists, and psychiatrists), and lawyers. During 1994, a significant decrease was observed in women's utilization of these official institutions and services: Requests for help made to the police dropped by one-half; requests for help to social work services, medical institutions, and attorneys dropped by two-thirds. In 1995, however, there was a slight increase in the number of requests for help made to these same institutions. Even so, the total was less than it had been during the first three years. Indeed, the reluctance and prejudice with which institutional representatives and authorities respond to women victims of domestic violence are perhaps best highlighted by the fact that significant numbers of abused women fail to turn to them for help. Women victims of domestic violence found that their cases were not only ignored, but also mishandled. In consequence, women have learned that substantive help from official quarters was not likely to be forthcoming.

Furthermore, cultural traditions—discussed earlier—have contributed to a failure on the part of individuals (e.g., family and relatives) to show support for the plight of women victims (although women did recognize that their private social networks tended to be more helpful than public institutions).[13] In view of both public and private reluctance to assist battered women, many of them never sought help from any source, nor did they initiate legal proceedings against the perpetrators of these offenses. Women explained their inaction as being a result of a combination of factors: feelings of shame, fear, and guilt; personal experiences with the ineffectiveness of official institutions; and their own lack of basic knowledge concerning legal provisions.

SOS's data consistently indicate that victims of violence are, in essence, forced to continue living with the perpetrator of violence against them. The most frequently cited reasons for remaining with a violent partner were the need for a place to live, other economic reasons, and fear of the perpetrator. These remained constant over the five-year period of research. Those women who did leave their violent partners were, in the end, consistently motivated to leave because of their constant sense of danger.

Domestic Violence and Feminist Politics:
Reproducing Ingrained "Ways of Seeing" and Behaving

As the data gathered by SOS demonstrate, there is a stable pattern to the kinds of domestic violence reported; variations across the years studied have been minimal. Partially as a consequence of the war (and, in particular, the rape camps) and partially as a consequence of international attention, domestic violence has

---

[13] Women nonetheless expressed overall dissatisfaction with the treatment they received from those to whom they appealed. This finding held throughout the course of the five-year study.

become a focus of interest. Among Belgrade feminists, it is widely held that domestic violence—specifically violence by men against women—has increased dramatically since the war began. However, no SOS data support such a claim with any degree of reliability. And before the war, no such information was collected. (SOS, of course, did not exist.) Nevertheless, feminists invoke the argument of increased violence because of its rhetorical force, its effectiveness in mobilizing support, and its utility for securing grants.[14]

Some feminists further assert that 80–90 percent of the victims of domestic violence suffer forms of sexual violence. Yet again, there is little evidence to support this assertion either. According to data collected for this study, approximately 10 percent of victims have been sexually abused. Sexual violence is a theme that attracts quick response from international funding sources. Indeed, as a result of such funding, centers have been established in Belgrade to specifically help sexually abused women, for example, the Autonomous Center against Sexual Violence and the SOS Hotline and Center for Girls (One and Two). In the interest of continuing financial support for services to assist victims of violence, feminists, whether intentionally or not, promote a myth of widespread sexual abuse.

Questions of effective responses to the traumas of sexual violence have divided feminists in a number of ways. In addition to disagreements about the actual incidence of sexual violence, there are also tensions around the provision of professional assistance. Some feminists believe it is sufficient to make available a sympathetic, supportive listener with no special training. They are suspicious of women with official degrees and question their ability to remain sensitive to feminist approaches to women's problems. Others hold the view that violations as serious as sexual abuse require professional therapy. They argue that university-trained women can be just as committed to feminist approaches and that there is no contradiction between higher learning and feminist practice.

The relationship between professionalization and feminist commitment has also been problematic in the case of legal assistance for victims of abuse. On the one hand, female lawyers have been willing to provide advice and to represent victims in court; on the other hand, they demand payment for certain of their services in contrast to most other SOS workers who volunteer their time and effort. The fees charged by some female lawyers (requested in foreign currency and at rates substantially higher than most professional salaries) have caused considerable tension and even anger among SOS workers. At the same time, payment for services is a bone of contention in the case of therapy as well. Those without professional training in psychology or medicine are nevertheless able to earn significant sums of money as self-proclaimed experts for survivors of sexual abuse.

All of us in SOS were born and raised under socialism. We are the children of socialism and, however inadvertently, have reproduced in the feminist movement familiar socialist political roles and responses. For example, to deal with "differ-

---

[14] It is beyond the scope of this discussion to treat any of these issues in depth.

ence," we have formulated categories of exclusion. We too have concepts delineat-
ing commitment to the feminist vision, such as the "veteran feminist" (similar
to the "communist veteran") and the "young feminist crusader" (like the "young
communist crusader"). The "veterans" are those few women who participated in
the original feminist group, Women and Society, and have remained active in
the feminist movement. For them, feminism is their livelihood; that is, the
movement serves as both work and a source of social status. The "young feminist
crusaders," on the other hand, are newcomers who, like the "young communist
crusaders" before them, are often poorly educated, lack expertise, and exhibit
zealous ideological commitment to and faith in their leaders. Among veterans
and newcomers alike, there are also the crusader types who, in their devotion
to feminist politics, promote feminism as they themselves understand it and seek
to banish anyone who does not share their view of "real" feminism. This said,
the newcomers tend to mimic the positions of the veterans so that their predecessors will believe them worthy of the movement's heritage or, more bluntly put,
the privileges associated with it. For example, and reiterating a certain form of
communist ideological rhetoric, "sinners" or "enemies" are those women who do
not put loyalty before personal integrity, who disagree rather than quietly accept
"the party line," or who pose questions that are not always welcome.

"Enemies" who hold critical views—for example, about the lack of transparency
pertaining to financial matters or the lack of democratic decision-making procedures—are considered menaces to the survival of "veterans" and "young crusaders"
who have no other place to go. One method of dealing with such "enemies" is
akin to the former communists' practice of "party cleansing." A public campaign
is mounted against those individuals whose behavior is allegedly unacceptable
for "true" feminists. Clearly, we in the feminist movement must ourselves learn
to address our differences in more democratic ways; despite our "emancipatory"
intentions, we remain captive to our upbringing.

Conclusion: SOS, Domestic Violence, and Public Awareness

Whatever the shortcomings of feminist politics, they have contributed importantly to the pursuit of democratic ideals and practices. As can be seen in this
chapter, the "herstory" of SOS—that is, the impetus behind its creation and the
nature of its daily operations—is not only that of the Hotline, but also of a
feminist social movement. Before SOS became engaged in the public discussion
about violence against women, public opinion on this topic was characterized
mainly by prejudice and misinformation. To review, women were variously blamed
for provoking violence and for not leaving their violent partners (thereby suggesting that they "must enjoy violence"). Existing legal provisions were claimed to
be adequate. Both victims and abusers were thought to be equally responsible
for violence, and men were considered to be victims of domestic violence to the
same extent as women. Furthermore, domestic violence was thought to be a
private matter that does not warrant outside intervention. When made public,

domestic violence was said to bring shame upon the family; hence, it should remain hidden from relatives, friends, and neighbors. Moreover, women should submit to a certain degree of violence in the interest of keeping the family together and providing their children with a father. It was believed that men are entitled to hold a superior position in the family and that they are to be obeyed and properly respected. The incidence of domestic violence was purported to be rare; that of sexual violence, even more so. Incest is allegedly nonexistent in Serbian culture (and any claims to the contrary are attributed to the false allegations of Western feminists). According to popular belief, domestic violence did not compare in "enormity" to the violence committed by criminal intruders who might enter an apartment by force and employ violence against family members in order to find their valuables.

Yet, as a result of SOS's daily work and publicity efforts, public opinion on the matter of domestic violence has gradually begun to change. Today, no one denies that domestic violence exists or that it is a legitimate matter of public concern. At the same time, it must be recognized that the war itself provided a context in which it was perhaps easier to speak of the problem. During these years, many people shared a need for a kind of solidarity against violence and suffering. The war raised awareness about all kinds of violence and made people more sensitive to women's daily burdens.

But as the war wore on and the activities of daily life during wartime became institutionalized, so SOS took on an existence of its own. The internal tensions between professionals and nonprofessionals, as well as the lack of transparency regarding financial as well as decision-making processes, intensified. The formal end of the war did not affect the work habits or attitudes of SOS members. It did make it possible for women to recognize their own state of "burn out" that had resulted from years of constant work without respite, as well as years of increasing internal dissatisfaction without resolution.

The multifaceted "burn-out syndrome" began to surface at the 1995 and 1996 training sessions that the afore-mentioned veterans and crusaders organized for new volunteers. In the end, few of the new volunteers stayed involved, and many "old" SOS volunteers left because of the tension-fraught dynamics of interaction. The negative consequence of these developments was that for the first time since its establishment in 1990, the SOS Hotline did not function during the summer of 1997. Volunteers no longer wanted to invest their time, energy, and goodwill during the summer holiday period. On the positive side, those women who left SOS formed various new groups, so that, in one respect, independent feminist activities have multiplied. As was revealed at the August 1996 conference "Women for Peace," attended by volunteers and feminist activists from Croatia, Macedonia, Bosnia, Kosovo, and Serbia, the problems that have beset SOS Belgrade are not specific to it, but rather, reflect similar issues with which feminist groups throughout the former Yugoslavia have been confronted. Whether these new, smaller groups will develop into broad-based feminist movements with different particular but overall feminist interests remains to be seen. In part, this is the challenge posed to all who seek more democratic ways of living throughout the former

Yugoslavia. As to the first seven years of Belgrade's SOS Hotline, whatever its shortcomings, this is the first time in Balkan history that women have been able to formulate their own "herstory"—to promote it, write about it, and assess its living legacy.

BIBLIOGRAPHY

Kligman, Gail
    1988   The Wedding of the Dead: Ritual, Poetics, and Popular Culture in Transylvania. Berkeley: University of California Press.
Mršević, Zorica
    1994   Ženska prava su ljudska prava [Women's Rights Are Human Rights]. Belgrade: Autonomous Women's Center against Sexual Violence and the Center for Women's Studies and Communication.
Mršević, Zorica and Donna Hughes
    1997   "Violence against Women in Belgrade, Serbia: SOS Hotline 1990–1993." *Violence Against Women*, April, 101–128.

CHAPTER 14

Media Representations of Men and Women in Times of War and Crisis: The Case of Serbia

JASMINA LUKIĆ

NUMEROUS EXPLANATIONS CONTINUE to be offered for the disintegration of Yugoslavia and the subsequent crises and ferocious war that followed. Although the flood of books on the subject differ significantly on many points, most comprehensive analyses agree upon one thing: The mass media were enormously important in creating and sustaining the atmosphere of intolerance and hatred that favored war and violence.[1] What has been noted less often is the prominent role of gendered images in shaping this new reality, which was largely constructed by the state-controlled media and contested by the small, independent media. The aim of this chapter is to explore some of the most important images of women and men that appeared in the former Yugoslav media during the early 1990s and to demonstrate the various ways in which newspapers and magazines used these images to advance different political agendas.

It has been suggested that the case of Yugoslavia added a new chapter to the history of modern mass media. Not only was the war closely followed by domestic and foreign media, it was also, in many ways, strongly influenced by newspapers and television. In *Forging War* (a telling title), Mark Thompson (1994) argues that the mass media, which people mistakenly accepted as trustworthy, twisted images of unfolding events and thus acted as an instrument of war. Furthermore, the largest media—state television and news dailies—became strongholds of the region's new regimes. For instance, as many observers have noted, state-controlled television proved to be Slobodan Milošević's most effective instrument of power.[2] Fulfilling what might seem to be paradoxical roles, the media fomented the chaos of war, while at the same time presenting a facade of normality, buttressed by—and legitimating—a strong, centralized regime. Raboy and Deganais elaborate on this paradox in general:

---

[1] This problem has been investigated by authors gathered around the Belgrade Circle of Intellectuals, the Center for Antiwar Action, and *Republika*, a journal supporting civic initiatives "against fear, hatred, and violence." Several volumes were subsequently published on these topics, including *Intellectuals and War, The Serbian Side of the War,* and *Toward the Language of Peace.*

[2] On the role of media in Serbia in 1990s, see Lalić 1995; Milivojević 1995; Nenadović 1995; and Marković 1996a, b, c.

As all social institutions, media thrive on stability, and are threatened by change. But the contradictions inherent to the relationship between their specifically ascribed function as agents of social discourse and their economic status as purveyors of commodified knowledge/information distinguish media from other social institutions: in a certain sense, media thrive on *crisis*, and are threatened by *normalcy*. The tendency is, therefore, for media to seek out crisis where it does not exist, and to obscure the actual forces of change that threaten media privilege along with entrenched social privilege in general. (1994:1–4)

These tendencies were only stronger in the state-controlled media.

The former Yugoslavia in the early 1990s provides an excellent illustration. In Serbia, both state TV and the large daily papers were controlled by the regime and were strongly dependent on it for financial support.[3] These media organs blamed any and all imaginable external, foreign factors to explain the crisis. For example, the media created an incident around the sanctions against Serbia, thus using them to explain literally everything that was wrong. On the other hand, the situation inside the country was made to seem safe, familiar, and stable— despite daily occurrences to the contrary. Coverage of events inside Serbia, particularly of anything unfavorable to the Milošević government, was downplayed to such an extent that it created a kind of virtual reality that had little to do with the actual situation in the country.[4]

Keeping in mind these different roles—media as provocateur and as custodian of normality—I have two motives for examining the ways in which women (and sometimes men) were represented in the media. First, by analyzing the presentation of crisis and war by state-controlled newspapers and magazines in Serbia, I hope to show how the regime's version of events was made persuasive, familiar, and palatable to a wide readership by appealing to popular, although implicit, highly conventional and historically rooted images of women and men. Often derived from patriarchal epic literature, these images have been repeatedly reinforced by their frequent association with more recent events. As Joan Scott (1988) and others have argued, gendered images are often and systematically invoked by those in power to "naturalize" political arrangements, to make them seem normal, justified, and even inevitable. In short, events are politicized by linking them, in locally recognizable ways, to gender images assumed to be natural and normal. I also set this process in a comparative context by looking

[3] With respect to regime control of state TV, an obligatory tax on subscriptions is included on monthly electricity bills. It should be noted nonetheless that privately owned TV stations, such as BK TV, owned by Braća Karić [the Karić brothers], may also support the regime.

[4] By the time this article was written, in January 1997, this practice had reached staggering proportions. Protests against the regime, provoked by the annulment of the local election results in November 1996, have been virtually ignored by both state TV and *Politika*, the government-controlled daily—despite the fact that people had been gathering in the streets for two months, with protesters occasionally numbering in the hundreds of thousands. As a result, many people refused to watch the main TV news and instead made public noise during the broadcast to show their indignation and revolt.

at several small, independent publications that also relied on gender images, but tried to undermine the stories and tropes in the mainstream press, thus providing different definitions of crisis.[5]

Second, if the intellectuals who produced the state-run media in former Yugoslavia must be held in part responsible for creating an atmosphere of intolerance, peril, ethnic paranoia, and hatred, then it is also important to document the efforts of those who tried to oppose these destructive forces. To this end, I will concentrate on one issue in particular. Since the beginning of the Yugoslav crisis, small groups of organized feminists have had an outstanding role in various kinds of civic resistance to the dominant forms of militaristic and nationalistic ideologies. I hope to show what they tried to achieve, but also the ways in which the mainstream and independent media reported on their activities. Significantly, state media coverage of feminists critical of nationalism differed in important ways from coverage, by the same media, of women's groups that supported the regime.

Thus, in this chapter I compare the mainstream media's framing of particular events with the way independent newspapers characterized men and women in the same events. Where possible, I juxtapose this to publications by various women's organizations during the same period. The first section describes the newspapers and magazines chosen for analysis. To provide a context for the rest of the discussion, I present a general overview of what kinds of women were noticed and deemed worthy of attention by state-controlled media. It turns out that although feminist political action existed, it was either ignored or severely marginalized. The image of the "Serbian mother" and related symbols of heroic militarism, on the other hand, were used repeatedly to divert attention away from, and blunt the effects of, a variety of protests against the war. Independent newspapers repeatedly tried to unmask these regime-inspired stories and to construct different ways of understanding the protest events. In showing how this kind of framing and counterframing worked, I consider the coverage, by newspapers with different political profiles, of the following events: (1) a feminist meeting and a pro-regime women's meeting in 1990, (2) the "Parents' Movement" against military recruitment in 1991, and (3) the influx of refugees into Serbia in 1991 and again in 1995.

CHOICE OF TEXTS

For this analysis, I have chosen publications with solid professional reputations. As such, they are generally assumed to be more "gender neutral" than popular, sensationalist publications. However, as will be clear throughout this chapter,

---

[5] Note that, in contrast to most "gender analysis of the media" (e.g., Wood 1994), I examine images of women only as a point of departure. I am interested, rather, in the way that such images made implicit claims about the meanings of events. For a similar approach, see Gal 1994.

the phenomena I highlight are very much evident in the professional media. I have included some papers that are clearly state-controlled and several others that are financially independent and vary in their shades of opinion.

Two daily newspapers, *Politika* and *Borba*, constitute my main focus: Each holds a different position in the newspaper market. The first, *Politika*, was founded in 1904[6] and has long been considered the national daily paper; it continues to enjoy the widest circulation, and its workforce is highly professional. Throughout the 1990s, *Politika* was a stronghold of the regime, presenting information in the way most favorable to the regime's policy (for a detailed analysis, see Nenadović 1995:i–xiv).

The second daily paper, *Borba* [Struggle], has a notably different history. Founded after World War II as "the organ of the Communist Party of Yugoslavia," it served for decades as the mouthpiece for official policy. With the political changes and collapse of the Communist Party in the late 1980s, however, *Borba* started to develop as an independent political paper. After gaining substantial influence, the paper was taken over by government officials in 1994, on the pretext of an irregularity in ownership rights. This action provoked loud protests by liberal segments of the population, including statements in other independent media as well as demonstrations in front of the *Borba* building. The unusual result was the creation of two essentially new papers. The regime continued to publish *Borba* under the same name and logo, but the paper had a completely new editorial board, editorial policy, and a new team of journalists; this new incarnation has very poor circulation and practically no influence. Meanwhile, *Borba*'s former editorial board founded another paper, *Naša Borba* [Our Struggle], which maintained the original paper's readership and continues to be influential, especially among the liberal intelligentsia. I will examine *Naša Borba* together with the original *Borba*, since both represent liberal, independent media; the new (regime-controlled) *Borba*, published since December 1994, will not be considered. I will briefly consider two other papers with a similarly wide circulation and official orientation: *Politika ekspres* (a popular daily paper by the same publishing house as *Politika*), and *Večernje novosti* [Evening News]. The latter is published by the *Borba* firm, but has a strong nationalist flavor.

Of the weeklies, I have chosen two political magazines for closer observation: NIN [*Nedeljne informativne novine*, or Weekly News Briefing] and *Vreme* [Time]. Zoran M. Marković (1996b:2) suggests that these magazines are

> practically the only two serious, politically-informative weeklies, which have quite different editorial concepts. For NIN it can be generally said that it belongs to the tradition of serious, analytical, politically balanced journalism. *Vreme*, a private journal, started at the beginning of the big transformations in the society; it is characterized by greater freedom, which also means a recognizable creativity, an outstanding authorial approach, and a clear political commitment.

---

[6] It was founded, owned and directed by the influential Ribnikar family until World War II, when the last owner joined the partisans. He remained the director after the war, until his death in 1955.

NIN has been well established for several decades. Although it lasted less than a year after its founding in 1935, it was resurrected in 1951 and became one of the most influential weeklies in the former Yugoslavia. Published by the state-controlled *Politika* company, the late 1980s were tempestuous for this news magazine. When it separated from its parent company in the early 1990s, many observers felt that the newly independent NIN was searching for its own voice and distinctive profile. Initially, the paper focused on nationalist issues, but in time it grew more liberal, and also decidedly critical of the regime. This was particularly obvious after 1993 when, with a new editorial board, NIN began to openly oppose Milošević's policies.

Vreme, on the other hand, began as an independent weekly; in fact, it was the first such news magazine in post-Titoist Yugoslavia. Founded in late 1990 with a clear all-Yugoslav orientation, *Vreme* supported Ante Marković as federal prime minister, and also his proposed reforms, which aimed at keeping the country together on the basis of common economic interests. Later, after Marković resigned and the war began, *Vreme* continued to cover events throughout the region, while it kept an equal distance from nationalisms of all kinds and stead-fastly supported civic and peace initiatives.[7] Highly critical from the beginning of Milošević's policies and ready to speak openly and critically about Serbian participation in the war, *Vreme* was appreciated by the liberal intelligentsia for its coverage of events and its clear and pointed political commentary.

Among the smaller media projects representing independent views and voices were *Republika*, which, in its subtitle, defines itself as the "journal for civic self-liberation, against the flood of fear and violence," and Radio B92. These small, independent media faced continued obstacles, most of which were technical and threatened to limit their potential audience. Radio B92, for instance, could only be heard in the immediate vicinity of Belgrade. Yet although the regime was able to restrict communications and broadcast frequencies, it could not easily manipulate or curtail the efforts of the independent media. Attempts to do so were often met with stiff resistance and popular protest. For instance, it took the government almost two years to take over the TV station Studio B (see Marković 1996c), which in March 1991 had reported on demonstrations against the regime in Belgrade. The influence of these broadcasting stations, as well as papers like *Republika*, often extended far beyond their relatively narrow range of distribution. Moreover, the independent media not only published important information and opinions, but was also often precisely the point around which civic activity, and alternatives to the regime's ideology, were preserved and developed.

Finally, I consider certain publications put out by various feminist groups.[8] Among these publications were several special journal issues as well as feminist

[7] In keeping with current usage throughout the former Yugoslavia, I designate as "civic initiatives" any political organizing or activity that is based on ideas of rights, civil society, and citizenship, as opposed to nationalism or ideological dogmatism.

[8] "Feminism" these days is a highly controversial term, especially in East Central Europe. I characterize these organizations as feminist because they identified themselves in this way. In the

commentaries on the war. For example, SOS Hotline-Belgrade,[9] an organization formed to help women deal with domestic violence, published a collection of documents in 1993 entitled *Žene za žene* [Women for Women]. In this compendium, one finds protests against war and violence, appeals, and statements of different autonomous women's groups, all issued in the period from 1990 to 1993. The Belgrade hotline also published other bulletins (SOS telefon za žene i decu žrtve nasilja 1993a, b). There is also a feminist review issued by the Autonomous Women's Center in Belgrade (*Feminističke sveske* [Feminist Notebooks]; Ženski Centar 1994, 1995) and the magazine *Žene protiv rata* [Women against the War], published by Women in Black, a protest group in Belgrade (Žene u crnom 1993, 1994a, b). The same group also released three issues of an anthology *Women for Peace* and a special issue on *Deserters from the War in Former Yugoslavia*. These publications cannot be covered in great detail, but as with the other independent and mainstream press, I will choose among them to illustrate contrasts in their coverage and commentary on events.

IMAGES OF WOMEN IN THE MEDIA

Before proceeding to an analysis of how particular events were presented in this range of publications, it is important to provide a broader context of how women were generally represented in the regime-controlled media in the early 1990s. What was the background against which readers could place the press reports I later discuss?

In general, women were more absent than present in the mass media of this period. Nevertheless, in looking at the largest circulation, most influential, and also regime-controlled daily papers in our sample—*Politika*, *Politika ekspres*, and *Večernje novosti*—it becomes clear that two kinds of women attracted the most attention. They belonged either to the sphere of politics or to the sphere of entertainment. They were sometimes promoted, and occasionally criticized, but always present.

The politically-oriented group is a fairly heterogeneous but small collection. First among them is Mirjana Marković, wife of President Slobodan Milošević, but also the leader of her own party, a "leftist" association named *Jugoslovenska udružena levica* (JUL) [Association of Yugoslav Leftists]. The abbreviation also means "July," the month that Mirjana Marković considers to be "the most beautiful of all." Marković was often on the front pages of both daily and weekly magazines. She has said that she wants to build an image of herself as a woman who is independent of her husband in public life. To this end, she wrote a column for the magazine *Duga*, a biweekly that covers topics from politics to fashion,

---

following sections, their own definition of themselves and their goals will become clear, as will their relative closeness to several forms of West European and American feminism.

[9] The SOS Hotline-Belgrade was founded on March 8, 1990; similar hotlines were founded in Zagreb and Ljubljana some months earlier. See Mršević, this volume.

in which she discusses everything from her personal feelings and impressions to her political beliefs and plans for her party. Her public position was intentionally controversial, for she was constantly shifting between different social roles and different political opinions. She sometimes even insinuates that she may be a "feminist." Generally, she declared herself to be a leftist, fighting for social equality. In reality, she was one of the strongest supporters of her husband's repressive, nationalist regime. She was a disturbing and ambiguous figure, much reproached by many for her activities and apparent duplicity.

Another such figure was Danica Drašković, wife of Vuk Drašković, the controversial leader of the SPO (*Srpski pokret obnove*, or Movement for Serbian Renewal), the strongly nationalist party that also claimed to seek the democratization of Serbia. Danica Drašković also held a prominent position in the party, supporting its hard-line, monarchist wing. The media used to attend to Biljana Plavšić as well, a prominent figure among Bosnian Serbs who was known for her extremely militant speeches; when she became the president of the Bosnian Serb government, however, she projected a radically different public image. Several other women who hold ministerial positions in the Serbian government were also quoted frequently in the media, including Bratislava Morina (in 1991, the president of the Initiative Council of the Women's Movement of Yugoslavia, and later the commissar for refugees), and Margit Savović, Minister of the Federal Ministry for National Minorities. The frequent presence of these figures in the press, however, is deceptive, for they are far from representative of women as a group. Rather than being active in politics or influential in public life, women's rates of participation in government actually fell in the 1990s, as compared to previous decades.[10]

The other category of women who regularly received media attention in this period were folk singers. They were particularly favored by TV, but were also fully present in the largest, regime-controlled newspapers. Some became national heroines. The music they produced was a mixture of oriental, Greek, Mexican, and national Serbian traditional forms, with a dash of MTV, although it was claimed that they were promoting Serbian "national traditions." The formula for such a young woman to be promoted into a popular starlet included songs about eternal love and eternal suffering, with a bit of patriotism and a lot of sexual allusions. Typically, a young girl in very sexy, revealing clothes would sing about her wish to live for "him" and for "his mother," to serve him, or wait for him and forgive him (what required forgiving was not often specified). Thus, somewhat ironically, open sexuality was harnessed to national values and patriarchal traditions that were otherwise quite repressive of sexuality. This particular

[10] As Kajošević (1995:164) points out, before the 1989 elections, 17 percent of the deputies in the Assembly of Yugoslavia were women. A quota system existed for women's representation in the parliaments of republics and autonomous regions, as well as at the federal level. In the Parliament of the Federal Republic of Yugoslavia elected in February 1993, there were only 4 women out of 138 deputies in the House of Citizens and only 1 out of 40 in the Chamber of Republics. In January 24, 1994, in the Republic of Serbia's Parliament, 14 women were elected out of a total of 250 deputy positions.

form of popular culture already existed before the 1990s, but it became more influential with the development of economic crisis and war (see Dragićević-Šešić 1994). It was promoted primarily by various small, private TV stations, which declared themselves to be "out of politics," caring only about people's entertainment. In fact, by diverting attention away from the deprivations of daily life and the implications of the war, they helped the mainstream media create an alternate picture of cheerful, lively, happy Serbians who cannot be harmed by anyone. It encouraged a common trend in Serbian life of the time: a narrow-minded self-sufficiency apathetic toward public events. Tabloid newspapers ("boulevard papers") also significantly helped promote these values.

If this was the basic coverage of individual women, there were also strategies for reporting on organized women's activities. There were some women's groups who accepted the new national ideology, promoted by the regime in the late 1980s and early 1990s. It is significant that their activities were followed by the big media not so much as activities of women's groups, but as activities of promoters of certain ideas. They often consisted of politicians or women akin to the ruling power structures. They were given a certain amount of space in big media, and their activities were used to imply that women as individuals, and women in groups, supported the official policy of the regime, or some aspect of it, such as the call for higher birthrates or ideas for the "salvation" of the nation. The best known of such women's organizations was *Kolo srpskih sestara* [Circle of Serbian Sisters], which claimed to keep up the national tradition of women's humanitarian work in Serbia, taking its name from a women's organization founded in 1903. They declared themselves to be concerned with *mothers* and children, emphasizing their nonfeminist orientation.

In contrast, there were women who opposed from the beginning both nationalism and the militarism of the official policy. Many of them became engaged in some kind of public activity, both as individuals and as members of groups that tried to promote peace, civic initiatives, or self-identified "feminist" issues (see Licht and Drakulić 1996). Women engaged in these activities were mainly ignored, or sometimes mocked, not only by the mainstream media that supported official policy but also by that part of the opposition press concerned with national interests. Even those independent papers that were liberal, supportive of civic initiatives, and sympathetic to feminism limited their coverage of these women's organizations.

Thus, as one might expect, *Politika* was mainly open to the voices of women who supported the regime, as was NIN, until a change in editor in 1993, when other women's activities also became visible in it. In 1994, NIN even devoted some separate pages to feminist topics. *Borba* largely ignored women altogether; *Vreme*, on the other hand, provided coverage of women of all types. It followed quite closely and critically those women who supported the regime, often using their actions as a clue for interpreting the intentions and hidden strategies of the regime. And it was quite open, at least for a while, to feminist issues, recognizing in them important allies of the civic policies *Vreme* itself promoted. But it should be emphasized here that only *Republika* steadfastly maintained a clear awareness of the alliance between peace and civic initiatives on the one hand and activities of feminist groups on the other, so this small journal took particular care to publish texts on women written by feminists. In the end, feminist perspectives and initiatives were fully presented only in the particular publications I have already listed, in other words, in pamphlets, letters to the editors, and specialized books that never entered the network of big bookstores.

FEMINISM IN THE MEDIA

To explore the contrasting images of self-identified feminist groups, as opposed to other women's organizations, it is revealing to contrast two events and the ways they were covered by different publications. The first was a feminist meeting held in Belgrade in March 1990, under the title I, You, She, For Us. The second was a meeting of the Initiative Council of the Women's Movement of Yugoslavia. Held in February 1991, it consisted mainly of women who had been officials of the Communist Party or other state structures.

I, You, She, For Us 1990 was the third meeting of feminists in what was still Yugoslavia. Some sixty representatives of feminist groups from Belgrade, Zagreb, and Ljubljana gathered to discuss a range of issues. In a concluding statement that summarized their main concerns, the participants called for the following: the formation of domestic violence hotlines, the affirmation of feminist theories in the social sciences, the introduction of Women's Studies in universities, the elimination of violence against women, the recognition of women's writing, or *écriture féminine*, and the rights of lesbians. Most importantly, they called for a new distribution of social power, one that would enable women to participate in political and social affairs more fully. The meeting was among the last all-Yugoslav gatherings, and it was in one sense a "private" one, since it was not open to either the general public or the media.

Politika, the regime's official paper, covered the meeting in a short article that merits attention. *Politika* interpreted the group's attempt at privacy as a hostile act, as suggested by the title, "Zabranjeno za muškarce" [Forbidden for Men]; the article was signed with initials only. Quoting the meeting's concluding document, the article accurately reported that "feminists of Yugoslavia do not accept the politics of nationalistic segregation, of nationalistic manipulation, supported by both official institutionalized policy, and most of the new, euphoric political parties" (G.P. 1990). It reported as well that feminists declared their willingness to strive for alternative power structures, for different values (such as anti-patriarchy, anti-authoritarianism, and nonviolence), and for solidarity not only between women, but with all who are socially marginalized groups. But then the article moved into a different, and characteristically hostile, tone: The journalist noted that despite the general acceptance of domestic violence hotlines, "nobody liked the fact that they were started by feminists." The text ended with a suggestion that feminists should reconsider their own behavior because their "aggressive manner" had already been superceded in their own movement. In reading this article, one is struck by its presumptuousness in instructing activists about how they "should" behave. Also, the accusation of aggressiveness, in the context of reporting on a closed, private meeting, is interesting. It reveals the hostile atmosphere in which feminist groups operated even before the war, when certain ideas and values supported by feminists, such as ethnic, gender, and national tolerance, as well as equality, were supposedly still respected by the public.

This hostile and condescending tone reflected a long-standing tendency of the mainstream media to treat feminists with suspicion and skepticism and to reproach them for being elitist. There had been ample time for this tendency to develop, since by the early 1990s feminist issues were no longer news in Yugoslavia. Indeed, since the 1970s they had been widely discussed in Belgrade, Zagreb, and Ljubljana (see Papić 1989; Jancar 1988). Out of the first feminist group Women and Society (founded in 1979 in Belgrade), several other groups developed in the 1990s. Among them were the SOS Hotline for Women and Children Victims of Violence, the Women's Lobby, and the women's political party Ženska stranka (ŽEST), which advocated a civic, anti-militaristic, and anti-nationalistic program. In October 1991 the Belgrade protest group Women in Black was formed, followed in 1992 by the Autonomous Women's Center against Sexual Violence, and finally the Belgrade Women's Studies Center. By 1996, there were already some fourteen feminist groups in Belgrade alone.[11] Yet despite this progress feminist activities were either not reported or were viewed with a conventional mockery and marginalized. Hardly noted, of course, was the fact that before the war, feminists were primarily concerned with general, theoretical issues; in the 1990s, many of the new groups adopted a more activist approach. Nationalism, war, and violence became the main focus of their interest. Ultimately their declarations, as well as accounts of their efforts to help war victims and to support civic action against violence, were available only in the publications of the feminist groups themselves.

The independent media took a very different tack in responding to feminist activities. For instance, in one of its first issues, *Vreme* published an article entitled "Women in Communism" (Ast 1991d). Although the article was ostensibly about other countries, the implications for Yugoslavia were clear. The message was that while women throughout Eastern Europe had fought for communism's end, they were the ones who bore the burden of the drastic social changes that followed. In a separate, framed interview on the same page, *Vreme* quoted Sonja Licht, a sociologist known for her commitment to civil society: "Pointing out the peril of

[11] It is hard to quantitatively estimate the influence of feminist groups in the early 1990s. Still, some examples might be illustrative. Since it was established, approximately 200 volunteers have worked with SOS Hotline, which had received over 10,000 calls by 1996. The Autonomous Women's Center against Sexual Violence had by that time received some 3,000 calls and visits, while Women in Black had organized six annual meetings attended by approximately 1,000 women. In five years, approximately 200 women enrolled in courses at the Women's Studies Center in Belgrade, and as many as 5,000 copies of feminist publications (see the Bibliography) were distributed to interested people.

nationalism and fascism must be the very essence of the new women's movements. Unfortunately, we are slow in recognizing the peril we are now in: We face the terrible danger of seeing one relatively weakened totalitarianism replaced by another even more horrifying." Relatedly, the article quotes Slavenka Drakulić, a feminist from Croatia who at that time was addressing the problem of democratic change in that region: "If women fail to participate in bringing political decisions, and in defending their rights, I am afraid that democracy in Eastern Europe will be of masculine gender. And, what is worse, it will wear boots" (see also Drakulić 1992). Written at a time when many people still hoped for peace despite the extensive preparations for war that had already been made, the *Vreme* article, as well as the magazine's general editorial policy, articulated a clear consciousness of the importance that women's voices could have in opposing the totalizing processes of nationalism.

Recognizing exactly this potential, in 1990 feminist groups began issuing public statements, many of which not only addressed the situation of women themselves, but also the general situation in the country. Warning against violence and growing militarism, these statements also backed any and all political initiatives for a peaceful resolution of an increasingly fragmented political situation. Ignored by the mainstream media, these statements were later gathered in a collection of documents "Women for Women" (*Žene za žene*). In retrospect, this publication constitutes an alternative chronicle of events associated with Yugoslavia's disintegration.[12] Many of these writings highlighted the link between violence in families and violence in the wider society, thus issuing a kind of warning against the coming brutality of the war. But there were also more direct forms of political action. In December 1990, Belgrade Women's Lobby (BWL) cautioned all citizens, male and female, against voting for either Slobodan Milošević and his Socialist Party of Serbia (SPS) or for Vuk Drašković and his Movement for Serbian Renewal. The former, the BWL warned, would retain a one-party system, while the latter advocated a radical nationalistic policy and the patriarchal ethos that went with it. "Vote for democracy, equality and solidarity with those who are different," they advised (SOS telefon za žene i decu žrtve nasilja 1993a, b).

In telling contrast to the paucity of coverage given to feminist activity was the extensive attention given to a 1991 gathering in which the Initiative Council of the Women's Movement of Yugoslavia, an organization in which former communist cadres took a leading role. The gathering, along with similar ones in smaller cities of Serbia and Bosnia-Herzegovina, was meant to support the Yugoslav National Army, whose name was then being invoked as the savior of the existing country. However, the YNA had already been instrumentalized by Milošević's aim to make a Serbia-centered Yugoslavia. These women demanded

---

[12] It is divided into three parts: "Stop Male Violence" (January 1990–May 1991); "Stop the War" (June 1991–October 1992); and "Stop Raping" (October 1992–October 1993). The first part contains the programs of feminist groups, public declarations concerning actual events in the country, and texts describing women's initiatives to raise general consciousness about the situation of women.

that all the other paramilitary organizations (which is to say, the military forces organized at that time in Slovenia and Croatia by their new governments) be disbanded so that the Yugoslav National Army, as the only "legitimate" army in the country, could keep or maintain control.

Politika devoted an entire page to this meeting, entitling it, "Protest Gatherings of Women in the Whole of Yugoslavia." At the center of the page was a photograph of numerous women sitting in a large auditorium attentively listening to an invisible speaker. The photo's message is obvious to anyone who has seen similar pictures of Communist Party gatherings in which a person in authority issues instructions to obedient cadres. The photograph skillfully blends two different images. On the one hand, the gathering evokes the tradition of organized meetings that characterized Communist Party rule. Such gatherings were used to demonstrate the "will of the people" in supporting centrally made decisions. On the other hand, the fact that these cadres were women makes the image even more compelling. The women emerge not simply as political subjects, but also as mythic *mothers*. As one participant explained in an interview with NIN, "It is not an issue of politics as such . . . but the whole of Yugoslavia, and the lives of our children. So it was only logical that we, women and mothers, should protest against those who prepare death for all the sons of this country" (Grubač 1991:16–17). Patriotism of a particular kind (pro-Milošević in this case) was thus equated with the naturalized fact of parental love.

Vreme's presentation of the same meeting suggests a very different story. Wryly asking how so many women had suddenly decided to go into politics when so few had participated in previous elections, the reporter suggested that the whole event was not so spontaneous as the leaders had claimed. Commenting on the meeting, the prominent feminist Nadežda Ćetković explained that the government, in a strategy taken from earlier regimes, had permitted women from certain companies to quit work early on the condition that they attended the meeting. She reminded readers that appeals for peace, released by alternative women's groups, did not receive any space in the media. In its next issue (February 18), *Vreme* pointedly published several pictures of leading women from the Initiative Council of the Women's Movement for Yugoslavia—all of them in fur coats. In the previously quoted *Vreme* piece (Ast 1991d), Sonja Licht characterized as excessive and manipulative the attention paid by mainstream media to such a militaristic gathering of "women in fur coats." Licht's phrase is both bitter and ironic. By alluding to expensive fur coats, a symbol of privilege, it highlights the economic and political privilege of the former *nomenklatura*, and thus their hypocrisy. Licht too was using the image of women to express her politics, in this case an anti-totalitarian and anti-militaristic critique.

I have used these examples not only to show that women's groups took different positions in the early 1990s, but also to emphasize the point that these groups were differently represented by the mainstream, as opposed to independent, media. By the early 1990s, the themes of (Serbian) motherhood and protection of children had already been used to make nationalist and militarist actions seem familiar, commonsensical, and natural. By contrast, feminist groups spoke of the same events in the language of nonviolence, civil rights, universalism, and anti-dogmatism. (These contrasts will be developed in examples of media reporting presented below.) In addition, it is noteworthy that the competing media organs paid close attention to each other's reporting. For instance, independent papers made ironic or subversive comments about the mainstream media, thus self-consciously drawing attention to the overall political and social context (meta level) I am emphasizing here: Regardless of their conflicting positions, *all* newspapers constructed reality by using images of women.

THE PARENTS' MOVEMENT IN PRINT

Without living people, there is no state . . .

Be brave, make peace . . .

Use words, not bullets . . .

Women, Ethics, Cooperation, Tolerance . . .

These slogans, chanted by women demonstrators in front of the Serbian Parliament on July 17, 1991, came to be identified with the Parents', or the Mothers', Movement—names used interchangeably by the press to refer to a series of protests that lasted for several months in 1991. Reacting to the onset of war, many people—mostly women—asked the authorities to return their children who had served their term but were still in the Army or who were drafted and sent to Slovenia and Croatia, regions where the war was already raging. My interest is not directly with the movement itself, but rather with the ways in which reports about it called on several powerful, long-entrenched images of ideal masculinity and femininity—images that went hand in hand with an emerging war culture and with the intensive repatriarchalization of society (see Čolović 1993). One of these is the brave young male soldier; the other is the heroic, self-sacrificing mother. Both are very old motifs in Balkan folk art, especially in the medieval epic genre, rewoven and continued in more recent popular culture.[13] It is relatively easy to show how the pro-Milošević media used these images to support his policy. Equally interesting, however, were the responses of the independent press and some feminist groups, which advanced their own distinctive and anti-heroic reinterpretations of motherhood. Before presenting the media analysis, I must say a few words about those aspects of the movement, which are not contested by any side.

The movement started as a spontaneous gathering of people who were concerned about the fate of their drafted children. It achieved its first success when, in the wake of several protest meetings held all around the city, a group of parents broke into the building of the Serbian Parliament. In a highly intense

---

[13] For examples of similar motifs in the epic genre, see Pennington 1984 and Subotić 1932. For the usage of these motifs in recent popular culture, see Čolović 1993.

and emotional atmosphere, they asked the deputies to secure the return of their children. The parents remained in and in front of the Parliament building all night and all the next day, when coaches were found to transport some 450 parents to Slovenia. The first stop was in Zagreb, where other parents joined them. After reaching Slovenia, where they were met by military authorities and sent to different camps to see their children, the parents returned to their homes. Still, the social turmoil persisted. Throughout the whole month of July there were different demonstrations, with one dominant slogan, that the war should stop immediately and that all problems should be solved peacefully. Ultimately, however, this pacifist aspect of the movement was destroyed, as mothers were soon divided along national lines. Evidently, the parents were a heterogeneous group and were clearly not uniformly anti-militarist. Thus as the movement expanded, the differences among the parents also grew as well—so much so that after their children returned, many parents gave up their demands for peace, thus proving that their motives were strictly private (Šušak 1996:546). The second and last high point of the movement came in late August and early September of 1991, when women from Sarajevo broke into the Sarajevo Parliament and demanded that their children be brought back home alive. Another convoy of parents, this time from Bosnia, Macedonia, and Croatia, then headed toward Belgrade to make similar demands. But the convoy was stopped outside the city, and through various means the general, nonnationally based solidarity of mothers/parents was eventually replaced by a form of parochial solidarity that operated within the newly created national borders (see Ugrešić 1996 for a moving account).

The twisted manner by which *Politika*, the regime-controlled daily, covered these events deserves close scrutiny. First, this paper construed the parents' protest to favor official policy. Given the parents' repeated demand for peace, this was no easy task. One tactic was to relegate detailed reports of the parents' demonstrations to the back of the paper and to highlight relatively innocuous slogans such as, "Serbia, Serbia" and, "Bring us back our children." Another was to argue that in fact the parents were not asking for any political change at all, only for the return of their children. Another response, voiced by the commanding officer of the Yugoslav Army, was juxtaposed to the parents' protest: "We are in a war which has been imposed on us, and we had to accept it . . . [but] we are doing everything in our power to protect the lives and dignity of members of our Army."

But most significant for our purposes are the ways that *Politika*'s reports drew on the image of the heroic mother, a set of ideas and ideals constructed upon the national epic tradition, as well as folk custom, and carefully preserved in remembrances of World War II: The patriotic mother is the one who bravely sends her soldier son to give his life for the homeland. Within the Balkan epics, the mother of a grownup son occupies an ambiguous position, that of strength and power and of weakness at the same time. Through her son, she can take some power reserved for men. As an old woman, she has control and power over the younger ones, and her word finally gets to be heard and even appreciated. On the other hand, being a woman and being old, she also has to be protected, and her son has to sacrifice for her, as she did for him when he was a child (for the rural tradition, see Denich 1974 and Kligman 1988). In that sense, the usual equation of a homeland with a mother—a stereotype very much employed by all sides in this war—underlines exactly this ultimate obligation.

In accordance with these images, one report on the women's protest before Parliament gave special place to one woman, a certain Nena Kunijević, the mother of twins serving their term in Slovenia, which was already a site of conflicts. Speaking "as a Serb," she asks that "the Serbian government should take care of her children" in the same way as Tuđman and Peterle, the leaders of Croatia and Slovenia, take care of "theirs." She stresses the legitimacy of the Yugoslav Army, asking that all other forces, those organized by Slovenian and Croatian governments at that time, be disarmed. However, her concern seems focused at least as much on the public relations benefits accruing from the parents' dramatic behavior in Parliament as with the Army or the fate of children. We should act with dignity, she advises: "Pictures are going to the world, and we do not want them to say that Serbs fight with each other." Kunijević is presented as "a mother of four" who is proud of her sons in the Army (Šuvaković 1991a). This heroic mother was supplemented, the next day, with the representation of a heroic sister, who places her destiny in the hands of her brother and his comrades: Describing the continuing occupation of the Parliament by enraged parents, *Politika* reported on a 19-year-old girl who came there to speak "instead of her mother, who had gone to Slovenia to find her son." Subtitled "Those We Did Not Hear in the Serbian Parliament" [*Oni koje nismo čuli u Skupštini Srbije*], the article stressed the girl's conviction that "her generation is not cowardly as their parents present them" and that they would know how to defend their own country (Šuvaković 1991b).

In analyzing these articles, what deserves attention is not merely the calculated use of interviewees. Rather, what is especially striking is how the imagery of women as mothers and sisters is placed in a discourse about national kinship (the *us* who is being watched by *them*), which is then used to legitimate the war as, ironically, a defensive struggle in which leaders "take care" of the children they send into battle. Numerous parallel stories about the "endangered brothers and sisters" in other parts of the country also justified such a "defensive" war. Moreover, there are implications here for men as well. Mothers may demand that their boys not fight and die, but as the young woman quoted in the last paragraph intimates, the young men themselves are implicitly threatened with accusations of cowardice if they are not ready to go into battle. That many were willing to risk such accusations is well demonstrated by the extremely high rate of deserters in Serbia. But here we are not concerned with acts but with images. And the question of cowardice brings up the fact that images of men were just as important in the presentation of the Mothers' Movement as images of women.

A significant element of the Balkan heroic tradition is the assumption that manhood is proved in battle, or at least in military service. It was a custom in recent years, particularly in rural parts of the country, to send off new recruits with a feast, a form of initiation into the world of adulthood. But note that this ritual of the "solemn oath" by which young men entered the army flourished in times of peace. It was a ritual that often served as an excuse for feasting and celebrating the youth and maturity of new generations. The ritual was generally supported by the authorities and was presented in the mass media because it sustained an image of the army as a "people's force."

Politika (July 23) played on such celebrations to make arguments about masculine bravery, arguments that were grotesquely transformed by the context of war. Alongside reports of the Parents' Movement ("Let Us Not Allow Our Children To Be Killed in Any Army"), *Politika* published an article entitled "Visiting the Family of a Fallen Soldier," subtitled "They Saw Him for the Last Time at the Solemn Oath" [*Poslednji susret na zakletvi*] (Ostojić 1991). It reports on a journalist's visit to a family of a young man killed in battle and praises the dead soldier's courage and patriotism. In the middle of the text, in a framed space, there is the boy's picture, taken at the feast in honor of his departure to the army, complete with a cake decorated with the initials of the Yugoslav Army. In the context of this article, a celebration usually linked with life and adulthood became a pathetic reminder of future death. By dramatizing and even romanticizing death in war by linking it to adulthood, heroism, and celebration, the *Politika* article in effect opposed the Parents' Movement. But this article also unwittingly reveals the basic mechanism of war propaganda and the paradox on which it is based.

In contrast to *Politika*, the independent magazine *Vreme* emphasized the parents' anguish and their anti-war potential. An article entitled "Parents as the Last Line of Defense: War among Us" (Milošević 1991) described desperate people, afraid for their children, who only wanted the war to stop so that their sons could return home. Perhaps most significantly, in contrast to the interviewees in *Politika* who compared "their" army with those of the "others," *Vreme* described an immense confusion and incomprehension about the break-up of Yugoslavia. For such people there was no clearly defined "us" and "them" at that point; they desperately hoped the fighting would end and that everything would somehow settle down. A person who read only *Politika* at this time, or populist-nationalist papers such as *Večernje novosti* or *Politika ekspres*, would invariably conclude that many were just waiting for the battles to start. But if we look at *Vreme's* reports, it becomes obvious how hard it was for people to abandon the idea of a normal life and accept the effects of war.

In the summer of 1991 *Vreme* continually emphasized a link between all the other peace initiatives and the parents' claims, as in a block of reportage on the peace events of summer 1991, entitled "Uprising for Peace: Let Us Give Peace a Chance" [*Mirovni ustanak: Dajmo šansu miru*] (Ast et al. 1991). It is noteworthy that in her text, included in this block, Rada Iveković, a philosopher and feminist from Zagreb, explicitly stated that the new nationalist euphoria is much more common for men than for women (Iveković 1991). In *Vreme*, there are no images of *heroic mothers*, but of *unhappy women*, desperate to help their children. Instead of nationalist ideas, emphasized in *Politika*'s presentation of the events, *Vreme* accentuated pacifist slogans, such as: "What am I going to do with a sovereign state, if my son has to be killed?" or "In whose name do they declare that they will fight to the last Serbian?" (Ast 1991b).

Vreme also paid attention to the meta issue of media effects. The same articles assess the media's reaction to the movement, showing how the major media simply ignore, or minimize, all events linked with peace initiatives. The same situation, they showed, could be found in Serbia, Croatia, and Slovenia. In another issue of *Vreme*, the prominent journalist Slobodanka Ast noted: "Peace activists are starting to shake unhealthy indifference, or maybe the desperate feeling of helplessness spread among the quiet majority, who did believe until yesterday that nothing could stop the war-tide any more. Mass media, on the contrary, are propagating those 'heroes' of war nationalism who despise life and who glorify the idea of more killing and more deaths" (Ast et al. 1991:33–36).

The parents' demands for peace were also strongly supported by feminist groups, but because such statements were ignored by the press, we must consult the publications of feminist groups to learn of their activities. When the Mothers' Movement started, feminist organizations marched together with the parents. But many feminists also knew that this movement could be used by "those who are in power in all the republics" to support their own agenda, as the Belgrade Women's Lobby stated in their "Support for Mothers' Movement" [*Podrška pokretu majki*] (Beogradski ženski lobi 1993). This fear was also evident in an appeal "Against Manipulation of Mothers" (*Protiv manipulacije majkama*), issued by the Women's Party ŽEST and Women's Parliament. The authors of the appeal warned against what they called "the new patriarchalization of society," evidenced in the revival of heroic ideals upon which, they said, any ideology of war is necessarily based (Ženska stranka i Ženski parlament 1993). Feminist statements also noted and criticized women's participation in this manipulation, as in the efforts of Nena Kunijević, who wanted to present the whole of the Mothers' Movement as supportive of the Yugoslav Army.

Despite such fears of manipulation, many feminists had high hopes for the effect of the Parents' Movement in gaining peace. One statement argued: "Mothers seek support from other peace organizations that have similar demands. There is nothing strange in the fact that women have leading roles in anti-war actions, and that mothers of soldiers joined such actions without any reservations." Indeed, they argued: "Mothers are a new force that has to be reckoned with" ("Statement of Support" [*Podrška majkama*] from August 1991, signed by Nadežda Ćetković in the name of Women's Parliament [Ćetković 1991; for the whole set of feminist documents on the Mothers' Movement, see SOS telefon za žene i decu žrtve nasilja 1993a, b]). In the given situation, although rejecting the traditional heroic ideal of the mother who sacrifices her son to war, the feminist statements recognize the potential strength of *mothers* as political (peace) activists. There is of course much historical precedent in many parts of the world for motherhood as a moral basis for public demands (see, for example, Koven and Michel 1990). The case of Yugoslavia in the early 1990s shows how the moral weight of motherhood was used by all sides—pro-peace and pro-military—but in different ways. Yet this use neglects the broader theme that feminists in

Belgrade invoked in other situations: women as citizens and individuals in their own name, not that of children, making political statements and taking public action. In short, while the maternalist position can be very powerful, especially against the backdrop of patriarchal assumptions, it also displays fundamental contradictions.

These tensions are clearly revealed by the subversive activities of Belgrade Women in Black. Formed in October 1991, on the model of Israeli, Argentinian, and Palestinian women's pacifist movements, Belgrade Women in Black tried to renounce the heroic ideal of motherhood and to publicly subvert some of its most recognizable signs. Dressed in black and maintaining total silence, they demonstrated against war and violence in public places. Traditionally, black dresses are used by women in the Balkans, as in many other regions, to signal mourning for close relatives. More specifically, although it is fundamentally a social convention, black for mourning can nevertheless be read as a sign that a woman wants to exclude herself from social, and especially public, life. In this sense it is a private gesture, a demand that the woman be left alone with her grief for a loved one. However, by making mourning a public event, they evoked the basic feminist claim that the personal is political. Using black dresses as a sign of mourning for *all* victims of the war, known and unknown, Women in Black changed the meaning of this ritual. Henceforth it became a specific anti-nationalist gesture. By refusing the distinction between "our" and "their" victims, it undermined exactly that kind of nationalist boundary that the *Politika* interviews tried to erect. The women's silence was an example of this same strategy of reversing symbolic meanings: "We have chosen SILENCE, refusing to pronounce excessive words which prevent us from thinking about ourselves and others. SILENCE determines the lives of the majority of women and men in our society. Mass media have silenced us, but black clothes and silence have become our ways to express our disagreement with this war, and with war in general." Thus, the explicit, general aim is *reversal* of the whole system on which militant patriarchy is based: "Women in Black want to initiate a creation of values which will be different from the presently dominant patriarchal ones—nonviolence against violence, solidarity against oppression, life instead of destruction, death, and necrophilia" (SOS telefon za žene i decu žrtve nasilja 1993a, b).

Women in Black later published two issues of a journal *Women against War*, both of which critically probed the topic of militarism. One issue included a section that addressed women's responsibility for supporting militaristic ideas and also examined the government's and mass media's role in manipulating the Mothers' Movement for militaristic purposes (Žene u crnom 1995b:5–71). The other issue was dedicated to supporting women's protests in Sarajevo, but also provided space for discussion about male anti-militarism, some of it written by men. This issue was powerfully subversive from the perspective adopted here: Advocating desertion from war rather than fighting, it directly violated and rejected the very logic of heroic militarism, notably the ideals of masculine bravery and worthy death, upon which it is based (Žene u crnom 1994b:51–75).

THE REFUGEE STORIES

My final examples are drawn from the movement of refugees within the borders of the former Yugoslavia. Here I only examine that fraction of the problem related to gendered aspects of the media's representation of refugees. My goal is to illuminate how this highly sensitive humanitarian problem was not only heavily politicized, but also strongly gendered (and this was the case on all the sides in the war).

Exact numbers are not available, but by some estimates more than 3.5 million people, mainly from Bosnia, Croatia, and Serbia, fled their homes between 1990 and 1995, becoming "displaced people" (see Appendix 14.1). Many simply left the country altogether. Before the war started, one of the strongest arguments against military action was the simple fact that people living in the territories of Yugoslavia were so mixed—with ethnic groups geographically dispersed and many marriages between individuals from different ethnic groups—that it would be impossible to make any ethnically homogeneous states. Tragically and notoriously, the displacement of people not only became one of the major strategies in making new nation-states: The very creation of ethnically homogeneous states was used to justify mass expulsions. Specifically, I focus on the way in which two separate episodes were framed, one taking place at the very beginning of the war, and the other near its end. From the media's vantage point, these two events can be compared and contrasted for various reasons. The first is the arrival of refugees from Slavonia (Croatia) to Serbia in spring and summer of 1991, the second is the enormous wave of Serbian refugees leaving Krajina (Croatia) in the summer of 1995, several months before the Dayton Peace Agreement was signed. In this case, as in my earlier examples, I must first provide a rough outline of the undisputed events.

The first major groups of refugees arrived in Serbia proper before the war started, while negotiations on a possible future for united Yugoslavia were still going on. Coming mainly from the Croatian region of Slavonia—soon to become one of the major battlefields in the war—these people were often put up in private homes within Serbia. The subsequent stream of refugees from Bosnia and Croatia (with peak points in 1992 and 1995; see Appendix 14.1) became so large that it became necessary to prepare long-term facilities for their stay and to provide care for them; many of them lodged with their families and friends.[14] But, together with the condition of the whole population, the situation of the

---

[14] NGOs have played a significant role in providing care for refugees, and women activists tend to be predominant within these organizations. Two major refugee assistance projects were also run by women. The Soros Fund of Yugoslavia, in operation since 1991, is run by Sonja Licht and has worked not only to improve refugees' living conditions but also to resocialize them. The "Hi Neighbor" project had a similar goal, but focused mainly on children and their mothers. It was initiated in 1992 by Vesna Ognjenović together with a group of independent psychologists. Sonja Drljević, a feminist who supported the project in its early work, later took over as its primary organizer. Vesna Pešić of the Center for Antiwar Action has also been an active supporter.

refugees soon worsened as a result of the sanctions and hyperinflation of 1993 and 1994. Refugees who had planned to return to their homes had to stay far longer than they wanted, or than their hosts had expected, creating considerable tension. The last major influx of refugees to Serbia occurred in August 1995, when more than 150,000 people left Kninska Krajina. The Serbian population from the region, dissatisfied with constitutional changes in Croatia in 1990, had proclaimed themselves "Serbian Krajina" and had asked for independence, refusing to submit to the authorities of the new Croatian state. When in 1995 the Croatian army defeated the local Serbian forces in a quick military campaign, the territory again came under Croatian control. The consequent exodus was sudden, consisting of entire families who traveled for days under difficult conditions and often in a state of utter confusion. This exodus left the region practically emptied of Serbian population.

During the spring and summer of 1991 the mainstream media closely followed the arrival of the first wave of refugees to Serbia. As I noted earlier, at this relatively early date the full implications of national categories were not firmly established in the minds of the general population. As some observers have astutely noted, a vague but widespread sense of danger among the Serbian population led to a readiness to accept war, while also providing the official justification for military operations. As I will show here, it was partly the media's presentation of the refugee problem—particularly through gendered images—that provoked this intense feeling of imperilment. *Politika* played a major part in this effort, together with some less serious, but high circulation and thus influential, daily papers like *Večernje novosti* and *Politika ekspres*.

Articles in these papers systematically presented refugees as women and children, portraying them as helpless, forced to leave their homes, and desperate for the kind of protection that they would only find in their "mother-homeland." Men were omitted, but photographs of women and children abounded, accompanied by dramatic titles: "Refugees are Running from Terror" [*U zbegu pred terorom*] (*Politika ekspres*, March 6, 1991). These papers highlighted the refugees' own simple stories and focused on their sense of menace, which was supposedly relieved only when they arrived in Serbia, where they did not feel like strangers, but rather as if they were coming home. The cause of danger was powerfully named in coded terms: "We should have known who *they* are," one article noted, alluding clearly to World War II and the genocidal policies of the Croatian Ustaša against Serbs in Croatia. Such comments echoed the intense use of history in the service of nationalist feeling throughout the 1980s. At the same time, it was either assumed or openly said that the men of the refugee families remained behind in order to fight. On March 6, *Politika* ran an article about 20,000 people leaving East Slavonia, noting dramatically, "only those who are willing to defend their homes are left there." The emphasis on this fact alone already strongly implied war, and thus prepared the way for it.

Paralleling these stories, and reinforcing oppositions of *us* against *them*, Serbs against Croats, were stories of ordinary Serbian people taking in refugees, being touched by their plight and willing to help in a dramatic show of hospitality that spoke of their common kinship. There is much evidence that such help was indeed forthcoming, but the mainstream media focus was not so much on what was done, but rather on the sense of unity among Serbs: common actions for a common cause.

In contrast to this coverage, the attitude of the independent magazine *Vreme* was quite different. In this early stage of the military conflict, journalists of *Vreme* considered some other aspects of the country's crisis much more important than the refugees. They wrote instead about the general political and economic situation, the perils of nationalism for the future of the common country; the nature of the Serbian regime; the massive anti-regime demonstrations in Belgrade on March 9, 1991, which were dispersed with violence; the negotiations among the six leaders of the ex-Yugoslav republics; and the strange situation of neither-peace-nor-war in which the country found itself. Thus, in sharp contrast to the mainstream press and despite clear signs of danger, *Vreme*'s journalists apparently did not believe, at this time, that the disintegration of the country and a real war were imminent.

Refugees were not entirely ignored by *Vreme*, but were handled instead as a problem whose solution depended on the disposition of other issues. In addition, the refugee issue provided the opportunity for *Vreme* to make meta-commentary on the nationalistic reporting of the other papers. On August 26, 1991, a *Vreme* journalist noted "refugees have become both a number, and arms, and their pains and sufferings are used for further arousing of hatred toward the other side. All warring sides are using them to heat up the atmosphere of war, and to call for general mobilization for the national cause" (Ast 1991a). This rhetoric was what *Vreme* considered the real problem, and it avoided such rhetoric in its own coverage. Instead, when writing of refugees, *Vreme* focused on children and implicitly took the plight of refugee children out of the context of ethno-national conflict by comparing Serbian children not to some other neighboring ethnic group, but to Western Europeans. For example, Ast's article, "Children of the War," was meta-commented with two pictures ironically juxtaposed under the single title, "Life of Teenagers." In one photo, we see boys from a Paris school, sitting at their computers; in the other we see boys in military uniforms with national Serbian symbols. The moral is clear: Instead of building knowledge, as such children do in happier countries, the Serbian boys are unfairly faced with war.

With the passing of time, another aspect of the continuous influx of refugees started to preoccupy the press. This was the increasingly palpable conflict between refugees and the rest of the Serb population, inevitably exacerbated by increasing economic difficulties and the outbreak of war. It is indisputable that such tensions existed (see Đurević 1991). The question here is how they were formulated and framed by the press. In the really big media, like state TV or *Politika*, the problem was mainly overlooked, but in popular papers like *Politika Ekspres* or *Večernje novosti* it was clearly recognizable. There, the familiar distinction between *us* and *them* was now applied to the refugees also, demonstrating clearly how the vast mechanisms of exclusion of the "other" operates on any level. The domestic *us* were described as modest, poor, honest, and heroic, fighting and dying for their country. The refugee *them*, in contrast, were arrogant, cowardly, rich, and exploitative of the domestics.

One article from *Politika Ekspres* is so clearly coded by gender that it deserves a detailed look. It tells the story of a refugee woman going to a store in the midst of the devastating hyperinflation of 1993. She is "heavily adorned with golden jewelry" and takes many valuable goods—high-quality food, expensive clothes, and even a short fur coat, again a symbol of luxury—and when she is told the price, she asks for a special discount for refugees. The story then describes the reactions of "poor domestic women" who see this and are enraged, since they must stay in line and do not have a refugee discount. Seizing the refugee, they "jump on her," and it is only with the help of guards that a "female lynching" is avoided (see Drašković 1994). This article is not typical for presentation of refugees, and is rather an excessive example, but I am using it here to indicate the ways in which the problem has been falsely presented. Although the cases of rich refugees were rare and insignificant, compared with misfortune of all the others, the article is only playing on irrational feelings of impoverished people that *they* are better off than *us*; what is even more important for this analysis, in underling this distinction, it is using misogynist images of women. This article scapegoats all refugees as the source of economic problems, while hiding the fact that the entire population, domestics and refugees, were suffering deprivations caused by systemic factors.

Refugee men, in particular, were also reproached with another set of negative traits that were also clearly gendered. As the regime conducted quiet but forced mobilization among male refugees, expecting them to go back to the front lines; as war deaths mounted; and as large numbers of the young men of the domestic population emigrated to avoid the draft, some popular newspapers characterized refugee men as unpatriotic and unwilling to fight. Indeed, male refugees were often presented as the unpatriotic, unmasculine, even cowardly and treasonous, negative examples that would shame the others into abiding by the heroic nationalist ideal of manly behavior.

Meanwhile *Borba*, and later *Naša Borba*, both independent papers, commented on exactly this rhetorical process, evident in the mainstream press. *Borba* pointed out that refugees were being written about in a way that would indirectly help support official policy and buttress national (heroic masculinist) ideology. The refugees at first were presented by the press of each national state as living proof of imminent danger and thus the rightness of nationalist policy, only later did they become "problems." Journalists of the independent press pointedly refrained from invidious comparisons of refugees and domestics. For instance, one article began, "Every sixth inhabitant of former Yugoslavia today is in a position of 'displaced person'" (Matić and Živković 1994). With this observation the journalist-authors turned the status of refugee into the universal problem of the whole population, rather than of only one subgroup, and refused to accept displacement as a factor that should distinguish and thus divide people.

The last large wave of refugees, coming this time from Krajina, was too large, and the problems involved were too pressing for any newspapers to downplay or ignore. But after significant change in the official policy of the regime, mainstream, regime-controlled media treated the refugee problem differently in 1995 than they had in previous years. Indeed, the previous approaches of the independent and state-controlled media were actually reversed, and with significant effect. People coming from Krajina were not greeted by the state-controlled media with the earlier emotional and pompous welcomes, nor the solemn declarations about the defense of national interests at any cost. In its reports on events from Krajina, *Politika* took a more emotionally muted, distanced approach, stressing the responsibility of the Croatian government for the exodus of Serbian people, and emphasized, in its own defense, that help offered to refugees in Serbia was well organized, despite serious economic problems in the country. Perhaps exactly to bolster this image, *Politika* tended to write about the problem in an impersonal way, describing events through numbers rather than through stories of individual people. Gone were the personal interviews and immediate pathos of the reports in 1991 and 1992. The same tendency was obvious in TV reports also, which gave most of the attention to the statements of officials dealing with refugees, and not so much to the plight of the people themselves. This conveniently allowed the mainstream press to ignore the problems with settlements. The great dissatisfaction of these refugees with some of the solutions offered to them—like going to Kosovo or remaining in Bosnia—were not closely covered by the state media.

In contrast, the independent press that had approached the earlier refugee wave as a general problem, attempting to drain it of personalistic and thus of nationalist pathos, now attempted to capture individual stories and something of the immediate drama of the events. In the given situation, this rhetorical strategy had some important effects. First, it encouraged direct help to the refugees, through the involvement of mass media figures as well as their organizations. For instance, independent Radio B92 devoted most of its programming to following the refugees and organized the collection of provisions for those on the road. Yet, while similarly personal and up-close, the stance of the independent media was strikingly at odds with the earlier ethnic-centered reporting of the mainstream media. Svetlana Lukić, one of the Radio B92 reporters who was involved in the relief effort, stated to NIN on August 18, 1995: "Now, it is necessary to help, all the rest comes after that. There are two kinds of people now; those who have seen all this and who cannot stop helping, and the other ones." Note how her allusion to two kinds of people echoes the us/them dichotomy of mainstream nationalist hostility, but then ironically undermines that by revealing the content of the dichotomy to be universalist, and far from ethnic (K.R. 1995).

A second effect of the personalized approach to the 1995 refugee wave was to provide documentation of the refugees' perspective, which was exactly what the mainstream media were trying to avoid with their distanced view. The refugee perspective undermined the official, nationalist stance. Through interviews and eyewitness reports on the roads and in shelters, *Naša Borba*, NIN, and *Vreme* were able to reveal that, far from "coming home" as heroic warriors, many of the refugees felt betrayed, manipulated by politicians, and very unhappy with the position in which they found themselves. It was even possible to suggest, through the voices of refugees, large-scale political collusion on the part of Serbian politicians. Dragan Banjac of *Naša Borba* reported the following comment from a woman on the road: "We did not come here because we wanted to do so; somebody planned it, and maybe even had some benefit out of it. We are little people and we cannot know it for sure, but I can see that we were are all deceived" (1995). Even more effective in undermining some of the main slogans of the war was an article by Mikloš Biro, another writer for *Vreme*. This piece was based on statements given by refugees to the Helsinki Committee for Human Rights in Belgrade (Biro 1996). He concluded, on the basis of interviews, that many people regretted the war, were nostalgic for their homes, and would have been glad to go back to Croatia as its loyal citizens, if they could have been granted security.

This difference in general approach was also observable in depictions of gender. Despite the personal approach to the refugee problem in both *Vreme* and *Naša Borba*, it was obvious that journalists in these papers tended to be as gender-neutral as possible. Instead of focusing on any particular age or gender, the emphasis was on the fact that the whole of the population was on the move, including males and females of all ages, in very hard conditions, sharing a feeling of common misfortune. Nevertheless, gendered perspectives could easily be detected from the statements of the refugees themselves, who often described the misfortunes of weak ones, broken families, children's sufferings, or pregnant women giving birth on the road. In such statements it was obvious that for many of these people, a heroic code and the gendered concepts firmly linked to it were seriously eroded.

On the other hand, mainstream media also appeared to be much more gender-neutral than in previous years, due to the very fact that they were operating more with statistics and figures than with personal stories. But there were some particular occasions in which the deepest roots of patriarchal culture and the heroic code inscribed in it were clearly revealed in striking images. There were several cases in which male children were the heroes. Both *Politika* and *Večernje novosti* published articles about a 10-year-old boy who drove his mother and sisters the whole way from Krajina, while his father was missing. In a followup, *Večernje novosti* made the patriarchal implication explicit, framing the whole story in a militaristic context; upon finally finding his father, the boy delivers "a report, a real soldier's report of a big small man," and explains that he had not eaten for days because "the food was needed for women." In another case, it was an 11-year-old boy who was featured for driving a tractor with nine female relatives and friends. On a photograph in the middle of the page the boy is surrounded by three generations of women, who in the crucial moment proved to be dependent on him.

But these examples are not used here only because they are so striking for a gender analysis. I am deeply convinced that, extreme as they are, these examples bear a subversive message, clearly revealing some basic assumptions of a patriarchal code that reduces women to the helpless status of children. And it is exactly the role that many women rejected in opposing the war and the patriarchal code on which the war culture necessarily relies. The development of a feminist movement and the participation of women in peace and civic activities offer the strongest proof of this rejection.

CONCLUSION

In this chapter, I have argued a number of points about the use of gendered images in the mass media presentation of crisis and war in former Yugoslavia. Examples have been taken from some of the most influential papers in Serbia, both the mainstream ones supporting the policy of the regime and the independent opposition papers that resisted the war and call for democratic reforms. In both cases, gender images were used to prove the points argued by the authors.

In the case of the mainstream media, gender images were used to cover up for the policy of the regime, as part of an inclusive process of selection and distortion of information. Speaking of women in particular, there was an obvious tendency to follow certain stereotypes. These categorized women into those acceptable for public presentation, namely, entertainers and politicians supportive of the regime, and those who did not have access to the media, namely, feminists and women in the democratic opposition. In cases of major social uprisings, for instance the Mothers' Movement, gendered images were used to shape the meaning of events and to present them in a manner more favorable for the regime. Examples from mainstream media showed that official justification and explanations of the social crisis necessarily relied on some familiar gender stereotypes deeply rooted in the patriarchal culture of the region. This included heroic men ready to sacrifice for their motherland and heroic women/mothers ready to sacrifice their children and themselves for the common cause. At an early stage of the crisis, gendered images were employed in creating and supporting the general feeling of imperilment among Serbian people, as well as the feeling of mutual solidarity among Serbs. A good example is the presentation of refugees at the beginning of the war in the region. Finally, in the case of the last big influx of refugees in 1995, it was possible to show how the mainstream media presentation of this problem changed with the formal change of official policy.

Contrary to the strategy of the mainstream media, the democratic independent media put their main effort into unmasking the hidden strategies of the regime and filling the gaps in missing information. Their use of gender images fits into this pattern as well. Their strategies often included meta-commentary, explicitly drawing attention to the tropes and figures used, and to the politically loaded impression that the mainstream articles worked to create. They also tried to directly undermine the rhetorical effects produced by the regime-controlled press to make their own anti-war political points. In presentation of women in general, they tended to be mainly interested in the same categories of women as the mainstream press—that is, politicians and entertainers—but they presented them from another perspective. In addition, the democratic press was much more open to reporting on a different kind of women's participation in public life, recognizing the importance of women's peace and civic initiatives, although not always in a sufficiently clear manner.

Finally, it is only in their own publications that women, and feminists in particular, managed to present their actions clearly and to oppose the gender stereotypes so strongly employed in mass media. Only in feminist publications was the participation of women in peace and civic initiatives made clear and visible. Only there did it emerge that women made up more than 80 percent of peace activists. Only in women's and feminist publications did it become really obvious that, generally speaking, war in the region was basically a male event, while considerable numbers of women were on the side of peace.

BIBLIOGRAPHY

Newspapers/Media

Ast, Slobodanka
  1991a   Deca rata [Children of War]. Vreme, August 26, 1991:24–27.
  1991b   Julski mirotvorni ustanak: Mir, odmah! [Uprising for Peace in July: Peace Now!]. Vreme, July 29, 1991:15–17.
  1991c   Mobilizacija majki [Mobilization of Mothers]. Vreme, February 11, 1991:34–35.
  1991d   Žene komunizma [Women in Communism]. Vreme, June 17, 1991:35–37.
Ast, Slobodanka et al.
  1991   Mirovni ustanak: Dajmo šansu miru [Uprising for Peace: Let's Give Peace a Chance]. Vreme, August 5, 1991:33–39.
Banjac, Dragan
  1995   Niko nije izašao pred narod [Nobody Came to Meet People]. Naša Borba, August 10, 1995:1, 7.
Biro, Mikloš
  1996   Krajišnici hoće kući [People from Krajina Want to Go Home]. Vreme, January 13, 1996:12–14.
Čolović, Ivan
  1996   Društvo mrtvih ratnika. Republika (August):145–146.
Drašković, Draško
  1994   "Izbeglica" kao nova profesija u glavnom gradu: Druga strana obraza ["Refugee" as a New Profession in the Capital: The Other Side of the Story]. Politika ekspres, January 21, 1994:13.
Đurević, Svetlana
  1991   Veseli početak rata [Funny Beginning of the War]. NIN, September 13, 1991:18–19.
G.P.
  1990   Zabranjeno za muškarce [Forbidden for Men]. Politika, April 4, 1990:16.
Grubač, Stefan
  1991   Intervju, Bratislava Buba Morina: "Zašto je mađarska vlada uradila više od naše" [Interview with B.B. Morina, "Why the Hungarian Government Did More Than Ours"]. NIN, February 15, 1991:16–17.

Iveković, Rada
1991   Pomračenje uma na Balkanu [Losing Minds in the Balkans]. Vreme, August
        5, 1991:38–39.
K.R.
1995   Više neće biti isto: Intervju, Svetlana Lukić [It Will Never Be The Same:
        Interview with Svetlana Lukić]. NIN, August:34.
Matić, Jovanka and Aleksandar Živković
1994   Od nacionalnog cveta do korova [From National Flower to Weed]. Borba,
        January 5, 1994:iv–v.
Milošević, Milan
1991   Roditelji, poslednja linija odbrane: Rat, među nama [Parents as the Last Line
        of Defense: War among Us]. Vreme, July 8, 1991:9–11.
Ostojić, Z.
1991   U poseti porodici poginulog vojnika Dejana Spasovskog: Poslednji susret na
        zakletvi [Visiting the Family of Fallen Soldier Dejan Spasovski: They Saw
        Him for the Last Time on the Solemn Oath]. Politika, July 23, 1991:9.
Šuvaković, Zorana
1991a   Priča Nene Kunijević, majke tenkista u Vrhnici [The Story of Nena Kunijević,
        Mother of Tank Drivers in Vrhnika]. Politika, July 3, 1991:11.
1991b   Oni koje nismo čuli u Skupštini Srbije: Ima da postoji Jugoslavija [Those We
        Did Not Hear in the Serbian Parliament: Yugoslavia Must Exist]. Politika,
        July 4, 1991:9.
Vujić, V. and M. Pešić
1991   Protestni mitinzi žena širom Jugoslavije [Protest Gatherings of Women
        throughout Yugoslavia]. Politika, February 5, 1991:7.

Books/General

Beogradski ženski lobi
1993   (July 1991) Podrška pokretu majki [Support for the Mothers' Movement].
        Žene za žene, vanredni bilten SOS-a (5):52–53.
Blagojević, Marina with Daša Duhaček and Jasmina Lukić, eds.
1995   What Can We Do for Ourselves? Proceedings from the East European Feminist
        Conference, June 1994. Belgrade: Women's Studies Center.
Ćetković, Nadežda
1993   (August 27, 1991) Podrška majkama [Statement of Support for Mothers].
        Žene za žene, vanredni bilten SOS-a (5):62.
Čolović, Ivan
1993   Bordel ratnika: Folklor, politika i rat. Beograd: XXvek.
Denich, Bette S.
1974   Sex and Power in the Balkans. *In* Women, Culture and Society. Michelle
        Zimbalist Rosaldo and Louise Lamphere, eds. Pp. 243–262. Palo Alto: Stanford
        University Press.
Dragićević-Šešić, Milena
1994   Neofolk kultura, Publika i njene zvezde. Sremski Karlovci: Izdavačka knjižar-
        nica Zorana Stojanovića.
Drakulić, Slavenka
1992   How We Survived Communism and Even Laughed. London: Hutchinson
        Press.

Gal, Susan
  1994   Gender in the Post-Socialist Transition: The Abortion Debate in Hungary.
          East European Politics and Societies 8(2):256–287.
Jancar, Barbara
  1988   Neofeminism in Yugoslavia: A Closer Look. Women and Politics 8(1):1–30.
Kajošević, Indira
  1995   Women of Yugoslavia in Parliament and Political Life after the Multiparty
          Elections of 1989. *In* Žene u crnom, eds. Annual Anthology. Pp. 164–165.
          Belgrade: Women in Black.
Kligman, Gail
  1988   The Wedding of the Dead: Ritual, Poetics, and Popular Culture in Transylva-
          nia. Berkeley: University of California Press.
Koven, Seth and Sonya Michel
  1993   Mothers of a New World: Maternalist Politics and the Origins of Welfare
          States. New York: Routledge.
Lalić, Lazar
  1995   Three TV Years in Serbia. Belgrade: Independent Media Union.
Licht, Sonja and Slobodan Drakulić
  1996   When the Word for Peacenik Was Woman: War and Gender in the Former
          Yugoslavia. Research on Russia and Eastern Europe 2:111–139.
Marković, Zoran M.
  1996a   Nacija—žrtva i osveta (prema revijalnoj štampi u Srbiji 1987–1991). Re-
          publika 139:1–12.
  1996b   Priča sa naslovne strane. Republika [Special issue] 19(141):1–8.
  1996c   Uspon i pad Studija B. Republika 147:15–22.
Milivojević, Zdenka
  1995   Mediji u Srbiji od 1985 do 1994. *In* Srbija izmedju prošlosti i budućnosti.
          Beograd: Radnička štampa.
Nenadović, Aleksandar
  1995   Politika u nacionalističkoj oluji, udeo i odgovornost Politike u proizvodnji
          trauma. Republika 114:1–16.
Papić, Žarana
  1989   Sociologija i feminizam. Beograd: IICSSOS.
Pennington, Anne and Peter Levi, trans.
  1984   Marko the Prince: Serbo-Croat Heroic Songs. London: Duckworth.
Popov, Nebojša
  1996   Srpska strana rata: Trauma i katarza u istorijskom pamćenju. Beograd: Vikom
          Grafik-Gradjanska čitaonica.
Roboy, Marc, and Bernard Dagenais, eds.
  1992   Media, Crisis, and Democracy: Mass Communication and the Disruption of
          Social Order. London: Sage.
Scott, Joan
  1988   Gender and the Politics of History. New York: Columbia University Press.
Snitow, Ann
  1995   Feminist Futures in the Former Eastern Block. *In* What Can We Do for
          Ourselves? Proceedings from the East European Feminist Conference, June
          1994. Marina Blagojević, Daša Duhaček, and Jasmina Lukić, eds. Pp. 141–154.
          Belgrade: Women's Studies Center.

SOS telefon za žene i decu žrtve nasilja [SOS Hotline for Women and Children Victims of War]
- 1993a   Anti-ratni bilten SOS-a. (4). [Anti-war bulletin of SOS].
- 1993b   Žene za žene, vanredni bilten SOS-a (5). [Women for women, special bulletin of SOS].

Subotić, Dragutin
- 1932   Yugoslav Popular Ballads, Their Origin and Development. Cambridge: Cambridge University Press.

Šušak, Bojana
- 1996   Alternativa ratu. *In* Srpska strana rata: Trauma i katarza u istorijskom pamćenju. Nebojša Popov, ed. Pp. 531–557. Beograd: Vikom Grafik-Gradjanska čitaonica.

Thompson, Mark
- 1994   Forging War: The Media in Serbia, Croatia and Bosnia-Herzegovina. London: International Centre Against Censorship.

Ugrešić, Dubravka
- 1995   Because We're Lads. *In* What Can We Do for Ourselves? Proceedings from the East European Feminist Conference, June 1994. Marina Blagojević, Daša Duhaček, and Jasmina Lukić, eds. Pp. 128–140. Belgrade: Women's Studies Center.

Wood, Julia
- 1994   Gendered Lives: Communication, Gender and Culture. Belmont, CA: Wadsworth.

Žene u crnom
- 1993   Women for Peace, Annual Anthology. Belgrade: Women in Black.
- 1994a   Women for Peace, Annual Anthology. Belgrade: Women in Black.
- 1994b   Žene protiv rata 1 & 2 [Women against War]. Belgrade: Women in Black.
- 1995a   Women for Peace, Annual Anthology. Belgrade: Women in Black.
- 1995b   Žene protiv rata 3 & 4. Belgrade: Women in Black.

Ženska stranka i Ženski parlament
- 1993   Protiv manipulacije majkama [Against the Manipulation of Mothers]. Žene za žene (September 6, 1991):54–55.

Ženski Centar
- 1994   Feminističke sveske 1 & 2. Beograd: Ženski Centar [Belgrade Women's Center].
- 1995   Feminističke sveske 3 & 4. Beograd: Ženski Centar [Belgrade Women's Center].

Selected Bibliography on the War and Crisis in Yugoslavia

Almond, Mark
- 1994   Europe's Backyard War: The War in the Balkans. London: William Heinemann Ltd.

Banac, Ivo
- 1984   The National Question in Yugoslavia: Origins, History, Politics. Ithaca, NY: Cornell University Press.

Beogradski krug
- 1994   Selected Bibliography on War and Nationalism in the Former Yugoslavia. Beogradski krug [Belgrade Circle] 1:235–248.

Bogdanović, Bogdan
 1993   Die Stadt und der Tod. Klagenfurt & Salzburg: Vieser Verlag.
Burg, Steven
 1993   Conflict and Cohesion in Socialist Yugoslavia. Princeton, NJ: Princeton University Press.
Cohen, Lenard J.
 1993   Broken Bonds: The Disintegration of Yugoslavia. Boulder, CO: Westview Press.
Dizdarević, Zlatko
 1993   Journal de guerre. Paris: Spengler.
Glenny, Misha
 1992   The Fall of Yugoslavia: The Third Balkan War. New York: Penguin Books.
Hall, Brian
 1994   The Impossible Country: A Journey through the Last Days of Yugoslavia. London: Secker & Warburg.
Iveković, Rada
 1994   La balkanizacione della regione: Il caso Jugoslavo. Roma: Manifesto libri.
Iveković, Rada et al.
 1993   Brieffe von Frauen über Krieg und Nationalismus. Frankfurt: Suhrkamp Verlag.
Kovačević, Slobodanka and Putnik Dajić
 1994   Hronologija jugoslovenske krize (1942–1993). Beograd: Institut za evropske studije.
 1995   Hronologija jugoslovenske krize (1994). Beograd: Institut za evropske studije.
 1996   Hronologija jugoslovenske krize (1995). Beograd: Institut za evropske studije.
Lampe, John R.
 1996   Yugoslavia as History: Twice There Was a Country. Cambridge: Cambridge University Press.
Matvejevich, Predrag
 1993   Epistolaire de l'autre Europe. Paris: Fayard.
Sekelj, Laslo
 1993   Yugoslavia: The Process of Disintegration. V. Vukelić, trans. Highland Lakes, NJ: Atlantic Research and Publications.
Silber, Laura and Allan Little
 1996   Yugoslavia: Death of a Nation. London: Penguin/BBC Books.
Udovički, Jasminka and James Ridgeway
 1997   Burn This House: The Making and Unmaking of Yugoslavia. Durham, NC: Duke University Press.
Ugrešić, Dubravka
 1995   Der Cultur der Lüge. Frankfurt: Suhrkamp Verlag.

APPENDIX 14.1

Refugee Arrivals in the Federal Republic of Yugoslavia, December 31, 1991 to September 6, 1996

Time of Arrival	Number of Refugees for the Period Specified	Total Number of Refugees
As of December 31, 1991	48,653	48,653
January 1, 1992, to December 31, 1992	133,863	182,516
January 1, 1993, to December 31, 1993	32,305	214,821
January 1, 1994, to December 31, 1994	24,060	238,881
January 1, 1995, to June 30, 1995	22,704	261,585
July 31, 1995, to December 31, 1995	253,482	515,067
January 1, 1996, to September 9, 1996	43,021	558,088

Source: Red Cross of FR Yugoslavia (Serbia and Montenegro).

Note: 53 percent of refugees are women; and 47 percent are men.

SUSAN GAL AND GAIL KLIGMAN

A DECADE AFTER THE fall of communism, the Hungarian Constitutional Court is again considering the question of restricting legal abortion; domestic violence has become a highly publicized issue in Poland; sexual harassment and the decriminalization of homosexuality are being debated in Romania; and the international trade in the sexual services of men, women, and children in and from the region has burgeoned. Clearly, the issues and themes with which we began this project continue to command the attention of people across East Central Europe.

Our goal has been to outline an agenda for research on post-socialist societies that puts gender at the center of analysis. We have argued that gender—as a set of practices and ideas about the differences between men and women—shapes many of the social changes that have followed the collapse of communism. Debates about reproduction contribute to making states and legitimating governments. Economic and political restructuring are not only recasting the boundaries of public and private but are also redefining forms of masculinity and femininity. At the same time, divisions of labor and routes toward mobility are shaped in part by a newly emerging system of gender differences. Finally, we have argued that political participation is also gendered; men and women are differently involved in international, national, and local politics as well as civil society.

Nevertheless, gender is not equally important at all times and places. Or, to put it another way, gender identities are foregrounded in some institutions, in some countries, and in some historical moments, but not necessarily at all times and in all places. This variability can be approached in a number of ways. In ethnographic studies of particular institutions such as schools, one can observe how gatekeeping practices may select on the basis of gender or ignore this distinction; one can note how managers in offices and shop floors make assumptions about what work is appropriate for men as opposed to women or select and distribute workers on the basis of other criteria. Fluctuation in the importance of gender can also be studied statistically so that gender as a variable is only sometimes significant in explaining large-scale trends such as changing patterns of unemployment.

Other variables such as age and generation may well be as significant as gender in shaping the ways in which the East Central Europeans have experienced the post-socialist transformations. Marketization has created vulnerability and insecurity for many, but it has also created opportunities. As a broad generalization, young people at the start of their work lives are in a better position to take advantage of new possibilities than those further on in the life cycle. The current fashioning of more competitive, individualized selves who are ready to take risks and initiative differs radically from the construction of the "new socialist man" of some forty years ago. Similarly, ethnic and racial factors may sometimes be more important than gender in facilitating or constraining access to employment, positions of authority, or vulnerability to poverty. For example, across the region, Roma regardless of gender are increasingly marginalized and impoverished.

Variability in the salience of gender is one strong indicator of the differing temporalities of transformation in the countries of East Central Europe. What in 1989 could be characterized as an identifiable geopolitical region has since experienced divergent trajectories and rates of change. To illustrate, the gendered division of labor under socialism in the state sector and in the domestic sphere was similar across these countries. However, since 1989, through marketization, new occupations have been created to which women and men have different access, while the gender composition of old occupations has changed in many instances. Relatedly, the domestic sphere is also being redefined. While these processes of labor market and domestic transformation are happening everywhere, they are not consistent across the region. Their gendering is affected in each country by different governmental policies and other factors such as pressures exerted by organized religious or nationalist interests.

The studies that grew out of our collaborative research project document the complexity of the ways in which gender is central in post-socialist transformation. Gender contributes to the reconfiguration of the meanings of public and private—with respect to selves, spheres, activities, and institutions. Ideas about the differences between men and women shape practices and social institutions, which, in turn, have brought changes in what it means to be a man or a woman after socialism.

CONTRIBUTORS

ADRIANA BĂBAN is Associate Professor in the Department of Psychology at Babeş-Bolyai University, Cluj-Napoca, Romania.

KRASSIMIRA DASKALOVA is Senior Lecturer in Modern Cultural History at St. Kliment Ohridski University of Sofia, Sofia, Bulgaria.

IRENE DÖLLING is Professor in the Department of Economics and Social Sciences at the University of Potsdam, Potsdam, Germany.

MYRA MARX FERREE is Professor of Sociology and of Women's Studies at the University of Connecticut, Storrs, Connecticut.

MAŁGORZATA FUSZARA is Director of the Center for Socio-Legal Studies on the Situation of Women and Assistant Professor at the Institute for Applied Social Sciences of the University of Warsaw, Warsaw, Poland.

SUSAN GAL is Professor of Anthropology and Linguistics at the University of Chicago, Chicago, Illinois.

ANNA GIZA-POLESZCZUK is Assistant Professor in the Institute of Sociology of the University of Warsaw, Warsaw, Poland.

JOANNA GOVEN is Lecturer in Political Science at the University of Canterbury, Christchurch, New Zealand.

LAURA GRUNBERG is a doctoral candidate in Sociology and Program Officer for UNESCO-CEPES, Bucharest, Romania.

DAPHNE HAHN is Senior Research Fellow at the Institute of the Sociology of Medicine in the Department of Medicine at Humboldt University, Berlin, Germany.

GAIL KLIGMAN is Professor of Sociology at the University of California, Los Angeles, Los Angeles, California.

KATALIN KOVÁCS is Senior Research Fellow at the Center for Regional Studies of the Hungarian Academy of Sciences, Budapest, Hungary.

JASMINA LUKIĆ is Lecturer at the Belgrade Women's Studies Center, Belgrade, Yugoslavia, and Visiting Lecturer at the Program on Gender and Culture of the Central European University, Budapest, Hungary.

EVA MALECK-LEWY holds a doctoral degree in philosophy. She taught for many years at the Humboldt University in Berlin. Her research focuses on German women's political participation and the East German women's movement.

MIRA MARODY is a Professor of Social Psychology in the Institute of Sociology at the University of Warsaw, Warsaw, Poland.

ZORICA MRŠEVIĆ is Senior Researcher at the Institute of Criminological and Sociological Research and Lecturer at the Belgrade Women's Studies Center, Belgrade, Yugoslavia.

SYLKA SCHOLZ is a doctoral candidate and Lecturer in the Department of Economics and Social Sciences at the University of Potsdam, Potsdam, Germany.

JÚLIA SZALAI is Professor of Sociology and Social History, John Wesley College, Budapest, and Senior Research Fellow at the Institute of Sociology, Budapest, Hungary.

MÓNIKA VÁRADI is Senior Research Fellow in the Center for Regional Studies of the Hungary Academy of Sciences, Budapest, Hungary.

SHARON WOLCHIK is Professor of Political Science and International Affairs at The George Washington University, Washington, D.C.

ELEONORA ZIELIŃSKA is Professor of Law in the Faculty of Law and Administration of the University of Warsaw, Warsaw, Poland.